Performance Management in Nonprofit Organizations

T0293712

With increased competition for external funding, technological advancement and public expectations for transparency, not-for-profit and non-governmental organizations are facing new challenges and pressures. While research has explored the roles of accounting, accountability and performance management in nonprofit organizations, we still lack evidence on the best practices these organizations implement in the areas of accountability and performance management. This book collects and presents that evidence for the first time, offering insights to help nonprofits face these new challenges head-on.

Performance Management in Nonprofit Organizations focuses on both conventional and contemporary issues facing nonprofits, presenting evidence-based insights from leading scholars in the field. Chapters examine the design, implementation and working of accounting, accountability, governance and performance management measures, providing both retrospective and contemporary views, as well as critical commentaries on accounting and performance-related issues in nonprofit organizations. The book's contributors also offer critical commentaries on the changing role of accounting and performance management in this sector.

This research-based collection is an interesting and useful read for academics, practitioners, students and consultants in nonprofit organizations, and is highly accessible to accounting and non-accounting audiences alike.

Zahirul Hoque is Professor of Accounting at La Trobe University Business School, Melbourne, Australia. He is the founding editor-in-chief of the *Journal of Accounting & Organizational Change*. He is author of three accounting text books and has published articles in a number of top-tiered accounting and public sector journals.

Lee Parker is a Professor in the School of Accounting at RMIT University, Melbourne, Australia and at Royal Holloway College, University of London. He has held posts in Australasia, UK, North America and Asia and has published in over 200 articles and books on management and accounting, including the nonprofit sector, internationally.

Routledge Studies in the Management of Voluntary and Nonprofit Organizations

Series Editor: Stephen P. Osborne (University of Edinburgh, UK)

This series presents innovative work grounded in new realities, addressing issues crucial to an understanding of the contemporary world. This is the world of organized societies, where boundaries between formal and informal, public and private, local and global organizations have been displaced or have vanished, along with other nineteenth-century dichotomies and oppositions. Management, apart from becoming a specialized profession for a growing number of people, is an everyday activity for most members of modern societies.

Similarly, at the level of enquiry, culture and technology, and literature and economics can no longer be conceived as isolated intellectual fields; conventional canons and established mainstreams are contested. Management, organization and society address these contemporary dynamics of transformation in a manner that transcends disciplinary boundaries, with books that will appeal to researchers, students and practitioners alike.

Performance Management in Nonprofit Organizations

Global Perspectives

Edited by Zahirul Hoque and Lee Parker

NEW YORK AND LONDON

First published 2015
by Routledge
711 Third Avenue, New York, NY 10017

and by Routledge
2 Park Square, Milton Park, Abingdon, Oxon OX14 4RN

First issued in paperback 2018

Routledge is an imprint of the Taylor & Francis Group, an informa business

Library of Congress Cataloging-in-Publication Data

Performance management in nonprofit organizations : global perspectives /
    edited by Zahirul Hoque and Lee Parker.
        pages cm — (Routledge studies in the management of voluntary and
non-profit organizations)
    Includes bibliographical references and index.
    (ebk)   1. Nonprofit organizations—Management.   2. Performance—
Management   I. Hoque, Zahirul.   II. Parker, Lee.
    HD62.6.P473 2014
    658.4'013—dc23

ISBN 13: 978-1-138-33994-1 (pbk)
ISBN 13: 978-1-138-78798-8 (hbk)

Typeset in Sabon
by Apex CoVantage, LLC

We dedicate this book to our long suffering wives *Shirin* and *Gloria* who deserve it . . . and more.

Contents

PART III
Issues in Accountability Processes and Governance

PART IV
Issues in Performance Management and Risk

Figures

Tables

Acknowledgments

The contributors and we (the editors) have been equal partners in the compilation of this volume. We are grateful to the contributors whose chapters are presented here. We would also like to thank Terry Clague (Publisher, Routledge: Business, Management & Accounting), Amy Laurens (Commission Editor, Routledge: Business, Management & Accounting), Dave Varley (Routledge) and Manjula Raman (Editorial Assistant, Routledge, Taylor & Francis (US): Business, Management & Accounting) for their support. Last, but not least, we also thank Mrs. Shirin Hoque (La Trobe Business School, La Trobe University) for her editorial assistance in producing this book.

Foreword

A considerable body of research has developed over many decades that examines accounting, accountability mechanisms, governance practices and performance management issues in commercial organizations. There is also a long-standing stream of research that has addressed many accounting, accountability, governance and performance management issues in public sector organizations. These issues are core to the effectiveness of organizations in both the public sector and the commercial sector because each encompasses a considerable amount of human productive activity and effort. Therefore, it is hardly surprising, and entirely appropriate, that so much intellectual effort has been devoted to better understanding these issues in both the commercial and public sectors.

In recent years the third sector, comprising non-governmental, nonprofit organizations, has grown considerably. Organizations in this sector range in scope from those delivering large-scale emergency aid and sustainable development in the most impoverished communities (both in less developed and in wealthy nations), through a variety of more local charity and community service organizations, to advocacy organizations campaigning on specific social, political and/or religious issues. In some societies third sector organizations now represent a substantial proportion of productive activity and community support. They also often have a privileged status in terms of the trust accorded to many charities and/or tax and other legislative privileges compared to commercial and public sector organizations. It is therefore perhaps surprising that research examining accounting, governance and performance management of nonprofit, non-governmental organizations has only recently begun to become more widespread. In comparison to the overall size and significance of this sector, it is clear that these issues have been under-researched—with scope for much greater research insights to be developed in future.

In this context, this book provides a very timely collection of impressive insights into aspects of performance management issues in a range of non-governmental, nonprofit organizations. These insights should help to provide a base for researchers interested in developing much-needed research into aspects of this diverse, economically and socially significant sector.

The book's four substantive sections (accountability challenges and practices; regulations, financial reporting and social and environmental accounting; performance measurement and risk management controls; governance, institutions and politics of development) each provide a collection of studies providing important insights into what we regard to be the key challenges of nonprofit accounting, accountability and performance management. We believe this book will rapidly become essential reading for anyone with a serious interest in a balanced understanding of the issues underlying these challenges to the future of a vibrant and effective nonprofit sector that is accountable and well governed.

Professor Brendan O'Dwyer
Faculty of Business and Economics
University of Amsterdam

Professor Jeffrey Unerman
School of Management
Royal Holloway, University of London

Preface

In recent years, increased competition for external funding, greater community involvement and programme assistance, technological advancement, the need to comply with complex government regulations and increased social/community expectations for greater transparency have placed more challenges and unanticipated pressures on organizations in the nonprofit or voluntary sector. In recent times, while there has been considerable academic research in exploring the role of performance management and accounting in nonprofit organizations, we still lack evidence on what kinds of best practices nonprofit organizations implement and use in the areas of accountability and performance management. Hence, the principal aims of this book are (1) to explore the changing nature and role of accounting, accountability and performance management in today's nonprofits and (2) to draw out evidence of what kinds of best practices nonprofit and non-government organizations implement and use in these areas.

The strengths of the edited collection elate to the variety of interesting topics, geographical diversity and mix of quality academic along with some practitioner inputs. All the chapters provide both retrospective and contemporary views and commentaries by knowledgeable scholars in the field, who offer unique insights on the changing role of accounting, accountability and performance management in today's nonprofit organizations. The work will be relevant to a wide range of audiences—academics, researchers, practitioners, graduate research students and consultants in the areas of nonprofit and non-government organizations.

Part I
Introduction and Context

1 Accountability, Governance and Performance Management in Nonprofit Organizations
An Overview

Zahirul Hoque and Lee Parker

INTRODUCTION

Nonprofit organizations represent a longstanding sector in many national economies and today have been generally growing in size, reach, scope and societal impact. They are to be found operating in education, welfare, sports, the arts, health and many other areas of national and international life in both developed and developing economies. Yet in the accounting and management research literatures, they have arguably been subject to a variety of misconceptions ranging from mistaken role definitions, to incorrectly assumed best practices, to inappropriate strategies and management tools imported from the private sector, to neglect of their unique characteristics and associated needs. These challenges are brought into sharp relief when the questions of nonprofit organization accountability, governance and performance management are put under the spotlight.

The purpose of this chapter is to open this book's examination of accountability, governance and performance management processes within nonprofit organizations. In doing so it presents a general overview of the nonprofit sector's societal positioning and role and goes on to consider the challenges to be managed by these organizations in dealing with their complex and dynamic national and international environments. The chapter draws upon the editors' experiences as researchers in this field, along with relevant research observations published in recent years and the contributions of the researchers who have authored the chapters appearing in this volume. The chapter is organized in the following manner. The next section highlights the importance of the nonprofit sector in a society. Section three presents a discussion about the challenges facing today's nonprofit organizations. Section four introduces the contributions to this book made by a group of experienced and emerging scholars in the field. The final section of the book offers conclusions and directs for future research in the nonprofit sector.

IMPORTANCE OF THE NONPROFIT SECTOR
IN A SOCIETY

Research shows that the nonprofit sector performs important social, economic and political functions in a society (O'Dwyer & Unerman, 2008, 2010; Unerman & O'Dwyer, 2006, 2010, 2012; Gray, Bebbington, & Collison, 2006). Nonprofit sector organizations include those that are distinct from government, self-governing, with ownership that is often vested in their members but does not distribute profits to them, and encompassing voluntary membership and service (Lyons, 1999; DCITA, 2005; Parker, 2007). Apart from being prevalent and significant in western, industrialized, developed countries, nonprofits have also gained popularity in less developed or emerging economies, including Asia and eastern European countries. They have become major providers of quasi-public goods and services (Smillie & Hailey, 2001; Lewis, 2004; Unerman & O'Dwyer, 2006, 2010, 2012; Gray et al., 2006). Salamon and Anheier (1996) see the nonprofit sector as a major economic force in a country and their study of nonprofits in seven developed countries (U.S., UK, France, Germany, Italy, Hungary and Japan) shows that at the time of their study the sector employed 11.8 million workers and in those countries overall, exceeded the combined employment of the largest private company in each country (General Motors, Hitachi, Alcatel-Alsthom, Daimler-Benz, Fiat and Unilever) by a factor of 6 to 1.

Further, Salamon and Anheier's (1996) study showed the sector making use of volunteer labour that is equivalent to another 4.7 million full-time workers. The operating expenditure of the nonprofits in their seven countries totalled $604.3 billion and represents 4.5% of the gross domestic product and 4 times the gross sales of General Motors, the world's largest private corporation. In France, Germany and the U.S. the nonprofit sector accounted for 13% of the new jobs added between 1980 and 1990. The U.S. nonprofit sector has the largest employment at 6.9% of total employment. France, Germany and the UK have a sizable nonprofit sector accounting for 3–4% of all jobs and 9–10% of employment in the service sector (Salamon & Anheier, 1996). Hungary has seen an unprecedented growth in the nonprofit sector with over 20,000 organizations registered across a period of five years accounting for 3.2% of all service jobs. The Japanese nonprofit sector employs more than its counterparts in the UK, Germany and France. In Australia, this sector employs people in the following proportions (Purdie, 2003): social services (26%), education and research (24%), culture and recreation (21%), health (15%), business, professional associations and unions (2.5%) and other (11.5%).

Salamon and Anheier also studied the nonprofit sector in five developing countries (Brazil, Ghana, Egypt, Thailand and India) and their findings revealed that at the time of their study, there were nearly 20,000 nonprofit organizations in Egypt, close to 200,000 in Brazil and over 15,000 registered organizations in Thailand. Another contrast is the predominant area of work by the nonprofit organizations. In Japan and UK the dominant field is education, whereas in Germany and U.S. it is health, in France and Italy it is social services, in Hungary it is culture and recreation and in developing countries it is work relating to development.

In understanding the nonprofit sector it is worth determining the underlying pressure for this extraordinary growth in the sector. Salamon (1994) suggests that the most basic force for the nonprofit sector is its ordinary people taking matters into their own hands and organizing to improve their conditions or seeking basic rights, as seen in the unprecedented growth of nonprofits in the Soviet Union and eastern Europe and South America, Asia and Africa.

A unique feature of the nonprofit sector is the way in which the sector is self-regulated with a marked difference in the motivation for self-regulation between the well-established developed countries and the emerging developing countries. Research centred around the specific national cases (Bies, 2010) reveals that in western Europe (Germany, Switzerland, the Netherlands and Austria) and the UK, where the nonprofit sector is long established and public regulation of the sector is weak, the nonprofit sector has a self-regulation design that builds on long-established self-regulation systems (Guet, 2002). Such activity serves variously to stimulate the nonprofit economy, to substitute or complement regulation by the state or to institutionalize nonprofit practices and enhance nonprofit legitimacy. In contrast, self-regulation efforts in Asia and Africa, where self-regulation is characteristically more recent and often the product of collective action, such nonprofit action is adversarial in nature and frequently motivated to defend organizations and communities against heavy-handed or repressive government intervention.

In understanding the importance of the nonprofit sector it is imperative to note the current challenges the sector is facing that may determine the future status of the sector. In the United States, some of the factors identified are: (1) public policy, particularly welfare reform and the devolution of increased responsibility to the states; (2) commercialism, competition and collaboration among sectors; (3) increased potential for giving and volunteering; and (4) new forms of philanthropy (Hodgkinson & Nelson, 2001). Collectively they have brought about major changes in the functioning of the nonprofit sector. The study by Hodgkinson and Nelson (2001) predicts that in coming decades part of the sector will be highly professionalized and indistinguishable from the corporate sector whereas the rest of the sector will try to maintain its mission of service and continue to build civil society.

The nonprofit sector in the developing world is commonly comprised of non-government organizations (NGOs) and has a different structure compared to the traditional nonprofit organizations (for details, see Ahmed & Hopper, this volume). Whatever their origins, the nonprofit sector and the NGOs of the developing world share the ideology to advance public purposes and address collective needs. They are identified in a distinctive social sphere and as a particular type of social institution even though their specific purposes may differ (Anheier & Salamon, 1998). Key features of the five developing countries studied by Anheier and Salamon included the contribution to the economy of the country. In Brazil, the organizations are small with a budget of less than $30 million engaged in education and health care. In Egypt 30% of the work carried out is in the rural areas. In Thailand traditional cremation societies form a large proportion of the NGOs and India has the most complex structure with over 2 million organizations, the largest proportion of which are engaged in education, development and environmental issues.

The nonprofit sector in developing countries, although large in absolute numbers, is relatively smaller than nonprofits in developed countries, where they form 4–5% of the work force. In developing countries they employ less than 2% of the work force. As mentioned before, these nonprofit organizations in developing countries collectively address 'developmental' activities and concentrate heavily on advocacy activities. Further, the nonprofit sector in developing countries attracts significant international funding and is less reliant on government funding than counterparts in the developed world (Anheier & Salamon, 1998). The emergence of the nonprofit institutions in the developing world has been a 'top-down' approach where the nonprofit is a direct product of the state-centred development policies and takes the role of agents in stimulating local development. More recently international aid has played a major role in the economy of the nonprofit sector with the nonprofit agenda being driven by broad 'developmental' activities in contrast to state-driven policies. Another factor that has contributed to the rapid growth of the nonprofit sector in developing countries is the unprecedented growth of the urban middle class. In comparison to the developed world that saw the growth of the urban commercial and professional middle class much earlier in time, developing countries have experienced rapid growth in the middle class in recent decades (Anheier & Salamon, 1998).

So there are marked differences between the nonprofit sector in the developed world and the developing countries. Accordingly we have highlighted some of the differences, drawing upon major studies by Anheier and Salamon into seven developed countries and five developing countries. Despite the differences, conceptually both nonprofit sectors work towards the betterment of society in general and are run by passionate people behind the cause.

CHALLENGES IN THE NONPROFIT SECTOR

To be able to fully understand the concepts of performance management, accountability and governance in the nonprofit sector, it is essential to briefly explain the trust placed by the public in the nonprofit sector, as well as its associated reputation. The perception of the public with regard to accountability and governance of the nonprofit sector is closely linked to the ethos of the nonprofit sector, which sets out to demonstrate that there are no incentives for opportunistic behaviour because there is no distribution of profits and hence no claim to any financial surplus that might motivate them to misrepresent their activities to stakeholders (Hansmann, 1980). If this non-distribution constraint is legitimate, accountability and governance in the nonprofit sector should be of the highest order because there is no incentive to erode accountability or governance due to a profit motive. Hence the principal-agent relationship will be one of compatibility rather than a watchdog over management that wants to maximize profits. However, will this prevent agents from behaving in their self-interest should there be performance-based remuneration? In the absence of profits, what drives the performance of the nonprofit sector and is there still an incentive for senior managers to act in their own self-interest (Ben-Ner & Gui, 2003)?

These questions can be addressed by examining the current status of the performance management, accountability and governance arrangements of the nonprofit sector. If financial surplus is not sought for distribution to members or shareholders, they can be consumed by the board, managers and other employees (e.g., in the form of perks). Some self-serving members can erode governance by misdirecting funds available for a specific purpose. This can result in substandard services being offered by the non-profit organizations. Performance management in nonprofit organizations is invariably focused on its services provided rather than on improving profit performance. Research suggests that the employees in the nonprofit sector are generally paid less than their counterparts in the for-profit sector (Bacchiega & Borzaga, 2003). If this is the case what are the incentives for employees in the nonprofit sector to meet their performance management criteria? The answer lies in the way performance incentives are structured in this sector. It becomes the responsibility of the employees, senior managers and co-workers alike to deliver the public goods and services for which donations, grants or sponsorships were received. In any nonprofit organization there are volunteers who significantly contribute to the work force. It becomes the responsibility of the paid workers to oversee the work done by the volunteers and to be accountable for their own performance and report to the board members. They have to do a balancing act between delivering quality services and utilizing funds wisely to deliver the services. The question remains as to whether performance targets help.

A 2005 study (Ostrower, 2007) of over 5,100 nonprofit organizations carried out in the US revealed that board performance management and accountability is particularly concerned with exercising financial oversight. Approximately 52% of the respondents said their boards were active in performance management and accountability in areas of financial oversight and organizational policy. This leads to the next question of governance (for details, see Ostrower, 2007). Further, only a minority of the respondents said their boards are active in monitoring their own board performance, implying there is lack of board member interest in self-evaluation. Findings reveal it is increasingly becoming difficult to recruit board members who can volunteer their time, which results in poor board performance. Although at present there is no conclusive evidence, poor board performance can cascade down to substandard performance at the organizational level. Overall there is thus a need to improve performance management and accountability at board level (Ostrower, 2007).

The current trends in board governance practices in the nonprofit sector that warrant attention can be summarized as: succession plans, board recruitment, skills assessment, expertise required, board member removal, orientation, training, governance spending, involvement, policies and procedures, goal setting, accountability, information requirements, board evaluation, oversight of the CEO, measures of success, strategic discussions and risk management (Bugg & Dalhoff, 2007).

More research done on NGOs and nonprofit organizations working across borders in the developing world suggest that these organizations face more complexities and have greater accountability challenges. An interview of 152 leaders of transnational NGOs reveals that demands on accountability have increased in the recent years (Schmitz, Raggo, & Vijfeijken, 2012). For 64% their view of accountability centres on financial management accountability and for 46% it centres on the mission of the organization and how they meet the expectations of the community. A sizeable proportion (38%) describes accountability as transparency, whereas some primarily associate accountability with contractual and legal obligations. When asked whom they are accountable to, the most common answer was the donor, identified as the key stakeholder, and when asked how they would strengthen accountability nearly 56% of NGO leaders quoted audits (Schmitz et al., 2012).

Financial accountability sits high on the agenda for nonprofit organizations, although they face more complexities in cross-border operations. Overall the measurement of performance is linked to financial indicators, although the key emphasis of the nonprofit organization is on service delivery rather than profit distribution to owners. In conclusion, financial viability is taken to be a measure of accountability and the governance aspects of nonprofit organizations are expanding from succession plans, to risk management and board recruitment.

THEMES AND SCOPE OF THIS VOLUME

Aimed at academics, practitioners, students and consultants in the areas of nonprofits and non-government organizations, this research-based book provides high-level insight into the design, implementation and working of accounting, accountability, governance and performance management in organizations in this sector. The book's contents are organized into four principal themes: (a) introduction and context; (2) issues in financial reporting and regulation; (3) issues in accountability processes and governance; and (4) issues in performance management and risk. We expand on them in turn.

Introduction and Context

We include a total of four chapters that provide an introduction and context to the remainder of the book. In the first chapter, we provide an overview of the role of nonprofit organizations in today's society where nonprofit organizations compete for funding. The chapter discusses the nature of current challenges the sector is facing and that will determine the future status of the sector. Chapter 2 by Ahmed and Hopper examines the growing activities, roles, power and accountability of development non-governmental organizations (NGOs) from a socio-political perspective. They discuss how accountability is linked to NGO growth, efficiency and the creation of hegemony. Ahmed and Hopper suggest that shifts in the scale and nature of NGO activities are strongly influenced by changing ideologies and policies of dominant western governments and transnational financial intuitions. This has brought greater attention to the accountability of NGOs, especially with respect to their mission to empower marginalized beneficiaries and influence political reform bottom-up with civil society. Next, the chapter by Oakes explores how the attacks on 11 September 2001 prompted U.S.-elected officials to ask whether tax-exempt charities were funnelling funds to terrorist organizations. The author suggests that although U.S. congressional hearings identified few donations traceable to suspect organizations, they also identified inadequate governance, mismanagement of resources and, in some cases, outright abuse of the tax-exempt status among the 1.2 million nonprofits in existence at the time. This chapter follows those hearings, documenting how the framing of this crisis shifted. It also documents that by stressing public transparency and enacting blunt, easy-to-enforce regulatory mechanisms, these hearings led to a dramatic reduction in the number of charitable organizations providing services in the United States. In a related theme, Costa, in Chapter 4, shows how the legal changes issued in 2005 by the Italian legislator, while designed to offer Italian social enterprises (SEs) the opportunity to obtain official accreditation, missed their objective (very limited number of accreditations since then). Based on extant literature about accountability in nonprofit organizations (NPOs), this chapter explains the inappropriateness of the accountability framework imposed by the new Italian legislation and, finally, provides insights on what should have been added to the framework to make the SE accreditation more relevant.

Research to date reflected in these opening chapters reveals a spectrum of fascinating and important challenges faced by the nonprofit sector. NPOs and NGOs operate in highly dynamic environments that continually shift in response to societal conventions and expectations, legislative and regulatory changes, economic circumstances and institutional structures. Indeed they typically have dual relationships with governments that range from adversarial stances to strategic alliances. As such, the interaction and interdependency between NPOs/NGOs and government imply that both parties maintain a watching brief on each other's strategies and actions, particularly as government agendas do change over time and NPO and NGO strategies invariably try to respond. Such interactive monitoring becomes even more important when governments impose accountability frameworks as conditions for grants or contracts that may intervene in NPO/NGO autonomy and require those organizations' constant monitoring, adaptation and managing.

Issues in Financial Reporting and Regulation

In 2011, the Australian government announced new arrangements for untaxed trading income after a High Court case drew attention to it. In Chapter 5, Brody, Breen, McGregor-Lowndes and Turnour identify issues experienced on a practical level in the U.S. and the UK, where unrelated business income is taxed, and offers directions for any future Australian attempt to tax this income.

Focusing on issues surrounding nonprofit reserves, Booth, McGregor-Lowndes, Ryan and Irvine explore in Chapter 6 whether it is desirable for organizations to hold reserves in the bank or as a net asset to hedge uncertainty and enhance financial sustainability, or whether all monies received should be spent on mission. Their chapter suggests that individuals within nonprofit organizations have a broad accountability for ensuring their organizations' financial sustainability and mission fulfilment in the longer term, but highlights uncertainties surrounding the issue. Further, they explore what reserves are, examine reasons for accumulating nonprofit reserves, review approaches adopted internationally across jurisdictions and report what is known about practice.

In an alternative context, Khan and Ahmed in Chapter 7 examine the existing institutional and regulatory environment for the financial reporting of microfinance institutions (MFIs) and the extent of information disclosed to various stakeholders in Bangladesh, a country that is credited with introducing microcredit to poor people to develop their entrepreneurial capacity in emerging nations. Further, the chapter assesses whether MFIs meet the information needs of users and preparers. Khan and Ahmed find that over the four-year reporting period, the reporting quality of MFIs in Bangladesh has not improved despite the introduction of regulations and the efforts of local and international funding and regulatory bodies. They further reveal significant differences between the perceived information needs of users and preparers and the actual amount of information disclosed by MFIs.

In the UK context, chapter 8 by Connolly, Hyndman and McConville summarizes some of the key themes, issues and research findings emanating from the UK in recent years. They suggest that requirements relating to accounting practice and broader reporting have evolved considerably, driven by influential stakeholder concerns. The chapter concludes that such considerations are critical in developing a more accountable charity sector, and such an objective should be vital for all those concerned with the health and growth of the sector.

All these four chapters share a similar view that government regulations and socio-political institutions significantly influence the development of accounting and performance management information for multi-stakeholders such as governments, communities and funding agencies. Those influences range across taxation policies, accountability for both financial outcomes and mission achievement and the ongoing imperative for generating and managing financial reserves. With respect to reporting and accountability, these organizations must still grapple with trends in quality of performance reporting, the challenge of more accurately identifying key report users, the task of trying to close the report preparer (user gap) and effectively delivering accountability to key stakeholders.

Issues in Accountability Process and Governance

Furneaux and Ryan, in Chapter 9, explore the relationship between a government as a purchaser and a nonprofit organization as a provider of social services. In this contractual context, Furneaux and Ryan argue that a clear accountability relationship between the purchaser and the provider needs to be developed. They suggest that the nonprofit organization must give an account for the use of the funds and achievement of outcomes to the funder. This chapter explores how accountability is enacted in two different types of funding relationships in the state of Queensland in Australia. Support has been found for the argument that different NPO-funder relationships have different approaches to accountability.

In Chapter 10, Pawson and Joannidès explore the consequences of accountability for mission and money on fundraising strategy in a charity setting. Using grounded theory principles, their interviews with seven U.S. fundraising managers expose a fundraising function that is both powerful and powerless, crucial to mission and subject to multiple, even schizophrenic, accountabilities. A limiting attitude to risk is also observed with a focus on efficiency and donor trust that could hamper the utility of the sector.

In another study, Joannidès, Jaumier and Hoque seek to identify patterns of boardroom discussions around the design and adoption of an accountability system in a French-based nonprofit entity. In Chapter 11, the authors show that collegiality and unanimity within their subject nonprofit organization are fostered by its board's discussions surrounding the predictability and manageability of the organization's social implications. Further, the chapter concludes that once an accountability system is decided upon and implemented by grassroots members, new issues arise and test the solution. This leads to its incremental adjustment and enrichment.

In a related theme, Parker and Hoque, in Chapter 12, address the processes of nonprofit, organizational, corporate governance and accountability from inside the boardroom. They argue for the importance of investigating and understanding corporate governance and accountability processes that occur within the top levels of organizational management and at the board of director level. Drawing on an albeit limited corpus of qualitative research into this top-level corporate governing community, their chapter examines the processes of planning and strategizing, operational and financial control, management of internal corporate governance processes and perspectives on accountability. In the course of addressing these key governance processes, particular attention is paid to the complexities and unique features of the nonprofit organizational environment, the internal and external influences that impact on governance processes and the importance of managing relationships in this setting.

Charity accountability has featured prominently in Australian policy debates for two decades. In 2010 the issue took centre stage with reforms that led to the establishment of Australia's first uniform charity-reporting framework in 2012. Chapter 13, by Saj, explores the development of Australian charity reporting by mapping its progress against theories of nonprofit accountability. He finds that accountability is highly contested, with some believing that mere compliance with funding contracts is sufficient, whereas others embrace a holistic approach that includes comprehensive audited financial reports and performance reports.

The evidence presented in these five chapters concentrates on boardroom governance, control, reporting and accountability processes and the role of top management therein. The chapters provide strong empirical evidence concerning the tensions between public accountability, reporting frameworks and processes and regulatory compliance. An accountability design that addresses the needs of service purchasers and resource providers remains a central NPO concern. It must encompass probity of process, efficiency of operations and funds usage and effectiveness of outcomes delivery. Defining and prioritizing these dimensions has a direct effect upon the scope and form of accountability rendered. The above researchers also demonstrate that the discharge of accountability by NPOs/NGOs can be highly variable and at times contested, being an emergent, negotiated and changing phenomenon that is subject to the vagaries of internal organizational dynamics set in their contextualized environment. At the same time, the discharge of accountability reflects the organization's stakeholder interface and is ultimately tied to both organizational strategy and control orientations.

Issues in Performance Management and Risk

The remainder chapters of this volume address issues in performance management and risk. Tucker in Chapter 14 seeks to provide insights into how performance may be viewed within a nonprofit context. Drawing on management control and nonprofit literature, Tucker considers nonprofit performance from the vantage point of two influential theoretical perspectives: contingency theory on the one hand, and neo-institutional sociology on the other. The chapter argues that these seemingly conflicting theoretical positions as they relate to nonprofit performance are quite reconcilable. In this chapter, conclusions presented provide guidance for researchers and practitioners in both conceptualizing and operationalizing the nature of performance in this important sector. Hough, McGregor-Lowndes and Ryan, in Chapter 15, discuss the role of the balanced scorecard (BSC) in nonprofit board monitoring. The chapter reports on case studies of five nonprofit boards following the imposition of a BSC-type performance-monitoring tool. Based on a field study of direct observation, interviews and documentary analysis, Hough et al. reported that the boards did not modify, or did not significantly modify, their existing monitoring routines. The chapter concludes that when a new monitoring tool such as BSC is adopted, attention should be given to how the preexisting routines might be changed to promote its active use.

Chapter 16, by Morris, McGregor-Lowndes and Tarr, focuses on financial risk involved in government grants in the new public management (NPM) context. NPM has accelerated governments' outsourcing of community services. A monopsony exists where government is almost the sole buyer or funder, which places governments in a powerful negotiating position. Seen in such a context, risk is a critical contractual term. Morris et al. suggest that it is important for risk to be allocated to the party best able to manage it, to maximize the benefits of outsourcing, particularly where the market is not informing risk allocation. The chapter examines Australian and UK model grant agreements for the allocation of risk. The authors offer a guiding principle for the apportionment of risk between the parties, based on risk being allocated to the party most able to manage it.

The final chapter 17, by Alawattage, Wickramasinghe and Tennakoon, attempts to examine how civil societies give shape to forms of accountability that, in turn, trigger civil society performance. In this chapter, the authors used the formative phase of the largest Sri Lankan civil society organization to explore how a particular social form of accountability functioned in its civil society context. Based on their ethnographic materials and associated secondary sources, they report how the country's Buddhist ideology gave shape to underprivileged villages, to a performing civil society and to a social form of accountability and performance.

Performance and risk management emerge as vital issues for nonprofit sector organizations in the above chapters. How these are operationalized and controlled is in the first instance, potentially affected by an organization's conceptual framing. However even then, when government emerges as the dominant resource provider, it exercises a powerful influence over nonprofit strategies, programmes, risk and ultimate viability. However, even when powerful external stakeholders like government impose or demand new formal monitoring and control systems, in actuality, nonprofit organization approaches in these functional areas may cling to or return to preexisting, internally valued financial and operational routines and related control processes. Finally, just as earlier chapters in this book have concluded, accountability and performance are identified as intrinsically interrelated, again reflecting the effects of their social, philosophical and institutional context.

CONCLUSIONS

Nonprofit organizations are today major players in national economies and societies. They are arguably more complex and forced to operate in and react to environments even more shifting and dynamic than their profit sector counterparts. Theirs is a challenge of managing and delivering financial and operational strategies, as well as outcomes in circumstances where resource providers, members, professional staff, volunteers and clients all may have differing expectations and agendas. Yet they are still charged with the responsibility of good governance and the rendering of appropriate accountability for this very complex field of stakeholders. Prior research and chapters in this volume suggest that nonprofit organizations face environmental uncertainties stemming from dependence on external funding, problems in the coordination of services, dealings with government and non-government agencies and difficulties addressing the divergent needs of a wide spectrum of stakeholders. Hence, the process of formalization and institutionalization of nonprofit, organizational, operational and financial accountability and management changes may change over time, responding to competing values and strategies, as well as dissonant discourses and practices (Cornforth and Edwards, 1999).

Not the least of the challenges faced by nonprofits is their at times complex relationship with national, regional and local governments. It could often be said to be an intimate relationship that will depend on the nonprofit's positioning as adversary, critic or strategic partner. This in many countries has been accentuated by nonprofits increasingly taking over direct community service delivery functions that have been abandoned by governments seeking to withdraw to a philosophy of indirect support via a small government model. In addition to their complex relationships with government, nonprofits face layers of stakeholders that include various groups of resource suppliers (e.g., donors, sponsors, grantors), service deliverers (e.g., professional staff, volunteers, community groups, subcontractors) and service recipients. All of these arguably need attention and management, but that task is complicated by their divergent perspectives, needs and expectations. Accordingly, 'good' governance requires the navigation of this competing spectrum of interests and agendas.

In support of good governance, the identification, measurement and assessment of performance emerges as a multidimensional task. Performance is not easily conceptualized or rendered calculable, especially when services are oftentimes intangible and the demands of stakeholders so variant. Both governance and associated management control systems call for an increasing plethora of support systems and disclosure processes, all demanding of resources, time and expertise.

Financial viability and delivery of service mission for the nonprofit organization are inevitably and uniquely intertwined. Any consideration of one requires the encompassing of the other. So it is for nonprofit accountability, governance and performance management, being intertwined and all essential to financial and operational management. In this book, we hope the reader will come to appreciate that accountability, governance and performance management are mutually reinforcing essentials for nonprofit organizational functioning. They are strategic, environmentally reactive, stakeholder negotiated and contextually situated. We invite the reader to explore these phenomena in the chapters that follow.

REFERENCES

Anheier, H., & Salamon, L. M. (1998). *The nonprofit sector in the developing world: A comparative analysis.* Manchester: Manchester University Press.

Bacchiega, A., & Borzaga, C. (2003). The economics of the third sector, toward a more comprehensive approach. In H. K. Anheier & A. Ben-Ner (Eds.), *The study of the nonprofit enterprise, theories and approaches.* New York: Plenum Publishers.

Ben-Ner, A., & Gui, B. (2003). The theory of nonprofit organizations revisited. In H. K. Anheier & A. Ben-Ner (Eds.), *The study of the nonprofit enterprise, theories and approaches.* New York: Plenum Publishers.

Bies, A. L. (2010). Evolution of nonprofit self-regulation in Europe. *Nonprofit and Voluntary Sector Quarterly, 39*(6), 1057–1086.

Bugg, G., & Dalhoff, S. (2007). *National Study of Board Governance Practices in the Nonprofit and Voluntary Sector in Canada.* CVSRD (Centre for Voluntary Sector Research and Development): Ottawa, Ontario, Canada and Strategic Leverage Partners Inc.: Toronto, Ontario, Canada.

Cornforth, C., & Edwards, C. (1999). Board roles in the strategic management of non-profit organisations: Theory and practice. *Corporate Governance: An International Review, 7*(4), 346–362.

Department of Communications, Information Technology and the Arts (DCITA). (2005). *Information economy: Sector 2—the nonprofit sector in Australia.* Retrieved from http://www.dcita.gov.au/ie/community_connectivity/information_and_comm unication_technologies_transforming_the_nonprofit_sector_a_discussion_paper/ section_2_the_nonprofit_sector_in_australia

Gray, R., Bebbington, J., & Collison, D. (2006). NGOs, civil society and account-ability: Making the people accountable to capital. *Accounting, Auditing and Accountability Journal, 19*(3), 319–348.

Guet, I. H. (2002). *Monitoring fundraising: A comparative survey of ICFO members and their countries.* Berlin: International Committee on Fundraising Organizations.

Hansmann, H. B. (1980). The role of nonprofit enterprise. *The Yale Law Journal, 89*(5), 835–901.

Hodgkinson, V. A., & Nelson, K. E. (2001). Major issues facing America's nonprofit sector. *The Nonprofit Review, 1*(2), 113–118.

Lewis, D. (2004). On the difficulty of studying civil society: NGOs, state and democ-racy in Bangladesh. *Contributions to Indian Sociology, 38*(3), 299–322.

Lyons, M. (1999). Australia's nonprofit sector. *Yearbook of Australia (1999)*, Australian Bureau of Statistics, ABS Catalogue No. 1301.01. Retrieved from http://www.abs.gov. au/Ausstats/abs@.nsf/0/5ebe1496169c5d31ca2569de002842b6?OpenDocument

O'Dwyer, B., & Unerman, J. (2008). The paradox of greater NGO accountability: A case study. *Accounting, Organizations and Society, 33*, 801–824.

O'Dwyer, B., & Unerman, J. (2010). Enhancing the role of accountability in pro-moting the rights of beneficiaries of development NGOs. *Accounting and Busi-ness Research, 40*(5), 451–471.

Ostrower, F. (2007). *Nonprofit governance in the United States: Findings on perfor-mance and accountability from the first national representative study.* Washing-ton, DC: Urban Institute. http://www.urban.org/publications/411479.html

Parker, L. D. (2007). Professional association boardroom strategising: Processual and institutional perspectives. *Journal of Management Studies, 44*(8), 1454–1480.

Purdie, J. (2003). *The nonprofit sector in Australia.* Philanthropy Australia. Retrieved from http://www.philanthropy.org.au/factsheets/7–05–03-nonprof.htm

Salamon, L. M. (1994). The rise of the nonprofit sector. *Foreign Affairs, 73*(4), 109–122.

Salamon, L. M., & Anheier, H. (1996). *The emerging nonprofit sector.* Manchester: Manchester University Press.

Schmitz, H. P., Raggo, P., & Vijfeijken, T. B. (2012). Accountability of transnational NGOs: Aspirations vs. practice. *Nonprofit and Voluntary Sector Quarterly, 41*, 1175–1194.

Smillie, I., & Hailey, J. (2001). *Managing for change: Leadership, strategy and man-agement in Asian NGO.* London: Earthscan.

Unerman, J., & O'Dwyer, B. (2006). On James Bond and the importance of NGO accountability. *Accounting, Auditing and Accountability Journal, 19*(3), 305–318.

Unerman, J., & O'Dwyer, B. (2010). NGO accountability and sustainability issues in the changing global environment. *Public Management Review, 12*(4), 475–486.

Unerman, J., & O'Dwyer, B. (2012). Accounting and accountability for NGOs. In T. Hopper, M. Tsamenyi, S. Uddin, & D. Wickramasinghe (Eds.), *Handbook of accounting and development.* Cheltenham, UK: Edward Elgar.

2 Politics, Development and NGO Accountability

Zahir Ahmed and Trevor Hopper

INTRODUCTION

Non-governmental organisations (NGOs) are not new. 'Philanthropy'—the ethical notion of giving to and serving those beyond one's immediate family—has existed in most cultures throughout history. However, NGOs now play a growing role in economic development and welfare, especially in poor countries (O'Dwyer & Unerman, 2008, 2010; Unerman & O'Dwyer, 2006a, 2010, 2012; Gray, Bebbington, & Collison, 2006). For example, they provide community development, assistance in national disasters, sustainable system development and assist social movements (Dixon, Ritchie, & Siwale, 2006; Smillie & Hailey, 2001; Lewis, 2004). This has precipitated a rapid increase of research on NGOs.

Support for NGOs stems from their proximity to remote communities and the poor (Awio, Northcott, & Lawrence, 2011); efficient low cost operations, e.g., microcredit programmes (Hulme & Moore, 2007); promotion of sustainable development (O'Dwyer & Unerman, 2007); and their potential for organising and representing civil society (Devine, 2006; Gray et al., 2006; Lehman, 2007). Their rapid growth is attributed to indigenous governments' failure to alleviate poverty, growing bureaucracy and corruption, and their lack of accountability (Haque, 2004; Stiles, 2002; Gauri & Galef, 2005). Despite differences in size, scope and approach, NGOs are no longer perceived as small bands of activists but rather as new 'super brands' serving consumers that grant them more esteem than major corporations, government bodies and even the media (Wootliff & Deri, 2001). This is especially pronounced with respect to Western aid agencies and transnational financial institutions such as the World Bank, especially since the cessation of the 'Cold War.' NGOs have become perceived as major agents in development and poverty reduction, but as will be discussed, their role and accountability has been shaped by significant changes in approaches to development by external agencies and the politics of aid. However, NGOs' activities are not universally acclaimed. Turner and Hulme (1997) call them 'Janus-like' organisations exhibiting 'mushroom growth'; Temple (1997) argues that they continue the missionary tradition and are handmaidens of capitalist change; Vivian and Maseko (1994) claim that evidence of their superior performance is scanty. Others criticise NGOs for being resource brokers rather than change agents (Pearce, 2006); providing palliatives to poverty rather than precipitating significant structural change (Tembo, 2003; Wright, 2012); serving so many divergent vested interests that fundamental development problems are denied (Rahmani, 2012; Wright, 2012); delivering projects with poor long-term effectiveness (Ati, 1993); and drifting from their original mission and even into financial corruption (Gibelman & Gelman, 2004; Townsend & Townsend, 2004). Independent information on NGOs' actual practices and whether the beliefs that underpin their rapid growth are justified is lacking (Jordan & Van Tuijl, 2000). The worry is that managers and/or promoters use the organisational form of NGOs as a cover to solicit donations for alleviating suffering but divert them towards their personal interests (Gibelman & Gelman, 2004).

This chapter examines the growing roles, power and activities of NGOs, which requires in-depth political economy analysis (Ward, 2005). Important topics include the potential of NGOs to deflect their accountability from their fundamental values, mission and obligations to grassroots clients; and the social, economic and political conditions and strategies that enable them to grow, sustain themselves and influence public policy. Initially the chapter focuses on describing the NGO sector and controversies surrounding it and after defining NGOs it examines the nature of their activities, their rapid expansion and the power and politics of NGO development. The final section summarises the conclusions and outlines topics worthy of further research.

WHAT IS AN NGO?

The term 'NGO' was officially created by Resolution 288 (X) of the United Nations Economic and Social Council on 27 February 1950. This referred to officially recognised organisations without governmental affiliations but with consultative status within the United Nations (Vakil, 1997). Nevertheless, local third sector organisations had worked relatively unnoticed in villages and towns in most societies for generations in the form of religious organisations, community groups and organised self-help ventures. Despite the expanding profile of NGOs within development, the lack of consensus on defining and classifying them creates confusion (Salamon & Anheier, 1992; Smillie, 1995; Najam, 1996; Martens, 2002; Burger & Owens, 2010)[1]. Salamon and Anheier (1992) suggest the term NGO represents a subset of nonprofit organisations (NPOs) that focus on social and economic development. They identify five critical features: *formal, private, nonprofit distributing, self-governing* and *voluntary*. The organisation is *formal* if it is institutionalised and has regular meetings, office bearers and some organisational permanence; it is *private* if it is institutionally separate from government, although it may receive government support; it is *non-profit distributing* if any financial surplus generated does not accrue to owners or directors; it is *self-governing* if it can control and manage its own affairs; and finally it is *voluntary* if there is some voluntary participation in the conduct or management of the organisation, such as a voluntary board of directors. However, this definition is not universally accepted. Gordenker and Weiss (1995) describe NGOs as private, self-governing, formal and nonprofit, but they omit the 'voluntary' aspect to acknowledge the increasing professionalism of the NGO sector. Martens is also more cautious, especially about altruism of NGOs and hence defines a NGO more generally '. . . as a formal (professionalized) independent societal organisation[2] whose primary aim is to promote common goals[3] at the national or international levels' (Martens, 2002, p. 282). The more constrained definitions may have merit with respect to the actual conduct of NGOs, but the authors believe a normative definition is required to capture altruism, self-governance and social accountability as features of NGOs.

Vakil (1997) emphasises altruism in his structural-operational definition of NGOs as '. . . *self-governing, private, not-for-profit organisations that are geared to improving the quality of life of disadvantaged people*' (p. 2060). Smillie and Hailey (2001) differentiate NGOs from NPOs by attributing a value-driven approach to NGOs that incorporates attaining justice, equity and empowerment for the poor, accompanied by promotion of full stakeholder participation, mutual learning, accountability and transparency, local self-governance, long-term sustainability and, perhaps above all, a people–centred approach (Korten, 1990). This is consistent with the World Bank definition of NGOs that includes informal organisations alongside altruistic goals;

> the myriad of organisations, some of them formally constituted, and some of them informal that are largely independent of government and that are characterised primarily by humanitarian or co-operative, rather than commercial, objectives, and that generally seek to relieve suffering, promote the interests of the poor, protect the environment, provide basic social services, or undertake community development.
>
> (World Bank, 1997a)

In summary, no consensus on defining and classifying NGOs exists: it remains notoriously vexed and resolving it has become an art form in its own right. The lack of unanimity in defining NGOs reflects different perceptions of highly ambiguous organisations working within contested moral and political domains of development policy and practice. They can exhibit a dualistic character, alternating between theoretical and practical activist discourse; public and private, and professional and amateur identities; market and non-market values; radicalism and pluralism; modernity and tradition; and ultimately, perhaps, even between good and evil. However, this chapter follows the World Bank definition to embrace a normative view of NGOs despite it possibly, not invariably, reflecting actuality.

NGOS, CIVIL SOCIETY AND GRASSROOTS ORGANISATIONS

The term NGO encompasses many types of organisations. In the development field they include research institutes, churches, professional associations and lobby groups. The World Bank classified NGOs into two main categories[4]: *operational*—where the primary purpose is designing and implementing development-related projects; and *advocacy*—where the primary purpose is defending or promoting a specific cause and influencing policies and practices. Their operational services include relief in emergencies, primary health care, non-formal education, housing and legal provision, access to microcredit and training. Advocacy NGOs purport to be agents for alleviating poverty by promoting equity and citizen participation through redistributions of economic and political power, and by expanding rural employment and income opportunities by integrating rural areas into national development initiatives and fostering democratic organisations of primary producers and rural workers by building farmers' associations, cooperatives and other voluntary, autonomous organisations. The operational and advocacy categories are not mutually exclusive: many NGOs engage in both activities, and some advocacy groups, while not directly involved in designing and implementing projects, focus on project-related concerns (Triffonova, 2005). Thus NGO activities border on and overlap with many other bodies involved in development reform, including civil society, social movements, grassroots organisations and the transnational development community.

A civil society organisation is formed by people freely associating to do something they all value and are prepared to act upon (Holloway, 1997). In other words, 'civil society' is a forum where social and environmental problems can be identified and solutions explored, shaped and formalised (Ward, 2005, p. 6). Recently the terms 'NGO' and 'civil society' are frequently used interchangeably (Ward, 2005; Howell, 2002; Frewer, 2013). This is an over-simplification, for civil society encompasses more organisations and associations beyond the state (including political parties) and the market than NGOs (Holloway, 1997). These include business associations, trade unions, NGOs, churches, human rights' groups, farmers' groups, environmental groups and women's organisations. Such long lists reflect the normative ideals of pluralism and social inclusion that are attractive to donors: their mere statement can encourage beliefs that they support a range of actors beyond merely NGOs (Howell, 2002; Lehman, 2007). Arguably every development intervention contains a welfare element (Buckland, 1999). However, whilst welfare is justifiably high when a natural disaster or civil conflict occurs, many contend that welfare aid should be minimised when poverty needs are less acute and chronic to avoid dependency. Instead NGOs should attack the underlying structural and political constraints inhibiting development (Buckland, 1999; Kaldor, 2002). This often requires working with elements of civil society.

Developmental NGOs, especially human rights and environmental ones (Clark, 1995), recognise the importance of social movements and grassroots organisations (GROs), often formed by poor and marginalised groups within civil society, to their mission (Otto, 1996). Social movements (loosely organised but sustained collective campaigns, typically directed at social change) vary in size and often emanate from spontaneous informal gatherings of people with similar views. When their collective behaviour produces sustained voluntary associations with predetermined, purposive, long-term aims a social movement is created. One or more organisations may provide leadership but their boundaries are permeable and not necessarily coterminous with those of participating organisations. Nevertheless they are political actors that shape public consciousness about social issues and political solutions (McCarthy & Zald, 1977; Unerman & O'Dwyer, 2006b), whether positively or negatively (Kebede, 2005; Buckland, 1999). Grassroots organisations (GROs) can resemble many NGOs but NGOs are officially established, run by employed staff and are often relatively large and well resourced, whereas GROs are usually smaller, membership-based organisations that operate without paid staff and rely upon donors or international/national agencies' support, which often is issue-based (Mercer, 2002).

Otto (1996) claims development NGOs evolve from operations to advocacy; i.e., move from delivering immediate relief projects to advocacy on behalf of clients over socio-economic politics and policy. Others contend that the cycle works conversely; i.e., 'new' social movements and GROs initially acting primarily as advocates transform themselves into service providers to gain credibility among local populations and/or to ensure their survival (see Kaldor, 2002; Kebede, 2005). Whatever, many development NGOs are closely involved with but distinct from social movements and GROs. NGOs claim that this widens (socially and geographically) and deepens (in terms of personal and organisational capacity) citizen participation; and the NGOs can represent and campaign within a wider public arena and thereby shift public policy towards ends sought by social movements and GROs. Such 'bottom-up democracy' can bring 'top-down political change' (Fisher, 1998, p. 126); e.g., grassroots mobilisation by the Undugu Society in a Nairobi slum empowered the local community organisations it supported to make the local state pursue their interests (Holloway, 1998; Fisher, 1998; Mercer, 2002) (see Devine (2006) and Jayasinghe and Wickramasinghe (2006) for other successful efforts).

A common belief is that NGOs represent 'civil society' whereas states represent elites.' The belief is that development NGOs can contribute to 'good governance,' particularly locally where 'the poor are normally much more concerned with, and affected by [this]' (Clark, 1995). Otto (1996) argues that NGOs represent a 'third system' between the state and the market, claiming, 'it is inevitable that the power of the non-governmental sector will at least mitigate the exercise of the economic and formal political power, and it may eventually provide an alternative that entirely transforms the cultural arrangements.' The presumption is that NGOs are more 'participatory' than the state and market structures, more 'accountable' to subordinate groups in society, that their democratic approach bolsters civil society and encourages it to challenge authoritarian states and question irregularities (Bratton, 1989; Kebede, 2005; Holloway, 1997). However, many commentators remain suspicious of claims that NGOs invariably represent civil society and promote its democratic development (Frewer, 2013; Rahmani, 2012; Lehman, 2007; Gray et al., 2006). They argue that the 'legitimacy' NGOs gain from such claims owes more to ideology and unproven assumptions of dominant institutions, which diverts attention from wider political debates about development. Understanding power within a society is crucial to understand the dynamics and philosophies of NGOs: they play a complex hegemonic role best seen as a contested image—a zone of conflict (Devine, 2006). They can further ideological struggles, build consensus within civil society, but may also reproduce prevailing, coercive political relations (Goddard, 2002). The boundaries between state and civil society are not impermeable and outcomes of their interaction remain essentially indeterminate. These debates need to be understood by the political context in which NGOs have grown.

In summary, NGOs have been and remain inextricably linked to civil society and within this GROs and social movements, with respect to advocacy and/or delivery of services especially to the marginalised and poor. Their activities are shaped not only by indigenous politics but also conditionalities of external aid and finance governed by changing fashions and policies for development.

NGO GROWTH: A SYNTHESIS

The apparent recent rise of NGOs is an illusion: NGOs or 'NGO-like organisations' are far from new. The concept of 'philanthropy'—'the ethical notions of giving and serving to those beyond one's immediate family'—has existed in different forms in most cultures throughout history, often driven by religious tradition (Ahmad & Jahan, 2002). Local 'third-sector organisations'[5] have worked relatively unnoticed in most societies for generations through religious and community groups, and organised self-help ventures in villages and towns. However, historical circumstances fashioned the growth and roles of NGOs within developing countries (Mitlin, Hickey, & Bebbington, 2007). Initially (up to the mid and late 1960s) NGOs were characterised by small organisations addressing the needs of disadvantaged poor people who lacked professional support. These NGOs, supported by public voluntary contributions, gained an institutional base and funding from a supporting organisation, often religious ones although sometimes wealthy family foundations[6] (Ahmad & Jahan, 2002; Fernando & Heston, 1997; Mitlin et al., 2007). This early non-governmental activity was alternative in that it was voluntary and normatively motivated, unlike many of the state and commercial sectors. The sponsors maintained relationships with the latter and transferred revenue through welfare development foundations (a model that continues today on a larger scale).

Many developing countries, upon gaining independence in the 1940s to 1960s, pursued socialist models of development based on central planning and industrialisation for ideological and pragmatic reasons, but also because external institutions and experts recommended this. These policies often failed and resulted in fiscal crises of the state. This heralded, in the 1980s, the rise of neoliberal development policies, often made conditions of aid by transnational financial institutions such as the World Bank. From the mid to late 1960s to the early 1980s, NGOs pursued changes in government policies and altered relations between the state, markets and civil society by developing and lobbying for new development strategies. Until the 1980s NGOs received little or no attention from governments, policy makers and researchers but subsequently they became an integral part of most poor countries' development, not least because they became fashionable amongst international aid agencies that diverted funds to them (Edwards & Hulme, 1996). Why is this so? Fortunately there is considerable research on NGO development and whilst scholars emphasise different aspects of this history, their interpretations tend to overlap.[7]

In the 1980s to early 1990s NGOs received growing recognition and increased funding of their activities, often via (sometimes contrived) relationships with the state and development agencies. Donors increasingly directed their funds for social services and welfare rather than to perceived ineffective and sometimes corrupt government agencies, and they were often perceived as potential sites of resistance to authoritarian rule. NGO collaboration with other political and social movements was often encouraged (e.g., in the Philippines, South Africa and El Salvador). Some European donors channelled resources to opposition movements via NGOs with few questions asked and without any explicit, traceable government knowledge (Mitlin et al., 2007). Governments and conservative forces used similar tactics to sustain the prevailing hegemony and resist ideas promulgated by NGOs and political movements. Channelling resources through NGOs for both ends still continues. Whatever, NGOs became important in civil society contestation of the role of the state (MacDonald, 1996; Howell & Pearce, 2001).

After the Cold War, neoliberals argued that NGOs are effective alternatives to the inefficiencies and waste of state economic planning in former socialist states and developing countries in the South. Perceptions that governments of both North and South had performed poorly in fighting poverty fed NGO development. Especially in developing countries, governments were deemed as unresponsive to people's needs, too bureaucratic, corrupt and lacking accountability (Fisher, 1998; Lewis, 2001). Established institutions such as government, churches and business often lacked popular trust. Donors' critique of 'poor governance' in the South became linked with a belief in the 'comparative advantages' of NGOs (Fowler, 1997). They were put on a pedestal as moral, people-led, less corrupt and more efficient, offering better channels for popular participation and giving more voice to marginalised people than the state, which was often depicted as venal, clientele-reliant and incompetent.

NGOs and multilateral organisations (such as World Bank, International Monetary Fund (IMF) and Asian Development Bank (ADB))—the major channels for development aid worldwide—came to dominate development discourse (Ward, 2005). The ensuing 'boom' period for NGOs must be understood in relation to structural transformations in capitalism involving state, markets and civil society relationships, namely: macroeconomic instability and crisis in many developing countries; shifts to formally liberal democracies by dictatorships and 'enlightened authoritarian' regimes; and concepts and practices such as 'civil society' and participation gaining greater centrality in dominant development discourse (Mitlin et al., 2007). Inspired by neoclassical economics, including agency theory and transaction cost economics, a widespread belief emerged that public sector reform and competition would better foster development. Put crudely, the state was seen as the problem, not the solution. Loans to rectify fiscal imbalances of Least Developed Countries (LDCs) often became conditional on adopting market-oriented reforms within structural adjustment programmes, normally involving privatisation of State-Owned Enterprises (SOEs), deregulation, reduced trade barriers and balanced budgets. 'New public sector' methods akin to private sector practices were advocated. Rather than the government directly delivering services it was recommended that private firms or NGOs be contracted to do so. Northern multilateral agencies and donors channelled their funds to Southern NGOs rather than to governments (see White, 1999; Stiles, 2002). In the 1990s, they published a flood of manuals and thousands of development workers from the South received education on the development industry in colleges in the North. Eventually though, big Southern NGOs became 'gatekeepers of knowledge' (Townsend, Porter, & Mawdsley, 2002), were well funded, could often bypass governments and deal directly with donors and assumed roles once restricted to Northern NGOs, leaving some Northern NGO employees feeling they had become managers rather than activists or development workers (Townsend et al., 2002; Malhotra, 2000). The belief was that seeing citizens as customers and reducing principal-agent conflicts through better planning and controls in the public sector would improve accountability, lessen corruption and thus increase economic growth.

However, the market-led reforms, often promulgated through structural adjustment programmes, became increasingly criticised. Judgments of such market-based reforms are divided and their results patchy and variable across jurisdictions. Nevertheless, they experienced difficulties; e.g., exacerbating inequalities; neglect of poverty reduction, social goals and environmental issues; diminished local democracy; and failures to deliver the economic growth promised. Economic growth was at best patchy. Some scholars link this and NGO growth to a theoretical 'impasse.' Mainstream macro-theories of 'modernisation' and radical 'dependency,' dominant in development economics for two decades, failed to explain low income countries' inability to develop (Booth, 1994; Lewis & Kanji, 2009). There was recognition that in the face of powerful forces, local project interventions alone cannot significantly and durably alleviate poverty: it requires changes to policy and wider norms.

Effective governance has always been deemed essential for effective development aid, but economic evidence supporting this only emerged in the late 1990s. A World Bank working paper found that aid only had a positive and significant impact in countries with sufficiently reformed policies and institutions; i.e., good governance (Burnside & Dollar, 2000). Other studies, mainly led by World Bank staff, supported this (Svensson, 1999; Collier & Dollar, 2004). Others claimed that aid may generate negative returns (Lensink & White, 2001; Guillaumont & Chauvet, 2001); e.g., high aid may erode the quality of governance of recipient countries (Brautigam, 2000; Stiles, 2002).

In the late 1990s external experts and institutions laid greater emphasis on linking economic development to 'good governance' and democracy. This has resurrected policies to strengthen the state whilst also making it more accountable to civil society. The emergence of good governance as a condition to aid in the 1990s had implications for governments, whether receivers or givers. It is difficult to achieve in practice and takes a long time to be effective. But most importantly, the political dimension of international development assistance increased. For example, World Bank Structural Adjustment Programmes (SAPs) were evaluated largely on a country's institutional and political features, such as whether the government was democratically elected and how long it had been in power (see Svensson, 1999; Collier & Dollar, 2004).

The turn to 'good governance' policies precipitated a search for alternative ideas and new participants in the development process (particularly in relation to states). The late 1990s saw a move from traditional economic and political development concerns to environmental, gender and social development issues—where a growing NGO presence and policy 'voice' were apparent (Pearce, 2006; Unerman & Bennet, 2004; O'Dwyer, 2005; Unerman & O'Dwyer, 2010). NGOs 'fitted the bill' (Booth, 1994; Clarke, 1998). Whatever, NGOs gained increased access to policy makers and got their ideas implemented through activism, campaigning and policy dialogue. Mitlin et al. (2007) has attributed the last 20 years' NGO growth (mid to late 1990s until the present) to the continued growth of the democratisation-neoliberalisation agenda; the hegemony of a poverty agenda in international aid, and more recently but perniciously, the coupling together of security and poverty agendas in strange ways. Major transnational institutions began to realise that downsizing the state was an error and attention turned to developing the 'capable state' to complement markets and broader development goals (World Bank, 1997b).

International financial institutions changed their focus, placing increased emphasis on the three components of 'triangle accountability' (World Bank, 2004). Here improved development is claimed to emanate from: the state (politicians and policy makers) through greater democracy and more effective internal and external controls; service providers (managers and frontline workers) through market disciplines and increased public choice; and citizens and clients of services through greater transparency, media and civil society involvement and elections. The aim is to build state supply-side capacity by strengthening the rule of law and protecting property rights; maintaining macroeconomic stability; investing in human resources and infrastructure; protecting the most vulnerable, especially the poor and women; and safeguarding natural resources and the environment, which arguably suffered under market-led approaches. It is recognised that states need greater capacity to deliver such ends, hence the switch of more donor funding directly into government coffers rather than to specific projects and delivery agencies such as NGOs; an emphasis on improved planning and control systems; securing better motivated, trained and remunerated civil servants; and often greater delegation of powers and resources to local government and communities. Although external funding for operational services provided by NGOs continued, the emphasis switched from welfare to microcredit, and services and advocacy that encourage and enable greater democracy, often on Western models. Increasingly Western governments linked aid to political reform, which has encouraged many NGOs to adopt a greater advocacy role.

Thus the further rise and development of NGOs marked what Edwards (2000) terms a shift from 'government' to 'governance' (see Gray et al., 2006, p. 328). Both left and right-wing theorists and practitioners, disillusioned with conventional ideas about development, became attracted to 'people-centred' approaches (Korten, 1990) and both Northern and Southern NGOs became associated with their delivery. NGOs offered opportunities for a wider range of civil interest groups to network, create alliances, gain a 'voice' and act as 'watchdogs' vis-à-vis the state and exert pressure for changes (Mercer, 2002). NGOs appeal across the political spectrum (Clarke, 1998). For liberals, NGOs help balance state and business interests and prevent them abusing their power (Lewis, 2001). For neoliberals, NGOs are private sector institutions that can encourage market behaviour (e.g., through microcredit) and privatisation through private, 'not-for-profit' action. For the left, NGOs promise a 'new politics' of social transformation with an alternative radical strategy for capturing state power and overcoming centralisation. NGOs can mean all things to people, which may explain their current ubiquity (see Clarke, 1998; Martens, 2002; Mayhew, 2005; Gray et al., 2006; Mitlin et al., 2007). Nevertheless, the major aid institutions' 'discovery' of NGOs, subsequent investment in them and their belief that NGOs deliver aid more effectively and enable civil society to secure political reform had elements of opportunism (Fisher, 1998, p. 2). It tallied with their growing promulgation of market forces alongside good governance (Edwards, 2000; Howell, 2002).

In summary, NGO sector activities gradually shifted from delivering services (now again deemed to be governments' responsibility) to more politically motivated advocacy and services. SustainAbility (2003) attribute the increased size and importance of the NGO sector to ex-communist and emerging nations embracing democracy and market-based hegemonic solutions, the communications revolution and continuing social inequality and environmental degradation (Gray et al., 2006). Others argue it filled the space left by the declining reach of the state, coupled to growing globalisation and emasculations of local political influence (Gray et al., 2006; Charnovitz, 1997; Edwards, 2000; Kaldor, Anheier, & Glasius, 2003). Globalised governance of national and everyday processes—even life and death—has become more marked—and NGOs are complicit in this (Duffield, 2005; Ferguson & Gupta, 2002; Mitlin et al., 2007). For example, transnational NGOs influence global governance and domestic social and political change (Glasius, 2006; Joachim, 2007; Koslinski & Reis, 2009). They primarily focus on the advancement of human rights, environmental protection, conflict resolution and sustainable development, but the relevance of transnational activism has created debate about the legitimacy and accountability of transitional NGOs (Collingwood & Logister, 2005), the alleged democratising influence of global civil society (Jaeger, 2007), harmful effects and limits of transnational activism (Carpenter, 2007; Fisher, 1997; Mendelson & Glenn, 2002) and its links to new forms of Western hegemony (Bob, 2005; Chandhoke, 2005). Whatever, shifts in the scale and nature of NGO activities are strongly influenced by changing ideologies and policies of Western governments and transnational financial institutions: some question whether many NGOs could stand by themselves (see Sobhan, 1997; Stiles, 2002; Mitlin et al., 2007). This has brought greater attention to the accountability of NGOs, especially with respect to their mission to empower marginalised beneficiaries and wreak popular political reform bottom-up with civil society.

NGO ACCOUNTABILITY

NGO accountability has received increasing research attention (Parker, 2005; Roberts & Scapens, 1985; Roberts, 1991; Kilby, 2006; Unerman & O'Dwyer,

2006a, 2006b; O'Dwyer & Unerman, 2007, 2008) from various per-spectives, although theoretical distinctions are not invariably clear (Gray, Kouhy, & Lavers, 1995). Some claim that: accounting representations of NGO actions affect accountability (Roberts & Scapens, 1985); demands for NGO accountability extend beyond financial procedures (Slim, 2002); and 'socialising forms of accountability' promote ethical stances (Roberts, 1991). O'Dwyer and Unerman (2007) demarcate two contrasting perspec-tives on accountability—the functional and the social. Functional account-ability in NGOs is often driven by 'patrons'—usually donors, governments and foundation trustees that concentrate on 'spending designated monies for designated purposes' (Najam, 1996, p. 342). This may bring rule-bound reports 'on mechanistic project ends' (Dillon, 2004, p. 107), prioritise effi-ciency over efficacy and assume logical and linear decision-making (John-ston & Gudergan, 2007), emphasising organisational predictability.

Such concerns produced more holistic formulations of 'social account-ability,' which presumes individuals have a moral right to participate in decisions affecting them irrespective of power (Edwards & Hulme, 2002; Najam, 1996; Ebrahim, 2003b; O'Dwyer & Unerman, 2008; Unerman & O'Dwyer, 2006b; Unerman & Bennett, 2004). These researchers recog-nise that accountability is linked to accounting representations (Roberts & Scapens, 1985), but they argue that accountability should be multifaceted. NGO accountability is more comprehensive and diverse than that for com-mercial organisations (Gray et al., 2006). NGOs are judged on both economic and non-economic criteria and have at least four categories of stakeholders to whom they should be accountable: those who shape an NGO's operat-ing environment (governments, donors); those internal to the organisation (staff, boards, supporters, subsidiaries, local partners); civil society (social movements, the general public, other NGOs); and those that NGOs often try to affect (beneficiaries, private sector, global institutions, governments) (Lee, 2004; Ebrahim, 2003b; Kovach, Neligan, & Burali, 2003; SustainAbil-ity and the Global Compact, 2003; Grant & Keohane, 2005). Some com-mentators find the tendency of functional accountability to reproduce NGOs and their clients as self-interested economic agents worrisome (Pearce, 2006) as they see their role as increasing the voice and influence to disadvan-taged groups; e.g., 'the poor, people whose rights have been violated, and the victims of war' (Slim, 2002, p. 5). For many NGO employees, mem-bers and supporters ethical and political aims are vital to their commitment (Ebrahim, 2003a, 2005; Najam, 1996) and the NGO's legitimacy rests on demonstrably helping constituents to reform the status quo. If accountabil-ity does not monitor the goals, aspirations, mission and values of all stake-holders or debars them from actively monitoring performance according to their needs, the NGO is vulnerable to charges of hypocrisy (Brown & Moore, 2001). Identifying stakeholders and their needs must go beyond functional accountability (Donaldson & Preston, 1995; Gray, Dey, Owen, Evans, & Zadek, 1997; Stoney & Winstanley, 2001; Unerman & Bennett, 2004; Unerman & O'Dwyer, 2006b).

Prior to the late 1980s many NGOs lacked rigorous, formal and systematic record keeping and accountability. They were often small; they and their employees had strong moral commitments to poverty reduction, they often were dealing with immediate humanitarian crises, they feared more upward accountability and formal performance measures would increase bureaucracy and costs, diminish internal control and flexibility and distance the NGO from its members and beneficiaries. However, as NGOs grew they tended to be less accountable towards beneficiaries, emphasising 'only' moral obligations and they became more accountable towards their donors, especially legal obligations to meet objective, predefined programme goals (Carothers & Ottaway, 2000). Even if beneficiaries wanted greater accountability they rarely had the legal or economic standing to demand it, especially when they did not pay for services received (Senbeta, 2003, p. 50).

The exponential increase in NGO funding and scale of service activities raised their individual and sector profile. Both domestic and foreign donors desired greater transparency to demonstrate effective and honest use of their contributions. They argued that this would improve future performance and make future funding more secure. Also, as funding recipients and distributors of aid, governments came to more closely regulate NGOs' activities to link them to an overall development strategy and to check that resources are distributed efficiently, honestly and effectively within legal guidelines. The declining aid trend from 1991 to 1998 (according to the 1999 Development Index, the real value of aid from the North dropped by 21%) meant that NGOs had to be more transparent to avoid a 'beyond aid scenario' where they cannot rely on Overseas Development Assistance. This produced calls for NGOs to find new funding locally and/or from business, and make 'organisational sustainability' their main goal. Previously many donor agencies were satisfied with annual narratives, financial reporting and occasional staff visits, but they increasingly emphasised results-based management. Changes in the sources, volume and conditions for funding required NGOs to gain new market-related skills regarding risk assessment, strategic planning, management and financial planning and control, along with good interpersonal, negotiating and networking skills to improve collaboration with the government and the private sector, while paying heed to public opinion (see Fowler, 2000; Malhotra, 2000). In short, the externally imposed, market-based development policies fed down to NGOs pressured them to adopt performance measures based on private sector practices. The drive for greater NGO accountability came especially from foreign donors and governments—the main disbursers of funds to NGOs.

Calls for better upward accountability were also associated with a growing 'crisis of legitimacy' of NGOs (Goddard, 2004), precipitated partly by financial scandals (see Lee, 2004; Gibelman & Gelman, 2001) and disputes over whether NGOs are more efficient, innovative, flexible and cost-effective service providers than the public sector (Smillie & Hailey, 2001; Ahmed, 2003, 2004; Fyvie & Ager, 1999; Uphoff, 1997; Carroll, 1992). Edwards and Hulme (1996, p. 963) complained that 'there is no empirical study that demonstrates a general case that NGO provision is "cheaper" than public provision' or if so, this is due to NGOs paying their employees less than government officials. In addition, the growth in scale and scope of many NGOs led them to introduce more conventional formal controls and performance management systems. For example, in researching BRAC, a large Bangladesh NGO, the authors found that its growth brought a growing emphasis on budgetary controls, performance measures and evaluation, hierarchical management and formal external reporting—especially to donors and governments—coupled to an increased emphasis on commercialisation.

The time and costs an NGO dedicates to its accountability are contentious (Lee, 2004). Greater emphasis on performance measures may decrease its tactical options (SustainAbility and The Global Compact, 2003); an emphasis on results can increase an NGO's insecurity due to fears of negative outcomes (Smillie, 1995; Carroll, 1992); greater transparency may conflict with expectations of sovereignty and confidentiality (Nelson, 1995); the agendas, time frames, goals and objectives of donor agencies and NGOs may not overlap with those of local civil society groups (Howell, 2002; Mercer, 2002); and increased stakeholder accountability may evoke tensions (not all stakeholders can be fully satisfied, and excessive bureaucracy can slow decision-making and render the benefits of involving more people lost). However, the prime worry is that the emphasis on achieving and demonstrating efficient delivery of services through formal performance measurements compounds NGO 'mission drift' from advocacy to services, denies development of downward accountability to poor and marginalised beneficiaries requiring more informal systems, prioritises commercial rather than social goals and renders clients as economic subjects; i.e., makes them customers or suppliers within the NGO's value chain rather than empowering them politically.

Becoming public service contractors may have tied NGOs into mainstream commercial approaches more, weakened the state and diminished its responsibility to provide services to the populace, transferred funds and responsibilities to institutions lacking democratic accountability to civil society and transferred delivery of welfare services normally provided by the state to organisations with insufficient capacity or financial security to provide them. NGOs may be 'flexible' but this may be because donors can manipulate them more easily than indigenous governments and NGOs will mould their activities to meet the donor's goals (Meyer, 1999). Problems can arise when NGOs get close to centres of power. Aid donors understandably want value for money, but their desire for objective demonstration of efficient delivery of projects can direct NGO activities towards measurable and easily achievable short-term targets at the expense of long-term impacts and the NGO's original mission (Desai & Howes, 1995). The growing dependency on foreign donors may render NGOs less accountable to local recipients, decrease NGOs' legitimacy within recipient communities, be detrimental to their programmes (Hulme & Edwards, 1997; Stirrat & Henkel,

1997; Shah & Shah, 1996), make NGOs compete with rather than learn from one another and be less innovative (Riddell & Robinson, 1995; White, 1999; Sanyal, 1994).

Such concerns have brought greater scrutiny of the advocacy undertaken by NGOs, whose interests they serve and their accountability (Unerman & O'Dwyer, 2006b; Fowler, 1997, 2000; Mitlin et al., 2007). The shift to good governance development policies by leading development agencies has made broader notions of accountability more central. SustainAbility (2003) identifies four major drivers of NGO accountability: *morality* (accountability is right in principle); *performance* (accountability improves effectiveness); *political space* (accountability increases credibility and thus influence), and *wider democratisation* (accountability of NGOs improves democracy in society). The belief is that better accountability will increase organisational performance and learning; demonstrate NGOs' effectiveness; improve the trust and commitment of stakeholders by demonstrating commitment to them (Brown, Moore, & Honan, 2004); and counter criticisms that NGOs practice secretive and undemocratic decision-making, lack rigorous standards of governance (Adair, 2000, p. 11) and thus become derailed from their mission and vision (Ahmad & Jahan, 2002). The drivers were derived pragmatically and inductively but they reflect the changing geo-political context in which accountability relationships operate, and their influence upon the relationship and its means of discharge (SustainAbility, 2003; Fries, 2003; Kamat, 2003; Lee, 2004).

The shift towards good governance brings increasingly acute challenges to NGOs registered in the North and the South alike over representation (Jordan & Van Tuijl, 2000; D'Cruz, 2003). Many question their right to represent social movements. In aid-dependent economies, civil society organisations and NGOs often depend on donor grants to hire staff, establish offices, organise practical activities and network. This creates tensions and constraints. The success of NGOs has increased people's envy of them and has attracted charlatans and fraud to the sector. Beliefs that they are over-reliant on public funds and 'official aid' has often damaged public perception of NGOs' nature, trustworthiness and effectiveness, leading to accusations that this has trapped many NGOs into the narrow confines and relative comfort of the aid system; diminished their accountability to civic society; rendered the transparency of their activities more opaque; made them prioritise programmes, values and agendas of donors over those of local organisations and the NGOs themselves.

The good governance route to development supplements rather than diminishes forms of accountability and performance measurement endorsed in market-led reforms. However, there is a greater emphasis on broader development goals encapsulated in the United Nations' Millennium Development Goals, namely to: eradicate extreme poverty and hunger; achieve universal primary education; promote gender equality and empower women; reduce child mortality rates; improve maternal health; combat

HIV/AIDS, malaria and other diseases; ensure environmental sustainability; and develop a global partnership for development (United Nations, 2013). Throughout, greater democracy and greater decentralisation to local levels is seen as essential as both a means and end to achieving development. Associated accounting reforms remain framed in terms of legal rational authority, but are coupled to greater democracy locally and nationally through free and fair elections and separated powers to provide checks and balances of power, and more recently, emphasis on strengthening the voice and involvement of civil society organisations, political parties, the media and external organisations such as NGOs to make public servants more accountable.

Put crudely, the new policies are akin to an adoption of social accountability principles described previously alongside strengthened functional accountability. This has brought the need for NGOs to readdress accountability and performance measure issues often neglected under previous development regimes, especially how to involve civil society in NGO's activities; being more accountable to them; developing performance measures for employees and external reporting that reflects broader development goals; increasing the participation of marginal poor clients through more informal channels; promoting democratic forces through transparent financial information; and through increased advocacy, strengthening media and civil society scrutiny of public servants.

CONCLUSIONS

This chapter discussed issues affecting the NGO sector. First, the problem of defining and classifying NGOs was seen to be vexed. Second, it has become commonplace in development discourse and practice to credit NGOs with several comparative advantages. In particular, that they are more innovative, flexible and cost-effective than government organisations (Townsend et al., 2002), are especially good at reaching and mobilising the poor in remote rural communities and they practice participatory project implementation that 'empowers' recipients rather than treating them as mere 'clients.' These claims are debatable. Similarly, the evidence that NGOs are more cost-effective than government institutions is questionable (Sanyal, 1994; Riddell & Robinson, 1995; Edwards & Hulme, 1996; Hulme & Edwards, 1997; Karim, 2001; Haque, 2002). Also, NGOs tend to fail to reach the poorest of the poor (Sanyal, 1994, p. 42; Arellano-Lopez & Petras, 1994).

Coopting NGOs into state service provision has also had repercussions for states, although the jury is out on whether they are strengthened or weakened. NGOs are considered to be capable of solving social problems, but this positive attribute is situated within the context of aid to support struggles against poverty or responses to need not covered by society. When NGOs move out of this perspective and support social or economic movements, they are regarded with mistrust, and political and economic powers try to control them or use them for their own ends (Houtart, 2001, p. 56). Besides doubting the effectiveness and efficiency of NGOs, some authors discuss the broader political consequences of NGO action. An important accusation against NGOs is collateralism with power. It is argued that to become more acceptable to governments, NGOs abandoned their early concerns with structural reform/transformation, instead retreating into the more hospitable and less politically contested territory of service provision. Many governments, wary of the political effects of NGOs, have had little choice but to concede the provision of development services to NGOs (Mercer, 2002).

However, handing over social welfare activities formerly undertaken by the state to the NGO sector can be damaging for state power. Diversion of funding from the state towards NGOs threatens state legitimacy, while continuing to undermine the ability of the state to play a role in social service provision (Tvedt, 1998; Haque, 2002, 2004). Moreover, strengthening civil society through NGOs can weaken the state. In Bangladesh, for example, the rise of NGOs has been accompanied by a decline in state legitimacy (White, 1999); Clarke (1998) describes them as a 'virtual parallel state,' whereas Wood (1997) refers to Bangladesh as a 'franchise state.' NGO accountability is increasingly considered to be upwards to the donor rather than downwards to the grassroots (Zaidi, 1999). As Gary asks, 'would not reformed state institutions be more efficient in providing social welfare services, let alone planning development, than scattered NGO efforts?' (1996, p. 163; cited by Mercer, 2002). Arellano-Lopez & Petras (1994) argue that NGOs are not agents of self-empowerment or grassroots democratisation, but rather 'Trojan horses' for a new imperialism. NGOs are accused of being economically and ideologically controlled by Western donors whose funds are conditional on the NGOs not challenging seriously the status quo; being politically unaccountable to the local populace and solely accountable to external donors; creating a new petite bourgeoisie of NGO bureaucrats benefiting from rich salaries and opportunities for international travel while grassroots, radical movements are deprived of potential leaders; actively contributing through their emphasis on 'self-help' to the dismantling of state services and protections; and being ineffectual in addressing the problems (e.g., eradication of poverty) they are concerned with (Arellano-Lopez & Petras, 1994).

The unilateral success claims made by NGOs require re-examination. Although NGOs are always praised for their positive societal roles by local and foreign advocates, a more objective analysis would demonstrate that under the facade of helping the poor, many NGOs are now guided by economic self-interest (Molla et al., 2008). Large NGOs (like BRAC, Proshika, ASA) in Bangladesh are turning into rent-seeking institutions, because they charge among the highest interest rates (20–30%) on loans given to the poor, while they themselves receive massive financial assistance from government and foreign donors at rates as low as 3% (Molla et al., 2008).

Moreover, these NGOs are now aggressively pursuing profit-making business enterprises in major economic sectors. Another important reason for the necessity of NGO is the possible distance between the high standards they publicly set for themselves and their actual practices. If the distance between goals and practices becomes very large, or very obvious, then the NGO will have a credibility gap (Fox & Brown, 1998; Edwards & Hulme, 1996; Meyer, 1999). This is a major potential source of accountability because most NGOs need credibility to survive. They need credibility with the media to have a public voice, with grassroots partners to give popular legitimacy, with elites to influence policy and with funders to gain the material support essential for institutional survival. Because different NGOs often share these same goals, there is an element of competition that creates an incentive for mutual oversight, and therefore mutual accountability. Many NGOs have also formed networks and coalitions, and these forays can serve to set at least some 'rules of the game' for NGO accountability. A detailed study in this area would enhance knowledge of accountability and credibility in this sector.

Moreover, further study is needed, with in-depth analysis of donors switching motive towards the NGO sector. NGOs often argue that they are overburdened with accountability requests while those who usually issue those requests—the donors—insist that accountability needs to be served. Much has been written about the problems of NGO management and internal accountability (Lewis, 2001; Fowler, 1997, 2000). The increased levels of bureaucracy involved in accountability often mean that the organisation loses some internal control, and results in a distancing from its members and beneficiaries. Comprehensive knowledge would enhance comprehension of the cost of accountability.

The debate about NGO accountability has been ongoing in the mainstream for more than a decade now, and is likely to continue. The nature of NGO sector accountability is a complex one as operations involve the attainment of various non-financial objectives in addition to the financial ones. The diversity of NGOs, fields of operation and stakeholders means that there can be no one, single standard by which NGOs can be judged. Several questions still require addressing, and the debate on how to best answer them is still continuing (Mitlin et al., 2007). Furthermore, the provenance of accountability mechanisms needs to be addressed in order to balance between internally driven and externally imposed accountability mechanisms (Ebrahim, 2003, p. 825).

NOTES

1 See Smillie (1995) and Najam (1996) for lists of different acronyms for NGOs use`d worldwide. These include 'non-governmental development organisation' (NGDO), 'non-profit organisation' (NPO), 'not-for-profit organisation'

(NFPO), 'private development organisation' (PDO), 'popular development agency' (PDA), 'voluntary organisation' (VO), 'voluntary agency' (sometimes shortened to 'volag'), 'private voluntary organisation' (PVO), 'charities' (commonly used in UK), 'membership organisation' (MO), 'grassroots organisation' (GRO), 'grassroots development organisation' (GRDO), 'private service organisation' (PSO), 'donor local organisation' (DLO), 'non-state actor' (NSA), 'private voluntary development organisation' (PVDO), 'voluntary development organisation' (VDO), 'community-based organisation' (CBO), 'people's organisation' (PO), 'grassroots support organisation' (GSO), 'public sector contractor' and 'value-driven organisation.'

2 They are societal actors because they originate from the private sphere. Members are individuals or local, regional, national branches of an association and not (or only to a limited extent) official members, such as governments, government representatives or government institutions (Martens, 2002).

3 NGOs promote common goals because they endeavour to provide public goods from which their members and/or the public will gain (Martens, 2002).

4 See World Bank report "NGO World Bank Collaboration" published online at www.worldbank.org.

5 Development scholars divide governments as first sector, businesses as second sector and the rest, including NGOs, as third sector (Fowler, 1997).

6 Examples are the Ford Foundation, the Aga Khan Foundation, the Gates Foundation, the Gordon Moore Foundation and the Soros Foundation.

7 For a detailed discussion of the development of NGOs, see Smillie (1995); Lewis (2001); Howell (2002); Mitlin et al. (2007) and Gray et al. (2006).

REFERENCES

Adair, A. (2000). *A code of conduct for NGOs—a necessary reform*. London: Institute of Economic Affairs.

Ahmad, M., & Jahan, R. (2002). *Investing in ourselves: Giving and fund raising in Bangladesh*. Manila, PH: Asian Development Bank.

Ahmed, S. (2003). Non-government organisations. In S. Islam (Ed.), *Banglapedia: National Encyclopaedia of Bangladesh* (pp. 325–328). Dhaka, BD: Asiatic Society of Bangladesh.

Ahmed, S. (2004). *Aid and NGOs in Bangladesh in revisiting foreign aid: A review of Bangladesh's development 2003*. Dhaka, BD: University Press Limited.

Arellano-Lopez, S., & Petras, J. (1994). Non-governmental organizations and poverty alleviation in Bolivia. *Development and Change, 25*(3), 555–568.

Ati, H. (1993). The development impact of NGO activities in the Red Sea province of Sudan: A critique. *Development and Change, 24*(1), 103–130.

Awio, G., Northcott, D., & Lawrence, S. (2011). Social capital and accountability in grass-roots NGOs. *Accounting, Auditing and Accountability Journal, 24*(1), 62–92.

Bob, C. (2005). *The marketing of rebellion: Insurgents, media, and international activism*. Cambridge, UK: Cambridge University Press.

Booth, D. (1994). How far beyond the impasse? A provisional summing-up. In D. Booth (Ed.), *Rethinking Social Development: Theory, Research and Practice*. London: Longman.

Bratton, M. (1989). The politics of government-NGO relations in Africa. *World Development, 17*(4), 407–430.

Brautigam, D. (2000). *Aid dependence and governance*. Stockholm: Almqvist and Wiksell International.

Brown, D., & Moore, M. (2001). Accountability, strategy, and international non-governmental organizations. *Nonprofit and Voluntary Sector Quarterly, 30*(3), 569–587.

Brown, D., Moore, M., & Honan, J. (2004). Building strategic accountability systems for international NGOs. *AccountAbility Forum*, 31–43.

Buckland, J. (1999). *Nongovernmental organizations as intermediaries of rural development for the poor.* New York: PACT Publications.

Burger, R., & Owens, T. (2010). Promoting transparency in the NGO sector: Examining the availability and reliability of self-reported data. *World Development, 38*(9), 1263–1277.

Burnside, C., & Dollar, D. (2000). Aid, policies and growth. *American Economic Review, 90*(4), 847–868.

Carothers, T., & Ottaway, M. (2000). The burgeoning world of civil society aid. In T. Carothers. & M. Ottaway (Eds.), *Funding Virtue, Civil Society Aid and Democracy Promotion.* Washington, DC: Carnegie Endowment for International Peace.

Carpenter, C. (2007). Setting the advocacy agenda: Theorizing issue emergence and nonemergence in transnational advocacy networks. *International Studies Quarterly, 51*(1), 99–120.

Carroll, T. (1992). *Intermediary NGOs: The supporting link in grassroots development.* West Hartford, CT: Kumarian.

Chandhoke, N. (2005). How global is global civil society? *Journal of World-Systems Research, 11*(2), 354–371.

Charnovitz, S. (1997). Two centuries of participation: NGOs and international governance. *Michigan Journal of International Law, 18*(2), 183–286.

Clark, A. (1995). Non-governmental organizations and their influence on international society. *Journal of International Affairs, 48*(2), 507–525.

Clarke, G. (1998). Nongovernmental organizations and politics in the developing world. *Political Studies, 46*(1), 36–52.

Collier, P., & Dollar, D. (2004). Development effectiveness: What have we learnt? *The Economic Journal, 114*(June), 244–271.

Collingwood, V., & Logister, L. (2005). State of the art. Addressing the INGO legitimacy deficit. *Political Studies Review, 3*(2), 175–192.

D'Cruz, D. (2003). NGOs: Chasing the corporate dollar. *Review-Institute of Public Affairs, 55*(3), 27–28.

Desai, V., & Howes, M. (1995). Accountability and participation: A case study from Bombay. In M. Edwards & D. Hulme (Eds.), *Non-government organisations: Performance and accountability beyond the magic bullet.* London: Earthscan Publications.

Devine, J. (2006). NGOs, politics and grassroots mobilisation: Evidence from Bangladesh. *Journal of South Asian Development, 1*(1), 77–99.

Dillon, E. (2004). Accountabilities and power in development relationships. *Trocaire Development Review, 4*, 105–117.

Dixon, R., Ritchie, J., & Siwale, J. (2006). Microfinance: Accountability from the grassroots. *Accounting, Auditing and Accountability Journal, 19*(3), 405–427.

Donaldson, T., & Preston, L. (1995). The stakeholder theory of the corporation: Concepts, evidence, and implications. *Academy of Management Review, 20*(1), 65–92.

Duffield, M. (2005). *Global governance and the new wars: The merger of development and security.* London: Zed Books.

Ebrahim, A. (2003a). Making sense of accountability: Conceptual perspectives for northern and southern nonprofits. *Nonprofit Management and Leadership, 14*(2), 191–212.

Ebrahim, A. (2003b). Accountability in practice: Mechanisms for NGOs. *World Development, 31*(5), 813–829.

Ebrahim, A. (2005). Accountability myopia: Losing sight of organizational learning. *Nonprofit and Voluntary Sector Quarterly, 34*(1), 56–87.

Edwards, M. (2000). *NGO rights and responsibilities: A new deal for global governance.* London: The Foreign Policy Centre/NCVO.

Edwards, M., & Hulme, D. (1996). Too close for comfort? The impact of official aid on nongovernmental organisations. *World Development, 24*(6), 961–973.

Edwards, M., & Hulme, D. (2002). Beyond the magic bullet? Lessons and conclusions. In M. Edwards. & A. Fowler (Eds.), *NGO Management.* London: Earthscan.

Ferguson, J., & Gupta, A. (2002). Spatializing states: Towards an ethnography of neoliberal governmentality. *American Ethnologist, 29*(4), 981–1002.

Fernando, J., & Heston, A. (1997). Between states, markets, and civil society. *The Annals of the American Academy of Political and Social Science, 554*, 8–21.

Fisher, F. (1997). Doing good? The politics and anti-politics of NGO practices. *Annual review of anthropology, 26*, 439–464.

Fisher, J. (1998). *Nongovernments: NGOs and the political development of the third world.* Hartford, CT: Kumarian.

Fowler, A. (1997). *Striking a balance: A guide to enhancing the effectiveness of nongovernmental organisations in international development.* London: Earthscan.

Fowler, A. (2000). *The virtuous spiral: A guide to sustainability for NGOs in international development.* London: Earthscan.

Fox, J., & Brown, L. (1998). *The struggle for accountability: The World Bank, NGOs, and grassroots movements.* Cambridge, MA: MIT Press.

Frewer, T. (2013). Doing NGO work: The politics of being 'civil society' and promoting 'good governance' in Cambodia. *Australian Geographer, 44*(1), 97–114.

Fries R. (2003). The legal environmental of civil society. In M. Kaldor, H. Anheier, & M. Glasius (Eds.), *Global Civil Society* (pp. 221–238). Oxford, UK: Oxford University Press.

Fyvie, C., & Ager, A. (1999). NGOs and innovation: Organizational characteristics and constraints in development assistance work in the Gambia. *World Development, 27*(8), 1383–1395.

Gary, I. (1996). Confrontation, co-operation or co-optation: NGOs and the Ghanaian state during structural adjustment. *Review of African Political Economy, 23*(68), 149–168.

Gauri, V., & Galef, J. (2005). NGOs in Bangladesh: Activities, resources, and governance. *World Development, 33*(12), 2045–2065.

Gibelman, M., & Gelman, S. (2001). Very public scandals: Nongovernmental organizations in trouble. *Voluntas, 12*(1), 49–61.

Gibelman, M., & Gelman, S. (2004). A loss of credibility: Patterns of wrongdoing among nongovernmental organizations. *Voluntas, 15*(4), 355–382.

Glasius, M. (2006). *The international criminal court: A global civil society achievement.* London: Routledge.

Goddard, A. (2002). Development of the accounting profession and practices in the public sector—a hegemonic analysis. *Accounting, Auditing, and Accountability Journal, 15*(5), 655–688.

Goddard, A. (2004). Budgetary practices and accountability habitus: A grounded theory. *Accounting, Auditing and Accountability Journal, 17*(4), 543–577.

Gordenker, L., & Weiss, T. (1995). Pluralising global governance: Analytical approaches and dimensions. *Third World Quarterly, 16*(3), 358–387.

Grant, R., & Keohane, R. (2005). Accountability and abuses of power in world politics. *American Political Science Review, 99*(1), 29–43.

Gray, E., Kouhy, R., & Lavers, S. (1995). Corporate social and environmental reporting: A review of the literature and a longitudinal study of UK disclosure. *Accounting, Auditing and Accountability Journal, 8*(2), 47–77.

Gray, R., Bebbington, J., & Collison, D. (2006). NGOs, civil society and accountability: Making the people accountable to capital. *Accounting, Auditing and Accountability Journal, 19*(3), 319–348.

Gray, R., Dey, C., Owen, D., Evans, R., & Zadek, S. (1997). Struggling with the praxis of social accounting: Stakeholders, accountability, audits and procedures. *Accounting, Auditing and Accountability Journal, 10*(3), 325–364.

Guillaumont P., & Chauvet, L. (2001). Aid and performance: A reassessment. In N. Hermes & R. Lensink (Eds.), *Changing Conditions for Development Aid: A New Paradigm?* London: Frank Cass.

Haque, M. S. (2002). The changing balance of power between the government and NGOs in Bangladesh. *International Political Science Review, 23*(4), 413–437.

Haque, M. S. (2004). Governance based on partnership with NGOs: Implications for development and empowerment in rural Bangladesh. *International Review of administrative Sciences, 70*(2), 271–290.

Holloway, R. (1997). *NGOs: Loosing the moral high ground—corruption and misrepresentation.* Paper presented at 8th International Anti-Corruption Conference, Lima, PE. Retrieved from http://www.8iacc.org/papers/holloway.html

Holloway, R. (1998). *Supporting citizens' initiatives: Bangladesh's NGOs and society.* Dhaka, BD: University Press Limited.

Houtart, F. (2001). Alternatives to the neoliberal model. In F. Houtart & F. Polet (Eds.), *The other Davos: The globalization of resistance to the world economic system* (pp. 47–59). London: Zed Books.

Howell, J. (2002). In their own image: Donor assistance to civil society. *Lusotopie, 1*, 117–130.

Howell, J., & Pearce, J. (2001). *Civil society and development: A critical exploration.* London: Lynne Rienner Publishers.

Hulme, D., & Edwards, M. (1997). *NGOs, states and donors: Too close for comfort?* London: Macmillan.

Hulme, D., & Moore, K. (2007). Why has microfinance been a policy success? Bangladesh (and beyond). In A. Bebbington & W. McCourt (Eds.), *Statecraft in the south: Public policy success in developing countries.* London: Palgrave Macmillan.

Jaeger, H. (2007). Global civil society and the political depoliticization of global governance. *International Political Sociology, 1*(3), 257–277.

Jayasinghe, K., & Wickramasinghe, D. (2006). Can NGOs deliver accountability? Realities, predictions and difficulties: The case of Sri Lanka. In H. Bhargava & D. Kumar (Eds.), *NGOs: Role and accountability: An introduction* (pp. 296–327). India: The ICFAI University Press.

Joachim, J. (2007). *Agenda setting, the UN, and NGOs. Gender violence and reproductive rights.* Washington, DC: Georgetown University Press.

Johnston, J., & Gudergan, S. P. (2007). Governance of public—private partnerships: Lessons learnt from an Australian case? *International Review of Administrative Sciences, 73*(4), 569–582.

Jordan, L., & Van Tuijl, P. (2000). Political responsibility in transnational NGO advocacy. *World Development, 28*(12), 2051–2065.

Kaldor, M. (2002). Civil society and accountability. *Human Development Report Office Occasional Paper.* Geneva: UNDP.

Kaldor, M., Anheier, H., & Glasius, M. (2003). Global civil society in an era of regressive globalisation. In Kaldor, M., Anheier, H., & Glasius, M. (Eds.), *Global Civil Society*, 3–33. Oxford, UK: Oxford University Press.

Kamat, S. (2003). NGOs and the new democracy. *Harvard International Review*, Spring, 65–69.

Karim, L. (2001). Politics of the poor? NGOs and grassroots political mobilization in Bangladesh. *Political and Legal Anthropology Review, 24*(1), 92–107.

Kebede, A. (2005). Grassroot environmental organizations in the United States: A Gramscian analysis. *Sociological Inquiry, 75*(1), 81–108.

Kilby, P. (2006). Accountability for empowerment: Dilemmas facing non-governmental organizations. *World Development, 34*(6), 951–963.

Korten, D. C. (1990). *Getting to the 21st century: Voluntary action and the global agenda.* West Hartford, CT: Kumarian Press.

Koslinski, C., & Reis, E. (2009). Transnational and domestic relations of NGOs in Brazil. *World Development, 37*(3), 714–725.

Kovach, H., Neligan, C., & Burali, S. (2003). *Power without accountability? The global accountability report 1.* London: One World Trust. Retrieved from http://www.globalpolicy.org/ngos/intro/general/2003/0120account.pdf

Lee, J. (2004). *NGO accountability: Rights and responsibilities, programme on NGOs and civil society.* Centre for Applied Studies in International Negotiations (CASIN). Retrieved from http://www.icomfloripa.org.br/transparencia/wp-cont ent/uploads/2009/06/ngo_accountability_rights_and_responsibilities.pdf

Lehman, G. (2007). The accountability of NGOs in civil society and its public spheres. *Critical Perspectives on Accounting, 18*(6), 645–669.

Lensink, R., & White, H. (2001). Are there negative returns to aid? In N. Hermes & R. Lensink (Eds.), *Changing conditions for development aid: A new paradigm?* London: Frank Cass.

Lewis, D. (2001). *The management of non-governmental development organisa-tions.* London: Routledge.

Lewis, D. (2004). On the difficulty of studying civil society: NGOs, state and democ-racy in Bangladesh. *Contributions to Indian Sociology, 38*(3), 299–322.

Lewis, D., & Kanji, N. (2009). *Non-governmental organizations and development.* London: Routledge.

MacDonald, L. (1996). Globalizing civil society: Interpreting NGOs in Central America. *Millennium: Journal of International Studies, 23*(2), 267–285.

Malhotra, K. (2000). NGOs without aid: Beyond the global soup kitchen. *Third World Quarterly, 21*(4), 669–683.

Martens, K. (2002). Mission impossible? Defining nongovernmental organizations. *Voluntas, 13*(3), 271–285.

Mayhew, S. H. (2005). Hegemony, politics and ideology: The role of legislation in NGO–government relations in Asia. *Journal of Development Studies, 41*(5), 727–758.

McCarthy, J. D., & Zald, M. N. (1977). Resource mobilization and social move-ments: A partial theory. *American Journal of Sociology, 82*(6), 1212–1241.

Mendelson, S., & Glenn, J. (2002). *The power and limits of NGOs.* New York: Columbia University Press.

Mercer, C. (2002). NGOs, civil society and democratization: A critical review of the literature. *Progress in Development Studies, 2*(1), 5–22.

Meyer, C. (1999). The economics and politics of NGOs in Latin America. Connecti-cut: Praeger.

Mitlin, D., Hickey, S., & Bebbington, T. (2007). Reclaiming development? NGOs and the challenge of alternatives. *World Development, 35*(10), 1699–1720.

Molla, R. I., Alam, M. M., & Wahid, A.N.M. (2008). Questioning Bangladesh's microcredit. *Challenge: The Magazine of Economic Affairs, 51*(6), 113–121.

Najam, A. (1996). NGO accountability: A conceptual framework. *Development Policy Review, 14*(4), 339–353.

Nelson, P. J. (1995). *The World Bank and nongovernmental organizations: The limits of apolitical development*. New York: St Martins Press.

O'Dwyer, B. (2005). The construction of a social account: A case study in an overseas aid agency. *Accounting, Organizations and Society, 30*(3), 279–296.

O'Dwyer, B., & Unerman, J. (2007). From functional to social accountability: Transforming the accountability relationship between funders and non-governmental development organisations. *Accounting, Auditing and Accountability Journal, 20*(3), 446–471.

O'Dwyer, B., & Unerman, J. (2008). The paradox of greater NGO accountability: A case study. *Accounting, Organizations and Society, 33*(7–8), 801–824.

O'Dwyer, B., & Unerman, J. (2010). Enhancing the role of accountability in promoting the rights of beneficiaries of development NGOs. *Accounting & Business Research, 40*(5), 451–471.

Otto, D. (1996). Nongovernmental organizations in the United Nations system: The emerging role of international civil society. *Human Rights Quarterly, 18*(1), 107–141.

Parker, L. (2005). Social and environmental accountability research: A view from the commentary box. *Accounting, Auditing and Accountability Journal, 18*(6), 842–860.

Pearce, J. (2006). Development, NGOs, and civil society: The debate and its future. In D. Eade (Ed.), *Development, NGOs, and Civil Society*. Oxford, UK: Oxfam.

Rahmani, R. (2012). Donors, beneficiaries, or NGOs: Whose needs come first? A dilemma in Afghanistan. *Development in Practice, 22*(3), 295–304.

Riddell, R., & Robinson, M. (1995). *NGOs and rural poverty alleviation*. Oxford, UK: Clarendon Press.

Roberts, J. (1991). The possibilities of accountability. *Accounting, Organizations and Society, 16*(4), 355–368.

Roberts, J., & Scapens, R. (1985). Accounting systems and systems of accountability. *Accounting, Organizations and Society, 10*(4), 443–456.

Salamon, L., & Anheier, H. (1992). In search of the non-profit sector: In search of definitions. *Voluntas, 13*(2), 125–152.

Sanyal, B. (1994). *Cooperative autonomy: The dialectic of state-NGOs relationship in developing countries* [Monograph]. Geneva: International Institute for Labour Studies.

Senbeta, A. (2003). Non governmental organizations and development with reference to the Benelux countries. *Document de travail No.19*. Leuven, BE: Université catholique de Louvain.

Shah, P., & Shah, M. (1996). Participatory methods for increasing NGO accountability. In M. Edwards & D. Hulme (Eds.), *Beyond the magic bullet* (pp. 215–225). West Hartford, CT: Kumarian.

Slim, H. (2002). *By what authority? The legitimacy and accountability of nongovernmental organisations*. International Meetings on Global Trends and Human Rights-Before and After September 11th, Geneva.

Smillie, I. (1995). *The Almas Bazar: Altruism under fire—non-profit organisations and international development*. London: Intermediate Technology Publications.

Smillie, I., & Hailey, J. (2001). *Managing for change: Leadership, strategy and management in Asian NGO*. London: Earthscan.

Sobhan, B. (1997). Partners or contractors? The relationship between official agencies and NGOs: Bangladesh. *Occasional Paper Series 14*, Oxford, UK: The International NGO Training and Research Centre.

Stiles, K. (2002). International support for NGOs in Bangladesh: Some unintended consequences. *World Development, 30*(5), 835–846.

Stirrat, R., & Henkel, H. (1997). The development gift: The problem of reciprocity in the NGO world. *Annals of the American Academy of Political and Social Science, 55*(4), 66–81.

Stoney, C., & Winstanley, D. (2001). Stakeholding: Confusion or utopia? Mapping the conceptual terrain. *Journal of Management Studies, 38*(5), 603–626.

SustainAbility. (2003). *The 21st Century NGO*. London: SustainAbility.

SustainAbility and the Global Compact. (2003). *Summary of the Workshop. Who Guards the Guardians?* New York: SustainAbility.

Svensson, J. (1999). Aid, growth and democracy. *Economics and Politics, 11*(3), 275–297.

Tembo, F. (2003). The multi-image development NGO: An agent of the new imperialism? *Development in Practice, 13*(5), 527–532.

Temple, D. (1997). NGOs: A Trojan horse. In M. Rahnema & V. Bawtree (Eds.), *The Post-Development Reader*. London: Zed Books.

Townsend, J. G., Porter, G., & Mawdsley, E. (2002). The role of the transnational community of non-government organisations: Governance or poverty reduction? *Journal of International Development, 14*(6), 829–839.

Townsend, J., & Townsend, A. (2004). Accountability, motivation and practice: NGOs north and south. *Social and Cultural Geography, 5*(2), 271–285.

Triffonova, E. (2005). Civil society—key element of post-cold war zeitgeist. In Güneş-Ayata. In A. Ergun & I. Çelimli (Eds.), *Black Sea politics: Political culture and civil society in an unstable region*. London: I. B. Tauris.

Turner, M., & Hulme, D. (1997). *Governance, administration and development: Making the state work*. London: Macmillan.

Tvedt, T. (1998). *Angels of mercy or development diplomats*. Oxford, UK: James Curry.

Unerman, J., & Bennett, M. (2004). Increased stakeholder dialogue and the internet: Towards greater corporate accountability or reinforcing capitalist hegemony? *Accounting, Organizations and Society, 29*(7), 685–707.

Unerman, J., & O'Dwyer, B. (2006a). On James Bond and the importance of NGO accountability. *Accounting, Auditing and Accountability Journal, 19*(3), 305–318.

Unerman, J., & O'Dwyer, B. (2006b). Theorising accountability for NGO advocacy. *Accounting, Auditing and Accountability Journal, 19*(3), 349–376.

Unerman, J., & O'Dwyer, B. (2010). NGO accountability and sustainability issues in the changing global environment. *Public Management Review, 12*(4), 475–486.

Unerman, J., & O'Dwyer, B. (2012). Accounting and accountability for NGOs. In T. Hopper, M. Tsamenyi, S. Uddin, & D. Wickramasinghe (Eds.), *Handbook of accounting and development*. Cheltenham, UK: Edward Elgar.

United Nations. (2013). *The Millennium Development Goals report 2013*, New York: United Nations. Retrieved from: http://www.undp.org/content/dam/undp/library/MDG/english/mdg-report-2013-english.pdf

Uphoff, N. (1997). Why NGOs are not a third sector: A sectoral analysis with some thoughts on accountability, sustainability and evaluation. In D. Hulme & M. Edwards (Eds.), *Too close for comfort? NGOs, states and donors* (pp. 17–30). London: Macmillan.

Vakil, A. (1997). Confronting the classification problem: Toward a taxonomy of NGOs. *World Development, 25*(12), 2057–2071.

Vivian, J., & Maseko, G. (1994). *NGOs, participation and rural development: Testing the assumptions with evidence from Zimbabwe*. Geneva: UN Research Institute for Social Development.

Ward, T. (2005). The political economy of NGOs. In J. Ward (Ed.), *Development, social justice and civil society: An introduction to the political economy of NGOs*. Minnesota: Paragon House.

White, S. (1999). NGOs, civil society, and the state in Bangladesh: The politics of representing the poor. *Development and Change, 30*(2), 307–326.

Wood, G. (1997). States without citizens: The problems of the franchise state in Bangladesh. In M. Edwards & D. Hulme (Eds.), *Too close for comfort? NGOs, states and donors*. London: Macmillan.

Wootliff, J., & Deri, C. (2001). NGOs: The new super brands. *Corporate Reputation Review, 4*(2), 157–165.

World Bank. (1997a). *Handbook of good practices for laws relating to NGOs: Discussion draft.* NGO Unit. Washington, DC: World Bank.

World Bank. (1997b). *World development report 1997: The state in a changing world.* New York: Oxford University Press.

World Bank. (2004). *World development report 2004: Making services work for poor people.* New York: Oxford University Press.

Wright, G. (2012). NGOs and Western hegemony: Causes for concern and ideas for change. *Development in Practice, 22*(1), 123–134.

Zaidi, S. (1999). NGO failure and the need to bring back the state. *Journal of International Development, 11*(2), 259–271.

3 Terrorists and Tax-Cheats
Transforming Accountability in U.S. Nonprofits

Leslie S. Oakes

INTRODUCTION

The attacks on the World Trade Center in 2001 had far-reaching consequences both inside and outside the United States. Major armed conflicts in Afghanistan and Iraq followed almost immediately. Within months, the United States government was granted expanded legal ability to conduct surveillance of private citizens. Airline safety measures were heightened and in some communities, most notably Arab-American communities, U.S. citizens and residents experienced increased government scrutiny and discrimination. These events could, perhaps, be expected given the dramatic loss of life and destruction of property on that day.

What could not be anticipated were the changes in the U.S. nonprofit sector triggered by the attacks, changes that are arguably the most significant in almost half a century. In the five years following 9/11, nonprofit regulatory scrutiny was expanded at both the federal and state level, creating a corresponding increase in the compliance burden placed on charities and other nonprofits. The Internal Revenue Service (IRS) Form 990 that most nonprofits are required to file annually was substantially altered to allow the IRS and the Treasury Department easier access to information about foreign donors and clients, executive compensation, conflicts of interest and lobbying activities. Most states increased filing requirements for both nonprofits and professional fundraisers. In some cases, audit requirements were tightened or expanded (Guidestar, 2011). Most significantly, newly enacted compliance regulations, coupled with expanded electronic access to documents submitted to state and federal regulators, created unpredictable vulnerability for nonprofit organizations.

The result of these changes has been dramatic. Few nonprofits were proven to have links to active terrorist organizations. Within a decade, however, the IRS, using its newly enacted powers, had revoked the essential 501(c) tax-exempt status of over 275,000 nonprofits (Blackwood & Roeger, 2011). This status allows donors to deduct donations from their own personal or corporate taxes. Many donors will not contribute to organizations lacking 501(c) status; most state and federal agencies will not fund nonprofits that do not have current status. Further, obtaining 501(c) status from the IRS is an arduous and expensive process. As a result, losing this status is costly financially and often leads to organizational demise. While some experts have argued that most of the organizations whose status was revoked were already defunct, over 50,000 nonprofits had filed for reinstatement as of 2013 (Lough, 2013). Some of the revoked organizations were significant in size. Each of the 50 largest revoked nonprofits had previously report over $10 million in annual revenue. Three revoked organizations had reported over $100 million in revenue in recent filings.

Perhaps more importantly, some organizations that lost their tax-exempt status played a significant role locally. Thousands of small nonprofits that provided meaningful services in some of the U.S.'s most vulnerable communities were swept up in the IRS regulations. For some nonprofits, losing their status has ended their ability to continue their valuable work. For others, the additional regulatory burden has caused them to curtail program activities and direct their energy toward meeting complex and changing federal and state compliance requirements.

Finally, and perhaps most troubling, the increased scrutiny came with few additional resources to assist nonprofits to improve their governance. In most cases, neither additional financial resources nor local expertise has emerged to solve long-running problems of inadequate accountability, abuse of the tax deductions allowed for donations and, in some cases, outright fraud in this sector that now accounts for at least 10% of the U.S. economy (Roeger, Blackwood, & Pettijohn, 2012).

This chapter reviews the discourse surrounding these dramatic events and documents the changes that occurred in that discourse, noting the lack of focus on traditional, accounting-based reports as a form of accountability. It begins with a review of the backdrop to the Senate hearings that became a driving force for increased scrutiny, but that failed to identify additional funding to help organizations meet heightened compliance requirements. The chapter reviews how the hearings were structured and how they promoted public discussion of nonprofit misbehavior. It reviews the reaction of the nonprofit sector that was primarily concerned with avoiding direct government oversight and the possibility of even more expensive regulations. Finally, the chapter draws several conclusions about the twin tracks that expanded surveillance has taken in the United States, one that uses blunt instruments amenable to electronic, low-cost enforcement and one that relies on public scrutiny instead of direct government oversight.

THE BACKDROP

The stories of nonprofit abuse and poor governance that followed the 9/11 attacks are not new. The federal tax deduction for charitable donations was first enacted in 1917; controversy around these donations commenced almost immediately. In fact, the hearings covered in this paper follow at least three earlier episodes of legislative displeasure over the role of nonprofits in the United States. The first occurred in 1912 when, following a bombing of the Los Angeles Times building, a special commission was struck to investigate the role of private foundations in creating poor labor conditions (Brilliant, 2001). In 1953, a second commission was charged with investigating the role of nonprofits in fermenting labor unrest and communist agitation. That commission, called the Reece Committee after the Congressman who led the investigations, argued that nonprofits played a central role in influencing legislation that Reece did not like. Although the Reece Commission was unsuccessful in proving leftist influence was widespread, the results were far reaching. For example, the Committee was able to stunt or eliminate organizations supporting women's right to birth control, immigrant rights and other groups advocating civil rights (Garcilazo, 2001). Legislation that followed those hearings limited the ability of nonprofits to advocate for specific policies and political candidates, issues that remain important and controversial today.

The third period in which nonprofit governance was challenged occurred in the late 1960s and early 1970s, another period of cultural unrest in the United States; although that episode seems to have been prompted by the need to generate revenue to fund war efforts in Vietnam. These earlier episodes provide lessons relevant to the events following 9/11 in that prior regulatory efforts were also prompted by 'calamities;' that is, events that are viewed as critical and unpredictable, yet that revealed chasms in the public life that appeared to demand repair.

THE LEADING EDGE OF THE PERFECT STORM

Within days of the 9/11 attacks, President George W. Bush signed an executive order freezing the U.S. assets of several nonprofit organizations, declaring, 'just to show you how insidious these terrorists are, they often times use nice sounding non-governmental organizations as fronts for their activities. We have targeted three such NGOs' (Bush, 2001). Within days, two important federal committees, the Senate Committee on Finance and the House Committee on Ways and Means, began holding hearings to explore the role of nonprofits in financing terrorists.

Charles Grassley, an influential Senator from Iowa, phrased their concern this way:

> Many of these groups not only enjoy tax-exempt status, but their reputations as charities and foundations often allows them to escape scrutiny, making it easier to hide and move their funds to other groups and individuals who threaten our national security. This support for the machinery of terrorism not only violates the law and tax regulations,

but it violates the trust that citizens have in the large majority of charities, foundations and other groups that do good works in the United States. Government officials, investigations by federal agencies and the Congress, and other reports have identified the crucial role that charities and foundations play in terror financing. While much attention has been paid to where their money ends up, the source of their funds is equally important. Often these groups are nothing more than shell companies for the same small group of people, moving funds from one charity to the next charity to hide the trail.

(Grassley, 2003)

In fact, the early hearings resulted in few actual regulatory changes. The Treasury Department, utilizing special powers granted by President Bush's Executive Order 13224, released 'Anti-Terrorist Financing Guidelines: Voluntary Best Practices for U.S.-Based Charities' in November 2002. These guidelines, which were revised in 2005, were intended 'to assist charities that attempt in good faith to protect themselves from terrorist abuse and are not intended to address the problems of organizations that intend to use the cover of charitable work, whether real or perceived, to provide support to terrorist groups' (U.S. Treasury Department, 2005, p. 1). This document reviews basic steps for good nonprofit governance and then suggests that nonprofits compare donor, client and employee lists against the State Department and United Nations' terror watch lists (Jarnal, 2011). Later, the IRS also provided guidance to nonprofits either accepting donations from or granting funds to non-domestic organizations (Office of Chief Counsel, Internal Revenue Service, 2004). This legal memorandum delineates the steps domestic nonprofits must follow when working outside of the United States. In order to protect their tax-exempt status and to allow donors to take a tax deduction for contributions that support foreign activities, the IRS requires organizations to certify that foreign organizations and individuals who receive their aid would satisfy IRS requirements for a domestic organization applying for 501(c) status. In other words, the domestic nonprofit must ensure activities are mission driven, comply with U.S. rules for nonprofit governance and account for the use of funds as they would domestically.

Despite the U.S. government's stated concerns about links between nonprofits and terrorist organizations, few connections were publically documented. The Treasury Department, utilizing special powers granted by President Bush's Executive Order 13224, targeted seven nonprofits publically, designating six charities as Specially Designated Global Terrorist, or SDGT, organizations. Ultimately, only two nonprofits were actually charged with aiding terrorism and in one case, those involved were acquitted (American Civil Liberties Union, 2009).

Although the issue of nonprofits supporting terrorism was often mentioned in media reports immediately following the actual attacks, it soon fell out of public reports all together. During the next four years, the U.S. media focused on the role of nonprofits in disaster relief, beginning with the controversy surrounding the distribution of over $1 billion in donations for victims of the 9/11 attacks. Although Congressional hearing intensified during this period, their focus shifted away from links to terrorists. For example, at a 2004 Senate hearing titled 'Charity Oversight and Reform: Keeping Bad Things from Happening to Good Charities,' Senator Max Baucaus listed the important topics for the hearing as inflated salaries, insider dealing, abusive tax shelters and, finally, 'charities serving as conduits to finance terrorist activities and operations' (Barnett, 2002, p. 1). Senator Charles Grassley of Iowa, who had been outspoken on the subject earlier, did not mention terrorist activities in his opening statement and terrorism was rarely mentioned in hearing testimony. Although the events of 9/11 prompted the renewed Congressional oversight, it served as the opening edge of a perfect storm. Other events including Hurricane Katrina and public scandals at the U.S. Red Cross and United Way—two of the largest charities in the United States—changed the way concerns about nonprofits were framed. As noted by Diana Aviv, President and CEO of the Independent Sector, in the year after the attacks, other indirect effects surpassed terrorism in 'catapulted the charitable sector into new heights of visibility resulting in media scrutiny and the expression of Congressional and public concerns regarding the distribution of some funds that had been collected' (quoted in Vartabedian, 2005, p. 6).

THE STORM SPREADS

Despite the futility of the Senate Finance Committee's search for terrorists, Senator Grassley, his staff and several large news outlets continued to argue that there was something very wrong in the world of U.S. nonprofits. The wording here is important. Events external to these hearings (specifically the collection of 9/11 donations and the massive destruction along the Gulf Coast following Hurricane Katrina) provided additional evidence of nonprofit mismanagement, but as noted earlier, the history of U.S. charities has been marked by periods of public anxiety over the role and operation of tax-exempt organizations. However, this public fretting has often led to little congressional legislation. The major difference between this period and earlier periods when hearings led to few changes in federal oversight was the stubborn persistence and finesse Senate Grassley exhibited in framing these debates as crisis.

The first of the 'framed' events involved the American Red Cross, which reported revenues of between $2 and $3 billion each year over the last two decades. The American Red Cross collected over $1.5 billion in donations following 9/11, an unprecedented amount given that the disaster did not require the Red Cross to house or feed displaced people in its normal manner.

Public outrage, supported by media accounts, grew as it was revealed that not every dollar collected would be contributed to the remaining efforts to retrieve human remains from the three disaster sites, nor would the dollars be passed on to survivors. In fact, the Red Cross planned to retain up to 25% of the donations for general administration and for smaller local disasters like house fires and limited regional flooding. These are both categories that are traditionally difficult to fund and there was never any substantive proof that the Red Cross wasted the additional dollars or that individuals benefited inappropriately. However, donors across the U.S. remained angry that their donations did not go where they intended (Wilhelm, 2002).

Concerned U.S. residents also donated so much blood following 9/11 that it is estimated that one in five donations was destroyed when the blood passed the 41-day shelf life. Smaller blood banks questioned the Red Cross's decision to continue to collect a perishable product when there were few injured survivors who could benefit from these supplies.

In response, Charles Grassley, who was not the chair of the Senate Finance Committee but its ranking republican, called for federal oversight of all 9/11 donations (Philanthropy News Digest, 2001). He also called for widening the hearings on nonprofits in general, arguing:

> It's obvious from the abuses we see that there's been no check on charities. Big money, tax-free, and no oversight have created a cesspool in too many cases. It's alarming to see tax-exempt organizations become willing partners in tax shelters used by corporations and wealthy individuals to avoid or minimize their taxes. We see powerful insiders using the assets of charities to line their own pockets instead of to help the needy. Donations and assets are being used for things like private jets and European vacations. We have to clean this up so charities keep the trust of the American people.
>
> (Senate Committee on Finance, 2004)

In addition to public outrage over the Red Cross's handling of both blood and dollars, other stories of nonprofit mismanagements emerged in these hearings. The United Way, a charity that distributes funds to other organizations and often tops *Forbes* list of the 50 largest U.S. charities, was accused of double counting donations to overstate its importance. The Nature Conservancy, an organization that purchases land to be kept undeveloped, was found to be making loans to its officers, board members and to the officers of several private companies from which it purchased land. Some of the Nature Conservancies donors were accused of taking tax exemptions for donated easements that greatly exceeded the actual market value of the donation. Witnesses from the IRS and other experts reported the widespread practice of overstating the value of used cars donated to charities, thereby overstating their deductions. Art collectors donated their collections to museums, but kept control over the artworks. Finally, the Make-a-wish

Foundation (Lipman, 2002) and several organizations that depend on professional fundraisers were accused of spending so much to raise dollars that few funds ever found their way into the hands of dying children.

In all of these cases, public attention was directed to nonprofit malfeasance by a delicate dance of public reporting and Senate action, usually in the form of a hearing or letter sent by Grassley to the entity in question (Johnson, 2005). Grassley's staff strategically released the letters he sent to the Red Cross, United Way and Nature Conservancy to the media (Senate Committee on Finance, 2007). This action essentially forced these organizations to respond formally in letters and documents that also found their way into the press. Grassley's letters kept the image of faltering (and in some cases, evil) nonprofits on the front page of major newspapers across the U.S. Because Grassley's letters were detailed and well researched, the letters in response were extensive and detailed—the letter to the Red Cross was 47 pages long, for example. Thus, the response letters provided significant meat for the national press (Strom, 2005).

As Pablo Eisenberg, a senior fellow at the Georgetown Public Policy, summarized in his 2004 Senate testimony:

> The rapid expansion of the [nonprofit] sector, the heightened focus on charities after September 11 and the investigative reporting of the *New York Times*, *Boston Globe* and other major newspapers have turned the spotlight on what was a well hidden facet of nonprofit life. There are many more "bad apples" than most of us believe exist.
>
> (2004)

THE STAFF DISCUSSION DRAFT

In addition to hearings and press releases, Grassley's staff produced a discussion draft in 2005 that was publically released by the Senate Committee on Finance. The recommendations contained in the draft were directed specifically at 501(c) organizations—those organizations that depend on receiving donations from donors who then take a personal tax deduction. The introductory paragraph describes the document this way:

> The document reflects proposals for reforms and best practices in the area of tax-exempt organizations based on staff investigations and research as well as proposals from practitioners, officers and directors of charities, academia and other interested parties. This document is a work-in-progress and is meant to encourage and foster additional comments and suggestions as the Finance Committee continues to consider possible legislation.
>
> (Senate Committee on Finance, 2005, p. 11)

Staff discussion papers rarely receive the kind of attention this draft received from both the media and the nonprofit sector itself. This focus resulted in part because the discussion draft's first recommendation threw down a gauntlet that shook the sector to its core. The first recommendation was that all tax-exempt organizations be required to reapply or renew their coveted 501(c) status every five years. This filing would be extensive, including much of the information in the original IRS Form 1023 or 1024 applications for 501(c) status. The renewal requests would be required to include articles of incorporation, bylaws and conflict of interest policies. Management would be required to provide detailed discussions of the organizations' 'practices' and, finally, would include financial statements. In addition, the discussion draft suggested that all the information contained in the renewal documents be made publically available. Further, the proposal threatened to revoke current tax-exempt status for failure to file this five-year review.

The Committee on Finance's staff document included a second proposal that created similar, if not greater, anxiety. The draft raised the issue of requiring government accreditation of nonprofits, accreditation that might be paid for by an existing excise tax on certain private foundation transactions. Although several non-governmental organizations provide voluntary accreditation (for example, the Better Business Bureau), the nonprofit sector has long resisted direct government accreditation.

The draft proposals included recommendations in several other areas seen as less controversial and, not coincidentally, much more costly to actually enact. These included expanding private foundation rules concerning transactions with 'disqualified persons'—that is, persons seen as having insider relationships with management or the board of directors. The document also called for limits to allowable administrative and travel expenses, for improving federal and state coordination of enforcement actions and expansion of the role of tax courts.

The draft proposal did not focus on improving financial reporting or auditing, concentrating instead on expanding reporting of compensation, conflicts of interest and other issues of governance. As noted in the introduction, the changes in accountability that flowed from this period rarely focused on accounting or even financial issues, except as the Sarbanes Oxley reforms were extended to cover nonprofits not explicitly covered by the original law. In particular, the draft recommended that chief financial officers be required to sign the tax forms submitted to the IRS. Further, boards of directors would be asked to review tax documents before they were submitted. Finally, the draft document proposed expanding public access to both IRS tax rulings and to the actual forms submitted by all tax-exempt organizations.

The importance of this set of draft proposals should not be missed. Experts reviewing the first decade of the new millennium often cite this document as one of the most important events of the period, along with the

9/11 attacks (see, for example, Takagi, 2009) These lists also cite Hurricane Katrina and the American Red Cross's mishandling of 9/11 donations.

In short order, however, the nonprofit sector mobilized in response to Grassley's staff proposal. This mobilization was not a grassroots response to the direct regulation recommended in the proposal, but rather a very orderly response organized in part by Senator Grassley himself when he encouraged an organization called the Independent Sector to convene a panel to respond officially to his staff's recommendations (Panel on the Nonprofit Sector, 2005). The Panel, which came to be called the Panel on the Nonprofit Sector, was highly selective in its membership and included CEOs and executive directors from large nonprofits and foundations, including the United Way and the American Red Cross, as well as representatives from the Kellogg, Charles Stewart Mott and Ford Foundations. Indeed, although Grassley's committee received response letters from small nonprofits across the country, these responses were usually from individuals acting on behalf of themselves or their individual charity; there was no organized or visible media response from organizations with less than $500,000 in revenue, more than half of all reporting charities (Roeger et al., 2012).

THE PANEL ON THE INDEPENDENT SECTOR'S RESPONSE

The Panel released its final report in June 2005 after holding hearings in 15 locations across the United States. Their report was titled 'Strengthening Transparency, Governance and Accountability of Charitable Organizations,' a title that indicates the way the issues were framed not only in the Grassley's staff draft, but also in the Panel's response. The Panel did not challenge the underlying belief that there was something wrong with nonprofits, nor did the Panel dispute the way the debate revolved around whether enforcement of 'ethical behavior and good government' should be expanded.

The Panel, however, rejected both of the most radical recommendations in the staff draft report—that tax-exempt status be re-examined every five years and that there be a formal accreditation process for nonprofits. This response was echoed by small, individual nonprofits that did respond publically, and widely rejected in the press.

The Panel did request additional federal funding in two areas. First, the Panel recommended that there be additional funding for federal enforcement. Second, it suggested that Congress explicitly authorize funds to establish or expand state agencies that could augment existing compliance enforcement, as well as supplement educational and training opportunities (p. 24).

The panel also noted the good work done by U.S. charities and remarked on the limited funds available for this work. The need for additional funding to the organizations themselves, however, was not a major theme in their final report.

The final report did make many recommendations that became part of the nonprofit reform legislation that was tacked onto a separate, unrelated bill called the Pension Protection Act of 2006. The Panel's recommendations and the final legislation are compared in the next section.

THE PENSION PROTECTION ACT OF 2006

Although the Panel on the Nonprofit Sector prioritized the need for additional federal funding for enforcement of existing rules and to expand education and training at the state level, the final enacted legislation focused instead on changes in the federal 990 forms that most tax-exempt organizations are required to file annually. The new legislation required that all nonprofits file one of three forms—the 990N (a simple form), a 990EZ which is slightly more complicated or the full 990. Only religious organizations were exempted. Further, failure to file for three years would result in automatic revocation of 501(c) status.

Previously, nonprofits with annual revenues of less than $25,000 were not required to file at all. This provision made it impossible for the IRS to know whether an organization that did not file fell into this category legitimately or was just lax in filing. In the Pension Protection Act, the federal government created a form called 990N specifically for small organizations reporting less than $50,000 in annual revenue. Form 990N is essentially an electronic postcard that lists the organization's total revenue, expenses and assets, but not much more. The final legislation required organizations with gross receipts of $200,000 or more and total assets of $500,000 or more to file the most complete and complex Form 990 annually. Organizations reporting between $50,000 and $250,000 were required to file Form 900EZ, a slightly reduced form of the longer filing.

The Panel made recommendations in several other areas that became part of the new law. It suggested that rules for donated property become stricter and that disclosure of these types of transactions be expanded. Grassley and his committee agreed, in part because of the problems raised by the Nature Conservancy. The new Form 990 included Schedule M requiring organizations that receive more than $25,000 in aggregate, non-cash donations to disclose information about quantity and type of goods. The form also required organizations to detail the method used and assumptions made to record the revenue associated with such gifts (Hopkins, Anning, Gross, & Schenkelberg, 2009). The new 990 Form also established special rules for disclosing items that had emerged as troublesome in Congressional hearings, including reporting of artwork, used vehicles, clothing and household goods, intellectual property and conservation easements.

Congress agreed with the Panel that self-dealing or what is called excess benefit transactions involving 'disqualified' people—executives and board members with conflicts of interest—needed to be disclosed and ultimately sanctioned. Congress expanded all disclosures concerning compensation and possible conflicts of interest. Section VII of the core form, and supplemented by Schedule J, was explicitly designed to make it easier for the IRS to identify, investigate and fine key employees, board members and contracts who receive inappropriate salaries, benefits or loans from a tax-exempt organization. Further, the definition of fringe benefits was expanded to include first-class or charter travel, discretionary spending accounts, tax indemnification, household allowances, health and social club dues and personal services. It also required reporting of benefits granted to the family members of key employees and board members.

A second new schedule targeted the excise taxes levied for excess benefit transactions that nonprofits paid on behalf of their executives. In other words, if the IRS fined a nonprofit for paying salaries in excess of community standards, providing appropriate benefits or purchasing assets from interested persons for more than a reasonable market value, the organization would be required to reveal these fines publically. Further, the nonprofit must reveal if the fines levied on individuals were actually paid by the organization. Schedule L also required disclosure of other transactions involving interest persons, including grants and loans to and from interested persons.

The new Form 990 expanded disclosure from donor-advised funds. These are donations for which the donor retains the ability to direct their use or benefit from their investment. The new legislation required organizations to identify donations to such funds (for example, museum collections, escrow accounts and certain endowment funds for which donors retain custodial arrangements) (Wylie, 2009).

The IRS went beyond the Panel's recommended actions in several areas. It expanded disclosure of political campaign activity by creating Schedule C (McRay, 2009). Disclosure rules for tax-exempt private schools and hospitals were expanded significantly, as was Schedule G, which asks about fundraising and gaming activities.

Finally, the new Form 990 asked detailed questions about organizations with fundraising, grant-making or other exempt activities outside the United States, additions many observers attribute to the 9/11 attacks that sparked Grassley's investigations (Hopkins et al., 2009.) Originally this information was to be listed by specific country of activity, but after discussion with nonprofits working overseas the disclosures were altered, asking only information about employees, agents and offices by region. This change was intended to protect the safety of individuals working in areas of conflict.

GOALS OF THE IRS REFORM

At a video webinar in which the IRS introduced the new 990 Form, an IRS representative commented that the new form was intended to force organizations to comply with federal rules and to expand transparency concerning all areas of nonprofit governance. The goal of the reforms was to alter troublesome behavior either through inexpensive, noncontroversial enforcement mechanisms or by revealing such improper behavior to donors, grantors and state regulators. Further, the IRS argues, just as the Panel on the Nonprofit Sector argued, that while the changes increased the reporting burden on tax-exempt organizations, it was a balanced approach that kept the cost of compliance in mind.

The IRS did not explain, neither did the new legislation reveal, how the additional information contained in the new Form 990 would be monitored. It is estimated that less than 1% of all tax-exempt organizations were audited by the IRS before these reforms. Indeed, the number of IRS agents working in the tax-exempt sector had not increased during the two decades before the Grassley hearings, despite the rapid growth in the number of nonprofits. Further, the small funding increase for enforcement granted to the IRS as part of the changes to Form 990 is not expected to greatly expand the number of individual agents monitoring 990 disclosures. In an era of federal budget tightening, the legislative actions that have proven most effective in forcing changes in the nonprofit world are the rules requiring public, electronic filing and the blunt, easy to enforce rule that requires revocation of tax-exempt status for failing to file. These two actions and their effects will be discussed in the next section.

THE BLUNT AND THE INDIRECT

The two changes that have had the most significant impact on the nonprofit sector emerged from both Grassley's staff recommendations and the Panel on the Nonprofit Sector's response, although not just as either body would have liked.

The first impactful rule change invested in the IRS the power to revoke the 501(c) status from any nonprofit that failed to file for three years. Revocation was automatic. If a functioning nonprofit wished to continue to operate after revocation, the nonprofit must re-file their original Form 1023 or 1024 with all supporting documents. In essence, the revoked organization must begin the extensive, time-consuming and difficult process of obtaining tax-exempt status in the same cumbersome, expensive process that new nonprofits expect to complete only once. In addition, the revocation rules require revoked organizations to pay substantial filing fees and significant fines to have their applications reviewed (Internal Revenue Service, 2013c).

This key provision in the new law is easy to enforce because it requires a binary decision. No judgment is involved because revocation is not based on the accuracy or even the completeness of filings. An organization either files or it doesn't; fail to file in three consecutive years and the organization's status is revoked. This rule fell somewhere between the staff recommendation that organizations be required to have their status reviewed formally every five years—a requirement that was opposed by nearly every nonprofit willing to go on record—and the suggestion from the Panel on the Nonprofit Sector that non-filers be fined as specified in the existing legislation.

The impact of the revocation rule has been immediate. As noted in the introduction, by 2011 over 275,000 organizations had their status revoked, a powerful motivator of at least filing behavior on the part of nonprofits (Blackwood & Roeger, 2011). Loss of this special status cripples charities by making it impossible for government agencies to extend grant funding, as most state agencies require their grantees to have an affirmative IRS ruling. Loss means donors are unable to declare a deduction for their donations, robbing small organizations of a main source of funding. Revocation also undermines the confidence of nonprofit grantors who might not have had explicit rules against funding such organizations in the past.

The second important change is the requirement that Form 990s, 990EZ and the postcard, along with most of the accompanying schedules, be filed electronically and made available upon request. The impact of this rule has been less clear but most experts believe that, at the very minimum, public disclosure will inspire symbolic compliance with good governance policies. There is good reason to believe the experts. Prior to this requirement, donors and grantees could ask whether an organization was in good standing with the IRS and current with state filing requirements, but verifying this information was difficult, costly and sometimes impossible. Many grantors choose to assume that their grantees were in compliance. Others required grantees to sign forms confirming their 501(c) status, something executive directors did regularly, although they themselves may never have reviewed the original documents and were not required to review the Form 990.

The new legislation required that the Form 990s and associate schedules (including compensation reports for key employees and disclosure of compensation for board members) be made *readily* available. Because they are electronic, several organizations including Guidestar and Charity Navigator are able to upload the information to their sites without requesting permission. Many states now require tax-exempt organizations to submit an electronic copy of the federal form as part of their compliance requirements. Further, the IRS has published lists of revoked organizations regularly, compiling the names of revoked organizations by state for easy access.

There is much we do not know about the organizations who have had their status revoked. Early studies, however, reveal how broadly revocations have hit the sector. In 2011, the Urban Institute reported that the revocations have been spread across all types of organizations, including education, environmental, arts and public benefit, although the largest percentage provide human services (Blackwood & Roeger, 2011). The Urban Institute also found that while 60% of organizations formed before 1950 were revoked, the majority of revocations were for organizations registered for 20 years or less. Ultimately, the Institute concluded that many of those revoked were defunct prior to the IRS's action, but a significant group were still functioning. This point was reinforced in a second study by the Taxpayer Advocate Service of the U.S. government that reported that over 50,000 organizations filed for reinstatement during the first three years of the new law and that these filings were on top of 60,000 new applications for tax-exempt status filed in the same period. The combination contributed to a significant backlog of organizations requesting re-evaluation, forcing some organizations to wait up to 18 months for certification or recertification (Lough, 2013).

Not surprisingly, even simple forms of enforcement turn out to be more complicated than anticipated. The Taxpayer Advocate Service estimated that 9,000 organizations received revocations in error, often because of the way the three-year window was measured.

Of the additional disclosure requirements, the disclosure of compensation has created the greatest stir, especially when accompanied by the requirement that nonprofit boards review all the federal filings. To ease this process, most of the large accounting services firms now provide board training on how to read and interpret the 990 (c.f. Grant Thornton's 'Form 990: A Board Member's Review Checklist'). Nonprofits also report that the cost of audits and of professional help preparing the 990 has gone up significantly, although the funds available for either preparation or enforcement have not.

CONCLUSION

The discourse of crisis that rippled through the nonprofit sector following the 9/11 attacks shifted as time passed, revealing how difficult it is to predict the outcome of regulatory efforts. The proposals that were finally enacted reflect the reality of nonprofit accountability and compliance—it is easy to advocate reform, more difficult to enact actual regulation and, perhaps most importantly, more costly than predicted to enforce.

This episode illustrates two important findings about electronic compliance filings at both the local and federal level, findings with importance beyond the nonprofit sector. First, this episode documents the power of targeted, easy to enforce rules to force organizational compliance with the letter of the regulations, although not necessarily guaranteeing improvement in overall legality or accountability. Further, even the simplest rules can become costly when, as in this case, organizations apply for reinstatement or are revoked in error

It is unclear whether public scrutiny of Form 990s will lead to better governance in the long-run, or if it reduces unethical behavior. It may be that these new requirements will only undermine public confidence as board members struggle to understand complex issues with little help, executive directors and others work to meet compliance rules without the skills or financial resources to competently report complete information, and as regulators try to monitor this growing sector without additional funds.

Increasing the cost of compliance has another indirect effect. Most U.S. states recognize that tax-exempt organizations conduct activities that are desirable, even necessary for the economic and social health of their populations. They provide services that for-profit businesses will not provide. Further, the organizations conduct these activities at costs that are significantly lower than if state or federal governments attempted to provide the same services. Increasing compliance requirements in a way that impinges on these low-cost providers is not seen as advantageous in many local arenas, especially after media attention has moved on to other issues. Some states, most notably New York, have begun to roll back or consolidate regulations in an attempt to encourage local non-profits to flourish (Boris, de Leon, Roeger & Nikolova, 2010). As the federal government continues to cut grants to the states, and states move to reduce their budgets, it is likely that additional efforts will be made to reduce the costs of compliance while attempting to avoid further public 'calamities.'

REFERENCES

American Civil Liberties Union. (2009). *Blocking faith, freezing charity: Chilling Muslim charitable giving.* Retrieved from https://www.aclu.org/human-rights/report-blocking-faith-freezing-charity

Barnett, P. (2002). Senators seek coordination in tracking terrorist funding. *Congressional Daily*, 1–5.

Blackwood, A. S., & Roeger, K. L. (2011). *Revoked: A snapshot of organizations that lost their tax-exempt status.* Retrieved from http://www.urban.org/publications/412386.html

Brilliant, E. (2001). *Private charity and public inquiry: A history of the filer and Peterson Commissions.* Bloomington: Indiana University Press.

Bush, G. (2001). *We will starve the terrorists.* Retrieved from http://edition.cnn.com/2001/US/09/24/ret.bush.transcript/index.html

Eisenberg, P. (2004, July 22). *Testimony before the U.S. Senate Finance Committee: Recommendations for the reform of the nonprofit sector.* Retrieved from www.finance.senate.gov/newsroom/chairman/download/?id=e9786146–54e

Garcilazo, J. M. (2001). McCarthyism, Mexican Americans, and the Los Angeles Committee for Protection of the Foreign-Born, 1950–1954. *The Western Historical Quarterly, 32*(3), 273–295.

Grant Thornton, 2011 "Form 990: A board member's review checklist". Retrieved from http://www.grantthornton.com

Grassley, C. (2003, December 22). *Record sought about tax-exempt organizations for committee's terror finance probe* [Press release]. Retrieved from http://www.grassley.senate.gov/news/Article.cfm?customel_dataPageID_1502=9937

Guidestar. (2011). *Roles and responsibilities of nonprofit audit committee members.* Retrieved from http://www.guidestar.org

Hopkins, B. R., Anning, D. K., Gross, V. C., & Schenkelberg, T. J. (2009). *The new form 990; Law, policy and preparation.* Hoboken, NJ: Wiley and Sons.

Internal Revenue Service. (2013a). *Current form 990 series—forms and instructions.* Retrieved from www.irs.gov/. . ./Current-Form-990-Series-Form

Internal Revenue Service. (2013b). *Form 990 instructions.* Retrieved from www.irs.gov/pub/irs-pdf/i990.pd

Internal Revenue Service. (2013c). *Instructions for form 1023—additional material.* Retrieved from http://www.irs.gove/instructions/i1023/ar.03.html

Jarnal, Z. (2011). *Charitable giving among Muslim Americans: Ten years after 9/11.* Institute for Social Policy and Understanding Policy Brief. Retrieved from: http://www.ispu.org

Johnson, C. (2005, April 6). Charities going beyond required controls to regain their donor's confidence. *The Washington Post*, p. E1.

Lipman, H. (2002). Making oversight a priority. *Chronicle of Philanthropy, 14*(17), 31.

Lough, S. B. (2013). *Exempt organizations: The IRS continues to struggle with revocation processes and erroneous revocations of exempt status* (MPS #15). Retrieved from http://www.taxpayeradvocate.irs.gov/

McRay, G. (2009). *Radical changes to form 990.* Retrieved from http://501c3.org/blog/radical-changes-to-form-990/

Office of Chief Counsel Internal Revenue Service. (2004, January 26). Memorandum: International grants and activities. Number 200504031.

Panel on the Nonprofit Sector. (2005). *Strengthening transparency, governance, accountability of charitable organizations: A final report to Congress and the nonprofit sector.* Retrieved from http://www.independentsector.org/uploads/Accountability_Documents/Panel_Final_Report.pdf

Philanthropy News Digest: The Foundation Center. (2001, November 2). *Grassley calls for federal oversight of September 11 donations.* Retrieved at http://philanthropynewsdigest.org/

Roeger, K. L., Blackwood, A. S., & Pettijohn, S. J. (2012). *The nonprofit almanac.* Washington, DC: The Urban Institute Press.

Senate Committee on Finance. (2004, June 22). Opening statement of Senator Chuck Grassley hearing on charitable giving. Retrieved from www.finance.senate.gov

Senate Committee on Finance. (2005). Staff discussion draft. Retrieved from http://www.finance.senate.gov/imo/media/doc/062204stfdis.pdf

Senate Committee on Finance. (2007, November 20). Summary of Senator Grassley's nonprofit oversight to date [Press release]. Retrieved from www.finance.senate.gov

Strom, S. (2005, April 6). Official cites tax abuses with charities. *The New York Times.* Retrieved from http://www.nytimes.com/2005/04/06/national/06charity.htm

Takagi, G. (2009). U.S. nonprofits: Top 10 events of the decade [Web log post]. Retrieved from http://www.nonprofitlawblog.com/home

U.S Treasury Department. (2005). *U.S. Department of the Treasury anti-terrorist financing guidelines.* Retrieved from: http://www. treasury.gov

Vartabedian, R. (2005, June 6.) IRS urges action on nonprofit tax abuse. *The Los Angeles Times.* Retrieved from http://articles.latimes.com/2005/apr/06/nation/na-taxfraud6

Wilhelm, I. (2002). Red Cross defends its fund rising in response to U.S. senator. *Chronicle of Philanthropy, 14*(18), 41.

Wylie, B. (2009). The redesigned form 990. *Journal of Accountancy, 207*(3). Retrieved from http://www.journalofaccountancy.com/issues/2009/mar/redsignedform990.htm

4 Social Reporting for Italian Social Enterprises
Did the Italian Legislature Miss an Opportunity?

Ericka Costa

INTRODUCTION

Over the past 15 years, a growing body of empirical and theoretical studies on the accountability of nonprofit organisations (NPOs) and non-governmental organisations (NGOs) has been published (Gandía, 2011; Benjamin, 2008; O'Dwyer & Unerman, 2007; Dixon, Ritchie, & Siwale, 2006; Goddard & Assad, 2006; Gray, Bebbington, & Collison, 2006; Unerman & O'Dwyer, 2006; Ebrahim, 2003a, 2003b, 2005; Ospina, Diaz, & O'Sullivan, 2002; Brown & Moore, 2001; Moore, 2000; Najam, 1996). Within extant literature on NPOs, few studies have dealt with the accountability mechanism for social enterprises (SEs) (Bagnoli & Megali, 2011; Nicholls, 2009, 2010; Diochon & Anderson, 2009; Gibbon & Affleck, 2008; Andreaus, 2007). According to the European definition, SEs are private NPOs oriented to creating social value, having dividend constraints and assuming an open and participatory governance model (Borzaga & Defourny, 2001).

From 1990 onwards, Italian SEs have assumed various legal forms such as the social cooperative (Law n. 381/1991). With the aim of encompassing under one unique umbrella the various legal forms of SEs, in 2005 a new legal framework for SEs was developed by introducing the concept of 'legal social enterprises' (Law 118/2005 and Legislative Decree Dlgs. no. 155/2006). This concept does not refer to a new legal form, or a new type of organisation; rather, it is only a 'brand/accreditation' in which all eligible organisations may be included (Fici, 2006). Therefore, this enables various types of organisations (not only cooperatives and traditional non-profit organisations) to obtain the 'legal brand' of SE when respecting the non-distribution constraint and the governance multi-stakeholder model provided by law. Finally, according to this law, 'legal social enterprises' must provide an annual, stand-alone social report according to the pro forma established by the legislator.

Recent studies have, however, highlighted that most Italian SEs continue to use the social cooperative form (Galera & Borzaga, 2009); indeed, Zandonai and Borzaga (2009) revealed that only 623 organisations out of almost

14,000 SEs have obtained the 'legal brand' of SE. The aim of this chapter is, therefore, to offer a possible explanation of the 'partial failure' of the recent Italian legal framework by explaining how SEs discharge accountability and by providing stimulating insights in light of the recent legal framework.

In order to deal with this purpose, the chapter is structured in the following way. The next section positions European SEs in a global context by comparing different definitions. Section 2 analyses the European legal framework for SEs and Section 3 makes a case of Italy by highlighting how Italian SEs currently voluntarily and compulsorily discharge accountability. Section 4 examines prior theoretical studies that have suggested, using a normative approach, how NPOs and SEs should be accountable to stakeholders by adopting a multidirectional system. Using these theories and comparing them with the current Italian experience presented in Section 3, Section 5 presents some critical remarks on the current status of Italian SEs by arguing that in light of SE behaviour, where social and environmental reporting have been addressed, Italian legislation was unable to design a new legal framework as an opportunity to create greater accountability. Finally, a conclusion and directions for future research are given.

POSITIONING SOCIAL ENTERPRISES: CONCEPTS AND DEFINITIONS

The notions of 'social entrepreneurship,' 'social entrepreneur' and 'social enterprise' were developed in different ways mainly by U.S. researchers (Dees, 1998a, 1998b) and are still emerging as subjects of academic investigation since the theoretical underpinning of these concepts has not yet been adequately developed (Defourny & Nyssen, 2010; Austin, Stevenson, & Skillern, 2006; Sud, VanSandt, & Baugous, 2009). Even if numerous studies have contributed to this debate by attempting to build an agreed theoretical model (Dees, 1998a; Dees & Elias, 1998; Seelos & Mair, 2005), these concepts remain fuzzy (Dart, 2004; Dorado, 2006) and many scholars call for a contribution both to theory and to practice that can define them more precisely (Dacin, Dacin, & Matear, 2010; Thompson, 2008; Dart, Clow, & Armstrong, 2010).

To simplify this somewhat, it could be argued that the definition of *social entrepreneurship* mainly refers to the innovative process undertaken by a *social entrepreneur* to develop *social enterprises*. These definitions highlight the intention of the entrepreneur to undertake innovative processes and to face challenging opportunities to serve a socially oriented mission (Bolton & Thompson, 2003). In this field, entrepreneurs are perceived as 'innovative, opportunity-oriented, resourceful, value-creating change agents' (Dees & Economy, 2001, p. 4). However, the concept of social entrepreneurship is still used in a very broad sense by various scholars (Austin et al., 2006; Sud et al., 2009; Seelos & Mair, 2005; Dorado, 2006; Dart, 2004) who represent a wide continuum from innovative nonprofit ventures to philanthropic initiatives taken by for-profit organisations (Dees, 1998b; Dees & Economy, 2001). In this wide spectrum, numerous categories can be developed, including hybrid organisations mixing nonprofit and for-profit elements (Battilana & Dorado, 2010; Sud et al., 2009; Dorado, 2005; Dees & Economy, 2001; Alter, 2006).

Despite some attempts to build a comprehensive picture of the social entrepreneurship spectrum (for some contributions, see Dacin et al., 2010; Boschee, 1995; Peredo & McLean, 2006; Thompson, 2008; Dart et al., 2010), an agreed-upon definition is lacking. However, by following Mair and Martì (2006), it is possible to consider social entrepreneurship as 'a process involving the innovative use and combination of resources to pursue opportunities to catalyze social changes and/or address social needs' (p. 37).

While in the U.S., the debate mainly involves the concepts of social entrepreneurship and social entrepreneur, in Europe, the notion of *social enterprise* has been investigated to a greater extent (Galera & Borzaga, 2009; Defourny & Nyssen, 2008a, 2008b; Borzaga & Defourny, 2001). More specifically, in Western Europe, two main approaches to SEs emerge. 'One school of thought stresses the social entrepreneurship dynamic developed by firms who seek to enhance the social impact of their productive activities. In this line, the literature often highlights the innovative approaches to tackling social needs that are developed as businesses are fostered (Grenier, 2003), mainly through nonprofit organisations but also in the for-profit sectors (Nicholls, 2005)' (Kerlin, 2006, p. 249).

Another school of thought includes the SEs within the third sector and also involves social cooperatives (Defourny & Nyssen, 2008c, 2010; Galera & Borzaga, 2009). The definition of this second stream has been developed by university researchers and scholars cooperating in the EMES Research Network[1]. EMES defines SEs as 'not-for-profit private organizations providing goods or services directly related to their explicit aim to benefit the community. They rely on a collective dynamic involving various types of stakeholders in their governing bodies, they place a high value on their autonomy and they bear economic risks linked to their activity' (Defourny & Nyssen, 2008b, p. 5). The conceptualization of social enterprise proposed by the EMES network is based on nine criteria (Defourny, 2001, pp. 16–18):

1. A continuous activity producing goods and/or selling services;
2. A high degree of autonomy;
3. A significant level of economic risk;
4. A minimum amount of paid work;
5. An explicit aim to benefit the community;
6. An initiative launched by a group of citizens;
7. A decision-making power not based on capital ownership;

8. A participatory nature, which involves the persons affected by the activity;
9. Limited profit distribution

'Those criteria do not represent a set of conditions that an organization should meet to qualify as a social enterprise; indeed, rather than constituting prescriptive criteria, these indicators describe an "ideal-type" (in Weber's terms) that enables researchers to position themselves within the "galaxy" of social enterprises' (Defourny & Nyssen, 2008a, p. 204). In such a perspective, the definition proposed by EMES is not intended to curtail the academic debate on social entrepreneurship and the social entrepreneur; on the contrary, it aims to build a common ground in which different existing European third sector organisations are able to recognise themselves. This concept differs from the U.S. definition of social entrepreneurship and social entrepreneurs (Dees & Elias, 1998; Seelos & Mair, 2005; Dart, 2004; Dacin et al., 2010) mainly because it situates SEs within the third sector and social economy sector and, therefore, embraces NPOs as well as cooperatives and related not-for-profit private forms of enterprises (Defourny & Nyssen, 2008c; Kerlin, 2006). In order to have a general frame of differences between the U.S. and Europe, see Kerlin (2006, p. 259).

Following this approach, European SEs (Galera and Borzaga, 2009):

1. *Are oriented to pursue a social end.* The goal pursued by SEs is explicitly other than profit, presupposing that the activity carried out is characterized by a merit or general-interest dimension. The activity carried out can either entail the promotion of the interests of specific categories of stakeholders—i.e., consumers that are unable to pay; disadvantaged workers, or of the community at large—i.e. regeneration of a depressed area.

2. *Have profit-distribution constraints.* The profits gained are mainly reinvested in the organisations as a mechanism of self-financing in order to support the future development of the SE. The non-profit distribution constraint can be either total or partial (e.g. with the possibility of distributing profits up to a certain percentage over the risk capital provided by members), as it is the case of some cooperative enterprises that display social functions.

3. *Adopt an open and participatory governance model* in which stakeholders, and not only the investors, have ownership rights and control power. Depending upon the type of SE under consideration, ownership rights and control power can be assigned to a single category of stakeholders (users, workers, or donors) or to more than one category at a time—hence giving ground to a multi-stakeholder ownership asset.

The European definition of SE, which is taken as a benchmark for the purposes of this study, denotes private NPOs whose mission is to produce goods and services in the pursuit of objectives in the general interests of local communities and/or persons or social groups (sometimes in states of fragility). This concept ranges between the nonprofit and the cooperative frame, but it does not overlap completely with them. Indeed, it excludes organisations, such as volunteer associations, grant-making foundations or charities that are not devoted to fulfilling a productive role, even if they belong to the nonprofit sector (Lohmann, 1992). It also excludes 'third sector organizations that do not carry out entrepreneurial activities and mainly perform advocacy or re-distributive functions, public institutions, and for profit enterprises engaged in social projects' (Galera & Borzaga, 2009, p. 216).

LEGAL FRAMEWORKS FOR EUROPEAN SOCIAL ENTERPRISES

The evolution of the legal frameworks for the European SEs can be divided into two main phases. During the *first phase*, most SEs were established as associations and cooperatives (and in several cases, this continues to be the most adopted legal form). European SEs were initially set up as associations in those countries where the legal definition of association allows for a degree of freedom in selling goods and services on the open market, i.e., France and Belgium. In countries such as Sweden, Finland, Spain and Italy where associations are more limited in this regard, SEs are more often established under the legal form of cooperatives (Borzaga & Defourny, 2001; Galera & Borzaga, 2009). Borzaga and Defourny (2001) note a possible convergence of associations and cooperatives as associations adopt more entrepreneurial activities and cooperatives increasingly offer social benefits to non-members.

During the *second phase*, some countries adopted specific legal forms for SEs both via the adaptation of the cooperative legal framework or through the introduction of legal brands and categories that recognise the social commitment taken on by certain economic entities (Galera & Borzaga, 2009). The idea to recognise SEs via the cooperative legal framework was marked by the acknowledgment of initiatives serving a broad community (not only the members) and putting great emphasis on the dimension of general interest (Defourny & Nyssen, 2010). This trend undermines the traditional model of cooperatives, which are primarily oriented toward members' interests and are single-stakeholder organisations (Levi, 1999).

This process formally began in Italy in 1991 when Law 381 on social cooperatives provided the basis for a legislative framework for the 'socially oriented' organisations that had spontaneously sprung up more than 20 years earlier (Borzaga & Ianes, 2006). According to this law, the purpose of a social cooperative is to: 'pursue the general interest of the community in promoting personal growth and in integrating people into society by providing social, welfare and educational services (A type) and carrying out different activities for the purposes of providing employment for disadvantaged people (B type)' (Law 381/1991). Caring activities—so-called type A—refer to social health care and educational services, cultural services, nurseries and initiatives aimed at environmental protection (Thomas, 2004). Training activities—so-called type B—introduce disadvantaged people to business activities and employment opportunities and an enterprise of this nature is referred to as a Work Integration Social Enterprise—WISE (Defourny & Nyssen, 2006). Both type A and type B organisations are privately owned and specifically member-owned, and they operate to create social value for their community.

After the pioneering Italian law adopted in 1991, other European countries later introduced new legal frameworks for the SE model, even though the term of 'social enterprise' was not always used, as shown in Table 4.1 (for a review see Kerlin, 2006; Galera & Borzaga, 2009; Defourny & Nyssen, 2008a, 2010; European Commission, 2013).

Historical and cultural reasons may be found to explain why it was in Italy that innovative organisational models which were able to deal with the unmet social needs emerged. Defourny and Nyssen (2008b, 2010) explain that the weak presence of the welfare state combined with the historical and Church-related tradition of the cooperative movement in Italy gave rise to new organisational forms, i.e., the *social cooperatives*. In a context where governments were unable to solve or ameliorate such failures, social cooperatives sprang up as a mechanism capable of offering social services to citizens (Austin et al., 2006).

The introduction of the Italian Law 381/1991 on social cooperatives was instrumental in increasing the number of organisations of this type over the years (Kerlin, 2006). According to ISTAT (2008), the national statistical office, the number of social cooperatives increased from 650 in 1985 to 7,400 in 2005 (estimation). These were mainly located in Northern Italy (46.8%). They drew in more than 262,000 members, 244,223 paid workers and 34,626 volunteers. More recently, the Observatory on Cooperatives and Social Enterprises—a project promoted by the European Research Institute on Cooperative and Social Enterprises (EURICSE)—identified 13,938 SEs in Italy in 2008 (54.5% type A and the remaining type B), with €8.97 billion in total turnover—65% of which was invested in the North—and 317,339 employees (Costa, Andreaus, Carini, & Carpita, 2012).

SOCIAL ENTERPRISES IN ITALY: THE LEGAL FRAMEWORKS AND THE ACCOUNTABILITY DUTIES

The Evolution of the Legal Framework

Recently in Italy and the UK, a shift towards more general legal forms—not just inspired by the cooperative tradition—was favoured by the legislators of both countries. In Italy[2], a new law was introduced (Law 118/2005 and

Table 4.1   European social enterprises and the legal form used, by country

Country	Legal forms used	Law/year	Activities
Italy	Social cooperative	381/1991	Social services (a-type) Work integration (b-type)
Spain	Social cooperative societies Labour integration Cooperative societies	National Law 27/1999 and regional laws in 12 autonomous regions (1993–2003)	Assistance services in the fields of health, education, culture or any activity of a social nature Work integration
Portugal	Social solidarity cooperatives	Cooperative code (Law No. 51/96 of 7 September 1996) and Legislative Decree No. 7/98 of 15 January 1998	Work integration of vulnerable groups
France	General interest cooperative societies	Law of 17 July 2001	Production or provision of goods and services of collective interest
Poland	Social cooperative	Law on Social Cooperative 2006	Work integration of a wide category of disadvantaged workers
Hungary	Social cooperative	Law 2006. X.	Create work opportunities and facilitate the improvement of other social needs of its disadvantaged members
Greece	Social cooperative	Law 4019/30-9-2011 on 'Social Economy and Social enterprises'	Engagement in three fields: i. work integration; ii. social care; iii. provision of services that satisfy collective needs/local development

Adapted from: European Commission. (2013). *Social economy and social entrepreneurship—social Europe guide* (Vol. 4), 42. Retrieved from http://ec.europa.eu/social/main.jsp?catId=738&langId=it&pubId=7523

Legislative Decree Dlgs.n. 155/2006) in order to 'cross the boundaries of all legal forms' (Defourny & Nyssen, 2010, p. 37).

According to the law, a social enterprise is defined as a nonprofit private organisation, which permanently and principally carries out an economic activity aimed at the production and distribution of social benefit goods and services, and pursues general interest goals (Galera & Borzaga, 2009). Indeed, this enables various types of organisations (not only cooperatives and traditional nonprofit organisations, but also investor-owned organisations, for instance) to obtain the 'legal brand' of SE, provided they comply with the non-distribution constraint and organise the representation of certain categories of stakeholders, including workers and beneficiaries (Defourny & Nyssen, 2008c). Therefore, not only social cooperatives— which are *naturally* SEs—could be encompassed under the 'umbrella' of legal SEs, but also other investor-owned organisations could obtain the legal brand of SE if they define an explicit social aim and they are not dedicated to the enrichment of their members (Defourny & Nyssen, 2010).

According to the current Italian law, an SE is not a new type of organization or new legal form; rather, it is only an 'accreditation' in which all eligible organisations that are respecting the requirements provided by law may be included, regardless of their organisational structure (Fici, 2006). 'Eligible organizations include cooperatives (i.e. worker- producer-, orconsumer-owned firms), investor-owned firms or traditional non-profit firms (i.e. associations and foundations)' (Galera & Borzaga, 2009, p. 222).

Social cooperatives thus fall *naturally*, but not *automatically*, under the banner of SEs. Their legal status only applies if: (1) they are indeed recognised by the Chamber of Commerce[3]; (2) engage both members and stakeholders in governance; and (3) follow pro forma legislative social reporting. Within the new legal framework (refer to figure 4.1), the legislator required SEs to draw up a compulsory, stand-alone social report. At the European level, this Italian experience is the first case of mandatory social reporting for 'legal social enterprises.'[4] In delineating this aspect, the political purpose of the new law (118/2005) was to determine a self-identifying brand which distinguishes between SEs and other organisational legal forms. This choice is consistent with the aim of promoting pluralism in the production of general interest services, especially in the welfare and health sectors. However, the law is quite new and (similar to the Belgian law) it is not supported by any fiscal advantages. 'Consequently, it is still too early to assess the impact

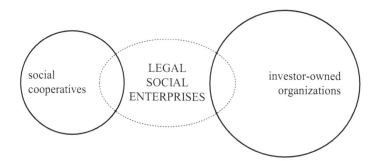

Figure 4.1   The new 'legal brand' for Italian Social Enterprises

of this new legal framework. Italian organisations performing social enterprise activities currently continue to use mainly the social cooperative form' (Borzaga & Galera, 2009, p. 223).

The Accountability Duties of Italian Social Enterprises

Given the understanding of what SEs are in Italy compared with other concepts developed on a worldwide basis, this section investigates why and how SEs discharge accountability, both compulsorily and voluntarily.

Before the new legal framework (Law 118/2005 and Legislative Decree Dlgs.n. 155/2006), which introduced a mandatory, stand-alone social report for 'legal' SEs, Italian regulation compelled all organisational SEs to draw up their annual report according to the pro forma provided for *for*-profit companies (art. 2516 Italian Civil Code). This annual report disseminates economic and financial data by representing both descriptive and quantitative information. Specifically, the quantitative information is provided by the financial statement, which is formed by the balance sheet and the income statement (Legislative Decree Dlgs.n. 127/1991). Moreover, according to the current Italian regulation, small companies can (but do not have to) draw up an abbreviated annual report which provides some simplification of the information gathered. Therefore, since Italian social cooperatives are mainly small organisations (Costa et al., 2012), they adopt an abbreviated annual report which contains economic and financial information. However, social cooperatives and SEs find it awkward to report on financial statements in the same manner as small, for-profit organisations, since their mission is socially oriented.

This scenario reveals the inconsistency between the social mission of the SEs and their compulsory accounting model which was basically economically oriented. As Gray et al. (2006) suggest, the 'calls for a financial performance reporting by NFPOs [not-for-profit organisations] are largely misdirected. After all what could it tell one other than at a simply "pocket money" stewardship sort of level?' (p. 341).

It was probably for these reasons that Italian SEs felt the need to enlarge their accountability and accounting systems by providing additional information closer to their identity (Unerman & O'Dwyer, 2006) and their activity mission purposes. Thus, some Italian SEs built up a social report in an attempt to go beyond the traditional economic and financial bottom line. Moreover, some Italian SEs also extended their accountability to social and environmental issues by forecasting the future impact of their activities, thereby using social reporting in an estimative manner.

Italian Case Studies

In order to better understand what motivates Italian SEs to voluntarily go beyond the traditional economic bottom line and to comprehend to what extent they discharge social and environmental accountability, some brief case studies are presented in an explorative (but certainly not exhaustive) manner. All three case studies adopt the legal form of social cooperative and are not accredited as 'legal social enterprises' (Galera & Borzaga, 2009). These case studies are useful for understanding the *rationales* which have supported the decision to enlarge their accountability system from the economic and financial statement to other forms of accountabilities.

Acli is a social enterprise, without the 'accreditation' but with the legal form of a type A social cooperative. The aim of Acli is to pursue the general interests of the community and to promote the human and social integration of citizens through the management of health care, social and educational services. From 2002, Acli voluntarily drew up a stand-alone social report in order to be more accountable to stakeholders and to be more operatively responsible in the community:

> Twenty years after it was set up, in a new scenario but with the same issues to be dealt with, the Acli Social Cooperative finds itself reviewing what must keep it connected to its founders. *What is our task? Are we faithful to it?* Answering these questions involves taking on the real responsibility of a social enterprise that puts itself to the test and that does not stop questioning what values are at the basis of its activities. The Social Report, which will be presented here, is the result of a process that the Board of Directors has promoted and supported. We are in no doubt that being transparent and accountable for our actions, as well as a duty, is a resource for the community where the Acli Cooperative knows it belongs.
>
> (Acli, 2002, Letter of the President, p. 3, emphasis added)

Acli has developed its stand-alone social report with the intention of giving further evidence of its widespread assumption of a shared social responsibility while explicitly contributing to the achievement of a global, social accounting of the territory where it works. This document mainly refers to the internal and external stakeholders by providing information about members, employees, customers, the local government and suppliers, as well as presenting stakeholder engagement practices which capture the perceptions and claims of the main recipients to the services offered by the social enterprise.

Bessimo is a social cooperative founded in 1976. It operates in Lombardy and works towards the recovery and reintegration of drug addicts.

Since 2006, Bessimo has integrated social and environmental issues into its economic and financial annual report, thus building up an integrated report. This document combines quantitative information related to economic/financial performance (balance sheet and net income statement), along with detailed descriptions of its relationships with beneficiaries and the community as a whole.

From 2008, Bessimo has drawn up an integrated report using the guide-lines provided by the new law on social enterprise, even though it has not acquired the 'accreditation' of a social enterprise. In addition, Bessimo fills its integrated report with voluntarily added information, which better explains the social value they are creating and promoting by taking care of weak, drug-addicted people. In their integrated social report, numerous pages are devoted to presenting projects and initiatives carried out during the year. Finally, the report incorporates this information with the financial statement and the CEO's letter to the members.

A third and final example is **Cadiai**, which is a social enterprise (with-out the 'legal accreditation') with the legal form of a socially oriented type A. Cadiai deals with social services, health and education with the aim of improving the quality of people's lives and contributing to the community in general. Since 1999, Cadiai has voluntarily produced a report called 'Social Activities,' which aims to provide stakeholders with a general overview of Cadiai and its activities/initiatives. In 2000, the report changed its name to 'Social Report' and it has been constantly enhanced in order to monitor the projects and services offered by Cadiai, thereby providing an account which is primarily geared towards its members. From 2006, Cadiai has also produced an 'Estimated Social Report,' a document that refers to the objec-tives set for the coming year by the Board of Directors. According to the organization,

> the introduction of the Estimated Social Report *closes the circle of accountability*. The Estimated Social Report 2006—which will be pre-sented in 2007—will be final and it will verify the degree of achievement of the forecasted goals for 2006. It implies a performance measurement useful for reflection on our aims and it becomes a necessary tool to implement actions and plans which are able to improve the performed outcomes.
>
> (Cadiai, 2006, p. 1, emphasis added)

Thus, from 2006, Cadiai has drawn up three types of reports: (1) the Annual Report (Financial Statement and Income Statement); (2) the Social Report; and (3) the Estimated Social Report. Cadiai asserts that 'to develop and to make available these reports is a duty to the members—as owners of the cooperative: it is their right/duty to receive/request information on oper-ations, objectives to be pursued and methods carried out' (Cadiai, 2006, p. 2). According to this view, social accounting and reporting seem to be considered strategic tools for organisational planning and stakeholder dia-logue (Ebrahim, 2003b).

These case studies provide an overview of different emergent and dynamic reporting practices (stand-alone, integrated or estimative social reporting) among Italian SEs, and represent an idea of the disclosure logics that Italian SEs exploit strategically in order to satisfy the accountabilities claims of their stakeholders. The development of these reporting practices is 'consistent with the *bricolage* evident in social entrepreneurs' attitude to problem-solving . . . Such reporting practices not only account for financial performance but also report more nuanced and contingent social and environmental impacts and outcomes' (Nicholls, 2009, p. 756).

These documents seem to demonstrate that SEs voluntarily engage in social and environmental reporting because they perceive this as a 'moral obligation' (Black, 2003) and responsibility towards different stakeholders, primarily the members (or internal stakeholders). Thus, these reports (stand-alone, integrated or estimative social reporting) struggle with self-reflexivity to enhance stakeholder dialogue rather than merely to respond to regulations.

ACCOUNTABILITY FOR SOCIAL ENTERPRISES: FROM A ONE-BOTTOM-LINE APPROACH TO A 'MULTIDIRECTIONAL' APPROACH

After defining SEs in Europe and specifically in Italy and presenting the current way they adopt to discharge accountability, both compulsorily and voluntarily, the aim of this section is to summarise prior studies that have argued for the importance of a multidirectional accountability system and, thus, also social accounting, for both NPOs and SEs.

Managing Social and Economic Value Creation

SEs are organisations focused on social value creation; thus, their mission is not oriented to creating economic value and wealth for the public good (Dart et al., 2010; Austin et al., 2006; Dees, 1998b). However, this does not mean that SEs should not undertake strategies able to guarantee net income earnings; on the contrary, they have to constantly create economic value in order to survive over time and to ensure that they are able to continue with their mission. In other words, while business organisations consider wealth creation as a way of measuring value creation, for SEs, wealth creation has to be considered as a means to an end, since this enables SEs to self-maintain over time (Dees, 1998a).

SEs have to pursue both social value creation (*primary objective*), as stated in their mission, and economic wealth creation (*secondary objective*— or *constraint*, as termed by Andreaus, 2006) in order to guarantee that they can pursue their mission statement in future years. According to this view, SEs are considered 'double bottom line' organisations (Dart et al., 2010), able to produce both social and economic value (Dees & Economy, 2001). Since they are social value oriented, they cannot be measured by traditional financial indicators or by market share (Austin et al., 2006), and the adoption of sole economic and financial indicators are meaningless in evaluating the performance of these organisations.

While the performance of a for-profit organisation is well summarised in its financial statements because shareholders consider this the mission achievement of the company, in contrast there is no automatic relationship between increments of achievement in the organisation's mission and financial performance in SEs (Moore, 2000). As a consequence, SEs should develop a more complex and 'multidirectional' accountability system that does not focus on only one economic bottom line, in order to be accountable to a great number of stakeholders and to satisfy their competing claims while simultaneously considering complexity in managing these relationships (Kanter & Summers, 1987).

Accountability for Social Enterprises: The 'Multidirectional' Approach

Literature on accountability for SEs is quite new (Nicholls, 2009; Matacena, 2007; Rusconi & Signori, 2007; Andreaus, 2007; Bagnoli & Megali, 2011), but to date many international scholars have offered insights with a view to contributing to the burgeoning debate on accountability for NPOs (Kearns, 1994; Edwards & Hulme, 1996). Accountability has been defined as 'the means by which individuals and organizations report to a recognized authority (or authorities) and are held responsible for their actions' (Edwards & Hulme, 1996, p. 967) or 'the process of holding actors responsible for actions' (Fox & Brown, 1998, p. 12). These definitions focus on an external approach; thus, they are primarily based on an agency theory perspective that recognises the presence of an external principal holding an agent to account. Other approaches stress both an external and an internal perspective (Cornwall, Lucas, & Pasteur, 2000; Gray, Owen, & Adams, 1996) by arguing that accountability is 'the duty to provide an account (by no means necessarily financial) or reckoning of those actions for which one is held responsible' (Gray et al., 1996, p. 38). This definition suggests that accountability involves two different but linked responsibilities: (1) the duty to undertake certain action (*internal responsibility*), and (2) the duty to provide an account for those actions (*external responsibility*). In both perspectives, accountability is often a relational concept (Brown & Moore, 2001; Ebrahim, 2005; Unerman & O'Dwyer, 2006) because many stakeholders call organisations (both for-profit and nonprofit) to account for their activities.

By following these perspectives of the accountability (both internal and external), many scholars have analysed *to whom* organisations have to be accountable and have provided significant conceptual frameworks to investigate the complex accountability system of NPOs, as well as describing the expectations and needs of stakeholders who are affected by or affect the organisations' activities (Avina, 1993; Kearns, 1994; Edwards & Hulme, 1996; Najam, 1996; Mitchell, Agle, & Wood, 1997; Brown & Moore, 2001; Ebrahim, 2003a, 2003b; Ospina et al., 2002). In analysing NGO accountability, Najam (1996) considers that these organisations have to be accountable to *patrons* (or 'upward,' as Edwards and Hulme, 1996 call it), *clients* (or 'downward,' Edwards and Hulme, 1996) and *themselves*, and provides insights aimed at investigating the 'difficulties they face in prioritizing and reconciling these multiple accountabilities' (p. 350; see also Stewart, 1984; Ebrahim, 2003a, 2003b, 2005; Christensen & Ebrahim, 2006).

While Najam (1996) and Ebrahim (2003a) focus on a relationship model by investigating the stakeholders to which NPOs have a moral duty to provide an account, other scholars propose a strategic approach to accountability. Moore (2000) reflects on the strategic worthiness of international NGOs' (INGOs) accountability and proposes a 'strategic triangle' developed to bolster leaders' calculations: social value creation, sustainable support by donors and founders and organisational survival. Using this approach, Brown and Moore (2001) proposed a multilevel accountability model aimed at linking and balancing these three dimensions simultaneously, because each of these issues can be seen as demanding accountability. They stated that 'in this sense, the choice of organizational strategy is a negotiated deal among the stakeholders to whom an INGO owes accountability. A successful strategy would be one that aligns these different kinds of accountability' (p. 587).

In reference to SEs, Matacena (2007) developed an accountability model in which he suggested a three-level accountability process that considers the social effectiveness (the ability to achieve social goals), the institutional (respect of legal and self-imposed rules) and the economic and financial dimension to evaluate the performance measurement and the long-run sustainability of the activity. This model was then set up and empirically tested by Bagnoli and Megali (2011). Moreover, Andreaus (2007) introduced social responsibility into the debate by offering a model that has since been empirically tested by Costa, Ramus, and Andreaus (2011). According to Andreaus (2007), if the institutional purpose of SEs is to maximise social value creation as defined by their mission and if accountability is the duty to provide an account of those actions for which a body is held responsible, SEs are primarily accountable to their stakeholders for the social value they create. Furthermore, SEs must also fulfil socially responsible and economic purposes in order to reinforce the achievement of their mission. In short, the SE has three types of responsibility, which are namely economic, social and mission-related.

Economic responsibility is a means to an end because SEs must be economically and financially accountable in order to guarantee the mission's achievement over time. *Social responsibility* refers to the SEs' accountability to stakeholders by providing them with information needed to react to the organisations' actions. This dimension is also called 'relational accountability' (Unerman & O'Dwyer, 2006). Finally, *mission responsibility* refers to accountability for the coherence of SE activities with the values underlying the mission. Unerman and O'Dwyer (2006) consider this dimension 'identity accountability' since it 'represents a means by which managers (or activists) running organizations take responsibility for shaping their organizational mission and values' (p. 356).

To recap, these theoretical contributions have highlighted how an accountability system solely focused on donors or patrons (upward accountability) is likely to encounter 'accountability myopia,' as Ebrahim (2005) calls it. An accountability mechanism that exclusively pays attention to one economic bottom line will likely be myopic, because: (1) it privileges the relationship with one stakeholder—usually the funders—by missing and hiding the possibility of being accountable to communities or the NPOs' own missions; and (2) it ignores the long-run and reduces the time span of projects by focusing on short-term efficiency criteria.

On the basis of this discussion, some authors have both theoretically (Gray et al., 2006; Ebrahim, 2005; Pearce, 2003) and empirically (Nicholls, 2009, 2010; Gibbon & Affleck, 2008; Diochon & Anderson, 2009) pointed out the relevance of enlarging accountability systems in NPOs and SEs by also adopting social and environmental accounting and reporting practices. Furthermore, as Gray et al. (2006) recall, 'Fowler (1995) recommended the use of multi-stakeholder social accounting for NGOs almost ten years ago [nineteen years from the present]' (p. 337). Similarly, Ebrahim (2003b) demonstrated the advantages and disadvantages that may occur when NPOs adopt the process of social accounting[5] by concluding that these innovative practices 'can increase organizational transparency if information that is collected and analyzed—including evidence of failure—is disclosed to stakeholders or the public' (p. 824).

DID THE ITALIAN LEGISLATOR MISS AN OPPORTUNITY? A CRITICAL DISSERTATION OF THE RECENT ITALIAN LAW (LAW 118/2005 AND LEGISLATIVE DECREE DLGS.N. 155/2006)

From the practical and theoretical considerations which emerged in the previous paragraph, this section reflects on the Italian context by offering critical and constructive insights into the recent Italian law on SEs (118/2005) in order to understand how the legislator has probably 'missed the opportunity' to accommodate the accountability needs of SEs to be more accountable to their stakeholder.

These observations emanate from data provided in 2009 from the IRIS Network, the Italian Association of Research Centre for Social Enterprises. Four years after the promulgation of the law, Zandonai and Borzaga (2009) highlighted that only 623 organisations[6] out of almost 14,000 possible organisational SEs obtained their 'legal brand' of SE by registering at the Chamber of Commerce.

These data seem to suggest a possible 'partial failure' of the recent legal Italian framework due to the inability to appeal to traditional social cooperatives in the new legal form of 'regulated social enterprises.' One simple question arises: how many regulated SEs belong to the category of organisational SEs, and how many of them have other organisational legal forms? The data are not robust enough, even if the IRIS Network reports the hypothesis that few regulated SEs belong to the organisational form of social cooperative. This means (refer to Figure 4.1) that regulated SEs are actually dominated by investor-owned organisations (the right side of the figure), which offer goods and services that meet the social welfare needs in an entrepreneurial way. They do so by respecting dividend constraints and adopting an organisational form that is very different from a cooperative one.

Both Italian academics and practitioners ask why the new legal framework was unable to act as a self-identifying brand to distinguish SEs from other organisations (Andreaus, 2007; Sacconi, 2006). In other words, they ask why non-regulated organisational SEs (primarily social cooperatives) did not become 'regulated social enterprises.' Reflections on the reasons for the 'partial failure' of the legislation come from many Italian scholars involved in different research fields. Lawyers (Fici & Galletti, 2007; Iamiceli, 2009), as well as economists (Ecchia & Viviani, 2006; Sacconi, 2006) and accountants (Andreaus, 2007; Marano, 2006; Rusconi & Signori, 2007; Travaglini, 2006, 2007), have contributed to the debate on SEs by analysing the limits and potential of the recent legislation. Simplifying the issue a little, they 'blame' the social reporting duty, and in particular, they criticise the compulsory content of the pro forma established on 24 January 2008 within the Implementing Decree[7]. By analysing the 38 items required by the law and trying to attribute an 'area of disclosure' for each one of these (Annex I), it is possible to see that few indicators refer to social and environmental issues; i.e., minimum and maximum value of compensation for workers, compensation for temporary workers, the total number of women workers, the total number of active volunteers in the organisation and the number and types of beneficiaries (many of these are related to governance, activities, general information and financial subjects). Thus, it seems that the legislator put a list of items rather unrelated to social and environmental disclosure under the 'social accounting umbrella.' If one considers social reporting as 'the process of communicating the social and environmental effects of organizations' economic actions to particular interest groups within society and to society at large' (Gray, Owen, & Mauders, 1987, p. ix), it is doubtful that the guidelines for social reporting proposed by the legislator can be accepted.

From this issue, two main concerns arise. First, the legislator gave too much attention to the details of the information, thus building a strictly formal accountability system. Since 'formal accountability may well be an unnecessary burden—and an improper imposition' (Gray et al., 2006, p. 335), in this case it probably discourages SEs from facing the challenging social accounting process (Iamiceli, 2009). As a consequence, for NPOs and thus SEs, it is better to suggest an informal and less 'heavy' system of accounting in order to properly understand the organisations' accountability and its application.

Second, the standard promoted by the new legal framework is primarily devoted to controlling the governance requirement demanded by the legislator. The main information is related to the governance and activities carried out as a formal control of the requirements to become a regulated SE. In this sense, two main areas of disclosure are underestimated/less considered: (1) the centrality of the mission, and (2) the stakeholders.

As Ebrahim (2003a, 2005) suggests, NPO accountability should be based on the ethical mission of the organisation and should not overemphasise rule-following. Since the mission has an ethical dimension that highlights the internal motivations of actors, it saves NPOs from the risk of privileging the accountability relationship with one type of stakeholder, namely funders, because of their greater power. Therefore, a first prerequisite for SE accountability seems to be the mission, its description and the outputs and outcomes resulting from the activities carried out. Moreover, the pro forma social report suggested by the legislator is not able to effectively take account of the relationship with stakeholders; it only requires a representation of the map of stakeholders. However, this information is not meaningful without an analysis of the stakeholders' needs and claims, resulting in the definition of SEs' responsibilities and duties of accountability (Gray et al., 1996; Unerman & O'Dwyer, 2006). If we accept the broadest view of accountability, then SEs should be accountable to all those who are affected or can affect the organisations. According to this view, the standard for social reporting proposed by the Italian legislator is poor in content and unsuitable to encourage a dialogue between SEs and their stakeholders.

In summation, if social and environmental accounting and reporting is considered a process through which SEs appraise, report and enhance their social and environmental performance, in particular by stakeholder engagement and dialogue, it is difficult to accept and agree with the compulsory standard of social reporting provided by the Italian regulation for 'legal' SEs. This guideline should be considered to include a 'minimum level' of transparency (Gray et al., 2006) due to the general information contained therein; i.e., what the organisation is, what it does, how its governance works. However, it can hardly be accepted as a 'complete framework' for social and environmental reporting. In this sense, I agree with Sacconi (2006) when he states that the social reporting required by law 'is defined as an instrument to verify the correspondence with the social aim required to be social enterprise . . . Thus, the guidelines suggest mainly to account for the quantity and quality of social-value goods and services provided. In this way, the social report is likely to be understood as a social statement of the core business and its results (production of a good social utility)' (p. 58).

The above considerations raise the question: *what would a social reporting standard for SEs look like?* Three main steps probably have to be considered.

1. *To simplify.* Generalisation is necessary. The regulation should provide the SEs with a more general-oriented reporting pro forma by avoiding counterproductive and unnecessary tools.
2. *To put mission at the core.* It is possible to restart from an 'enhanced social audit' (Nicholls, 2009) or 'identity' report (Unerman & O'Dwyer, 2006), which is mission-focused and provides narratives on the activities and actions that SEs carry out.
3. *To enlarge accountability towards stakeholders.* This last step is consistent with a broad conceptualisation of stakeholder accountability and assumes that SEs have a moral duty (Black, 2003) to provide an account towards all stakeholders (not only members).

CONCLUSIONS AND FURTHER RESEARCH

This chapter, by presenting the Italian scenario on SEs and also by considering the recent Italian regulation (Law 118/2005 and Legislative Decree Dlgs.n. 155/2006), has critically argued that organisational SEs are not encouraged to acquire the 'legal brand' of a social enterprise because after the accreditation they have to draw up a stand-alone social report on a compulsory basis. These constructive concerns do not criticise the adoption of the mandatory social report a priori; on the contrary, they reflect on the content proposed by the Italian legislator.

The main points that are missing in the pro forma report are the centrality of the mission and the relationship with the stakeholders. The law is, thus, unable to highlight the central role of the mission, which is a distinctive feature of every NPO (Kanter & Summers, 1987; Johnston, 2001). Moreover, the guidelines proposed by the legislator do not take into account the legitimate needs of the stakeholders (Unerman & O'Dwyer, 2006; Bouckaert & Vandenhove, 1998). In this sense, the social report seems to be more a 'cost' and a 'constraint' than a strength, and an opportunity for an NPO willing to acquire the status of 'regulated social enterprise'; this could be a disincentive.

In conclusion, after the promulgation of the Legislative Decree Dlgs.n. 155/2006 in Italy, which introduced a compulsory standard for delivering social reports, many Italian authors have pointed out that the 'bureaucratic' approach adopted by the legislator might be one reason for the partial failure of the law (Andreaus, 2006, 2007; Rusconi & Signori, 2007). Indeed, this chapter argues that the model of social reporting proposed by the legislator is neither able to measure the achievement of the institutional purposes of the SEs (mission) nor the means by which those objectives are pursued in accordance with the legitimate interests of all stakeholders involved and under the constraint of long-term sustainability (efficiency). As a result, social reporting is characterised as being essentially an additional 'cost' and inherently bureaucratic for the SEs, rather than an opportunity for self-evaluation or clear communication to the relevant stakeholders.

In order to better comprehend the role of the Italian social reporting standard as a disincentive to acquire the legal status of an SE, more empirical studies have to be developed. In particular, further quantitative and qualitative research could evaluate how SEs are discharging accountability, both financial and social. Furthermore, some in-depth content analysis might evaluate whether the legislation had an impact on SEs' accountability and reporting systems. Finally, future research could look at the accountability frameworks that are developed in other countries where similar or nearly similar organisations are put in place.

APPENDIX

Appendix 1: Compulsory pro forma standard required by the Decree, 24 January 2008

		Area of disclosure
1	Introduction. Description of the methodology used for the social report	General
A. General information about the institution/organisation and the administrator(s)		
2	Name of the organisation	General
3	Registered office	General
4	Secondary office	General
5	Name of the administrator(s)	General
6	Names of people in charge as an institutional office	General
7	Sector of activity	General
B. Structure and corporate governance		
8	Mission	General
9	Information about the social/legal form adopted	General
10	Corporate governance information required from statute	Governance

(*Continued*)

Appendix I   (Continued)

		Area of disclosure
11	Appointment of directors criteria	Governance
12	Appointing directors with delegated powers	Governance
13	Number of members	Governance
14	Summary of associative life (number of meetings, etc.)	Governance
15	Map of stakeholders	Governance
16	Payments to directors	Governance
17	Payments to financial controller	Governance
18	Min and max value of compensation for workers	Social: workers
19	Compensation for temporary workers	Social: workers
20	The total number of women workers	Social: workers
21	Analysis of the subsidiaries	Consolidated
22	Major networks and collaborations with third parties	Context
23	The total number of active volunteers in the organisation	Social: workers
24	Number and types of beneficiaries	Social: beneficiaries
25	Evaluation of the economic and financial risk provided by the directors	Financial
	C. Aims and activity	
26	Main objectives	Activities
27	Summary of main activities	Activities
28	Analysis of the relevant factors to achieve the objectives	Activities
29	Evaluation of achieved results and analysis of the impact on the social value created	Social: beneficiaries
30	Engagement with employees and beneficiaries	Social: beneficiaries + workers
31	Description of fundraising activities	Financial
32	Indication of long-term strategies and outline of future plans	Activities
	Economic and financial information	
33	Analysis of revenue and income	Financial
34	Analysis of costs and expenses	Financial

		Area of disclosure
35	Analysis of how the costs have supported the key objectives of the institution	Financial
36	Analysis of the availability of funds—budget and constraints	Financial
37	Costs related to fundraising activities, income obtained through fundraising activities and the percentage of this revenue used to defray the costs of fundraising	Financial
38	Analysis of the investment carried out and analysis of their funding	Financial

NOTES

1 The EMES (Emergence of Social Enterprise in Europe) Project, begun in 1996, conducts research on social enterprise in European Union countries with funds from the European Commission. It is the basis for the European EMES Network that annually holds international conferences on social enterprise in Trento, Italy.

2 For an in-depth investigation of the UK experience, see Borzaga and Defourny (2001) and Defourny and Nyssen (2008b).

3 The Chamber of Commerce in Italy is organised as a national body with regional networks/chapters. Each regional Chamber of Commerce is aimed at carrying out functions of general interest within the private business system. One of the functions of the regional Chamber of Commerce is to manage the 'official business register,' a register where all enterprises belonging to that region must be enrolled.

4 New legislation has also been set up for SEs in the UK. In July 2005, the Community Interest Company (CIC) was established as the legal form for SEs (Defourny & Nyssen, 2008b, 2008c). CICs are required to present their financial account annually, along with the CIC34, a Community Interest Company Report that contains information about activities carried out, stakeholder engagement and other economic information (transfer of assets, dividends offered, interest paid) (Nicholls, 2009).

5 To be precise, Ebrahim (2005) refers to social auditing practices; however, according to Gray (2002), social accounting, social responsibility accounting and social auditing are only different 'labels' that describe the extension of accounting reports to include information about products, employee claims, community initiatives and environmental impact.

6 The list of these organisations was not available at the time of this study because the National Centre of the Chamber of Commerce has to coordinate with each regional body to build an integrated and complete database. However, the complete database for the 'non-regulated' social enterprises (SEs) is available because, historically, they play an important role in the economic tissue of Italy.

7 See Appendix 1 for a complete list of the items required by law.

REFERENCES

Acli. (2002). *Bilancio Sociale 2002*. Servizi Socio-Assistenziali ed Educativi. Organizzazione Non Lucativa di Utilità Sociale. Cordenons.

Alter, S. (2006). Social enterprise models and their mission and money. In A. Nicholls (Ed.), *Social entrepreneurship* (pp. 205–232). Oxford: Oxford University Press.

Andreaus, M. (2006). La legge delega sull'impresa sociale: Quali implicazioni dal punto di vista aziendale. *Impresa Sociale, 75*(3), 100–113.

Andreaus, M. (2007). Quale modello di rendicontazione per l'impresa sociale? *Impresa Sociale, 76*(1), 59–78.

Austin, J., Stevenson, H., & Skillern, J. W. (2006). Social and commercial entrepreneurship: Same, different, or both? *Entrepreneurship Theory and Practice*, January, 1–22.

Avina, J. (1993). The evolutionary life cycles of non-governmental development organizations. *Public Administration and Development, 13*, 453–474.

Bagnoli, L., & Megali, C. (2011). Measuring performance in social enterprises. *Nonprofit and Voluntary Sector Quarterly, 40*(1), 149–165.

Battilana, J., & Dorado, S. (2010). Building sustainable hybrid organizations: The case of commercial microfinance organizations. *Academy of Management Journal, 53*(6), 1419–1440.

Benjamin, L. M. (2008). Account space: How accountability requirements shape nonprofit practice. *Nonprofit and Voluntary Sector Quarterly, 37*(2), 201–223.

Black, L. (2003, May 20). *Archive: Liam Black*. Ethical Corporation. Retrieved from http://www.ethicalcorp.com/content.asp?ContentID=622

Bolton, B., & Thompson, J. (2003). *The entrepreneur in focus*. Boston, MA: Thomson Learning.

Borzaga, C., & Ianes, A. (2006). L'Economia della solidarietà. Storia e prospettive della cooperazione sociale. Rome: Donzelli Editore.

Borzaga, C., & Defourny, J. (2001). *The emergence of social enterprise*. London: Routledge.

Boschee, J. (1995). Social entrepreneurship. *Across the Board, 32*(3), 20–25.

Bouckaert, L., & Vandenhove, J. (1998). Business ethics and the management of non-profit institutions. *Journal of Business Ethics, 17*, 1073–1081.

Brown, L. D., & Moore, M. H. (2001). Accountability, strategy and international non-governmental organizations. *Nonprofit and Voluntary Sector Quarterly, 30*, 569–587.

Cadiai. (2006). *Bilancio Sociale Preventivo 2006*. Bologna.

Christensen, R. A., & Ebrahim, A. (2006). How does accountability affect mission? *Nonprofit Management and Leadership, 17*(2), 195–209.

Cornwall, A., Lucas, H., & Pasteur, K. (2000). Introduction. Accountability through participation: Developing workable partnership models in the health sector. *IDS Bulletin, 31*, 1–13.

Costa, E., Andreaus, M., Carini, C., & Carpita, M. (2012). Exploring the efficiency of Italian social cooperatives by descriptive and principal component analysis. *Service Business, 6*(1), 117–136.

Costa, E., Ramus, T., & Andreaus, M. (2011). Accountability as a managerial tool in non-profit organizations: Evidence from Italian CSVs. *Voluntas: International Journal of Voluntary and Nonprofit Organizations, 22*(3), 470–493.

Dacin, P. A., Dacin, M. T., & Matear, M. (2010). Social entrepreneurship: Why we don't need a new theory and how we move forward from here. *Academy of Management Perspectives, 24*(3), 37–57.

Dart, R. (2004). The legitimacy of social enterprise. *Nonprofit Management & Leadership, 14*(4), 411–424.

Dart, R., Clow, E., & Armstrong, A. (2010). Meaningful difficulties in the mapping of social enterprises. *Social Enterprise Journal, 6*(3), 186–193.

Dees, J. G. (1998a). *The meaning of social entrepreneurship.* Retrieved from http://www.fuqua.duke.edu/centers/case/documents/dees_SE.pdf

Dees, J. G. (1998b). Enterprising nonprofits. *Harvard Business Review, 76*(1), 55–66.

Dees, J. G., & Elias, L. (1998). The challenges of combining social and commercial enterprise. *Business Ethics Quarterly, 8*(1), 165–178.

Dees, J. G., & Economy, P. (2001). Social entrepreneurship. In J. G Dees, J. Emerson, & P. Economy (Eds.), *Enterprising nonprofits: A toolkit for social entrepreneurship* (pp. 1–18). Canada: John Wiley & Sons, Inc.

Defourny, J. (2001). Introduction: From third sector to social enterprise. In C. Borzaga & J. Defourny (Eds.), *The emergence of social enterprise* (pp. 1–28). London: Routledge.

Defourny, J., & Nyssen, M. (2006). Defining social enterprises. In M. Nyssen (Ed.), *Social enterprise: At the crossroads of market, public policies and civil society* (pp. 3–27). New York: Routledge.

Defourny, J., & Nyssen, M. (2008a). Social enterprise in Europe: Recent trends and developments. *Social Enterprise Journal, 4*(3), 203–228.

Defourny, J, & Nyssen, M. (2008b). *Conceptions of social enterprises in Europe and the United States: Convergences and divergences.* Paper presented at the Second EMES International Conference on Social Enterprise, University of Trento, IT, July 1–4, 2009. Retrieved from http://www.emes.net/fileadmin/emes/PDF_files/Conferences/JD_MN_EU-US_final_Trento_2009.pdf

Defourny, J., & Nyssen, M. (Eds.). (2008c). *Social enterprise in Europe: Recent trends and developments.* EMES Working paper, 08/01.

Defourny, J., & Nyssen, M. (2010). Conceptions of social enterprise and social entrepreneurship in Europe and the United States: Convergences and divergences. *Journal of Social Entrepreneurship, 1*(1), 32–53.

Diochon, M., & Anderson, A. R. (2009). Social enterprise and effectiveness: A process typology. *Social Enterprise Journal, 5*(1), 7–29.

Dixon, R., Ritchie, J., & Siwale, J. (2006). Microfinance: Accountability from the grassroots. *Accounting, Auditing & Accountability Journal, 19*(3), 405–427.

Dorado, S. (2005). Institutional entrepreneurship, partaking, and convening. *Organization Studies, 26*(3), 383–413.

Dorado, S. (2006). Social entrepreneurial ventures: Different values so different process of creations, no? *Journal of Developmental Entrepreneurship, 11*(4), 319–343.

Ebrahim, A. (2003a). Making sense of accountability: Conceptual perspectives for northern and southern nonprofits. *Nonprofit Management & Leadership, 14*(2), 191–212.

Ebrahim, A. (2003b). Accountability in practice: Mechanisms for NGOs. *World Development, 31*(5), 813–829.

Ebrahim, A. (2005). Accountability myopia: Losing sight of organizational learning. *Nonprofit and Voluntary Sector Quarterly, 34*(1), 56–87.

Ecchia, G., & Viviani, M. (2006). *Responsabilità sociale e impresa sociale.* AICCON Working paper, no. 34. Retrieved from http://www.aiccon.it/working_paper.cfm

Edwards, M., & Hulme, D. (1996). Too close for comfort? The impact of official aid on nongovernmental organizations. *World Development, 24*(6), 961–973.

European Commission. (2013). *Social economy and social entrepreneurship—social Europe guide* (Vol. 4). Retrieved from http://ec.europa.eu/social/main.jsp?-catId=738&langId=it&pubId =7523

Fici, A. (2006). La nozione di impresa sociale e le finalità della disciplina. *Impresa Sociale*, 75(3), 23–41.

Fici, A. & Galletti, D. (2007). *Commentario al decreto sull'impresa sociale* (D.lgs. 24 marzo 2006, n. 155). Torino, IT: Giappichelli.

Fowler, A. (1995). Assessing NGO performance: Difficulties, dilemmas and a way forward. In M. Edwards & D. Hulme (Eds.), *Non-governmental organisations—performance and accountability: Beyond the magic bullet* (pp. 143–156). London: Earthscan.

Fox, J. A., & Brown, L. D. (Eds.). (1998). *The struggle for accountability: The World Bank, NGOs and grassroots movements*. London: MIT Press.

Galera, G., & Borzaga, C. (2009). Social enterprise: An international overview of its conceptual evolution and legal implementation. *Social Enterprise Journal*, 5(3), 210–228.

Gandía, J. L. (2011). Internet disclosure by nonprofit organizations: Empirical evidence of nongovernmental organizations for development in Spain. *Nonprofit and Voluntary Sector Quarterly*, 40(1), 57–78.

Gibbon, J., & Affleck, A. (2008). Social enterprise resisting social accounting: Reflecting on lived experiences. *Social Enterprise Journal*, 4(1), 41–56.

Goddard, A., & Assad, M. J. (2006). Accounting and navigating legitimacy in Tanzanian NGOs. *Accounting, Auditing & Accountability Journal*, 19(3), 377–404.

Gray, R., Bebbington, J., & Collison, D. (2006). NGOs, civil society and accountability: Making the people accountable to capital. *Accounting, Auditing & Accountability Journal*, 19(3), 319–348.

Gray, R. H. (2002). The social accounting project and accounting organizations and society privileging engagement, imaginings, new accountings and pragmatism over critique? *Accounting, Organizations and Society*, 27, 687–708.

Gray, R. H., Owen, D. L., & Adams, C. (1996). *Accounting and accountability: Changes and challenges in corporate social and environmental reporting*. London: Prentice Hall.

Gray, R. H., Owen, D. L., & Mauders, K. T. (1987). *Corporate social reporting: Accounting and accountability*. Hemel Hempstead, UK: Prentice Hall.

Grenier, P. (2003). Reclaiming enterprise for the social good: The political climate for social entrepreneurship in UK. Paper presented at the 32nd Annual ARNOVA Conference, Denver, CO.

Iamiceli, P. (2009). La disciplina dell'impresa sociale: Potenzialità, limiti e prospettive. In C. Borzaga & F. Zandonai (Eds.), *L'impresa sociale in Italia* (pp. 87–102). Rome: Donzelli Editore.

ISTAT. (2008). *Le cooperative sociali in Italia—anno 2005*. Informazioni, n. 4, Roma. Retrieved from: http://www3.istat.it/dati/catalogo/20080807_03/inf_08_04le_cooperative_sociali_italia05.pdf

Johnston, R. (2001). Defining your mission. In J. G. Dees, J. Emerson, & P. Economy (Eds.), *Enterprising nonprofits: A toolkit for social entrepreneurship* (pp. 19–42). Canada: John Wiley & Sons, Inc.

Kanter, R. M., & Summers, D. V. (1987). Doing well while doing good: Dilemmas of performance measurement in nonprofit organizations and the need for a multiple-constituency approach. In W. W. Powell (Ed.), *The non-profit sector—a research handbook* (pp. 154–164). New Haven, CT: Yale University Press.

Kearns, K. P. (1994). The strategic management of accountability in nonprofit organizations: An analytical framework. *Public Administration Review*, 54(2), 185–192.

Kerlin, J. A. (2006). Social enterprise in the United States and Europe: Understanding and learning from the differences. *Voluntas: International Journal of Voluntary and Nonprofit Organizations*, 17, 247–263.

Levi, Y. (1999). Community and hybrid multi-stakeholder co-operatives: A comparison. *Review of International Co-operation, 92,* 83–94.

Lohmann, R. (1992). The commons: A multidisciplinary approach to nonprofit organization, voluntary action, and philanthropy. *Nonprofit and Voluntary Sector Quarterly, 21*(3), 309–323.

Mair, J., & Martì, I. (2006). Social entrepreneurship research: A source of explanation, prediction, and delight. *Journal of World Business, 41*(1), 36–44.

Marano, M. (2006). *L'accountability e i processi informativi dell'impresa sociale alla luce del* (D.lgs. 155/2006). AICCON Working paper, no. 38. Retrieved from http://www.aiccon.it/file/convdoc/n.38.pdf

Matacena, A. (2007). Accountability e social reporting nelle imprese sociali. *Impresa Sociale, 76*(1), 12–39.

Mitchell, R., Agle, B., & Wood, D. (1997). Towards a theory of stakeholder identification and salience: Defining the principle of who and what really counts. *Academy of Management Review, 22*(4), 853–886.

Moore, M. H. (2000). Managing for value: Organizational strategy in for-profit, nonprofit and governmental organizations. *Nonprofit and Voluntary Sector Quarterly, 29*(1), 183–204.

Najam, A. (1996). NGO accountability: A conceptual framework. *Development Policy Review, 46,* 339–353.

Nicholls, A. (2005). Measuring impact in social entrepreneurship: New accountabilities to stakeholders and investors? Seminar on Social Enterprise, Milton Keynes University.

Nicholls, A. (2009). 'We do good things, don't we?': 'Blended value accounting' in social entrepreneurship. *Accounting, Organizations and Society, 34,* 755–769.

Nicholls, A. (2010). Institutionalizing social entrepreneurship in regulatory space: Reporting and disclosure by community interest companies. *Accounting, Organizations and Society, 35,* 394–415.

O'Dwyer, B., & Unerman, J. (2007). From functional to social accountability. Transforming the accountability relationship between funders and non-governmental development organisations. *Accounting, Auditing & Accountability Journal, 20*(3), 446–471.

Ospina, S., Diaz, W., & O'Sullivan, J. F. (2002). Negotiating accountability: Managerial lessons from identity-based nonprofit organizations. *Nonprofit and Voluntary Sector Quarterly, 31*(1), 5–31.

Pearce, J. (2003). *Social enterprise in anytown.* London: Calouste Gulbenkian Foundation.

Peredo, A. M., & McLean, M. (2006). Social entrepreneurship: A critical review of the concept. *Journal of World Business, 41*(1), 56–65.

Rusconi, G., & Signori, S. (2007). Responsabilità sociale e aziende nonprofit: Quale declinazione? *Impresa Sociale, 76*(1), 39–58.

Sacconi, L. (2006). La legge sull'impresa sociale come selettore di organizzazioni con motivazioni necessarie all'efficienza: Quasi un'occasione mancata. *Impresa Sociale, 75*(3), 42–65.

Seelos, C., & Mair, J. (2005). Social entrepreneurship: Creating new business models to serve the poor. *Business Horizons, 48,* 241–246.

Stewart, J. (1984). The role of information in public accountability. In A. Hopwood & C. Tomkins (Eds.), *Issues in public sector accountability* (pp. 13–34). Oxford: Phillip Allan.

Sud, M., VanSandt, C. V., & Baugous, A. M. (2009). Social entrepreneurship: The role of institutions. *Journal of Business Ethics, 85,* 201–216.

Thomas, A. (2004). The rise of social cooperatives in Italy. *Voluntas: International Journal of Voluntary and Nonprofit Organizations, 15*(3), 243–263.

Thompson, J. L. (2008). Social enterprise and social entrepreneurship: Where have we reached? A summary of issues and discussion points. *Social Enterprise Journal, 4*(2), 149–161.

Travaglini, C. (2006). L'informazione contabile nell'impresa sociale. *Impresa Sociale, 75*(3), 88–99.

Travaglini, C. (2007). Dal gruppo nonprofit al gruppo dell'impresa sociale: Dieci anni di sviluppo delle attività e di accountability nonprofit. *Impresa Sociale, 76*(1), 79–90.

Unerman, J., & O'Dwyer, B. (2006). Theorising accountability for NGO advocacy. *Accounting, Auditing & Accountability Journal, 19*(3), 349–376.

Zandonai, F., & Borzaga, C. (Eds.). (2009). *L'impresa sociale in Italia. Economia e Istituzione dei beni Comuni*. Rapporto Iris Network. Rome: Donzelli Editore.

Part II

Issues in Financial Reporting and Regulation

5 An Unrelated Income Tax for Australia?

Evelyn Brody, Oonagh B. Breen, Myles McGregor-Lowndes and Matthew Turnour

INTRODUCTION

Australia, unlike other developed economies, does not tax the unrelated business income of tax-exempt charitable organisations. It has been estimated that 'the value of tax concessions given by all Australian governments to [NFPs] could be at least $4 billion in 2008–09 and that it could realistically be twice this amount when non-estimated expenditures are included' (Productivity Commission, 2010, p. 78). In the 2011 federal budget (Australian Government, The Treasury, 2011a, p. 36), the Australian government announced the introduction of what amounts to an unrelated business income tax (UBIT) on the income of not-for-profit (NFP) entities, commencing from 1 July 2011. It broadly proposed that NFPs pay tax on any retained earnings not annually remitted and applied to the purposes of the tax concession entity, and that existing input tax concessions (such as Fringe Benefits Tax and Goods and Services Tax) would not be available for unrelated commercial activities. The government postponed the commencement date to 1 July 2012 to allow for more consultation (Bradbury, 2012). Unrelated activities begun before that date will be covered by transitional arrangements amounting to a phase-out over an unspecified period. However, the bill was not introduced into Parliament before the 2013 election and the new government has formally indicated that it will not proceed with the bill, 'but will explore simpler alternatives to address the risks to revenue' (Assistant Treasurer, 2013).

This chapter will examine the Australian government's proposals to establish the desired policy outcomes and the models suggested for implementation of the policy. While there appear to be multiple bases for the policy, the government's intention is clearly to use taxation tools to achieve its purposes. However, it offers a number of models—drawn from the experiences of two jurisdictions, the United States of America and the United Kingdom—to implement the policy. Each is examined in turn.

In addition, the broad policy that has developed over decades in the U.S. is described, before examining the lessons that might inform future policy implementation in Australia. The U.S. introduced a UBIT in 1950 (Simon,

Dale, & Chisolm, 2006, p. 267; Burch, 2012) in response to unfair competition claims. The tax framework for NFP commercial activity in that
country includes both federal and state-level tax-exemption regimes. The
federal rules also apply the regular income tax to certain business activities
that do not otherwise jeopardise exemption. Under UBIT, tax-exempt NFP
organisations are taxed at the corporate tax rate on income not related to
their exempt purposes. While income tax-exempt NFP organisations generate taxable income by regularly carrying on unrelated business activities
(Brody, 2009, p. 93–94), an IRS statistical report on UBIT in 2013 established that, in fact, little unrelated income of NFPs was actually taxed (Jackson, 2013, p. 169). The low amount of collections is attributed to a number
of factors, including the width of exemptions, sophisticated tax planning,
errors and ignorance of the specific provisions (Brody, 2009; Sansing, 1998;
Yetman, 2005).

Finally, we examine the position in the UK, where a different structural approach is taken with unrelated business income—it also results
in little revenue being collected, but substantial administration and compliance costs. The Charity Commission for England and Wales (CCEW)
will refuse to register charities with objects for trading, because trading is
not a charitable object (Luxton, 2001, p. 20.2). This stance has promoted
the use of charity-trading subsidiaries which are controlled by the charity, but which separate risk from the charity's assets. The profits from a
trading subsidiary do not qualify for charity tax exemption and are liable
to corporation tax. However, payments (Gift Aid contributions) made by
the trading subsidiary to the controlling charity reduce the level of profits
which are taxable in the trading subsidiary. Tax exemption is available to
the recipient charity in respect of the income which it receives from the
trading subsidiary. Any dual use of assets or staff must be apportioned.
The net result is that there are additional costs of establishment and maintenance of the separate legal structures, tax administration and compliance
costs, but little additional income tax revenue (Breen, 2010, p. 136).

THE AUSTRALIAN PROPOSALS

The Australian government's formal announcement of its intention to enact
legislation to tax unrelated business income of charitable bodies heralded a
reform journey contorted with hairpin turns. This may partly explain why
the underlying problem to be addressed is difficult to establish with any cer-
tainty. Once they qualify as being income tax exempt, Australian nonprofits
are not required to file income tax returns or pay income tax on any income,
even if it was generated from sources unrelated to its primary purpose, in
order to cross-subsidise its mission.

A High Court case was funded as a test case by the Australian Taxation Office (ATO) on the theory that at a certain point unrelated income

imperilled the income tax-exempt status of a nonprofit organisation. That case was Commissioner of Taxation v Word Investments Ltd (2008) 236 CLR 204 (Word Investments), which made its way through the appeal courts, eventually reaching the High Court. The Court held that the income of a charitable organisation conducting business activities to fund charitable purposes conducted by another organisation was exempt from income tax. The consequence is that charities are defined by reference to a charitable purpose, not their activities or legal form. The organisation involved had at various times operated a funeral business, land subdivision and charged for financial services advice, to generate funds to support a religious organisation that translated the bible into foreign languages. Its activities reflect an international trend of NFPs generating additional revenues from social purpose enterprise which may be technically 'for-profit' or hybrid in legal structure.

The decision appears identical to the 'destination of income' test, which had been the initial position in the United States (Trinidad v Sagrada Orden de Predicadores 263 US 578 (1924)). Legal commentary written immediately after the High Court decision foreshadowed the possibility of legislation to reverse or reform the situation (Murray, 2008, 2009; Mortimer, 2010; Sadiq & Richardson, 2010).

The Australian government indicated that it would monitor the situation and await the recommendations of the Australia's Future Tax System Review (2009) (the Henry Review), which was specifically tasked to examine tax expenditures such as the income tax exemption for NFPs, but warned that it would act sooner if there were 'adverse implications' (Bowen, 2009). The Henry Review, headed by the then Head of Treasury, surprisingly recommended that the exemption continue to apply not only to charities but all NFPs and that unrelated business income continue to be exempt in the following terms:

> Categories of NFP organisations that currently receive income tax or GST [Goods and Services Tax] concessions should retain these concessions. NFP organisations should be permitted to apply their income concessions to their commercial activities.
> (Australia's Future Tax System Review Panel, 2009, p. 88)

Reporting after the Henry Review, although having conducted its inquiry in parallel, the Productivity Commission also concluded that NFP income tax exemptions should remain and should cover all income, include unrelated business income (Productivity Commission, 2010, p. 203). A decade and a half ago, the Industry Commission, predecessor of the Productivity Commission, reached the same conclusion (Industry Commission, 1995, appendix K). These three substantial report findings would ordinarily be expected to put the matter to rest until another situation arose to reopen the debate. However, the federal election in 2010 saw the government elected on a policy of charity law reform having a central regulator as its core feature (O'Connell, Martin, & Chan, 2013). The Treasury noted of the election commitment that scope existed for 'ensuring that the assets of charities are adequately protected when organisations undertake risky activities' (Australian Government, The Treasury, 2010, p. 6).

The 2011 federal budget contained a number of reforms concerning the NFP sector, including removing tax concessions from income generated by, and retained in, new unrelated commercial activities commencing after 10 May 2011 (budget night). Initially only applying to new commercial activities, the application to existing activities will be phased in over time, after consultation (Australian Government, The Treasury, 2011a, p. 36). Shortly afterwards, the Treasury released a consultation paper about reforming the use of tax concessions by businesses operated by NFP entities (Australian Government, The Treasury, 2011b). Broadly it proposed that NFP entities pay tax on any retained earnings not annually remitted to it and applied to the purposes of the tax concession entity. Existing input tax concessions such as FBT (Fringe Benefits Tax) and Goods and Services Tax (GST) would not be available for unrelated commercial activities, which would be a serious impost on nonprofit organisations. The Productivity Commission (2010, p. 76) estimates FBT concession at about $1 billion annually, with many organisations completely exempt. The paper further explained that the proposed reforms were not to alter the current state of the law in relation to mutuality. Australia, unlike other common law jurisdictions, has not statutorily altered the doctrine of mutuality whereby an organisation cannot gain income from itself (Australian Taxation Office, 2010). The case of Bohemians Club v Acting Federal Commissioner of Taxation (1918) 24 CLR 334 confirmed the application of English common law in Australia, so that receipts from members, which are pooled funds, are not treated as taxable income. Clearly the policy sought not to tangle directly with the politically powerful machine gaming clubs, who have a vested interest in maintaining the doctrine of mutuality.

The proposed reforms would not alter the situation in respect of passive income for income tax-exempt organisations. Passive income (rather than trading income) generated from the holding of shares or equities is not regarded as assessable income and is viewed differently from income generated directly from a business, despite the absence of a bright line in many cases (Australian Taxation Office, 2005, para. 91). The consultation paper also carved out small-scale commercial activity and gave the example of UK tax law where a turnover threshold operates to exclude income from miscellaneous trading activities. There was no apparent discussion of why the government decided not to heed the advice of the previous inquiries, even those which had considered the impact of the Word Investments decision. Those inquiries had already exhaustively considered the policy reasons given in the consultation paper and had rejected any taxation response. The consultation policy rationale was couched in terms of:

a. 'Competitive neutrality' or level playing field;
b. Protecting NFPs from unnecessary commercial risks;
c. Ensuring only the specified tax subsidy purpose was supported by government concessions;
d. Encouraging NFPs to direct profits from unrelated commercial activities to their specified tax subsidy purpose

(Australian Government, The Treasury, 2011b;
Chia & Stewart, 2012, p. 337)

The competitive neutrality arguments mirror the principal concerns driving the U.S. provisions, and the risk argument draws strongly on the UK experience. The focus on ensuring that taxation concessions are targeted on a specific, narrow purpose is a characteristic of the Australia taxation system. It is illustrated by the awarding of gift deductibility status to a limited class of direct public benefit organisations and certain specifically named organisations, not to charities broadly defined, as occurs in the U.S., UK and most other Organisation for Economic Co-operation and Development (OECD) economies.

These U.S. and UK influences can be seen in the three broad options for implementing the reforms, suggested in the consultation paper. Two options require NFPs to create separate entities to carry on the unrelated business activities, as occurs in the UK; the other allows the unrelated activities to be carried on within the NFP, as can occur in the U.S., although, as conceded in the paper, in the U.S. there is often separation of the unrelated business.

The first option would have a separate entity—a company or a trust— created to conduct the unrelated business income. These entities would be subject to taxes, as would any comparable commercial business. NFPs which are charities or deductible gift recipients would be able either to have a separate company donate profits back, generating a taxation deduction, or use the franking credits system to repatriate profits. If a trust were used to carry on the business, a distribution to a charity would not trigger taxable income provisions. NFPs which do not fall into Australia's narrow definitions of charitable or deductible gift recipients would not be able to escape the full liability of taxation for unrelated business income. A number of advantages of this option were put forward, including transparency, consistency with for-profit commercial taxation and simplicity of administration for the Treasury. There was no analysis of potential disadvantages, apart from the need to take account of adverse consequences for state taxation, particularly stamp duties.

The second option is a variation of the first, with profits at the end of the year being taxed if they have not been distributed to the NFP. It was said to differ from the first option by having a cash flow advantage for the NFP, and also being more complex to administer and implement.

The third option would have the unrelated activity carried on within the NFP, which would need to account separately for unrelated business activity, the profits of which would be taxed if they were not directed to the tax-endorsed purposes. While this option would minimise the costs of establishing and maintaining a separate trading entity, it was seen as complex to administer with significant compliance costs for the NFP. It would also not achieve the risk exposure policy objectives.

The consultation paper's authors signalled their preference for the first option by devoting considerable detail to it and focusing on its advantages, giving little consideration to its disadvantages either to the regulators or NFPs; e.g., the paper lacks detail about costs and economic distortions from the perspective of NFPs. A considered analysis of these options in relation to the UK and U.S. experiences can inform this deficiency, as those jurisdictions have had distinct regulatory mechanisms for NFPs generating income through unrelated business activities for some time.

UNITED STATES

Federal Income Tax Exemption

Since 1950, federal income tax exemption is not available to 'feeder organizations'—those NFPs whose purpose is to operate a business and transfer its profits to an exempt organisation. While a taxable corporation may deduct charitable contributions, a cap of 10% of income applies in any given year. In regulations that apply to charities (tax exempt under Internal Revenue Code § 501(c)(3)), the Treasury Department distinguishes between purpose and activities, effectively providing that the 'destination of income' test for exemption survives if the charity engages in business activities for the right reasons. Specifically, exemption is not in jeopardy, 'although [the organisation] operates a trade or business as a substantial part of its activities, if the operation of such trade or business is in furtherance of the organization's exempt purpose or purposes and if the organization is not organized or operated for the primary purpose of carrying on an unrelated trade or business . . .' (26 CFR § 1.501(c) (3)-1(e)). In applying this 'primary purpose' test, the regulations add, 'all the circumstances must be considered, including the size and extent of the trade or business and the size and extent of the activities which are in furtherance of one or more exempt purposes' (26 CFR § 1.501(c)(3)-1(e)). While the primary purpose test might save overall exemption, separate provisions of the Code (described below) tax the exempt organisation on profits from an 'unrelated' trade or business.

In the last few decades, some courts have begun to embrace a position asserted by the IRS that a business purpose can be inferred if the NFP follows sound commercial practices. As one federal appeals court ruled: 'The particular manner in which an organization's activities are conducted, the commercial hue of those activities, competition with commercial firms, and the existence and amount of annual or accumulated profits, are all relevant evidence in determining whether an organization has a substantial nonexempt purpose' (Living Faith, Inc. v Commissioner, 950 F.2d 365, 371 (7th Cir. 1991)). Hopkins (1992) dubbed the approach epitomised by Living Faith as the 'commerciality doctrine,' and harshly criticised it: 'The commerciality doctrine was (1) conjured up by the courts, (2) never defined, but rather just asserted (as if everyone knew it was there all along), and (3) born out of the courts' concern over factors such as sizable net profits, accumulated funds, aggressive marketing, and competition between nonprofit and for-profit organizations. . . . The doctrine just evolved, growing from loose language in court opinions, which in turn seems to have reflected judges' personal views as to what the law ought to be (rather than what it is).' Simon et al. also question whether concerns about distortion of purpose or public trust due to erosion of the border between 'the nonprofit and the for-profit territories' are 'properly addressed by the tax system' (2006, p. 292).

Nevertheless, on a case-by-case basis, the IRS has increasingly denied exemption to NFP entities engaged in a variety of activities—including adoption, insurance, financial services, religious publishing, restaurants and conference centres, low-income housing and retreats for caretakers—generally due to their resemblance to similar for-profit businesses (see, e.g., Family Trust of Massachusetts, Inc, 892 F. Supp. 2d 149 (D.D.C. 2012)) (following Living Faith). Kelley observes that American society has been moving 'toward a results-oriented, quasi-commercial, social engineer's conception of charity, while our law has continued to encourage, and often insist upon, a compassionate brand of "vulgar" charity' (2005, p. 2439).

From time to time, Congress has amended the Code to repeal exemption for specified types of NFPs that have found their commercial feet (notably, savings and loan associations, and Blue Cross/Blue Shield and similar health insurance organisations), or to impose additional conditions for exemption (such as for NFP credit-counselling organisations and hospitals).

The Unrelated Business Income Tax (UBIT)

Congress created the UBIT in the same legislation that replaced the destination-of-income test with denial of exemption for feeder organisations. The UBIT is designed to provide for one level of tax regardless of whether an NFP conducts an unrelated business directly or invests in the stock of a taxable corporation (Hansmann, 1989). The amount of potential tax could be significant: in estimating the profit earned on unrelated activities undertaken to earn income to support mission-related activities, Cordes and Brody (2006) found, assuming a combined federal and state tax rate of 40%, that exemption increases the resources of NFP organisations by roughly $10 billion in the aggregate. However, as described below, actual UBIT collections are a small fraction of this amount.

As defined in the statute and regulations, income from a business activity that is substantially related—aside from the production of funds—to the exempt purposes of the organisation is still tax exempt, but income from an unrelated trade or business is subject to normal corporate (or trust) tax. However, Congress specifically exempts most forms of passive investment income, such as dividends, interest, rents and royalties. Because of an automatic $1,000 deduction, an exempt organisation with a small amount of unrelated business income (UBI) need not file a Form 990-T. Note that since 2006, this form (in contrast to the return filed by taxable subsidiaries) must be publicly disclosed.

Importantly, under the UBIT, the significant term is not 'business,' but rather 'unrelated.' A given activity is exempt or taxable depending on the purposes of the entity conducting it. The IRS applies a 'fragmentation' approach to determining relatedness to a particular NFP's purpose. For example, if the museum shop of an art museum also sells science books, those would be taxable, even though they are, broadly considered, educational. To be taxable, the unrelated business activity must be 'regularly carried on,' but the UBIT contains numerous carve-outs and allowances. Notable exceptions include businesses that are run entirely by volunteers, sell donated goods or are conducted for the 'convenience' of members, students, patients or employees. The exemptions for most forms of passive investment income do not extend to investments that are debt-financed (with exceptions for educational institutions) or to certain income from controlled subsidiaries. Additional special rules apply, including benefits for research and hospital medical services.

UBIT applies only to unrelated business income net of connected expenses. Many unrelated businesses make use of assets or employees that are also devoted to exempt activities, and the allocation to the taxable activity of a portion of deductions attributable to these 'dual-use assets' reduces (and may even eliminate) net taxable income. (Tax reasons aside, charities tend not to engage in businesses drastically unrelated to their existing activities or beyond the excess capacity of their charitable assets.) Separately, to conform to the rule for business corporations described above, an NFP earning UBI can deduct charitable contributions of up to 10% of UBI annually.

The trickiest disputes between the IRS and charities occur over the tax treatment of income from the use of an NFP's intangible assets, because royalties are among the excepted passive investment income categories. An exempt organisation might license its name, trademark and other intangible assets for a fee, and the income will be excludable as long as the organisation's contractual rights do not rise to the level of performing services. (Of course, even if a product endorsement or logo licensing could produce tax-free income, an NFP might decide that monetising its name in a particular fashion is inconsistent with its charitable purpose.) Even a gift to a charity can result in UBI—again, the question is whether the charity is performing services for a private party. Sponsorship that simply recognises a donor by name does not render a gift taxable, but UBIT would result if the arrangement rises to the level of advertising services. The poster child for this type of arrangement was Mobil Corporation's detailed contract to brand the Mobil Cotton Bowl, an annual championship college football match. Recognising the significant revenue at stake, particularly for educational and arts and cultural organisations, in 1997 Congress created a safe harbour for 'qualified sponsorship payments.'

Due to all of these exclusions and allowances, the amount of UBIT collected overall remains small. The most recent study by the Internal Revenue Service's Statistics of Income Division (Jackson, 2013, p. 169) reported that for tax year 2009, in the aggregate, $9.7 billion in gross UBI was offset by $9.8 billion in deductions; only about half of all Form 990-T filers declared any tax liability. In total, filers declared $266.4 million in UBIT, a 22% drop from the previous year. The 14,000 Form 990-T filers exempt under Code § 501(c)(3) represented about one-third of total Form 990-T filers—but a minuscule percentage of the 1.24 million § 501(c)(3) organisations on the IRS master file for 2009 (Arnsberger, 2012, p. 170), and still a negligible 4% of the 320,000 § 501(c)(3) organisations large enough to file Form 990 or Form 990-EZ in 2009 (Arnsberger, 2012, p. 169). These filing charities 'reported 65 percent of all gross unrelated business income for the year, claimed nearly 66 percent of deductions, and accounted for a little more than half of all unrelated business income tax liability' (Jackson, 2013, p. 175).

Recently the IRS asserted a new strategy to attack the low level of UBIT collections. In a broad (although unscientific) compliance project focused on 34 colleges and universities for years 2006 to 2008 (Internal Revenue Service (U.S.), 2013), the agency explicitly identified 'lack of profit motive' as a legal basis for challenge:

> The IRS found that organizations were claiming losses from activities that did not qualify as a trade or business. Nearly 70 percent of examined colleges and universities reported losses from activities for which expenses had consistently exceeded UBI for many years. UBI must be generated by a "trade or business." An activity qualifies as a "trade or business" only if, among other things, the taxpayer engaged in the activity with the intent to make a profit. A pattern of recurring losses indicates a lack of profit motive. The IRS disallowed reporting of activities for which the taxpayer failed to show a profit motive. Those losses no longer offset profits from other activities in the current year or in future years, with more than $150 million of NOLs disallowed.
>
> (Internal Revenue Service (U.S.), 2013, p. 3)

Separately, the IRS study found

that on nearly 60% of the Form 990-Ts we examined, colleges and universities had misallocated expenses to offset UBI for specific activities. Organisations may allocate expenses that are used to carry on both exempt and unrelated business activities, but they must do so on a reasonable basis and the expenses offsetting UBI must be directly connected to the UBI activities. In many cases, the IRS found that claimed expenses, which generated losses, were not connected to the unrelated business activity.

(Internal Revenue Service (U.S.), 2013, p. 3)

In commenting on the low level of UBIT collections, one academic accountant observed: 'The commercial revenues that do slip through the exclusion webbing are not necessarily the most 'objectionable', or even the most 'commercial', but are quite possibly those . . . which . . . Congress did not think to exclude or those for which there was no political champion to promote a specific exclusion' (Yetman, 2005, p. 17). Indeed, a sustained congressional effort in the late 1980s and early 1990s to tighten the UBIT regime—undertaken at the urging of the small business sector concerned about unfair competition from NFPs—ended with no proposal, even making it to the House Ways and Means Committee (Brody, 2009). That effort would have addressed, among other issues, the concerns quoted above from the IRS's colleges and universities compliance project. One reform would have prevented an exempt parent organisation from dropping a money-losing exempt activity down into a taxable subsidiary in order to soak up otherwise taxable profit; another would have limited deductions for dual-use assets (such as a university football stadium leased for unrelated activities) to a proportionate share of only their marginal costs, thus denying deductions for depreciation and general overhead (United States Congress, Oversight Subcommittee, 1988).

Highlighting the relatively few UBIT dollars assessed in the 'massive audit of colleges of universities,' one prominent legal academic asks whether 'the UBIT has outlived its usefulness,' suggesting a 15-year moratorium accompanied by 'another comprehensive review by the IRS at the 10-year mark . . . to see if bad things really do happen' (Colombo, 2013, pp. 42–43). Colombo instead proposes taxing all commercial activity, related or not, defining a commercial activity as one competing with for-profit firms providing similar goods or services (Colombo, 2007, 2013). While he cites college athletic ticket revenue as vulnerable under his proposal, once enough for-profit businesses enter the market for higher education, under such an approach even college tuition income would be taxable. Ominously, Hansmann (2013, p. 9) reports that, as of 2009, for-profit institutions of higher education enrol one-third of all students enrolled in private colleges and universities (and 10% of all students at both public and private institutions).

Joint Ventures with Private Parties

As cumbersome as it appears, the current regime has the desirable goal of trying to separate exempt from taxable business activity. Compare the recent interest in 'hybrid' organisations—not (yet?) eligible for tax benefits— for which operational transparency would be difficult, if not unattainable. When an NFP pools resources with other investors (taxable or exempt) through an unincorporated vehicle, for federal tax purposes the entity is treated as a partnership. Being a pass-through entity for tax purposes, a partnership is not itself eligible for exemption. Rather, a tax-exempt partner's share of income is treated as exempt or unrelated business income depending on what the tax result would be if that partner had earned the income directly. Accordingly, if all partners are charitable entities and the enterprise is engaged in charitable activities, the partners' exemptions are not in jeopardy, and the income will not be taxable. Special rules apply, however, if exempt organisations enter into partnerships with taxable participants; notably, these rules reduce the tax benefits of making certain disproportionate allocations of income to the exempt partners and of deductions to the taxable partners (see Brody, 2009).

Taxable Subsidiaries

In part because the IRS encouraged NFPs to spin off exempt and taxable activities for clarity of governance and reporting, exempt organisations often conduct unrelated business activities through separate, for-profit subsidiaries. However, under the 'excess business holding' limits of Code § 4943, a charity classified as a private foundation generally may own no more than 20% of an unrelated business. For all other exempt organisations, UBIT has long applied to interest, royalties, rents and annuities received from a controlled' (more than 50% owned) corporation or partnership. Congress feared that the affiliated group could reduce or eliminate taxable income by making inflated payments of these tax-deductible items, while the exempt parent would claim the corresponding UBIT exclusions for such classically passive items. By contrast, dividends are not deductible by the paying corporation (Halperin, 2005). Note that temporary legislation (expiring after 2013) replaces the 'automatic UBIT' regime with one that treats deductible payments from controlled subsidiaries as UBI only to the extent they exceed the amount that would be paid in an arm's-length transaction.

Exemption from State-Level Property Taxes

At the subnational level, state income tax rules generally follow the federal model. By contrast, state property tax exemption typically is narrower, being generally available only for property owned by a charitable NFP that uses the property for charitable purposes. In some states, charities forfeit property tax exemption by using the property, even in part, for an unrelated business, while in other states the exemption is apportioned. Uniquely, a 1997 Pennsylvania statute declared a policy that exemption should not allow charities 'to compete unfairly with small business,' providing: 'An institution of purely public charity may not fund, capitalize, guarantee the indebtedness of, lease obligations of or subsidize a commercial business that is unrelated to the institution's charitable purpose as stated in the institution's charter or governing legal documents.' Particular uses of property (notably, housing and health care) and practices (such as paying high compensation or simply earning profits) have prompted some municipalities to ask charities to make 'voluntary' 'payments in lieu of taxes' (PILOTs) on legally exempt property (Brody, 2010).

THE UNITED KINGDOM

Charitable engagement in trading activities and social enterprise continues to grow in the United Kingdom. The 2012 National Council for Voluntary Organisations (NCVO) Almanac reveals that 1,800 charities set up a trading subsidiary, generating £566 million in income during 2009–2010 (NCVO, 2012). According to the recent 'Managing in a Downturn' survey series, 55% of the 400 charity respondents had increased charitable trading or social enterprise activities since the onset of the recession with a further 39% of respondents planning to increase trading during 2013. For 31% of respondents, trading was cited as one of their most important income sources (PwC, 2013, p. 31).

Common Law and Tax Law Approaches and Exceptions

At common law, an organisation wishing to register as a charity must have exclusively charitable purposes, a requirement reiterated in section 1(1) of the Charities Act 2011. The Charity Commission for England and Wales will not register an organisation as a charity when its purpose is, or includes, the carrying out of trade (Luxton, 2001, p. 20.2; Warburton, Morris, & Riddle, 2003, p. 7.039). However, a charity can engage in trade that either directly supports its charitable purposes ('primary purpose trading') or that complements its charitable purposes ('ancillary trading'), provided that its governing instrument empowers it to do so and the scale of such activities (in the context of ancillary trading) is deemed acceptable. In essence, therefore, charities may trade in pursuit of their charitable objectives.

Charity law prohibits a charity from engaging in non-primary purpose trading (so called unrelated business activity)—even when the purpose of such trading is to fundraise for the charity—if engagement in such activity would place the assets of the charity at risk. Such a risk could arise if the costs of these unrelated activities were to exceed the turnover real-ised, thereby forcing the charity to finance the shortfall from charitable assets. Exposure of a charity's assets to the risks of unrelated trading could adversely affect the charity in two ways: first, by undermining its ability to deliver its charitable mission as effectively as it might otherwise have done, and second, by discouraging future donations if donors feared their gifts were used for commercial speculation rather than programme support. Charity law therefore restricts charities to low-risk ventures when engaging directly in trade that is not primary purpose trade. An organisation wishing to engage in substantial trading in order to raise funds for the charity is best advised to achieve this objective by setting up a separate trading subsidiary (CCEW, 2007, p. 16). The trading subsidiary does not enjoy charitable sta-tus or charitable tax-exempt status but is free to trade, and can donate its profits to the charity in a tax efficient manner through the Gift Aid scheme (HM Revenue and Customs (HMRC), 2013d).

What Constitutes 'Trade'?

Whether an activity qualifies as 'trading' depends on a number of factors, including: the presence or absence of a profit-seeking motive, how many transactions are carried out, the nature of the asset, the method of its acqui-sition and whether any changes were made to it to facilitate trade. Con-sideration will also be paid to the source of finance for the asset and the interval between its purchase and sale, as well as whether the transaction is similar to that of an existing trade (HMRC, 2013a). HMRC starts from the premise that provision of goods or services to customers on a commercial basis constitutes trade (HMRC, 2013b). Sponsorship may constitute tax-able trading income if a charity provides goods or services for the payments received, which may occur if a charity's acknowledgment of thanks becomes an advertisement for the sponsor, or the charity shares its mailing list or charity logo with a sponsor or endorses its products (Framjee, 2010, p. 32).

Neither the ultimate destination of any profits made (even if charitable) nor the fact that the venture is a 'one off' prevents the activity being classi-fied as 'trade' for tax purposes. However, passive income earned from invest-ments has escaped such labelling (HMRC, 2013b). The ability to distinguish trade from investment becomes ever more important as many charities begin to consider social investment as a new avenue of finance. According to the CCEW (2011, p. 16), 'this distinction is particularly important when look-ing at derivatives, property, commodities and other opportunities which can be regarded either as an investment or as trading, depending on the context in which they are made. Trustees should be able to demonstrate their inten-tion through their decision-making.'

A charity engaging in trade is liable for tax on the resulting profits unless they are expressly exempted and it is at this point that HMRC dis-tinguishes between primary purpose, non-primary purpose and ancillary trading. Profits earned in the course of carrying on a primary purpose trade are exempt from tax once the resulting income is applied solely to the purposes of the charity (Income Tax Act, 2007, s. 525; Corporation Tax Act, 2010, s. 479). Common examples would include tuition fees earned by a charitable educational institution or charges for medical procedures carried out at a charitable hospital. If the trade in question is carried out 'mainly' by the beneficiaries of the charity and has a remedial or educational purpose, such activities will often qualify as primary purpose activity and be exempt.

Ancillary purpose trading may also qualify for tax exemption. In its charity guidance, HMRC views ancillary trading as trading which, while not overtly amounting to primary purpose trading, nevertheless is exercised in the course of carrying out the primary purpose, e.g., university provision of student rental accommodation (HMRC, 2013b). When there is a nexus between the ancillary trading activity and the primary charitable purpose, HMRC treats the ancillary trading as falling within the primary purpose trading exemption. As to whether such grey area trading contravenes charity law, the CCEW adopts a qualitative as opposed to mathematical approach—in classifying this activity it treats the level of annual turnover of purported ancillary trading as a factor, but not determinative. Trading conducted for the purposes of raising charitable funds, per se, does not qualify as ancillary trading (CCEW, 2007).

Finally, the tax treatment of non-primary purpose trading activity (unrelated business activity) is such that, subject to the two exceptions outlined below, any resulting profit is taxable regardless of its ultimate destination. For periods on and after 21 March 2006, UK law allows for differentiation to be drawn between primary and non-primary purpose trade carried out by a charity: primary purpose profits are tax exempt once applied for charitable purposes; non-primary purpose profits are taxable, subject to an extraordinary fundraising concession and an exemption for small-scale trading (Finance Act, 2006, s. 56). The Finance Act (2006) treats primary and non-primary purpose trading separately and, for the first time, allows a charity to apportion receipts and expenses between the two. The effect of such apportionment is that it is permissible under UK tax law for charities to carry on non-primary purpose trading directly alongside primary purpose trading (even if it exceeds the small-scale statutory exemption), subject to the payment of tax on the unrelated business activity.

Small-Scale Trade

The first tax exemption relates to small-scale trading. This statutory tax exemption (Corporation Tax Act, 2010, s. 480; Income Tax Act, 2007, s. 526) applies to profits on small-scale, non-primary purpose trading and other 'miscellaneous incoming resources,' provided the annual turnover does not exceed £5,000 or 25% of the charity's total incoming resources up to a maximum threshold of £50,000 (Corporation Tax Act, 2010, s. 482(6)). To qualify, the profits must be applied for the charity's purpose.

Extraordinary Fundraising Concession

The second exemption concerns fundraising. If the profits arise from the holding of a fundraising event, exemption from tax may be possible under section 483 of the Corporation Tax Act (2010) or section 529 of the Income Tax Act (2007). To qualify, the profits must arise from an event that is Value Added Tax (VAT) exempt in relation to the charity and be applied to charitable purposes or transferred to another charity (HMRC, 2013c). There is a limit of 15 events that a charity may run each year in a given location. If this threshold is exceeded, the profits from *all* events become liable to taxation and the concession is lost.

Consequences of the UK Approach to Charitable Trading

Although the tax treatment of charitable trading has improved with the introduction of apportionment rules in 2006, charity law imposes limitations on a charity wishing to engage directly and substantially in unrelated business activity. For this reason, many charities choose to establish a wholly owned trading subsidiary which, although liable for taxes on any trading profits it makes, can get tax relief for any donations it makes to its parent charity under the Gift Aid scheme. Such donations must comply with sections 191 to 198 of the Corporation Tax Act (2010), but if a company donates all of its taxable profits to a charity it will benefit from a tax deduction equal to that amount, essentially avoiding corporation tax. Moreover, the separate legal identity of the trading subsidiary protects the parent charity from liability.

Although this provides organisational clarity and protection of charitable assets from trading liability, establishing and maintaining a trading subsidiary can be costly for charities. While a subsidiary limited by shares provides an excellent structure for declaring dividends, it may not constitute an eligible body for VAT purposes, in which case a company limited by guarantee or a community interest company (CIC) may be a better choice (Framjee, 2010, p. 53). From a governance perspective, often the charity and trading company will share staff, premises and facilities. Tax law requires a reasonable apportionment of shared costs to be made in the books of both parent and subsidiary (Corporation Tax Act, 2010, s. 479(4)). From a capital requirement perspective, the trading company will require working capital by way of charitable or commercial loan or by the issue of share capital. There would be a valid reason for investing in share capital if a loan from the parent charity would expose the trading company to the risk of, or actual, insolvency. The downside of shares, of course, is that charity is not a creditor and share capital is only normally repaid upon dissolution once creditors have been repaid.

As a shareholder, the charity has a duty to monitor the subsidiary's performance in order to protect the charity's investment. However, shareholders have only a limited right to request information on the subsidiary's commercial ventures and cannot interfere in the running of the business. To do so could expose charity trustees to the charge of acting as shadow directors (Companies Act, 2006, s. 251), thereby defeating one of the main reasons for establishing a trading subsidiary (Rowley, 2010). A typical solution to the information/control deficit is to appoint charity trustees to the trading subsidiary's board. Although solving the information asymmetry problems, this dual role, with trustees owing duties of care to both the charity and the trading company, may create conflicts of interest which then need to be managed in a careful and transparent manner.

Whether a charity invests or lends funds to a trading company, the investment must be an expedient one and the CCEW and HRMC expect charities to consider carefully their investment powers, issues of portfolio diversification and the risk profile of the trading activity before investing (CCEW, 2011; HMRC, 2013e). Any such investment, even if made within the powers of the charity, runs the risk of being viewed as non-charitable expenditure (Corporation Tax Act, 2010, s. 496) and jeopardising the charity's tax exemption. To avoid such an outcome, the trustees must prove that the investment is for the benefit of the charity and not to avoid tax. HMRC has interpreted this to mean investments are commercially sound, carry a fair rate of return (which is actually paid) and, in the case of loans, provide for recovery of the amount invested (HMRC, 2013e).

The 2004 introduction of the community interest company (CIC)—a limited liability company with the specific aim of providing benefit to the community—has proved to be an increasingly popular option with social enterprises and charities seeking a legal vehicle with separate legal personality. There are currently 8,428 CICs, a 20% increase on 2011–2012 figures (CIC Regulator, 2013a). An organisation cannot simultaneously be a charity and a CIC (Companies (Audit, Investigations and Community Enterprise) Act, 2004, s. 26(3)), but a CIC can form part of the group that includes a charity, for example, its trading wing. CICs, which may be limited by shares or guarantee, are more lightly regulated than charities and do not enjoy charitable status, even if their activities are entirely charitable in nature. Primary features of the CIC include an 'asset lock' and a 'community interest' test, ensuring the CIC is established for community purposes and its assets and profits are dedicated to those purposes. Once registered, exiting the CIC structure requires either the dissolution of the company entirely or its conversion to a charitable company. CIC dissolutions remain common. In 2012, there were 766 dissolutions—a loss of 10% of the register. Of those dissolutions, over 72% had traded for less than three years and 70% had been dormant and were struck off by the Registrar of Companies for not filing their statutory documents. Less than 1% were subject to compulsory liquidation. The key reasons for the companies dissolving were lack of funding, no trading activity and poor corporate governance (CIC Regulator, 2013a).

The Future Direction of Charitable Trading

It is now 10 years since the UK's Strategy Unit Report recommended amending the law to allow charities to trade directly without the need for a separate trading company but subject to a specific statutory duty of care (HM Strategy Unit, 2002, p. 4.47), a recommendation that remains unimplemented to this date. Neither of the recent reviews of charity law in the UK (Hodgson, 2012; Public Administration Select Committee, 2013) nor the ongoing Law Commission Consultation on charity law (2013) address the issue of charitable trading.

The new buzzword in the government's lexicon is 'social investment,' i.e., investment in social enterprise. It should be remembered that 'social enterprise' is simply a popular term for trading activities that in some way benefit the community, often engaged in by charities as either primary purpose or ancillary trading. It is estimated that total investment inflows into the UK social investment market were only £165 million in the financial year 2010–2011 while the demand for such investment by social enterprises is likely to exceed £750 million by 2015 (Bates, Wells, & Braithwaite, 2012, p. 5). Following the enactment of the Dormant Bank and Building Society Accounts Act (2008), the UK government committed in 2010 to using all dormant accounts' money available for spending in England to establish a social investment wholesale institution, a decision which culminated in the Financial Service Authority's authorisation of Big Society Capital (BSC) in 2012. Since it became operational in April 2012, BSC has committed £56 million in 20 investments to social investment financial intermediaries, exceeding its £50 million target for 2012–2013 (HM Treasury, 2013a).

Social investment encompasses investment in the activities of CICs, community benefit societies (Bencoms) and registered charities, and is an area Westminster remains keen to encourage (HM Treasury, 2013a, p. 3). The decision to create a new tax incentive to encourage direct private investment in social enterprise is the next phase in the Government's broader plan to open up and decentralise public service opportunities for social enterprises to deliver public contracts. Problems generally experienced by charities in entering this market relate to capital requirement difficulties. Lack of security for loans and an inability to issue shares result in charities being unable to access existing venture capital schemes. Under the Treasury's current proposal, the consultation period for which closed in September 2013, individual investors who invest in CICs, registered charities or Bencoms for a minimum period of five years will earn income tax relief on their qualifying investment and roll-over relief (in the form of capital gains tax relief) on funds reinvested thereafter. The initial investment cannot be secured against charitable assets or subject to any guarantee of repayment and any dividend/ interest paid should be broadly consistent with a commercial rate of return and linked to the financial performance of the enterprise. One of the government's concerns is to distinguish properly between 'investment in' and 'donation to' a charity so that the donor/investor cannot claim tax relief twice (HM Treasury, 2013a). The extent of the existing dividend cap, which limits the rate at which private investors in CICs can be rewarded, is also up for discussion (HM Treasury, 2013a, p. 18). In its recently issued response to the consultation (HM Treasury, 2013b), the government has, inter alia, reduced the minimum period of investment from five to three years and has dropped the requirement for investor returns to be linked to the financial performance of the company, changes which will take effect in the Finance Act (2014). For its part, the CIC Regulator now proposes to remove the maximum dividend per share cap and to maintain but increase the interest cap in place for performance-related interest from 10% to 20% for CICs (CIC Regulator, 2013b).

In considering charities' participation in social investment, both Lord Hodgson (2012, p. 106) and the CCEW (2011) focused on the legal constraints on charities engaging in this area. In its review of charity law, the Law Commission has recently added the issue of whether trustees could be given new powers to make mixed-motive investments (Mason, 2013). The scope of the review, however, will not extend to the potential for social investment by charities to confer any 'private benefit' to investors.

CONCLUSION

The Australia's Future Tax System Review (2009) and Productivity Commission Research Report (2010) confirmed the Industry Commission's considered opinion that 'unrelated business income is a concept that is too difficult to define and too costly to enforce, and consequently the costs [of taxing it] are likely to outweigh the benefits' (1995, p. 316). The Treasury proposals do not offer options to avoid these pitfalls by borrowing policies from the regimes in place in the U.S. and the UK. The experiences in these jurisdictions offer some lessons for Australia. First, the regulation requires careful design to conceptualise unrelated business income without complex and potentially tax abusive weaknesses in areas such as passive income, sponsorships, quid pro quo advertising, intangible property and fundraising. The U.S. example—books sold in a museum's shop having different tax treatments depending on their subject—is an exemplar of distorting behaviour with little public benefit.

Second, the compliance costs placed on NFPs appears to be significant if organisations comply with the law. The creation of a separate trading entity, as occurs in the UK and often in the U.S., provides a series of transaction costs and governance risk exposures for no discernible advantage in tax collections. Whether there are other advantages and whether these are best achieved through the tax system have not been made explicit. The internal segregation of trading from other income is replete with allocation issues which are costly and introduce significant risk of genuine misapplication or tax abusive behaviour. Dual use of staff and assets for both related and unrelated income generation presents conceptual and actual difficulties, as well as driving up compliance costs.

Third, the risk argument of protecting dedicated charitable assets from high-risk trading requires further exploration and analysis. The evidence from the UK shows very little default amongst charitable trading entities and no evidence was given in the Australian Treasury paper (2011b) that this is a problem in Australia. The evidence from the U.S. indicates that NFPs tend to be cautious and constrained to business opportunities allied to their purpose and activities.

The rise of social investing and social enterprise hybrids which blur the boundary between not-for-profit and for-profit is increasing, and in the case of the UK and Australia, is driven by government policy. The taxation treatment of this growing class of enterprise needs to be given due consideration in any proposed UBIT.

The application of the regulation, even if the design features are honed, is critical. As Thomas Kelley (2005, p. 2475) notes in the U.S., what 'appears simple in the regulation has become muddled in the execution' by the IRS, descending into 'an unprincipled, unpredictable test that amounts to an examination of whether the organization "smell[s] like" a charity to whomever is inquiring.' Such a situation quickly drives up tax administration and compliance costs, and would promote tax system gaming, which has significant adverse costs for charities, which require high levels of trust and esteem from the general community to attract philanthropic contributions, volunteers and licence to work in vulnerable communities.

REFERENCES

Arnsberger, P. (2012). Nonprofit charitable organizations, 2009. *Statistics of Income Bulletin*, Fall, 169–181. Retrieved from http://www.irs.gov/PUP/taxstats/pro ductsandpubs/12eofallbulteorg.pdf

Assistant Treasurer. (2013, December 14). *Integrity restored to Australia's taxation system* [Media release].

Australian Government, The Treasury. (2010). *Incoming government brief: Election commitments*. Retrieved from http://www.treasury.gov.au/Access-to-Information/ DisclosureLog/2010/2010-Red-Book

Australian Government, The Treasury. (2011a). *Budget Measures 2011–12* (Budget paper no. 2).

Australian Government, The Treasury. (2011b). *Better targeting of not-for-profit tax concessions*. Canberra, AU: The Treasury.

Australian Taxation Office. (2005). *Income tax: Companies controlled by exempt entities* (Taxation ruling TR2005/22).

Australian Taxation Office. (2010). *Mutuality and taxable income* (Guide no. NAT 73436–07.2010).

Australia's Future Tax System Review Panel. (2009). *Australia's Future Tax System: Report to the treasurer.* Australian Government, The Treasury: Canberra, ACT: Australia.

Bates, Wells, & Braithwaite, LLP. (2012). *Ten reforms to grow the social investment market.* London: BWB.

Bowen, C. (2009, May 12). *Government's interim response to High Court's decision in word investments case* [Media release], no. 043.

Bradbury, D. (2012, March 30). *Extended start date for 2011–12 budget measure to better target not-for-profit tax concessions* [Media release], no. 009.

Breen, O. (2010). Holding the line: Regulatory challenges in Ireland and England when business and charity collide. In M. McGregor-Lowndes & K. O'Halloran (Eds.), *Modernising charity law: Recent developments and future directions* (pp. 136–163). Cheltenham, UK: Edward Elgar Publishing.

Brody, E. (2009). Business activities of nonprofit organizations: Legal boundary problems. In J. J. Cordes & C. E. Steuerle (Eds.), *Nonprofits and business* (pp. 83–97). Washington, DC: Urban Institute Press.

Brody, E. (2010). All charities are property-tax exempt, but some charities are more exempt than others. *New England Law Review, 44*(3), 621–732.

Burch, M. (2012). Australia's proposed unrelated commercial activities tax: Lessons from the U.S. UBIT. *Journal of the Australasian Tax Teachers Association, 7*(1), 21–30.

Charity Commission for England and Wales (CCEW). (2007). *Trustees, trading and tax: How charities may lawfully trade* (CC35).

Charity Commission for England and Wales (CCEW). (2011). *Charities and investment matters: A guide for trustees* (CC14).Chia, J., & Stewart, M. (2012). Doing business to do good: Should we tax the business profits of not-for-profits? *Adelaide Law Review, 33*, 335–370.

Colombo, J. (2007). Reforming Internal Revenue Code provisions on commercial activity by charities. *Fordham Law Review, 76*(2), 667–692.

Colombo, J. (2013). *The IRS university compliance project report on UBIT issues: Roadmap for enforcement . . . reform . . . or repeal?* Paper presented at National Center on Philanthropy and the Law, Conference on Colleges and Universities: Legal Issues in the Halls of Ivy, New York City, October 24–25.

Community Interest Company (CIC) Regulator (UK). (2013a). *Regulator of Community Interest Companies Annual Report 2012/2013.*

Community Interest Company (CIC) Regulator (UK). (2013b, December). *Changes to the Dividend and Interest Caps for Community Interest Companies: Response to the CIC consultation on the dividend and interest caps.*

Cordes, J., & Brody, E. (2006). Tax treatment of nonprofit organizations: A two-edged sword? In E. Boris & C. E. Steuerle (Eds.), *Nonprofits and government: Collaboration and conflict*, 2nd ed. (pp. 141–180). Washington, DC: The Urban Institute Press.

Framjee, P. (2010). *The tax implications of charity trading.* London: Charity Finance Directors Group.

Halperin, D. (2005). The unrelated business income tax and payments from controlled entities. *Tax Notes, 109* (12 December), 1443–1449.

Hansmann, H. (1989). Unfair competition and the unrelated business income tax. *Virginia Law Review, 75*(3), 605–635.

Hansmann, H. (2013). *Why are colleges and universities exempt from taxes?* Paper presented at National Center on Philanthropy and the Law, Conference on Colleges and Universities: Legal Issues in the Halls of Ivy, New York City, October 24–25.

HM Revenue and Customs (HMRC). (2013a). *Trade: Badges of trade: Summary*. Retrieved from http://www.hmrc.gov.uk/manuals/bimmanual/bim20205.htm

HM Revenue and Customs (HMRC). (2013b). *Charities—trading and business activities* (Detailed guidance notes: Annex IV). Retrieved from http://www.hmrc. gov.uk/charities/guidance-notes/annex4/sectiona.htm

HM Revenue and Customs (HMRC). (2013c). *Fund-raising events: Exemption for charities and other qualifying bodies*. Retrieved from http://www.hmrc.gov.uk/ charities/fund-raising-events.htm

HM Revenue and Customs (HMRC). (2013d). *The gift aid toolkit*. Retrieved from http://www.hmrc.gov.uk/charities/gift-aid-toolkit.htm

HM Revenue and Customs (HMRC). (2013e). *Financing the trading company* (Detailed guidance notes: Annex IV). Retrieved from http://www.hmrc.gov.uk/ charities/guidance-notes/annex4/sectionh.htm

HM Strategy Unit. (2002). *Private action, public benefit: A review of charities and the wider not for profit sector*. London: Cabinet Office.

HM Treasury. (2013a). *Consultation on social investment tax*. London: The Stationery Office.

HM Treasury. (2013b, December). *Social investment tax relief: Summary of responses*. London: The Stationery Office.

Hodgson, Lord of Astley Abbotts. (2012). *Trusted and independent: Giving charity back to charities—review of the Charities Act 2006*. London: The Stationery Office.

Hopkins, B. (1992). The most important concept in the law of organizations today: The commerciality doctrine. *Exempt Organization Tax Review, 5* (March), 459–467.

Industry Commission. (1995). *Charitable organisations in Australia* (Report no. 45). Melbourne: Australian Government Publishing Service.

Internal Revenue Service (U.S.). (2013). *Colleges and universities compliance project: Final report*. Retrieved from http://www.irs.gov/pub/irs-tege/CUCP_FinalRpt_042513.pdf

Jackson, J. (2013). Unrelated business income tax returns, 2009. *Statistics of Income Bulletin*, Summer, 169–189. Retrieved from http://www.irs.gov/pub/irs-soi/13e osumbulunrelateintax.pdf

Kelley, T. (2005). Rediscovering vulgar charity: A historical analysis of America's tangled nonprofit law. *Fordham Law Review, 73*(6), 2437–2499.

Law Commission. (2013). *Selected issues in charity law: Terms of reference*. Retrieved from http://lawcommission.justice.gov.uk/areas/charity-law.htm

Luxton, P. (2001). *The law of charities*. Oxford: Oxford University Press.

Mason, T. (2013). Law Commission adds mixed-motive investment to its review. *Civil Society*, (25 October).

Mortimer, D. (2010). A word about charity. *Law Institute Journal, 84*(4), 50–53.

Murray, I. (2008). Charitable fundraising through commercial activities: The final word or a pyrrhic victory? *Journal of Australian Taxation, 11*, 138–207.

Murray, I. (2009). Charity means business—Commissioner of Taxation v Word Investments Ltd. *Sydney Law Review, 31*(2), 309–329.

National Council for Voluntary Organisations (NCVO). (2012). How much do organisations generate from their trading subsidiaries. *The UK Civil Society Almanac 2012*. Retrieved from http://data.ncvo-vol.org.uk/a/almanac12/almanac/voluntary-sector/income-in-focus/how-much-do-organisations-generate-from-their-trading-subsidiaries/

O'Connell, A., Martin, F., & Chan, J. (2013). Law, policy and politics in Australia's recent not-for-profit sector reforms. *Australian Tax Forum, 28*, 289–315.

Productivity Commission. (2010). *Contribution of the not-for-profit sector: Research report*. Melbourne: Productivity Commission.

Public Administration Select Committee. (2013). *The role of the Charity Commission and 'public benefit': Post-legislative scrutiny of the Charities Act 2006.* London: The Stationery Office.

PwC Charity Finance Group and Institute of Fundraising. (2013). Managing in the "new normal"—adapting to uncertainty. *Managing in the Downturn Series.* Retrieved from: http://www.cfg.org.uk/~/media/Files/Policy/Have%20your%20 Say/Managing_in_the_new_normal_adapting_to_uncertainty_report2013.ashx

Rowley, S. (2010). Two's company. *Solicitors Journal*, (Spring).

Sadiq, K., & Richardson, C. (2010). Tax concessions for charities: Competitive neutrality, the tax base and "public goods" choice. *Australian Tax Forum, 25*, 113–128.

Sansing, R. (1998). The unrelated business income tax, cost allocation and productive efficiency. *National Tax Journal, 51*(2), 291–302.

Simon, J. G., Dale, H., & Chisolm, L. (2006). The federal tax treatment of charitable organizations. In W. W. Powell & R. Steinberg (Eds.), *The nonprofit sector: A research handbook* (pp. 267–306). New Haven, CT: Yale University Press.

United States Congress, Oversight Subcommittee, House Ways and Means Committee. (1988). *UBIT Recommendations* (24 June).

Warburton, J., Morris, D., & Riddle, N. F. (2003). *Tudor on charities*, 9th ed. London: Sweet & Maxwell.

Yetman, R. J. (2005). *Causes and consequences of the unrelated business income tax*. Paper presented at National Tax Association meeting, Miami, December.

6 Financial Reserves

A Necessary Condition for Not-for-Profit Sustainability?

Michael S. Booth, Myles McGregor-Lowndes, Christine M. Ryan and Helen Irvine

INTRODUCTION

Should not-for-profit (NFP) organisations hold reserves to hedge uncertainty and protect mission delivery? This chapter outlines the nature and context of NFP reserves. Many would accept that actors within NFP organisations have a broad accountability to ensure sustainability where an appropriate mission exists, and that sustainability is assisted or ensured through the purposeful accumulation of reserves.

This chapter examines current relevant literature on reserves, reviews various approaches to reserves accumulation across jurisdictions and reports what is known about practice. We highlight the tension faced by NFP organisations, balancing mission spending against the need to hedge uncertainty. We investigate the role of reserves, and how an appropriate level is determined to ensure a NFP board's accountability for organisational sustainability. This issue is particularly significant in the period following the global financial crisis, and while practitioner interest is evident, there has been little academic attention paid to the topic of NFP reserves, and 'very few [articles] have even focused on related topics' (Calabrese, 2011, p. 282).

This is an important issue for NFP stakeholders. For management boards, there is a need to communicate the level of reserves, and balance the prudent hedging of uncertainty against donors' perception of resource hoarding (Charity Commission, 2006, 2008, 2012; NORI, 2008). For the public, NFP reserves are a significant indicator of commitment to purpose and organisational effectiveness. Funders, especially governments, are interested in knowing the appropriate level of reserves to facilitate the ongoing sustainability of organisations and the sector, particularly when organisations provide essential public goods and services (Productivity Commission, 2010; Akingbola, 2004; Brock, 2000; Golensky & DeRuiter, 1999).

Early frameworks attempted to explain the savings behaviour of NFP organisations and the contribution of reserves to organisational sustainability (Weisbrod, 1975; Hansmann, 1980, 1987, 1990; Chang & Tuckman, 1990; Steinberg & Gray, 1993). Its treatment has usually been purely descriptive, peripheral to a broader prediction of financial vulnerability, or issue specific (Chang & Tuckman, 1990; Tuckman & Chang, 1991, 1992; Gilbert, Menon, & Schwartz, 1990; Greenlee & Trussel, 2000; Trussel, 2002; Keating, Fischer, Gordon, & Greenlee, 2005; Core, Guay, & Verdi, 2006; Petrovits, 2006; Calabrese, 2009; Besel, Williams, & Klak, 2011; Bowman, 2011).

Acknowledging this lack of clarity, we examine regulatory frameworks about NFP reserves accumulation in various jurisdictions: the heavily regulated approach of the Charity Commission for England and Wales (Charity Commission, 2006, 2008, 2012); voluntary practice suggested by the U.S. National Operating Reserves Initiative (NORI, 2008); emerging views of the Australian Charities and Not-for-Profits Commission (ACNC)[1]; the changing environment faced by Canadian NFP organisations (Broder, 2010; Drache, 2012); and recommendations of the former Charities Commission of New Zealand (now part of the Department of Internal Affairs) (Hanley, 2006). We conclude by identifying the implications of these approaches for ensuring organisational sustainability.

The NFP sector is comprised of a wide variety of organisational forms, missions and governance models, each influenced by its jurisdiction. This chapter recognises this complexity but does not attempt to capture it. Instead, we take a broad view of the sector as a whole, acknowledging that the management of NFP organisations embodies complexities similar to the for-profit sector: issues of people, finance, technology and resources. Specific to the NFP community however is the complexity surrounding the issue of accumulating surpluses and building reserves:

> Most charities are keenly aware of the need to secure their viability beyond the immediate future. To provide reliable services or funding over the longer term, charities must be able to absorb setbacks and to take advantage of change and opportunity.
>
> (Charity Commission, 2008, p. 1)

This is achieved by 'putting aside, when they can afford it, some of their current income as a reserve against future uncertainties' (Charity Commission, 2008, p. 1). While the term financial sustainability is contested (see, for example, Struthers, 2004; Gold, 2008; Hunter, 2006; Leviton, Herrera, Pepper, Fishman, & Racine, 2006; National Audit Office (UK), 2009; Gregory & Howard, 2009; Besel et al., 2011; Bowman, 2011; Bingham & Walters, 2013), we adopt the concept of 'viability beyond the immediate future,' as cited above (Charity Commission, 2008, p. 1).

Counterbalancing this are negative perceptions of hoarding when charities hold large reserves (Charity Commission, 2008). The view that when NFP organisations seek funding from government grants or public donation they should expend monies received exclusively and immediately on mission highlights the tension identified above. The view that a NFP organisation plans to earn a yearly surplus, and accumulate surpluses, does not comfortably align with general expectations about NFP roles and behaviours, but has attracted academic attention (e.g., Weisbrod, 1975, 1988; Hansmann, 1980).

Hansmann (1980, p. 838) defined the non-distribution constraint, noting that a NFP organisation is not barred from earning profits but is prohibited from distributing them. He examined the theoretical basis for asset accumulation in his study of endowments held by U.S. universities, but did not offer 'a single, simple theory' (Hansmann, 1990, p. 5). Limited scholarly attention by a number of other authors (Chang & Tuckman, 1990; Tuckman & Chang, 1991; Keating et al., 2005; Bowman, 2011) has measured the level of such surpluses in a range of (primarily U.S.) demographics. While in practice it would appear that savings are essential to the ongoing viability and sustainability of NFP entities, many organisations have survived in the long term with very limited savings. Bowman (2011), in a U.S. study of 97,500 'ordinary nonprofits'[2] reported that 25% had coverage of 20 days or less of normal operating expenses, and 16% had negative short-term capacity, i.e., their liabilities exceeded their assets.

Internationally, governments increasingly rely on NFP organisations to deliver core community services and infrastructure. The need for reserves to underpin sustainability therefore becomes more important. It is thus both timely and relevant to explore the role of reserves in undergirding NFP financial sustainability.

DEFINING NFP RESERVES

The concept of NFP reserves seems simple; however, the technical meaning of reserves for the preparation of formal financial statements and consequent discourse is not straightforward. A review of literature and regulatory frameworks suggests no coherent definition is available. For example, IAS 1 Presentation of Financial Statements requires the disaggregation of reserves and a description of the nature and purpose of each reserve (IFRS Foundation, 2011), but the International Accounting Standards Board (IASB) nowhere defines what a reserve is. Similarly, the Conceptual Framework of the IASB defines equity as a residual interest (i.e., the net assets remaining after deducting liabilities), but does not define reserves (IFRS Foundation, 2010). Leo, Hoggett, and Sweeting (2012, p. 110) suggested that a reserve may be thought of simply as a 'direct adjustment to equity plus the retained earnings of the entity.' Hoggett, Edwards, Medlin, and Tilling (2009, p. 673) noted that 'reserves are not defined in Australian legislation, accounting standards or in the Framework' and observed that they represent equity other than capital contributed by owners. In ordinary use in a financial context, a 'reserve' is '[a stock of] funds kept available by a bank, insurance company, etc., to meet ordinary or probable demand' (Oxford English Dictionary, 2014). Even at this level the definition has implications regarding the long or short term.

This lack of definition has resulted in inconsistent reporting of reserve, which in turn has caused difficulties in understanding and comparing reserves, and in some cases has led the sector to develop its own interpretations and guidelines[3]. The Charity Commission noted the contextual nature of reserves, adopting the definition of the Charities (Accounts and Reports) Regulations (2008) to describe that part of a charity's income funds that is freely available for its general purposes. Reflecting the Commission's focus on accountability, reserves are therefore the resources the charity has, or can make, available to spend, for all or any of its purposes, once it has met its commitments and covered its planned expenditure. This defines reserves as income which is available to the charity and is to be spent at the trustees' discretion to further any of the charity's objects (sometimes referred to as 'general purpose' income), but which is not yet spent, committed or designated (i.e., is 'free') (Charity Commission, 2012).

Scholars examining the accumulation of reserves have not separately considered the elements of the equity accounts beyond the specific issues of restricted reserves and endowments or savings (see, for example, Bowman, Tuckman, & Young, 2012). As already noted, equity represents an entity's net worth, and may be restricted in the short term, but is rarely restricted in the longer term. If necessary, fixed assets can be sold over time, presumably at their carrying amount. Thus all elements of equity will be available for deployment if required. It would only be where an asset (usually cash) needs to be returned if it cannot be spent on its intended purpose that it would need to be excluded as a net asset. Thus while a NFP management board may decide to separately identify an element of equity as representing, for example, asset replacement, nevertheless all elements of equity, unless legally restricted, will be available for deployment.

Noting the breadth of definition of reserves, and acknowledging the specific issue of restricted reserves, we adopt a broad definition of reserves to include all equity or net assets. In some areas this will be varied, where appropriate, to exclude restricted equity.

DEFINING NFP FINANCIAL SUSTAINABILITY

We now consider the issue of financial sustainability. If reserves are built to ensure sustainability then what does it mean? Financial sustainability has been defined as 'the ability of nonprofits to diversify their funding base and subsequently grow their operating budget over a five-year period' (Besel et al., 2011, p. 54). This incorporates the notion of financial capacity, which Bowman defined as consisting of resources that give an organisation 'the wherewithal to seize opportunities and react to unexpected threats' (2011,

p. 38). Other authors, as evident in Table 6.1, define organisational sustainability differently, or do not define it at all (Bingham & Walters, 2013; Struthers, 2004; Gold, 2008; Hunter, 2006; Leviton et al., 2006; National Audit Office (UK), 2009; Gregory & Howard, 2009).

The Oxford English Dictionary (2014) defines 'sustainable' as meaning '[c]apable of being maintained or continued at a certain rate or level,' highlighting the long-term focus. In an organisational context, durability is thus key, as identified by Weerawardena, McDonald, and Mort (2010, p. 2), who defined a NFP organisation's sustainability as its ability to survive, 'so that it can continue to serve its constituency.'

Bowman (2011) emphasised the importance of long and short-term timeframes in allowing different degrees of managerial flexibility to reallocate assets in response to opportunities and threats. He proposed the rate of change in capacity in each period as a quantitative measure of financial sustainability, requiring 'consistency between short-term sustainability, as

Table 6.1 Definitions of sustainability

Author	Definition
Weerawardena et al., 2010	An organisation's ability to survive so that it can continue to serve its constituency.
Besel et al., 2011	The ability of not-for-profit organisations to develop a diversified funding base and in consequence to grow their operating budget over five years.
Bingham and Walters, 2013	A lack of sustainability results in a decline in an organisation's financial position.
Bowman, 2008, 2011	The ability of an organisation to maintain its capacity.
	An organisation's long-term financial capacity is sustainable if its rate of change is sufficient to maintain assets at their replacement cost.
Struthers, 2004	The ability to meet present needs without compromising the ability to meet needs in the future.
Gold, 2008; Hunter, 2006; Leviton et al., 2006; National Audit Office (UK), 2009; Gregory and Howard, 2009	No definition or similar construct.

measured in terms of annual surpluses, and long-term sustainability, as measured by asset growth, which must stay ahead of the long-run rate of inflation' (Bowman, 2011, p. 38).

This long-term focus is in contrast to the related concepts of financial 'viability' and 'vulnerability,' which have also attracted scholarly attention. With viability being the 'capacity for living; the ability to live under certain conditions,' and vulnerability implying 'open to attack or assault' (Oxford English Dictionary, 2014), both these constructs would appear to have a shorter time horizon than those implied by sustainability. It is the twin issues of viability or vulnerability rather than sustainability that are most prevalent in academic literature.

Except for Bowman's (2011) study, the temporal nature of financial sustainability, viability and health have been addressed only as 'through a glass darkly.' Greenlee and Tuckman (2007, p. 316) posited that an assessment of financial health needs to consider constructs beyond income and expenditure, to include the relationship between assets and liabilities, measures of organisational efficiency and surpluses (reserves) accumulated over time. They identified the need for such analysis to consider trend information as well as static measures (Greenlee & Tuckman, 2007, p. 316). This concept of NFP financial health or sustainability goes beyond most studies, which focus on vulnerability or viability and consequently fail to consider an organisation's ability to financially sustain its operations in the longer term.[4]

The literature has taken two paths in examining the factors which describe or predict a NFP entity's financial health and/or viability. These approaches either model financial data (Tuckman & Chang, 1991; Greenlee & Trussel, 2000; Hager, 2001; Trussel, 2002) or take a qualitative approach, examining relationships within entities to explain financial performance, and in some cases financial vulnerability (Crittenden, 2000; Baber, Roberts, & Visyanathan, 2001; Callen, Klein, & Tinkelman, 2003; Hodge, 2006; Tinkelman & Donabedian, 2007, 2009). These relationships can include factors and activities which are organisationally, rather than financially, grounded, such as the use of formal planning tools to measure NFP board quality. Predicting financial vulnerability to avoid a reduction in programme expenditure has been identified as 'the most difficult challenge' facing NFP organisations, due to their desire 'to protect program services at all costs and find ways to fund mission-related activities even in the face of declining revenues or net assets' (Keating et al., 2005, pp. 22–23).

While it appears intuitively obvious that reserves would be a factor in mitigating risk, facilitating innovation and ensuring viability, research findings are mixed. Some studies use equity (a surrogate for reserves) as a measure of viability, whereas others use annual surplus. Tuckman and Chang (1991) found both operating margin and equity balance to be effective descriptors of financial viability, whereas Greenlee and Trussel (2000) found that operating margin, but not the equity ratio, was a viability predictor. Hager (2001), using the Tuckman and Chang (1991) model, preferred both variables as significant descriptors, whereas Trussel (2002) confirmed operating reserves as a significant viability predictor. Finally Hodge (2006), in seeking to use a Board Self-Assessment Questionnaire as an indicator of board effectiveness, included the level of reserves as an important measure of success. These indicators of financial vulnerability are summarised in Table 6.2.

Table 6.2 Studies identifying indicators of financial viability/vulnerability

Authors	Conditions of financial vulnerability	Measures of financial vulnerability	Purpose
Tuckman and Chang (1991)	Financially vulnerable if likely to cut back services immediately when it suffers a financial shock	Equity balance; revenue concentration, administration costs, operating ratios	Descriptive
Greenlee and Trussel (2000)	Decrease on programme expenditure scaled by total revenue in three consecutive years	As above	Equity balance *not predictive*. The others were
Hager (2001)	Demise of the organisation	Tuckman and Chang parameters	Varies by type of organisation but *did predict* vulnerability for some
Trussel (2002)	More than a 20% decrease in fund balance over three years	Several measures, including Total Liabilities and Total Assets	Predictive
Trussel and Greenlee (2004)	Decrease in net assets over three years	Tuckman and Chang parameters plus Size, Sector, Time	Predictive
Keating et al. (2005)	Bankruptcy/ financial distress	Used Ohlson for-profit model 15 parameters including EBIT	Net Asset/Total Asset ratio was not predictive but Total Liability/Total Asset ratio was predictive

The core question of what financial vulnerability is and how it is measured is clearly complex, with limited agreement between researchers, although the Tuckman and Chang (1991) parameters have been accepted by scholars as primary indicators of NFP viability. For the purposes of this chapter it is worth noting that net assets are used as both antecedents of vulnerability (Tuckman & Chang, 1991; Greenlee & Trussel, 2000; Hager, 2001; Keating et al., 2005) and as a measure/condition of vulnerability (Trussel, 2002; Trussel & Greenlee, 2004).

THEORETICAL FRAMEWORK

While the previous discussion has focused on studies that explore the relationship between reserves accumulation and financial health, we now turn to broader frameworks that focus on reserve-accumulating behaviour. Pioneering studies by Weisbrod (1975) and Hansmann (1980) provide a framework for understanding NFP roles and behaviour, but a recent review observed that the literature is silent on 'the actual financial operations of the sector' (Calabrese, 2009, p. 78)[5]. Chang and Tuckman (1990) accepted that NFP organisations can be defined by their inability to distribute their profits (Hansmann, 1980), and prior to the Tuckman and Chang (1992) study, presented empirical evidence that NFPs 'consistently accumulate' reserves over time (Chang & Tuckman, 1990, p. 117). Other studies have treated NFP surpluses and consequent accumulations as either expected to be nil, because all funds received would necessarily be spent on mission, or alternatively, that any residual was simply a result of poor forecasting of income and expenditure over time. However, Chang and Tuckman (1990) proposed that

- NFP managers and decision makers found value in increasing equity, i.e., in accumulating reserves.
- Current theories do not provide guidance about movements in accumulated surpluses.
- If all revenue is used, NFP organisations will arguably maximise market share and dominate industries where they compete with for-profit entities (see also Rose-Ackerman, 1986).
- Theories about reserve accumulation do not provide guidance about public policy issues concerning NFP accumulation of surplus.

Contemporaneously, Hansmann (1990) examined the role of endowments in U.S. universities and tested a number of possible reasons for their accumulation. He observed the conflict between increasing endowments at the expense of research or educational services, and questioned why universities save, rather than spend, a considerable amount of their income. Focusing on Yale University, he examined a number of generally held views, mostly around the question of intergenerational equity (i.e., the protection of the perceived needs of the future against the requirements and demands of the present) and found them unpersuasive. He identified several compelling reasons for the accumulation of reserves: to ensure the long term preservation of reputational capital, to preserve the institution's intellectual freedom, to pass on values prized by the current generation and to act as a financial buffer against periods of adversity.

Hansmann's (1990) findings aligned with those of Chang and Tuckman (1990), who proposed a number of potential benefits for NFP organisations that accumulate equity. First, they suggested that having a level of deployable assets or reserves allowed the subsidisation of programme products and services to people who would otherwise be unable to afford them. Second, having reserves ensured the continuation of existing programmes and expansion into new areas. The presence of strong equity would not only provide internal capital as a source of expansion but also potentially facilitate access to lending facilities. Third, the availability of internal funds allowed a NFP manager to implement a long-term vision. The larger the unrestricted equity balance of a NFP organisation relative to its revenues, the greater its independence from the marketplace. The equity balance also served as a tangible measure of financial success, both internally and externally. Finally, Chang and Tuckman (1990) posited that the accumulation of equity might provide a hedge against uncertainty and risk and enhance long-term sustainability, particularly in cases of temporary downturns in revenue and unexpected spikes in expenditures.

These authors' subsequent analysis demonstrated that NFP organisations do accumulate surpluses over time, even after adjusting for inflation. This was observed in almost all organisation size categories, and for each NFP type. The fact that an organisation already had a large equity base was found not to be a deterrent to further accumulation. Indeed, for some organisational categories, and for the entire sample, those NFP organisations with the most equity also accumulated additional surpluses at the greatest rate for the period examined, indicating an instinct for 'organisational survival' (Chang & Tuckman, 1990, p. 133).

Continuing on from previous studies, Tuckman and Chang's (1992) research hypothesised that NFP organisations deliberately tried to accumulate surpluses and increase equity over time. The authors tested this using a model based on the assumption that NFP managers' satisfaction is dependent on levels of programme operations and equity. In addition they acknowledged the views of other researchers that 'equity growth may be seen as an end in itself, particularly if the NFP is run by persons who have fund-raising backgrounds, and enthusiasm for raising gifts and donations' (Tuckman & Chang, 1992, p. 79). The study modelled end-of-year equity, informed by operating margin/unit of product, interest rate on borrowed funds and surplus. The results supported the hypothesis that equity growth is deliberate and predictable: 'a nonprofit may seek to accumulate equity without necessarily planning to use it in direct support of its mission' (Tuckman & Chang, 1992, p. 77).

In summary, researchers noted the importance of reserves accumulation as a financial buffer, as protection against downturns, and as an end in itself. However, the literature developed as a general theory of NFP reserves behaviour has limited use for further exploring the theoretical nature and role of reserves.

By incorporating a time dimension to the study of NFP financial sustainability, Bowman (2011, p. 39) offered the 'first comprehensive alternative' to the Tuckman and Chang model. Where Tuckman and Chang (1992) used a predictive modelling approach, Bowman (2011) took a normative approach, proposing the need for a NFP organisation to maintain its asset base in real terms in order to ensure longer term financial sustainability. His model considered a long-run objective as maintaining or expanding services, and a short-run objective as developing resilience to occasional economic shocks while making progress toward meeting long-term objectives. Long-term sustainability required total assets to grow at a rate no less than the long-term rate of inflation (Anthony & Young, 2005), whereas short-term resilience required unrestricted cash-convertible assets. Because long-term sustainability is reached through successive short terms, consistency is required between short-term (annual surpluses) and long-term (asset growth) measures (Bowman, 2011).

Other research considered the issue of organisational viability through different lenses. Studies by Crittenden (2000), Baber et al. (2001), Callen et al. (2003), Hodge and Piccolo (2005), Hodge (2006) and Tinkelman and Donabedian (2007, 2009) informed and contextualised the constructs of financial viability/vulnerability/sustainability. They are peripheral to financial sustainability, except for the work by Crittenden (2000), Hodge and Piccolo (2005) and Hodge (2006). Nevertheless, each of these approaches is relevant as they include surplus accumulation as an element in determining financial vulnerability and/or financial performance, emphasising

- The link between strategy, funding and financial performance in NFP social service organisations (Crittenden, 2000);
- Programme spending ratios as a predictor of effectiveness of strategy (Baber et al., 2001);
- Board composition and organisational efficiency (Callen et al., 2003);
- The relationship between funding source, board involvement and financial vulnerability (Hodge & Piccolo, 2005);
- The relationship between board effectiveness and financial vulnerability (Hodge, 2006);
- The use of traditional ratio analysis and standard cost/pricing to predict organisational efficiency (Tinkelman & Donabedian 2007, 2009).

This research leads us to conclude that there is no overarching framework to assist NFP organisations to develop a reserves policy, to enable us to identify whether reserves are a necessary condition for ensuring financial sustainability, and if so, to determine whether there is an optimal level of reserves. However, there is support for the view that hedging risk and uncertainty is an important driver in reserves accumulation. We now review the NFP regulatory frameworks of several jurisdictions to identify reserves policies.

LEGAL RULES AND REGULATORY POLICIES ABOUT NFP RESERVES ACROSS JURISDICTIONS

NFP organisations exist in a complex regulatory and practice environment, where reserves accumulation may be expressed in government regulation or industry advice rather than the economics of business and desires of management. Given the strong history and tradition flowing from English charity law, the approaches adopted by these jurisdictions have substantial commonality in their treatment of charities and NFP organisations.

England and Wales

While the jurisdiction of England and Wales arguably offers the most comprehensive guidance with respect to reserves, it is at best broad and generalised:

> Setting the level of reserves depends entirely on the unique circumstances of each charity—no universal formula applies when deciding on an appropriate amount to either hold back or aspire to. It will normally depend on what the charity is established to do and whom it seeks to assist and should take into account any opportunities, risks, scale and growth of charitable activity, financial commitments and plans, and the likelihood of those risks affecting the charity.
>
> (Charity Commission, 2006, p. 16)

The Commission advised that a charity's reserves policy should be informed by forecasts of level of income and expenditure for future year, considering the reliability of each source of income as well as opportunities for new sources (Charity Commission, 2008, para. 48). An analysis of unfunded opportunities and contingencies should be provided, along with a risk assessment which should include the potential consequences for the charity of not being able to meet them. Further, emphasising the importance of disclosure, the Charities Statement of Recommended Practice (Charities Commission, 2005) requires trustees to include in their Annual Report information about their charity's reserves policy, the level of reserves held and reasons for those levels. In addition, trustees are required to quantify and explain the purpose of any material designated funds, and where set aside for future expenditure, the likely timing of that expenditure (Charity Commission, 2008).

Moving from disclosure guidance, the Commission observed that there is no specific legal rule which determines the amount or proportion of a charity's income funds it is allowed to hold as a reserve (Charity Commission, 2008, para. 29). Trustees are under a general legal duty to apply charity funds within a reasonable time of receiving them (Charity Commission, 2008, para. 30) and therefore need a legal power to hold income funds in reserve (Charity Commission, 2008, para. 31). While in some cases trustees have an express legal power in their charity's governing document to hold income in reserve instead of expending it promptly, more frequently that power will be implied. As with all discretionary powers, the decision to hold reserves cannot be exercised arbitrarily, and trustees must demonstrate their accountability for the accumulation of reserves by demonstrating that it is in the charity's best interests to do so (Charity Commission, 2008, para. 32).

U.S.

Simon, Dale, and Chisolm (2006) noted the close relationship between U.S. charities and the taxation regime, a connection unmatched elsewhere in the world. The purpose of this chapter is not to summarise the tax regime in jurisdictions generally, but we note their statement that rather than one single federal tax treatment existing there is in fact a multiplicity sharing the two tenets of the non-distribution constraint (Hansmann, 1980) and federal income tax exemption.

Considering the general law, Brody commented (2006, p. 243) that U.S. law operates quite differently in relation to NFP organisations, providing 'at best an incomplete solution to problems of nonprofit governance and the protection of public interest,' with no laws telling the entity or its managers how 'to do' charity. Further, NFP organisations operate within broadly bounded charitable purposes, subject only to a general proposition against insider self-dealing: 'No law requires charities to serve only the poor, bars charities from paying (reasonably) high salaries or requires charities to be democratically run' (Brody, 2006, p. 243). There is no law preventing a NFP organisation from accumulating reserves and no law determining the amount of reserves which should be held. However, the Nonprofit Operating Reserves Initiative workgroup (NORI, 2008) suggests a minimum operating reserves ratio and recommends that NFP boards establish operating reserves policies for their organisations, providing more operational than the Charity Commission for England and Wales about

- The determination of a normal circumstance minimum operating reserves ratio with an associated formulae to derive this metric
- The development of policies for investment, replenishment, frequency of measurement and reporting of reserves (NORI, 2008)

While recognising that the level of reserves will be entity specific, NORI recommends that the minimum board-established operating reserves ratio be *no less than three months* of operating expenses.

Australia

In Australia, the commencement in 2012 of the ACNC indicates a NFP regulatory environment that is not yet mature. In the absence of a Statement of Recommended Practice (SORP) equivalent or set of guidance documents such as those produced by the Charities Commission for England and Wales, there is as yet no detailed guidance on reserves accumulation. Indeed, with the major exception of NFP organisations structured as companies limited by guarantee (a federal responsibility), an understanding of the regulatory framework still requires attention to be given to national law as well as the laws of six states and two territories.

Ali and Gold (2002), in examining the question of socially responsible investing, observed that a fiduciary empowered to invest funds must exercise that power in a prudent manner. This duty of prudence arises through individual state statute, supplementing the duties of care, skill and diligence imposed by the Corporations Act 2001 (Commonwealth). This specific accountability mechanism deals with the duty owed by the fiduciary to its beneficiaries with respect to the need to derive an optimum return on funds in accordance with the fund's investment objectives, for an acceptable level of risk. A fiduciary who sacrifices an adequate rate of return on fund assets or places them in jeopardy, in the pursuit of a non-financial objective, risks being in breach of the duty of prudence.

Arguably this duty imposes a requirement on a NFP organisation to ensure that, consistent with its mission, it remains a 'going concern,' providing for uncertainty through, for example, an appropriate reserves policy. In a related sense, and recognising that NFP organisations will often have potentially substantial ongoing financial expenditures which cannot be quickly terminated, it is important that they ensure appropriate planning to reduce the possibility of insolvent trading; i.e., that they ensure their financial sustainability.

In Australia, in common with the legal systems in other jurisdictions, once a company becomes insolvent, the directors have specific responsibilities. Section 588G of the Corporations Act 2001 (Commonwealth) places a duty on directors to prevent the company incurring debts where they have grounds for suspecting that it is insolvent. In practice, only two Australian states have provisions in their legislation covering NFP organisations formed as incorporated associations that specifically address this issue.

Canada

In common with the U.S. model, the Canadian charity sector is regulated by the Charities Directorate of the Canada Revenue Agency (CRA). Again in common with the U.S., Australia and New Zealand, there is no detailed guidance with respect to reserves accumulation. Of particular interest, however, is the specification of a disbursement quota, which is the minimum amount a registered charity is required to spend each year on its own charitable activities, or on gifts to qualified donees.

Broder (2010) noted two recent rulings from the CRA which suggested that NFP organisations, which are defined as distinct from charities for purposes of the Income Tax Act (ITA) and not regulated through the Charities Directorate, cannot intentionally generate surpluses and retain their Income Tax Act NFP status. He further noted that if they earn revenues in excess of their costs, CRA has, at times, taken the position that they are only entitled to have those revenues as tax exempt if they earn them accidentally. That calls into question the ability of NFP organisations to accumulate reserves for which they have no specified purpose, and highlights the risk to their taxation status if they accumulate reserves (Drache, 2012).

New Zealand

Since 2012, regulation of charities in New Zealand, carried out from 2005 by the Charities Commission, has been performed by the Charities and Services Business Group within the Department of Internal Affairs. Best practice, as well as an exposition of the relevant law relating to charity, is provided by free access to an internally developed book on New Zealand charity law (Poirier, 2013). Two points are of particular relevance to the issue of reserves, both being highlighted in Poirier's (2013) book: charities have the express power, confirmed by NZ's High Court, to accumulate reserves, and there is a general requirement that surplus assets be exclusively directed to charitable purposes upon liquidation or winding up.

The above examination of the legal and regulatory frameworks of England and Wales, the U.S., Australia, Canada and New Zealand suggests that within all those jurisdictions except New Zealand, the power of NFP organisations to accumulate reserves where there are opportunities for the funds to be deployed to their mission is, at best, unclear. However, generally there is at least a framework to work with. While the power to accumulate reserves is unclear, there is, with the exception of the NORI (2008) guideline, a general absence of any concrete advice about the appropriate level of reserves to achieve relevant goals (i.e., insure against financial uncertainty, provide for innovation). In a number of jurisdictions, policy comments outline at least the need to report the amount of reserves held along with explanations of key issues, such as the base for calculation and accumulation replenishment. Given the lack of clarity on these matters, the next issue to be considered is the extent to which NFP organisations hold reserves in these jurisdictions.

LEVELS OF RESERVES HELD

As noted previously, there is compelling research supporting a view that the accumulation of reserves supports ongoing viability and sustainability. Previous discussion also noted the lack of clarity as to both legal authority and guidance generally on both the ability to accumulate reserves and the appropriate level of reserves to be held. We now turn to a number of studies which provide some understanding of the extent of reserves held by NFP organisations in a number of jurisdictions, as well as arguments about why such reserves might be held. Note that no comparative data has been identified for Canada.

England and Wales

An analysis of some 62,000 registered charities with an income of £10,000 and over, providing information for financial years ending in 2004, was undertaken by the Charity Commission (2006). This research shows that reserves totalling £35.5 billion (£26 billion in 2002) were held by charities in the sample, with 75% of the total reserves held by very large charities (7% of the sample). The study revealed that medium-sized charities held reserves covering more months' expenditure than larger charities, but the total amount medium-sized charities held in reserve had remained relatively static since 2002. While the 35% growth in the charity sector's reserves appears to be a major increase in holdings, it was in fact less than equivalent rises in income and expenditure, with medium-sized charities in particular facing shortfalls in the amounts available to them to put aside for the future (Charity Commission, 2006). The survey indicated that on average charities held 11.4 months" coverage, with very large, large and medium charities holding 10.2, 16.6 and 18 months' coverage, respectively (Charity Commission, 2006).

On the question of reserves policy, the Charity Commission study reported that 40% of all charities stated that they had a reserves policy, an increase from 27% in 2002. The study also sought to establish whether there was a perception by funders that the maintenance of reserves was equivalent to hoarding and hence undesirable (Charity Commission, 2006). While the casework showed that some charities believed funders would penalise them if they had large reserves, this was true in only a minority of cases. 88% said that having reserves had not been a barrier to attracting funding. A similar percentage highlighted that having reserves and a policy about reserves provided their charity with more security for their charity and also enhanced donor perceptions of accountability, whereas funding bodies also viewed reserves positively as contributing to a charity's long-term security (Charity Commission, 2006).

In commenting on its survey of 127 predominantly small and medium-sized charities, the Charities Aid Foundation (CAF) noted that 'charities have often been uncomfortable talking to donors about reserves, so it is reassuring that there is widespread understanding that well run charities need reserves' (CAF, 2009). The CAF (2009) survey also revealed widespread differences in the levels of financial reserves held by charities, with 5% holding no reserves at all, nearly a quarter holding less than three months of reserves, 20% holding between four and six months of reserves and almost half holding more. In addition, it was noted that 40% of charities reported their levels of reserves as being lower than the previous year, while a similar proportion had increased their reserves. The survey found that although most charities held reserves in cash, some were held in stocks and shares and these had been affected by falls in the stock market (CAF, 2009).

There are several trends noticeable in this research. Data available indicates a higher overall accumulation level than in the U.S., with almost one years coverage held among medium and large organisations. Further, based on survey data, 25% of UK organisations hold less than three months' (12 weeks') coverage compared with a similar percentage holding less than three weeks' coverage in the U.S. The UK focus on encouraging organisations to develop a reserves policy (and perhaps to hold reserves) thus appears to be successful.

U.S.

Chang and Tuckman (1990) examined the question of why NFP managers accumulated reserves, and noted that adjusted for inflation, total NFP equity in the U.S. was estimated at $60.9 billion in 1975 and $65.9 billion in 1983. Fremont-Smith (2004) noted the increase in the value of financial holdings of NFP organisations (other than churches) in real terms between 1988 and 1998, from $777 billion to $1.77 trillion, a rate of 7.8% annually. Most of the wealth was held by hospitals and related health care organisations, and also colleges and universities, leading to her observation of the need to:

> Pay continued attention to the problems of wealth in the charitable sector, and particularly to understand and articulate the purposes for maintaining and expanding wealth and the costs associated with excessive accumulation.

> (Fremont-Smith, 2004, p. 3)

Fremont-Smith (2004) further inferred that little had changed since Hansmann (1990) challenged universities and other endowed institutions to satisfy themselves and others that their policies toward accumulation were reasonable in light of the ends to which their institutions are dedicated. Trussel, Greenlee, and Brady (2002), in a study including 10,000 organisations, identified a total equity of in excess of $100 billion for those entities.

In a study of 97,500 U.S. entities defined as 'ordinary nonprofits' (i.e., excluding groupings such as membership associations and grant makers), Bowman (2011) removed from his data entities with life spans of less than six years, inactive and shell organisations and those that did not use accrual accounting, His study provided insights about financial sustainability.

- The median equity ratio was 0.72. Although nine out of 10 NFP organisations had a positive equity ratio, one in 10 was balance-sheet insolvent (i.e., total liabilities exceed total assets).
- The return on assets of the median organisation was 1%. Long-term sustainability requires growth of total assets faster than the long-term rate of inflation of 3.4%, but more than half (62%) were unsustainable in the long term and 45% actually had negative returns.
- The median organisation had reserves to cover 2.7 months of spending, which is very close to the recommended NORI (2008) level, but one-quarter had only 20 days or less and 16% had negative short-term capacity.
- Only 56% of the entities were considered sustainable in the sense that they were accumulating enough cash to guarantee a return on assets of 3.4% in the long term.

In summarising his research, Bowman (2011, p. 48) described the data as telling 'a familiar story: ordinary NFPs stretching their resources to the limit and exposing themselves to long- and short term risks to serve their clients.'

Insights can also be drawn from studies done at more local levels. Blackwood and Pollack (2009) examined the operating reserves of 2,648 organisations from soup kitchens to schools in the greater Washington area:

> If you have some money in the bank—an operating reserve—you can survive. If not, you could be in dire straits. This is the current predicament faced by many public charities in the Greater Washington area. Major foundations lost a median value of 28 percent of their endowments between 2007 and 2008.
>
> (Blackwood & Pollack, 2009, p. 1)

The study calculated an operating reserves ratio using data from IRS Form 990, made available through the National Centre for Charitable Statistics. It revealed that these charities had a median operating reserve of 2.1 months, with 57% having operating reserves of less than three months of operating expenses. The study reported that '28 percent of organisations appear to be operating hand to mouth, reporting no operating reserves whatsoever'

(Blackwood & Pollack, 2009, p. 2). This research also analysed reserves held by demographic or other characteristics:

- Operating reserves by age—entities regardless of age can have low operating reserves.
- Operating reserves by organisational expenses—an inverse relationship was found; i.e., the larger the expense base, the lower the reserves.
- Operating reserves by primary source of revenue—the lowest level of reserves were held where funding was from government grants or programme service revenue. The government grants and programme service revenue categories had a much higher percentage of organisations with no operating reserves (about one-third), compared to the private contributions category, where only 20% of organisations that relied primarily on private contributions reported no operating reserves.
- Operating reserves by organisational mission (or type)—no specific relationship was found.

In addition to researching the level of reserves held, the Blackwood and Pollack (2009) study also examined the situation over the 2000–2006 period, finding that 16% of organisations which had filed returns in 2000 did not file in 2006. Further, it was noted that those that did not file in 2006 looked substantially different from those that survived. In particular, their 2,000 median operating reserve was 0.7 months, approximately one-third the level (2.0 months) of those that filed in all three years. 52% of those that ceased filing had operating reserves of one month or less, compared to 40% reserves held by organisations that filed in all three years. Further characteristics of the non-filers revealed (Blackwood & Pollack, 2009):

- Age—organisations older than 30 years had median reserves covering at least a month more than younger organisations that filed in all three years.
- Organisational expenses—mean operating reserve ratios dropped 30% across all sizes.
- Primary revenue source—there were no substantial changes in median ratios regardless of revenue source.
- Mission—environment and animal organisations appeared to have dipped more into their operating reserves during these years, with their median operating reserves ratio dropping by a fifth from 2000 to 2003 before rebounding strongly in 2006.

The U.S. experience is that NFP organisations hold very large financial reserves in total, with most held within the health care and educational subsectors. There is no national picture of reserves holdings across the sector, however the studies reviewed reported median operating reserves of two to three months' equivalent of operating expenditure. Of concern, substantial numbers (between one in six and one in four) had no operating reserves at all.

Australia

Until 2012, Australia lacked both a national regulator and the availability of national accounting data, with studies on the level of reserves held consequently very limited. An exception is a study by Booth (2012) using Australian data from non-government organisations (NGOs) involved in delivering overseas aid and development. The study consisted of two phases, the first analysing all NGOs who filed financial statements with the Australian Council for International Development (ACFID) for the 2009 year, and the second analysing those NGOs who filed continuously from 2006 to 2010.

Booth (2012) reported that 38% (more than one in three) of entities had less than the three-month level recommended by the Charity Commission for England and Wales and the U.S. NORI group (see Table 6.3). The average of each entity's months covered was 6.87, while the median was 3.81.

The study revealed further that while the average Net Assets/Total Asset ratio was 0.22 compared with Bowman's (2011) recommendation of 0.50, the median was a high 0.79. This suggested that generally, the organisations had little debt (see Table 6.4).

In terms of long-term sustainability, the story was quite different. With the Australian long-term inflation rate at 3%, the median rate of return on assets for the organisations was a low 1.8%. In addition, 39 organisations had negative rates of return, while another eight had rates greater

Table 6.3 Entities' level of reserves held measured by 'months covered' (2009)

Months covered	Number of entities	Percentage (%)
Over 12 months	15	17
6 to 12 months	15	17
3 to 6 months	23	27
0 to 3 months	32*	37
Less than 0	1	1

*Includes 3 with 0 months covered.

Table 6.4 Bowman's (2011) measures of sustainability

	Net assets/Total assets	Change in Net assets/Total assets
Average	22%	17%
Median	79%	2%

Booth (2012)

than zero but less than the 3% recommended (Booth, 2012). Using programme expenditure/total revenue and programme expenditure/total expenditure as metrics measuring relative mission orientation, the study also examined behaviours for those NGOs which held reserves above and below the NORI recommended three months for all of the five years from 2006 to 2010. The results, summarised in Table 6.5, reveal observable difference between these measures for the two groups over the period.

In Booth's (2012) longitudinal study, entities with fewer than three months' reserves reported higher levels of programme expenditure as a percentage of total revenue (PE/TR). This indicated that more of their resources were spent on mission, and further, that the lack of reserves did not preclude the maintenance of a relatively higher level of programme expenditure. Supporting this view were the metrics for programme expenditure as a percentage of total expenditure (PE/TE), which showed that entities with fewer than three months' coverage had equal or higher spending on mission for four of the five years. Thus arguably, based on these findings, NGOs with lower levels of reserves demonstrated a higher level of mission sustainability.

New Zealand

New Zealand data is limited, however media reports of charities with assets of more than $NZ 100 million (a total of 32, excluding universities) indicated that $NZ 2 billion was held in investments from a total asset base of $NZ 7.7 billion. The average investment holding was 27% of total assets, however with a median of 11%, a high level of skew was evident (Stock,

Table 6.5   Comparative mission-oriented measures

	Group	2006	2007	2008	2009	2010	Comment
PE/TR	<3 months (MC-NORI)	83%	78%	79%	82%	78%	Observable difference for all years with entities with fewer than 3 months reserves having higher levels of total revenue expended on programme.
	≥3 months (MC-NORI)	75%	75%	75%	73%	73%	
PE/TE	<3 months (MC-NORI)	80%	78%	79%	82%	77%	Observable difference is mixed for all years with entities with fewer than 3 months reserves having higher levels of total expenditure expended on programme.
	≥3 months (MC-NORI)	76%	78%	78%	75%	78%	

2011). The same source indicated that for the eight charitable groups identified with assets over $NZ 100 million (total assets of $NZ 3 billion and investments of $NZ 1.5 billion), the average investment holding was 50% with a median of 55%. Interestingly, these statistics hide a high level of skewing as well, with three of the eight groups holding 85% of assets as investments and three holding 12% or less.

Cross-Jurisdictional Comparison

The studies conducted in these five jurisdictions indicate that the richest and most extensive readily available data on NFP reserves is in the U.S., due to its regulatory arrangements. As evident in Table 6.6, there are many U.S. studies, few from Australia, England and Wales, and none from Canada or New Zealand, making comparison difficult.

Based on the studies available, we note that the level of reserves held by Australian NFP organisations appears to sit between the U.S., with the

Table 6.6 Reserves measured as months of total expenditure covered in U.S., Australia and England and Wales

U.S.	Australia	England and Wales
Bowman (2011) national study		Charity Commission (medium to very large)
Blackwood and Pollack (2009) Washington study		CAF (small to medium)
Average 2.7 months (Bowman, 2011)	6.87 months (average) 3.81 months (median)	11.4 months (CC)
16% zero or negative (Bowman, 2011)	1%	5% zero or negative (CAF)
25% less than 21 days (Bowman, 2011)		
Average 2.1 months (Blackwood & Pollack, 2009)		
28% zero or negative (Blackwood & Pollack, 2009)		
57% less than 3 months (Blackwood & Pollack, 2009)	38% less than 3 months	25% less than 3 months (CAF)

Note: no comparative data is available for Canada and New Zealand lowest levels of reserves generally, and England and Wales with the highest level. U.S. studies indicate that lower levels of reserves are evident in organisations that have a higher reliance on government revenue and larger expenditure bases. U.S. reserve patterns appear not to be affected by age or organisational mission, and entities that cease operations generally have lower reserves.

The sole Australian study indicated that organisations' revenue streams were the only explanation for differences in reserve levels. Further, when defining sustainability as the maintenance of relative programme expenditure over time there was no support for the view that high relative programme expenditure is supported by high relative levels of reserves. A direct comparison of this Australian study with U.S. studies is problematic, due to the dramatic difference in scope. Charities in England and Wales were found to have fewer entities with low levels of reserves than those in the U.S. or Australia. This may reflect the Charity Commission's active stance on promoting the importance of reserves.

Finally, in examining the inter-jurisdictional discussion, there is very little mention of the reasons for accumulating reserves, the exception being the comment by the Charity Commission (2006, p. 4) that, 'the majority of respondents (88%) said that having reserves and a policy made their charity more secure and protected it against risks and that donors now regarded the charity as more accountable.'

CONCLUSION

In attempting to understand the role of reserves in ensuring NFP organisational sustainability and underlying accountability for long-term mission delivery, it rapidly becomes clear that there is a lack of definition and understanding of the key constructs of reserves and sustainability, in both theory and practice. The notion of sustainability is rarely addressed, with the primary focus on vulnerability or viability. These measures focus only on the short term, however, rather than offering a longer term focus.

There is an overarching commonality of approach across jurisdictions, reflecting the history and tradition of treatment of NFP organisations, and charities in particular, flowing from early English law and an inherent recognition that trustees and boards are accountable for operational matters, including their organisations' ability to continue to survive. However, despite this commonality, in practice jurisdictional regulatory systems, particularly as they relate to the availability of NFP data, inevitably skew research and understanding of the issue of NFP reserves. While there is a high emphasis on the accountability of NFP organisations, there is little coherent guidance offered about either the need for reserves or what constitutes acceptable levels of reserves. The purpose of this chapter has not been to provide a normative framework for determining what this level may be, but rather to highlight the need for NFP boards and managers to be acquainted with reserves policies, and to work, under their own jurisdictional guidelines, on developing a unique reserves policy appropriate to the structural and mission imperatives of their organisation.

Notwithstanding the limitations of this chapter, which does not consider the variety and complexity of the NFP sector, we can, however, state that where data is available, there appears to be a core belief that some reserves should be kept as a hedge against uncertainty and to enhance financial sustainability, while at the same time continuing to expend resources on mission activities. On the other hand, there is evidence that some NFP organisations operate with very low levels of reserves in both the U.S. and Australia, indicating their ability to operate under conditions of limited resources and high uncertainty. Further research investigating the specificities of individual jurisdictions or types of NFP organisations would provide additional valuable insights into reserves practice.

NOTES

1 The ACNC obtained legislative authority in December 2012 under the then Labour government, and plans to close it as a separate body were announced by the new Australian Coalition government in December 2013.
2 This excludes groupings such as membership associations, grant makers, NFP organisations with lifespans of less than six years, inactive and shell organisations, as well as those that did not use accrual accounting.
3 The Australian Council for International Development (ACFID) Code of Conduct Guidance document refines the requirements of Australian accounting standards, noting that reserves (i.e., any monies specifically set aside by the governing body for the future) can be classified as restricted (allocated for a specific purpose) or unrestricted (any other reserve established by the organisation) (ACFID, 2010).
4 In an unpublished paper, Tuckman (2006) argued that traditional frameworks for measuring organisational viability should be contextually based, particularly with regard to an organisation's position in the organisational life cycle (cited in Greenlee & Tuckman, 2007).
5 Calabrese (2009) observed that only Tuckman and Chang (1992) actually modelled net asset accumulation as a NFP goal.

REFERENCES

Akingbola, K. (2004). Staffing, retention, and government funding: a case study. *Nonprofit Management and Leadership, 14*(4), 453–465.
Ali, P. U., & Gold, M. (2002). *An appraisal of socially responsible investments and implications for trustees and other investment fiduciaries, centre for corporate law and securities regulation.* Melbourne: University of Melbourne.
Anthony, R. N., & Young, D. W. (2005). Financial accounting and financial management. In R. G. Herman & Associates (Eds.), *Jossey-Bass handbook of nonprofit leadership and management* (pp. 466–512). San Francisco: Jossey-Bass.

Australian Council for International Development (ACFID). (2010). *ACFID Code of Conduct Guidance Document.* Retrieved 27 February 2012 from http://www.acfid.asn.au/code-of-conduct/implementation-guidance

Baber, W. R., Roberts, A. A., & Visvanathan, G. (2001). Charitable organizations' strategies and program-spending ratios. *Accounting Horizons, 15*(4), 329–343.

Besel, K., Williams, C. L., & Klak, J. (2011). Nonprofit sustainability during times of uncertainty. *Nonprofit Management and Leadership, 22*(1), 53–65.

Bingham, T., & Walters, G. (2013). Financial sustainability within UK charities: Community sport trusts and corporate social responsibility partnerships. *Voluntas, 24*(3), 606–629.

Blackwood, A., & Pollack, T. H. (2009). *Washington-area nonprofit operating reserves. Charting civil society series.* Centre on Nonprofits and Philanthropy, The Urban Institute. Retrieved 10 April 2013 from www.urban.org/publications/411913.htm

Booth, M. S. (2012). *In the bank or on the ground: An examination of financial reserves in Australian international aid organisations* (Masters thesis). Retrieved 6 February 2014 from http://eprints.qut.edu.au/54669/

Bowman, W. (2008). *Beyond the bottom line: Understanding and promoting nonprofit financial sustainability.* Retrieved 4 February 2014 from www4.uwm.edu/milwaukeeidea/hbi/docs/Dec4advancematerials.pdf

Bowman, W. (2011). Financial capacity and sustainability of ordinary nonprofits. *Nonprofits Management and Leadership, 22*(1), 37–51.

Bowman, W., Tuckman, H. P., & Young, D. R. (2012). Issues in nonprofit finance research: Surplus, endowment, and endowment portfolios. *Nonprofit and Voluntary Sector Quarterly, 41,* 560–579.

Brock, K. L. (2000). Sustaining a relationship: Insights from Canada on linking the government and third sector. In W. Powell & R. Steinberg (Eds.), *The Fourth Conference of the International Society for Third Sector Research,* Dublin, IE. Retrieved 13 July 2014 from www.queensu.ca/sps/publications/workingpapers/01.pdf

Broder, P. (2010). *Not-for-law.* Retrieved 27 November 2012 from http://www.charitycentral.ca/docs/34-5broder-en.pdf

Brody, E. (2006). The legal framework for nonprofit organisations. In W. Powell & R. Steinberg (Eds.), *The nonprofit sector: A research handbook,* 2nd ed. (pp. 243–266). New Haven, CT: Yale University Press.

Calabrese, T. D. (2009). *Three essays on nonprofit net assets* (PhD thesis). New York University, New York.

Calabrese, T. D. (2011). Running on empty: The operating reserves of US nonprofit organizations. *Nonprofit Management & Leadership, 23*(3), 281–302.

Callen, J. L., Klein, A., & Tinkelman, D. (2003). Board composition, committees, and organizational efficiency: The case of nonprofits. *Nonprofit and Voluntary Sector Quarterly, 32*(4), 493–520.

Chang, C. F., & Tuckman, H. P. (1990). Why do nonprofit managers accumulate surpluses, and how much do they accumulate? *Nonprofit Management and Leadership, 1*(2), 117–136.

Charities Aid Foundation (CAF). (2009). *Public backs charities building up reserves to see them through difficult economic times.* Retrieved 11 June 2010 from http://www.cafonline.org/Default.aspx?page=18277andWT.mc_id=914

Charity Commission. (2005). *Accounting and reporting by charities: Statement of recommended practice.* Retrieved 5 February 2014 from https://www.charitycommission.gov.uk/media/95505/sorp05textcolour.pdf

Charity Commission. (2006). *Tell it like it is: The extent of charity reserves and reserves policies.* Retrieved 7 June 2010 from http://www.charitycommission.gov.uk/media/95265/rs13text.pdf

Charity Commission. (2008). *CC19—charities' reserves.* Retrieved 7 June 2010 from http://www.charity-commission.gov.uk/publications/cc19.asp

Charity Commission. (2012). *Glossary of terms used*. Retrieved 4 February 2010 from http://www.charitycommission.gov.uk/About_/OGs/glossary.aspx

Core, J., Guay, W. R., & Verdi, R. S. (2006). Agency problems of excess endowment holdings in not-for-profit firms. *Journal of Accounting and Economics, 41*, 307–333.

Crittenden, W. F. (2000). Spinning straw into gold: The tenuous strategy, funding, and financial performance linkage. *Nonprofit and Voluntary Sector Quarterly, 29*(1), 164–182.

Drache, A. (2012). *Accumulation of profits in a non-profit organization*. Retrieved 15 October 2013 from http://www.drache.ca/articles/charities/accumulation-of-profits/

Fremont-Smith, M. R. (2004). *Accumulations of wealth by nonprofits*. Emerging issues in philanthropy seminar series, in the Urban Institute, Centre on Nonprofits and Philanthropy, Washington, DC. Retrieved 26 November 2009 from http://www.urban.org/publications/311022.html

Gilbert, L. R., Menon, K., & Schwartz, K. B. (1990). Predicting bankruptcy for firms in financial distress. *Journal of Business Finance and Accounting, 17*(1), 161–171.

Gold, M. (2008). Financial sustainability and the imperative for reform in investment organisation in Australia's local government sector. *Accounting, Accountability & Performance, 14*(1), 35–56.

Golensky, M., & DeRuiter, G. L. (1999). Merger as a strategic response to government contracting pressures. *Nonprofit Management and Leadership, 10*(2), 137–152.

Greenlee, J. S., & Trussel, J. M. (2000). Predicting the financial vulnerability of charitable organisations. *Nonprofit Management and Leadership, 11*(2), 199–210.

Greenlee, J. S., & Tuckman, H. P. (2007). Financial health. In D. R. Young (Ed.), *Financing nonprofits: Putting theory into practice* (pp. 315–335). Lanham, MD: AltaMira Press.

Gregory, A. G., & Howard, D. (2009). *The nonprofit starvation cycle*. Retrieved 6 June 2011 from http://www.ssireview.org/images/articles/2009FA_feature_Gregory_Howard.pdf

Hager, M. (2001). Financial vulnerability among Arts Organizations: A test of the Tuckman-Chang measures. *Nonprofit and Voluntary Sector Quarterly, 31*(2), 376–392.

Hanley, P. (2006). *Why your organisation should consider developing a Financial Reserves Policy*. Wellington, NZ: Social & Civic Policy Institute. Retrieved 27 November 2012 from http://www.community.net.nz/how-toguides/finance/publicationsresources/

Hansmann, H. B. (1980). The role of nonprofit enterprise. *The Yale Law Journal, 89*(5), 835–901.

Hansmann, H. B. (1987). Economic theories of nonprofit organization. In *Nonprofit sector: A research handbook*, 2nd ed. (pp. 27–42). New Haven, CT: Yale University Press.

Hansmann, H. B. (1990). Why do universities have endowments? *The Journal of Legal Studies, 19*(1), 3–42.

Hodge, M. M. (2006). *Nonprofit board effectiveness, funding source, and financial vulnerability* (PhD thesis). College of Health and Public Affairs, University of Central Florida, Orlando, FL.

Hodge, M. M., & Piccolo, R. F. (2005). Funding source, board involvement techniques, and financial vulnerability in nonprofit organisations. A test of resource dependence. *Nonprofit Management and Leadership, 16*(2), 171–190.

Hoggett, J., Edwards, L., Medlin, J., & Tilling, M. (2009). *Financial accounting*, 7th ed. Milton, QLD: John Wiley and Sons Ltd.

Hunter, D. E. (2006). Using a theory of change approach to build organizational strength, capacity and sustainability with not-for-profit organizations in the human services sector. *Evaluation and Program Planning, 29*(2), 193–200.

IFRS Foundation. (2010). *The conceptual framework for financial reporting, IFRS Foundation.* Retrieved 31 October 2013 from http://eifrs.ifrs.org/eifrs/bnstandards/en/2013/conceptualframework.pdf

IFRS Foundation. (2011). *IAS1 Presentation of Financial Statements.* Retrieved 31 October 2013) from: http://www.ifrs.org/Current-Projects/IASB-Projects/Financial-Statement-Presentation/Phase-B-OCI/IAS-1-Presentation-of-Financial-Statments/Pages/IAS-1-Presentation-of-Financial-Statements.aspx

Keating, E. K., Fischer, M., Gordon, T. P., & Greenlee, J. (2005). *Assessing financial vulnerability in the nonprofit sector* (Paper no. 27) . Faculty Research Working Papers Series, The Hauser Centre for Nonprofit Organisations.

Leo, K., Hoggett, J., & Sweeting, J. (2012). *Company accounting*, 9th ed. John Wiley and Sons Australia, Ltd.

Leviton, L. C., Herrera, C., Pepper, S. K., Fishman, N., & Racine, D. P. (2006). Faith in action: Capacity and sustainability of volunteer organizations. *Evaluation and Program Planning, 29*(2), 201–207.

National Audit Office (UK). (2009). *Building the capacity of the third sector.* Retrieved 12 July 2013 from http://www.nao.org.uk/publications/0809/builing_the_capacity_of_the_t.aspx

Nonprofit Operating Reserve Initiative Workgroup (NORI). (2008). *Maintaining nonprofit operating reserves: An organisational imperative for nonprofit financial stability.* Retrieved 5 February 2012 from http://www.nccs2.org/wiki/imaes/3/3c/OperatingReservesWhitePaper2009.pdf

Oxford English Dictionary. (2014). *Welcome.* Retrieved 2 February 2014 from http://www.oed.com.ezp01.library.qut.edu.au/

Petrovits, C. M. (2006). Corporate-sponsored foundations and earnings management. *Journal of Accounting and Economics, 41*(3), 335–362.

Poirier, D. (2013). *Charity law in New Zealand.* Department of the Charities Commission. Retrieved 4 February 2014 from http://www.charities.govt.nz/assets/docs/media/Charity-Law-in-New-Zealand.pdf

Productivity Commission. (2010). *Contribution of the not-for-profit sector.* Retrieved 31 May 2010 from http://www.pc.gov.au/projects/study/not-for-profit

Rose-Ackerman, S. (1986). Altruism, nonprofits, and economic theory. *Journal of Economic Literature, XXXIV*(34), 701–728.

Simon, J., Dale, H., & Chisolm, L. (2006). The federal tax treatment of charitable organizations. In W. Powell & R. Steinberg (Eds.), *The nonprofit sector: A research handbook,* 2nd ed. (pp. 267–306). New Haven, CT: Yale University Press.

Steinberg, R. & Gray, B. H. (1993). The role of nonprofit enterprise in Hansmann revisited. *Nonprofit and Voluntary Sector Quarterly, 22*(4), 297–316.

Stock, R. (2011, May 8). Some charities sitting on a heap of assets, *Sunday Star Times*, D4.

Struthers, M. (2004). Supporting financial vibrancy in the quest for sustainability in the not-for-profit sector. *The Philanthropist, 19*(4), 241–260.

Tinkelman, D., & Donabedian, B. (2007). Street lamps, alleys, ratio analysis, and nonprofit organizations. *Nonprofit Management and Leadership, 18*(1), 5–18.

Tinkelman, D., & Donabedian, B. (2009). Decomposing the elements of nonprofit organisational performance. *Research in Governmental and Nonprofit Accounting, 12*(1), 75–98.

Trussel, J. M. (2002). Revisiting the prediction of financial vulnerability. *Nonprofit Management and Leadership, 13*(1), 17–31.

Trussel, J., & Greenlee, J. (2004). A financial rating system for nonprofit organizations. *Research in Government and Nonprofit Accounting, 11*(1), 105–128.

Trussel, J. M., Greenlee, J. S., & Brady, T. (2002). Predicting financial vulnerability in charitable organisations. *The CPA Journal, 72*(6), 66–69.

Tuckman, H. P. (2006). The various stages of development of a nonprofit organization and their implications for its financial health (Unpublished paper). Rutgers University, NJ.

Tuckman, H. P., & Chang, C. F. (1991). A methodology for measuring the financial vulnerability of charitable nonprofit organisations. *Nonprofit and Voluntary Sector Quarterly, 20*(1), 445–460.

Tuckman, H. P., & Chang, C. F. (1992). Nonprofit equity: A behavioral model and its policy implications. *Journal of Policy Analysis and Management, 111*(1), 76–87.

Weerawardena, J., McDonald, R. E., & Mort, G. S. (2010). Sustainability of nonprofit organizations: An empirical investigation. *Journal of World Business, 45*(4), 346–356.

Weisbrod, B. A. (1975). Towards a theory of the voluntary nonprofit sector in a three-sector economy. In S. Rose-Ackerman (Ed.), *The economics of nonprofit organisations: Studies in structure and policy*. New York: Oxford University Press.

Weisbrod, B. A. (1988). *The nonprofit economy*. Cambridge, MA: Harvard University Press.

7 Regulations and Financial Reporting Practices of Microfinance Institutions in Bangladesh

Rakib Khan and Kamran Ahmed

INTRODUCTION

In recent years, the world has witnessed a significant growth in microfinance institutions (MFIs).[1] MFIs are specialised entities that provide a small amount of business credit (popularly known as microcredit or microfinance), usually without collateral, to very poor people who lack steady employment and a verifiable credit history. The objectives of these institutions are to build the entrepreneurial capacity of borrowers (micro-entrepreneurs) by providing small (micro) finance with a view to generating employment opportunities and assisting them with training and education to sustain entrepreneurial activities. It is estimated that at the end of 2010, there were 3,625 MFIs of which 1,746 were located in Asia, 1,009 were in Sub-Saharan Africa, 647 were in Latin America and the Caribbean and the remaining 223 in the Middle East and North Africa (Reed & Maes, 2012). Due to significant growth in the number of MFIs, the United Nations declared 2005 the 'International Year of Microfinance.'

Along with other emerging nations, Bangladesh also witnessed exponential growth in MFIs in terms of number, size, membership and finance (Devine, 2006). These organisations are well known for pioneering microcredit programmes, reaching as many as 37% of all Bangladeshi households and around 60% of poor households in 2008 (Siddiquee & Faroqi, 2009). For example, the World Bank alone has reached more than 6 million poor people in Bangladesh through microfinance projects worth over $0.26 million since 1996 (World Bank Report, 2006). According to the Institute of Microfinance surveys 2009–2010, the cumulative disbursement of loans to the individual borrowers stood at Tk. 1,790.03 ($23.87) billion as of December 2009, reaching Tk. 2,174.86 ($29.1) billion as of December 2010. This shows that the annual loan disbursement was Tk. 384.83 ($5.12) billion, an increase in loan disbursement by 21.50% in 2010 from 2009 (MRA, 2011). With this significant growth in microfinance, MFIs are facing the problem of accountability and financial reporting, not only in Bangladesh but also in other countries in the world. The quality of financial reporting and information disclosures of MFIs has been highlighted by several global donor agencies, such as the World Bank and the United Nations Capital Development Fund (UNCDF) (Khan, 2003; Bala & Mir, 2006). The Centre for the Study of Financial Innovation (CSFI) also observes that the lack of effective governance structures and financial transparencies in MFIs has created important obstacles to their growth and sustainability (CSFI, 2008; CGAP, 2012).

To date, academic research with respect to MFIs' accountability and performance is mostly confined to assessing the effectiveness of microfinance relating to loan repayment, utilisation of funds, poverty alleviation and empowerment of women (Hashemi, Schuler, & Riley, 1996; Murdoch, 1999; BIDS, 2001; Khandaker & Cartwright, 2003). Some have examined the role of their governance structure in outreach to the poor and their financial performance internationally (Hartarska, 2005; Mersland & Strøm, 2009).

Most accounting research on non-governmental organisations (NGOs) (MFIs included) is based on an accountability framework with particular focus on service delivery and effectiveness in achieving intended social goals. Gray, Dey, Evans, and Zadek (1997) view accountability as 'the duty to provide an account (by no means necessarily a financial account) or reckoning of those actions for which one is held responsible.' Some researchers use agency theory to define and measure accountability for NGOs on the basis of contractual relationships between principal and agent (Yetman & Yetman, 2009). The focus of the theory is the contract governing the relationship between principal and agent and determining how the contract can be made as efficient as possible (Eisenhardt, 1989). Laughlin (1996), studying religious organisations, talks about *contractual accountability* as a relationship where expectations are formally recorded, and for Roberts (1991), the relationship is called *hierarchical accountability* based on subordinates accounting to their superiors. The information disclosure about how resources are being used via financial reporting becomes an integral part of discharging the accountability function.

The use of relationship based on principal and agents as the primary basis of agency theory has been seen as being too narrow and hierarchical and emphasises formal processes and channels for reporting to a higher authority. Najam (1996), Bryson, Cunningham, and Lokkesmoe (2002) and Ebrahim (2003a, 2003b) conceptualised accountability for NGOs in a broader and more inclusive manner through the stakeholder theory framework. Here, for an organisation to continue to succeed, it requires the support of *all* its stakeholders, and in order to engender this support it needs to account to all its stakeholder groups. Ebrahim (2003b) reports that disclosure statements and reports are among the most widely used tools of accountability (about 95%) and frequently required by the funding body or regulatory authority of NGOs. This framework supports the traditional decision usefulness framework in which all purpose financial reporting is issued by organisations, in addition to specific reports to meet demand from funds providers (Dhanani, 2009). This decision usefulness framework for reporting has also been accepted as one way of discharging accountability not only in the private sector but also in the public sector (Ryan, Stanley, & Nelson, 2002).

However, despite the importance of MFIs in the economic development of emerging countries, very little information is available, as there has been no substantive study, to date, to assess how these organisations report to various stakeholders, despite the recognition that quality financial reporting is a sine qua non to improve MFI accountability to stakeholders. Further, there has been no attempt to seek the perception of users and preparers as to what information items an MFI financial statement should contain to assess the quality of its reporting.

Gutiérrez-Nieto, Fuertes-Callén, and Serrano-Cinca's 2008 study is the only study to our knowledge that has focused on the financial reporting of MFIs in different countries from a database of MFIs, known as the Microfinance Information eXchange (MIX) Market, a web-based platform that compiles information on MFIs worldwide and whose membership is voluntary. They examined the incidence of voluntary financial and social information disclosure on the Internet and the contents of those reports in 2006. Using a sample of 273 MFIs, Gutiérrez-Nieto et al. (2008) found that MFIs' Internet presence overall was very limited and that large MFIs with a high degree of public online exposure disclosed larger amounts of information than smaller MFIs with a low degree of public exposure. Because the study examined the incidence of reporting on the Internet using a secondary source whose membership is voluntary, their results lack the depth to help understand the entity-specific determinants and the quality of disclosures. Additionally, self-selection bias was evident. For example, Nelson (2007) noted that efficient, well-managed programmes with high disclosure standards that are looking to attract investors provide data to international databases, such as the MIX Market. More recently, Mersland and Strøm (2009) examined the role of the governance structure of MFIs, using a panel dataset of 278 MFIs of 60 countries between 2000 and 2007, reporting that financial performance improved with the use of local directors, an internal board auditor and a female CEO. However, these studies suffer from selection bias as the samples represent commercial and professionally oriented institutions that have decided to be rated to improve access to funding. In Bangladesh, Bala & Mir (2006), using a case study approach, found that accounting reports and disclosure statements of MFIs emphasised 'upward' and 'external' accountability to donors while 'downward' and 'internal' mechanisms remained comparatively underdeveloped. They also noted that NGO literature in Bangladesh provides non-empirical, recommendation-type discussion on administration and activities and lacks substantive analysis of how they discharge their accountability functions via financial reporting. Overall, the above review suggests that the financial reporting practices of MFIs have been under-researched. There is a gap in our understanding of how they undertake their reporting function via the provision of information in annual financial statements.

Our study, to the best of our knowledge, is the first attempt to provide insights into the financial reporting practices of MFIs in Bangladesh, a country which has been credited with microfinance development in emerging countries, by examining the extent of information disclosure by MFIs by utilising a large sample of 654 firm-year reports of MFIs between 2004 and 2010. The financial reporting practices of these institutions are analysed by developing an index comprising 82 disclosure items appropriate for MFIs, based on the recommendations of the World Bank, IASB and government and non-government bodies engaged in monitoring and reporting on the performance of these entities. Further, a large questionnaire survey of 104 officials of donor agencies, government regulatory officials, accountants and auditors was undertaken in 2007 to determine the appropriateness of selecting the items. This approach to developing an index and measuring reporting practice is well established in accounting and business reporting (Cerf, 1961; Marston & Shrives, 1991; Ahmed & Courtis, 1999; Palepu & Healy, 2001; Beattie, McInnes, & Fearnley, 2004).

The results show that between 2004 and 2010, the extent of information disclosed has not improved and information disclosure is low on accounting policy choice, and other issues and information items. For example, the overall disclosure index in 2004 was 69.3, with the index for liability items being the highest at 0.886 and the lowest being 40.4 for other information. In 2010, the overall index remained the same at 69.9, with the highest being 89.4 for liability items and the lowest being 44.2 for other information items. We also find MFIs have not disclosed enough to meet the information needs of users and preparers both in 2006 and 2010. The result of this study contributes significantly to our understanding of the disclosure practices of MFIs in Bangladesh and internationally, and generates a greater level of awareness among the regulators, donors and other stakeholders on policy-making in improving the reporting standards of MFIs/NGOs across the world, because very little information is currently available.

The remainder of this chapter is structured as follows. After the introduction, section 2 presents institutional and legal frameworks in Bangladesh. Section 3 describes the research methods and data collection procedures. In section 4, the results of the study are presented, followed by concluding remarks.

INSTITUTIONAL AND LEGAL PROVISIONS FOR THE FORMATION AND REGULATION OF MFI/NGOS IN BANGLADESH

Institutional Structure

The institutional setting in Bangladesh is comprised of four types of institutions involved in microfinance activities in the country. These are: (1)

MFI-NGOs, (2) specialised MFIs such as Grameen Bank, (3) commercial and specialised banks with microfinance portfolios and (4) government departments and government-sponsored microfinance projects. Institutionally, microfinance is provided at two stages: direct providers and apex lenders. Direct providers are usually non-government organisations (NGOs) and are called MFI-NGOs. Grameen Bank, Bangladesh Rural Advancement Committee (BRAC) and the Association for Social Advancement (ASA) are the three major MFIs in terms of loan disbursements, outstanding loans and savings mobilisation.

Apex lenders such as the Palli Karma-Sahayak Foundation (PKSF)[2] do not engage in the provision of loans directly to eligible borrowers; instead, loans are given to its member organisations, called partner organisations (POs), for disbursement to the borrowers. PKSF is the most important organisation for the regulation and financing of MFIs in Bangladesh (Hulme & Moore, 2006). PKSF itself was created in 1990 under the old Companies Act 1913 (amended in 1994) with funds from the government of Bangladesh and the United States Aid for International Development (USAID) to support and assist, financially and institutionally, its eligible partner MFIs (POs) and monitor their performance, including financial reporting. At the end of 2011, PKSF had 271 partner organisations and the total cumulative disbursement of loans stood at Tk. 805.884 billion ($10.06 billion) (PKSF, 2012).

The other regulatory body formed by the government is the NGO Affairs Bureau (NGOAB), which requires all NGOs (including MFIs) seeking or receiving foreign funds to register with it under the Foreign Contributions (Regulation) Ordinance, 1982 and to renew the registration every five years. The Bureau is concerned with the receipt and utilisation of foreign funds for projects, and evaluating statements and reports submitted by NGOs, including verifying income and expenditure accounts by external auditors. However, unlike the PKSF, it has not developed any guidelines for financial reporting. Organisations are only required to submit a partial report for the utilisation of foreign donations/funds (World Bank, 2006). To improve the institutional and regulatory framework for MFIs, the government of Bangladesh promulgated the Microcredit Regulatory Authority Act 2006 (Act number 32 of the year 2006) in August 2006 (partially implemented in 2008) and established the Microcredit Regulatory Authority (MRA) to improve the transparency and accountability of microcredit activities within the country.

Legal Provisions for Formation and Regulation of MFI/NGOs in Bangladesh

Although there has been an unprecedented growth of microfinance NGOs in Bangladesh, the legal framework for NGOs has not gone through a major reform. At present, NGOs can be registered under one or more Acts of

Parliament. These provisions apply to NGOs in general and do not specifically address microfinance activities. The following are the Acts that deal with the formation and accountability reporting of NGOs within Bangladesh.

The Societies Registration Act 1860 (Act XXI of 1860)

Under the provision of the Societies Registration Act 1860 (Act XXI of 1860), the Registrar of Joint Stock Companies (RJSC) within the Ministry of Commerce is responsible for any society formed for any 'literary, science, or charitable purpose' (World Bank, 2006). A great majority of nonprofit organisations in Bangladesh are formed and registered under this Act because of its wide scope and flexibility to permit a range of activities. Under this Act, each society must have a formal governing body which is responsible for managing the society (section 16). Societies must hold annual general meetings except where their rules allow otherwise, and any person may inspect the documents of a society filed with the registrar (section 19). However, the Act does not specify whether a society is required to maintain the accounts and have them audited.

The Trust Act 1882

A nonprofit organisation can also be formed under the Trust Act 1882. A Board of Trustees is responsible for the management of the trust and is bound under the Act to maintain clear and accurate accounts of the trust property. Whenever the beneficiary requests, the trustee shall furnish him/her with detailed information of the amount and state of the trust property, but it does not require submission of annual accounts or an audit report to the beneficiaries (section 19).

Voluntary Social Welfare Agencies (VSWA) (Registration and Control) Ordinance 1961

Under the Registration and Control Ordinance 1961, the registration of voluntary associations is mandatory. The Ordinance is administered by the Social Welfare Department within the Ministry of Social Welfare and it has broad power to suspend or dissolve an NGO without recourse to judicial appeal. A large number of NGOs are registered under the ordinance. Every agency registered under the Registration and Control Ordinance 1961 shall maintain accounts as required by the registration authority, submit annual reports and audited accounts, pay money into separate accounts in approved banks and furnish any other information required. The VSWA registration authority may inspect books and records, including any financial information (section 7). In addition, any person may, on payment of a prescribed fee, inspect any document relating to a registered agency or obtain a copy or extract thereof (section 13).

The Companies Act 1994

Although the Companies Act 1994 deals mainly with private trading companies, it also contains provisions that permit formation of a not-for-profit organisation with limited liability, provided that the organisation applies any income to promote its objectives and prohibits the payment of any dividends to its members. An entity wishing to register under the Companies Act seeks approval from the Registrar of Joint Stock companies. Forming a not-for-profit company under the Companies Act requires the preparation of the Memorandum of Association and the Articles of Association (section 22).

Nonprofit companies registered under this Act are required to maintain proper books of accounts, in order to provide a free and fair view of the state of affairs (section 18). Detailed financial reports and reports on company activities must be made available to shareholders before and at the annual general meeting (section 183). However, the number of NGOs registered under this law is significantly lower than under any other laws, possibly due to its more rigorous legal requirements (World Bank, 2006).

Cooperative Societies Act 2001

Cooperative societies can be formed under the Cooperative Societies Act 2001 with the objective of producing and/or disposing of goods as collective property and performing services for cooperative members. Under the Act, societies are permitted to receive savings from the general public (members). The Registrar of cooperatives has little power, either preventive or protective, and conducts minimal supervision. The Societies Act includes a requirement for an annual meeting, but does not require the submission of annual accounts or external audits.

Financial Reporting Provisions for MFIs in Bangladesh

As stated earlier, there are several legislation and regulatory bodies, but their monitoring of MFI reporting is minimal. Most of the small NGOs do not prepare annual reports; rather, they prepare a management report showing only receipts and payments. Some organisations prepare financial reports and their financial accounts are also audited, but these reports provide minimum information for assessing their financial position. Some financial statements, for example, limit performance analysis by not separating microfinance operations from the institution's other activities, such as health or training services. Audits are generally conducted to comply with donor requirements. To satisfy the requirements of different donor organisations, MFIs sometimes undertake multiple audits and in some cases, even close their books twice a year (Irish & Simon, 2005). The production of multiple audited accounts creates an additional strain on limited resources and results in showing a partial picture of the MFIs, because donors usually ask for audited accounts covering only the utilisation of their funds within the institution.

The Consultative Group to Assist the Poor (CGAP) of the World Bank, in association with the PKSF, has issued a set of disclosure guidelines on MFI financial reporting requirements, based on International Financial Reporting Standards (Rosenberg, Mwangi, Christen, & Nasr, 2003)[3]. These disclosure guidelines were developed in consultation with microfinance practitioners and the donor members of CGAP, which is a consortium of bilateral foreign aid agencies from 16 countries, 12 multilateral agencies and two private foundations. This final version (July 2003) is based on the results of field testing and input from the Financial Services Working Group (FSWG) of the Small Enterprise and Education and Promotion Network (SEEP). The CGAP encourages MFIs to adopt International Accounting Reporting Standards (IFRS 1, 30 and 32) issued by the International Accounting Standards Board (IASB) and the industry-specific Consensus Guidelines on Disclosure for Financial Reporting. However, these guidelines are not accounting policies and do not command any particular format for financial reporting. Instead, they simply indicate the minimum information that should be included in MFI's financial reports.

PKSF, with support from the World Bank, has moved towards consolidated, audited accounts for the microfinance operations of its POs. PKSF has developed guidelines for accountants on how to prepare financial statements on accrual basis accounting and information to be contained within these statements; the management of information systems; business planning for POs; and internal and external audit procedures, including their appointments (Miah, 2006). In collaboration with the World Bank, PKSF has introduced certain International Accounting Standards for financial reporting (World Bank, 2006).

The MRA, apart from authorising operations, the audit of accounts and policy formation, requires MFIs (under section 27 of the Act) to maintain their accounts in the manner prescribed by the Authority, prepare annual budgets for the next financial year and prepare the Balance Sheet, the Profit & Loss Account annually, and submit it to the Authority. The Authority also promulgated rules in 2010 to improve reporting standards further, but these reporting requirements have not yet been fully implemented at the time of developing this chapter.

RESEARCH METHODS AND DATA COLLECTION

Operationalisation of Financial Disclosure

While corporate investors and users often can obtain information from many alternative sources in addition to the published reports, this is not so for microfinance institutions because there is no alternative market for information generation, such as analysts and management forecasts, and financial newspapers. Although international donor agencies, banks and regulators receive the necessary amount of information from MFIs through direct contacts and directives, the financial statements remain the only formal method of communication to all of their stakeholders.

The literature on disclosure provides a number of proxies for the amount of information disclosed: the number of words, sentences and pages; the frequency of disclosure releases; financial analysts' perceptions about the firm disclosure practices; and the disclosure index (for a review, see Marston & Shrives, 1991; Hackston & Milne, 1996).

In this study, because we use financial statements to determine the type and extent of information by constructing a disclosure index, it is very important that informational items included in the index are useful to the stakeholders (such as users, preparers and regulators), without including too many items in the index, so as to reduce the problems associated with information redundancy. Content analysis validity and reliability are very important considerations (Weber, 1990). To address these issues, first we read all the disclosure provisions of CGAP, PKSF and the Bangladesh Bank and reviewed the disclosure literature focusing on NGOs. Second, with the help of PKSF, we obtained a list of people representing international donor agencies such as the World Bank, senior administrators of all regulatory bodies for microfinance organisations such as PKSF and NGOAB and the accountants involved in the preparation of the financial statements of MFIs. On this basis, a questionnaire was then mailed to 200 of them in order to obtain their opinion on the importance of information items on a five-point Likert scale, with one being not important and five being the most important. 104 responses (52% response rate) were received, of which 32 were from auditors and regulators and 72 were from accountants. We undertook non-response bias tests and did not find material difference between early responses and late responses (responses received after two weeks, following a second reminder). The demographic profile of the respondents shows that they are highly educated, with all users holding a professional accounting degree and 79% of preparers holding a Masters degree. 34% of the user group have received overseas training and 62% have work experience of more than 10 years (users). In the case of preparers, 6% have overseas training, 53% have local training and 36% have more than 10 years' work experience.

The index was then constructed based on 82 items, comprising five items for financial statements, nine for revenue items, 16 items for expenses, 11 items for assets, 11 items for liabilities, five items for other statements, 12 items for accounting policies and 13 items for other information. The mean values of these 82 items ranged between 3.34 and 4.41, suggesting that users and preparers consider them to be important and justify their inclusion in the index. To increase the reliability of the index, a pre-test was conducted and the coding schedule was prepared around mid-2007 and applied to a small number of financial statements.

We employed an unweighted approach to index construction because prior reviews do not show difference in results between weighted and unweighted items (Marston & Shrives, 1991; Ahmed & Courtis, 1999). For each item of information disclosed in the annual reports of the sampled MFIs, the value one was assigned and zero otherwise. In order to mitigate concern about the lack of reliability in determining whether an item was disclosed or not, we applied well-accepted methods, such as counting and cross-checking several financial statements by an independent rater. In the event of variation between the researchers and the independent rater, further discussions were held to find the sources of errors to improve the index construction process. The overall disclosure index is calculated by the following formula (TDI), where

$$I_j = \frac{\sum_{i=1}^{n_j} x_y}{n_j}$$

I_j = disclosure index
n_j = number of relevant items for j for the MFI, $n_j \leq 82$
  x_{ij} = 1 if ¡ the (relevant) item is disclosed
  x_{ij} = 0 if ¡ the (relevant) item is not disclosed
    So that $0 \leq I_j \leq 1$.

Data Collection

The annual reports of microfinance organisations mostly contain descriptions of projects and activities, yet they present very little financial information. The audited financial statements are prepared separately and lodged with regulatory bodies. We prepared a list of licenced MFIs from the MRA website at the end of 2007 and contacted the senior management of PKSF and the Bangladesh Bank. We obtained the financial statements of all MFIs that received some funds from PKSF, because they are required to submit copies to these institutions. Through this process, the financial statements of 435 MFI-NGOs, comprising 160 (2006), 136 (2005) and 139 (2004) were collected, which represent about 50% of the total licenced MFIs in Bangladesh for 2007. A disclosure index for each of these MFIs was developed for analysis. Around the same period, the questionnaire survey was conducted as described earlier. To update the dataset, one researcher went to Dhaka again in 2011 and obtained a further 129 MFI financial statements for the year 2009–2010 from PKSF and the Bangladesh Bank libraries. This provided a total of 564 MFI-year observations over the period under study. The latest dataset is then used to determine if the extent of disclosure has increased following the promulgation of the MRA.

RESULTS

Disclosure Index

This section presents some descriptive statistics of the MFIs included in the analysis. It is found that the average total assets of the firms are Tk. 17.36 ($0.25) million with a median value of Tk. 17.29 (USD $0.25) million, the smallest firm having total assets of Tk. 0.72 ($0.01) million and the largest having total assets of Tk. 2,759.38 ($39.52) million. The size of the board of the firms varies between four and 25 members, with the frequency of board meetings ranging from one to 28 meetings per year. The average age of the firms was 17 years, the maximum being 44 years, suggesting that some firms have been undertaking microfinance operations from the late sixties.

Table 7.1 shows disclosure levels over the four years 2004, 2005, 2006 and 2010. The results show that the total disclosure index in 2004 was 69.3% and slightly increased to 72.7% in 2006, but declined to 69.9% in 2010. While there has been marginal increase over the years, this improvement in disclosure levels is not significant. The disclosure levels are relatively

Table 7.1 Distribution of average sectional and overall disclosure index during 2004–2010

	2004	2005	2006	2010
Financial statement	0.776	0.786	0.764	0.774
Revenue	0.763	0.807	0.816	0.758
Expense	0.809	0.844	0.870	0.784
Asset	0.747	0.741	0.748	0.740
Liability	0.886	0.896	0.898	0.894
Other statement	0.596	0.599	0.603	0.601
Accounting policy	0.56	0.582	0.582	0.596
Other information	0.404	0.538	0.535	0.442
Overall	0.693	0.724	0.727	0.699

high for asset and liability items (around 74%), whereas low for other informational items (40%). It is noted that while the disclosure index for other statements and financial statements has remained steady at 60% and 77%, the index has slightly declined for expense items.

Panel A of Table 7.2 presents the distribution of disclosure indices according to the number of MFIs in 2006. It shows that of the 160 firms, only 65 firms have a score above 90% and 90 firms scored between 60% and 70% for financial statement items. Scores for the other items are quite low. The next levels of disclosure are on revenue, expense and liability items, with 66, 66 and 137 firms, respectively, having disclosure indices above 80%. These results indicate that microfinance firms prepare and disclose traditional financial statements, such as the balance sheet and income statement, more than other items which are voluntary.

Perceived Information Needs of Users and Preparers and Information Disclosure by MFIs

As 104 users and preparers were surveyed at the end of 2007, the constructed disclosure index is compared to assess if there are gaps between their perceived information needs and actual disclosure practices during 2006 and 2010. The years 2006 and 2010 are chosen because the Bangladesh government established the MRA in 2006 to improve the accountability, performance and financial reporting standards of MFIs in Bangladesh. In this way, regulators can determine disclosure adequacy and can take action to redress this if there are expectation gaps. They can also indirectly assess the effectiveness of the MRA in improving disclosure standards in the country.

Panel A of Table 7.3 shows that overall, the users' information need is 0.889 compared to the MFIs' actual disclosure score of 0.727 in 2006, and this gap is significant (P<0.05). MFIs disclose more information on liability, expense and revenue items, but less information is disclosed on other information, accounting policies and information relating to other statements. The sectional comparison shows that there is a gap between the actual disclosure practice and the users' expected information needs. The results reveal that more expectation gaps occur in relation to accounting policy, other statements and other information items, whereas there are less gaps in expectation in relation to revenue, expense, asset and liability items. The Mann-Whitney U tests reveal that there are significant differences between actual disclosure practices and users' expected information needs in every section of the financial statement, except expense and liability items. MFIs disclose more information on expense and liability items because of their conservative accounting policies. The table also shows that the overall actual disclosure practice is 0.727, whereas the preparers' perception of this disclosed information is 0.766. The sectional comparisons show that there

Panel A

Disclosure index	Financial statement	Revenue	Expenses	Assets	Liabilities	Other statement	Accounting policy	Other information
91–100	65	36	81	–	20	–	–	–
81–90	–	66	66	1	137	–	–	–
71–80	2	20	8	79	3	–	–	2
61–70	90	29	2	78	–	–	66	–
51–60	–	–	3	2	–	160	93	80
41–50	3	8	–	–	–	–	1	77
31–40	–	1	–	–	–	–	–	1
21–30	–	–	–	–	–	–	–	–
11–20	–	–	–	–	–	–	–	–
0–10	–	–	–	–	–	–	–	–
Total	160	160	160	160	160	160	160	160
Lowest (%)	40	40	58.3	60	77.8	60	45.45	37.5
Highest (%)	100	100	100	90	100	60	63.6	71.4
Average (%)	76.4	81.6	87	74.8	89.8	60.0	58.2	53.5

Panel B

Disclosure index	Financial statement	Revenue	Expenses	Assets	Liabilities	Other statement	Accounting policy	Other information
91–100	57	14	6	–	16	–	–	–
81–90	–	45	44	44	107	–	–	–
71–80	–	48	50	41	2	4	–	1
61–70	72	4	24	41	4	–	34	35
51–60	–	15	5	3	–	125	81	6
41–50	–	2	–	–	–	–	14	84
31–40	–	1	–	–	–	–	–	3
21–30	–	–	–	–	–	–	–	–
11–20	–	–	–	–	–	–	–	–
0–10	–	–	–	–	–	–	–	–
Total	129	129	129	129	129	129	129	129
Lowest (%)	60	28.5	35.3	54.5	66.7	60	50	25
Highest (%)	100	100	100	81.8	100	80	66.7	63.6
Average (%)	77.4	75.8	78.4	74.0	89.4	60.1	59.6	44.2

Table 7.3   Disclosure indices and users' and preparers' perceived needs

Panel A: 2006

	Disclosure index 2006	Users' perception	Difference	Preparers' perception	Difference
Financial Statement	0.764	0.959	0.195	0.817	0.053
Revenue	0.816	0.938	0.122	0.771	(0.045)
Expense	0.870	0.890	0.020	0.819	(0.051)
Asset	0.748	0.0891	0.143	0.726	(0.022)
Liability	0.898	0.876	(0.020)	0.796	(0.102)
Other statements	0.600	0.881	0.281	0.805	0.205
Accounting policy	0.582	0.886	0.304	0.716	0.134
Other information	0.535	0.795	0.260	0.674	0.139
Overall	0.727	0.889	0.162	0.766	0.039

Panel B: 2010

	Disclosure index 2010	Users' perception	Difference	Preparers' perception	Difference
Financial Statement	0.774	0.959	0.185	0.817	0.043
Revenue	0.758	0.938	0.180	0.771	(0.013)
Expense	0.784	0.890	0.180	0.819	0.0510
Asset	0.740	0.891	0.151	0.726	(0.014)
Liability	0.894	0.876	(0.018)	0.796	(0.098)
Other statements	0.601	0.881	0.281	0.805	0.205
Accounting policy	0.596	0.886	0.290	0.716	0.120
Other information	0.442	0.795	0.353	0.674	0.232
Overall	0.699	0.889	0.190	0.766	0.067

are more gaps in other statements, accounting policy and other information, whereas there are less gaps in revenue, expense, assets and liabilities.

In 2010, the same perceived needs are compared with actual disclosures and tabulated in Table 7.3, panel B. As stated earlier, actual disclosure practices have not improved in 2010; there are expectation gaps in the areas of financial statements, revenue, other statements, accounting policy and other information sections, whereas MFIs have disclosed more in the liability section for both the user and preparer groups.

SUMMARY AND CONCLUSIONS

Prior studies of not-for-profit entities including microfinance institutions have focused on the effects of economic and social welfare on the fund recipients and operating and financial performance of these organisations to the neglect of how they discharge their accountability functions to various stakeholders. Due to the significant growth of microfinance over the last decade, microfinance institutions face several challenges, including their sustainability and discharging accountability functions to various stakeholders. However, there has been a lack of understanding of the financial reporting practices in any emerging country despite the importance of financial reporting as the most important communication channel for MFIs to their stakeholders, including depositors, borrowers, regulatory bodies and internal donor agencies. In this chapter, we examined the existing institutional and regulatory environment for the financial reporting of microfinance institutions (MFIs) and the extent of information disclosed to various stakeholders to assess whether MFIs meet the information needs of users and preparers in Bangladesh. Although some studies have examined the financial performance and accountability of MFIs across the world using a formatted database, no substantial empirical research on the financial reporting of MFIs has been undertaken using primary data. We developed a disclosure index comprising 82 information items based on the recommendation of the World Bank, PKSF and an opinion survey of 104 accountants, auditors and regulators, and applied this to the financial statements of 564 MFI-NGOs for the years 2004–2010.

We find that between 2004 and 2010, the extent of information disclosed has not improved and information disclosure is low on accounting policy choice, and other issues and information items. The overall disclosure index in 2004 was 69.3% and in 2010, the overall index remained the same at 69.9. We also found that MFIs have not disclosed enough to meet the information needs of users and preparers in both the pre and post-implementation of the Microfinance Regulatory Authority (MRA).

The static nature of information disclosure between 2004 and 2010, despite the promulgation of MRA in Bangladesh, suggests the need for more effective monitoring of reporting by various regulating bodies in the countries. The results of this study contribute significantly to our understanding of disclosure practices of MFIs in Bangladesh and internationally, and generate a greater level of awareness among the regulators, donors and other stakeholders on policy-making in order to improve the reporting standards of MFIs/NGOs across the world, because very little information is currently available. Other countries where MFIs have emerged as alternatives to traditional institutions (such as banks and development banks) should take notice of the weaknesses and outdated nature of prevailing regulation relating to formation, monitoring and reporting practices in Bangladesh, and should consider updating the institutional structure having outdated provisions.

ACKNOWLEDGMENTS

The authors are grateful to Andrei Filip, John Hillier, Zahirul Hoque, Robert Nyamori and seminar participants at the Department of Accounting, La Trobe University, and conference participants at the International Association for Accounting Education and Research, November, 2010 in Singapore, and at the Annual Public Sector and Nonprofit Symposium, November 2013 in Melbourne.

NOTES

1 Microcredit is not a new concept and has been practised at various times in modern history (Cons & Paprocki, 2008). The provision of microcredit was initially operationalised by Dr. Akhther Hamid Khan during the late sixties in Comilla, Bangladesh. Later, through the formation of Grameen (village) Bank in Chittagong, Bangladesh in 1972, Professor Muhammad Yunus (a Nobel laureate for his contribution to poverty alleviation) popularised the concept, not only in emerging countries but also in many developed countries, including the U.S.
2 Palli Karma-Sahayak Foundation (PKSF) means Rural (Palli) Employment (Karma) Support (Sahayak) Foundation (Foundation) in English.
3 These disclosure guidelines were developed in consultation with microfinance practitioners and the member donors of the Consultative Group to Assist the Poor (CGAP). CGAP is a consortium of bilateral foreign aid agencies from 16 countries, 12 multilateral agencies and two private foundations. This final version (July 2003) is based on the results of field testing and input from the Financial Services Working Group (FSWG) of the Small Enterprise and Education and Promotion Network (SEEP).

REFERENCES

Ahmed, K., & Courtis, J. K. (1999). Association between corporate characteristics on mandatory disclosure compliance in annual reports: A meta analysis. *British Accounting Review, 31,* 35–61.
Bala, K. S., & Mir, Z. M. (2006). *'Overaccount' to 'underaccount'? A study of the third sector accountability and accounting in action in a developing country.* Working paper, University of Canberra, ACT.
Bangladesh Institute of Development Studies (BIDS). (2001). *BIDS Survey.*

Beattie, V., McInnes, B., & Fearnley, S. (2004). A methodology for analysing and evaluating narrative in annual reports: A comprehensive descriptive profile and metrics for disclosure quality attributes. *Accounting Forum, 28*(3), 205–236.

Bryson, J., Cunningham, G., & Lokkesmoe, K. (2002). What to do when stakeholders matter: The case of problem formation for the African American Men Project of Hennepin County, Minnesota. *Public Administration Review, 62,* 568–584.

Cerf, A.R. (1961). *Corporate reporting and investment decision.* Berkley, CA: University of California Press.

Cons, J., & Paprocki, K. (2008). The limits of microcredit—A Bangladesh case. *Institute for Food and Development Policy, 14*(4), 1–4.

Consultative Group to Assist the Poor (CGAP). (2012). *Current Trends in Cross-Border Funding for Microfinance.* Retrieved from: http://www.cgap.org/publications/current-trends-cross-border-funding-microfinance

CSFI. (2008). Microfinance banana skins—risk in a booming industry. In A. Hilton (Ed.), *Banking banana skins report.* New York: Centre for the Study of Financial Innovation.

Devine, J. (2006). NGOs, politics and grassroots mobilisation: Evidence from Bangladesh. *Journal of South Asian Development, 1*(1), 77–99.

Dhanani, A. (2009). Accountability of UK Charities. *Public Money & Management, 29,* 183–190.

Ebrahim, A. (2003a). Accountability in practice: Mechanisms for NGOs. *World Development, 31*(5), 813–829.

Ebrahim, A. (2003b). Making sense of accountability: Conceptual perspectives for Northern and Southern nonprofits. *Nonprofit Management and Leadership, 14*(2), 191–212.

Eisenhardt, K. (1989). Agency theory: An assessment and review. *Academy of Management Review, 14,* 57–74.

Gray, R., Dey, C. O., Evans, R., & Zadek, S. (1997). Struggling with the praxis of social accounting: Stakeholder's accountability, audits and procedures. *Accounting, Auditing and Accountability Journal, 10,* 325–364.

Gutiérrez-Nieto, B., Fuertes-Callén, Y., & Serrano-Cinca, C. (2008). Internet reporting in microfinance institutions. *Online Information Review, 32*(3), 415–436.

Hackston, D., & Milne, M. J. (1996). Some determinants of social environment disclosure in New Zealand companies. *Accounting, Auditing and Accountability Journal, 9*(1), 77–108.

Hartarska, V. (2005). Governance and performance of microfinance institutions in Central and Eastern Europe and the newly independent states. *World Development, 33*(10), 1627–1648.

Hashemi, S., Schuler, S. R., & Riley, A. P. (1996). Rural credit programs and women's employment in Bangladesh. *World Development, 24*(4), 635–653.

Hulme, D., & Moore, K. (2006). *Why has microfinance been a policy success in Bangladesh (and beyond)?* Working paper, University of Manchester.

Irish, E. L., & Simon, W. K. (2005). *Legal and regulatory environment for NGOs in Bangladesh.* Washington, DC: International Center for Civil Society Law, Catholic University of America.

Khan, M. M. (2003). Accountability of NGOs in Bangladesh, a critical review. *Public Management Review, 5*(2), 267–278.

Khandaker, S., & Cartwright, J. (2003). Does micro-credit empower women? Evidence from Bangladesh. *Demography, 36*(1), 1–21.

Laughlin, R. (1996). Principals and higher principals: Accounting for accountability in the caring professions. In R. Munro & J. Mouritsen (Eds.), *Accountability: Power, ethos and the technologies of managing.* London: Thomson Business Press.

Marston, C. L., & Shrives, P. J. (1991). The use of disclosure indices in accounting research: A review article. *British Accounting Review, 23,* 195–210.

Mersland, R., & Strøm, R. Ø. (2009). Performance and governance in microfinance institutions. *Journal of Banking and Finance, 33*(4), 662–669.

Miah, M. A. (2006). Bangladesh. In *Regulatory architecture for microfinance in Asia.* Tokyo: Asian Productivity Organization.

Microcredit Regulatory Authority (MRA). (2011). NGO-MFls in Bangladesh. *A Statistical Publication VIII,* June.

Ministry of Finance. (1913). *The Companies Act 1913 (amended in 1994).* Government of People's Republic of Bangladesh.

Ministry of Social Welfare. (1860). *The Societies Registration Act 1860 (Act XXI of 1860).* Government of People's Republic of Bangladesh.

Ministry of Social Welfare. (1961). *Voluntary Social Welfare Agencies (VSWA) (Registration and Control) Ordinance 1961.* Government of People's Republic of Bangladesh.

Murdoch, J. (1999). The microfinance promise. *Journal of Economic Literature, 37* (December), 1569–1614.

Najam, A. (1996). NGO accountability: A conceptual framework. *Development Policy Review, 14,* 339–353.

Nelson, E. (2007). *Microcapital story: What are the total global assets in microfinance?* Retrieved from http://www.microcapital.org

Palepu, G., & Healy, M. P. (2001). Information asymmetry, corporate disclosure, and the capital markets: A review of the empirical disclosure literature. *Journal of Accounting and Economics, 31,* 405–440.

PKSF. (2006, 2007, 2012). *Annual Reports.* Retrieved from Palli Karma-Sahayak Foundation website: www.pksf-bd.org

Reed, L., & Maes, J. (2012). *State of the Microcredit Summit Campaign Report 2012.* Retrieved from Microcredit Summit Campaign website: http://www.micr ocreditsummit.org/resource/46/state-of-the-microcredit-summit.html

Roberts, J. (1991). The possibilities of accountability. *Accounting Organizations and Society, 16,* 355–368.

Rosenberg, R., Mwangi, P., Christen, R. P., & Nasr, M. (2003). Microfinance consensus guidelines: Disclosure guidelines for financial reporting by microfinance institutions. *CGAP/The World Bank Group*, July, 1–61.

Ryan, C., Stanley, T., & Nelson, M. (2002). Accountability disclosures by Queensland local government councils: 1997–1999. *Financial Accountability & Management, 18*(3), 261–289.

Siddiquee, N. A., & Faroqi, M. G. (2009). Holding the giants to account? Constraints on NGO accountability in Bangladesh. *Asian Journal of Political Science, 17*(3), 243–264.

Weber, R. P. (1990). *Basic content analysis,* 2nd ed. Newbury Park, CA: Sage.

World Bank. (2006). *The economic and governance of non governmental organizations (NGOs) in Bangladesh.* World Bank Report 2006.

Yetman, J. R., & Yetman, M. (2009). *The effects of governance on the financial reporting quality of non-profit organizations.* American Accounting Association, Western Regional Meeting, April.

8 UK Charity Accounting
Developments, Issues and Recent Research

Ciaran Connolly, Noel Hyndman and Danielle McConville

INTRODUCTION

The charity sector represents the sphere of social activity undertaken by organisations that are nonprofit and non-governmental. It is quite different from either the private or the public sectors in terms of its orientation and motivation, the nature of its activities, its resource availability to engage in these activities and the manner of its contribution to the public good. The charity sector in the United Kingdom (UK)[1] is significant economically. Individual charities range in size from large international organisations with sizeable incomes, substantial assets, significant numbers of employees and complex and extensive structures, to small, locally based groups run by volunteers, with limited income and assets, and few paid employees. Regardless of their size, charities play a significant and vital role in society, often serving and helping those who are most disadvantaged and marginalised, and increasingly are delivering public services to tackle social exclusion. As a result, they make a unique and widely recognised contribution to the public good by building social capital in civil society. However, the rise in the visibility and influence of the charity sector in recent years, together with adverse publicity surrounding a number of high-profile scandals (Beattie, McInnes, & Fearnley, 2002; Home Office, 2003; Charity Commission, 2004; Milmo, 2013), has highlighted the need for an increased focus on charity accounting and accountability. This could be seen as a basis for ensuring greater confidence in the control processes within charities (which may encourage greater willingness on the part of donors to provide funding), as well as providing further legitimisation of the sector's activities. These conditions can be seen as crucial to ensuring the health and growth of the sector.

It is a sector in which the fact and perception of accountability is particularly important. Calls for increased sector visibility and scrutiny have been widespread, with the need for it to operate transparently and discharge accountability being widely articulated (Brody, 2002; Ebrahim, 2003a; Home Office, 2003). To support this, several initiatives, both regulatory and voluntary, to encourage and promote UK charity accountability and better governance have been launched. For instance, under the Charities Act 2006, the Charity Commission in England and Wales has been charged with the responsibility of: enhancing charity accountability, increasing public trust and confidence and promoting the effective use of charitable funds. In Scotland and Northern Ireland, major changes in the regulatory environment have emphasised similar themes. Since the late 1980s, the development of, and ongoing revisions to, a charity Statement of Recommended Practice (SORP)[2] to improve the accounting and reporting of charities has massively changed the look and standardisation of charity reports. Moreover, the establishment of the ImpACT Coalition by the Association of Chief Executives of Voluntary Organisations (to improve accountability, clarity and transparency in the charity sector) and the development of organisations (such as New Philanthropy Capital) which seek to support existing and potential donors in steering them towards effective and efficient charities, are further examples of this emerging support. Yet substantial challenges in terms of accounting and accountability are faced by charities (and the sector as a whole) as they strive to engage with stakeholders in meaningful ways (often seen as a key aspect of good governance). The aims of this chapter are to: outline the features of the various iterations of required charity reporting practice in the UK (as contained in the SORP) and explain the rationale behind the SORP's development; to present and analyse continuing major issues of concern with respect to accounting and accountability processes in charities; and, in the context of the identified issues, explore some key themes of research that are central to charity accounting and accountability (and have been a focus of the authors' interests over many years). The remainder of the chapter proceeds as follows. The next section briefly profiles the charity sector in the UK as a basis for understanding context. This is followed by an overview of the reasons behind the creation of the first SORP, together with an examination of the development of the SORP through time and an analysis of a number of key issues relating to charity accountability. This is presented as a basis for appreciating the subsequent research included later in the chapter. The penultimate section details some major themes of past research, utilising selected studies under the headings of financial accountability, performance accountability and stakeholder engagement. Finally, the chapter concludes with the identification of possible areas for future research.

THE CHARITY SECTOR IN THE UK

Charities exist to provide public benefit (such as the relief of poverty, the expansion of education, the advancement of religion or other purposes considered beneficial to the community), benefits that may perhaps not be provided, or not provided to the same extent, without charitable recognition. They exist in most societies and are facilitated through the various legal

and administrative frameworks by, for example, major tax benefits and differing, and possibly lighter-touch, legal and regulatory frameworks. They
vary from general not-for-profit organisations in that they focus on goals of
a philanthropic nature that are deemed by individual societies to serve the
public interest or common good. As a result, the precise legal definition of
a charity can vary according to the country in which the charitable organisation operates. In the UK, a major reference point in deciding whether a
particular purpose is charitable or not is the preamble to the 1601 Elizabe-
than Statute of Charitable Uses. More recently, in England and Wales, the
Charities Act 2011[3] provides guidance on whether an organisation can be
deemed charitable by specifying 13 'charitable purposes.'[4] An organisation
seeking charitable status must have as its main goal at least one of these
purposes and, in addition, fulfil a 'public benefit' test (there must be an
identifiable benefit or benefits, and that benefit must be to the public or a
section of the public).

The charity sector in the UK comprises a vast and growing segment of
economic activity with substantial assets at its disposal. There are over
200,000 registered charities with an estimated total annual income over
£60 billion. In addition, there are many exempt charities (mostly universities, educational institutions and national museums) and excepted charities
(including religious charities), which are not required to register. Therefore
the total number of charities, and their economic impact, is considerably
higher. While the size of the charity sector has grown considerably over
time, the income distribution is skewed, with a small number of large charities accounting for a significant proportion of the total sector income. For
example, in England and Wales, 958 large registered charities (just over
one-half of 1% of total registered charities) account for 57.3% of the total
income of registered charities, with the British Council having the largest
income (£739 million, and assets of £578 million), and Cancer Research
UK (income £576 million, assets £463 million) and Oxfam (income £386
million, assets £138 million) being in the 'Top 10' by income (Charity
Commission, 2013a). The National Council for Voluntary Organisations
(NCVO) (2013) estimates that over one-third of the total income of charities is derived from statutory sources, with the vast majority of this emanating from government contracts. Other sources of charitable income are
large institutional funders, trusts and members of the public responding to
fundraising campaigns or gifting legacies.

DEVELOPMENT OF A CHARITY STATEMENT OF
RECOMMENDED PRACTICE

Since the early 1980s, considerable efforts have been made to improve the
quality and consistency of charity accounting and reporting in the UK. It
has been argued that while significant improvement has been made over

time, this improvement would not have been seen without the sector-specific guidance and disciplining influence of a charity-specific SORP (see, for example, Connolly, Hyndman, and McConville, 2013a). This section sets out the development of that SORP from the identification of a significant problem within the sector in the 1980s, through the four iterations of the SORP to the current (2005-issued) SORP.

Bird and Morgan-Jones (1981) and the Development of the Original Charity SORP

In 1981, Bird and Morgan-Jones' seminal study of charities' annual reports and accounts cast significant doubt on their usefulness as a means of providing accurate, reliable and comparable information to stakeholders. Focusing primarily on financial reporting, it revealed a sector where non-compliance with accounting standards was prevalent and where wide disparity in accounting practices between charities was observed. Among some of the contentious accounting treatments found were: legacies—the majority of charities which received legacies either credited them directly to capital or split the credit between revenue and capital; deferred expenses—a number of charities made use of a provision or reserve for deferred expenses and charged the amount 'above the line'; and fixed assets—in a significant number of charities fixed assets (including freehold property) were written off on acquisition. These treatments, and other widely adopted accounting ploys, had a significant impact on a reader's assessment of the financial statements of the charity and on the reader's ability to compare charities. Bird and Morgan-Jones suggested that the financial accounts of many charities were misleading, with an apparent objective of the preparers often being the understating of the revenue result in order to motivate donors to provide funds.

The findings of the Bird and Morgan-Jones (1981) research were widely regarded as a 'wake-up call' for the UK charity sector. Indeed, it is clear from the discussions relating to many subsequent developments in UK charity reporting, this work is often used as a major point of reference by those promoting change. In April 1982, in a stated response to Bird and Morgan-Jones, the Accounting Standards Committee (ASC), the regulator and standard-setting body of the UK accounting profession at that time, undertook a lengthy consultation on the issues raised and in 1988 released a SORP on charity accounting (ASC, 1988).[5] This focused on addressing the financial reporting deficiencies identified in Bird and Morgan-Jones' report, often closely following that report's recommendations and interpreting the then existing UK reporting standards. In the majority of cases it clarified best practice—for example, that donated assets should be included as incoming resources at a reasonable estimate of their value to the charity and that fixed assets should be capitalised and depreciated. Nonetheless, in a number of cases, the SORP allowed discretion and emphasised that presentation should be made in a manner appropriate to the charity. This, coupled with the fact that the SORP contained 'recommendations' that were clearly not mandatory, allowed preparers to use considerable judgment in the presentation of their financial statements.

The Development of the Charity SORP from 1995 Onwards

This first charity SORP largely applied existing, commercially based standards to charities. Yet while it was, by its existence and in some of its suggestions, ground breaking, compliance was entirely voluntary and, as a result, the impact of this SORP was described as marginal (Charity Commission, 2009a). Over time, it became generally accepted that the sector's poor response necessitated the development of a more rigid regulatory framework to ensure proper accountability in the sector. A key element of this was the further development of the SORP. From 1990, responsibility for preparing the SORP passed to the SORP Committee of the Charity Commission, the regulatory body for charities in England and Wales, which had been established and continues to be funded by government. Subsequent SORPs were issued by this body (Charity Commission, 1995, 2000, 2005).

Since 1995 the SORP has developed virtually beyond recognition. One notable modification was the name change in 2000 from 'Accounting' to 'Accounting and Reporting,' reflecting the much greater emphasis on the trustees' annual report in later versions. Other significant changes (as summarised in Figure 8.1) were its: increased legislative weight, increased charity specificity, shift in focus and reduced preparer discretion (these are

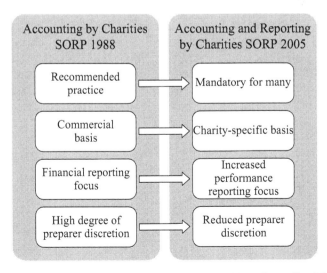

Figure 8.1 Evolution of the charity SORP, 1988–2005 (Connolly, Dhanani & Hyndman, 2013, reproduced with permission)

discussed below, with a fuller explanation provided in Connolly, Dhanani, and Hyndman, 2013).

Charities in the UK were encouraged to apply the recommendations of the 1988 SORP (ASC, 1988), although they were not required to do so. However, since the 1995 SORP (Charity Commission, 1995), legislative changes have made compliance with the SORP mandatory for many larger charities. In England and Wales, the Charities Acts in 1992 and 1993, together with new charity accounting regulations (in 1995, 2000 and 2005), have made compliance with the SORP a legal requirement for many large charities. In 2006, compliance with the SORP was required for the first time in Scotland (for all charities preparing accruals-based financial statements). Although no such requirement was made in the Charities Act (Northern Ireland) 2008, the position is still under discussion with an expectation that the SORP will be compulsory for the biggest charities. In effect, at the time of writing (April 2014), compliance with the SORP is now mandatory for large charities in England, Scotland and Wales, where the vast majority of UK charity spending takes place and where over 95% of UK charities are located (NCVO, 2013). The 'recommendations' have become 'requirements' for these charities.

The 1988 SORP (ASC, 1988), rather than create a set of charity reporting standards, focused on interpreting the existing commercial reporting standards. The SORP remains an interpretation of those standards. However, through time, charity financial statements have become substantially different from commercial financial statements as the SORP has evolved. One of the most radical changes was the introduction of the Statement of Financial Activities (SOFA) in place of the income and expenditure statement in the 1995 SORP (Charity Commission, 1995). The SOFA, which has evolved since its introduction, is unlike the income and expenditure statements of companies; for example, it is columnar, separately showing income and expenses related to restricted and unrestricted funds (an important distinction under UK trust law). Additionally, it shows income of different types together with the expenditure associated with that income (rather than showing only one type of income and many types of expenditure in 'natural categories'—such as wage costs and interest costs).

Over time, recommendations on performance and governance reporting (arguably having greater importance to many charity stakeholders than traditional financial statements) have been progressively added to the SORP. Most notably, following the publication of *Private Action, Public Benefit* (Cabinet Office, 2002), which was a government report based on a review of charities and the wider not-for-profit sector, the Charity Commission formed a subcommittee (the Annual Reporting Advisory Group), with a wider membership than the SORP Committee, to focus on such reporting. This group was instrumental in helping to develop the details for the trustees' annual report that were included in the revised SORP (Charity Commission, 2005), the most comprehensive recommendations on performance reporting yet seen. This SORP advocated more disclosure on the adminis-tration, governance and management of the charity, and additional infor-mation in the financial review and on plans for future periods. In addition, it also contained detailed recommendations on (Charity Commission, 2005, paras. 47–54):

- The need to explain the charity's main objectives for the year and pro-vide a description of the strategies for achieving those objectives;
- The provision of qualitative and quantitative information about the achievements and performance of the charity in the year, to include sum-maries of any measures used by the charity to assess its performance;
- Disclosure of sufficient information to allow readers to understand the role and contribution of volunteers

Subsequent to the 1988 SORP (ASC, 1988), the various iterations of the SORP have become progressively more prescriptive. For example, the 1995 SORP required investments to be shown on the balance sheet at market value, whereas the 1988 SORP (ASC, 1988) had made no specific refer-ence to investment valuation (allowing preparers to use a variety of valua-tion bases). Over time, the SORPs have provided more clarification, more detailed technical guidance and more examples, reducing reliance on the judgment of the preparing accountant and lessening the scope for variability in charity accounting practices.

Formal consultation with stakeholders has always been an integral part of the SORP development process. As a basis for reviewing the present SORP (issued in 2005), in 2008 and 2009 the SORP Committee undertook its largest ever consultation on a charity accounting pronouncement, with the aim of ensuring that any further development of the SORP reflected best practice and was relevant to the needs of the key stakeholders in the sector. This significant engagement process lasted well over a year and involved approximately 1,000 stakeholders, including preparers and auditors of charity accounts, funders, beneficiaries and academics. This resulted in a draft-revised SORP (Charity Commission, 2013b), drawing heavily on this consultation process, which is expected to progress to a final document (expected in 2015). For more detail of the consultation process, see Charity Commission (2009b).

KEY ISSUES RELATING TO CHARITY REPORTING

Charity Accounting and Accountability

Good governance is often a leitmotif in discussions on how organisations in general, and charities in particular, should operate (Hyndman & McDonnell, 2009). However, although what is meant by governance is rather fuzzy and a myriad of ideas are often placed under the umbrella of 'good governance,' themes that often emerge relate to 'good' accounting and appropriate accountability. The conventional view of accounting is that it is a purposive activity, directed towards a specified end (that is, the meeting of users' information needs) (AAA, 1966; CICA, 1980; Macve, 1981; ASB, 1999). While the main focus of these publications was on corporate accounting issues, they helped stimulate debate on user needs with respect to the charity sector. The user-needs emphasis was evident in the *Trueblood Report* (AICPA, 1973) and the Statement of Financial Accounting Concepts No. 4 *Objectives of Financial Reporting by Non-Business Organisations* (FASB, 1980) in the United States of America. As was seen above, this theme was also central in the work of Bird and Morgan-Jones (1981) in the UK, which provided the impetus that ultimately led to the publication of the first charity SORP (ASC, 1988).

Whilst accepting the argument that accountability, in its widest sense, is more than accounting (however widely accounting is defined), focusing on the information needs of users seems clearly linked with ideas relating to accountability (a key aspect of a contemporary definition of accounting). Jackson (1982) and the Government Accounting Standards Board (GASB) (1987) describe accountability as being responsible to someone or for some event and as explaining one's actions and justifying what has been done respectively. Rutherford (1983) views accountability as being related to the requirement to be answerable for one's conduct and responsibilities. However, despite accountability being a much-debated topic in the literature, the concept remains an abstract construct that lacks a clear definition (Munro & Mouritsen, 1996; Ebrahim, 2003a; Geer, Maher, & Cole, 2008). Various conceptualisations and measures of the construct are offered (Roberts, 1991; Sinclair, 1995), and the concept has been studied from different perspectives and in different contexts. For example, previous research has considered accountability in the context of: principal-agent theory (Laughlin, 1990; Edwards & Hulme, 1995); stakeholder theory (Gray, Kouhy, & Lavers, 1995; Mäkelä & Näsi, 2010); and legitimacy theory (Deegan, 2002; Campbell, Moore, & Shrives, 2006; Tilling & Tilt, 2010). It has also been examined in terms of the role and value of the different mechanisms of accountability (O'Dwyer, 2005; O'Dwyer & Unerman, 2007), the play-out of accountability in organisations (Panozzo, 1996; Ezzamel, Robson, Stapleton, & McLean, 2007) and the discharge of accountability through public discourse (Connolly & Dhanani, 2009; Dhanani, 2009). Operationally, Ebrahim (2003b), Lloyd (2005) and Bendell (2006) reviewed a number of different mechanisms of accountability. These related to, among other things, disclosure reports, performance assessments and evaluations, reviews of participation, social audits and the use of codes of practice.

It is argued that disclosure reports serve as a key tool of accountability as they enable organisations to communicate with their constituents and account to them (i.e., demonstrate that they are operating responsibly)

(Ebrahim, 2003b; Samkin & Schneider, 2010). Often these are prepared in response to an external obligation and/or as an internal felt responsibility (Fry, 1995). Examples of disclosure reports include: publicly available statutory annual reports; voluntary annual reviews; mandatory, but private, reports to large donors and grantors; and less formal vehicles such as organisational websites and newsletters. Of these different disclosure mechanisms, the annual report is the most widely used tool that occupies a prominent position as a statutory document in most Western economies (Gray, Bebbington, & Collison, 2006). Moreover, it serves an important source of information as a systematically produced document that attracts a degree of authenticity not associated with other media utilised by organisations (Neu, Warsame, & Pedwell, 1998; Kamla & Rammal, 2013).

Performance evaluation systems refer to organisational efforts to assess their activities. Together with offering indicators of what measures organisations view as critical in terms of advancing societal development, such systems can also provide benchmarks against which to assess the extent to which these advancements have taken place. Participation, aimed principally at beneficiary groups and viewed as an aspect of accounting downwards, seeks involvement from constituents in designing and implementing projects. While the types and levels of engagement may vary (ranging from consultation and implementation, to enabling negotiations between the beneficiaries and organisations), often the ultimate intention of participation is to ensure that projects undertaken target the appropriate areas of need (Ebrahim, 2003b; O'Dwyer & Unerman, 2010). Social auditing, a mechanism with its roots in the corporate sector, refers to the framework that enables organisations to assess the extent to which their social and ethical performance lives up to their values through systematic and regular monitoring and stakeholder dialogue (Ebrahim, 2003b; Lloyd, 2005). Further, it is suggested that the development and adoption of codes of conduct, at both the sector and organisational levels, reflects a commitment to accountable and ethical practices aimed at enhancing the standards of accountability practice (Ebrahim, 2003b).

In practice, the various accountability mechanisms function collectively and connectedly. Codes of conduct may, for example, encourage wider beneficiary participation in organisational decision-making, whereas (self-imposed) pressures to account through disclosure reports may promote the broader adoption of specific standards. Similarly, the social auditing process and participatory mechanisms should influence the content of annual reports, informing external stakeholders about organisational performance in terms of their mission and also their ethical practices in terms of how they conduct their operations. Ultimately, the mechanisms function together to address the needs and interests of different stakeholder groups and offer learning opportunities which, in turn, encourage continual improvement and accountability. Such can provide a springboard for social change (Ebrahim, 2005; Lloyd, 2005). This said, it is perhaps important to note that organisations run a risk of over-accounting. Gray et al. (2006), for example, believe that the actions of not-for-profit organisations in themselves constitute accountability and thus there is little need to report on it, whereas Messner (2009) adds that the (self-imposed) demands to account may become problematic if they are overly burdensome. Moreover, Ebrahim (2003b) and Walden (2006) suggest that concern for performance and performance assessment may stifle creativity and innovation if management fears having to record failures.

Financial Accountability and Performance Accountability

Given the above discussion, two main types of information that may be particularly important in discharging accountability are: financial information as contained in traditional financial statements (to indicate, for example, that the money raised has been used for the appropriate purposes, that the charity has 'lived within its means' and the level of resources available to the charity for future service provision); and wider performance information, often of a non-financial nature, relating to the goals, objectives, efficiency and effectiveness of the charity. Engaging in fine-grained analyses of accountability, Goodin (2003), Brody (2002) and Taylor and Rosair (2000) identify and distinguish between different themes or states of affairs for which one may be responsible and may in turn (be made to) account for. Goodin's (2003) states of affairs include: one's intentions, which for charities translate into the missions, visions and objectives that the organisations are working towards; one's actions, that is, the actual activities and programmes undertaken by charities to fulfil their visions and objectives; and one's results, that is the extent to which the organisations have achieved their mission and objectives. Brody (2002) and Taylor and Rosair (2000), who classify Goodin's themes as managerial accountability (or, as Connolly and Hyndman (2004) classify them, as performance accountability), add that charities also need to discharge fiduciary (or financial) accountability. As was seen in the earlier section on the development of a charity SORP, each of these themes has been highlighted as critical in a UK charity reporting context; financial accountability, particularly in the earlier iterations, with performance accountability increasingly coming to the fore in later versions. With fiduciary (or financial) accountability, it is assumed that appropriate systems and measures, such as good compliance, control and governance practices, are in place to ensure financial probity. This is emphasised to assure organisational stakeholders that the funds, assets and future of the organisation are safeguarded (Taylor & Rosair, 2000; Brody, 2002). In this regard, it is analogous to the stewardship function that financial accounting fulfils, whereby there is confirmation and, in turn, confidence that the funds and assets of the organisation are not misappropriated.

On the other hand, performance (or managerial) accountability refers to managerial effectiveness and the impact of the organisation on society (i.e., organisational success). With respect to performance accountability, there has been considerable debate as to how performance can be measured and how such accountability can be discharged. In a range of studies, performance reporting and the components of that reporting have been explained using a production model of performance utilising such terms as input, process, output, outcome and impact (AAA, 1989; Carter, Klein, & Day, 1992; Breckell, Harrison, & Robert, 2011). Perhaps the best-known outworking of this is the logic model (or logical framework), developed to be used to evaluate the effectiveness of programmes. Logic models are usually graphical depictions of the relationships between the resources, activities, outputs and outcomes of a programme. They consist of inputs, activities, outputs, outcomes (which are long term and individual) and impacts (which are long term and societal) (see, for example, The W. K. Kellogg Foundation, 2004).

The importance of outcome or impact measurement and reporting (impact, arguably, being the ultimate expression of the performance of a charity) has, despite major measurement difficulties, gained high profile. For larger funders (and particularly those commissioning public services) information on outcomes and outcome-based effectiveness is demanded as a basis for the effective targeting of resources at proven solutions to social problems (Lumley et al., 2011). In addition, the UK government has highlighted the importance of focusing on societal outcomes in government decision-making, and in funding non-government activities in the delivery of social programmes (HM Treasury, 2011). Moreover, the UK government has also funded a cross-sector group known as 'Inspiring Impact', which seeks to encourage and support good practice in reporting on outcomes and impacts (Lumley, Rickey, & Pike, 2011) and has developed a 'Code of Good Impact Practice' (Inspiring Impact, 2013).

Accountability: Contractual or Communal?

Laughlin (1996) suggests that an organisation's style of accountability will depend upon the relationship between the organisation's principals and agents, categorising accountability as either contractual or communal. Contractual accountability exists in formal relationships, where expectations of action, and information demand and supply are clearly defined and specified. It involves entering into a legally binding agreement over standards of performance by laying them down in writing and in specific enforceable terms, often through the judicial process (Dubnick, 1998). In contrast, it is argued that communal accountability occurs in less formal relationships, where expectations over conduct and information demand and supply are less structured and defined (Laughlin, 1996). The communal accountability process involves meeting stakeholders' needs through consultation and seeking their involvement in the decision-making process.

Laughlin (1996) attributes the different forms of accountability to the potential for trust and value conflict between principals and agents. He contends that formal mechanisms are less central where there is a high level of trust between parties, as it is assumed that the agent will fulfil the expectations of the principal. In contrast, if there is a low level of trust, the principal is likely to place much greater reliance on formal and contractual mechanisms to exert control over the behaviour of the agent. Similarly, with respect to value conflict, if there is relative alignment of values between principals and agents, communal accountability is more likely; in contrast, if this is not the case, the principal may employ more contractual forms of accountability. Laughlin asserts that as the principal has transferred resources to the agent, the principal has the right to demand from the agent reasons for actions taken and that the agent should meet the principal's expectations.

CHARITY ACCOUNTING AND ACCOUNTABILITY RESEARCH IN THE UK

Some major themes of past research relating to the key issues previously presented are considered here. These focus on the accountability of charities and the extent to which accountability mechanisms are influenced by stakeholder views (areas that have been of particular interest to a number of researchers). Such issues are viewed as critical in legitimising the sector and building confidence in terms of the actions and control processes of charities. While a range of studies on charity accounting and accountability have been undertaken in the UK and elsewhere, the research presented here is largely UK-based and restricted to selected studies that have investigated financial accountability and compliance with the extant SORP, and performance accountability and stakeholder engagement with respect to reporting frameworks for charities. Because of space constraints, it is not, and cannot be, exhaustive. The categorisations used are a convenient way to organise the material, although many of the studies themselves impact across the three categories and more widely.

Financial Accountability

As was presented above, Bird and Morgan-Jones' (1981) seminal work reviewed the financial reporting practices of UK charities in the late 1970s and exposed substantial poor reporting practice in a sector which was, even at that time, important in the context of the economy as a whole and highly visible in the public consciousness. Moreover, as was seen, this research provided the catalyst for the development of the first charity SORP (ASC, 1988) and for its subsequent iterations. Following this, a number of studies have explored the extent to which UK charity financial statements comply with the financial accounting recommendations of these SORPs. These studies were often based on the presumption that best-practice financial accounting, as embedded in the extant SORP, is important to users from both accountability and legitimacy viewpoints. Whether such financial accounts are of interest to the public (evidenced by an extensive and interested readership, perhaps an unlikely event) or whether such publication is in the public interest (whereby a few interested parties will/may explore the detail) is often at the heart of such discussions. Indeed, it may be that, although the general public has limited interest (and probably imperfect understanding) of the meaning and technical detail of SORP-compliant accounts, it is in the public interest that such accounts are produced and audited (and, at the very least, have the potential to be scrutinised by a limited number of informed and interested individuals). These recurring themes show themselves in many of the studies.

Ashford (1989), Gambling, Jones, Kunz, and Pendlebury (1990) and Hines and Jones (1992)

Three very different studies completed shortly after the publication of the 1988 SORP concluded that that SORP had had very limited impact on the financial statements of the charities studied. Ashford (1989) investigated the compliance of the financial statements of large charities with the recommendations of the SORP, and highlighted that, notwithstanding some examples of good practice, many charities were continuing to use accounting practices contrary to the recommendations (and, it was suggested, the spirit) of the SORP. They did this, he argued, to present their position in a way which made those charities seem to be more in need of funds; examples included failing to recognise income from legacies in the income statement, and recording the value of investments at the (usually lower) cost rather than market value.

In a study of six small charities, Gambling et al. (1990) identified, through a series of semi-structured interviews, that not only were these smaller charities not applying the recommendations of the SORP, but that awareness of the existence of the SORP was low. In addition, the recommendations were seen as increasing compliance costs with little or no perceived benefit to the charity. The authors suggested that this lack of awareness and perceived irrelevance, combined with the lack of resources then available to the Charity Commission to monitor or to enforce compliance, made it unlikely that the SORP would impact significantly on the sector.

In a longitudinal study of the financial statements of large charities, Hines and Jones (1992) found that while the vast majority of charities prepared the statements recommended by the SORP, dubious accounting practices in the preparation of those statements remained pervasive, citing such basic examples as failure to capitalise and depreciate assets. They argued that non-compliance with the mere recommendations of the SORP was unsurprising and opined that if this position was to change, then legislation or mandating of the SORP would be required.

Williams and Palmer (1998), Connolly and Hyndman (2000) and Palmer, Isaacs, and D'Silva (2001)

The poor response of the sector to the 1988 SORP necessitated the development of a more rigid regulatory framework and strengthening of the SORP to ensure proper accountability in the sector. After further review and con-sultation, a revised SORP was published in 1995 (Charity Commission, 1995) (as outlined above, at about this time changes in legislation progres-sively made adherence to the SORP mandatory for larger charities). Fol-lowing this, Williams and Palmer (1998), in a study reviewing the financial statements of a sample of small, medium and large charities, identified some improvement in compliance with the 1995 SORP. They observed significant increased compliance with the SORP among larger charities since the early 1980s, but fairly extensive failure to comply among small and medium-sized charities.

Connolly and Hyndman (2000) analysed the financial statements of the top 100 fundraising charities before and after the publication of the 1995 SORP. Referencing earlier studies, they commented that the 1988 SORP had had a significant, but lagged, impact over time on charity accounting practices. They argued that this delayed impact was as a result of a 'fairly gradual learning curve' (p. 96) in the accounting profession on the recom-mendations of the SORP. However, in respect of the 1995 SORP only partial compliance was seen. Non-compliance was particularly observed in respect of some of the most significant changes, such as reporting on costs, and Connolly and Hyndman commented that given the 'radical' nature of the 1995 SORP changes and the lagged impact of earlier recommendations, change would perhaps again be seen, but it was likely to be later. Overall, they concluded that 'charity accounts have improved significantly since the early 1980s, where improvement is seen in terms of increasing compliance with recommended practice' (p. 95).

Palmer et al. (2001) examined the first year of adoption of the 1995 SORP (Charity Commission, 1995) by 125 'major' UK charities (all of whom were registered with the Charity Commission in England and Wales, statutorily required to comply with the SORP and subject to full profes-sional audit). The research found a number of major departures from the SORP financial accounting requirements, few of which were disclosed as such. The authors concluded that charities and their auditors were aware of the SORP and that divergence seemed to occur because it suited the charity. Consistent with prior research, areas of non-compliance included the treat-ment of legacies, income being taken directly to capital, investment income being recorded on a receipts rather than an accruals basis and subsidiaries not being consolidated. On the basis of the research, Palmer et al. (2001) questioned whether auditors understood the requirements of the SORP or, if they did, why auditors did not report non-compliance. As a consequence, doubts were raised about the apparent reliance of the Charity Commission on the adequacy of auditors' reports. Palmer et al. agreed with Connolly and Hyndman (2000) that while charity accounting had improved there was still considerable diversity in practices which needed to be reduced.

Given the findings of the above research relating to financial account-ability, and in particular the limited compliance with SORP requirements, it is perhaps of little surprise that the accounting profession and the charity regulator moved to change the financial accounting guidance in the SORP from 'recommendations' to 'requirements' for the largest charities (as was detailed earlier). Genuine concerns relating to transparency and legitimacy (Cabinet Office, 2002; Charity Commission, 2004) as a basis for ensuring stakeholder confidence encouraged government and the accounting profession to exercise power and influence.

Performance Accountability

Over time, the focus of much empirical work on UK charities has shifted away from financial accountability to accountability for performance and the provision of additional background information valuable to the users of accounts. The potential importance of such information had been identified by Bird and Morgan-Jones (1981) but was not the focus of either their work or the 1988 SORP. However, progressively, the performance and governance aspects of charities came more to the fore, mirroring, at least to some extent, what was viewed by government (an increasingly important funder of charity activities) and others as central. As is seen above, while the SORP was evolving, the performance and governance aspects were strengthened considerably. A key theme in a number of these studies was that while financial accountability is important, such accounts are likely only to be of secondary importance to both external users and internal managers. Other, wider information, particularly relating to performance, is probably paramount in discharging accountability to a range of stakeholders and in providing managers with appropriate information to support decision-making. This will often require the telling of 'the story' of the charity in a way that is truthful, consequential and engages with donors. In the studies outlined below, how performance is (or is not) measured and reported comes to the fore, as do issues of how it might be measured.

Hyndman (1990, 1991)
Based upon an analysis of the annual reports of 163 large UK charities and a survey of 133 donors to such charities, Hyndman (1990) sought to identify the information that was routinely made available to donors through the annual report, and the most important information sought by donors to charities. In the study, donors were asked to rank 14 types of financial and non-financial information, including frequently disclosed information, in terms of importance to them. This was compared with the information routinely made available to them in the annual report. He found that while audited financial statements dominated reporting by charities, donors viewed other information, particularly that relating to performance, as most important.

In a related study, Hyndman (1991) investigated whether the identified 'relevance gap,' the difference between the information disclosed by charities in their annual reports (mainly audited financial statement information) and the information required by donors (mainly performance-related information), was due to a lack of awareness on the part of the providers of the information. The objectives of Hyndman's (1991) research were to identify the views of providers of information regarding the importance of donors as users of charity reports, and to ascertain the perceptions of such providers concerning the importance to donors of the 14 information types used as the basis for previous study (Hyndman, 1990). Two key groups involved in the provision of information to donors (charity officials and auditors) were surveyed. As well as identifying the perceived importance of donors as users of charity annual reports (with both groups of providers overwhelmingly identifying donors as the user group to whom the annual report is primarily directed), the major part of each questionnaire asked charity officials and auditors to rate the 14 information types in terms of perception of importance to donors. These perceptions were then compared with the actual importance to donors identified in the previous study. It was found that while providers of information are aware of the most important information required by donors (performance-related information), and donors are identified as the most important user of the annual report, the majority of charities do not disclose such information. Overall, the research discounted the possibility that the 'relevance gap' was caused by providers of information being unaware of the information needs of donors. Rather, it was argued that accountability to donors was not discharged in the most effective manner, particularly reflected in the limited reporting of performance information. In addition, it was suggested that there may be a general complacency among the providers of information with respect to the adequacy of existing reporting procedures, given that they know what is important but do not disclose, and limited motivation to improve accountability to donors.

Connolly and Hyndman (2003)
In a study of the annual reports of large UK charities over two accounting periods, Connolly and Hyndman (2003), aware of the changes in SORP 2000 and the emerging pressure from various sources for charities to improve performance reporting, sought to identify the extent to which performance accountability was discharged. Annual reports were analysed using a checklist developed from the recommendations of the SORPs, the information types identified by Hyndman (1990) as being important to donors and other sector guidance of the time. Categorising disclosures on this basis and comparing to the Hyndman (1990) study, they identified that many charities were providing extensive background information (for example, on how the charity was constituted, the mission and the need area addressed) and that there had been some limited improvement over time in performance reporting (such as reporting on goals, objectives and outputs). However, their primary conclusion was that, despite the recognised

importance of performance information to the users of accounts, it was still not widely disclosed by charities.

A number of examples of charities' failings in this regard were given, including that a significant proportion of charities did not disclose a single measure of efficiency or of effectiveness (two of the key criteria for judging performance). Reporting of efficiency and effectiveness measures actually decreased in the two periods studied, against an increase in the reporting of more 'marketing-focused' information. The authors contrasted this situation with significant improvements in reporting in the UK public sector in the same time period, and suggested this deterioration might be due to a number of factors including a lack of willingness and pressure to report in the charity sector, combined with a paucity of guidance on performance reporting in charities. They also suggested that the focus of the charity reporting debate on financial accounting matters 'may have detracted from a meaningful debate relating to the relevance of the information content of charity annual reports' (p. 117).

Connolly and Dhanani (2006)

Connolly and Dhanani (2006) investigated narrative reporting practices in the top 100 fundraising charities in the UK, including the disclosure of organisational information, financial management policies, financial information, operational information and non-financial performance information. They found that while charities readily disclosed organisational information and financial management policies, the quantity and quality of disclosure tended to decrease in the reporting of financial information, decreasing again in respect of operational information (including measures of fundraising efficiency), and lowest in respect of performance information. Performance reporting tended to be dominated by information on charitable activities (with 91% of the sample reporting at least one measure), reporting on inputs (73%), volunteer contributions (67%) and outputs (66%). Significantly lower levels of disclosure were seen in respect of reporting on results (17%) and on effectiveness (3%). Moreover, the authors commented that the charities tended to report using quantitative or monetary measures (depending on what was being reported), but that ratio analysis presentations were uncommon. Where the information was disclosed, a key concern in respect of this reporting was that 'charities seldom provided disclosures of comparative information, explanations of results and plans for the future, indicating that there is considerable scope to improve reporting practices' (p. 59).

Dhanani (2009)

On the basis of reviewing the practices of 73 of the largest charities reporting on the GuideStar UK website, Dhanani (2009) applied content analysis to those charities' records. She sought to identify the existence and quantity of reporting across four key disclosure types: charitable intent (or aims and objectives), charitable activities (or programmes), charitable performance (subdivided into outputs, results, efficiency and effectiveness) and future intentions (or plans/strategy). The study found that while all but one charity provided information on aims and objectives, and 89% provided information on their activities, reporting on performance and future plans was much less common. She highlighted that while 75% of charities provided some performance measures, these tended to be the 'lower order' measures, such as simple quantifications of the services provided, rather than measures of efficiency or effectiveness. Additionally, only a third of the sample provided any information on future plans, indicating 'a willingness to provide descriptive information but hold back information that organisations may be held to or questioned about' (p. 189). Dhanani argued that this lack of reporting was particularly concerning given the high levels of media attention and public scrutiny being focused on higher-order measures of performance, particularly on efficiency and effectiveness. While these results demonstrated some improvement in comparison with earlier studies (albeit acknowledging difficulties in that comparison), they also suggested wide variations in practice between the charities investigated. For example, fundraising charities were more likely to provide information on charitable activities, performance information and future plans (concurring with the findings of Connolly and Hyndman, 2003).

Connolly and Dhanani (2009)

Connolly and Dhanani (2009) carried out content analysis of the annual reports and annual reviews of the largest UK charities, an examination of their websites and a series of interviews with representatives of those charities. Their results identified continuing problems with the discharge of accountability in the sector—at the most basic level, 36% of charities asked to supply a copy of their annual report failed to do so and therefore contravened a statutory requirement. Comparing their analysis with earlier research, they commented that the demonstration of accountability in the annual reports of charities had weakened over time. They contrasted the increasing length and perceived importance of these reports to lower disclosure levels of information relating to fiduciary accountability, financial managerial accountability and operational managerial accountability. Considering operational management disclosures in more detail, they found that reporting was dominated by information on the charity's activities, rather than on their performance or impact on society. They commented that 'charities appear to seek legitimacy for their actions on the basis of the nature of their work (i.e. charitable activities and projects) rather than from evidence of the resulting societal change' (p. 7).

From the interviews, conducted in tandem with their survey, they concluded that this was an identified problem among interviewees, who highlighted an information gap that existed both internally within charities in terms of how they assessed their performance, and externally in respect of their reporting of that performance. The authors acknowledged some attempts to improve reporting on the impact of charity activities, and recommended that these be supported through efforts to put in place holistic and formal systems of performance measurement within charities.

Jetty and Beattie (2009)

Jetty and Beattie (2009) conducted an in-depth analysis of the narrative element of the annual reports and annual reviews of 10 charities, together with interviews with the preparers of these documents to explore the motivations, drivers and constraints relating to public charity disclosure. Consistent with the findings of previous studies reported here (for example, Hyndman, 1990, 1991; Connolly & Hyndman, 2000, 2003; Connolly & Dhanani, 2006), the authors reported variations in charity reporting practices and a continuing lack of forward-looking information, especially in the annual report; although there was evidence that charities were beginning to provide more non-financial, non-quantitative and narrative information. However, in contrast to Connolly and Hyndman (2003), Jetty and Beattie's findings suggested that charities were disclosing more performance-related information than background data, with the former often being presented in a narrative form (perhaps due to difficulties in measuring impact).

As called for by Bird and Morgan-Jones (1981) and Hyndman (1990, 1991), the authors presented a framework towards understanding the drivers and motivations for charity disclosure. They posited that there appeared to be various motivations for disclosure other than the accountability and user-needs arguments; for example, motivations relating to stakeholder influence (salience) and socio-political drivers, such as a desire to create a sense of empathy for the charity. Jetty and Beattie suggested that the main hindrance to improved charity annual reports and accounts was not only the lack of agreement about their content, but also the extent of the enthusiasm and engagement of preparers. They also advised that the annual review, the document favoured by users, should be subject to regulatory oversight, albeit one that was 'light-touch,' to alleviate the risk of it becoming a clone of the annual report.

Engagement with Stakeholders

In discussions on accountability (whether financial or performance), a connection to stakeholders is often highlighted. For example, the Charity Commission (2004), in making this clear link, argues that accountability is a charity's response to the legitimate information needs of its stakeholders, a response commonly made through annual reports and accounts which should provide 'adequate information to allow stakeholders to assess the overall performance of the charity' (p. 2). A stakeholder could be defined as any 'group or individual who can affect or is affected by' an organisation's achievements (Freeman, 1984, p. 46). It is this language that has been much in evidence from the Charity Commission (and other charity sector bodies) in recent years in discussions of governance in charities. Specifically with respect to accountability and accounting, the meeting of stakeholders' information needs is a key theme in both *Transparency and Accountability* (Charity Commission, 2004) and *Charity Reporting and Accounting: Taking Stock and Future Reform* (Charity Commission, 2009b). The central argument advanced is that if charities (or other organisations) engage with stakeholders on a basis of mutual trust and cooperation, they will build legitimacy and reputation. However, it is realised that, often in such a scheme, all stakeholders may not be equally important from a charity's perspective. To allow organisations to evaluate 'who or what really counts' and prioritise competing stakeholder claims, Mitchell, Agle, and Wood (1997) introduced the concept of stakeholder salience. They argued that the salience of stakeholders (or the degree to which they and their arguments were perceived to count) depended upon the stakeholder possessing three attributes: power, legitimacy and urgency. These themes provide a focus for the research outlined below.

Hyndman and McMahon (2010, 2011)

The objective of Hyndman and McMahon (2010) was to analyse the evolution of the UK charity SORP with insights from stakeholder theory. It was argued that for an accounting pronouncement such as a SORP, stakeholders might include groups or individuals who impact on, or are impacted upon by, a sector's reporting regime. They opined that these considerations have been central in discussions on accounting principles both in the commercial and charitable sectors over many years. Drawing on ideas of stakeholder salience, they explored competing stakeholder claims as they impacted on the evolution of the SORP since the mid-1980s.

Analysing a period of almost 20 years, they contended that the SORP had developed from the rather limited 1988 version to a much more significant accounting and reporting document by 2005. From their analysis, it was suggested that the two most salient and continuing stakeholders in this process have been government and the accounting profession. Furthermore, with each of these stakeholder groups, it was argued that they began as rather passive and inactive with respect to charity accounting and reporting issues, but, through time, as discussion built and awareness of the importance of the issues became clearer, they each engaged vigorously in shaping the SORP. Moreover, it was suggested that the perspectives of these two stakeholder groups had different focuses, with government being more concerned with performance and governance reporting, while the accounting profession's primary interest was more related to technical financial accounting issues.

This theme was extended in empirical work by Hyndman and McMahon (2011), which, using data from interviews with members of the various SORP Committees, focused on the influence of one highly salient stakeholder—government—in developing a regime of quality accounting and reporting in the charity sector. It was argued that, over time, government as a stakeholder became much more vigorous and demonstrated considerable power and legitimacy as it has sought to push through agendas it perceived as urgent. In addition, the authors contended that government's influence has been partly coercive (in creating the regulatory framework, through legislation requiring SORP compliance and as an increasingly important resource provider exercising a direct disciplining effect on those charities to whom it provides funds) and partly persuasive (in encouraging greater prominence to measuring and reporting performance, and in facilitating the basis for the drafting of best-practice financial reporting). The authors claimed that the field data from the research suggested that government's increasing engagement over time with the charitable sector, often on the basis of a customer-provider relationship, has certainly influenced government's demands relating to the 'giving of accounts' to themselves (and more widely to other stakeholders) and is evidence of the powerful hand of government shaping accounting and reporting. Moreover, it was argued that much of this had to do with government's view with respect to the correct conduit through which certain services should be delivered to the public, and the increased prominence afforded the charity sector was evidence of it being viewed in a progressively more favourable light.

Connolly et al. (2013a)

Utilising data from a major consultation on a revised future charity SORP, Connolly et al. (2013a) explored stakeholder engagement with respect to this future publication. This consultation lasted for more than a year and involved approximately 1,000 stakeholders, including funders (such as charitable trusts, government agencies and individual donors), accounting professionals involved in preparing and auditing charity accounts and academics. Data was generated from 28 roundtable events conducted throughout the UK, and evidence was presented of how this data had influenced the SORP Committee's deliberations. The researchers concluded that this ambitious consultation exercise facilitated much wider stakeholder engagement than had previously been observed (particularly with funders), and the extensive and much broader stakeholder engagement that was achieved has the potential to further legitimise the process and make the UK's unique sector-specific reporting framework (the SORP) an even more powerful tool with respect to charity reporting and accounting.

AREAS FOR FURTHER RESEARCH AND CONCLUDING COMMENTS

This chapter focuses on a range of research themes and specific material that has been the hub of the authors' interests over a number of years (which is largely based in the UK). Many of the specific studies referred to focus on large charities, which, numerically in the UK, are a small part of the entire sector, albeit representing a large proportion of the economic activity of the sector. It is highly likely that accountability and governance mechanisms are much less developed in smaller charities, and the means through which accountability is discharged may be much less formal (because, for example, smaller charities are closer to their donor and beneficiary bases). Studies comparing accountability processes across different size groupings of charity would aid understanding in these areas. Moreover, more international comparative research (not considered in this chapter), possibly comparing countries with different control and regulation regimes, and at different stages of maturity, would aid a more complete understanding. It may be that in those countries with greater control and regulation, and better accountability, charitable activity is supported by reducing information asymmetry problems, possibly resulting in a growth in charitable giving.

Beneficiaries are viewed as an important stakeholder group to whom charities owe accountability and, with whom charities should engage vigorously in order to sharpen their service delivery and avoid mission drift. In addition, such engagement, which could be viewed as 'ethical' and 'right,' has the potential to build trust and strengthen what Laughlin (1996) would describe as communal accountability, or what O'Dwyer and Unerman (2007) would describe as social accountability. The possible benefits from such discharges of accountability, what these might look like in practice and how they would impact on a charity's operations, would seem fruitful areas for further research. This is particularly the case given that studies have found beneficiaries often unwilling (or perhaps unable) to engage with a charity in any way other than as a recipient of a service. Indeed, in some areas of activity, it is difficult even to identify a beneficiary who could engage with the charity. In a related vein, and given the importance placed by a range of stakeholders on performance information, further studies relating to what is meant by 'performance,' how it might be measured and reported and what emphasis stakeholders place on it, would seem appropriate. A range of questions might flow from such considerations. What does 'impact' actually mean, what does it look like and can it be 'measured'? How does a charity 'tell its story'? While some useful research has been done in the broad area of performance measurement (see, for example, Cordery & Sinclair, 2013), detailed case studies focusing on impact in specific contexts would aid understanding and have the potential to support charities in delivering their core mission and improving their discharge of accountability.

What are the difficulties in generating meaningful conversion (or pass-through) ratios, and can using them to compare 'performance' across charities mean anything useful? The significance of such ratios, the dangers of misinterpretation and misunderstanding by donors and the impact of changed accounting requirements are subjects where some research has already been conducted (Tinkelman, 2006; Connolly, Hyndman, & McConville, 2013b).

However, given the importance often placed on conversion ratio information by donors, and the obvious sensitivities of charities to the headlining of such numbers, further work is needed, particularly relating to how charities manage both disclosure and donor understanding. Furthermore, how do we (or should we) account for the input of volunteers? Given the significant contribution of volunteers to many charities, what is appropriate recording, valuing and reporting, and how does it affect management decision-making and the discharge of accountability? Again, these are areas where some work has been done (Narraway & Cordery, 2009; Cordery, Proctor-Thomson, & Smith, 2011; O'Brien & Tooley, 2013), but further research, especially to support accounting standard-setters and charity regulators, would seem appropriate. And finally, in an era where government (in the UK and elsewhere) is an increasingly important provider of funding to charities (often by way of contracts), research into the effects of this would seem necessary. For example, how does increasing reliance on government funding affect charity operations and charity reporting?

Good accounting and accountability (and, more widely, good governance) processes are vital to support management decision-making within charities and appropriate accountability by charities. Such may be desirable, or indeed necessary, for the continuing health and growth of the sector. In this chapter it is argued that charities have an accountability to stakeholders, and accounting information can play a key role in the discharge of such accountability. Good accounting and good accountability can increase the confidence of stakeholders, legitimise the operations of charities and provide a basis for stability and growth in the flow of funding. Overall, more research into what passes for good accounting and good accountability (and good governance), and, as a result, greater debate of the issues, has the potential to support charities (and the sector as a whole) as they seek to relate to their communities and increase public confidence in what they are doing. The net result of such debate, if conducted with key stakeholder input and reflecting the context in which charities operate, can provide the basis for a more accountable charity sector, surely a desire of all those with a heart for the varied, valuable and socially desirable activity in which charities engage. Indeed, the empirical studies reported in this chapter present some evidence of the ability of past researchers in this area to influence both policy and practice relating to charity reporting.

NOTES

1 The UK consists of four separate countries (England, Northern Ireland (NI), Scotland and Wales) within one main political unit.
2 SORPs are recommendations on accounting practice for specialised industries or sectors, and they supplement other legal and regulatory requirements. The first charity SORP was issued in 1988, with subsequent revisions in 1995, 2000 and 2005. More detail is provided later in the chapter.

3   The Charities Act 2011 came into effect in March 2012 and consolidated the law by replacing four Acts of Parliament (Charities Acts 1992, 1993 and 2006, and the Recreational Charities Act 1958) with one. It made no changes to the law.
4   The Charities Act 2011 provides detailed guidance in terms of what is deemed charitable and, with the support of Charity Commission publications, what constitutes public benefit.
5   At this time, SORPs were new instruments of accounting rule-making, allowing the accountancy profession to continue to develop rules in controversial areas but with reduced status so as to preempt enforcement problems. SORPs make recommendations for accounting and reporting to provide consistency of accounting treatment within specialised industries or sectors. They supplement accounting standards and other legal and regulatory requirements in the light of the special factors prevailing or transactions undertaken in the particular industry or sector. Since 1994 SORPs have no longer been issued by the ASC/Accounting Standards Board (ASB) (the successor to the ASC), but by industry or sectoral bodies recognised for the purpose by the ASB. Although not issued by the ASB, each SORP must carry a statement by the ASB confirming that it does not appear to contain any fundamental points of principle that are unacceptable within current accounting practice and does not conflict with an accounting standard or the ASB's plans for future standards.

REFERENCES

Accounting Standards Board (ASB). (1999). *Statement of principles for financial reporting*. London: ASB.
Accounting Standards Committee (ASC). (1988). *Accounting by charities: Statement of recommended practice 2*. London: ASC.
American Accounting Association (AAA). (1966). *A statement of basic accounting theory*. Chicago, IL: AAA.
American Accounting Association (AAA). (1989). *Measuring the performance of non-profit organisations: The state of the art*. Sarasota, FL: AAA.
American Institute of Certified Public Accountants (AICPA). (1973). *Objectives of financial statements: Report of the study group on the objectives of financial statements (Trueblood report)*. New York: AICPA.
Ashford, J. K. (1989). Charity accounts. In L.C.L. Skerratt & D. J. Tonkins (Eds.), *Financial reporting 1989–90: A survey of UK reporting practice* (pp. 23–48). London: Institute of Chartered Accountants in England and Wales.
Beattie, V., McInnes, B., & Fearnley, S. (2002). *Through the eyes of management: A study of narrative disclosures, interim report*. London: Institute of Chartered Accountants in England and Wales.
Bendell, J. (2006). *Debating NGO accountability*. New York: United Nations Non-Governmental Liaison Service.
Bird, P., & Morgan-Jones, P. (1981). *Financial reporting by charities*. London: Institute of Chartered Accountants in England and Wales.
Breckell, P., Harrison, K., & Robert, N. (2011). *Impact reporting in the UK charity sector*. Retrieved 24 May 2011 from http://www.cfdg.org.uk/resources/̅/media/Files/Resources/Impact%20Reporting%20in%20the%20UK%20Charity%20Sector.ashx
Brody, E. (2002). Accountability and public trust. In L. M. Salamon (Ed.), *The state of America's non-profit sector* (pp. 471–498). Aspen, CO: Aspen Institute and Brookings Institution.

Cabinet Office. (2002). *Private action, public benefit: A review of charities and the wider not-for-profit sector.* London: Cabinet Office.

Campbell, D., Moore, G., & Shrives, P. (2006). Cross-sectional effects in community disclosure. *Accounting, Auditing and Accountability Journal, 19*(1), 96–114.

Canadian Institute of Chartered Accountants (CICA). (1980). *Financial reporting for non-profit organizations (a research study).* Toronto: CICA.

Carter, N., Klein, K., & Day, P. (1992). *How organisations measure success: The use of performance indicators in government.* London: Routledge.

Charity Commission. (1995). *Accounting by charities: Statement of recommended practice.* London: Charity Commission.

Charity Commission. (2000). *Accounting and reporting by charities: Statement of recommended practice.* London: Charity Commission.

Charity Commission. (2004). *RS8: Transparency and accountability.* London: Charity Commission.

Charity Commission. (2005). *Accounting and reporting by charities: Statement of recommended practice.* London: Charity Commission.

Charity Commission. (2009a). *Operational guidance: Charity accounts and reports.* London: Charity Commission.

Charity Commission. (2009b). *Charity reporting and accounting: Taking stock and future reform.* London: Charity Commission/Office of the Scottish Charity Regulator.

Charity Commission. (2013a). *Facts and figures.* Retrieved 11 November 2013 from http://www.charity-commission.gov.uk/About_us/About_charities/factfigures.aspx

Charity Commission. (2013b). *Accounting and reporting by charities: Statement of recommended practice (exposure draft).* London: Charity Commission/Office of the Scottish Charity Regulator.

Connolly, C., & Dhanani, A. (2006). Accounting narratives: The reporting practices of British charities. *Journal for Public and Nonprofit Services, 35*(1), 39–62.

Connolly, C., & Dhanani, A. (2009). *Research report 109: Narrative reporting by UK charities.* London: Association of Chartered Certified Accountants.

Connolly, C., Dhanani, A., & Hyndman, N. (2013). *Research report 132: The accountability mechanisms and needs of external charity stakeholders.* London: Association of Chartered Certified Accountants.

Connolly, C., & Hyndman, N. (2000). Charity accounting: An empirical analysis of the impact of recent changes. *British Accounting Review, 32*(1), 77–100.

Connolly, C., & Hyndman, N. (2003). *Performance reporting by UK charities: Approaches, difficulties and current practice.* Edinburgh: Institute of Chartered Accountants of Scotland.

Connolly, C., & Hyndman, N. (2004). Performance reporting: A comparative study of British and Irish charities. *British Accounting Review, 36*(2), 127–154.

Connolly, C., Hyndman, N., & McConville, D. (2013a). UK charity accounting: An exercise in widening stakeholder engagement. *British Accounting Review, 45*(1), 58–69.

Connolly, C., Hyndman, N., & McConville, D. (2013b). Conversion ratios, efficiency and obfuscation: A study of the impact of changed UK charity accounting requirements on external stakeholders. *Voluntas, 24*(3), 785–804.

Cordery, C., Proctor-Thomson, S., & Smith, K. (2011). Valuing volunteer contributions to charities. *Public Money & Management, 31*(3), 193–200.

Cordery, C., & Sinclair, R. (2013). Measuring performance in the third sector. *Qualitative Research in Accounting and Management, 10*(3/4), 196–212.

Deegan, C. (2002). The legitimising effect of social and environmental disclosures—a theoretical foundation. *Accounting, Auditing and Accountability Journal, 1*(3), 282–311.

Dhanani, A. (2009). Accountability of UK charities. *Public Money & Management, 29*(3), 183–190.

Dubnick, M. (1998). Clarifying accountability: An ethical theory framework. In N. Preston & C. A. Bois (Eds.), *Public sector ethics: Finding and implementing values* (pp. 68–81). London: Routledge.

Ebrahim, A. (2003a). Making sense of accountability: Conceptual perspectives for northern and southern nonprofits. *Nonprofit Management and Leadership, 14*(2), 191–212.

Ebrahim, A. (2003b). Accountability in practice: Mechanisms for NGOs. *World Development, 31*(5), 813–829.

Ebrahim, A. (2005). Accountability myopia: Losing sight of organizational learning. *Nonprofit and Voluntary Sector Quarterly, 34*(1), 56–87.

Edwards, M., & Hulme, D. (1995). *Non-governmental organisations—performance and accountability (beyond the magic bullet).* London: Earthscan Publications.

Ezzamel, M., Robson, K., Stapleton, P., & McLean, C. (2007). Discourse and institutional change: 'Giving accounts' and accountability. *Management Accounting Research, 18*(2), 150–171.

Financial Accounting Standards Board (FASB). (1980). *SFAC no. 4 objectives of financial reporting by non-business organisations.* Norwalk, CT: FASB.

Freeman, R. E. (1984). *Strategic management: A stakeholder approach.* Boston, MA: Pitman.

Fry, R. (1995). Accountability in organizational life: Problem or opportunity for nonprofits? *Nonprofit Management and Leadership, 6*(2), 181–195.

Gambling, T., Jones, R., Kunz, C., & Pendlebury, M. (1990). *Accounting by charities: The application of SORP2: Certified research report no. 21.* London: Association of Chartered Certified Accountants.

Geer, B., Maher, J., & Cole, M. (2008). Managing nonprofit organizations: The importance of transformational leadership and commitment to operating standards for nonprofit accountability. *Public Performance and Management Review, 32*(1), 51–75.

Goodin, R. (2003). Democratic accountability: The distinctiveness of the third sector. *European Journal of Sociology, 44*(3), 359–371.

Government Accounting Standards Board (GASB). (1987). *Concepts statement no. 1: Objectives of financial reporting.* Stamford, CT: GASB.

Gray, R., Bebbington, J., & Collison, D. (2006). NGOs, civil society and accountability: Making the people accountable to capital. *Accounting, Auditing and Accountability Journal, 19*(3), 319–348.

Gray, R., Kouhy, R., & Lavers, S. (1995). Corporate social and environmental reporting: A review of the literature and a longitudinal study of UK disclosure. *Accounting, Auditing and Accountability Journal, 8*(2), 47–77.

Hines, A., & Jones, M. J. (1992). The impact of SORP on the UK charitable sector: An empirical study. *Financial Accountability & Management, 8*(1), 49–67.

HM Treasury. (2011). *HM Treasury and Department for Work and Pensions: Green Book discussion paper on valuing social impacts.* London: HM Treasury.

Home Office. (2003). *Charities and not for profits: A modern legal framework: The government's response to private action—public benefit.* London: Home Office.

Hyndman, N. (1990). Charity accounting: An empirical study of the information needs of contributors to UK fundraising charities. *Financial Accountability & Management, 6*(4), 295–307.

Hyndman, N. (1991). Contributors to charities—a comparison of their information needs and the perceptions of such by the providers of information. *Financial Accountability & Management, 7*(2), 69–82.

Hyndman, N., & McDonnell, P. (2009). Governance and charities: An exploration of key themes and the development of a research agenda. *Financial Accountability & Management, 25*(1), 5–31.

Hyndman, N., & McMahon, D. (2010). The evolution of the UK charity statement of recommended practice: The influence of key stakeholders. *European Management Journal, 28*(6), 255–266.

Hyndman, N., & McMahon, D. (2011). The hand of government in shaping accounting and reporting in the UK charity sector. *Public Money & Management, 31*(3), 167–174.

Inspiring Impact. (2013). *Our vision.* Retrieved 21 November 2013 from http://inspiringimpact.org/about/our-vision/

Jackson, P. M. (1982). *The political economy of bureaucracy.* London: Philip Allan.

Jetty, J., & Beattie, V. (2009). *Research report 108: Charity reporting—a study of disclosure practices and policies of UK charities.* London: Association of Chartered Certified Accountants.

Kamla, R., & Rammal, H. (2013). Social reporting by Islamic banks: Does social justice matter? *Accounting, Auditing and Accountability Journal, 26*(6), 911–945.

Laughlin, R. (1990). A model of financial accountability and the Church of England. *Financial Accountability & Management, 6*(2), 93–114.

Laughlin, R. (1996). Principals and higher principals: Accounting for accountability in the caring profession. In R. Munro & J. Mouritsen (Eds.), *Accountability: Power, ethos and the technologies of managing* (pp. 225–244). London: International Thomson Business Press.

Lloyd, R. (2005). *The role of NGO self regulation in increasing stakeholder accountability.* London: One World Trust.

Lumley, T., Rickey, B., & Pike, M. (2011). Inspiring impact: Working together for a bigger impact. In *The UK social sector.* Retrieved 21 November 2013 from http://inspiringimpact.org/wp-content/uploads/2012/06/inspiring_impact.pdf

Macve, R. (1981). *A conceptual framework for financial accounting and reporting: The possibilities for an agreed structure.* London: Institute of Chartered Accountants in England and Wales.

Mäkelä, H., & Näsi, S. (2010). Social responsibilities of MNCs in downsizing operations: A Finnish forest sector case analyzed from the stakeholder, social contract and legitimacy theory point of view. *Accounting, Auditing and Accountability Journal, 23*(2), 149–174.

Messner, M. (2009). The limits of accountability. *Accounting, Organizations and Society, 34*(8), 918–938.

Milmo, C. (2013, June 4). Charities watchdog under fire over tax avoidance scandal. *Independent Newspaper.* Retrieved 21 November 2013 from http://www.independent.co.uk/news/uk/home-news/charities-watchdog-under-fire-over-tax-avoidance-scandal-failed-to-stop-abuse-of-system-8643070.html

Mitchell, R. K., Agle, B. R., & Wood, D. J. (1997). Toward a theory of stakeholder identification and salience: Defining the principle of who and what really counts. *Academy of Management Review, 22*(4), 853–886.

Munro, R., & Mouritsen, J. (1996). *Accountability: Power, ethos and the technologies of managing.* London: International Thomson Business Press.

Narraway, G., & Cordery, C. (2009). Volunteers, valuable but invisible to accountants? *Third Sector Review, 15*(1), 11–29.

National Council for Voluntary Organisations (NCVO). (2013). *The UK civil society almanac.* London: NCVO.

Neu, D., Warsame, H., & Pedwell, K. (1998). Managing public impressions: Environmental disclosures in annual reports. *Accounting, Organizations and Society, 23*(3), 265–282.

O'Brien, E., & Tooley, S. (2013). Accounting for volunteer services: A deficiency in accountability. *Qualitative Research in Accounting and Management, 10*(3/4), 279–294.

O'Dwyer, B. (2005). The construction of a social account: A case study in an overseas aid agency. *Accounting, Organizations and Society, 30*(3), 279–296.

O'Dwyer, B., & Unerman, J. (2007). From functional to social accountability: Transforming the accountability relationship between funders and non-governmental development organisations. *Accounting, Auditing and Accountability Journal, 20*(3), 446–471.

O'Dwyer, B., & Unerman, J. (2010). Enhancing the role of accountability in promoting the rights of beneficiaries of development NGOs. *Accounting and Business Research, 40*(5), 451–471.

Palmer, P., Isaacs, M., & D'Silva, K. (2001). Charity SORP compliance—findings of a research study. *Managerial Auditing Journal, 16*(5), 255–262.

Panozzo, F. (1996). Accountability and identity: Accounting and the democratic organization. In R. Munro & J. Mouritsen (Eds.), *Accountability: Power, ethos and the technologies of managing* (pp. 182–197). London: International Thomson Business Press.

Roberts, J. (1991). The possibilities of accountability. *Accounting, Organizations and Society, 16*(4), 355–368.

Rutherford, B. A. (1983). *Financial reporting in the public sector.* London: Butterworths.

Samkin, G., & Schneider, A. (2010). Accountability, narrative reporting and legitimation: The case of a New Zealand public benefit entity. *Accounting, Auditing and Accountability Journal, 23*(2), 256–289.

Sinclair, A. (1995). The chameleon of accountability: Forms and discourses. *Accounting, Organizations and Society, 20*(2/3), 219–237.

Taylor, D., & Rosair, M. (2000). Effects of participating parties, the public and size on government departments' accountability disclosure in annual reports. *Accounting, Accountability and Performance, 6*(1), 77–98.

The W. K. Kellogg Foundation. (2004). *Using logic models to bring together planning, evaluation, and action: Logic model development guide.* Battle Creek, MI: The W. K. Kellogg Foundation.

Tilling, M., & Tilt, C. (2010). The edge of legitimacy: Voluntary social and environmental reporting in Rothmans' 1956–1999 annual reports. *Accounting, Auditing and Accountability Journal, 23*(1), 55–81.

Tinkelman, D. (2006). The decision-usefulness of nonprofit fundraising ratios: Some contrary evidence. *Journal of Accounting, Auditing and Finance, 21*(4), 441–462.

Walden, G. (2006). Who's watching us now? The nonprofit sector and the new government by surveillance. *Nonprofit and Voluntary Sector Quarterly, 35*(4), 715–720.

Williams, S., & Palmer, P. (1998). The state of charity accounting—developments, improvements and continuing problems. *Financial Accountability & Management, 14*(4), 265–279.

Part III

Issues in Accountability Processes and Governance

9 Nonprofit Service Delivery for Government
Accountability Relationships and Mechanisms[1]

Craig Furneaux and Neal Ryan

INTRODUCTION

Interest in the accountability of nonprofit organisations (NPOs) has increased considerably in recent decades, particularly since 1990, driven by increased delivery by these organisations of services on behalf of government (Catlaw & Chapman, 2007; Dunleavy & Hood, 1994; Kettl, 2000; Spicer, 2004), together with public concern about scandals involving NPOs (Ebrahim, 2003a). The mutual reliance of NPOs on government funding, and governments on NPOs for service delivery (Ebrahim, 2005) means that NPOs are not just providers of public goods and services, but have 'become the providers of public funded, public goods' and services (Candler & Dumont, 2010, p. 260). The sorts of services provided by NPOs in Australia typically include education, health, social services, housing, disability, rehabilitation and counselling (Lyons, 1998). This widespread practice of contracting out government services carries specific risks, as accountability can decrease (Mulgan, 1997), or at least become problematic (Mulgan, 2000a, 2000b). In fact, the accountability of NPO to government under service delivery contracts is considered by many to be not just problematic, but even adversarial (Menefee, 1997; Young, 2000), with good examples quite rare (Brown & Troutt, 2004).

However, as Roberts and Scapens (1985) note, accountability is not a simple construct and tends to be approached from either of two main perspectives: that of *accountability systems* or alternatively, *systems of accountability*. Generally, research into the accountability of NPOs to government has been obsessed (O'Dwyer & Unerman, 2007) with *accountability systems*: focusing on how resources have been used and the immediate, measurable impact of service delivery. By focusing on the mechanisms of accountability, such as financial reports and performance evaluation, research and practice has tended to underscore a principal/agent view of relationships between government funding agencies and NPOs (Ebrahim, 2003a, 2003b, 2009). This has led to a privileging of the external oversight of government (Ebrahim, 2003b, p. 193), and focusing on *what* NPO profits are accountable for (Candler & Dumont, 2010).

The alternative approach is *systems of accountability* (Roberts & Scapens, 1985), where the focus is on the institutional relationships between organisations, or to whom organisations are accountable (Candler & Dumont, 2010). In the nonprofit context this is potentially valuable, as it takes into account the complex multiple accountability relationships of NPOs (Candler & Dumont, 2010; Ebrahim, 2003a, 2003b, 2005, 2009; Najam, 1996).

Contextually sensitive empirical examination of accountability in the nonprofit context has been called for by Ebrahim (2009), and this work helps to partially fill this gap. This chapter undertakes a qualitative analysis, involving 94 organisational representatives who participated in interviews and focus groups, exploring the various government/NPO funding relationships in Queensland. What emerged from these conversations was a dichotomy between what could be termed a 'controlling accountability relationship,' which was characterised by conflicted and strained relationships and onerous reporting arrangements, and a few cases of what we have termed the 'collaborative accountability relationship,' which had vastly different reporting arrangements. Specific mechanisms of accountability (such as financial reporting and performance assessment) were also discussed by participants, in the context of these relationships.

It is evident from the data that the nature of the funding relationship (controlling as opposed to collaborative) between government and nonprofit organisations involves different approaches to accountability. The research supports the assertion of some authors that accountability mechanisms in the nonprofit sector are most properly understood in the context of relationships between organisations (Ebrahim, 2005, p. 60; see also Cordery, Baskerville, & Porter, 2010; O'Dwyer & Unerman, 2007).

THEORETICAL FRAMEWORK

The notion of accountability can be approached from many perspectives (Mulgan, 2000a). So first, a definition of accountability is needed.

Definition of Accountability

As Mulgan (2000a) wryly notes, the concept of accountability is an ever-expanding one, or as Sinclair (1995) suggests, it has a chameleon-like quality. Thus there are many perspectives on accountability, which makes the adoption of a particular definition essentially pragmatic. March and Olsen (1995) note that the core element of accountability is the giving of an 'account' itself. Any act of calling someone to account for their actions involves an invitation for explanation and justification for those actions. Accountability in the NPO context is most often understood as a 'social mechanism whereby an agent or organisation can be held to account by another agent or institution' (Bovens, 2010, p. 948).

Accountability involves not just the giving of an account, but interpretation of what the report means, which often occurs via a 'dialectical exchange' (Mulgan, 2000a, p. 569), and is thus a product of relationships (Ebrahim, 2003b). As Schillemans (2008, p. 177) notes: 'The communicative interaction between accountor and accountee presupposes a relationship . . . Accountability is first of all based on a formalized relationship that stipulates the rights, authorities and available sanctions of the accountee.' Given the importance of relationships in understanding and defining accountability, an overarching interest of this chapter is to explore how different types of relationships might influence how accountability is enacted (Messner, 2009; Roberts, 2001, 2003, 2009).

CORE ELEMENTS OF ACCOUNTABILITY

A number of core elements that can be used to analyse accountability have been articulated clearly, and utilised by many authors. These elements include accountability *for what*—what is the account to be made about; *to whom* must the account be given; and *how* is the account to be made— or what are the mechanisms by which the account is made? (Candler & Dumont, 2010; Ebrahim, 2003a, 2003b, 2010; Najam, 1996; Scott, 2000). These elements of accountability are examined in detail below, in particular the relationship to government/NPO funding relationships.

FOR WHAT IS A NPO ACCOUNTABLE UNDER GOVERNMENT FUNDING ARRANGEMENTS?

Accountability to government by a NPO is a most pertinent obligation (Najam, 1996), as this is a key accountability relationship that a nonprofit has (Ebrahim, 2003b). Broadly, in government/NPO funding arrangements, governments want to know not just whether money has been spent, but also require detailed descriptions of how the money was applied (Najam, 1996). As Ebrahim notes, 'funders provide money to NGOs[2] in exchange for regular reports and evaluations that confirm the legitimate use of those funds' (2003b, p. 201). Another key area of accountability is in terms of the social impact of NPO activities, particularly when these are undertaken with funding from government (Ebrahim, 2003a, 2003b). A third area is more about the processes and actions of the organisation (Ebrahim, 2010). Thus, in terms of the accountability framework, the 'for what' in this chapter is focused particularly on the acquittal of funds for designated purposes, the activities which were undertaken and the reporting of social outputs and outcomes from services delivered via this funding.

HOW IS A NPO ACCOUNTABLE TO GOVERNMENT FUNDING AGENCIES?

According to Ebrahim (2010), one key type of accounting mechanisms typically involves formal reports and disclosures, which can be required periodically or at the end of the project. Disclosures and reports are widely used accountability tools and are often required by government (Ebrahim, 2003a). An alternative is to use accountability mechanisms such as participation and learning, which Ebrahim (2010) terms process mechanisms.

TO WHOM ARE NPOS ACCOUNTABLE UNDER GOVERNMENT FUNDING ARRANGEMENTS?

Mulgan (2003) asserts accountability is inevitably about a relationship with an external party who has some form of authority, and 'can make demands on the person being held to account' (Willems & Van Dooren, 2011, p. 507). The array of stakeholders to whom NPOs account is typically huge (Romzek, 2010). Three main stakeholder groups stand out though: funders, clients and communities and regulators (Ebrahim, 2003b)[3]. Giving a tailored account to each of these groups is essential for the NPO to maintain legitimacy with these stakeholders (Benjamin, 2008).

Accountability to government is almost ubiquitous when discussing NPO accountability (e.g., Demirag, 2004; Ebrahim, 2003a; Kearns, 1994; Koppell, 2005; Mulgan, 1997; Najam, 1996; O'Dwyer & Unerman, 2007), and is typically seen as an 'upward' form of accountability (Ebrahim, 2010). However, government tends to be treated as an 'omnibus' construct (Candler & Dumont, 2010, p. 265) in much of the accountability literature and this can stifle good analysis. Government in fact has a multifaceted role in relation to the third sector, and can be seen as a financial stakeholder (funder), regulator and contractor (Kearns, 1994). Bode (2012, p. 137) suggests that this makes the relationship somewhat schizophrenic. As noted in the introduction, the relationship between NPO as service provider and government as funder is the one which will be explored in more detail here.

Historically, Australian governments provided grants to third sector organisations with little or no attached accountability requirements (Lyons, 1993, 1998). This scenario has shifted over time, particularly with the introduction of new public management (NPM) where the logic moved from (effectively) a gift to the purchasing of services by government from NPOs (Lyons & Dalton, 2012; Lyons & Passey, 2006; Maas & Liket, 2010). Statistical data on the funding of the sector reflects this situation. The Australian Bureau of Statistics (ABS, 2009) reports this by noting that funding can be either in the form of volume-based contracts[4] or grants[5]. A contract involves specification and accountability for services, whereas a grant typically has little accountability.

Najam (1996) reinforces these two main funding sources by differentiating between the accountability practices for projects funded via designated (restricted) funding, which need to deliver specific outcomes, and the accountability arrangements for general NPO funding by government, what we have termed grants above. Where the funding involves the delivery of outcomes on behalf of government, Brown and Ryan (2003) suggest government maintains strong control over resources, priority setting and service delivery through reporting. This form of a relationship between government and NPO is very much a purchaser/provider relationship, and carries with it the concerns about 'conditionalities or onerous reporting requirements being attached to the funding' (Ebrahim, 2003a, p. 814). Grants, however, are a different form of relationship, as government does not see itself responsible for delivering services via a NPO, but instead acts as a benevolent and wealthy body providing support for a delivery of a particular service by a community group (Brown & Ryan, 2003). The government funding discussed in this chapter is specifically related to contractual agreements with specified performance arrangements, as grants do not typically have associated performance reporting.

While focusing on a single relationship where government is funder, and the NPO is the service deliverer, it is important to note that even this very specific relationship can vary (Cordery et al., 2010; O'Dwyer & Unerman, 2007), even when government is viewed as principal providing funds and NPO as agent delivering services and giving an account (Broadbent, Dietrich, & Laughlin, 1996). This is important, as types of information provided with which to give an account are strongly related to the type of relationship within which such accountability is enacted (Laughlin, 1990). In effect, the nature of the relationship affects the form of accountability (Seal, 2004). Thus different types of relationships involve different ways in which accountability is exercised, as there are differing levels of trust in each relationship (Broadbent et al., 1996). This understanding is reflected in Figure 9.1.

As this figure suggests, we will argue that while government as the principal provides finances to an agent (in our case, NPOs), and the agent gives an account for finances and outcomes, the nature of the relationship can affect how accountability is requested and provided. The following section explores the two main types of accountability relationships identified in the literature in more detail.

Two Main Types of Accountability Relationship

A number of authors have identified two major ways that accountability is enacted, based on different types of relationships (Broadbent et al., 1996). For example, Laughlin (1990) distinguishes between contractual and communal approaches to accountability, whereas Roberts (1991) discusses hierarchical and socialising forms of accountability. Broadbent et al. (1996) argue that the contractual of Laughlin (1990) is the same as Roberts's (1991) hierarchical; and the communal of Laughlin (1990) is the same

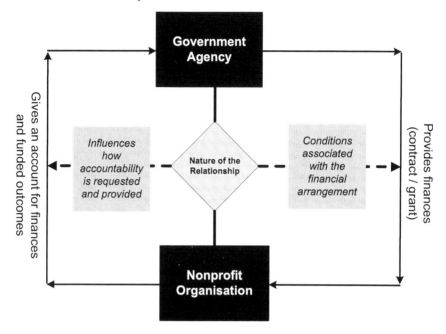

Figure 9.1   Diagram depicting government/nonprofit accountability relationships (developed by the authors)

as Roberts's (1991) socialising. Broadbent et al. (1996) then go on to discuss how in relationships with high trust and similarity of values, there is likely to be a communal/socialising form of accountability, which are contrasted with relationships characterised by low trust and high dissimilarity in values, in which the accountability is likely to be contractual/hierarchical. This approach to differentiating between two main types of relationships and discussing how accountability might be undertaken differently in each has been followed by O'Dwyer and Unerman (2007), and more recently by Cordery et al. (2010), although again, slightly different words are used.

For the sake of internal consistency in this paper, this chapter will follow the terminology of Cordery et al. (2010) by terming accountability relationship as *controlling*, when there is low trust between the parties, resulting in highly prescriptive accountability; and *collaborative* when there is high trust between the parties and therefore accountability is likely to be more negotiated. This is discussed in detail below.

Controlling Accountability Relationships in Government/NPO Funding Arrangements

What Laughlin (1990) terms the contractual approach to accountability involves a fairly prescriptive set of expectations. Broadbent et al. (1996)

argue that this contractual approach equates to Roberts's (1991) hierarchical form of accountability. One key reason for this is that this accountability is understood to occur in a way that strongly reflects principal-agent logic, and therefore involves vertical accountability (Broadbent et al., 1996).

Under a controlling approach to accountability, given its principal-agent theoretical underpinnings, the a priori assumption is that agents will behave opportunistically if they are able to (Broadbent & Laughlin, 2003; Cordery et al., 2010). Consequently, significant reporting obligations are typically established in the contract (Seal, 2004) to ensure that NPOs utilise the funds for the purposes that they have been given (Ebrahim, 2003a). This form of principal-agent relationship is characterised by low trust, as the economic rationale is that the agent (NPO) is very likely to 'do the wrong thing,' unless steps are put in place (accountability mechanisms) to ensure that they are highly accountable to the principal (the government funder) (Broadbent et al., 1996, p. 275; Cordery et al., 2010). In these types of relationships the principal is privileged and a high degree of prescriptive reporting is required (Laughlin, 1990). The external control is very much mandated, the demanding of an account is focused on compliance and the intent is on controlling the actions of the accountee (Roberts, 2001, 2003, 2009).

The response from NPO to government demands for accountability can be described as compliance (Kearns, 1996), as there is virtually no discretion on how to acquit the accountability requirements which have been demanded (Broadbent & Laughlin, 2003). Given the hierarchical accountability (Roberts, 1991) from the agent to the principal (Broadbent et al., 1996), the only way in which a NGO is capable of holding government to account for its actions under such arrangements is when the NGO has multiple sources of income, (Ebrahim, 2003b, p. 201) or there is 'a long-established and deeply interdependent relation with its funder' (see also Ebrahim, 2002)[6].

In summary, the controlling approach to accountability (Cordery et al., 2010) in government/nonprofit funding relationships is often framed in terms of principal-agent theory, with a hierarchical (Roberts, 1991) form of accountability due to the giving of a formal and structured account for the activities undertaken with the funds provided (Broadbent et al., 1996). Trust is low in these relationships, which are viewed from a very short-term perspective (Broadbent et al., 1996).

Critique of the Logic Underpinning the Controlling Accountability Relationship

A key difficulty with the principal-agent logic underpinning the controlling approach to accountability is that only two stakeholders are acknowledged (see, for example, Laughlin, 1990). This belies the reality that there are a number of key stakeholders such as communities to whom nonprofits have to account for the services they deliver, even if these are partly funded by government (Ebrahim, 2003a). Tenbensel, Dwyer, and Lavoie (2013, p. 9) argue that 'the tension between accountability to funders and accountability to community is likely to be most marked when government agencies demand rigorous accounting for resources used and quantifiable outcomes in terms that are not aligned with the financial accounting and activity monitoring needs of the organizations themselves . . . or those required for reporting to community boards.' In other words, the controlling approach to accountability while attending to government needs does not always match the internal processes of nonprofit organisations, or the needs of the communities they serve.

A further and deeper critique is to examine the assumptions that underlie the principal-agent approach to contracting. 'One key assumption of economic theory is that the transfer of financial resources from someone (a "principal") to another (an "agent") allows the former to have certain rights over the behaviour of the latter' (Broadbent & Laughlin, 2003, p. 25).

The principal-agent logic underpinning much of government purchasing of services from the third sector provides the conceptual basis by which the provider of resources (e.g., government) can act as the principal in a relationship, and demand and account from the agent (e.g., the NPO) (Broadbent & Laughlin, 2003). This set of assumptions under new public management (NPM) (Hood, 1996; Mulgan, 1997) may relate to what Suchman (1995) terms cognitive legitimacy, given the 'taken for grantedness' that they have the right to impose conditions on the contracts. Unfortunately, 'over precise specifications of obligations and performance may *destroy* rather than create trust' (Seal, 2004; see also Broadbent et al., 1996). McGregor-Lowndes and McBratney (2011) note that the chronic underfunding and onerous reporting requirements typically involved in this controlling approach have resulted in considerable distrust between government and NPOs. While NPOs would naturally want to be accountable in order to appear legitimate (Benjamin, 2008), such legitimacy is likely to be essentially pragmatic (Suchman, 1995), given the reality that governments need NPOs to deliver services, and NPOs need governments for funding. Consequently, a 'game' is played according to the 'rules' (Koppenjan & Klijn, 2004), with accountability undertaken to ensure compliance (Kearns, 1996), but little more.

The principal-agent assumptions are not unassailable however, and under certain circumstances, can be challenged. Indeed, Broadbent et al. (1996, p. 277) emphasise 'the need to probe the unquestioned moral right of the economic principal *in all circumstances*, even though being a supplier of financial resources, to make contractual requirements of an agent' (original emphasis). McGregor-Lowndes (2008) helps us to understand the appropriateness of different forms of contracting in different situations, concluding that the classical contracting approach, driven by principal-agent theory, is not well suited to structuring government funding arrangements with NPOs to deliver services. A key reason for this unsuitability is that governments typically do not pay the full amount for the service delivery, and consequently, as the services are effectively jointly funded by NPOs and government agencies, contractual arrangements such as joint ventures, public-private partnerships (PPPs) and trusts would be more appropriate (McGregor-Lowndes, 2008). In situations where there is joint government/NPO funding, there are, in fact, a number of principals in the project. In such situations collaborative types of arrangements are arguably more appropriate, with mutual agreement on outcomes and roles. These more collaborative approaches to government/NPO funding relationships are discussed next.

Collaborative Accountability Relationships in Government/NPO Funding Arrangements

Numerous commentators have already noted that the introduction of classic contracting, driven by principal-agent logic, and a heavy prescriptive approach to accountability requirements led to a souring in government/NPO relationships in many parts of the world, including Queensland (McGregor-Lowndes & McBratney, 2011). McGregor-Lowndes (2008) lists this set of discontents in the Australian context as at least partly arising from the imposition of performance measurement by government, and the erosion of trust as a result. Much of the discontent, in Australia at least, is due to the classical form of contract and instead, workers 'hanker for positive relationships with government funders' (McGregor-Lowndes, 2008, p. 51)[7]. This call is echoed in other nations where dissatisfaction with principal-agent approaches to government/NPO funding relationships, and the attendant hierarchically mandated functional reporting regimes, led to calls for alternative approaches to accountability (O'Dwyer & Unerman, 2007, p. 447).

The a priori assumption of what we are terming a collaborative approach to accountability, (following Cordery et al., 2010) is that the agent can be trusted to do what is right (Broadbent & Laughlin, 2003, p. 27), which means that the form of accountability may not be as rigid as under more controlling approaches. As noted above, principal-agent reasoning underpinning the controlling approach assumes low trust and a likelihood of wrongdoing by the agent. In contrast, 'where there is high trust the agent is anticipated to fulfil the expectations of the principal, and it follows that sophisticated and formal contracts are invariably not seen as necessary' (Broadbent et al., 1996, p. 274; see also Seal & Vincent-Jones, 1997). It is this fundamental shift in the assumptions underpinning the relationship which lead to differing ways of enacting accountability.

Under collaborative forms of accountability, reporting on outcomes is more negotiated, and there is therefore opportunity to report to multiple stakeholders—what Cordery et al. (2010) refer to as holistic accountability.

Here the approach to accountability involves attempts to build mutual understanding (O'Dwyer & Unerman, 2007; Laughlin, 1990) and goes beyond mere demands for an account (Messner, 2009). What we are terming the collaborative form of accountability goes beyond that functional reporting of numbers, and instead enables the significance and meaning of those numbers to be negotiated and discussed (Roberts & Scapens, 1985). The approach is not one of compliance, but more responsive and negotiated (Kearns, 1996). The legitimacy that arises from accountability (Benjamin, 2008) in these high trust relationships is likely to be a moral form of legitimacy where both government and NPO recognise and respect each other. The external control is implicit, the demanding of an account more negotiated and discourse around actions of the accountee is more communicative (Roberts, 2001, 2003, 2009). So, in reference to Figure 9.1, while an account is demanded and given in highly collaborative relationships, accountability is likely to be negotiated, given the higher levels of mutual respect.

While Roberts (1991) suggests more formal types of accountability are stronger than informal types, Broadbent et al. (1996, p. 269) strongly argue that '*both* are forms of accountability and *both* can be equally powerful in their control intentions with neither raising fundamental questions about the "right" of the principal to control the agent's behaviour' (original emphasis).

Following a review of the literature, it is possible to contrast these two differing types of accountability relationships. Table 9.1 summarises the literature that considers these dichotomous perspectives.

The Appropriateness of Accountability Demands

A focus on the nature of the funding relationship and how this affects accountability has not been a significant research stream to date (Seal, 2004), although much of the early conceptualisation of what this might look like was undertaken by Broadbent et al. (1996). O'Dwyer and Unerman (2007) and Cordery et al. (2010) are good contemporary examples, though. Both contrast the hierarchical approach to accountability with an approach in which there is a higher degree in collaboration and negotiation, and a broader array of people acknowledged in the accountability processes.

As noted above, government funds significant activity by NPOs in Australia. Theoretically at least two main forms of relationship noted by other authors are likely to exist here—the controlling and the collaborative. As Ebrahim concludes, 'if accountability is about relationships between organizational actors, then accountability mechanisms . . . cannot be properly understood without some consideration of for whom and for what purpose they are employed' (2005, p. 73). While intuitively sound, how different funding relationships might affect accountability practices needs empirical

Table 9.1   Summary of two different funding relationships and accountability

Type of accountability relationship	Controlling	Collaborative
Accountability is seen as . . . (Laughlin, 1990) (Roberts, 1991) (O'Dwyer & Unerman, 2007) (Cordery et al., 2011)	Contractual Hierarchical/ individualising Functional Hierarchical	Communal Socialising Social Holistic
Level of trust in relationship (Broadbent et al., 1996; Cordery et al., 2011)	Low	High
Underlying economic assumptions (Broadbent et al., 1996; Cordery et al., 2011)	Principal-agent Principal seeks to control agent, as it is likely to do wrong	Transaction cost theory/ sociology—agent can be trusted
Time frames (O'Dwyer & Unerman, 2007)	Typically short term	Longer term
Mandate for external control (Roberts, 2001, 2003, 2009)	Explicit	Implicit
Style (Roberts, 2001, 2003, 2009)	Compliance	Negotiation
Accounting for funds (Ebrahim, 2003a, 2010)	Detailed, exhaustive reports	Simple
Accounting for social impact (Ebrahim, 2003a, 2010)	Detailed reporting of outputs, set by the principal	Longer term or negotiated to meet multiple stakeholders
Accounting for actions (Ebrahim, 2003a, 2010)	Prescriptive accounts of activities	Negotiated

examination in specific contexts (Ebrahim, 2009) and it is here that this chapter contributes, by answering the following research question:

Research Question: *How do differing relationships* between government as principal (funder) and NPO as service deliver *affect the way in which accountability is exercised?*

METHODOLOGY

A qualitative research methodology was followed with primary data sources being interviews and focus groups involving 94 individuals, although some documentary data was also collected. Some 24 semi-structured interviews were conducted with peak organisations in Queensland. Interviews are typical data collection strategies in qualitative research, and are 'a highly efficient way to gather rich, empirical data' (Eisenhardt & Graebner, 2007, p. 28), as they provide a personal view of what happens in practice (Saunders, Lewis, & Thornhill, 2000).

Interviews with peak organisations sought to identify the key general components of a funding programme that was well regarded by the sector, although the dysfunctionality of many others was also discussed. Additionally, the peak organisations were asked to nominate a small and a large NPO, who were well regarded, to participate in subsequent focus groups. CEOs, or delegates, then nominated line managers who could participate meaningfully in a focus group to discuss the nature of the funding relationship, as well as the accountability aspects of these relationships. While the researchers thus set up the sample frame, the informed actors, rather than researchers, choose the final participants in the focus groups.

Three focus groups were conducted (two in the capital city and one regionally) with a total of 68 participants.[8] Focus groups are structured discussions with a group of people, where their collective views are focused on a particular topic (Kitzinger, 1994). Importantly, focus groups differ from interviews in that an individual's views are discussed in interaction with others, thereby creating discussion and debate about a particular issue (Morgan, 1998). A number of potential programmes were suggested within the focus groups and two were agreed upon. Again, while discussion in the focus groups was intent on identifying what was working well, which, as will be seen, was the collaborative accountability relationship, a large amount of data was collected about what was not working in other programmes, which, as will be seen, is the controlling accountability relationship.

These two well-regarded funding arrangements were investigated with an additional six interviews of both the funders (government agencies) and two funded NPOs. The data was coded into themes and a comparison made between the controlling accountability relationships, and the more collaborative accountability relationship, which was evident in the data. Given that the general trend in research to date has been the fixation (O'Dwyer & Unerman, 2007) on hierarchical reporting and the onerous implications this has for the sector, the data here provide a counterpoint to this discussion. Thus, the two examples are important, as they provide data on a phenomenon of interest (Patton, 2002)—something seen to be working well by both government and NPOs involved. Table 9.2 summarises the data collection method.

Table 9.2   Summary of data collection: Methods, participants and purposes

Organisations involved	Participants	Data collection method	Purpose
Peak groups ↓	CEOs of peak agencies	Interviews	To nominate two organisations (one large, one small) to participate in focus groups. Data collected on controlling accountability relationship.
Agencies ↓	CEOs or representatives	Focus groups	To identify two funding programmes considered to be working well. Also gathered data on controlling accountability relationships.
Programme	Managers of funding programme (government and nonprofit agency)	Interviews	Data collected on the collaborative accountability relationships.

FINDINGS

The focus groups and interviews with peak groups aimed at identifying a programme working well (collaborative accountability relationships). However, in order to identify these two cases, a large amount of data in relation to examples of situations which were not perceived to be functioning well was also gathered (controlling accountability relationships).

The nomenclature for the qualitative data is: PG = Peak Group; FG = Focus Group;

GO = Government Organisation; SP = Nonprofit Service Provider.

Accountability in Controlling Relationships between Government and NPOs

The specific relationships being examined here are where government contracts and pays for services from the third sector. Other authors have raised concerns about the onerous nature of reporting in such arrangements

(Ebrahim, 2003a) and this issue is supported in the findings. Specifically how accountability for finances and social outcomes was undertaken was investigated, along with what the mechanisms were.

ACCOUNTABILITY FOR FINANCES

When considering funding, Broadbent and Laughlin (2003) argue that an assumption is often made that the principal has the right to demand an account of the agent when funds are provided. What was surprising in the findings was that the government was not paying the full costs for the services being delivered. As the peak bodies argued, there is a tendency to see the community sector as a cheap way of getting something done (PG9), although without full funding, outcomes cannot be achieved (PG6, PG16, PG12). Oncosts, (e.g., sitting on government committees) were generally not funded (PG9), neither were capacity building, infrastructure, insurance and administration costs, and chronic underfunding of the specific service delivery tendered for was evident (PG4, PG11, PG12, PG7, PG6 and PG8). As one peak group noted, 'we have not been game to ask for what something actually costs' (PG17). Additionally, the lack of indexation to the Consumer Price Index (CPI) means many agencies effectively receive a funding cut every year (PG13, PG2, PG12, PG3). This deficient funding regime has a number of perverse effects on the ability of NPOs to report.

This inadequate funding coverage is a common theme in competitive tendering arrangements in Australia, with 85% of NPOs indicating in a recent survey that they *disagreed* or *strongly disagreed* with the comment: 'Government funding covers the true cost of delivering contracted services' (ACOSS, 2009, as cited in Productivity Commission, 2010, p. 21, appendix C). Likewise, Lyons (2003) observed that many programmes only *partly* fund the delivery of community services by nonprofit agencies. This reality was supported in the interviews and focus groups. This will be discussed further below, but in many cases, the controlling accountability relationship involved an assumption that a full account could be made, even though the full amount was not being paid for the service delivery.

The requirement to report on every single line item is taxing on small organisations (PG 19). Despite underfunding, there were strong requirements for reporting financial expenditure, albeit inconsistent ones. 'There is one department that has really good arrangements—they only require reporting on one line budget and outcomes, and yet another officer from the same department requires us to account for everything' (PG19). Thus, while there were no challenges to the notion of the need to report on the acquittal of funds, what was questioned was the manner in which the reporting was done.

ACCOUNTABILITY FOR ACTIVITIES

There was some major disjuncture in relation to the accountability of activities. Participants asserted that having established objectives, government agencies should not micromanage organisations, but allow flexibility in how outcomes are achieved (PG2, PG6). An overzealous intrusion into service delivery can have a negative impact on relationships (PG1). There needs to be recognition and respect for professionals engaged in community organisations (PG8). Thus, there is evidence of attempts to control NPO.

Much of this concern was driven by a lack of understanding by government departments about how community organisations are run, and how they can meet the results required in service contracts (PG8). High mobility in certain government departments and appointment of people who have no understanding of the sector create problems in the application and reporting process (PG8, PG19). Government agencies need to take the time to understand the organisation that they are funding (PG3, PG12, PG19). 'Government agencies could be far more productive if they were to build relationship, and work with us to achieve objectives. This probably won't happen as a lot of people in the bureaucracy are just protecting their jobs— seeing themselves as auditors, rather than facilitators' (PG19). Thus, there was a clear lack of mutual understanding between government and NPO.

In summary, in terms of accountability for activities, while nonprofits were generally supportive of the notion of being accountable, the lack of flexibility to adjust to the needs of clients, coupled with a lack of understanding by government officials of the organisations they were funding, was a source of considerable NPO vexation.

ACCOUNTABILITY FOR OUTCOMES AND OUTPUTS

Government agencies tend to have high-reporting requirements, coupled with tight service delivery agreements and low payments for services (PG11). Additionally, there are difficulties in specifying all outcomes in advance in service agreements (PG4), as the needs of communities can shift markedly in a short period of time, particularly with high-need clients (PG10, PG18); so, flexibility in how outcomes are met (PG6) would be helpful, and would allow for local responsiveness, innovation and viability (PG11).

Reporting requirements should not be onerous on NPOs (PG3, PG11), and there should be mutual agreement to the evaluation and reporting process (PG11). Government agencies often seek quite complex information from organisations that often do not have the wherewithal to gather that information (PG12). Qualitative, as well as quantitative, measures of success are necessary when evaluating funding programmes (PG4, PG12 and PG19). While government agencies are perceived as wanting quantitative measures in their evaluations (such as how many people attended a programme), community organisations are primarily interested in qualitative measures (such as how lives have been changed) (PG12), although some government departments do allow for qualitative measures (PG19).

The priorities of NPOs and the priorities of government agencies are not often matched. In fact, some organisations perceive a major discrepancy between government objectives and NPO objectives (PG6). Government agencies are often perceived as being more interested in achieving their programme's outcomes, rather than achieving good outcomes for communities (PG12). Other agencies were seen as preferring to account for the last dollar spent, rather than being concerned about whether the programme met needs and fulfilled its objectives (PG19).

Numerous participants commented on the controlling accountability relationship often resorting to hierarchical accountability to government, at the expense of other stakeholders.

The disaggregation of data and finances is difficult when reporting back to separate government agencies (FG1); there are multiple service agreements, and multiple government agencies. This multiplication of reporting, contracting and relating creates its own set of tensions and additional stresses for NPOs (FG3). There are problems with managing these multiple expectations and overlapping agreements, all of which involve different time frames, reporting requirements and data collection (FG3). This notion of 'multiple accountability disorder' has been noted elsewhere (Koppell, 2005).

Tenbensel et al. (2013, p. 9) note that this situation is not one restricted to Queensland: 'The tension between accountability to funders and accountability to community is likely to be most marked when government agencies demand rigorous accounting for resources used and quantifiable outcomes in terms that are not aligned with the financial accounting and activity monitoring needs of the organisation themselves.'

Accountability and compliance were argued as needing to be *appropriate* and negotiated between the organisations involved (FG2). Strong recommendations were made for mutual accountability between government agencies and NPOs (FG2), where government agencies could be held accountable for their decisions in the same way that NPOs could be held accountable for their delivery of services. As noted above, this is unlikely unless the NPO has a diverse income base and/or has a strong relationship with government (Ebrahim, 2002, 2003b).

In summary, these findings support other researchers who have examined, or theorised, a controlling form of relationship, with low trust, short time frames, high levels of reporting a lack of agreement on what the goals should be and explicit compliance expected. A very large number of participants voiced a desire for a very different type of accountability relationship—one based on trust, and where there were negotiated outcomes and shared understanding.

Accountability in Collaborative Relationships between Government and NPOs

Two funding programmes were identified which were well regarded by participants in focus groups.

ACCOUNTABILITY FOR FINANCES

Funding programme #1 allocates funds to the families of persons with a disability (GO1). The goals and services provided through the programme are agreed upon by the government agency, the families and the service agencies (GO1). The overall process is driven by trying to collaborate to determine client goals, and maximise the hours for clients (SP1), while individuals with a disability have control over the funding (SP2). Funding agreements are negotiated and include hours, services provided, cost and transport and administration charges. Additionally, oncosts, supervision and coordination are included in funding (GO1, SP2). The funding is recurrent and linked to 2.5% CPI increases (SP2). While these have not fully kept up with award increases, there is an acknowledgment of increased costs of service provision due to inflation (GO1).

The funding level of funding programme #2 is considered fantastic (SP3), and government acknowledges that the funding programme is generous (GO2, GO3); expenditure is legislated (SP4), allowing for a CPI increase of 3% every year (GO2, GO3). As one service provider noted, it is 'at the top of the tree' (SP4). The full funding requirements of the organisation are a key part of the funding process (SP3). Assessment is also transparent, with a reference group from the industry involved in peer reviewing applications and the development of the programme overall (GO2, GO3).

For programme #1 there is a need to report quarterly on expenditure (SP1), according to the funding agreement, but agencies do not need to report on line items (GO1). In programme #2, there is single line item reporting for annual reports with audited financials at the end of the year (GO2, GO3). Thus there is a simplified reporting requirement that could not be conceived as onerous.

ACCOUNTABILITY FOR ACTIVITIES

Programme #1 sees a shared understanding of the importance of providing post-school services to people with a disability. This understanding is enhanced with forums/conferences around the programmes in which the NPOs participate (GO1). Individualised funding is based on a fundamental desire to empower people with a disability. This ethos is strongly shared by the government agency and service providers (GO1). The values of putting the client first are important (SP2). The forums and conference provide a venue for sharing information and learning, while agreement on the outcomes of the funding (helping people with a disability) set up a more collaborative arrangement from the start. This shared set of values points to a high-trust relationship (Broadbent et al., 1996).

Programme #2 reflects an ongoing process of relationship building across the state throughout the year (GO2, GO3), with one-on-one contact between the departmental officials and sporting organisations in order to provide support, to learn about the organisation and to develop the capacity of the organisation (GO2, GO3). If the officers find organisational development and governance needs, they will seek funding to address the issues (GO2, GO3). There are a range of other initiatives and programmes (workshops and information sessions around the state) and forums on topical issues (GO2, GO3) that facilitate communication. Therefore the government agency is engaged at a peak, state and grassroots level with sports in QLD (GO2, GO3). The Minister also has a good understanding of sport and recreation in QLD, a solid knowledge of his portfolio (GO2, GO3). There is a shared ethos between the department and the sports organisations and a common commitment to the development of sport in Queensland (GO2, GO3). While government is purchasing outcomes, at the same time it is seeking to achieve organisational growth in the agencies funded (GO2, GO3).

In programme 2, regional officers act as advisors to sporting clubs in regional areas—working one-on-one to develop them (GO2, GO3). 'In some ways the entire funding process is seen as an organisational development tool for delivering and achieving outcomes' (GO2, GO3). There is a research and development unit in the government agency that seeks to address the organisational development needs of organisations (GO2, GO3). This points to mechanisms which are more about process and learning (Ebrahim, 2010).

OUTPUTS

In terms of other outcomes, there has been a real reduction of red tape reporting, with reporting occurring yearly (SP4). The organisations self-assess against the funding objectives, which are based on their strategic plan anyway, and indicate why they were or were not able to achieve the objectives (SP4). The department is not concerned about micromanagement—as long as the outcomes are achieved (GO2, GO3). 'I mean they have generic objectives, but they are really similar to what we want to achieve anyway' (SP3). The key agendas have been identified by the government agency and these are addressed by organisations in their applications and strategic plans (SP4). However, they use the strategic plans of organisations as the justification for the funding need (SP3).

Performance is reported using both quantitative and qualitative reporting (GO2, GO3). Some outcomes are hard to quantify, but have benefits (e.g., working with a government agency/local council and providing some benefit to communities) (GO2, GO3). Increase in numbers is only part of the issue, as there may be a need to increase the capacity of the organisation in the first place, helping it to establish and fulfil its strategic plan (GO2, GO3).

In summary, this research finds the collaborative accountability approach is one involving high trust, mutual goal setting and an enabling of goals to meet a wider array of stakeholder, with negotiation allowed on a number of matters.

DISCUSSION AND CONCLUSION

Clearly there is a large difference between these two funding arrangements and the nature of the accountability enacted under each. This supports the assertion by Ebrahim that 'accountability is a relational concept; it varies according the relationships among actors' (2010, p. 104).

NPOs express considerable angst on multiple points concerning what we have termed the controlling accountability approach. Accountability to government in these sorts of relationships seems to typically operate from a principal-agent perspective, with accountability enacted in a hierarchical manner. The reality of much contracting in the third sector is that it occurs under the shadow of hierarchy (Héritier & Lehmkuhl, 2008; Schillemans, 2008), even though some of the ways that this is undertaken are likely to be ineffective (Romzek & Johnston, 2005).

The findings of this study concur with much of the literature on the controlling approaches to relationships where accountability often involves formal reporting of expenditure (Broadbent et al., 1996), onerous reporting of outcomes (Ebrahim, 2003a, p. 814) and a short-term focus (Seal, 2004; McGregor-Lowndes, 2008). Conflicted, controlling approaches had much more hierarchical accountability arrangements, whereas the collaborative approaches had far less onerous reporting, a pattern that Broadbent et al. (1996) predicted.

Thus the argument that accountability is enacted and structured in relationships (Bovens, 2010) would be supported by the findings of this study. Unfortunately, narrow focus on informational reporting in projects (Ebrahim, 2002) misses the learning, which should be inherent in the accountability process (Ebrahim, 2005).

The majority of government funding relationships evidenced strong differences in the beliefs and norms around what should happen. In contrast, in the two collaborative examples, there was an absolute, up front agreement—sport is good, and helping people with a disability is good, and the rest seemed to fall into place. This finding also supports Broadbent et al.'s (1996) understanding that congruence on values is related to higher trust in relationships, although it is difficult to determine causality.

While it may be tempting to ascribe poor relationships due to poor funding alone, this was not the tenor of the interviews and focus groups. Government historically subsidised, rather than paid for, the operations of NPOs (Lyons, 1993, 1998), so the shortfall in funding was not the critical issue. The larger issues noted in the findings were mismatch of objectives, understanding and philosophically how to achieve operations which affect each other, in addition to the resulting lack of trust. This too is reflected in the literature, as there is an underlying assumption inherent in the various definitions that NPOs have an obligation to provide an account to government for funding (Bovens, 2007, 2010). Broadbent et al. note the 'need to probe the unquestioned moral right of the economic principal *in all circumstances*' (1996, p. 277, original emphasis) to require an account. In order for a NPO to accept that it had to give an account, their accountee must be seen to have *legitimate* authority (Fung, 2003). Legitimacy is always accorded by others (Grafstein, 1981). The legitimacy of the claim made by government, or their right to enforce accountability for funds, when full cost is not paid, is in essence contested by NPO.

In terms of cognitive legitimacy (Suchman, 1995) with the competitive tendering, government seems to assume a cognitive taken for grantedness that they have the right to impose conditions on the contracts, and a principal/agent relationship, based as it is in NPM logic (Adams, 2000; Boyne, Gould-Williams, Law, & Walker, 1999; Hood, 1996; Mulgan, 1997). However, as in most cases where the full price for the services is not being paid, such assumptions are not necessarily warranted. One can hardly imagine a situation in which a government agency would contract a civil contractor to build a bridge, refuse to pay full price for the bridge, require the contractor to foot the rest of the bill and then place onerous, unfunded reporting expectations on the civil contractor. Such a situation would be laughed at, or end up in court. In fact, where another party is asked to pay for part of the asset, this would inevitably be set up as a form of relational contract (such as a PPP or alliance), as claims for control are not warranted (Deloitte, 2006; Infrastructure Australia, 2008; Willems & Van Dooren, 2011). It is for these reasons that McGregor-Lowndes (2008) argues more collaborative contractual relationships, such as joint ventures, are needed in the third sector as opposed to classic forms of contracting. The best that this competitive situation seems to hold is a pragmatic approach to legitimacy (Suchman, 1995), in that governments need NPOs to deliver services, and NPOs need governments for funding; so, a 'game' is played, although neither party is happy with the way the game is played (Koppenjan & Klijn, 2004).

These findings of conflicted accountability stand in stark contrast to the two cases perceived to be functioning well. In these cases, there was strong agreement on goals and values, implying that there was a moral legitimacy (Suchman, 1995) based on the high respect accorded by government and

Table 9.3 Summary of legitimacy issues in government/NPO accountability

	Controlling approaches	Collaborative approaches
Moral legitimacy	Lack of agreement means that this has not been achieved by government nor by nonprofits.	The agreement on goals seems to be the basis on which the relationship is built and the trust is formed.
Cognitive legitimacy	Assumed by both government and nonprofits, but not automatically afforded to each other.	Having agreed on the main goal, both parties accord each other an assumption that they both have a role.
Pragmatic legitimacy	Governments need NPO to deliver services and NPO needs government funding.	In order to help sport or disability, both government and NPO work together.

NPO to each other. Once this mutual respect was created, then cognitive and pragmatic legitimacy was not a problem, or at least was not contested. However, where there is low trust or where government is not acting truly as a principal, as they only partly fund the services being purchased, then the legitimacy of the claim being made is contested. The following table (Table 9.3) summarises this finding:

This chapter set out to explore how different types of accountability relationships involve different accountability mechanisms. First, the findings show that in highly collaborative accountability relationships, accountability mechanisms are often negotiated, while in relationships where there is low collaboration and high power differences, accountability mechanisms tend to be imposed by government. The research thus empirically supports the assertion of some authors that accountability mechanisms in the nonprofit sector are most properly understood in the context of relationships between organisations (Broadbent et al., 1996; Ebrahim, 2005, p. 60; see also O'Dwyer & Unerman, 2007).

Second, it supports the two main types of relationships that other authors have theorised (Broadbent et al., 1996), or found (Cordery at al., 2010): a controlling accountability relationship, or a collaborative accountability relationship. These two different types of accountability relationships exhibited markedly different accountability mechanisms, in a similar fashion to those found by Cordery at al. (2010). We would argue that the findings support our understanding of how relationships affect accountability between government and NPOs, as depicted in Figure 9.1.

Third, there is support for the argument that the way accountability is enacted in these different relationships will have an impact on legitimacy.

Finally, the suggestion that the demand for an account by the principal of an agent relationship can in some cases be questioned (Broadbent et al., 1996) finds an empirical voice here with a strong critique of the ability of government to make the demands it does, when not paying full price for services. In such circumstances the legitimacy of the claim of the principal over the agent is contested, as the principal is jointly funding the activity with the nonprofit organisation.

ACKNOWLEDGMENTS

Funding for this project was provided by the Myer Foundation. Our thanks also to two reviewers for their helpful feedback on earlier versions of the document.

NOTES

1   This chapter is dedicated to Professor Mark Lyons, who was a driving force in third sector research for a great many years and will be sadly missed.
2   NGOs are non-government organisations and are used by some authors in preference to NPO—nonprofit organisations. As these are quotations, the term NGO is retained.
3   Najam (1996b) lists patrons, clients and themselves, so properly Ebrahim's (2003) framework is one focusing on external accountability.
4   Contracts are termed in this report 'volume based funding,' which is funding provided subject to an agreement or contract specifying the volume of services to be delivered, and paid in proportion to the volume of services delivered.
5   Grants are termed 'transfers' in this report, and can be for general or capital expenditure, which may be provided under a funding agreement, but is not dependent on the delivery of a specified volume of services.
6   Pfeffer and Salancik (1978) discuss this point in some detail.
7   See McGregor-Lowndes (2008) for a discussion of these forms of contracts in government/NPO funding arrangements. See Seal (2004) for an extended discussion on accounting and accountability in these differing forms of contracts.
8   The regional focus group included additional representatives of organisations not necessarily nominated by peak groups.

REFERENCES

Adams, G. B. (2000). Uncovering the politcal philosophy of the new public management. *Administrative Theory & Praxis, 22*(3), 498–499.
Australian Bureau of Statistics (ABS). (2009). *Australian national accounts: Nonprofit institutions satellite account—2006/07* (Report No. 5256.0). Retrieved from http://www.ausstats.abs.gov.au/ausstats/subscriber.nsf/0/661F486077ACD 72BCA2576340019C6C8/$File/52560_2006-07.pdf
Benjamin, L. M. (2008). Account space: How accountability requirements shape nonprofit practice. *Nonprofit and Voluntary Sector Quarterly, 37*, 201–223.

Bode, I. (2012). Creeping marketization and post-corporatist governance: The transformation of state-nonprofit relations in Continental Europe. In S. Phillips & S. R. Smith (Eds.), *Governance and regulation in the third sector* (pp. 115–141). Hoboken, NJ: Taylor and Francis.

Bovens, M. (2007). Analysing and assessing accountability: A conceptual framework. *European Law Journal, 13*(4), 447–468.

Bovens, M. (2010). Two concepts of accountability: Accountability as a virtue and as a mechanism. *West European Politics, 33*(5), 946–967.

Boyne, G., Gould-Williams, J., Law, J., & Walker, R. (1999, October–December). Markets, bureaucracy and public management: Competitive tendering and best value in government. *Public Money & Management, 19*(4), 23–29.

Broadbent, J., Dietrich, M., & Laughlin, R. (1996). The development of principal-agent, contracting and accountability relationships in the public sector: Conceptual and cultural problems. *Critical Perspectives on Accounting, 7*(3), 259–284. doi: 10.1006/cpac.1996.0033

Broadbent, J., & Laughlin, R. (2003). Control and legitimation in government accountability processes: The private finance initiative in the UK. *Critical Perspectives on Accounting, 14*, 23–48.

Brown, K. A., & Ryan, N. (2003). Redefining government: Community relations through service agreements. *The Journal of Contemporary Issues in Business and Government, 9*(1), 15–24.

Brown, L. K., & Troutt, E. (2004). Funding relations between nonprofits and government: A positive example. *Nonprofit and Voluntary Sector Quarterly, 33*(1), 5–27.

Candler, G., & Dumont, G. (2010). A non-profit accountability framework. *Canadian Public Administration, 53*(2), 259–279.

Catlaw, T., & Chapman, J. (2007). A comment on Stephen Page's 'What's New about the New Public Management.' *Public Administration Review, 67*(2), 341–342.

Cordery, C., Baskerville, R., & Porter, B. (2010). Control or collaboration: Contrasting accountability relationships in the primary health sector. *Accounting, Auditing and Accountability, 23*(6), 793–813.

Deloitte. (2006). *Closing the infrastructure gap: The role of public-private partnerships*. NPD, Deloitte Research. Retrieved from http://www.infrastructureaustralia.gov.au/publications/files/Closing_the_Infrastructure_Gap-The_role_of_PPPs_Deloitte_2006.pdf

Demirag, I. (2004). Towards better governance and accountability: Exploring the relationships between the public, private and the community. *Journal of Corporate Citizenship, 15*, 19–26.

Dunleavy, P., & Hood, C. (1994). From old public administration to new public management. *Public Money & Management, 14*(3), 9–16.

Ebrahim, A. (2002). Information struggles: The role of information in the reproduction of NGO-funder relationships. *Nonprofit and Voluntary Sector Quarterly, 31*(1), 84–114.

Ebrahim, A. (2003a). Accountability in practice: Mechanisms for NGOs. *World Development, 31*(5), 813–829.

Ebrahim, A. (2003b). Making sense of accountability: Conceptual perspectives for northern and southern nonprofits. *Nonprofit Management and Leadership, 14*(2), 191–212.

Ebrahim, A. (2005). Accountability myopia: Losing sight of organizational learning. *Nonprofit and Voluntary Sector Quarterly, 34*(1), 56–87.

Ebrahim, A. (2009). Placing the normative logics of accountability in 'thick' perspective. *American Behavioral Scientist, 52*, 885–904.

Ebrahim, A. (2010). The many faces of nonprofits accountability. In D. O. Renz (Ed.), *The Jossey-Bass handbook of nonprofit leadership and management* (pp. 101–121). Hoboken, NJ: Wiley.

208 Furneaux and Ryan

Eisenhardt, K. M., & Graebner, M. E. (2007). Theory building from cases: Opportunity and challenges. *Academy of Management Journal, 50*(1), 25–32.

Fung, A. (2003). Associations and democracy: Between theories, hopes, and realities. *Annual Review of Sociology, 29,* 515–539.

Grafstein, R. (1981). The failure of Weber's conception of legitimacy: Its causes and implications. *The Journal of Politics, 43*(2), 456–472.

Héritier, A., & Lehmkuhl, D. (2008). The shadow of hierarchy and new modes of governance. *Journal of Public Policy, 28*(1), 1–17.

Hood, C. (1996). Beyond 'progressiveism': A new 'global paradigm' in public management? *International Journal of Public Administration, 19*(2), 151–177.

Infrastructure Australia. (2008). *National public private partnership guidelines.* Canberra: Australian Government. Retrived from: http://www.infrastructureau tralia.gov.au/public_private/files/National_PPP_Guidelines_Overview_Dec_08. pdf

Kearns, K. P. (1994). The strategic management of accountability in nonprofit organizations: An analytical framework. *Public Administration Review, 54*(2), 185–192.

Kearns, K. P. (1996). *Managing for accountability: Preserving public trust in public and nonprofit organisations.* San Francisco: Jossey-Bass.

Kettl, D. F. (2000). Public administration at the millenium: The state of the field. *Journal of Public Administration Research and Theory, 10*(1), 7–34.

Kitzinger, J. (1994). The methodology of focus groups: The importance of interaction between research participants. *Sociology of Health and Illness, 16*(1), 103–121.

Koppell, J.G.S. (2005). Pathologies of accountability: ICANN and the challenge of "multiple accountabilities disorder." *Public Administration Review, 65*(1), 94–108.

Koppenjan, J., & Klijn, E. H. (2004). *Managing uncertainties in networks.* London: Routledge.

Laughlin, R. C. (1990). A model of financial accountability and the Church of England. *Financial Accountability & Management, 6*(2), 93–114.

Lyons, M. (1993). The history of nonprofit organisations in Australia as a test of some recent nonprofit theory. *Voluntas, 4*(3), 301–325.

Lyons, M. (1998). Defining the nonprofit sector: Australia. In L. M. Salamon & H. K. Anheier (Eds.), *Working papers of the Johns Hopkins comparative nonprofit sector project: Comparative nonprofit sector project.* Baltimore: John Hopkins University. Retrieved from http://www.adm-cf.com/jhu/pdfs/CNP_Working_ Papers/CNP_WP30_Australia_1998.pdf

Lyons, M. (2003). Improving government-community sector relations. *Journal of Contemporary Issues in Business and Government, 9*(1), 31–42.

Lyons, M., & Dalton, B. (2012). A continuing love affair with the new public management. In S. Phillips & S. R. Smith (Eds.), *Governance and regulation in the third sector* (pp. 238–259). Hoboken, NJ: Taylor and Francis.

Lyons, M., & Passey, A. (2006). Need public policy ignore the third sector? Government policy in Australia and the United Kingdom. *Australian Journal of Public Administration, 65*(3), 90–102.

Maas, K.E.H., & Liket, K. C. (2010). Social impact measurement: Classification of methods. In R. L. Burritt, S. Schaltegger, M. Bennett, T. Pohjola, & M. Csutora (Eds.), *Environmental management accounting, supply chain management, and corporate responsibility accounting* (pp. 171–202). Dordrecht, NL: Springer Publishers.

March, J. G., & Olsen, J. P. (1995). *Democratic governance.* New York: New York Free Press.McGregor-Lowndes, M. (2008). Is there something better than partnership. In J. Barraket (Ed.), *Strategic issues for the not-for-profit sector* (pp. 45–73). Sydney: UNSW Press.

McGregor-Lowndes, M., & McBratney, A. (2011). Government community service contracts: Restraining abuse of power. *Public Law Review,* 22(4), 279–297.

Menefee, D. (1997). Strategic administration of nonprofit human service organizations. *Administration in Social Work,* 21(2), 1–19. doi: 10.1300/J147v21n02_01

Messner, M. (2009). The limits of accountability. *Accounting, Organizations & Society,* 34, 918–938.

Morgan, D. L. (1998). *Planning focus groups: Focus group kit 2.* Thousand Oaks, CA: Sage.

Mulgan, R. (1997). Contracting out and accountability. *Australian Journal of Public Administration,* 56(4), 106–116.

Mulgan, R. (2000a). Accountability: An ever expanding concept. *Public Administration,* 78, 555–573.

Mulgan, R. (2000b). Comparing accountability in the public and private sectors. *Australian Journal of Public Administration,* 59(1), 87–97.

Mulgan, R. (2003). *Holding power to account.* New York: Palgrave.

Najam, A. (1996). NGO accountability: A conceptual framework. *Development Policy Review,* 14(4), 339–354.

O'Dwyer, B., & Unerman, J. (2007). From functional to social accountability: Transforming the accountability relationship between funding and non-governmental development organisations. *Accounting, Auditing and Accountability Journal,* 20(3), 446–471.

Patton, M. Q. (2002). *Qualitative research and evaluation methods,* 3rd ed. Thousand Oaks, CA: Sage.

Pfeffer, J., & Salancik, G. R. (1978). *The external control of organizations: A resource dependence perspective.* New York: Harper Collins.

Productivity Commission. (2010). *Contribution of the not-for-profit sector.* Canberra, AU: PC.

Roberts, J. (1991). The possibilities of accountability. *Accounting, Organizations and Society,* 16(4), 355–368.

Roberts, J. (2001). Trust and control in Anglo-American systems of coporate governance: The individualising and socialising affects of process of ccountabilty. *Human Relations,* 54(12), 1547–1572.

Roberts, J. (2003). The manufacture of corporate social responsiblity: Constructing corporate sensibility. *Organization,* 10(2), 249–265.

Roberts, J. (2009). No one is perfect: The limits of transparency and an ethic for "intelligent" accountability. *Accounting, Organizations & Society,* 34(8), 957–970.

Roberts, J., & Scapens, R. (1985). Accounting systems and systems of accountability: Understanding accounting practices in their organisational contexts. *Accounting, Organizations and Society,* 10(4), 443–456.

Romzek, B. S. (2010). The tangled web of accountability in contracting networks: The case of welfare reform. In M. Dubnick & H. G. Frederickson (Eds.), *Accountable governance: Problems and promises* (pp. 22–41). Armonk, NY: M. E. Sharpe. Retrieved from http://site.elibrary.com/lib/qut/Doc?id=10448729& ppg=55http://site.elibrary.com/lib/qut/Doc?id=10448729&ppg=55

Romzek, B. S., & Johnston, J. M. (2005). State social services contracting: Exploring the determinants of effective contract accountability. *Public Administration Review,* 65(4), 436–449.

Saunders, M., Lewis, P., & Thornhill, A. (2000). *Research methods for business students,* 2nd ed. Harlow, UK: Pearson Education Ltd.

Schillemans, T. (2008). Accountability in the shadow of hierarchy: The horizontal accountability of agencies. *Public Organization Review,* 8(2), 175–194.

Scott, C. (2000). Accountability in the regulatory state. *Journal of Law and Society,* 27(1), 38–60.

Seal, W. (2004). Towards an enabling research agenda for the accounting/contracting nexus. *Accounting Forum, 28*(4), 329–348.

Seal, W., & Vincent-Jones, P. (1997). Accounting and trust in the enabling of long-term relationships. *Accounting, Auditing and Accountability, 10*(3), 406–431.

Sinclair, A. (1995). The chameleon of accountability: Forms and discourses. *Accounting, Organizations and Society, 20*(2–3), 219–237.

Spicer, M. (2004). Public administration, the history of ideas, and the reinventing government movement. *Public Administration Review, 64*(3), 353–362.

Suchman, M. C. (1995). Managing legitimacy: Strategic and institutional approaches. *Academy of Management Review, 20*, 571–610.

Tenbensel, T., Dwyer, J., & Lavoie, J. (2013). How not to kill the golden goose: Reconceptualizing accountability environments of third-sector organizations. *Public Management Review, 15*(2), 1–20. doi: 10.1080/14719037.2013.770054

Willems, T., & Van Dooren, W. (2011). Lost in diffusion? How collaborative arrangements lead to an accountability paradox. *International Review of Administrative Sciences, 77*(3), 505–530.

Young, D. R. (2000). Alternative models of government-nonprofit sector relations: Theoretical and international perspectives. *Nonprofit and Voluntary Sector Quarterly, 29*(1), 149–172.

10 What Costs Accountability? Financial Accountability, Mission and Fundraising in Nonprofits

*Benjamin J. Pawson and
Vassili Joannidès*

INTRODUCTION

Although greater calls for accountability have been articulated by academics, policy makers and donors in the recent years, a stream of thought has been questioning where the giving of an account should stop. In conveying limits to the giving of an account (Messner, 2009) and associated transparency (Roberts, 2009), critical accounting scholars have also pointed to as yet unresolved contradictions intrinsic to accountability (McKernan, 2012), especially when it comes to be operationalised (Joannidès, 2012). The impact of accountability's discharging on nonprofits' strategy or operations has to date been underexplored (Dhanani & Connelly, 2012; Tucker & Parker, 2013). Accordingly, this chapter seeks to contribute to this body of literature on the consequences of accountability on fundraising strategies in nonprofits, questioning whether accountability practice may hamper the effectiveness of the nonprofit sector by restraining the fundraising profession.

Our chapter seeks to fill a dual theoretical gap. Firstly, only a limited number of publications have investigated the interplay between accountability and the making of organisational strategy (Parker, 2002, 2003b, 2011, 2012, 2013; Tucker & Parker, 2013). Therefore, we seek to fill a theoretical gap as to the impact of accountability on the conduct of strategic operations. By questioning whether accountability hampers fundraising strategy in nonprofits we are also contributing to the literature balancing accountability and the mission. In this literature, it appears that money and the mission are often conflictual, financial managers being often seen by mission advocates as guardians shielding organisational resources (Chiapello, 1993, 1998; Lightbody, 2000, 2003). Another approach shows that making nonprofits accountable to capital and multiple stakeholders (donors, public authorities) leads to changes in organisational culture (O'Dwyer & Unerman, 2007; Unerman & Bennett, 2004; Unerman & O'Dwyer, 2006a, 2006b, 2008). By examining a small number of cases we show how accountability practices result in fundraising adapting and adjusting under such external pressures and constraints. We also show accountability systems may have a direct impact on the conduct of strategic operations, which might hamper mission conduct.

Our aim here, then, is to ask, 'what are the consequences of accountability to both money and mission for fundraising strategies'? To this aim, this chapter presents a small-scale exploratory qualitative study of seven fundraising managers selected from the state of Minnesota in the Unites States of America. This state has a history of concern with nonprofit accountability, particularly through the Minnesota Charities Review Council, who are active on a local and national policy level. Minnesota also presented the researchers ready access to quality sources of primary and secondary information from a wide, but not exhaustive, range of nonprofits. Our analysis is informed with grounded theory principles but does not claim to strictly follow the four canons of grounded theory, which, like Parker (2001, 2002), we take as: the interrelated collection of data and its analysis, the use of codes, concepts and categories; coding openly, axially and selectively, and the evaluation of resulting theories. This methodology revealed the cost of accountability may be a pervasive conservative and cautious attitude to fundraising, to the extent that we question if this is impoverishing the sector by inhibiting the ability to fulfil the stated missions.

The chapter is structured as follows. In the first section we position ourselves within the literature on accountability, fundraising and mission in nonprofits. Section two exposes our empirical findings, followed by a discussion thereof in section three and our conclusion.

CHAPTER POSITIONING

The knowledge debates addressed in this chapter and the means by which the study is conducted are exposed here.

Literature Review and Knowledge Debates

It is now well established in the literature that accountability is the 'giving and demanding of reasons for conduct' (Roberts & Scapens, 1985, p. 447). This relationship by which an organisation justifies the reasonableness of its actions and their outcomes can be built on conventional accounting systems and procedures as well as any other narrative practices (Roberts & Scapens, 1985; Scapens & Roberts, 1993). This practice includes meetings and talks with funders (Roberts, Sanderson, Barker, & Hendry, 2006). Whilst financial accountability in a private sector organisation seems to be commonly understood as addressed to its funders in the first place and then to society and the environment, the grounding of nonprofits in the community at large makes them accountable to a broad set of stakeholders (Gray, Bebbington, & Collison, 2006; Hulme & Edwards, 1997; Jayasinghe & Wickramasinghe, 2006; Lehman, 2007). These stakeholders are undoubtedly public, private and corporate donors (Unerman & O'Dwyer, 2006a, 2008), but also the 'public' at large (Lehman, 2007). It is commonly accepted that private sponsors donate so as to make sense of their CSR policy (Breman, 2006; Cooper & Owen, 2007; Unerman & O'Dwyer, 2007, 2008). Local governments donate to sustain territory dynamism through the discharging of public policy (Allen, 2009; Kreander, Beattie, & Mcphail, 2009; Rouse & Putterill, 2005). Supposedly, local governments, funding nonprofit benefits through taxes raised from citizens, focus on economy, efficiency and effectiveness of their donations (Reiden, 2001). Lastly, individuals can donate for altruistic reasons, especially when the project is social (Breman, 2006). Individuals may also donate because they like or believe in the purpose for which money is raised; e.g., acquisition policy or exhibition organisation in a museum (Christensen & Mohr, 1995, 1999, 2003; Thompson, 2001).

Nonprofits' accountability is multifaceted, addressed to numerous stakeholders with different agendas (Connolly, Hyndman, & McConville, 2013; Hyndman & McDonnell, 2009). Contrary to their raison d'être, serving the community, accountability demands on nonprofits drive more and more of those to spend time, energy and resources doing impression management in order to show a good image of their organisation and their actions (Dhanani & Connelly, 2012). The contents of the account addressed to these multiple donors can be summarised as the giving of evidence that the monies entrusted have been stewarded in an economical, effective and efficient way (Kluvers & Tippett, 2011; Reiden, 2001) with a particular emphasis placed on the match between origin, destination and actual use (Joannidès, Jaumier, & Hoque, 2014).

Accountability in nonprofits is therefore strongly associated with organisation mission (Chiapello, 1993, 1998; Lightbody, 2000, 2003; Parker, 2001, 2003a, 2003b, 2013; Tucker & Parker, 2013). Thus far, the balancing of mission and money has proved to be problematic in nonprofits because of conflicts and tensions between occupational groups with different agendas (Chiapello, 1993, 1998; Lightbody, 2000, 2003). On one hand, Lightbody (2000, 2003) shows that mission advocates in a church setting often see money and financial management as an undue constraint over the religious mission itself. On the other, Chiapello (1993, 1998) arrives at a similar conclusion, observing an artist's critique addressed to money, control and accountability in cultural institutions. Both Lightbody (2000, 2003) and Chiapello (1993, 1998) implicitly suggest that accountability in its essence and practice can affect how the mission is conducted. Apart from studies showing the interplay between financing and mission (Parker, 2003b, 2013; Tucker & Parker, 2013), this intuition has not been much further investigated since. Therefore, by extending Chiapello (1993, 1998) and Lightbody's (2000, 2003) intuitions, this chapter contributes to the understanding of how accountability can affect the conduct of strategic operations in nonprofits. Also, fundraising has not been much studied in the accounting literature, although this is a vital and strategic activity of nonprofits (Parker, 2012, 2013).

Mission is understood here as the societal need identified by the nonprofit but currently unserved by the market (Rosso, 2003). The satisfaction of that need is then the mission of that organisation. Donors whose interests align with the nonprofit's mission are targeted, acquired and asked to contribute time, talent or a gift (Sargeant & Shang, 2010). When soliciting these potential or recurrent donors, fundraisers explicitly cite that mission in the course of their work, exploiting psychological and sales tactics (Sargeant & Shang, 2010). The closure of a nonprofit due to mission satisfaction (Hager, 2001) being, one assumes, a desirable endpoint. Fidelity to that mission gives the fundraisers 'the privilege to ask for philanthropic support' (Rosso, 2003). As long as that mission remains unfulfilled by the activities of the nonprofit, fundraising and the mission are locked in a dance of ever increasing need. The mission-focused members of the organisation are constrained in achieving their goals principally by the resources supplied by the fundraisers.

Restraining the ability of fundraisers to solicit resources to execute the mission are the strict bounds of operation laid down by laws and the concept of donor trust (Bryce, 2007). The fundraiser has freedom within those bounds to exploit emotive factors such as sympathy, empathy, fear, pity and guilt, and the means to disseminate those messages via appetitive and aversive communications (Sargeant & Shang, 2010, p. 78); however, the fundraiser will meet consequences—declining donations, lack of support or legal sanctions for straying into either unpalatable or illegal methods (Kelly, 2012).

Implicit in all voluntarily donated resources is the promise that the donated funds will be used to further the mission of the organisation; even though the fundraiser is not explicitly responsible for the actions that satisfy the mission, 'fundraising cannot function apart from the organization; apart from the organization's mission, goals, objective, and programs; or apart from a willingness to be held accountable for all of the organization's actions' (Rosso, 2003).

Fundraisers therefore find themselves subject to an array of accountabilities, but divorced from the means to operationalise the mission the donors have subscribed to support. Both exhorted to raise the maximum resources possible to fund the mission and to do so efficiently and without breaking the law of the state or upsetting a fragile donor trust.

In spite of the vital nature of fundraising, the way these varied and sometimes conflicting accountabilities affect the formulation of fundraising strategy has been overlooked. This chapter therefore contributes an exploratory study toward filling this void.

Empirical Site and Research Methodology

The research topic is explored through the examination of fundraising practice and accountability demands in seven nonprofits, including a museum in

Minnesota, U.S. Minnesota presents a number of compelling practical, cultural and legislative reasons to situate a study there, as well as a history of nonprofit research (Bielefeld, 1992; Bies, 2001; Stone, Bigelow, & Crittenden, 1999). Willing participants were readily found by the researchers. Minnesota is also among states that require a high level of nonprofit reporting (Keating & Frumkin, 2003). We take this site as an *expressive case* (Berry, 2005), bringing to light phenomena or interrelations that are not equally visible in other settings. As such, the U.S. case serves to help reveal issues in fundraising and accountability in nonprofits more generally.

The study is informed with grounded theory principles (Strauss & Corbin, 1990, 1994, 1998). As grounded theory is more of a mindset than a research method (Efferin & Hopper, 2007; Joannidès & Berland, 2008; Parker, 2001; Parker & Roffey, 1997), we do not claim to strictly follow its four canons as outlined above. The questions asked were not influenced by any commitment to prior theory. They were the offspring of a pilot study revealing practitioners' concerns as to the intertwining of fundraising, mission and operations. In our questions we avoided the suggestion of a result or conclusion based in accountability. The open-ended questions addressed generic subjects around fundraising:

1. How did you come to be working as a fundraising professional?
2. How is fundraising strategy planned in your organisation?
3. What are the main methods of fundraising used?
4. What kind of reporting do you do and to whom?
5. Have you ever had to stop a fundraising method?
6. Have review agencies ever had any consequences for fundraising?

A wide range of answers was elicited, but recurrent responses readily emerged, indicating a degree of, but not complete, theoretical saturation.

Eight nonprofits were approached, seven responded. This resulted in a total of seven interviews, three face-to-face interviews and four telephone interviews conducted around a weeklong visit to Minneapolis in March of 2011. All interviews except one lasted a little less than one hour. Responses were anonymised using a correspondence table (manager 1, manager 2, etc.), with the authors retaining the key to track responses. Interviews were supplemented with secondary research on the seven organisations: annual reports, mission statements, a recent IRS Form 990 and data from Guidestar.com.

Table 10.1 gives an overview of the organisations by whom the fundraising managers interviewed are employed. The types of fundraising used are included, however it should be noted that there are large variations within these types. All organisations stated they had a yearly goal planning process.

The scope of the sample was tightly defined without losing contextual sensitivity, thus allowing open interview questions. Analysis and interpretation

Table 10.1 Fundraising methods used

				Fundraising methods used									
Ref	Income ($ M)	Mission area	FTE staff	Grants	Individual	Community	Statutory	Corporate	Earned	Interest on capital	Legacy	Years in fundraising	Careers before fundraising
1	1.8	Youth development	78	X	X	X	X	X	X		X	8	yes
2	23.4	Charitable foundation	3							X		8	yes
3	78.5	Theatrical venue	600	X	X		X	X	X			6	yes
4	67	Food bank	108	X	X	X	X	X	X		X	19	yes
5	21	Homelessness	166	X	X	X	X	X	X		X	12	yes
7	52.2	Art museum	261	X	X	X	X	X	X	X	X	20	yes
8	11.4	Care of the elderly	390	X	X	X	X	X	X		X	16	yes

should reveal the social properties of the mechanisms that are created by—and best observed in—those involved with them (Burr, 1995); later research may approach these issues from additional points of view. The analysis of the interview transcriptions roughly followed the spirit of the analytical process outlined by Strauss & Corbin (1990, 1994, 1998).

Of the seven interviews conducted, managers 2 and 3 provided the least pertinent data, manager 3 corroborating the climate of accountability; however, as a foundation, they are both a generator of funds and a funder to other nonprofits, demanding accountability, efficiency and adherence to mission. Manager 3 had only recently changed to a fundraising role. Therefore, five interviews provided the most pertinent data in this investigative study.

The data analysis phase used a sensitive reflection on the words, phrases and sentences used by the subjects. A mixture of a priori and inductive open codes were first used to assign units of meaning to the data; 'moral compass,' 'learning organization,' 'arrogance' and 'public trust' were some of the codes to emerge frequently. The most interesting codes emerged during the creation of reflective notes. For example, the code 'reflexive accountability' was attached to unprompted, sometimes insistent, responses from six of the eight interviewees declaring that annual financial reporting was available online.

Other codes were drawn from 'in vivo' words used by the subjects to represent important concepts or ideas; 'best practice,' for example, was mentioned by three subjects to legitimise choices. The central theme in the study emerged easily, but was not easily labelled; that of a pervasive sense of conservatism in reaction to perceived forces of financial accountability. This concept emerged in codes labelled 'caution,' 'restrictions' and 'humility.' Although in frequent (but not constant) conjunction with fundraising choices, these codes, finally labelled 'conservative,' often surrounded the rationalisations for making inclusion or exclusion choices about fundraising methods.

Outlying concepts, such as the idea of fundraising as a game, whilst interesting, were not related to our core concept and were rejected. There followed an iterative and recursive process of axial coding, facilitated using an online 'mind map' tool to visually organise concepts, categories and their properties and thus identify primary themes; this helped eliminate non-critical variations and duplications. Finally, selective coding refined and identified a strong cross-case theme of conservative fundraising choices and a notion of 'stewardship,' which extended to involve ideas of donor trust. These ideas manifested themselves in often anticipatory choices made to maintain a level of fundraising expense and thus efficiency that was deemed appropriate to a confected notion of the standards held by the multiple sources they felt accountable to.

Analysis was halted soon after new codes ceased to add any definition or utility, although with such a limited sample theoretical saturation cannot be claimed; for an exploratory study, a good level of data was attained.

EMPIRICAL FINDINGS

Role of Fundraising in Mission

In tracing the role of accountability to mission in fundraising policy we see the clearest evidence of impact in the internal planning and goal-setting negotiations. Here the mission advocates set the desired activities to be funded (this constitutes the 'for what' the fundraiser is accountable for). Yet this mission-oriented work is translated into monetary amounts that should be raised, in order for the mission-related goals to be accomplished in the given time period. Here a contradiction is raised; the fundraiser is judged almost purely in monetary terms, of amounts raised. However, the organisation is judged in terms of its mission success, a difficult notion to measure (Sawhill, 2001).

A spectrum of negotiations emerged between the mission advocates' desires, as a museum fundraiser stated when asked about the fundraising goal negotiation: 'curators may have dreams and big appetites about how much they would like to spend to curate 13 exhibitions in a year' (manager 7). This is countered with the fundraisers' follow-on anticipatory accounts of what could be plausibly achieved in respect of raising funds to enable those mission-achieving activities, as the same manager continued: 'some of those shows you are proposing have some potential, some of those have some limitations, based on the content' (manager 7). This must be achieved while remaining within the scope of acceptable fundraising choices, as outlined during a response to the reporting question: 'obviously if you don't meet the [Minnesota] charity review [council] standards that can have a bad effect on your fundraising' (manager 1). This negotiated planning process, elucidated by the questions on strategy setting, is entered knowing that they will be accountable during the report-giving phase to both the internal mission advocates and external stakeholders for the narrative of both generation and use of these donated resources: 'we make sure there's a very strong paper trail of donor intent and how we spend the money' (manager 7). Thus the fundraiser is burdened with additional accountabilities outside of its control.

The observed negotiations resemble an annual goal-setting process predicated on the primacy of the mission (Stone et al., 1999), but operationalised in monetary terms, a process familiar from for-profit, goal-setting exercises (Locke & Latham, 2002). This process has been found to encourage parties to under-promise anticipated performance in order to be able to more easily achieve the negotiated goals.

This process is framed within a fundraising function described as 'irrelevant and secondary' (Lightbody, 2000), yet strategically crucial to the accomplishment of the mission objectives. Fundraising is viewed as both strategic to the mission and yet secondary, a contradictory situation.

The observed range of negotiation approaches described when planning a fundraising strategy range from a dictatorial attitude ('there are some institutions where it's very top down, where the head of fundraising is told by the head of the organization or a CFO, someone 'this is what you need to raise') (manager 7) to those grounded in mission ('always start with a growth focus, because we have a mission growth focus you know, we always need to be growing the financial resources') (manager 5). Both attitudes relegate the fundraiser to a secondary support function. However, if this mandated growth is not delivered, the mission will not be accomplished. Other fundraising managers seek to enter into a more equitable negotiation during strategy formation:

> So we do have a conversation about it and we come to consensus, mutual consensus about what the goal is . . . we decide on the goals for each area and if we know we have to raise X amount for exhibitions this year how can we do it?
>
> (manager 7)

During these strategy negotiations we see, from the same source, that fundraisers next consider the choices about the ways that funding is sourced, the 'how' mentioned above. Key to this, we propose, is what various funders will accept as a plausible use of donated resources, which can cause friction from the mission advocates within the organisation:

> I remember once, one chief curator described the exhibition he was going to do and we told him that was not necessarily an exhibition that a corporation was likely to align their support with and we'd probably focus on individual support or a few foundations and he looked at us and he said 'you just told me my baby's ugly!'
>
> (manager 7)

Variants of this negotiation process were found in a majority of cases, and therefore it may have the capability of informing the manner by which the mission is executed, as Lightbody (2000, 2003) and Chiapello (1993, 1998) intuit. The fundraisers influence mission by raising or lowering blocks or modifiers to mission-focused activities when being tasked to solicit funds within a framework of accountability they are charged with operationalising. When asked about how strategy is formed one fundraiser responded:

> All of our fundraising goals are set in that budgeting process and then we create a fundraising plan to try and, you know, meet those goals.
>
> (manager 1)

By 'trying' to meet these goals there is an acknowledgment of the possibility of not being able to raise the funds as expected, which, purposefully or not, would have an effect on how the mission is conducted. An inverse method also observed is soliciting funds restricted to a specific project not included in the planned core budget. These project-only funding opportunities would bind the organisation to deliver specific services for the funder, and potentially result in 'mission creep' (Dolnicar et al., 2008), as portrayed here while listing the types of fundraising carried out:

> We do occasionally secure state federal grants for programs, we typically don't budget for those, and if we get them then we build the budget out for the particular program and that secures the work.
>
> (manager 1)

These ad hoc funding initiatives bring in revenue, but also require activities and accountabilities that may affect the mission's conduct after funding is secured by the fundraiser. As Lightbody (2000, 2003) and Chiapello (1993, 1998) intuit, accountability through fundraising can affect mission conduct. From mission-dictating fundraising goals, to fundraising influencing mission, fundraising is both powerful and powerless when it comes to mission.

Efficiency and Other Influences

The theme of efficiency is universal across all cases examined. Efficiency was elevated to such a stature that we believe it may act as a brake on the desires of the 'mission side of the house' (manager 5), as mentioned immediately in response to the strategy question:

> So, every year we go through a process to do our budgeting and planning not only what do we anticipate being able to raise but what will it cost us to raise it?
>
> (manager 4)

Including this efficiency factor in such early stages would seem to inherently limit methodological choices to those known and reproducible methods of fundraising, something we see confirmed later, as the same manager continues:

> . . . so that process begins with our budgeting. We as a team in advancement are doing an earlier process, done previously, so I am proactively engaging the organization earlier in that process. It's a part of how we make choices about where we spend our dollars, impacts what the advancement team can do in terms of bringing in new resources to the organization.
>
> (manager 4)

This then outlines another duality that fundraisers are accountable for both raising as much money as possible, but also doing so within ambiguous efficiency targets. In the scenario of the above mission-growth advocate quote, both growing resources and being efficient, we can see this as talking, as Messner (2009) suggests, in 'several different languages at the same time,' and we have to ask if it is moral to hold fundraisers to these 'multiple and conflicting accountabilities' (p. 919).

Moving to examine the rendering of accounts for behaviour *after* elapsed periods of time to internal users, we encounter three distinct demands for efficiency, first when asked what reporting they do:

> We certainly most definitely have a series of reports that we provide them each board meeting and one of the main ones of course is the fiscal year data both revenue and expenses closed, we'll sort of go back and show them how we do it.
>
> (manager 5)

Here the demands of meeting two kinds of targets are seen as being met by one person. Second, we see a demand for a different form of efficiency, as the same respondent continues:

> On a subset of that I have a development committee of the board and they're more interested in how we raised the money and what individual pieces are working well .
>
> (manager 5)

Third, we see a further demand for accounts of the constructed narrative of individual methods of fundraising, highlighting the importance of the choices the fundraiser has made:

> . . . and then I guess within our organization I guess there a partnership between myself and the chief financial officer to make sure that my revenue and my expense based on my income are aligned, does that make sense? In other words to make sure my return on investment is strong.
>
> (manager 5)

This third source holds the manager accountable to a standard that was not readily defined. Contrasting this with for-profit scenarios where Return On Investment (ROI) levels can be compared with internal rates of return, or external interest rates, makes this type of examination in a nonprofit environment fraught with disparate and subjective conceptions of acceptable levels of performance.

These levels of performance (financial, efficiency and mission attainment) are also exposed to and informed by a nebulous array of public stakeholders via public reporting. Although uniform financial reports are required by Minnesota state law and are available freely (they were included in background research for every organisation interviewed), every interviewer but one mentioned (unprompted) their annual report and/or audited accounts, and their availability online. This almost defensive impression of management to an interviewer with almost no stakeholder rights perhaps tells of a crippling level of fear of being seen to not be wholly accountable and transparent. Offering an explanation of this anticipatory level of accountability (Kearns, 1994), proactive industry bodies are highlighted during a discussion of other issues outside the main questions:

> Independent Sector does some great work, they've been really proactive. So when I talk about some of that stuff that came into nonprofit work with, well . . . alignment to Sarbanes Oxley for example they are very proactive in taking the nonprofit community and saying you know folks, we need to be front of this or we're going to have stuff imposed on us that we don't like and we want to be better at our jobs, and we want our donors to trust us so were gonna do the right thing.
>
> (manager 4)

This is perhaps a manifestation of a concern with projecting an image of efficiency. One subject, when asked about these bodies, explicitly draws the link between an external examining body and fundraising performance, stating that

> obviously if you don't meet the [Minnesota] charity review [council] standards that can have a bad effect on your fundraising .
>
> (manager 1)

Although the literature is inconclusive about the effect of standards compliance on donation levels (Tinkelman & Mankaney, 2007), deference to these external review bodies was exhibited. The flawed methodology used by these examiners was highlighted by two subjects whose organisations had unorthodox financial structures. The elevated stature of the Minnesota Charities Review Council could be a consequence of the smaller distance between demander and provider of accounts (Roberts & Scapens, 1985). The Council's voluntary standards of conduct contain loose recommendations for operational efficiency (70–90% of funds used for mission programmes) and make a demand for compliance accountability (Kearns, 1994).

The Minnesota Charities Review Council is a vocal proxy for that most diffuse stakeholder, the public, which contributes to the economic benefit of tax exemption that is given to all qualifying nonprofits. Focused advocacy, press attention and the attitude of fundraisers however lend it a direct impact on fundraising and via that, the conduct of organisational mission. Similarly, funders with a higher stakeholder role attained through the size of their gifts also have an impact and receive individual explanatory accounts (Benjamin, 2008), summarised well here:

That board of trustees of 40 people, we put an enormous amount of effort and energy and are transparent to the point where we do lunch tutorials for our board members.

(manager 7)

One fundraising manager also expressed that during reporting: 'we hope to engage these funders in the real conversation of what's going on' (manager 1). This infers another level of dialog beyond the reporting of financial accounts to a complex, human narrative of change (Dhanani & Connelly, 2012), and a personal dialog of social impact and of helping achieve the mission with those donated resources. Thus the choices made by a fundraiser and the impacts of those choices are scrutinised in multiple ways, by multiple examiners, often with disparate agendas of efficiency, stewardship and mission attainment.

Impact on Fundraising Strategy

This leads us to ask how those fundraising choices are made and what factors (mission, income level, efficiency or perception of efficiency) determine the fundraising choices that form the narrative that is accounted for. If we see the factors of accountability eclipsing mission-oriented motivations in the strategic activities of fundraising, does this diminish the utility of the fundraiser in pursuit of a mission?

All of our fundraising goals are set in that budgeting process and then we create a fundraising plan to try and, you know, meet those goals.

(manager 1)

Looking again at this statement we now see an acknowledgment of the plurality of 'those goals,' some of which we have outlined here. Analysing the data in search of a response to this reconciliation of mission-driven goals and multiple accountabilities, we see a theme of conservative choices emerge from the data. For example, when asked how a strategy is formulated one fundraising manager responded, 'so we look at the money and we try to make educated bets, you know, to what's going to be reproducible' (manager 4). This recurrent dependency on reliable results from fundraising strategy readily emerged from the research data. With little variation, 'cautious optimisation' of existing fundraising methods seemed to be the dominant model of meeting the multiple and conflicting accountability demands placed on the fundraiser; to mission, to donors, to management and to a nebulous public via a range of public and industry agencies. This is summarised succinctly in the following quotes about the way choices are made: 'finding what we do well and doing it better' (manager 4), 'you have to pick the things that you know can have a big impact' (Manager 5), 'don't break things that work' (manager 4) and 'how we make choices, we look at our history, what we're good at what we're strong at, how do we invest more and get more value out of that which we're already good at' (manager 4).

To examine the mechanism of these decisions and to determine the role of accountabilities in them the interviewed managers were asked about individual choices regarding specific fundraising methods. When asked about decisions by nonprofits to stop some forms of fundraising, responses highlighted the axiomatic need for fundraising efficiency. This was prompted, we propose, by the financial accountabilities named earlier, for example:

> At one point we did telemarketing out of house, then we hired people and they came into the [building] itself and we did that from our office versus an external firm then we stopped that as well when the rate of return wasn't high enough for the work involved, we decided that's not worth our energy so that's something we have not done for years.
>
> (manager 7)

The rate of return, we assume, is that required to maintain acceptable notions of efficiency. Most fundraising managers had examples of stopping fundraising vehicles, and cited similar reasons. Events, printing annual reports and donor gifts all were explicitly curtailed with an explanation of reduced return in the face of expectations of efficiency. New fundraising vehicles were chosen only if a clear precedent existed and procedural guidance from others could be taken and used to provide an anticipatory account of an acceptable level of return. Themes of benchmarking and best practice also emerged in this area. For example, here we see reticence to launch a new form of fundraising from within the fundraising team, and best practices being used to reassure staff internally that returns would be high enough to satisfy the demands created by the needs of accountability, to make this new form of fundraising 'work':

> I need to do a little bit more homework on my side because my team is a little sceptical, I mean they're open, they just wanna understand just what is really the investment were gonna need to make this work, that said I think we could be looking at some very high six figure regular annual revenue streams for this organization, and it could be secured— you know if I look at some of the kind of best practices in that area— within a four or five year window.
>
> (manager 4)

Other sources used to assure success and avert failure include industry bodies, affiliates and industry press. Best practice was again referenced when one subject talked about a new planned giving programme in response to the question on fundraising methods used:

> Obviously universities and larger institutions are very good at planned giving, they often have a full staffs of people and that's all that they do,

so we're going to be working this year on putting together materials and just letting people know that they can make plans to give .

(manager 1)

The observance of best practices in the process of selecting new fundraising forms could be seen as a form of professional accountability (Sinclair, 1995), a lateral duty to a set of 'approved' behaviours defined in the body of professional knowledge. This lateral accountability may restrict experimentation and innovation by only endorsing forms of fundraising that will succeed, and therefore avoid the risk of high fundraising costs and the ensuing internal and external censure.

Another emergent theme used to rationalise conservative choices was branded 'stewardship' by one respondent, an apt summarisation of the type of behaviours and attitudes exhibited by many managers questioned. Responses demonstrating these 'stewardship' characteristics (and thus motivations for conservative behaviour) range from information security, to exhibiting a personal accountability discourse (Sinclair, 1995). This personal discourse is exhibited in a statement about stopping types of fundraising, specifically discontinuing a donor 'thank you' gift that was deemed unacceptable: 'I just couldn't stomach spending 2000 dollars on gifts, I just didn't think it was good stewardship' (manager 8). This clearly personal discourse, 'stomaching' actions, is expanded on by the following quote regarding a question about any other current accountability issues of note. This personal discourse is used to justify actions above that are required by organisational policy, or legislation; again, anticipatory conservative actions to preserve donor trust:

A lot of my day is about transcribing conversations. What do I transcribe? What do I store? I only store information that's immediately pertinent A) information that the donor has shared in a way indicating that the donor is comfortable with, self revealing that information B) that it's absolutely relevant to the discussion of the gift and that it's not hearsay, it's not a story that they are telling me about somebody else, it's not documenting gossip as it were. So there's some of that stuff as well, which isn't necessarily policy per say but it's how we start to think about work and how we protect our greatest asset, which is donors trust. Which is the only way that we can do our work.

(manager 4)

This very personal and complete rendering of a fundraising manager's conduct is above any external legal requirement of data capture and is not defined in an organisational policy. Here we are in the realm of individual anticipatory standards of behaviour, a model of idealised moral behaviour and 'just in case' actions enacted to maintain donor trust, but at what cost? The same respondent goes on to add:

> I mean there certainly are costs to documenting and processing infor-
> mation, you know to the extent that it's things that reinforce peoples'
> trust in the organization, that's to the good to the extent that it rein-
> forces good practices and behaviours on the part of organizations and
> individuals within them, that's to the good I think.
>
> (manager 4)

Here we may have arrived at a core motivation for the conservative measures we have seen in the nonprofits studied. Donor trust is perceived as too
valuable to even contemplate losing. Therefore, actions which may endanger it are excluded. Donor trust is present in the literature as a key factor
driving accountability (Bryce, 2007; Sloan, 2009). Donor trust seems to be
a universally valuable asset, yet is undefined and unquantified outside of
personal impression but seems to be a valued input for decision-making.

These anticipatory actions are interpreted as examples of what Benjamin
sees as funders 're-establishing their legitimacy in the face of some crisis,'
and 'one concrete way in which structures or institutionalized aspects of
behaviour or practice are affirmed' (2008, p. 208). However, although the
form of the account given here is different to that which Benjamin describes,
the role remains the same; to maintain or re-establish credibility in the face
of the media, academic and legal calls for increased accountability.

We have observed a concern for accountability manifested in a desire to
portray efficiency and to uphold a notion of external, reactive, yet undefined
donor trust. In other words, we see that 'the concern for accountability
ends up "colonizing" the conduct of the accountable self' (Messner, 2009,
p. 919).

Although we saw a wide spectrum of methods for rendering accounts and
some varying attitudes caused by organisational size, brand and character,
the same range of accountabilities affected all nonprofits studied. Regardless
of these differences, all the nonprofits demonstrate caution and low-risk
tolerance in fundraising policy.

DISCUSSION AND CONCLUDING THOUGHTS

The role of fundraisers in accountability relationships between nonprofits
and their donors seems not to have attracted much academic interest. Correlatively, the impact of accountability demands on fundraisers' work has
to date been underexplored. This chapter fills this dual gap in the literature
and makes two contributions to knowledge.

Fundraiser's Schizophrenic Accountability

Our first contribution to knowledge lies in two paradoxes surrounding
fundraisers' perceptions of their own accountability. First, as the fundraising

literature abundantly suggests, fundraising managers see their activity as strategic to the mission: they must prove that they are capable of raising funds enabling it to conduct its mission (Anheier & Salamon, 1996; Anthony & Herzlinger, 1975; Anthony & Young, 1984; Brown & Caughlin, 2009; Kearns, 1994; Niven, 2008; Zietlow, 1989). This is expected to be visible in the amount of money raised by the organisation on one hand and its individual fundraisers on the other (Anthony & Herzlinger, 1975; Anthony & Young, 1984), in terms of efficiency; i.e., measures of funds raised over the cost of fundraising with an upper limit that should not be exceeded (Anheier & Salamon, 1994, 1996). Or, more rarely, accountability is discussed as their capability of raising exactly the amount of money needed for the purpose of the mission (Joannidès et al., 2014).

As well as internal negotiations we have shown it is fear of these stakeholders, and their potential impact on fundraising operations and thus mission conduct, that discourages risky behaviour. Repeatable fundraising methods and vehicles with known or proven results and efficiencies are preferred. These accountability pressures come down to the fundraisers from nearly all directions, above from financial directors, from subordinate colleges, sideways from a profession and externally from a spectrum of sources, most concernedly from a media keen to report abuse but disinterested in stories of efficient and exemplary nonprofit conduct. Thus, fundraisers find themselves talking multiple languages with numerous internal and external stakeholders. Inevitably pressure from external stakeholders also makes them accountable to capital (Gray et al., 2006). Our case also outlines that the contribution of external donors, vital to a nonprofit organisation, leads fundraising managers to not only speak their language but embrace their concerns. That is, whilst fundraising is central and strategic to the conduct of the mission, fundraisers tend to be more and more focused on the efficiency of their activity. This phenomenon is particularly vivid in that they view their accountability in terms of return on assets, equity or investment, viz. measures resonating with operations in for-profit organisations.

The second paradox we observe is the fundraising managers' impression to be perceived by mission advocates as strategic and irrelevant at the same time. From their viewpoint, their activity is deemed to enable the mission at the same time as it undermines it. In other words, the paradox is that fundraising is the condition of possibility for the mission's execution at the same time as the condition of its impossibility. The literature usually arrives at either conclusion, showing how fundraising is central to the mission (Anthony & Herzlinger, 1975; Anthony & Young, 1984; Sargeant & Shang, 2010; Van Der Heijden, 2013). Or, when tensions between mission advocates and a financial occupational group occur, these are often ascribed to the recent extensive financialisation of accountability, even in nonprofits where calls for greater accountability have resulted in a shift from operational to financial accountability to donors seen as quasi-investors (Chiapello, 1993,

1997, 1998; Lehman, 2007; Lightbody, 2000, 2003; Unerman & O'Dwyer, 2006a, 2006b).

Our case furnishes a possible explanation of this paradox: fundraisers see their activity as strategic to the mission. But, in essence, their duties give them a dual identity and therefore dual accountability—internally to organisation members for the mission and externally to donors for efficiency. This forces them to talk in many languages (Messner, 2009) to engage and assure an array of supporters, addressing internal voices and the concerns of their own profession. Given nonprofits' reliance on donations, they find themselves adopting an outwardly oriented financial stance, but find it difficult to reconnect inwardly to other voices' concerns, i.e., mission advocates'. Increasing accountability demands cause a form of professional schizophrenia (Roberts, 2009) among fundraising managers who, confronted with those unresolved contradictions, find themselves talking the language of finance and efficiency knowing, albeit, it is not always appropriate or desirable.

The Impact of Accountability on Fundraising Strategies

Our second contribution can be found in the accountability pressures that affect fundraising strategies and ultimately the conduct of mission. We first observe that innovative projects are discouraged, as some conventional donors are unlikely to fund them. Fundraising managers, in their now schizophrenic behaviour, are confronted with a major dilemma. One option is that they privilege accountability to the mission and engage in fundraising strategies for innovative and brave projects. In this case, conventional solicitation practices are unlikely to be appropriate, leading them to develop alternative ways of collecting resources, risking efficiency. This proves very risky as they would be navigating in a swamp with lurking crocodiles. Failing at collecting sufficient funds would ultimately endanger the mission. The second option is that they privilege accountability to known donors and negotiate for the mission to be conventional and audible to traditional stakeholders. In this case, the quasi-guarantee of collecting sufficient resources hampers mission innovativeness and may reduce the likelihood of success.

It is their reaction to this dilemma that shows how multiple accountability demands affect fundraising strategies and the choice of methods as well as vehicles. Fear of these stakeholders and their potential impact on fundraising operations, and thus mission conduct, discourages a risky mission. Our case does not show the other side of the coin where fear of internal stakeholders would lead to the opposite response. This concurs with the idea that external stakeholders, by being capital holders and providers, tend to be hegemonic over nonprofits, imposing their accountability agenda (Gray et al., 2006; Unerman & O'Dwyer, 2008). Consequently, the choice of fundraising methods and vehicles appears to be dictated more by external stakeholders' agendas than by the mission itself. This observation enables us to further understand the aforementioned paradoxes surrounding fundraising activities: if fundraising strategy precedes the mission and this latter is subordinated, soliciting external financial support is irrelevant.

CONCLUSION

This chapter seeks to answer the question of whether accountability practice, to both money and mission, is hampering the effectiveness of nonprofit practice by restraining the fundraising profession. In other words, we are addressing what the cost of accountability is for the nonprofit organisation. So doing enables us to contribute to a debate initiated by Messner (2009) on whether accountability is always unambiguously desirable. Whilst this discussion has been initiated at a macro-social and philosophical level, this issue has to date not been addressed in the specific case of nonprofits. Beyond traditional discussions surrounding tensions, conflicts or misunderstandings between a financial occupational group and mission advocates, the exploratory cases studied here show how accountability demands cause these frictions. Hence, in the guise of an answer to the question asked in this chapter, we can say that accountability has two costs. On one hand, accountability demands, especially when they are multiple, lead to the impoverishment of the mission conduct. On the other hand, the pressures on fundraising managers from accountability demands result in tensions between them and mission advocates, ultimately resulting in conservative fundraising choices.

These two contributions to exposing the costs of accountability to both money and mission call for further research in three areas. First, our conclusions should be taken cautiously as they result from an exploratory study based predominantly on only five of the seven respondents interviewed. Accordingly, we call for further research on the interplay between accountability, fundraising and mission in a much broader perspective. Second, we call for further exploratory research on other types of nonprofits in sports or social work in order to verify the reach of our conclusions. Third, our case study is circumscribed within a particular cultural and legal setting, Minnesota, where pressures exerted by donors might be exacerbated as compared to other locales. Accordingly, we suggest further research should explore the interplay between accountability, fundraising and mission in varied cultural settings.

REFERENCES

Allen, P. (2009), Restructuring the NHS again: Supply side reform in recent English health care policy. *Financial Accountability & Management*, 25(4), 373–389.

Anheier, H., & Salamon, L. (1994). *The emerging sector: The nonprofit sector in comparative perspective. An overview.* Baltimore: The John Hopkins Sector Series.

Anheier, H., & Salamon, L. (1996). *The emerging nonprofit sector: An overview*. Manchester: Manchester University Press.

Anthony, R. N., & Herzlinger, M. (1975). *Management control in nonprofit organizations*. Homewood, IL: Richard D Irwin, Inc.

Anthony, R. N., & Young, D. W. (1984). *Management control in nonprofit organizations*. Homewood, IL: Richard D Irwin, Inc.

Benjamin, L. M. (2008). Account space: How accountability requirements shape nonprofit practice. *Nonprofit and Voluntary Sector Quarterly, 37*(2), 201–223.

Berry, A. (2005). Accountability and control in a cat's cradle. *Accounting, Auditing & Accountability Journal, 18*(2), 255–297.

Bielefeld, W. (1992). Funding uncertainty and nonprofit strategies in the 1980s. *Nonprofit Management and Leadership, 2*(4), 381–401.

Bies, A. L. (2001). Accountability, organizational capacity, and continuous improvement: Findings from Minnesota's nonprofit sector. *New Directions for Philanthropic Fundraising*, 51–80.

Breman, A. (2006). *The economics of altruism, paternalism and self-control* (PhD dissertation). Stockholm School of Economics, Stockholm, SE.

Brown, E., & Caughlin, K. (2009). Donors, ideologues, and bureaucrats: Government objectives and the performance of the nonprofit sector. *Financial Accountability & Management, 25*(1), 99–114.

Bryce, H. J. (2007). The public's trust in nonprofit organizations: The role of relationship marketing and management. *California Management Review, 49*(4), 112.

Burr, V. (1995). *An introduction to social constructionism*. London: Routledge.

Chiapello, E. (1993). *Le contrôle de gestion dans les organisations artistiques*. Paris: Université Paris Dauphine.

Chiapello, E. (1997). Les organisations et le travail artistiques sont-ils contrôlables? *Réseaux, 86*, 77–113.

Chiapello, E. (1998). *Artistes vs. managers: Le management culturel face à la critique artiste*. Paris: Seuil.

Christensen, A. L., & Mohr, R. M. (1995). Testing a positive theory model of museum accounting practices. *Financial Accountability & Management, 11*(4), 317–335.

Christensen, A. L., & Mohr, R. M. (1999). Nonprofit lobbying: Museums and collections capitalization. *Financial Accountability & Management, 15*(2), 115–133.

Christensen, A. L., & Mohr, R. M. (2003). Not-for-profit annual reports: What do museum managers communicate? *Financial Accountability & Management, 19*(2), 139–158.

Connolly, C., Hyndman, N., & McConville, D. (2013). UK charity accounting: An exercise in widening stakeholder engagement. *The British Accounting Review, 45*(1), 58–69.

Cooper, S. M., & Owen, D. L. (2007). Corporate social reporting and stakeholder accountability: The missing link. *Accounting, Organizations and Society, 32*(7–8), 649–667.

Dhanani, A., & Connelly, C. (2012). Discharging not-for-profit accountability: UK charities and public discourse. *Accounting, Auditing & Accountability Journal, 25*(7), 1140–1169.

Dolnicar, S., Irvine, H., & Lazarevski, K. (2008). Mission or money? Competitive challenges facing public sector nonprofit organisations in an institutionalised environment. *International Journal of Nonprofit and Voluntary Sector Marketing, 13*(2), 107–117.

Efferin, S., & Hopper, T. (2007). Management control, culture and ethnicity in a Chinese Indonesian company. *Accounting, Organizations and Society, 32*(3), 223–262.

Gray, R., Bebbington, J., & Collison, D. (2006). NGOs, civil society and accountability: Making the people accountable to capital. *Accounting, Auditing & Accountability Journal, 19*(3), 319–348.

Hager, M. A. (2001). Explaining demise among nonprofit organizations abstract. *Nonprofit and Voluntary Sector Quarterly, 30*(4), 795–796.

Hulme, D., & Edwards, M. (Eds.). (1997). *NGOs, states and donors: Too close for comfort?* Basingstoke, UK: MacMillan in association with Save the Children.

Hyndman, N., & Mcdonnell, P. (2009). Governance and charities: An exploration of key themes and the development of a research agenda. *Financial Accountability & Management, 25*(1), 5–31.

Jayasinghe, K., & Wickramasinghe, D. (2006). Can NGOs deliver accountability? Predictions, realities and difficulties. In M. Abdel-Kader (Ed.), *NGOs: Roles and accountability: Introduction*. Delhi, IN: Institute of Chartered Financial Analysts (ICFAI).

Joannidès, V. (2012). Accounterability and the problematics of accountability. *Critical Perspectives on Accounting, 23*(3), 244–257.

Joannidès, V., & Berland, N. (2008). Reactions to reading 'remaining consistent with methods? An analysis of grounded theory research in accounting'—a comment on Gurd. *Qualitative Research in Accounting & Management, 5*(3), 253–261.

Joannidès, V., Jaumier, S., & Hoque, Z. (2014). The making of accountability: An ethnography of the Salvation Army. In Z. Hoque & L. D. Parker (Eds.), *NGO's accountability and performance*. Melbourne: Emerald Group Publishing.

Kearns, K. P. (1994). The strategic management of accountability in nonprofit organizations: An analytical framework. *Public Administration Review*, 185–192.

Keating, E. K., & Frumkin, P., (2003), Reengineering nonprofit financial accountability: Toward a more reliable foundation for regulation. *Public Administration Review, 63*(1), 3–15.

Kelly, K. S. (2012). *Effective fundraising*. London: Routledge.

Kluvers, R., & Tippett, J. (2011). An exploration of stewardship theory in a not-for-profit organisation. *Accounting Forum, 35*(4), 275–284.

Kreander, N., Beattie, V., & Mcphail, K. (2009). Putting out money where their mouth is: Alignment of charitable aims with charitable investments—tensions in policy and practice. *The British Accounting Review*, in press.

Lehman, G. (2007). The accountability of NGOs in civil society and its public spheres. *Critical Perspectives on Accounting, 18*(6), 645–669.

Lightbody, M. (2000). Storing and shielding: Financial management behaviour in a church organization. *Accounting, Auditing & Accountability Journal, 13*(2), 156–174.

Lightbody, M. (2003). On being a financial manager in a church organisation: Understanding the experience. *Financial Accountability & Management, 19*(2), 117–138.

Locke, E. A., & Latham, G. P. (2002). Building a practically useful theory of goal setting and task motivation: A 35-year odyssey. *American Psychologist, 57*(9), 705.

McKernan, J. (2012). Accountability as aporia, testimony and gift. *Critical Perspectives on Accounting, 23*(3), 258–278.

Messner, M. (2009). The limits of accountability. *Accounting, Organizations and Society, 34*(8), 918–938.

Niven, P. R. (2008). *Balanced scorecard step-by-step for government and nonprofit agencies*. London: Wiley and Sons.

O'Dwyer, B., & Unerman, J. (2007). From functional to social accountability: Transforming the accountability relationship between funders and non-governmental development organisations. *Accounting, Auditing & Accountability Journal, 20*(3), 446–471.

Parker, L. D. (2001). Reactive planning in a Christian bureaucracy. *Management Accounting Research, 12*(3), 321–356.

Parker, L. D. (2002). It's been a pleasure doing business with you: A strategic analysis and critique of university change management. *Critical Perspectives on Accounting, 13*(5–6), 603–619.

Parker, L. D. (2003a). Financial management strategy in a community welfare organisation: A boardroom perspective. *Financial Accountability & Management, 19*(4), 341–374.

Parker, L. D. (2003b). Financial strategic management in a community welfare organisation: A Boardroom Perspective. *Financial Accountability & Management, 19*(4), 341–374.

Parker, L. D. (2011). University corporatisation: Driving redefinition. *Critical Perspectives on Accounting, 22*(4), 434–450.

Parker, L. D. (2012). From privatised to hybrid corporatised higher education: A global financial management discourse. *Financial Accountability & Management, 28*(3), 247–268.

Parker, L. D. (2013). Contemporary university strategising: The financial imperative. *Financial Accountability & Management, 29*(1), 1–25.

Parker, L. D., & Roffey, B. (1997). Methodological themes: Back to the drawing board: Revisiting grounded theory and the everyday accountant's and manager's reality. *Accounting, Auditing & Accountability Journal, 10*(2), 212–247.

Reiden, R. (2001). *Improving the economy, efficiency, and effectiveness of not-for-profits: Conducting operational reviews.* London: Wiley and Sons.

Roberts, J. (2009). No one is perfect: The limits of transparency and an ethic for 'intelligent' accountability. *Accounting, Organizations and Society, 34*(8), 957–970.

Roberts, J., Sanderson, P., Barker, R., & Hendry, J. (2006). In the mirror of the market: The disciplinary effects of company/fund manager meetings. *Accounting, Organizations and Society, 31*(3), 277–294.

Roberts, J., & Scapens, R. (1985). Accounting systems and systems of accountability—understanding accounting practices in their organisational contexts. *Accounting, Organizations and Society, 10*(4), 443–456.

Rosso, H. (2003). A philosophy of fund raising. In H. Rosso (Ed.), *Achieving excellence in fund raising.* San Francisco: Jossey-Bass.

Rouse, P., & Putterill, M. (2005). Local government amalgamation policy: A highway maintenance evaluation. *Management Accounting Research, 16*(4), 438–463.

Sargeant, A. (1999). Charitable giving: Towards a model of donor behaviour. *Journal of Marketing Management, 15*(4), 215–238.

Sargeant, A., & Shang, J. (2010). *Fundraising principles and practice.* San Francisco: Jossey-Bass.

Sawhill, J. C. (2001). Mission impossible?: Measuring success in nonprofit organizations. *Nonprofit Management and Leadership, 11*(3), 371–386.

Scapens, R. W., & Roberts, J. (1993). Accounting and control: A case study of resistance to accounting change. *Management Accounting Research, 4*(1), 1–32.

Sinclair, A. (1995). The chameleon of accountability: Forms and discourses. *Accounting, Organizations and Society, 20*(2–3), 219–237.

Sloan, M. F. (2009). The effects of nonprofit accountability ratings on donor behavior. *Nonprofit and Voluntary Sector Quarterly, 38*(2), 220–236.

Stone, M. M., Bigelow, B., & Crittenden, W. (1999). Research on strategic management in nonprofit organizations synthesis, analysis, and future directions. *Administration and Society, 31*(3), 378–423.

Strauss, A., & Corbin, J. (1990). *Basics of qualitative research: Techniques and procedures for developing grounded theory.* Newbury Park, CA: Sage Publishing.

Strauss, A., & Corbin, J. (1994). Grounded theory methodology: An overview. In N. K. Denzin & Y. S. Lincoln (Eds.), *Handbook of qualitative research*. Thousand Oaks, CA: Sage Publishing.

Strauss, A., & Corbin, J. (1998). *Basics of qualitative research: Techniques and procedures for developing grounded theory*. Thousand Oaks, CA: Sage Publishing.

Thompson, G. D. (2001). The impact of New Zealand's public sector accounting reforms on performance control in museums. *Financial Accountability & Management, 17*(1), 5–21.

Tinkelman, D., & Mankaney, K. (2007). When is administrative efficiency associated with charitable donations? *Nonprofit and Voluntary Sector Quarterly, 36*(1), 41–64.

Tucker, B., & Parker, L. (2013). Out of control? Strategy in the NFP sector: The implications for management control. *Accounting, Auditing & Accountability Journal, 26*(2), 234–266.

Unerman, J., & Bennett, M. (2004). Increased stakeholder dialogue and the internet: Towards greater corporate accountability or reinforcing capitalist hegemony? *Accounting, Organizations and Society, 29*(7), 685–707.

Unerman, J., & O'Dwyer, B. (2006a). On James Bond and the importance of NGO accountability. *Accounting, Auditing & Accountability Journal, 19*(3), 305–318.

Unerman, J., & O'Dwyer, B. (2006b). Theorising accountability for NGO advocacy. *Accounting, Auditing & Accountability Journal, 19*(3), 349–376.

Unerman, J., & O'Dwyer, B. (2007). The business case for regulation of corporate social responsibility and accountability. *Accounting Forum, 31*(4), 332–353.

Unerman, J., & O'Dwyer, B. (2008). The paradox of greater NGO accountability: A case study of Amnesty Ireland. *Accounting, Organizations & Society*, in press.

Van Der Heijden, H. (2013). Small is beautiful? Financial efficiency of small fundraising charities. *The British Accounting Review, 45*(1), 50–57.

Zietlow, J. T. (1989). Capital operating and budgeting practices in pure nonprofit organizations. *Financial Accountability & Management, 5*(4), 219–232.

11 Patterns of Boardroom Discussions Around the Accountability Process in a Nonprofit Organisation

Vassili Joannidès, Stéphane Jaumier and Zahirul Hoque

INTRODUCTION

This chapter sets out to identify patterns at play in boardroom discussions around the design and adoption of an accountability system in a nonprofit organisation. To this end, it contributes to the scarce literature showing the backstage of management accounting systems (Berry, 2005), investment policy determining (Kreander, Beattie, & Mcphail, 2009; Kreander, Mcphail, & Molyneaux, 2004) and financial planning strategizing (Parker, 2003) or budgeting (Irvine, 2005). The paucity of publications is due to issues raised by confidentiality preventing attendance at those meetings (Irvine, 2003; Irvine & Gaffikin, 2006). However, often, the implementation of a new control technology occurs over a long period of time that might exceed the duration of a research project (Quattrone & Hopper, 2001, 2005). Recent trends consisting of having research funded by grants from private institutions or charities have tended to reduce the length of such undertakings to a few months or rarely more than a couple of years (Parker, 2013; Parker & Guthrie, 2005). It is structurally difficult to conduct such research projects, unless the researcher is a field actor and attends meetings and discussions in that capacity (Berry, 2005; Irvine, 2005; Joannidès, 2012; Joannidès & Berland, 2013; Parker, 2003). As research usually studies existing accountability systems, this chapter contributes to knowledge by showing how an accountability process within a nonprofit organisation is decided upon, tested and enriched until it is implemented effectively.

This study draws on *The Making of Law: An Ethnography of the Conseil d'État* (Latour, 2002, 2009)[1] as a theoretical framework and is informed with an ethnography of the Salvation Army in France. Like Parker (2003), Kreander et al. (2004, 2009), Berry (2005) or Irvine (2005), this study relies on the involvement of one of its authors in a faith-based charity. More precisely, this chapter borrows from his experience in the making of an accountability system to public authorities between 2000 and 2008 in the French Salvation Army. Accordingly, this research was done in the triple capacity of researcher, Salvationist and personal counsellor[2] on accountability to the organisation's CEO ('Territorial Commander' in Salvationist terms). Interested in discussions and decisions, we consider the accountability system's implementation phases and working do not fall within our remit and should not be discussed in this study. Latour's (2002, 2009) insights enable us to show how a problem is *qualified* in order for solutions to be collectively discussed. In the making of law as applied to the making of accountability, collegiality and unanimity are fostered by discussions surrounding, not the technical merits of a solution, but the predictability and manageability of its implications. Once an accountability system is decided upon, its actual implementation and function are left to those who will practice it on a day-to-day basis. The solution is tested at each stage as new concerns arise, enabling its makers to reconsider it, alter it or enrich it until no new issues emerge.

The remainder of this chapter is organised in the following way. Section two positions the theoretical basis of the chapter. Section three outlines the research methodology adopted. Section four reveals the findings of the study. The final section discusses the findings and presents its conclusion.

THEORETICAL FRAMEWORK

Latour's (2009) ethnography of the *Conseil d'État* (the French Supreme Court) sets out to understand how jurisprudence is formed; i.e., what the state of discussions among judges and attorneys are. Contrary to first instance tribunals or courts of appeal, discussions at the *Conseil d'État* are conducted behind closed doors. Latour's (2009) work, through borrowing several concepts from actor-network theory, does not fit into the traditional canons of this otherwise well-known approach (Callon, 1985, 2009; Callon & Rabeharisoa, 2008; Latour, 1996, 2005). In particular, notions of human or nonhuman actors, as well as controversies, are absent, for Latour seeks to understand how magistrates make a collective decision that will be enforced by others and will be universally applied.

The making of law by the *Conseil d'État* is a process by which some actors share their construing of a normative project and come to a consensus as to how this interpretation should be delineated into a general and universally enforceable rule. This process commences with a question relating to the litigation of a *problematic case*: i.e., a new case that finds no solution in the existing laws or jurisprudence. It is a case that apparently first instance tribunals or courts of appeal have not been able to solve. It resorts to the *Conseil d'État* that a practical and perennial solution should be found. Latour (2009) observes that all counsellors involved are driven by the same objective to find that holy grail.

The solution is subject to the constraint that law is a consistent whole reflecting society's political orientations and must therefore remain consistent with prior legislation as to fit into the current legal system. As a consequence, the problem must first be *qualified*: the judges and attorneys must conceptualise the problem beyond the submitted case. That is, they identify why it is a problem and what are the concerns to society. Interviews conducted with the institution's members reveal that it is the condition under which commissioners can envisage a general and generic solution that will apply to all subsequent similar cases. Latour (2009) observes how a future taken-for-granted solution (i.e., a blackbox) is being made.

Latour (2009) finds that society's interest is superior to that of those actors who altogether serve the public good. Probably because a superior interest is threatened, institution members do not pursue any individual strategy. They rather tend to perpetuate the *Conseil d'État* as a *nonhuman* actor capable of enrolling ministers and MPs. This means the *Conseil d'État* 'cannot be incarnated by one person. A nonhuman may be a group of humans who cannot be identified individually and cannot have an individual existence per se. Functioning as a black box the group has its own identity and can enrol new allies or interact with other actors' (Joannidès & Berland, 2013). This means, Latour (2009) notes, any solution found by the *Conseil d'État* is the offspring of a collegial decision accentuated by the fact that the judgment is rendered 'in the name of the French People' without the names of those who partook in the decision being known.

Once the problem is collectively qualified and understood by *the Conseil d'État*, two rapporteurs are appointed to examine the case and propose technical solutions presented for discussion. A technical solution has two aspects: the jurisdiction's doctrine expressed in legal terms justified by explicit references to the philosophical assumptions that drive French values. The justification can thereby be so a-temporal that the solution will apply without risking it to be obsolete.

When gathered as a formation, the judges collegially test each rapporteur's solution against current thinking. In the first place, the proposal's technical robustness is discussed: judges test its consistency with the current French legal system and philosophy. If the solution successfully passes that step, its possible consequences for society and citizens' day-to-day life are envisaged. As discussions progress, either solution becomes detached from the rapporteur who articulated it and becomes the *Conseil d'État's* work in progress. A proposal whose consequences are too uncertain or unmanageable is commonly rejected because it is viewed as a possible cause for a new case. Conversely, when social, economic, political and legal consequences and ways of coping with those have been identified, the solution is adopted without a vote; it is a gentlemen's agreement.

The final solution appears as a judgment rendered *in the name of the French People* and commences with general philosophical concerns relating to the problem as qualified in the boardroom. Proceeding from these general concerns the case is described and the problems are qualified. Subsequently, the motives are revealed. At the end of the bill, the decision is rendered: a general and universal statement is articulated and followed by the *Conseil d'État's* interpretation thereof with some suggestions relating to its enforcing. Through this process, Latour (2009) notes that discussions are always courteous and reveal neither ambiguities, nor controversies or translation processes as in other contexts, like the production of scientific knowledge.

Although a-temporal and universal, the solution to the problem is not cast in stone. Until the *Conseil d'État* admits it can be taken for granted and then worked like a blackbox, the adopted solution needs to go through a more or less lengthy probation. As new cases occur, these trial the reasonableness of the solution's applicability. This new case either significantly challenges the initial settling, thereby calling for a very different solution and causing a shift in case law, whereby the new decision will go through the same process. Or, the new case raises new questions, calling for clarification or enrichment of the decision made. In response to this new case, the *Conseil d'État* articulates complementary solutions which unsurprisingly make marginal changes, specifications or nuances to the originally rendered case law.

The *Conseil d'État* never suggests clear, working practicalities as to the implementing and enforcing of the judgment thence rendered. Doing so would make the decision context-bound and no longer a-temporal and universal. Therefore, its operationalisation is the responsibility of grassroots civil servants, elected representatives and magistrates confronted with similar cases. As a consequence, Latour (2009) notes that the making of law is a non-linear but incremental process based on simulations and real-life trial-errors.

By drawing on the notion of law's making, this chapter follows Latour's (2009) steps and focuses on how the need for an accountability system arises. We thereby assume that a problematic case confronts an organisation urged to find a practical and sustainable solution. We then emphasise how the problem is *qualified* and how solutions are discussed, decided upon, tested and ultimately adopted by those at whom it is directed. Like Latour (2009), we deliberately consider practical implementation beyond the scope of our study. Also, consistent with Latour's leitmotif, we follow the actors and tell the story as subject matters and surrounding issues (Latour, 1996). That is, the empirical tale chronologically revolves around the emergence of a problem, the discussing, testing and adopting of an accountability system.

RESEARCH METHODOLOGY

Ethnography

Like Latour (2002, 2009) with the making of law, we have rested this research project on a rich ethnography of one single organisation: the Paris Salvation Army's Headquarters between 2000 and 2008. Our research slightly differs from Latour's (2002, 2009) as one of these research team members was involved in the making of accountability where *The Making of Law*'s author was an observer rather than an active participant. This co-author spent two days each week at the Salvation Army Territorial Headquarters in Paris for the entire period where he volunteered as a counsellor to successive Territorial Commanders. This was possible because he was a Salvation Army member attending a Parisian congregation, as well as a graduate in public policy and law and an emerging scholar working on accountability. In this triple capacity, that author was initially responsible for informally advising the Territorial Commander on legal issues specific to France, which could affect the functioning of the Salvation Army in its domestic environment. In this capacity, he attended numerous meetings organised by the Territorial Commander's cabinet. Soon after he started volunteering for the cabinet, the Salvation Army was urged by the government to adopt an accountability system, so that our colleague found himself involved from the beginning as a response to this need.

When any concerns were raised by the Salvation Army management at the time of reporting to public authorities, the researcher found himself involved from 2000 onwards in discussions surrounding the choice and follow-up of an accountability system. As such, he proposed an agenda, and organised numerous meetings with all actors directly concerned in finance and accountability issues, namely the Chief Operations Officer, Chief Finance Officer (CFO), Chief Accountant, Secretary for Quality, Secretary for Volunteering, Secretary for Evangelisation, Secretary for Social Work and a representative from the congregations. He also duly reported these meetings to the Territorial Commander and discussed with him the possible consequences of decisions that had been made. Also, as a soldier committed to a congregation in Paris, this researcher volunteered another two days every week for the day-to-day coordination of activities and people at the grassroots. In this capacity, he had privileged and unlimited access to most of the Salvation Army's volunteers, churchgoers and employees, accumulating thousands of hours of valuable interactions.

In this capacity of a Salvationist-researcher-counsellor, he attended numerous meetings with all actors involved in the making of accountability. He also gave workshops on the issue within the Salvation Army in France and overseas. After attendance at each event, he drafted memos summarising what had occurred and giving his fresh impression in the joint capacity of a counsellor, regular member and researcher. He also conducted hundreds of informal talks with other churchgoers, ministers, former ministers, volunteers, social workers and social home managers. Most talks revolved around the accountability demand articulated by French authorities.

Dataset

The researcher kept a research diary daily which consisted of memos relating to every single event, meeting and informal or formal talk with actors.

Furthermore, every meeting organised at the Headquarters was recorded, transcribed and then stored in the Salvation Army's library. Mail and email exchanges with the Territorial Commander and the various actors involved, as well as internal documents relating to the coordination of people and activities, were also compiled.

A total of 26 open-ended interviews were conducted with Salvation Army leaders, ministers, managers, employees and other volunteers. Interviewees were asked to explain their accountability practices and the extent to which these could fit with accountability requirements from public authorities. We sought to confirm with our interviewees that we clearly understood the issues confronting the Salvation Army.

This step consisted of periodically submitting our work to our informants, inviting them to explain how they had formed their opinion and adopted this or that stance on accountability during those meetings. The arguments received from these interviews were then compared to those transcribed in the meetings' minutes. If our interpretation of facts differed from that of our informants in such a way they would not recognise themselves, the situation or the Salvation Army, we asked for arbitration from another Salvationist. If that third party confirmed our interpretation, we considered it fair to the organisation. If he or she confirmed our informant's interpretation, we revised our text with them accordingly. Secondly, the arguments developed in this chapter were intended to provide an explicit and direct account of these boardroom discussions of the choice and follow-up of a system of accountability to public authorities.

The Research Site

The Salvation Army was founded in 1867 in London's poor districts by a Methodist pastor, William Booth. His life as a Methodist minister was driven by his past apprenticeship at a pawnbroker's shop where he could see how people fall into social trouble and could barely rise above such hardship. Disgusted by these social ravages, he was appointed as a minister in the UK Methodist Church, and concerned himself about helping those in need. Over time, as the church was attended by the higher-middle class and some upper-class people, he was shocked to see that poor people were perceived as troublemakers and no longer welcome. He therefore quit the UK Methodist Church and decided to found a congregation to save their soul, salvation being freely offered by God to everybody, provided they respond to His calling (Booth, 1890; Le Leu, 2001; Sandall, 1947; Walker, 2001; Watson, 1964). To this end, the Salvation Army furnishes temporary emergency aid with its 'soldiers' offering food to the poor so that they do not starve and may hear the Gospel (Sandall, 1947, 1950, 1955). This mission was expanded to provide broader material emergency support, including catering, clothing and temporary accommodation (Winston, 2000). Vocational social work allows social 'outcasts' to recover their dignity and hygiene as human beings. Nowadays, it includes all kinds of actions aimed at restoring people's dignity and humanity (Brigou, 1994).

In this dual capacity as a denomination and registered charity, the Salvation Army has historically organised its activities around spiritual coaching and social work such as soup kitchens, social housing, training and coaching holiday camps (Watson, 1964; Wiggins, 1960, 1968). According to its founder's theology, churchgoers must be involved in their church's social work either as volunteers or employees (Booth, 1890; Joannidès, 2012). Social work with no religious foundation would make very little sense to the Salvation Army, as that would not align with its identity. In turn, spiritual coaching with no social work would also not be consistent with the Salvation Army's identity. Over decades, the organisation has accumulated substantial know-how and expertise in the provision of social work, so that numerous governments in the world rely on its ministers, social workers and employees to delineate national social policies. Conscious that funding social work is highly reliant on private donors or government agencies, William Booth rested his theology on a religious and moral imperative of financial stewardship and accountability to those third parties. He thereby argued that accountability to God can be discharged on earth through financial discipline and accountability to donors (Howson, 2005; Irvine, 2002). This led the Salvation Army year after year to erect accountability as part of its belief system and accounting as part of day-to-day religious conduct (Joannidès, 2009, 2012), like Ferguson has in the Iona Community (Jacobs & Walker, 2004).

In 2012 the Salvation Army had 5 million soldiers with 10 million churchgoers attending 77,000 congregations worldwide. Consistent with its theology, the Salvation Army is a registered charity in these countries and aids 50 million needy people every year (Salvation Army, 2012). As a major partner of governments, the Salvation Army is financed mostly through public funding, amounting up to 76% of its resources in countries like France, where public money accounts for about €98 million of a total of about €130 million in funding (Salvation Army, 2012).

FINDINGS

Problem Identification: Management and Laïcité

The story begins in June 2000; the Territorial Commander organises a meeting with members of his cabinet; i.e., the CFO, the Chief Operations Officer, the Chief Accountant, the Secretary for Volunteering and the academic counselling him. At the opening of the meeting, he shares with us a major concern of his:

> As you know, auditors from the Home Office visited us last month. They dissected all our processes, namely inspecting our homes in order to see how we manage to keep religious matters in a strictly private

realm. In their report to the Home Minister and the Minister for Social Affairs, they stressed a major ambiguity in how we do things and conduct our mission . . . *Laïcité* is our legal constraint. Supposedly the Salvation Army should no longer be funded by public authorities. But, in our capacity as a major partner of the Ministry for Social Affairs, the government has found a solution: our social work can still be funded but our religious activities cannot. This will be the case under the condition we find a way of proving that the money we received is used for social work only. Accordingly, this meeting's purpose is to reflect on such a solution. The good news is that auditors still commend our way of doing conventional financial reporting. I must admit the Salvation Army has been used to doing that since it was founded.

Until that day, accountability for *laïcité* seemed not be a concern for the French Salvation Army, as none of the government's auditors ever raised the issue. Based on the day-to-day implications of the organisation founder's theology, they had already been producing financial statements. Unexpectedly, *laïcité* emerged as an issue central to Salvationist accountability and therefore required an appropriate response from the organisation. Used to producing financial reports, the Salvation Army could find such a solution in accounting procedures and technologies.

Accountability did no longer appear as the mere formal disclosure of financial figures but compliance with and accounting for French *laïcité*, a philosophy unique to France (Rémond, 1999, 2005, 2006). This principle has been erected as a constitutional principle since 9 December 1905, when the French Parliament issued a bill separating state from religion. This bill's first paragraph states,

> the Republic does neither recognise, nor employ nor fund any worship. Consequently, every expense related to the practice of a religion will be hidden from the budget of the State, counties and municipalities.

Recognising no religion results in the French authorities granting no monies to religious denominations, whatever the purpose is. This principle was reaffirmed by a bill passed by the French Parliament on 10 February 2004 and numerous court cases where the *Conseil d'État* had to clarify this philosophy's reach, and arbitrated cases (Latour, 2009).

A religious organisation, the Salvation Army must adhere to the 1905 bill and apply it. Given that organisation practices had been deviating from this principle's prescriptions, one could have expected the government would stop funding the Salvation Army. Due to the Army's know-how and expertise in undertaking social work, cutting its resources could endanger government social policy. This could explain why auditors acknowledged the quality of conventional financial reporting as an encouragement to find practical solutions proving at all times that public money is used just for social work.

In the case of the Salvation Army, religious and secular activities are intimately intertwined, as visible in its motto: *Soup, Soap, and Salvation* (Booth, 1890). Social work is not devoid of religious proselytism because the provisions of food (*soup*) and care (*soap*) are actually considered a prerequisite for souls in difficulty to become receptive to God's message (*salvation*).

However, this, in the minds of the representatives of the Ministry for Social Affairs, can be considered social work and thus deemed as secular. This would determine any activity that should be provided for by any other non-religious charity. Anything which would not fall within this scope would be seen as religious. French Salvationists rely on such distinction in order to make sense of the Ministry's expectations regarding public funding, a distinction that their familiarity with the concept of *laïcité* contributes to make palpable.

Problem Qualification: Need to Account for Laïcité

As the problem was identified, board members were to understand its general implications beyond the mere legal or technical issue raised by the auditors. They were to conceptualise it in such generic terms that a perennial solution could be found, rather than one that is just scratching the surface. A legal and quasi-constitutional constraint, *laïcité* could not be conceived as a problem. Rather, it is the extent to which operations comply with it and the way this is proved in a systematic manner that was problematic to auditors. Based on the Army's experience at producing financial reports, it seems that the pertinence of such conventional means of accountability are ineffective at responding to the demand and cannot operate as a valid solution; the CFO commented,

> for my part, there is nothing more I can do. I prepare financial statements complying with financial reporting standards for non-profits. As these apply to all charities there is no way we can prove how money is used . . . For the past two years, I have prepared a more comprehensive annual report in which all our activities and their budgets are detailed. But I must confess I can't tell which of these are religious or social.

Problem qualification revealed that financial reporting qua the conventional means of accountability was in this situation not appropriate for discharging accountability to public authorities. Whilst in this case the government is concerned about *laïcité*, conventional reporting standards apply to the not-for-profit sector as a whole and do not take the Salvation Army's specifics. Therefore, an additional report had been produced for two years to clarify some of these, but apparently not sufficiently to fulfil auditors' demands, as it was still impossible to distinguish between social and religious activities. Detail about these seemed to be critical to the Salvation Army situation. The CFO further explained the situation:

If we want to be exhaustive, we will be unintelligible. We have so many programmes that the report would be too long and not clear. . . Definitely, I confirm we must find some other way of proving that public money was used for social work only.

Apparently, conventional financial reporting and annual reports were part of the problem and not the solution, as these did not give a clear and pertinent account of the Salvation Army's actions. Addressing the Chief Accountant and his team, the CFO suggested,

obviously, the solution is beyond my realm . . . I am sure management accounting can provide us with a solution. I don't know how as yet but have good hope they can do it.

Once *identified*, the problem was conceived as the need for proving, through management accounting technologies, the effectiveness of public money use. *Laïcité* was not the problem in itself but the case raising it. *Qualified*, the problem was that an alternative to traditional financial reporting is needed. As no solution could be found on the spot, the Territorial Commander decided to form two groups of four people headed by one rapporteur. The researcher was not involved in either of these; but in his capacity as a counsellor and soldier interested in accountability he had discussed these issues with the Territorial Commander and advised him on their implications for the Salvation Army. Three months later, another meeting was held where the two groups revealed their solutions to the *laïcité* issue and had their options discussed.

Solutions to Problems

Each solution was discussed immediately after being revealed, so the board could make a collegial decision and disincarnate them. The two options were never compared, each of them being discussed for its own virtues regardless of other possibilities. Ultimately, however, it is the one deemed optimal by the board that is accepted.

OPTION 1: DIFFERENTIATION OF ACTIVITIES AND DIRECT ACCOUNTING

The first group, whose rapporteur was the Secretary for Social Work, articulated a solution directly addressing the problem as collectively *qualified*:

We suggest splitting the Salvation Army into two legal entities: a denomination funded by its members, soldiers and visitors, and focusing on evangelisation on one hand and a registered charity collecting public money and using it for social work only on the other.

Differentiating these activities through two legal bodies (*denomination* and *charity*) would result in no overlap between them, assuming that would make any misuse of public resources impossible. The Secretary for Volunteering supported his explanations by describing the new accountability structure and classification of territorial activities. According to his explanations, the Salvation Army should entirely reconsider its organisation, the conduct of its dual mission—*denomination* and *charity*—and the coordination of its activities. The solution would lie in a major change in organisational form.

Such a differentiation would make distinguishing between religious and social activities clear. An activity relating to religious purposes would be under the direct auspices and sole responsibility of the denomination whilst vocational or volunteer social work would be supervised by the charity. Participants all agreed that this would also perfectly match the scope of the two auditors' concerns. Home Office auditors would easily trace the use of public monies for social work. For their part, auditors from the Ministry for Social Affairs would follow up the completion of social work.

Participants viewed management accounting as a natural offspring of this solution: direct resources and costs would be associated with the concerned entity. Public monies would be directed to the charity and its social work whereas congregations would collect money for the denomination from their members (soldiers and other visitors). As funds would be separately raised and spent by each body, any expense would be incurred by a programme managed by the body that raised the monies needed for its completion. Although none of the participants called this solution such, it would resemble a form of direct accounting for resources and expenses.

Notwithstanding its capability of fixing the *laïcité* issue, the new accountability structure had major implications that had not yet been envisaged. Three questions were left unanswered, a soldier representing the Parisian congregations at those meeting highlights:

> I see three issues in what you suggest we should do. Firstly, is it normal that the daughter [charity] replace and order the mother [denomination]? What will happen is that the denomination is subordinated to the charity, which is not consistent at all with what William Booth wanted. The second problem I see is that the denomination and the charity will no longer be working together, making the Salvation Army a charity like any other. Lastly, I can see how the charity is funded, fair enough; I see how the denomination is funded. But I do not understand how you consider funding the Headquarters—or at least the Territorial Commander's Cabinet.

All participants suddenly became conscious of new problems that would arise if these consequences were not averted. In response to the first two concerns, the Territorial Commander took promise before the assembly, expecting to reassure them concerning the risk of Salvationist identity being undermined by loose or absent cooperation between social work and religious activities: 'under my responsibility, the Territorial Headquarters will direct and coordinate the two bodies.' However, this general promise accompanied with no concrete, working practicalities left some participants perplexed and others unconvinced. Ambivalence vis-à-vis that promise was aggravated by the third implication of solution as highlighted by the soldier: common expenses and indirect costs, especially those incurred by the Headquarters, would remain unfunded. It was a breakthrough in the discussion when the Territorial Commander guaranteed a solution for the interim:

> The International Salvation Army can subsidise Territorial Headquarters and fixed overheads in countries where they cannot find resources on their own. I have spoken to the General and he agrees to fund us until the end of his term within 5 years. But this solution is not perennial.

This third source of funding would be the condition of possibility for the differentiation of activities and thus the implementation of direct accounting. Although this option provided a solution to the *qualified* problem, it put the Salvation Army at risk of losing its identity and was subject not to be financially viable in the long term. This solution was therefore not deemed optimal; its long-term consequences could not be envisaged. Participants agreed not to adopt it. It was now time for the second rapporteur to present his solution.

OPTION 2: LABELLING AND ACCOUNTING FOR SOCIAL AND RELIGIOUS PROGRAMMES

The second group, whose rapporteur was a former consultant in strategy now working as the Secretary for Quality, commenced by reassuring the audience:

> With our solution, there is no change in terms of how we do our work. We guarantee that Salvationist identity is preserved. Our solution has no impact on the Salvation Army's structure. We suggest we should list all our activities and labelling them either *social* or *religious*. Let's take a concrete case where we can comply with *laïcité*: chaplaincy in social homes is clearly *religious* whereas a holiday camp organised by a congregation is obviously *social*. Here, it doesn't matter who is doing what; we care about the nature of the activity considered: *social* or *religious*.

Worries relating to the first option's implications are immediately dismissed: unsustainable funding over time and risk of losing organisation identity would be of no concern. This second option would have other implications for the Salvation Army as the Secretary for Quality explains, displaying on a screen the value chain as he talked. *Social* and *religious* are two strategic links that must be intertwined, hence the Salvation Army's value chain must be upheld by a comprehensive, working accounting of its various activities organised in clearly identifiable responsibility centres. This would commence with an exhaustive list of these activities and assigning of *Social* or *Religious* labels in a database accessible to everybody. The Headquarters would raise funds for the Salvation Army as a whole and allocate public monies for all activities labelled *social* in the database. In turn, monies collected from non-governmental sources would be allocated for activities labelled *religious*, and common expenses. Although apparently complex, this solution borrows from the logic of activity-based accounting insofar as activities consumed by the processes constituting the organisation's value chain need to be clearly identified as cost drivers. In this case, cost drivers would be the label associated with a programme and the origin of its funding. Although not calling this management accounting solution activity-based accounting, this option's practicalities resonated with that approach. The Secretary for Quality further explained that utilising this methodology, the Salvation Army would be in a capacity of accounting for the way its activities use public resources:

> Concretely, each of the religious and social labels should be separately accounted for by the CFO. That is, the *social account* is credited with monies given by public authorities or donors specifying they are donating for social work. On the other hand, funds granted with no purpose or donated by our soldiers go into the *religious account*. It will then be easy to make both budgets comply with *laïcité* principles. That of religious activities can be based only on resources available on the *religious account*. In turn, the budget for social work will rest on the monies held in the *social account* . . . Our solution also envisages the possibility of cooperation between the charity and the denomination. As we have labels driving programmes, these latter, may they be *social* or *religious*, can be conducted indifferently by the denomination or the charity. The difference would lie in the origin of funds and the expenses authorised only within these two accounts. In order to make sure there is no overlap at all, it is crucial to make transfers from one account to the other impossible.

By labelling activities and programmes *social* or *religious* and assigning them to a separate account at the Headquarters, money allocation would be aligned with fundraising, regardless of who applies for which resources. In this way, activities would be funded on the basis of their label, not of the applicant itself, so that the *qualified problem* could have a working solution. Salvationist identity would not be undermined, as the two pillars of its action would cooperate. This solution would not prohibit joint activities, as each would be accounted for and financed separately. Thus a minister could undertake *social* activities financed by public monies, just as a social worker could consume *religious* activities (e.g., chaplaincy in a home) funded by private funds. All participants saw as an immediate consequence the need for implementing another layer of accounting matching origins and use of resources based upon the activity consuming them, thereby envisaging the implications of this solution.

Although option 2 seemed to respond to the problem initially *qualified* and anticipate all its major implications for the Salvation Army, its practical working would be left to congregations and homes. As this would not go without saying, the Secretary for Evangelisation was asked to explain how he viewed the eventual working of such a subtle and complex management accounting system:

> Congregation officers should make sure that all their activities fit within the *religious* or *social* labels. To this end they would have to fill in the Salvation Army's management accounting system with their own data. Any expense should be ascribed to the appropriate titles. Congregations' *religious* activities would be funded by monies available on the *religious* account at Headquarters and their *social* activities by resources taken from *social* account . . . Then, the Secretaries for Social Work, Evangelisation and Volunteering should together verify that, for every single home or corps [congregation], activities have the same label. They would then be in charge of harmonising the whole thing in order to avoid any return to the lack of compliance with *laïcité* previously highlighted by the Ministry for Social Affairs' auditors . . . All this should be done before year end. So, the Territorial Headquarters can be advised of how much money in total is required for both *social* work and *religious* activities. All this, although complex, will make resource allocation easier when preparing the budget to be submitted to the Ministry for Social Affairs.

This option would leave organisational structure and mission completion unchanged. Its implications would mostly be that every middle manager in homes and congregations should have the appropriate training to the new system and become a hybrid (Kurunmäki & Miller, 2006; Miller, Kurunmäki, & O'Leary, 2008): beyond the day-to-day tasks associated with their organisational role, they would also keep management accounting records. This would be facilitated if, at Headquarters, the three secretaries in charge of the religious and social mission validated *ex-ante* procedures and management accounting data; i.e., how grassroots actors intend to assign activities to a label. All this preliminary work would ease the making of budgets, as these could be almost automated, matching fund origin and destination with existing programmes.

Regardless of option 1 that had been rejected, all participants acknowledged that option 2 would definitely enable compliance with *laïcité* prescriptions, guarantee the Salvation Army's identity through on-going cooperation between *religious* and *social* activities and secure its long-term financial viability. As they saw no other major implication for this option, they deemed it was optimal and unanimously decided to implement it.

Probing, Testing and Enriching Option 2

Everybody worked on option 2 to render it applicable on 1 January 2001. The Secretary for Quality was managing the project; the researcher maintained his activity as a counsellor to the Territorial Commander until the auditors' next visit in April 2002. This implied some regular follow-up meetings with both of them. When auditors from the Home Office and the Ministry for Social Affairs inspected the new accountability system based upon a comprehensive labelling of activities, they found that there were still major ambiguities resulting in insufficient compliance with *laïcité* and proof of how public monies are used. Either the solution found was inappropriate, or the problem had not been properly *qualified*.

INCONCLUSIVE TEST: NEED FOR QUALIFYING THE PROBLEM ANEW

As all possible implications of the solution had been envisaged, it is not its merits that were called into question but the way the problem had been *qualified*. This means, operations' compliance with *laïcité* and accounting for this was not the core *problem*. This is what emerged from a new meeting organised by the Territorial Commander with those involved immediately after the auditors left. It showed in his face that his initial worries and concerns had been revived:

> The auditors do not like our response to their demand for proving the use of public monies for social work only. They reasoned that our management accounting systems fail to perfectly trace the destination of public monies received. According to them, this is particularly vivid in the case of missions that could have either label [*social* and *religious*], such as a summer camp organised by a corps [congregation]. As in 2000, there is some good news, though. The good news is that they stressed the effort we have made by developing a sort of activity-based accounting and encourage us to build upon this. We therefore have to find a working solution until their next visit next year. No need to remind you that if we fail to do so, we can get into big trouble. I count on all of you to help the Salvation Army improve our accountability systems.

This resulted in refining problem *qualification*: finding an alternative to financial accounting that proves the origin of public money, destination and effective use, the *laïcité* case remaining unchanged. Refinement through new *qualification* lies in the term 'unambiguously.' In response to that opening, the General heading the International Salvation Army, to whom these issues had been reported, announced the appointment of a new Territorial Commander commencing the following week. This person was widely known in the Salvation Army for solving similar crises in other countries, such as Denmark and Norway. Confronted with similar issues, he was deemed able to *qualify* the problem and anticipate the implications of the new solutions. The General commissioned the researcher to keep counselling the new Territorial Commander on *laïcité*'s legal, political and social implications. Beginning with his new appointment, the new Territorial Commander organised a meeting with the taskforce on his first day. His opening was straightforward:

> Ladies and gentlemen, we have a *problem*. As you know, the IGAS [auditors from the Ministry for Social Affairs] have threatened to no longer support the Salvation Army financially if, on their next audit, we do not completely fulfil their demands. I took the past ten days to examine the situation and understand what had been done prior to my joining. Obviously, if we maintain the wonderful management accounting system you have designed, we must entirely revise our structure and processes. I think the problem does not just lie in having activities and accounting that reflect *laïcité* but in our ability to do this in a self-evident way. The problem, as I understand it, is what you have found before plus the fact that our processes and accounting systems are ambiguous . . . Although this would be a big thing for us, I concur with Colonel Duchêne [the previous Territorial Commander] and reckon we should build upon what we already have and probably borrow from the other option that was rejected in 2000. As I know you cannot arrive at a solution today, I give you a week to produce one.

Evidently, although the auditors liked the labelling of activities as either *social* or *religious*, ambiguity remained. All participants agreed on this analysis and admit they had underestimated the extent of *ambiguity* and that it is the core of the problem. Building on option 1 rejected two years prior would be suggestive that splitting the Salvation Army into two legal bodies would make operations and financial flows totally clear, viz. unambiguous.

This new *qualification* called for a different solution. Yet, the next solution would be expected not to be radically different but to address the ambiguity problem. Accordingly, rather than totally relinquishing the option eventually adopted two years prior, utilising the 'best parts' from the two options initially presented could result in a mix of activity-based accounting, labelling and having two separate bodies. The following week, the CFO, acting qua the taskforce's rapporteur, summarised in a meeting his new solution:

> We think we have found a model enabling us to address the two con-
> straints on the Salvation Army. On *laïcité*, we believe that splitting the
> Salvation Army into two and having an activity-based accounting system
> is appropriate. We recommend that, as with the option rejected in 2000,
> we establish a charity on one hand and a denomination on the other. On
> the other aspect—our identity—we do believe the two bodies, although
> separate, must cooperate. For this, we suggest extending the mechanism
> to homes and the corps constituting each of these two bodies.

As he speaks, the CFO addresses the audience, speaking in the plural form,
thereby disincarnating the proposal. All participants would recognise themselves in it and therefore discuss it as if it were a collective offspring. With
this solution, activities would remain differentiated and organised around
a direct accounting system, as with the option rejected in 2000. Such splitting would unambiguously differentiate the scope, realm, responsibility and
accountability of each body. Public monies would be raised by the charity
whereas the denomination would be privately funded and the Headquarters subsidised by the International Salvation Army. The proposed solution
would come in addition to the activity-based costing system adopted in
2000, so that cooperation would be made possible by a clear mechanism of
application for funding. Homes or congregations could apply for resources
whose origins would depend not on who the applicant was, but on their
use: *social* or *religious*. Having two layers of accounting upheld by a new
organisational form would obviously not have the same implications as
each option taken separately; also, implications could not be the sum of
what characterised the two options. Therefore, prior to making any decision
on this solution, all participants were to envisage the possible consequences
the new solution would have.

IMPLICATIONS: ACTIVITIES' COORDINATING
THROUGH TRANSFER PRICING

As with the option eventually selected in 2000, the new solution to the
laïcité and ambiguity issues, and need for preserving the Salvation Army's
identity, could be implemented at the grassroots level only by ministers,
social workers and home managers. Thus the investment they had made to
be trained in management accounting would not be wasted and could be
systematically applied. The concrete meaning, beyond accounting, would
be that labels could be operated indifferently by one entity or the other and
be supervised by the one who funds it. Engaging in the discussion, the Chief
Accountant, who was also a pastor, expresses his thoughts:

> I supposed that public money should be raised and accounted for by the
> charity *only*. In this way, by default, any activities run by the charity
> are social work. On the other hand, the denomination should raise only

private money and run, again by default, religious programmes. The new thing is that each of the two bodies should be encouraged to buy some programmes from each other. For instance, the charity could buy social programmes from the denomination and conversely the denomination could buy religious programmes from the charity. I know this would be complex but I reckon we can't do otherwise.

Although not openly calling it such, the management accountant suggested that a major implication of this solution under the dual constraint (i.e., complying with *laïcité*, and cooperating) would be solved through cross-contracting and subsequently transfer pricing systems. In this way, as two legal bodies and two separate sets of accounts and accounting systems would exist, cooperation would only be possible when one entity applied for programmes delivered by the other. All other participants in the meeting nodded. The representative from the Parisian congregations intervened and extended his colleague's thought:

> Cooperation would eventuate through the potential subcontracting of some of each other's programmes. In the charity, employees doing social work must be paid with public money only and religious people with resources from the denomination. In turn, ministers in the denomination must be paid with private resources while social workers are paid with resources from the charity. Fair enough!

The implication is that the frontier between transfer pricing and cross-subsidising is very thin and must therefore be unambiguously defined and secured. Trespassing on it, as the Chief Accountant stressed, would sabotage all the efforts made since 2000 to overcome the *laïcité* issue:

> The charity would not be allowed to subsidise any religious activity conducted by the denomination. The system can work if and only if it rests upon very strict and rigid labels. Really, we must be very specific and unyielding with the titles of every single programme. This is the condition in order for us to be highly transparent. Please note that the denomination must charge the charity the same cost as the charity would incur if it did the social work itself. Conversely, the charity must pay the same amount for chaplaincy as the denomination would pay its ministers. Regardless of overheads, the issue is that we must make sure that each of the two entities can pay for the wage of the worker or minister operating in the other. I insist, if any surplus is made by either the charity or the denomination, this is called cross-subsidising and we would be breaching the law.

Understanding these implications, participants needed a few minutes to absorb them and envisage the solution's feasibility. Apparently, although not calling it such, they saw transfer pricing and subcontracting as a necessary means of coordinating inter-organisational relations specific to its dual identity. Therefore, accepted implications included the need for cross-contracting, a standard price list for the two legal bodies, no margin on sales (to avoid cross-subsidising, which would return to the initial problem), as well as clear and rigid labels operationalised through an inter-organisational management accounting system. As no other implications and future problems seem to arise, all participants adopted this solution, stressing that some minor technical adjustments would be needed over time.

ENRICHING THE CHOSEN SOLUTION OVER TIME

The inter-organisational, relationships-focused management accounting system would eventually respond to most of the demands relating to unambiguous compliance with *laïcité* and the need for protecting the Salvation Army's identity. In order for accountability to be fully discharged, further controls were anticipated, the Chief Accountant warned:

> All figures will be reported to the Territorial Headquarters where we consolidate them for the denomination on one hand and the charity on the other. Reconciling these cross-section transactions, we will produce another statement with actual funds and expenses for each entity. At the end of the day, total funds raised and total expenses for both *social* and *religious* bodies and activities *must* match the funds we commenced with at the outset.

Clear labelling of each activity would be set in place before operations were undertaken and monies allocated. Keeping records of exactly which anticipated activities in homes and congregations were *religious* or *social* made it possible to know in advance the destination of public and private funds. While operations were conducted, periodic reporting of the funding and expenses of local activities would enable the Territorial Headquarters to be permanently informed of the eventual destination of funds, be they public or private. After operations are conducted, internal controllers and the management accountant would double-check the ex post facto systematic match between public money and *social* work, as well as private resources and *religious* activities. Participants all agreed that, in order for cross-contracting to eventually contribute to discharging accountability, clear budgeting and budgetary control systems would be required. Budgetary control would be the condition of proving that no surplus has been made by any entity when subcontracting programmes to the other.

Convinced by this accountability system's capability of fulfilling all demands articulated by auditors, participants acclaimed the solution and decided to implement it after summer break, i.e., in September 2002. The new solution was then tested for another two years until the next audit in

November 2004. That time, auditors from the Home Office and the Ministry for Social Affairs approved the new accountability system without reservation and agreed to perpetuate it. On 1 January 2005, the Territorial Commander was appointed to a new role in the Netherlands, confronted with similar issues. On his first day, his successor in France, who had attended every meeting since 2000, announced in a meeting congregating all Salvation Army stakeholders that he would continue in the same direction:

> Thanks to Dick Krommenhoek [the former Territorial Commander] and your work, we have managed to cope with the *laïcité* issue and the imperative of cooperation between the charity and the denomination. Our processes and accounting system have fixed the ambiguities from which our operations had been suffering for too long. Hallelujah! To reinforce the link with the Home Minister and the Minister for Social Affairs, I have invited them to join the Salvation Army board of directors in person to discuss and approve our budget even before we undertake operations. Madame Charbonnier[3] has approved this and encourages us to do this. God bless you!

Various follow-up meetings between November 2004 and June 2011 with the Territorial Commander and the other actors involved in the discharge of accountability have revealed that the management control system implemented has continued to function effectively. The solution found to overcome the crisis confronting the Salvation Army between 2000 and 2002 has interested Territorial Commanders in other countries facing similar problems. In 2009, one of us was consulted by the New Zealand Salvation Army to advise the board on a similar issue. Upon request from the Canadian and UK Territorial Commanders, a report synthesising what had been done in France and New Zealand was produced and is now used as pedagogical material at the Salvation Army William Booth Training College in London.

DISCUSSION AND CONCLUSION

The Salvation Army was supposed to find an accounting solution allowing it to respond to an issue of the same kind. This is therefore without surprise that the first exchanges are about the delineations of an accounting system allowing to account for the religious or social use of public funds. First of all, as the *Conseil d'État* does in a plenary session, the Salvation Army board discussed to *qualify* the problem; that is, to conceptualise it in generic terms. Then, as at the *Conseil d'État*, articulating a solution was left to two distinct rapporteurs who could then present their suggestions. Motivated by the common goal of finding an institutional solution to the issue at stake, as in the case of the *Conseil d'État* rapporteurs and judges, members of the two working groups see their identity substituting for the one of the organisation. Options 1 and 2, although formulated by two distinct working groups, are progressively disembodied so as to become the work object of the organisation. As the *Conseil d'État*'s judgments rendered *in the name of the French People*, the accountability system adopted in 2000 and then revised in 2002 was that of the board *in the name of the Salvation Army*.

It is altogether that board members first adhere to option 2, which perfectly preserves the identity of the Salvation Army, with neither opposition nor reservation. It is interesting to see that even those who articulated option 1 did not object to its collective rejection nor did they try to defend it. Members of the *Conseil d'État* are all experienced lawyers driven by an interest in intellectually complex cases. In other settings, such as the Salvation Army, this is not necessarily the case, which could lead to controversies and possible disagreements or tensions between actors. Especially when it comes to balancing money and the mission, in particular in a church setting, a form of sacred-secular divide can oppose different occupational groups (Booth, 1993), such as financial managers and religious people (Lightbody, 2000, 2003). In other nonprofits, mission people could feel forced to be accountable to capital and therefore uncomfortable with this. However, in the Salvation Army, such is not the case, which could be ascribed to its specifics. Since it was founded in the mid-nineteenth century, the Salvation Army has made accounting and financial accountability part of its belief system and religious day-to-day conduct (Howson, 2005; Irvine, 2002; Joannidès, 2012). The accounting culture driving this organisation is unlikely to be found as vividly in others; albeit, it reflects similar patterns as with the *Conseil d'État*. The similarity between cultures at the *Conseil d'État* and the Salvation Army can also be explained by the presence of Madame Charbonnier at the board, into which she might have brought the Supreme Court's culture. This might reinforce the specifics of this case.

Other features may similarly be invoked so as to convey some idiosyncrasies in the case studied. First, the success of the iterative method adopted by the French Salvation Army—and thus mirroring the deliberations of the *Conseil d'État*—certainly pertains to the broad acceptance of the separation between church and state, i.e., the *laïcité* principle in France (Furet, 1996; Latour, 2013; Rémond, 2005). This confers French Salvationists greater flexibility than other organisations in accepting how *Soup* and *Soap* are articulated with *Salvation*. Second, the Salvation Army's intrinsic acceptance of its need to be accountable in specific and direct ways to society (Joannidès, 2012) facilitated the overall process of devising a solution ultimately fulfilling government representatives' demands. Lastly, government auditors' recourse to coercive power—through the threat of defunding—left the French Salvation Army with no other option except to arrive at a workable solution.

Admittedly, these three elements played an important role in the successful remediation of this specific case. What can be generalised however is the principle that the success of a technology or a management accounting idea is linked to the collective support it gets, rather than its incarnation by some actors (Alcouffe, Berland, & Levant, 2008; Jones & Dugdale, 2002). Because the solution has been collegially adopted it can be visibly evident outside the organisation as an institutional response to a demand articulated by third parties.

As with the making of law, we see in the making of accountability no individual strategies followed by actors. As Latour (2009) argues, it is for three reasons. First, the rapporteurs' identity vanishes as discussions commence. Second, the nature of these discussions does not lead to controversies as all actors try to envisage all possible, practical implications of either option under the purview of arriving an optimal solution. Third, these discussions are based on the common sense of the time as understood by the institution, so that the ultimate judgment rendered should reflect it. Eventually, the options proposed by the two working groups are discussed collegially with regards to their organisational, operational, legal and financial consequences, and the way those can be handled. These take place under *laïcité* as the common sense of the time: religious affairs are private matters and must not be brought into the public realm. This is how the option consisting of splitting the Salvation Army into two legal entities and applying direct accounting was collectively rejected: its organisational implications (cooperation between the two bodies) were deemed uncertain, thereby making responses to potential problems even more uncertain.

As with the *Conseil d'État*'s case law, the Salvation Army situation reveals that an accountability system, once approved, is not cast in stone. It is subjected to tests and its resistance to trials is proofed. The activity-based accounting system implemented in 2000 is tested in 2002 when auditors from the Home Office and the Ministry for Social Affairs trial it prior to approval. Where Latour (2009) sees no major failures in the trials of the *Conseil d'État* decisions, the Salvation Army situation reveals one: option 2 did not fully respond to the initial problem. Accordingly, discussions were to recommence from the start: the option adopted in 2002 followed the same process and was then tested for another two years until final approval. The case studied in this chapter unveils one essential error, but reveals neither minor errors nor their potency for further discussion. This is particularly vivid regarding issues in budgeting and budgetary control. We know how they should be practiced and what they should reveal, but ignore what could happen in case of a mismatch between control stages. We can assume, although cannot substantiate, the claim that further controls would be implemented if at any time there were a doubt as to how public resources had been used.

The making of accountability in the Salvation Army reveals, as in the making of law at the *Conseil d'État*, that new rounds of discussion in the trial-error process do not lead to radical changes in the final solution. Like the *Conseil d'État* concerned about its decisions' temporal continuity in making law, the accountability system eventually approved by the Salvation

Army's auditors built on option 2, which had been previously adopted. Re-*qualifying* a problem does not lead to radically rejecting prior solutions, but to adjusting them. This concurs with Latour's (2009) observation that the *Conseil d'État*'s decisions never revolutionise the existing legal order. Breakthroughs in their decisions over time are very rare and become a political matter often leading to revising the constitution or issuing new laws. However, whether borrowing from the option initially rejected contributes to making the final decision consensual or why the new Territorial Commander insisted to borrow from option 1 is not revealed in this case. As the initial problem *qualification* was insufficient, we cannot conjecture to what extent the existing solution would have been built upon if that case had arisen.

Those boardroom perspectives on the making of accountability in non-profits, informed with Latour's (2002, 2009) insights into the making of law, enable us to contribute to knowledge in the following way. The Salvation Army case highlights issues pertinent to other nonprofits in the making of an accountability system. First, discussions focus not on the solution's technical aspects and merits, but its organisational and managerial implications' modelling. Provided those remain foreseeable and manageable, the solution is collectively acceptable. Second, arriving at an accountability system is the offspring of collegial work in which actors' identity vanishes. The final accountability system can be taken for granted because it is not incarnated by one person but operates in its own capacity, i.e., like a nonhuman actor (Joannidès & Berland, 2013). Lastly, an accountability system is never a finished product. Once accepted, it first needs to be tested, in order to ensure that the problem was properly *qualified* and the solution found is a working response to it. Once the accountability system has been trialled and proven to be robust, it is still prone to evolve over time. It is subject to later enrichments with new technologies responding to new needs once it is deemed stable (How & Alawattage, 2012). It can then become self-referential and be taken for granted, until the next crisis. In sum, the making of accountability is an incremental and ongoing process based on trials and errors.

This chapter aligns itself with other publications dealing with very similar types of organisations, i.e., faith-based charities. It offers insights into boardroom decision-making processes, and from within the organisation, often due to the researchers' association and involvement with the board. As this chapter does not address the actual implementing and working of an accountability system by grassroots actors, knowledge could be advanced through further research addressing this from any type of nonprofit organisation, such as sport clubs, cultural charities, schools or hospitals, and not only faith-based charities. Correlatively, the boardroom perspectives offered here, although insightful, do not show interactions between those who make accountability and those who practice it. Therefore, further research would make significant contributions to knowledge by addressing that issue. As Latour's (2002, 2009) insights are very helpful to understand the making of accountability in a nonprofit, we suggest further research on the making of performance management systems; in addition, governance institutions in nonprofits would enhance accounting knowledge. Lastly, the case of the French Salvation Army seems to reveal a form of mimicry of the institutional environment operating in its domestic environment. Accordingly, we could consider that new institutional sociology could be applied to envisage how nonprofits in their given country reproduce national accountability institutions.

NOTES

1 The book was originally published in French in 2002 and then translated into English in 2009. Accordingly, there is no anachronism in this research project formally started in November 2005.
2 The first-named author played these multiple roles in this research project.
3 Madame Charbonnier is a permanent member of the Salvation Army's board of directors, a Supreme Court judge and the daughter of Professor Charbonnier, one of the most influential law thinkers in France. In that triple capacity, she has been advising the board since she was invited to join.

REFERENCES

Alcouffe, S., Berland, N., & Levant, Y. (2008). Actor-networks and the diffusion of management accounting innovations: A comparative study. *Management Accounting Research, 19*(1), 1–17.

Berry, A. (2005). Accountability and control in a cat's cradle. *Accounting, Auditing & Accountability Journal, 18*(2), 255–297.

Booth, P. (1993). Accounting in churches: A research framework and agenda. *Accounting, Auditing & Accountability Journal, 6*(4), 37–67.

Booth, W. (1890). *In darkest England and the way out.* London: International Headquarters of the Salvation Army.

Brigou, D. (1994). *La maison du partage.* Yens sur Morge, CH: Cabédita.

Callon, M. (1985). Éléments pour une sociologie de la traduction: La domestication des coquilles St. Jacques et des marins pêcheurs dans la baie de St. Brieuc. *L'Année Sociologique, 36*, 169–208.

Callon, M. (2009). Civilizing markets: Carbon trading between in vitro and in vivo experiments. *Accounting, Organizations and Society, 34*(3–4), 535–548.

Callon, M., & Rabeharisoa, V. (2008). The growing engagement of emergent concerned groups in political and economic life: Lessons from the French Association of Neuromuscular Disease patients. *Science Technology Human Values, 33*, 230–261.

Furet, F. (1996). *The French revolution.* London: Blackwell.

How, S. M., & Alawattage, C. (2012). Accounting decoupled: A case study of accounting regime change in a Malaysian company. *Critical Perspectives on Accounting, 23*(6), 403–419.

Howson, K. (2005). The Salvation Army: Aspects of their financial administration: Success and failure. *Managerial Auditing Journal, 20*(7), 649–662.

Irvine, H. (2002). The legitimizing power of financial statements in the Salvation Army in England, 1865–1892. *Accounting Historians Journal, 29*(1), 1–36.

Irvine, H. (2003). Trust me! A personal account of confidentiality issues in an organisational research project. *Accounting Forum, 27*(1), 111–131.

Irvine, H. (2005). Balancing money and mission in a local church budget. *Accounting, Auditing & Accountability Journal, 18*(2), 211–237.

Irvine, H., & Gaffikin, M. (2006). Getting in, getting on and getting out: Reflections on a qualitative research project. *Accounting, Auditing & Accountability Journal, 19*(1), 115–145.

Jacobs, K., & Walker, S. P. (2004). Accounting and accountability in the Iona Community. *Accounting, Auditing & Accountability Journal, 17*(3), 361–381.

Joannidès, V. (2009). *Accountability and ethnicity in a religious setting: The Salvation Army in France, Switzerland, the United Kingdom and Sweden* (Unpublished PhD dissertation). Université Paris Dauphine, Paris, FR.

Joannidès, V. (2012). Accounterability and the problematics of accountability. *Critical Perspectives on Accounting, 23*(3), 244–257.

Joannidès, V., & Berland, N. (2013). Constructing a research network—accounting knowledge in production. *Accounting, Auditing & Accountability Journal, 26*(4), 512–538.

Jones, C. T., & Dugdale, D. (2002). The ABC bandwagon and the juggernaut of modernity. *Accounting, Organizations and Society, 27*(1–2), 121–163.

Kreander, N., Beattie, V., & Mcphail, K. (2009). Putting out money where their mouth is: Alignment of charitable aims with charitable investments—tensions in policy and practice. *The British Accounting Review*, in press.

Kreander, N., Mcphail, K., & Molyneaux, D. (2004). God's fund managers: A critical study of stock market investment practices of the Church of England and UK Methodists. *Accounting, Auditing & Accountability Journal, 17*(3), 408–441.

Kurunmäki, L., & Miller, P. (2006). Modernising government: The calculating self, hybridisation and performance measurement. *Financial Accountability & Management, 22*(1), 87–106.

Latour, B. (1996). *Aramis or the love of technology*. Boston, MA: Harvard University Press.

Latour, B. (2002). *La fabrique du droit: Une ethnographie du Conseil D'état*. Paris: La Découverte.

Latour, B. (2005). *Reassembling the social—An introduction to actor-network theory*. Oxford, Oxford University Press.

Latour, B. (2009). *The making of law: An ethnography of the Conseil D'état*. London: Polity Press.

Latour, B. (2013). *An inquiry into modes of existence: An anthropology of the moderns*. Boston, MA: Harvard University Press.

Le Leu, S. (2001). *The Salvation Army and the poor—voices from the past—lessons from our recent history, with special reference to IHQ Development Services*. Paper presented at The Salvation Army's International Summit on Poverty, London.

Lightbody, M. (2000). Storing and shielding: Financial management behaviour in a church organization. *Accounting, Auditing & Accountability Journal, 13*(2), 156–174.

Lightbody, M. (2003). On being a financial manager in a church organisation: Understanding the experience. *Financial Accountability & Management, 19*(2), 117–138.

Miller, P., Kurunmäki, L., & O'Leary, T. (2008). Accounting, hybrids and the management of risk. *Accounting, Organizations and Society, 33*(7–8), 942–967.

Parker, L. D. (2003). Financial strategic management in a community welfare organisation: A boardroom perspective. *Financial Accountability & Management, 19*(4), 341–374.

Parker, L. D. (2013). Contemporary university strategising: The financial imperative. *Financial Accountability & Management, 29*(1), 1–25.

Parker, L. D., & Guthrie, J. (2005). Welcome to "the rough and tumble": Managing accounting research in a corporatised university world. *Accounting, Auditing & Accountability Journal, 18*(1), 5–13.

Quattrone, P., & Hopper, T. (2001). What does organizational change mean? Speculations on a taken for granted category. *Management Accounting Research, 12*(4), 403–435.

Quattrone, P., & Hopper, T. (2005). A 'time-space odyssey': Management control systems in two multinational organisations. *Accounting, Organizations and Society, 30*(7–8), 735–764.

Rémond, R. (1999). *Religion and society in modern Europe.* London: Blackwell.

Rémond, R. (2005). *L'invention de la laïcité française: De 1789 à demain.* Paris: Bayard Centurion.

Rémond, R. (2006). *Quand l'etat se mêle de l'histoire.* Paris: Essais Stock.

Salvation Army. (2012). *Annual review (2011).* London: The Salvation Army Publishing.

Sandall, R. (1947). *The history of the Salvation Army, Vol. 1: 1865–1878.* London: Thomas Nelson and Sons.

Sandall, R. (1950). *The history of the Salvation Army, Vol. 2: 1878–1886.* London: Thomas Nelson and Sons.

Sandall, R. (1955). *The history of the Salvation Army, Vol. 3: Social reform and welfare work.* London: Thomas Nelson and Sons.

Walker, P. J. (2001). *Pulling the devil's kingdom down: The Salvation Army in Victorian Britain.* Los Angeles: University of California Press.

Watson, B. (1964). *A hundred years' war: The Salvation Army, 1865–1965.* New York: Hodder & Stoughton.

Wiggins, A. R. (1960). *The history of the Salvation Army, Vol. 4: 1886–1904.* London: Thomas Nelson and Sons.

Wiggins, A. R. (1968). *The history of the Salvation Army, Vol. 5: 1904–1914.* London: Thomas Nelson and Sons.

Winston, D. (2000). *Red-hot and righteous: The urban religion of the Salvation Army.* Boston, MA: Harvard University Press.

12 Boardroom Governance
Interrogating, Strategising, Control and Accountability Processes

Lee Parker and Zahirul Hoque

INTRODUCTION

In recent decades, the issues of effective and failed corporate governance have increasingly attracted the attention of corporate and accounting policy makers, legislators, regulators, the accounting profession, researchers and the media (Harford, Sattar, & Maxwell, 2012; Heracleous, 2001). In accounting, such concerns have focused upon aspects of financial reporting, audit committee roles, earnings manipulation, accounting information quality, investor protection, financial and stock price performance (Beasley, Carcello, Hermanson, & Lapides, 2000; Eng & Mak, 2003; Parker, 2007a). In contrast, the pivotal governance issues of boardroom decision-making, governance, control and accountability have been relatively neglected by the accounting literature. This chapter addresses these issues at the highest organizational level, contending that accounting and accountability research literature has largely ignored corporate governance and accountability processes inside the boardroom level of organizational leadership. Accounting information and external market reactions to accounting disclosures are not the sole, or even most critical, keys to stakeholders achieving more effective corporate governance. They arguably constitute post-event reflections of decisions often made within the boardroom. For a more comprehensive and early interventionist approach to enhancing corporate governance, accounting researchers need to address the context, relationships, decisions and actions at the top level of the organizational hierarchy, and it is this level that is addressed by this chapter. Furthermore, this chapter focuses upon the issues of board-level strategising, control and accountability in the nonprofit sector, which in recent decades has grown significantly in size and social and economic impact, particularly as it has increasingly taken on social, educational, health and welfare delivery roles formerly directly delivered by governments.

A further deficiency in the accounting literature's approach to the study of corporate governance has been its obsession with statistical analyses and predictions using quantifiable proxies for factors that try to track relationships between largely input factors and externally observable organizational strategies, reported profits, stock prices and other performance proxies. These neglect the crucial internal processes at the top levels of organization that determine how governance and accountability are pursued, executed or undermined. This chapter explores the albeit limited evidence on such internal governance and accountability processes within nonprofit organizations to provide a closer understanding of how decisions are actually made and how nonprofit organizational leaders reflect and impact on their surrounding context and organizations.

To this end, the chapter discusses the processes of planning and strategising, the exercise of operational and financial control, the management of internal boardroom governance processes and the related dimensions of accountability. In so doing, particular attention is given to the idiosyncrasies and complexities of the nonprofit organizational environment, the internal and external influences that impact on governance processes and the importance of managing relationships in this setting. Finally, the chapter offers a further research agenda for developing our knowledge of nonprofit corporate governance processes at the highest levels of organizational leadership.

A MATTER OF NEGLECT

As already indicated above, the corpus of published research into boardroom level governance processes is still relatively sparse. This lacuna is even more evident with respect to nonprofit boards and their internal operations and contexts. Qualitative research methodologies are uniquely suited to penetrating and unpacking such processes, their conditioning influences and rationales. This has accentuated the problem in that most accounting and management researchers are quantitatively, rather than qualitatively, trained and oriented. This has led to the preponderance of survey questionnaire studies and those that attempt to correlate proxies for governance influences against supposed governance outcomes (Parker, 2007a). So there are multiple underlying causes for the neglect and consequent lack of knowledge about board-level governance and accountability processes in the nonprofit sector. As Bansal puts it, '. . . corporate governance relies heavily on hypothetico-deductive quantitative research which fuels path-dependent theorizing' (2013, p. 127). In this sort of environment then, we end up knowing very little about what nonprofit boards do and how they do it. Most studies, analyses and discussions are based on secondary data, rather than direct interview or observation (Leatherwood & O'Neal, 1996; Miller, 2002). While qualitative studies of governance have been growing in number, they remain a very small proportion of the total corpus of corporate governance research literature, still dominated by an overwhelming majority of quantitative studies (McNulty, Zattoni, & Douglas, 2013).

Even in the relevant management literature on nonprofit boards, not only has there been a preponderance of quantitative studies, but also a strong reliance on normative discussions and opinion pieces. Such a lack of qualitative empirical data on board-level governance extends to director recruitment, selection and tenure, skills, roles and performance appraisal. Even less is known about internal boardroom meeting processes which have an arguably important bearing upon governance and accountability processes and effectiveness (Parker, 2007a). Why has this lacuna emerged? A number of reasons can be posited (Parker, 2007a). Parker's (2005) interviews of Australian and New Zealand financial accounting researchers revealed that they resisted what they perceived to be the time required for detailed qualitative examinations of corporate governance and corporate failures, and that they were reluctant to pursue required methodologies that are not generally accepted by leading North American economics and statistics-focused accounting research journals. So, rationing of personal research time and aspirations towards perceived journal esteem indicators drove their research choices, rather than importance of subject, gaps in knowledge or objectives-related methodology choice.

So why bother? The answer lies in the repeated failures in corporate governance and accountability at the board level in both profit and nonprofit organizations, and the ongoing concerns of regulators, professional associations and the public about these matters. This apparent vacuum in our knowledge set, where the issues appear to be represented by nothing more than relative silence in the accounting and management literatures, beckons our research attention. We have a capacity and duty to investigate and grapple with these lacunae, with their unobserved and unremarked functions and dysfunctions (Hines, 1992; Choudhury, 1988; Arrington & Francis, 1989; Inkpen & Choudhury, 1995). It is these empty spaces that this chapter addresses.

THE QUALITATIVE OFFERING

The qualitative approach offers us the opportunity to penetrate and understand boardroom decision-making, planning, control and accountability *processes*. This can provide a significant advance in our understanding of how corporate governance and accountability at the highest levels of nonprofit organizations work, and therefore *why* we observe some of the patterns of behaviour, disclosure, non-disclosure, regulatory compliance and non-compliance and voluntary initiatives that may become evident through the application of quantitative methodologies (Parker, 2003). Bansal (2013) sees qualitative data contributing to our corporate governance knowledge in three respects. First, it can inductively identify and articulate hitherto unrecognized governance phenomena, through its engagement in the field. Second, it can critique and challenge previous assumptions deduced from prior theories and empirics that are not reflected in the field data being collected through qualitative inquiry. Third, the application of qualitative methodologies can unearth quite new constructs or provide new perspectives on previously identified and discussed governance issues. The agenda is probably best summarized by Clarke (1998), who argues that the most critical challenge facing corporate governance research is to get through the boardroom door.

Heracleous (2001) has critiqued studies of the impact of corporate governance on organizational performance as being limited by a narrow focus on trying to directly relate board attributes to organizational performance. In an earlier study, he instead argued that the best way to understand those factors influencing board effectiveness is to secure primary longitudinal data through observation of actual board meetings (Heracleous, 1999). Pye reflects on her past qualitative research into boards and CEOs and reaches similar conclusions, arguing that 'organizational analysis is best done from an interpretive perspective which allows for change over time' (2001, p. 43). Cornforth (2012) also observes that the majority of non-profit organizational governance research has been conducted from a positivist epistemology and using cross-sectional data. He laments the relative dearth of studies of change over time, and of processes occurring within nonprofit boards. As Samra-Fredericks (2000a, 2000b) argues, we need better insights into boardroom processes from close examination of directors' skills, dialogue and interactions. This includes unravelling complex and layered behaviours and experiences that are crucial components of nonprofit, board-level governance and accountability. This offers the prospect of far deeper and more nuanced understandings of the corporate governance and accountability process than simplistic statistical correlations or normative reflections. Furthermore, we need greater deployment of longitudinal case studies and historical studies of nonprofit director-governance behaviour and decision-making, as well as much more heavily contextualized studies that reflect upon board behaviours, both conditioned by and conditioning their surrounding institutional contexts (Cornforth, 2012).

Bansal (2013) sees qualitative methodology being equally applicable to governance research subjects both where no prior theory exists and where theory does exist, but in a setting of conflicting or unclear empirical data. What the qualitative approach also offers is variety and flexibility in research design, focus and types of data sought out. Rather than only focusing upon routine typical cases, the atypical, deviant, abnormal cases and scenarios can reveal much more than otherwise possible from the representative survey sample (Brennan & Solomon, 2008). Data sources can extend across interviews, historical archives, participant observation and more. These are particularly suited to the investigation of processes, where we want to know more about how and why decisions are made (or not made) and actions taken (or not taken) (Bansal, 2013).

These possibilities also extend to researching accountability and its processes and mechanisms at the board level of nonprofit corporate governance. What little there has been, has tended towards a financial and external reporting focus. Yet, the nonprofit sector is not only significant in size, and economic and social reach, but is oftentimes in strategic alliance with government and, indeed, with business. Thus its complexities, uniqueness, wide-ranging constituents, purchaser-provider-funder splits and other salient features present significant governance and accountability questions and challenges that call for researcher attention (Brennan & Solomon, 2008; Parker, 2005, 2007c).

A QUESTION OF ROLE

In nonprofit, governance-related accounting and accountability research, the role and significance of the board of directors and the chief executive officer (CEO) has deserved rather more consideration. They have major impacts across the organization, ranging from their effects on management philosophies and modus operandi, to organizational strategies and approaches to management control, to support and accountability relationships with stakeholders (Parker, 2008b). Research across both profit and nonprofit organizational boards has found that major director roles include organizational control, advice to senior executives, assistance with the development of strategic plans and identifying pathways to accessing resources. From the contemporary research literature, Van den Berghe and Levrau (2004) identify six main board roles in corporate governance. They include the support role, linking role, strategic role, maintenance role, coordinating role and the control role.

These roles have arguably moved to centre stage as over the decades, corporate governance research has found that boards have moved from being predominantly ceremonial, to becoming much more directly and actively engaged in organizational leadership. This has in part been a response to more demanding societal expectations of board responsibility and accountability for organizational performance and impacts (Nicholson & Kiel, 2004). Hyndman and McDonnell (2009) point to the guide for nonprofit sector governance issued by the ACEVO (2005) which recommends that the primary role of the board should be strategic—focused on maximizing organizational performance, delegating to staff and volunteers, maintaining high ethical standards and pursuing a policy of transparency and accountability.

Role prescriptions are all very well, but research to date has demonstrated that the prescriptions can vary from practice to practice and, indeed, across actual boards (Stone & Ostrower, 2007). For example, Hyndman and McDonnell (2009) see boards operating along a continuum between partnering and supporting senior management and controlling them. Even in their attitudes to board roles and responsibilities, individual directors can differ quite widely (Stone & Ostrower, 2007). For example, Cornforth and Edwards's (1999) case study of four nonprofit organization boards found that the four boards varied considerably in their interpretation of their roles and the degree to which they contributed to organizational strategy. These variations were conditioned by such factors as how each organization was regulated, the organization's own history and governance philosophies, the selection of directors and their own skills, plus the manner in which the boards were operated and managed.

Studies of directors' perceptions of board roles have revealed a range of responsibilities being identified. Steane and Christie's (2001) survey of 118 nonprofit boards covering 1,405 directors in Australia found them allocating highest priority to strategic planning, government and public policy issues, management of programmes, human resources and industrial relations issues, organizational philosophy and values, managing the board itself and relationships with networks, affiliated organizations and strategic partners. Leatherwood and O'Neal's (1996) study of profit and nonprofit directors ascertained what they saw as their individual responsibilities as directors. They generally considered that they had a duty to apply their experience and competence, to be questioning, to attend to the concerns of stakeholders and to not merely be a 'rubber stamp' for executives' decisions. When it comes to the question of what boards actually do, Machold and Farquhar's (2013) study of six UK boards discovered that most time was spent on monitoring and control issues and discussions, including routine, detailed scrutiny of budgets, market, employee and financial performance, risk management and policy and procedure reviews. Service and strategy roles appeared to consume lesser amounts of board time and attention in comparison with monitoring and control. Nonetheless, they also found that boards were not uniform in the tasks to which they devoted most time. In terms of to whom both profit and nonprofit boards see themselves accountable, Leatherwood and O'Neal (1996) found that nonprofit directors differed considerably in identifying their primary stakeholder priority groups. Clients and service users were prioritized by 32% of directors, individual donors were first ranked by 28%, the community at large was prioritized by 25% and 11% ranked large donors as top priority. This arguably reflects the complexity of nonprofit organizations' missions, structures, environments and stakeholders. This range of attitudes to board roles spans directors operating across a range of national environments.

A RELATIONSHIPS-BASED ENVIRONMENT

It is generally acknowledged that in many countries today, the nonprofit sector is large, as an employer, and in terms of its total expenditures, its command over property and investment assets and in the reach of its social impact. Such organizations are politically, socially and economically important, and both reflect and drive their national, institutional and social environments. In doing so, they typically face a wider set of organizational stakeholders and their demands, balance a more complex set of objectives, address a more complex set of revenue resources and face more intricate relationships between service providers and recipients than for-profit organizations (Parker, 2001). In balancing relationships with key stakeholders in their environment, nonprofits must oftentimes deal with governments intent on outsourcing services to them but demanding associated accountability, donors and sponsors ranging from large corporations to individuals, regulators monitoring the services they deliver, beneficiaries and service users who have their own idiosyncratic views of what should be provided, and both professional and volunteer staff who often are driven by personal norms and agendas that motivate their involvement. This is a highly complex mix that nonprofit boards must continually take into account. That brings with it a risk that boards will become overly obsessed with monitoring regulatory compliance, or privileging particular stakeholder groups who provide significant revenues (Hyndmann & McDonnell, 2009).

Furthermore, it is important to recognize that nonprofit boards have in many countries been responding to significant changes in their environmental landscape over the past 10–20 years, as governments have progressively commercialized, privatized and outsourced many of their own former direct-delivery activities. This has directly engaged nonprofit organizations as replacement deliverers on behalf of government. While this has provided streams of revenues not previously available, it has also made nonprofits subject to the vagaries of sudden changes in government priorities and policy, imposed government priorities upon their organizational missions and strategic directions and required at times quite intrusive accountability reporting and key performance indicators (KPIs) that begin to drive organizational strategy and identity changes. It has also meant that the boundaries between public, private and nonprofit sectors and constituent organizations can become rather blurred. For nonprofits this can result in strategic piggy-backing as they develop commercial profit centres to generate further revenues, and in their also becoming surrogate 'arms' of government, thereby intruding into their own independence and autonomy (Cornforth, 2001; Parker, 2001, 2002, 2003).

So what sort of factors condition nonprofit board strategies? Chew and Osborne (2009a, 2009b) have studied this in the UK charity sector, and find that government was the strongest external influence, driving nonprofits' core strategies and strategic positioning. This effect was moderated by whether government acted as policy maker or legitimizer of the organization's activities, and by the type of services in which the organization was involved. Further complicating variables in the nonprofit environment include demographic changes in the population being targeted, changes in service-user needs, changes in public and donor attitudes and concerns, as well as economic and technological changes. Chew and Osborne (2009a, 2009b) also observed the increasing competition amongst charity nonprofits for financial and other resources. In addition to these arenas of competition, Parker (2001, 2002, 2003) has also noted that at times these nonprofits compete for clients! Finally, Parker's (2001) study of a large, religious, non-profit organization in Australia found that four major internal and external environmental factors conditioned board strategising. First were the values held within the nonprofit's own organizational community and those held by the community at large outside the organization, both becoming intertwined. Second was the pressure upon organizational resources due to the multiple and growing demands for services, the continuing search for sources of funding and the challenges of dealing with budgetary deficits or threats thereof. Third was the consultative bureaucracy that reflected the need to consult with a wider range of stakeholders than often required of a for-profit organization. Fourth was a tendency for production of historical, compliance-focused accounting information not well designed for providing early warning signals or facilitating anticipation of financial impacts of present or proposed strategies.

The above outline of the nonprofit organization's environmental relationships strongly implies a relationship-led approach to board strategising. This has been reported in an interview study conducted by Sosin (2012), who found that they most frequently rely on relationship-based strategies, a phenomenon largely ignored by the nonprofit governance research community. These strategies include liaising with and meeting government requirements, modifying programmes and tracking results to suit and maintain government and other key funders' support, and pursuing general social recognition and legitimacy for delivery of services valued by the state and the community. All of these relationship-based strategies had major foci upon maintaining sources of existing revenue streams and attracting new revenue streams to serve existing and new programmes. Parker's (2003) participant-observer study of a nonprofit social welfare organization board revealed an even broader specification of relationships management being employed at board level. These included paying attention to and managing relationships with affiliated supporting or ownership organizations, monitoring the activities of competitors and maintaining relationships important to the organization's competitive positioning, managing public and media relations and developing relationships with national, regional and local government through strategic alliances, lobbying and personal linkages. Of course, as already observed above, the nonprofit organization increasingly can play a direct public policy implementation role on behalf of government through its delivery of services formerly directly delivered by government (Stone & Ostrower, 2007). This in itself, Cornforth and Edwards (1999) argue, can reinforce the nonprofit board's focus on its managerial and compliance roles, as also observed above.

BOARDROOM STRATEGY

Qualitative research into boardroom strategising reveals unique insights into strategising orientations, approaches and conditioners from within the boardroom that are completely ignored by the predominant, quantitative, predictive studies that focus on external proxies for board profiles and behaviours. In the first instance, empirical evidence reveals a spectrum of degrees of board involvement in organizational strategising. This ranges from directors who engage in all stages of strategy formulation, implementation and control. Others restrict their roles to reviewing management-initiated strategies and their outcomes. Most often, board members become involved in mission, vision and objectives formulation, with management taking responsibility for developing associated, detailed business plans and implementation thereof. However, there is also a significant cadre of boards that limit their involvement to broad approval of management-developed strategies and plans (Cornforth & Edwards, 1999; Heracleous, 1999; Ingley & Van der Walt, 2001; Parker, 2008b). Ravasi and Zattoni's (2006) study of the boards of nine organizations echoed this general picture in finding similar variations in board-strategising engagement, with three boards simply approving or rejecting management strategy proposals, whereas the six others became involved in all phases of the strategic management process. The manner in which boards do engage in strategising can take the forms of advising management on strategic management methodology, reviewing mission and strategic direction, setting parameters for potential strategies and their discussion, as well as monitoring and authorizing priority strategies (McNulty & Pettigrew, 1999; Stiles, 2001; Stiles & Taylor, 2001; Parker, 2008b).

What factors appear to condition degrees of board involvement? There are quite a number of factors that have been observed. They include directors' knowledge and expertise in both the sector and strategic management itself (Ravasi & Zattoni, 2006; Parker, 2008b), the size of the board (a lesser size facilitating greater strategic involvement) (Collier, 2008; Parker, 2008b) and significant executive membership of the board (Zahra & Pearce, 1990; Parker, 2008b). Further influences have been identified as the organization's past performance, board meeting format, time for strategic discussions, directors' understanding of the strategic role and responsibilities and communications between directors outside the actual board meetings (Cornforth, 2001; McNulty & Pettigrew, 1999; Parker, 2008b).

Research has also revealed a further neglected dimension of boardroom strategic activity. Boards have been observed to pay particular attention to navigating organizational politics and to facilitating the reconciliation of diverging stakeholder interest and objectives. Ravasi and Zattoni (2006) found this reconciling role in evidence in their subject organizations manifesting itself as boards worked at reconciling conflicting views on strategic issues and trying to develop common goals to inform managements' actions. For these boards, strategic plans were evaluated not only in terms of their operational and financial viability, but also in terms of their impact on goals and interests of stakeholders. Parker's (2007b) study of two non-profit boards also found them paying considerable attention to navigating and managing the politics within their organizations, championing selected strategies and ensuring their implementation.

While nonprofit boards have significant operational mission and objectives concerns, particularly given the oftentimes societally significant roles their organizations play, nonetheless research reveals their ongoing focus on financial and commercial strategies and results. This is exemplified in Parker's (2003, 2007b) longitudinal participant-observer studies of nonprofit boards. For both reasons of organizational viability and ability to pursue its operational objectives, boards paid great attention to their means of financing the organizational mission. Given the ever-expanding demands these organizations faced, and their boards' staff and members' commitment, and calling to their service objectives, the need and desire for financial resources continually commanded boardroom attention and discussion. This meant that for these boards, financial strategy became a core phenomenon. Indeed, in pursuit of financial resources, a pronounced commercial focus was evident in boardroom deliberations. Directors imported private sector philosophies and attitudes, employed commercial and financial language and aimed for profit generation to support their organization's other nonprofit strategies.

One further dimension of boardroom strategising merits attention and has been identified in Parker's (2007b, 2008ab) participant-observer boardroom studies. Particularly in nonprofit boards, directors can grapple with the balances they strike between a strategic or compliance focus, and between their scope of responsibility across strategic and operational matters. Other researchers as well (Stone, 1991; Leatherwood & O'Neal, 1996; Cornforth & Edwards, 1999; Steane & Christie, 2001; Spear, Cornforth, & Aiken, 2009) have identified these two sets of pressures as commonly experienced by nonprofit boards. The temptation for boards of nonprofits—where directors are often also members or other types of stakeholders and have a sense of personal connection and calling to the organization's mission—is to transgress across the line between strategic and policy matters, into operational management detail, which is properly the province of management. In doing so, they can become distracted from central corporate-governance responsibilities and embroiled in routine, daily operational detail which is not their province and for which they are not equipped (Parker, 2007b, 2008ab). In addition, and not unrelated, is the risk that they may become focused upon legal and regulatory compliance monitoring, to the neglect of their strategic responsibilities (Parker, 2007c).

STRUGGLING WITH CONTROL

Being positioned at the nexus between the organization and its stakeholders, including government, owners and community, the board is widely acknowledged to have a significant responsibility for and role in the organizational control process—operational and financial (Cadbury, 2000;

Vinten, 2001). This remit has been recognized by the Treadway commission report, the Hampel committee, the Turnbull report and the Cadbury Committee code (Vinten, 2001). Research at board level has been revealing an increasing concern amongst directors with risk management. Such increasing sensitivity and attention has been reported by Dulewicz and Herbert (1999), Mackay and Sweeting (2000), and Parker (2008a). However, board approaches to their control responsibility have been far less evident. As with strategising, board approaches to this responsibility vary from the highly developed and sophisticated to the almost naïve. This is despite directors often rating the responsibility very highly when surveyed or interviewed (Dulewicz & Herbert, 1999).

Stiles and Taylor's (2001) extensive study of UK directors reported limited boardroom time spent on monthly budget control and performance reviews, and a predominantly informal approach to strategic control. This is also borne out by studies such as Parker's (2008a), who found that directors' attention to and discussion of operational and financial control matters were triggered by informal directors' reports or issues verbally raised in the board meeting, rather than by any formal budgetary or strategic control reports in the board meeting agenda papers. In addition, his case studies similarly revealed infrequent and limited levels of director questioning of formally tabled control reports at board meetings. Further qualitative boardroom studies that also support these findings can be found in Parker (2003) and Collier (2005). While encompassing both board and executive levels, Parker's (2002) nonprofit field study also reported a highly variable degree of budgetary control monitoring over time in a loosely coupled budgetary control system. Operational priorities appeared to be decoupled from the budgetary control system, with often contradictory control attitudes and practices being observed.

Factors accounting for this variability in approach to the board's exercising of its control remit are still being investigated and identified. Factors may include directors' uncertainty as to whether they should leave detailed control to senior executives, occasional lack of confidence or difficulties in comprehending control information provided to the board, distraction towards strategy development rather than strategy control and a tendency towards advice and support to senior executives, rather than monitoring and controlling their activities (Parker, 2008a; Peck, 1995). This can be compounded by the inherent difficulties in measuring and assessing the often qualitative and intangible outcomes and performance of nonprofit organizational operations. In these circumstances, directors may fall back on measures of performance with which they are familiar in other circumstances or which are employed in their own personal professional domain, but which may not be appropriate to the organization and its strategic objectives (Miller, 2002; Saj, 2013). Alternatively, they may opt for informal approaches to control, effectively decoupled from the formal management control system (Tucker & Parker, 2013, 2014).

Finally, it is important to recognize the ongoing question of the interrelated board and executive roles in nonprofit organizational control. Oftentimes the board focuses upon the control of financial resourcing, whereas senior executives focus on control of programme delivery (Parker, 2003; Ostrower, 2007; Saj, 2013). This is complicated however by the power relationships between the board and chief executive officer (CEO), thereby influencing who really exercises control over what. Where significant power accrues to the CEO, directors may sometimes lose the ability to discharge their control responsibilities, becoming merely information recipients and tacit approvers of CEO recommendations and decisions (Miller- Millesen, 2003). This is particularly possible given that board members invariably rely upon the nonprofit executives to supply them with information required for their decision-making and control functions. Thus the CEO may effectively control any control-related information flowing to the board (Hoye & Cuskelly, 2003). Indeed, as Spear et al. (2009) point out, it is senior management that has access to the main levers of organizational control and the information, skills, resources and time to access and exercise control functions. Thus the power of boards to control their own management can be subject to significant limitations. Monitoring and challenging senior management requires a board attitude that goes beyond consultation and advice to the CEO (Spear et al., 2009).

INTERNAL BOARD GOVERNANCE

The style and process of internal management and governance of boardroom proceedings is another important component of general governance of nonprofit organizations. These dimensions of corporate governance are often ignored by researchers, and yet they influence approaches to and effectiveness of governance right down through the organizational hierarchy (Parker, 2008b). In the first instance, the role of the board chair and the relationship with the CEO is a crucial input to board governance and its effectiveness. A number of studies point to this. Directors interviewed by Van den Berghe and Levrau (2004) observed that a board chair needed to be a good leader, controlling but not dominating board meetings, acting as an impartial monitor of directors and meeting processes and driving them from the front.

However, it is the relationship between the board chair and the CEO which is crucial to the exercise of internal governance within the board. Either or both can become the drivers of the board's agenda, the nature and strength of their relationship having a profound impact, depending on whether one or the other takes the lead or whether it is some form of mutual, cooperative partnership. Studies reveal the importance of their establishing a clear mutual understanding of their roles and partnership, thereby laying the foundation for the boardroom culture, and modus operandi (Stiles &

Taylor, 2001; Mole, 2003; Rochester, 2003). A number of empirical studies unpack this relationship. Golensky (1993) found that the board and the organizational executive may work in cooperative partnership or become embroiled in a power struggle, noting however that such relationships do not always fall into either of these simplistic categories but can exhibit variant combinations (Hoye & Cuskelly, 2003). Parker's (2003) study revealed that executive and non-executive directors can interpret the board's role differently, and can therefore differ in their approaches to the proposal, initiation and limitation of new strategies. In this study, executive directors tended to think of the board as a house of review for their initiatives, whereas non-executive directors wanted a more proactive board role. This created tensions between the two groups, with non-executive directors considering some executive director proposals and initiatives to be preemptive. Thus non-executive directors continually fought rear-guard actions by trying to set limits on proposed initiatives.

Cornforth and Edwards (1999) report that it is important for the board chair and CEO to consult over managing the board meeting's agenda so as to focus directors' attention and effort on key issues rather than straying into operational management detail. In a further nonprofit boardrooms' participant-observer study, Parker (2007b) found that boards could differ significantly in styles of operation and leadership delivered by the CEO. This could vary from direct and vocal leadership within board meetings to subtler leadership delivered through lobbying, informal discussions with directors and agenda setting before and after board meetings. Maitlis (2004) has identified four behavioural processes exploited by CEOs in influencing directors. First is their exploiting relationships with key directors to influence board decisions. Second is their use of impression management whereby they create an image of competence and legitimacy in influencing director support. Third is their information strategy of gathering, holding, disseminating and concealing information selectively between various directors. Fourth is CEOs' strategies to protect the formal authority of their own position, ensuring their authority over decision-making within meetings.

Board committees are also a key dimension of boardroom corporate governance. Only limited attention has been paid to these by researchers. Yet many board members of nonprofit organizations do find themselves also serving on a board committee, ranging from audit committee, to executive remuneration, to policy and strategy and more. Brown and Iverson (2004) argue that we are often unclear as to what functions these committees actually serve and how influential they are. Parker's (2007b) study of two nonprofit boards found that there were numerous occasions where board committees tabled recommendations to board meetings and expected uncritical board approval, while at the board meeting directors often did indeed passively accept committee recommendations. This raises questions about the effectiveness of main board governance and due diligence in evaluating proposals and making strategic and control decisions.

Boardroom agenda structuring is another aspect of nonprofit boardroom internal governance that appears to influence the board's governance processes and effectiveness. Studies reveal that poorly structured agendas can lead to directors becoming embroiled in short-term operational issues to the neglect of their longer-term strategy, policy and control responsibilities. In contrast, agendas that prioritize strategic issues have been found to maintain directors' focus on high-priority governance responsibilities (Holland, 2002; Parker, 2008b). Cornforth and Edwards's (1999) study found that long, unstructured agendas were accompanied by few attempts to prioritize issues for discussion or manage time allocated to their consideration. As a result, important priority strategic issues were squeezed for time or not addressed at all. Parker's (2007b) study found that structuring of board agendas with strategic issues being given priority and routine operational items relegated to the end of agendas reoriented director discussions towards a strategic and policy issues focus. Failure to structure the agenda in this way conversely produced functionally and operationally focused meetings that tended towards micromanagement of lesser operational management issues by directors.

Quality of boardroom governance has also been found to relate to information made available to the board. Researchers observe that board effectiveness appears to reflect in part the timing and quality of information supplied to directors (Cornforth, 2001; Parker, 2008b). This has also been observed by Cornforth and Edwards (1999), and Van den Berghe and Levrau (2004). Both Parker (2008a) and Cornforth and Edwards (1999) have empirically observed that too little or too much information supplied to directors can impede their analysis and decision-making, particularly at strategic and control levels. This feeds into the quality of boardroom critique, discussion and debate. The latter has been identified in their research findings by Van den Berghe and Levrau (2004) as essential for effective board meetings, maintaining a critical but constructive boardroom climate. Parker's (2007b) study observed directors switching between active and passive involvement in board meetings, at times taking initiatives and strong positions in debates and at other times acceding to executive proposals and views. Relating to Van den Berghe and Levrau's (2004) concern with boardroom climate, Parker's (2007b) study also revealed the importance of boardroom culture in how a board discharges its governance and accountability responsibilities. He observed the use of respect, informality and humour as social lubricants that facilitated and moderated at times intense debates on crucial matters, thereby preserving board cohesion. In both the cases studied, attention was paid to maintaining a cohesive board culture, managing searching inquiries, critical questioning and vigorous discussions. This at times included social networking before and after board meetings, directors' reflections on meeting processes and occasional dinners.

A final dimension of internal board governance is that of directors' evaluation of their own performance as directors, individually and as a whole board, including its processes and quality of decision-making. Research into nonprofit boards suggests that there has been a tendency towards informal rather than formal approaches to this performance evaluation. Reasons for this include board reservations about the value of such exercises, director nervousness about potential conclusions, the challenges of designing appropriate evaluative measures and pressures of time (for example, see Leatherwood & O'Neal, 1996; Conger, Finegold, & Lawler, 1998; Holland, 2002). However, Parker's (2007b) study revealed in those cases examined a trend towards more formal evaluations, including a questionnaire filled out by directors, follow-up verbal discussions with the board chair and then an overall, interactive review discussion by the whole board in the presence of the CEO and board chair.

DISCHARGING BOARD ACCOUNTABILITY

Nonprofit organization accountability and the accountability roles of their boards are a complex issue that requires reflection both at the organization-wide level and the board level. Collier (2005) offers a perspective on these accountabilities that are particularly germane to the nonprofit environment. He sees accounting as a technique, accountability as a state of mind and governance as a means of control and legitimation. This also relates to Roberts' (1990, 1991) concepts of accountability that incorporate both a formalized, hierarchical schemata based on accounting measures and reports that offer a degree of visibility for evaluating actions and performance, plus a socializing accountability enacted through a sense-making narrative or dialogue. The latter incorporates the building of shared understandings and reciprocal rights and responsibilities. Knutsen and Brower (2010) add further dimensions, arguing that further conceptualizations are needed since nonprofits are accountable to multiple stakeholders who may have multiple and differing accountability agendas. Their concepts include recognizing a nonprofit's instrumental accountability to internal, organizational resource providers such as staff members, volunteers and sponsors, and to external resource providers such as donors, government, etc. They also identify what they term expressive accountability through their self-perceived, value-driven, altruistic community roles, through their commitment to their mission and its underlying beliefs and values and through their service delivery to patrons such as clients and members. Oftentimes, nonprofits will engage in both forms of accountability enactment, and indeed Knutsen and Brower (2010) warn that privileging one form over the other risks ignoring or marginalizing some part of the organization's constituency.

This broadening of the accountability vision is also reflected in Anheier's (2009) advocacy of social accountability to complement traditional forms of accountability so that internal and external accountabilities become mutually reinforcing. Brennan and Solomon (2008) also see social accountability as an expanding responsibility of nonprofit organizations and their boards. This also relates to discussions of nonprofit accountability to the public interest. Jepson (2005) sees this pursued simultaneously through structural accountability via systems and procedures and public accountability through perceptions and meanings, both working together in the institutional and social domains to ensure public trust in a legitimate organization. The concern with the public interest is argued to be particularly important for nonprofit organizations as moral institutions committed to nonprofit objectives in the social, welfare, educational, medical, sporting and other societal fields. Invariably their commitments and responsibilities go beyond the economic and self-interest of owners in pursuit of a moral and social agenda with a strong moralistic underpinning (Hodgkin, 1993).

Returning to the board level of nonprofit organizations, Roberts, McNulty, and Stiles (2005) argue that traditional hierarchical accountability whereby executives' actions are scrutinized and monitored by non-executives (for example, on the board) is of itself insufficient for delivering broad-scope accountability within and beyond the organization. Instead they advocate moving beyond a defensive calling to account, to incorporate open dialogue and reciprocal exchanges that promote creative thinking and mutual understanding, plans and actions being thereby developed, evaluated, challenged and refined. Developing a broader-scope concept of accountability at both board and organizational levels is important for nonprofit organizations, since these impact directly upon organizational effectiveness overall, influencing public perceptions of organizational viability, good governance and reputation (Radbourne, 2003). Of course, this also poses the challenging question of 'accountable for what'? Stone and Ostrower (2007) suggest a variety of possibilities including programme delivery, outcomes of strategies, collaboration with strategic partners, improved civil democracy and more. Radbourne (2003) would add financial viability. Parker's (2003) boardroom participant-observer study of one nonprofit organization revealed the board's grappling with a desire to fully disclose financial status and performance while trying to manage other stakeholder perceptions that risked limiting donations and sponsorships. The point being made here is that a broadened scope of accountabilities can deliver more effective accountability to a full range of stakeholders, but at the same time can risk misperceptions and support amongst some of them when they view and try to interpret the full spectrum of organizational disclosures.

So to which stakeholders should nonprofit organizations' accountability-exercising be directed? This involves both the board's identification of the key stakeholder groups and the extent to which accountability is owed to each (Leatherwood & O'Neal, 1996; Hyndman & McDonnell, 2009). Brennan and Solomon (2008) argue that the set of stakeholders includes an expanding number of groups to whom nonprofits are becoming accountable, with stakeholder inclusivity becoming a more pervasive theme in contemporary nonprofit governance. The challenge is that of trying to balance the differing interests and agendas of these groups, such as funders versus beneficiaries or service users, present users versus future users, donors and sponsors versus professional staff and so on (Spear et al., 2009). This can be quite a complex and political issue (Stone & Ostrower, 2007), arguably more convoluted and risk-laden than the stakeholder environment faced by for-profit organizations.

A number of researchers have identified the temptation for nonprofits and their boards to prioritize their accountability to donors, since they can be major fund providers. This of course may also extend to sponsors. In terms of organizational viability assurance, that prioritization can also include regulators. While it may be argued that these stakeholders merit legal, moral and providential priority for accountability rendering, the underlying organizational motivation may be one of preserving these stakeholders' approval as a key to ongoing organizational funding and survival (Miller, 2002; Hyndman & McDonnell, 2009; Brown & Moore, 2001). However, if the above are being treated as surrogates for 'owners,' Miller (2002) argues that there are other stakeholder groups who can equally be regarded as 'owners': staff, taxpayers, other peer organizations, clients, suppliers and the general community. Jepson (2005), Ebrahim (2003) and Awio, Northcott, and Lawrence (2011) also point to the tendency in nonprofit organizations towards tactically or unconsciously directing their accountability efforts upwards and outwards towards the powerful stakeholders such as donors, sponsors and governments. This, they warn, risks producing imbalances in their accountability relationships that ignore the less powerful or less able stakeholders and those who they profess to serve. This has been revealed in Hermann et al.'s (2012) study, and the tendency was also reflected in Parker's (2003, 2008a) nonprofit boardroom studies that revealed pronounced boardroom focus upon financial strategies and their disclosure.

From the perspective of the board's own engagement with its accountabilities, Miller (2002) found that at times some nonprofit directors feel they are only accountable to themselves and many fail to be able to clearly identify just to whom they are accountable. Board accountability is a crucial concern, since Collier's (2005) study points out in his observation that nonprofit boards have a dual set of accountabilities, on one hand to stakeholders and on the other hand to hold management accountable. This duality was exhibited in Parker's (2003) study of a religious, social welfare, nonprofit organizational board which paid constant attention both to monitoring staff and executive accountability and to the organization's accountability relationship to its religious denomination 'owner.' Holland's (2002) qualitative study of 34 nonprofit organizations found that six groups of practices facilitated board accountability: maintaining focus on strategic priorities, pursuing two-way communications with stakeholder groups, setting clear expectations for the board members, activating policies in relation to conflicts of interest, regularly evaluating board and director performance and trialling new approaches to their work. However, he also found that many nonprofit boards ignored their basic responsibilities and accountabilities, thereby undermining public trust. Nowak and McCabe (2003) add to the slate of director responsibilities and accountabilities in pointing to their accountability for 'information harvesting' in order to obtain adequate information and to build their knowledge of the organization (Roberts et al., 2005) for fulfilling their responsibilities and accountabilities. Roberts et al. (2005) also argue for directors' responsibility to bring both independent judgment and close involvement in the organization as both critical evaluators and supporters of the organization's aspirations and actions in pursuit of its objectives. This requires accountability being pursued by them through their 'challenging, questioning, probing, discussing, testing, informing, debating and exploring' (Roberts et al., 2005, p. S12).

Where do accounting information and reports fit in the nonprofit board's exercise of its accountability obligations? The news is not necessarily good. Parker's (2003) participant-observer study of a social welfare organization board found that accounting reports and budget results monitoring were largely absent from boardroom discussions, being accorded a peripheral place in their attention. Instead they employed informal, self-triggered dialogues and only accorded accounting reports a central place in their deliberations when discussing the draft annual budget and discussing how to manage their public financial disclosures. In a further study of nonprofit professional association boards, Parker (2007b) similarly found that strategic development, monitoring and related discussions were again reactively triggered by informal director dialogue. This also applied to his observations of their monitoring performance against business plans and budgets. These were not generally triggered by formal reports but by directors' raising of issues ad hoc Parker (2008a). Thus, as Dhanani and Connolly (2012) have observed, formalized financial accountability appears to be largely expedited annually through the board's attention to the annual report, with an associated annual review developed as a public relations exercise. Collier's (2005) nonprofit board study points to a risk in this approach, namely that a vacant space in director's deliberations may occur between the limitations of accounting reports tabled and their narrative sense-making in boardroom discussions. That vacant space may allow a failure to raise appropriate accountability questions, questions raised to be left unanswered and acceptance of information which may be 'incomplete, ambiguous or misleading' (Collier, 2005, p. 948).

RESEARCH ISSUES IN NONPROFIT BOARD GOVERNANCE

The qualitative research to date that has addressed nonprofit organizational and board-level governance already reveals much about such governance processes that remain largely opaque to the vast majority of quantitative researchers engaging in the corporate governance research field. We see boards grappling with a set of potential roles that stretch across advice and support to the executive, mission and strategy development and approval, policy input and monitoring, control of strategic action, compliance with regulatory requirements and linkages to external constituencies. However, directors' attitudes to and understandings of these roles and responsibilities remain highly variable. We still need to learn more about what they prioritize and what they spend the bulk of their time discussing and deciding. Who they really see and address as their key stakeholders merits even further investigation.

Contemporary research reveals nonprofit directors engaged in a web of relationships, trying to manage these as part of their governance responsibilities and accountabilities. Dealing with and catering for their wide range of stakeholder groups presents a challenging task of trying to balance this complex mix. This is fraught with the dangers of excessive focus on one or more groups, to the exclusion of others. Oftentimes prominent in this mix is the nonprofit organization's relationship with government, either as a resource provider, or as an outsourcer or as a regulator. This also carries the risk of the board and its organization becoming a mere agent of the public sector and losing its identity, original mission and even losing or failing to adequately serve clients and members.

Evidence is emerging of a gradual change in the involvement of nonprofit boards as many move towards more active engagement with strategic development and management. Nonetheless, there is still evidence of the tendency towards passive monitoring and approval of executive proposals and initiatives, rather than directors offering independent input, critique and strategic advice. What does become clear is that for the nonprofit board overseeing often complex organizational operations and associated stakeholders, attention is often paid to organizational and external politics which must be monitored and navigated. At the same time boards continue to wrestle with their focus as it may oscillate between strategy/policy and compliance/control. It remains a question of balance. In relation to control, there appears to be an ever-present tendency for nonprofit boards to encroach upon executive management prerogatives and slip into micromanagement of daily operations. Yet on the other hand, due to information asymmetry, directors are invariably at the behest of senior executives with the latter's superior access to organizational information.

Crucial to the actual practice and ultimate effectiveness of nonprofit organizational governance is the board's own governance of its internal workings and responsibilities. The accounting research community has barely even considered this, likely being excessively focused upon measurable, quantifiable performance indicators and accounting systems and possibly considering such matters as 'soft,' irrelevant human behaviour. They could not be more mistaken. Available qualitative governance research reveals the CEO and board chair roles and relationship to be vital to how the board operates and how effectively it discharges its governance remit.

Both in terms of that relationship and how board members interact, we still need to know much more: what do they do and how do they do it? Already we have strong evidence that what a board focuses upon, how strategically oriented it is and whether it descends into routine operational minutiae is directly impacted by the manner in which its meeting agendas are structured and how the board chair drives those meetings. Furthermore, we also have some clear indications that the manner in which the board operates and the extent to which it successfully discharges its governance and accountability responsibilities reflects not only what transpires within the boardroom meetings but in various interactions and communications outside the boardroom.

For the nonprofit organization and its board, accountability is a much broader and more complex issue than accounting researchers have generally recognized or addressed. It is not a mere matter of receipt and scrutiny of formal reports and KPIs. Qualitative research reveals it to be a highly interactive, dialogical, socialized discourse that creates, generates, drives and determines accountability construction and ultimate shape and effectiveness or otherwise. For the board it is a relationship that runs in two directions, upwards and outwards to external parties and internally and downwards to organizational staff and members. Both must be addressed. Yet this involves a complex mix of stakeholder groups, each with their own perspectives and agendas: financial, social, community, economic, political and institutional. At the same time, working in an environment where there is often an unlimited demand for a nonprofit organization's services in a usually resource-constrained environment, there is an incessant temptation for boards to focus on their accountability to resource providers to the exclusion of other important and often less powerful groups. However, effective governance also requires board members to be accountable to each other.

The research agenda remains almost unlimited in scope. We need to know much more about how governance operates when nonprofit organizations enter into strategic alliances with government or other for-profit or nonprofit organizations (Cornforth, 2013). There is much more need for observation-based research into board operations, and research into board-level governance that adopts a longitudinal design rather than the convenient momentary snapshot at a point in time so characteristic of cross-sectional designs (Cornforth, 2013). There is also a case for pursuing the questions of how boards relate to government, to professional and volunteer staff and to users of their services, in terms of consultation, communication, reporting and accountability (Hyndman & McDonnell, 2009). Much more needs to be understood about whether, how and why nonprofit boards may be focused upon the strategies and performance of their own organization and/ or upon the extent to which the organization is serving its wider mission and the public interest. One suspects that with the pressures of regulation, government outsourcing to nonprofits and the competition for resources, boards may be erring towards a preoccupation with their own organization's internal operations and survival. So the question remains, how does the board relate to its wider environment (Stone & Ostrower, 2007)? While the sanctuary of the boardroom has been penetrated, there is much more we need to know.

REFERENCES

Anheier, H. K. (2009). What kind of nonprofit sector, what kind of society? Comparative policy reflections. *American Behavioural Scientist, 52*(7), 1082–1094.

Arrington, C.E., & Francis, J. R. (1989). Letting the chat out of the bag: Deconstruction, privilege and accounting research. *Accounting, Organizations and Society, 21*,1–28.

Association of Chief Executives of Voluntary Organisations (ACEVO). (2005). *Good governance: A code for the voluntary and community sector.* London: National Council For Voluntary Organizations.

Awio, G., Northcott, D., & Lawrence, S. (2011). Social capital and accountability in grass-roots NGOs: The case of the Ugandan community-led HIV/AIDS initiative. *Accounting, Auditing and Accountability Journal, 24*(1), 63–92.

Bansal, P. (2013). Commentary: Inducing frame-breaking insights through qualitative research. *Corporate Governance: An International Review, 21*(2), 127–130.

Beasley, M. S., Carcello, J. V., Hermanson, D. R., & Lapides, P. D. (2000). Fraudulent financial reporting: Consideration of industry traits and corporate governance mechanisms. *Accounting Horizons, 14*(4), 441–454.

Brennan, N. M., & Solomon, J. (2008). Guest editorial: Corporate governance, accountability and mechanisms of accountability: An overview. *Accounting, Auditing and Accountability Journal, 21*(7), 885–906.

Brown, L. D., & Moore, M. H. (2001). Symposium: New roles and challenges for NGOs: Accountability, strategy, and international nongovernmental organizations. *Nonprofit and Voluntary Sector Quarterly, 30*(3), 569–587.

Brown, W. A., & Iverson, J. O. (2004). Exploring strategy and board structure in nonprofit organizations. *Nonprofit and Voluntary Sector Quarterly, 33*, 377–400.

Cadbury, A. (2000). The corporate governance agenda. *Corporate Governance, 8*(1), 7–15.

Chew, C., & Osborne, S. P. (2009a). Exploring strategic positioning in the UK charitable sector: Emerging evidence from charitable organizations that provide public services. *British Journal of Management, 20*, 90–105.

Chew, C., & Osborne, S. P. (2009b). Identifying the factors that influence positioning strategy in U.K. charitable organizations that provide public services: Toward an integrating model. *Nonprofit and Voluntary Sector Quarterly, 38*(1), 29–50.

Choudhury, N. (1988). The seeking of accounting where it is not: Towards a theory of non-accounting in organizational settings. *Accounting, Organizations and Society, 13*(6), 549–558.

Clarke, T. (1998). Research on corporate governance. *Corporate Governance: An International Review, 6*(1), 57–66.

Collier, P. M. (2005). Governance and the quasi-public organization: A case study of social housing. *Critical Perspectives on Accounting, 16*, 929–949.

Collier, P. M. (2008). Stakeholder accountability: A field study of the implementation of a governance improvement plan. *Accounting, Auditing & Accountability Journal, 21*(7), 933–954.

Conger, J., Finegold, D., & Lawler, E., III. (1998). Appraising boardroom performance. *Harvard Business Review, 76*, 136–148.

Cornforth, C. (2001). What makes boards effective? An examination of the relationships between board inputs, structure, processes and effectiveness on non-profit organizations. *Corporate Governance, 9*, 217–227.

Cornforth, C. (2012). Nonprofit governance research: Limitations of the focus on boards and suggestions for new directions. *Nonprofit and Voluntary Sector Quarterly, 41*(6), 1116–1135.

Cornforth, C., & Edwards, C. (1999). Board roles in the strategic management of non-profit organisations: Theory and practice. *Corporate Governance: An International Review, 7*(4), 346–362.

Dhanani, A., & Connolly, C. (2012). Discharging not-for-profit accountability: UK charities and public discourse. *Accounting, Auditing and Accountability Journal, 25*(7), 1140–1169.

Dulewicz, V., & Herbert, P. (1999). The priorities and performance of boards in UK public companies. *Corporate Governance, 7*(2), 178–189.

Ebrahim, A. (2003). Accountability in practice: Mechanisms for NGOs. *World Development, 31*(5), 813–829.

Eng, L. L, & Mak, Y. T. (2003). Corporate governance and voluntary disclosure. *Journal of Accounting and Public Policy, 22*(4), 325–346.

Golensky, M. (1993). The board—executive relationship in nonprofit organizations: Partnership or power struggle? *Nonprofit Management and Leadership, 4*, 177–191.

Harford, J., Sattar, A. M., & Maxwell, W. F. (2012). Corporate governance and firm cash holdings in the U.S. *Corporate Governance*, Springer Berlin Hiedelberg, 107–138.

Heracleous, L. (1999). The board of directors as leaders of the organisation. *Corporate Governance: An International Review, 7*(3), 256–265.

Heracleous, L. (2001). What is the impact of corporate governance on organisational performance? *Corporate Governance: An International Review, 9*(3), 165–173.

Hermann, M. G., Lecy, J. D., Mitchell, G. E., Page, C., Raggo, P., Schmitz, H. P., & Vinuela, L. (2012). *Transnational NGOs: A cross-sectoral analysis of leadership perspectives*. New York: Moynihan Institute of Global Affairs, Syracuse University. Retrieved 6 September 2013 from http://ssrn.com/abstract=2191082

Hines, R. D. (1992). Accounting: Filling the negative space. *Accounting, Organizations and Society, 17*(3/4), 313–341.

Hodgkin, C. (1993). Policy *and* paper clips: Rejecting the lure of the corporate model. *Nonprofit Management & Leadership, 3*(4), 415–428.

Holland, T. (2002). Board accountability: Lessons from the field. *Nonprofit Management & Leadership, 12*(4), 409–428.

Hoye, R., & Cuskelly, G. (2003). Board-executive relationships within voluntary sport organisations. *Sport Management Review, 6*, 53–74.

Hyndman, N., & McDonnell, P. (2009). Governance and charities: An exploration of key themes and the development of a research agenda. *Financial Accountability and Management, 25*(1), 5–31.

Ingley, C. B., & Van der Walt, N. T. (2001). The strategic board: The changing role of directors in developing and maintaining corporate capability. *Corporate Governance: An International Review, 9*(3), 174–185.

Inkpen, A., & Choudhury, N. (1995). The seeking of strategy where it is not: Towards a theory of strategy absence. *Strategic Management Journal, 16*(4), 313–323.

Jepson, P. (2005). Commentary: Governance and accountability of environmental NGOs. *Environmental Science and Policy, 8*, 515–524.

Knutsen, W. L., & Brower, R. S. (2010). Managing expressive and instrumental accountabilities in nonprofit and voluntary organizations: A qualitative investigation. *Nonprofit and Voluntary Sector Quarterly, 39*(4), 588–610.

Leatherwood, M. L., & O'Neal, D. (1996). The transformation of boards in corporate and not-for-profit sectors: Diminishing differences and converging contexts. *Corporate Governance: An International Review, 4*(3), 180–192.

Machold, S., & Farquhar, S. (2013). Board task evolution: A longitudinal field study in the UK. *Corporate Governance: An International Review, 21*(2), 147–164.

Mackay, I. L., & Sweeting, R. C. (2000). Perspectives on integrated business risk management (BRM) and the implications for corporate governance. *Corporate Governance: An International Review, 8*(4), 367–375.

Maitlis, S. (2004). Taking it from the top: How CEOs influence (and fail to influence) their boards. *Organization Studies, 25*(8), 1275–1311.

McNulty, T., & Pettigrew, A. (1999). Strategists on the board. *Organization Studies, 20*(1), 47–74.

McNulty, T., Zattoni, A., & Douglas, T. (2013). Developing corporate governance research through qualitative methods: A review of previous studies. *Corporate Governance: An International Review, 21*(2), 183–198.

Miller, J. L. (2002). The board as a monitor of organizational activity: The applicability of agency theory to nonprofit boards. *Nonprofit Management and Leadership, 12*(4), 429–450.

Miller-Millesen, J. L. (2003). Understanding the behaviour of nonprofit boards of directors: A theory-based approach. *Nonprofit and Voluntary Sector Quarterly, 32*, 521–547.

Mole, V. (2003). What are the chief executive's expectations and experiences of their board? In C. Cornforth (Ed.), *The governance of public and non-profit organisations: What do boards do?* (pp. 150–163). London: Routledge.

Nicholson, G. J., & Kiel, G. C. (2004). A framework for diagnosing board effectiveness. *Corporate Governance: An International Review, 12*(4), 442–460.

Nowak, M. J., & McCabe, M. (2003). Information costs and the role of the independent corporate director. *Corporate Governance: An International Review, 11*(4), 300–307.

Ostrower, F. (2007). *Nonprofit governance in the United States: Findings on performance and accountability from the first national representative study.* Washington, DC: Urban Institute.

Parker, L. D. (2001). Reactive planning in a Christian bureaucracy. *Management Accounting Research, 12*(3), 321–356.

Parker, L. D. (2002). Budgetary incrementalism in a Christian bureaucracy. *Management Accounting Research, 13*(1), 71–100.

Parker, L. D. (2003). Financial management strategy in a community welfare organisation: A boardroom perspective. *Financial Accountability and Management, 19*(4), 341–374.

Parker, L. D. (2005). Corporate governance crisis down under: Post-Enron accounting education and research inertia. *European Accounting Review, 14*(2), 383–394.

Parker, L. D. (2007a). Financial and external reporting research: The broadening corporate governance challenge. *Accounting and Business Research, 37*(1), 39–54.

Parker, L. D. (2007b). Boardroom strategizing in professional associations: Processual and institutional perspectives. *Journal of Management Studies, 44*(8), 1454–1480.

Parker, L. D. (2007c). Internal governance in the nonprofit boardroom: A participant observer study. *Corporate Governance: An International Review, 15*(5), 923–934.

Parker, L. D. (2008a). Boardroom operational and financial control: An insider view. *British Journal of Management, 19*, 65–88.

Parker, L. D. (2008b). Towards understanding corporate governance processes: Life at the top. *Indonesian Management and Accounting Research, 7*(1), 1–15.

Peck, E. (1995). The performance of an NHS trust board: Actors' accounts, minutes and observation. *British Journal of Management, 6*(2), 135–156.

Pye, A. (2001). A study in studying corporate boards over time: Looking backwards to move forwards. *British Journal of Management, 12,* 33–45.

Radbourne, J. (2003). Performing on boards: The link between governance and corporate reputation in nonprofit arts boards. *Corporate Reputation Review, 6*(3), 212–222.

Ravasi, D., & Zattoni, A. (2006). Exploring the political side of board involvement in strategy: A study of mixed-ownership institutions. *Journal of Management Studies, 43*(8), 1671–1702.

Roberts, J. (1990). Strategy and accounting in a UK conglomerate. *Accounting, Organizations & Society, 15*(1/2), 107–126.

Roberts, J. (1991). The possibilities of accountability. *Accounting, Organizations & Society, 16,* 355–368.

Roberts, J., McNulty, T., & Stiles, P. (2005). Beyond agency conceptions of the work of the non-executive director: Creating accountability in the boardroom. *British Journal of Management, 16,* S5–S26.

Rochester, C. (2003). The role of boards in small voluntary organisations. In C. Cornforth (Ed.), *The governance of public and non-profit organisations: What do boards do?* (pp. 115–130). London: Routledge.

Saj, P. (2013). Charity performance reporting: Comparing board and executive roles. *Accounting, Auditing and Accountability Journal, 10*(3/4), 347–368.

Samra-Fredericks, D. (2000a). An analysis of the behavioural dynamics of corporate governance—a talk-based ethnography of a UK manufacturing 'board-in-action.' *Corporate Governance: An International Review, 8*(4), 311–326.

Samra-Fredericks, D. (2000b). Doing "boards-in-action" research—an ethnographic approach for the capture and analysis of directors' and senior managers' interactive routines. *Corporate Governance: An International Review, 8*(3), 244–257.

Sosin, M. R. (2012). Social expectations, constraints, and their effect on nonprofit strategies. *Nonprofit and Voluntary Sector Quarterly, 41*(6), 1231–1250.

Spear, R., Cornforth, C., & Aiken, M. (2009). The governance challenges of social enterprises: Evidence from a UK empirical study. *Annals of Public and Cooperative Economics, 80*(2), 247–273.

Steane, P. D., & Christie, M. (2001). Nonprofit boards in Australia: A distinctive governance approach. *Corporate Governance: An International Review, 9*(1), 48–58.

Stiles, P. (2001). The impact of the board on strategy: An empirical examination. *Journal of Management Studies, 38*(5), 627–650.

Stiles, P., & Taylor, B. (2001). *Boards at work: How directors view their roles and responsibilities.* Oxford: Oxford University Press.

Stone, M. (1991). The propensity of governing boards to plan. *Nonprofit Management and Leadership, 1*(3), 203–215.

Stone, M. M., & Ostrower, F. (2007). Acting in the public interest? Another look at research on nonprofit governance. *Nonprofit and Voluntary Sector Quarterly, 36,* 416–438.

Tucker, B., & Parker, L. D. (2013). Out of control? Strategy in the NFP sector: The implications for management control. *Accounting, Auditing & Accountability Journal, 26*(2), 234–266.

Tucker, B., & Parker, L. D. (2014, forthcoming). Business as usual? An institutional view of the relationship between management control systems and strategy. *Financial Accountability and Management.*

Van den Berghe, L.A.A., & Levrau, A. (2004). Evaluating boards of directors: What constitutes a good corporate board? *Corporate Governance: An International Review, 12*(4), 461–478.

Vinten, G. (2001). Corporate governance and the sons of Cadbury. *Corporate Governance, 1*(4), 4–8.

Zahra, S. A., & Pearce, J. A., II. (1990). Determinants of board directors' strategic involvement. *European Management Journal, 8*(2), 164–173.

13 Australian Charity Reporting Reforms

Serving Private or Public Interests?

Phil Saj

INTRODUCTION

In June 2013, the proclamation of the Financial Reporting Regulations (the ACNC Regulations) associated with the Australian Charities Not-for-Profit Commission Act 2012 (the ACNC Act), marked the end point of the Rudd/Gillard/Rudd Labor government's fast-paced legislative programme of comprehensive national regulation of charities, which had commenced in earnest in 2010. It was also a watershed in the development of an Australian public policy issue that has attracted considerable attention over two decades since the landmark report of Industry Commission (IC) Inquiry into Charitable Organisations in Australia in 1995. This chapter explores a major aspect of that reform: the development of reporting requirements for Australian charities.

The chapter is structured as follows: in the following section, the relevant literature on not-for-profit accountability is reviewed. Next a brief overview of the Australian charity sector is provided. Having established a conceptual and historical context, the chapter then traces the development of reporting requirements for Australian charities. This is done in two stages: first to be considered are the developments that occurred up to the commencement of the recent reforms; second, and dealt with in greater detail, are the reforms of 2010–2013. The analysis concludes with a reflection on the development of Australian charity reporting requirements by reference to the literature. A postscript concerning recent developments in charity reform that have been announced (but not yet completed) following a change in government in September 2013 completes the chapter.

LITERATURE REVIEW

It is something of an understatement to say that the concept of accountability has been thoroughly debated in the accounting literature and beyond. Always, the questions in relation to accountability are: to whom? for what?

and by what means? (Gray, Bebbington, & Collison, 2006). Mulgan (2000, p. 555) cuts to the chase by contrasting a narrow, or 'core,' definition with a wider, or 'extended,' definition, with the former comprising the mere reporting on one's actions to a higher authority who can impose sanctions, and the latter, the adoption of a more holistic approach where the party rendering account embraces a responsibility for their actions.

Charities typically have multiple narrow accountabilities imposed on them by corporate regulators (for example, an annual requirement to lodge audited financial reports), by industry accreditation agencies (for example, the requirement of residential aged-care providers to meet quality standards) and funders (for example, the provision of acquittal reports to government funders, or outcome evaluations to private donors). That the acquittal of multiple accountabilities is onerous and resource consuming has been well documented in the literature (cf. Kanter & Summers, 1987; Cutt & Murray, 2000), and was universally evidenced in countless submissions to Australian inquiries into the third sector over the past two decades (cf. Smith, 2008; Independent Schools Council of Australia, 2011).

Balancing multiple accountabilities and, in particular, acquitting a public accountability is often problematic, with some charity managers viewing the acquittal of accountabilities through specific contractual relationships as a proxy for acquitting a public accountability (Saj, 2012).

However, many have argued (cf. Jeavons, 1992; Coy, Fischer, & Gordon, 2001; Brody, 2003; Lee, 2004; Choudhury & Ahmed, 2002) that while, at law, charities are private organisations, the nature of their accountability is closer to that of government than to the private sector. That is, they are not only accountable to identifiable stakeholders like clients and funders with whom they have a contractual relationship, but also have a broader accountability to the community because of the essential nature of the roles they assume and the impact they have on people's lives, and the financial support and trust they receive from the public. Kearns, for example, described such accountability as

> much more than just the formal processes and channels for reporting to a higher authority. Instead, the term accountability generally refers to a wide spectrum of public expectations dealing with organizational performance, responsiveness, and even morality of government and nonprofit organizations. These expectations often include implicit performance criteria—related to obligations and responsibilities—that are subjectively interpreted and sometimes even contradictory. And in this broad conception of accountability, the range of people and institutions to whom public and nonprofit organizations must account includes not only higher authorities in the institutional chain of command but also the general public.

> (1996, p. 9)

Such an expansive definition of accountability has also been applied within the wider accounting literature. Normanton, for example, opined,

> it is not accountability merely to submit a certified financial account each year. To be accountable means to give reasons for, and explanations of, actions taken; but an account rarely provides explanations and it never gives reasons . . . Any major financial account hides far more than it reveals. It is a protection against fraud, and the law provides that it may not conceal criminal sins; but other kinds of sins may be lost without trace within it.
>
> (1971, p. 314)

In the private sector too, the narrow approach to accountability has been eschewed. In its landmark publication, *The Corporate Report*, the Accounting Standards Steering Committee (ASSC) provided a useful contrast between public accountability and compliance, holding that

> there is an implicit responsibility to report publicly (whether or not required by law or regulation) incumbent on every economic entity whose size and format renders it significant . . . The responsibility to report publicly (referred to later as public accountability) is separate from and broader than the legal obligation to report and arises from the custodial role played in the community by economic entities.
>
> (1975, p. 15)

Such a view embraces the notion of stewardship (Jeavons, 1992); a concept that Chen demonstrates is necessarily embedded in 'the prevailing social philosophy' (1975, p. 542). The views of Kearns (1996), Normanton (1971), the ASSC (1975), Jeavons (1992) and Chen (1975) exemplify the concept of accountability posited by Lee as 'a dialogue about shared values rather than the aggregation of individual self-interests' (2004, p. 70). That is, the party rendering an account is not divorced from the party to which the report is provided, but is engaged cooperatively.

In summary, the review of the literature has demonstrated that there is a significant public interest dimension to charity accountability, which extends well beyond mere private concerns for meeting compliance and contractual obligations in order to continue operations. In the following section, which provides a brief overview of the Australian charity sector, it is demonstrated that charities have developed together with, and at some times, in advance of, government, with a salient characteristic of the Australian welfare state being that of co-responsibility between the state and charities, one which Lyons (2001) differentiates from systems that have developed in similar jurisdictions. As such, Australian charities are integral to the social whole whereby the 'extended' notions of accountability, as put forward by writers such as Normanton (1971), Kearns (1996), Coy et al. (2001) and

Lee (2004), are clearly appropriate. In analysing the development of charity reporting in Australia during 1993–2012, this chapter provides strong empirical evidence, and thus understanding of the tension between public and private accountability of charities. In so doing it provides a basis for addressing the question posed in its title: have recent reforms served private or public interests?

THE AUSTRALIAN CHARITY SECTOR

To qualify as a charity, an organisation must meet the common law requirements of the Commissioners for Special Purposes of Income Tax v Pemsel [1891–1894] All ER Rep 28 case (the Pemsel case), or those specified by the Extension of Charitable Purpose Act 2004, which extended the common law meaning to include child care, self-help bodies and closed or contemplative religious orders. Thus the Australian charity sector comprises a wide range of organisations active in the fields of welfare, health, education and religion. In both social and economic terms the charity sector is significant. Charities have been active in the Australian community since European settlement (Dickey, 1986; Rogan & Moore, 1999) and 'have contributed significantly to community building and ultimately nation building' (IC, 1995, p. 1). Such is the significance of the role played by Australian charities that it has been acknowledged to be one of co-responsibility with government (Beilharz, Considine & Watts, 1993; Graycar & Jamrozic, 1989; IC, 1995; Robbins, 1997), which the Industry Commission noted, 'has been established by convention and by law' (1995, p. xx). As such, Australian charities operate within a welfare state, with responsibility for providing the social infrastructure assigned to the state, and the delivery of services to government departments, private operators and charities (Graycar & Jamrozic, 1989).

In 2012, 56,073 entities were endorsed by the Australian Taxation Office as charities (ACNC, 2013a). 43% have social and community welfare as their main purpose, with religious charities making up about 22% of these, a further 17% identifying their main purpose as education (ACNC, 2013a). The charity sector is constantly growing and changing. While 70% of charities have been active for over 10 years, the ACNC registered over 1,600 new charities in its first year (ACNC, 2013b). Indeed charities comprise the oldest of Australian organisations with some more than 100 years old (IC, 1995). Charities comprise a large part of the broader not-for-profit (NFP) sector, which contributed 4.1% to gross domestic product and in 2006 employed approximately 890,000 people (ABS, 2009). In 2010–2011 quantifiable tax expenditures provided to NFPs were approximately $3.3 billion, with a similar amount estimated to have been contributed from unquantifiable tax expenditures (Treasury, 2011).

In summary, the charity sector is thoroughly integrated into the fabric of Australian political, social and economic life. In economic terms it gives to the community and receives funding directly and indirectly from taxpayers. In practical ways it provides essential daily services that would otherwise not be provided. In times of crisis it is quick to garner resources and provide support. Charities perform their work, not just with resources provided by the government, but through individual donors and through their own, often considerable, resources. As well, they contribute significantly to the development of social capital through marshalling the effort of volunteers, and by participating strongly in the public policy debate. In these ways, charities perform very public roles, for which, as noted in the above review of the literature, it has been suggested that the nature of their accountability is closer to that of government than to the private sector.

Determining exactly how best charity accountability should be defined in Australia has attracted the attention of a wide range of stakeholders for two decades. It is to this policy debate that we now turn. In the following section the development of charity reporting requirements from 1993 to the commencement of the recent active reform programme that took place between 2010 and 2013 is considered. The data on which this analysis is based comprises reports of statutory inquiries, media reports, the work of professional accounting bodies and the Australian Accounting Standards Board and the views of charities and other stakeholders.

THE DEVELOPMENT OF CHARITY REPORTING REQUIREMENTS: PART 1—PRECURSORS TO THE REFORMS OF 2010–2013

Charity reporting has received considerable attention over the past 20 years. In some cases the issue has been raised directly, as in the 2008 Senate Standing Committee on Economics inquiry into disclosure regimes by charities and not-for-profit organisations. In others, it has been debated within a wider remit, as with the Industry Commission's 1995 Inquiry into Charitable Organisations in Australia. In addition to such government-initiated inquiries, the matter has received significant attention from the media (cf. Ferguson, 2006; Australian Consumers Association, 2008), the Australian Accounting Standards Board, the accounting profession and some charities. Since 2010, charity reporting has been debated intensely during the period of unprecedented reform that resulted in comprehensive national regulation of charities through the ACNC Act. The following provides an overview of the development of charity reporting requirements.

The 1995 Industry Commission Report

In December 1993, the Australian government asked the Industry Commission, a body charged with the carriage of microeconomic reform in Australia, to inquire into the provision of social welfare by that subset of charities that provided direct welfare services. The Commission undertook a wide-ranging inquiry that examined the size, scope, efficiency and effectiveness of services provided by the charitable sector; in particular, the nature and sources of fundraising, relations with government programmes and assistance, industrial agreements and arrangements, taxation issues, government regulation and the accountability and performance of organisations within the charitable sector. It produced a draft report in 1993 and a final report in 1995. The final report evidenced concerns from charities and professional accounting bodies over the then current state of public accountability. In particular, the Commission identified the following problems: (1) lack of consistent data collection processes, (2) lack of public access to information and (3) lack of standardisation of financial reporting and other information (IC, 1995). One large charity, the Brotherhood of St Laurence, said that 'openness and disclosure of information should be an essential operational principle of all community welfare organisations' (IC, 1995, p. 201). A number of charities highlighted the need for a sector-specific accounting standard, because

> existing accounting standards developed for for-profit entities, although applicable to CSWOs, do not address some issues, such as which expenditures should be reported as fundraising costs, which are particular to CSWOs and relevant for supporters or donors to CSWOs.
>
> (IC, 1995, p. 215)

The country's (then two) professional accounting bodies, the Australian Society of Certified Practising Accountants and the Institute of Chartered Accountants in Australia, also called for reform, suggesting that

> the reporting framework and its requirements should be standardised across all legislation enabling the formation of charitable organisations so that relevant, reliable and comparable financial reporting practices are adopted by all charitable organisations.
>
> (IC, 1995, p. 206)

In responding to submissions on the issue of public accountability, the Commission acknowledged the inadequacies of the situation by making two specific recommendations: the development of a sector-specific accounting standard, and uniform incorporation rules and a requirement for charities to report using the sector-specific accounting standard (IC, 1995).

While the 1995 Industry Commission of Inquiry marked a watershed in the development of public policy, its recommendations were never adopted, partly, according to McGregor-Lowndes (2009), due to the report being released at a time of a change of government, whereby nine months after its release, the 13-year period of the reforming Hawke/Keating Labor government ended with the election of a conservative government lead by John Howard. While regulatory reform was largely removed from the public agenda during the 10 years of the Howard government, one inquiry established in 2001 provided a forum through which the development of charity accountability was further developed.

The 2001 Inquiry into the Definition of Charities and Related Organisations

In 2000, as a result of pressure exerted by the liberal democratic party, the Australian Democrats, in response to their concerns that charities may suffer from the major reform to Australia's tax system as a result of bringing in a value-added tax (McGregor-Lowndes, 2009), the Prime Minister announced the establishment of an Inquiry into the Definition of Charities and Related Organisations (IDC). While the inquiry did not focus directly on the issue of disclosure, the matter was nonetheless raised explicitly in many submissions and in the final report. As such, the IDC provided a forum for the continuing development of ideas as to what is appropriate by way of charity reporting.

Submissions to the inquiry covered a wide range of issues, including the centralised, uniform regulation of charities and the provision of information to the public. Those in favour of public accountability included the major national charity, Mission Australia, which argued that all charities should 'provide high standards of accountability, ownership and purpose as well as transparency in their use of funds and distribution of assets' (Commonwealth of Australia, 2001, p. 94). Other major charities, such as Jobs Australia and Anglicare, made similar submissions, while the peak body, the Fundraising Institute of Australia, emphasised the importance of public disclosures by calling for the 'provision of a central information resource on charitable activities, including comparative performance data' (Commonwealth of Australia, 2001, p. 282). However, some opposed such a change. For example, the Catholic Church stated a preference for maintaining a common law approach to regulation rather than a legislative one; and the Asthma Foundation of Queensland opposed change for fear that it may actually increase the compliance burden (Commonwealth of Australia, 2001).

Overall there was majority support, from across the political spectrum, for improved charity disclosures with the final report stating that 'a clear and consistent accountability framework would help to maintain and enhance public confidence in the integrity of charities and related entities' (Commonwealth of Australia, 2001, p. 292). However, few of the committee's recommendations came to fruition, largely because of concerns over the unworkability of proposed legislation on the definition of a charity, and the potential diminution of charities' freedom to engage in political debate (McGregor-Lowndes, 2009). In 2004, the government passed legislation (the Extension of Charitable Purpose Act, 2004) that extended the definition of a charity to include child care, self-help groups and closed religious orders.

2004, A Better Framework: Reforming Not-for-Profit Regulation

In 2004, a study undertaken by Woodward and Marshall from the University of Melbourne's Centre for Corporate Law and Securities Regulation, titled *A Better Framework: Reforming Not-for-Profit Regulation*, which surveyed over 1,700 not-for-profits, concluded that the sector's value to the community was undermined through regulatory (including reporting) inefficiencies (Woodward & Marshall, 2004). Amongst the recommendations of the report were: (1) a single Commonwealth statutory regime should be introduced for all corporate bodies; (2) the introduction of a not-for-profit-specific accounting standard; (3) a review of overall NFP disclosure obligations because they were duplicative, often onerous, especially for smaller organisations, and did not facilitate transparency; (4) consideration of the desirability of developing a Standard Information Return, through which organisations would disclose their main purposes and activities, corporate information, how the objectives of the organisation are met and about how accountability to stakeholders is achieved; and (5) consideration of a fundraising accounting standard to promote transparency of and comparability between not-for-profits. As such, *A Better Framework* provided further evidence of the problems with charity accountability that were highlighted in the earlier inquiries and the media reports noted above. Further important research on charity reporting over the past 10 years has also been undertaken by the Institute of Chartered Accountants in Australia.

2003–2013 The Institute of Chartered Accountants in Australia

The Institute of Chartered Accountants in Australia (ICAA), one of Australia's three professional accounting bodies, has played a significant role in the policy discussion around not-for-profit accountability by undertaking research, developing guidance statements on financial and non-financial reporting, promoting best-practice reporting and making submissions to the many inquiries and consultation processes that have taken place since 1993.

In 2003, the ICAA surveyed 39 annual reports of not-for-profit entities. It found considerable inconsistency and lack of disclosure on some key issues. Four issues were highlighted: (1) a lack of consistency in accounting for grants; (2) insufficient disclosures on how funds were generated, administered and expended on core activities; (3) inadequate disclosures over inventories distributed at no or nominal cost; and (4) inadequate disclosures relating to economic dependency, especially where the not-for-profit organisation was in receipt of significant government grants or subsidies. The report concluded that 'it is unlikely a not-for-profit can satisfy the reporting obligations imposed by the current financial reporting framework by providing Special Purpose Financial Reports' (ICAA, 2003, p. 4) and suggested that not-for-profits would benefit from the development of a financial reporting framework that met their specific requirements. It also supported disclosure of service performance, plans and governance information.

The ICAA repeated the study in 2006, and, while finding that the not-for-profits in their sample largely complied with basic statutory reporting requirements, these fell short of best practice. The 2006 report reiterated the main concerns and put forward the same suggestions as the 2003 report did; but it also suggested the need for a not-for-profit-specific financial reporting standard, as it had in its submission to the Industry Commission Inquiry some 13 years earlier. This, it held, should be based on the Statement of Recommend Practice followed by charities and regulated by the Charities Commission of England and Wales. From 2007 to 2013, the ICAA has issued a series of biennial good practice guides for not-for-profit financial reporting, titled *Enhancing Not-for-Profit Annual and Financial Reporting—Best Practice Reporting*.

The accounting profession, academics and not-for-profit organisations were not the only voices expressing concern over the state of charity accountability. A series of well-publicised media stories between 2005 and 2008 also highlighted significant anomalies and community concerns.

2005–2008 Media Reports

In 2005 and 2006, charity accountability featured prominently in a series of articles published in the premier business journal, *Business Review Weekly*. The first article observed that, despite the issues of taxation and accountability across the economy being high-priority matters for the government, the Australian Taxation Office and the Department of Treasury 'have no idea what the sector is worth or how many organisations operate in it. Nor do they know how much tax is foregone each year' (Ferguson, 2005a, p. 46). The second article, also published in 2005, reported the journal's research into the size of the charity sector, estimating annual revenue in 2004 to have been $70 billion, making it a very significant player in the Australian economy (Ferguson, 2005b). Furthermore, charities were major recipients of government funding, which they used to deliver services (Ferguson, 2005b). This article also noted consistent calls from the sector for improved regulation and accountability, and concern over the adequacy of reporting requirements by the accounting profession, major philanthropists and academics (Ferguson, 2005b).

The third article (Ferguson, 2006) focused on the largest part of the charity sector, religions, the 2004 revenue of which was estimated to have been $23 billion. The article pointed out that, despite a significant part of this revenue having been derived from the public purse either directly as payments from government for service delivery, or indirectly through concessional taxation treatments, there was a significant lack of transparency in reporting by religious organisations.

In 2008 the Australian Consumers Association (now renamed CHOICE), a member-based not-for-profit organisation with the objective of empowering consumers through the provision of quality information (CHOICE, 2014), also investigated charity accountability. While finding that the vast majority of Australians donated to charity, they reported that 81% of respondents did not know what proportion of their donation reached the charity's beneficiaries, and 97% stated that it was 'very' or 'somewhat' important to be provided with information about the effectiveness of charities' work. Significantly, the article reported that many charities saw the lack of uniform accountability requirements as problematic, with, once again, some calling for a national charity regulator similar to that of England and Wales (Australian Consumers Association, 2008, p. 14).

2007–2013 PwC Transparency Awards

The PwC Transparency Awards are an annual competition aimed at improving the quality and transparency of charity reporting. They were first held in Australia in 2007, following success with similar competitions overseas. The awards are jointly sponsored by PwC, the ICAA and the Centre for Social Impact. One of the main reasons for holding the awards is to reduce the variability in charity reporting (PwC, 2012), which, as this chapter evidences, has been a widely held concern for some time. Since 2007, 253 not-for-profits have entered the awards. Each year the jury presents a report which includes their observations on trends and reporting issues across the sector. An example of accountability as dialogue is provided by the following statement from the 2012 winner:

> When we first submitted an entry to the PwC awards five years ago, we recognised that the awards represented best practice across the not-for-profit sector and provided a benchmark for complete and quality reporting. As an organisation committed to transparency and quality in all our systems, operations and reporting, we felt the PwC awards reflected our ethos and our win this year confirms just that.
>
> (Cancer Council of NSW, 2012)

2008 Disclosure Regimes for Charities and Not-for-Profit Organisations

On 18 June 2008, the Australian Democrats successfully moved a motion in the Senate to establish an inquiry by the Senate Standing Committee on Economics (the Committee) to investigate the relevance and appropriateness of (then) current disclosure regimes for charities and all other not-for-profit organisations; to identify models of regulation and legal forms that would improve governance and management of charities and not-for-profit organisations and cater for emerging social enterprises; and to identify other measures that can be taken by government and the not-for-profit sector to assist the sector to improve governance, standards, accountability and transparency in its use of public and government funds. In justifying the inquiry, the leader of the Australian Democrats, Senator Alison, tendered the article by CHOICE of March 2008 (see above), which evidenced 'wide variability and inconsistency in the way that charities disclose information to the public' (Commonwealth of Australia, 2008, p. 2729), and noted that the 27 recommendations from the 2001 Inquiry into the Definition of Charities had not been implemented. The Committee received 178 written submissions and heard directly from 85 witnesses. Charities continued to demonstrate their concern over reporting through the volume of their submissions: almost half the submissions to the Committee were from charities.

The Committee made 15 recommendations, including the establishment of a national regulator of not-for-profits similar to that operating in England and Wales, and a requirement for transparent public reporting by not-for-profit entities that permitted comparability across the sector, with the level of reporting proportionate to the size of the organisation (Commonwealth of Australia, 2008). In particular, the Committee acknowledged that stakeholders of not-for-profit organisations would want different information to that of shareholders in the business sector, such as the disclosure of non-financial (both narrative and quantitative) information (Commonwealth of Australia, 2008). To improve public accountability further, the Committee also recommended that a cost benefit analysis of implementing a GuideStar-type system (a website portal that publishes information on the aims and activities of all not-for-profit organisations) be undertaken (Commonwealth of Australia, 2008). With respect to fundraising, the Committee recommended annual reporting on fundraising by all not-for-profits that undertake fundraising, with the level of reporting commensurate with the size of the organisation or the amount raised (Commonwealth of Australia, 2008).

2009 Australia's Future Tax System: Report to the Treasurer

In 2009, the Australian Treasurer initiated a comprehensive review of Australia's tax system, including taxation arrangements relating to not-for-profits. The report noted the sector's contribution to the community and that, amongst other things, it received significant support from the public indirectly through tax concessions. The report also noted the complexity of tax arrangements for not-for-profits and inconsistencies in the regulations applied at the state, territory and local government levels. As other inquiries had done beforehand, the review panel recommended,

> the establishment of a national charities commission to monitor, regulate and provide advice to the sector, suggesting that such a body would address the issues that prove problematic to the sector.
>
> (Commonwealth of Australia, 2010, p. 43)

2009 The Australian Accounting Standards Board

In July 2009 the Australian Accounting Standards Board (AASB) initiated a project titled *Disclosures by Private Sector Not-for-Profit Entities*, with the aim of developing a standard on reporting service performance by not-for-profit entities (AASB, 2012). In its project outline, the AASB justified its decision by recourse to the recommendation on this subject by the Senate Standing Committee on Economics, which was discussed above, and other (then recent) reports that had identified the need to consider financial reporting issues specific to private sector, not-for profit entities, including the Institute of Chartered Accountants in Australia's document, *Enhancing Not-for-Profit Annual and Financial Reporting—Best Practice Reporting* (March 2009), and the PwC Transparency Awards.

In the background paper to this project, the AASB noted that Australian accounting standards were derived from International Financial Reporting Standards, which were not written with the needs of private sector, not-for-profit entities in mind. Consequently, it stated,

> there is a high risk that other information specific to private sector not-for-profit entities and needed by users is not being disclosed, or is not being disclosed in a consistent manner.
>
> (AASB, 2009, p. 1)

It is noteworthy that the AASB questioned the suitability of Australian accounting standards for application by not-for-profit entities (as have many charities and representatives of the accounting profession, as noted above), given their policy on sector neutrality, which was reaffirmed through acceptance of the Financial Reporting Council's review of the policy of transaction-neutral accounting standard-setting in Australia (Simpkins, 2006), and the perennial questioning by charities and the profession on the exitence of sector-specific accounting standards on government grants (Leslie, 2006).

2010 Contribution of the Not-for-Profit Sector: Productivity Commission Report

In 2009, the Australian government asked the Productivity Commission (PC) to examine the contribution of the not-for-profit sector to Australian society. In so doing, the government fulfilled a (2007) election commitment to maximise the sector's contribution to social inclusion, employment and economic growth (Bowen, 2009). While charity reporting per se was not specifically included in the terms of reference, the Commission addressed the matter of regulation, which included compliance and public reporting.

The recommendations contained in the report made a number of references to external reporting, including the alignment of not-for-profit organisations' public corporate and financial reporting requirements (which then varied significantly between states, territories and the Commonwealth), and the development of a single, publicly accessible, reporting portal through which corporate and financial information and information on service effort and fundraising would be disclosed.

In its report, the Productivity Commission noted the significant inadequacies in charity reporting that were highlighted in the 1995 report of the Industry Commission (referred to above), noting that, despite the efforts of many not-for-profit organisations to voluntarily adopt best practice, progress has been limited (PC, 2010). Submissions to the Productivity Commission Inquiry emphasised the inadequacy of charity reporting. For example, one peak body, the National Roundtable of Nonprofit Organisations, argued that inconsistencies between jurisdictions provided 'compelling arguments . . . for reform of accounting and reporting requirements' (PC, 2010, p. 132).

While one of the (then) two professional accounting bodies submitted that the legislation that governed not-for-profits had failed to keep up with developments in accounting practice and corporate governance, noting the overwhelming support for harmonisation of not-for-profit reporting requirements across the nine Australian jurisdictions that was evidenced in the 2007 Treasury consultation, *Improving Corporate Reporting and Accountability* (PC, 2010). Significantly, a major accounting firm with a large, not-for-profit client base, Grant Thornton, argued that there was a need for a sector-specific accounting standard for not-for-profits because of the special characteristics of not-for-profits, and that the information needs of those who used the reports of not-for-profits differed from those who used the reports of for-profit entities (PC, 2010).

2010 Inquiry into the Tax Laws Amendment (Public Benefit Test) Bill 2010

In May 2010, the Tax Laws Amendment (Public Benefit Test) Bill 2010 was introduced into the Senate as a private member's bill. The bill proposed a test that, in addition to meeting the common law definition of a charity, organisations would have to demonstrate that they operated for the public benefit in order to receive taxation concessions. During its passage through the legislature, the bill was referred to the Senate Standing Committee on Economics (the Committee), which, after taking submissions from the public, reported in September 2010. In particular, it noted that, despite the recommendations of the previous inquiries referred to in this chapter, there remains a serious lack of information in relation to the not-for-profit sector; for example, estimates of the value of tax concessions range from $1 billion to $8 billion (Senate Standing Committee on Economics, 2010, p. 1).

Consequently, the Committee suggested there should be an increase in transparency and accountability in the sector. In so doing, it recommended the establishment of a national commission that would incorporate a public benefit test in the broader regulatory framework. This, it said, would be in line with international best practice, such as that provided by the Charity Commissions in the United Kingdom and New Zealand (Senate Standing Committee on Economics, 2010). Amongst other things, the committee recommended that a national commission should 'develop and maintain an accessible, searchable public interface' (Senate Standing Committee on Economics, 2010, p. 2).

Summary

By 2010, the public record clearly evidenced an inadequate framework for charity reporting. Mandatory requirements varied significantly between state, territory and Commonwealth jurisdictions, and so they did not permit comparisons between charities. There was a lack of transparency and inadequate knowledge of charity economics. Furthermore, accounting standards did not capture many of the important aspects of charity performance. There was widespread desire for reform, with some progressive developments by parts of the accounting profession and standard setters, and voluntary initiatives by some charities to adopt best-practice reporting. Furthermore, the 2010 Productivity Commission Report acknowledged and comprehensively documented the significant role played in Australian society by charities (and other not-for-profit entities). It was against this background that the regulatory reforms of 2010–2013 took place.

THE DEVELOPMENT OF CHARITY REPORTING REQUIREMENTS: PART 2—THE REFORMS OF 2010–2013

In 2010, the Australian government went to the general election with a 'major reform agenda for Australia's non-profit sector to deliver smarter regulation, reduce red tape and improve transparency and accountability of the sector' (Australian Labor Party, 2007). In so doing, it built on the social inclusion policy agenda it had developed in 2006, which led, in 2010, to the National Compact, a government initiative aimed at strengthening the relationship between the not-for-profit sector and the state. The reform process commenced in January 2011, with the release of the consultation paper, *Scoping Study for a National Not-for-Profit Regulator*.

The 2011 Scoping Study for a National Not-for-Profit Regulator

The Treasury scoping study sought to determine the role functions, feasibility and design options for a 'one-stop shop' not-for-profit regulator. The consultation paper discussed the features of a best-practice regulatory framework and sought the views of stakeholders. It explored the issue of accountability by seeking information about current reporting requirements and practices and on the desirability or otherwise of a public information portal.

The scoping study received 161 submissions, 154 of which were made public. 75 % of public submissions were in favour of a uniform national regulator of not-for-profits, 18 % were opposed and 7% did not indicate a preference. That there should be such support for uniform national regulation of charities reflects the findings of preceding inquiries that were noted above. Those supporting reform were overwhelmingly of the view that current reporting requirements were onerous, duplicative and did not reflect the needs of charities or external users of information. The issue of transparency was particularly important to philanthropists and many welfare agencies, while more pragmatic concerns were reflected in the submissions of professional bodies and professional service providers who advised not-for-profits and their managers on reporting. Amongst those who supported reform many cited the success of reform overseas, in particular the Charity Commission of England and Wales proposed as a suitable model.

Of those who did not support reform, the strongest argument was provided by religious organisations and independent schools. In general, religious organisations were opposed to reform because, in their view, the sort of framework within prospect of the scoping study was not suitable for religious organisations. Furthermore, they argued, the administration of church affairs was a matter of cannon law. Religious organisations did, however, support the regulation of welfare, health and educational services (of which they are significant providers), but saw the present jurisdictional and industry-based regulation as satisfactory (cf. Australian Catholic Bishops Conference, 2011; Anglican Church Diocese of Sydney, 2011). The two submissions from peak bodies representing independent schools strongly opposed reform on the grounds that the present compliance-oriented reporting to funders was sufficient (cf. Independent Schools Council of Australia, 2011). Those in the category of other not-for-profit organisations who opposed reform were mainly not-for-profit organisations that were formed to represent commercial interests and were satisfied with the present compliance-oriented reporting framework (cf. Master Builders Association, 2011).

Stakeholders' views on the issue of public accountability were indicated in responses to a question on the establishment of a public portal by a national regulator through which not-for-profits would disclose information to the public. While only 40% of submissions included comment on this, 75% of those submissions were in favour. However, there was considerable variation in the extent of public disclosures. All were in favour of basic corporate information and information about the organisation's activities, most favoured the inclusion of governance information, with some in favour of disclosure of full financial information and management discussion and analysis of risk, operations, impact and future plans (cf. Australian Council of Social Services, 2011). Some who were generally in favour of greater public disclosures were concerned about the potential threat to their competitive position where they provided services in the same market as for-profit providers (cf. Mission Australia, 2011).

Notably, all religious organisations and independent schools were opposed to a national regulator hosting a public portal through which meaningful information could be disclosed. For religious organisations, opposition to a public portal was on the grounds that unless reports were standardised, they would not be meaningful (cf. Australian Catholic Bishops Conference, 2011). Independent schools were opposed because they saw no need to duplicate the existing public portal that had been established by the government for all schools (private and public) in 2008 (cf. Association of Independent Schools of Western Australia, 2011). However, this portal, titled, 'My School,' provides only summary financial information. The final report acknowledged the strong support for regulatory reform, recommending that 'a single regulator should be established for the purposes of governance, accountability and transparency (Treasury, 2011, p. 3). With respect to reporting, the final report noted the lack of uniformity and burdensome reporting requirements of not-for-profits, which were often concerned with particular activities, such as the acquittal of grants, but did not provide information about the activities of not-for-profits. As such, the final report recommended harmonised, uniform (subject to differentiation by size, risk factors and level of government support) financial reporting, and that the proposed regulator work with the AASB to ensure that accounting standards are relevant to the sector. In particular, the final report noted that, despite recent reviews of not-for-profit sector reporting calling for significant improvements, and not-for-profits receiving strong support from government and the wider Australia community, 'the Australian public and Australian governments know very little about the operations of this growing sector' (Treasury, 2011, p. 49).

Furthermore, the final report noted that there did not exist, 'a single source of information about charities and other concessionally taxed not-for-profit entities' (Treasury, 2011, p. 53), and that comparable jurisdictions overseas, such as the UK, New Zealand and the U.S., had improved accountability and transparency of charities through the use of public information portals. The report thus recommended the establishment of a not-for-profit public information portal and went on to suggest that a public information portal would advantage not-for-profits, the public and government by improving public confidence and permitting informed decision-making by the public. The report recommended that information reported through such a portal would include the sphere of operation, current and historical financial reports, governing documents, annual reports and trustees' reports. Seven months after the release of the final report, its recommendations were incorporated into the first draft of the Australian Charities and Not-for-Profits Commission Bill (the ACNC Bill).

The Australian Charities and Not-for-Profit Act 2012

The ACNC Bill was introduced into Parliament in December 2011 and was immediately released for public comment. The explanatory memorandum of the ACNC Bill referenced the inquiries that had preceded it (and are discussed in this chapter), and clearly set its purposes within the context of that policy debate. The bill proposed the establishment of a charity regulator, the Australian Charities and Not-for-Profits Commission (ACNC), the office of a commissioner and a full suite of regulatory mechanisms that would be applied to all not-for-profits that registered with the ACNC. (While registration was voluntary, tax concessions and government funding were to be made available only to registered entities.) Included in the bill were provisions for record keeping and reporting audit. The bill defined the reporting entity as the individual, registered not-for-profit entity, and was applicable to all types of not-for-profit entities across all fields of activity. The principle of differential reporting was applied such that entities were classified as small, medium or large (according to revenue and tax status), with reporting and audit requirements increasing in rigour as size increased. It proposed two types of reporting: an annual financial report and an annual information statement. Both reports were to be made available to the public through a web-based portal.

Financial reports were to be prepared by applying the full suite of relevant accounting standards. In justification of this requirement, the explanatory memorandum stated,

> this ensures that the information within the public domain is up-to-date and accurate, and reflects the true position of the entity. This will help promote public confidence and trust in [the] sector.
>
> (Commonwealth of Australia, 2012, p. 30)

Small entities were not required to prepare and lodge financial reports, while large entities were required to prepare and lodge annual financial reports that were audited by a registered company auditor. Medium entities were required to prepare and lodge annual financial reports, but could choose whether to have them reviewed or audited. The bill also gave the commissioner authority to seek additional information from an individual not-for-profit or class of not-for-profits.

The annual information statement was a statement in which registered charities disclosed basic corporate information, an outline of their activities and summary financial information. While details of the information to be included in the annual information statement were not given, the explanatory memorandum for the bill stated that NFPs

> generally operate for a broad public benefit, and are relied on by many Australians, often by those individuals who are the most vulnerable in

our community . . . It is therefore appropriate that registered entities provide some level of accountability to the public, and meet community expectations in relation to entities in receipt of public monies and support.

(Commonwealth of Australia, 2012, p. 28)

The bill thus appeared to accommodate much of what a wide range of stakeholders, including charity service providers, the accounting profession, standard setters and the media, had been calling for over the preceding two decades. It was released for public comment immediately and attracted 108 submissions, 23 of which were confidential. As a result of this consultation, the bill was revised. On re-introduction to the Parliament, the revised bill was sent for simultaneous consideration by committees (which also received stakeholder submissions) of both houses of Parliament. The revised bill returned to the Parliament in November 2012 and was passed by both houses of Parliament with only minor amendments. Also passed was legislation dealing with transitional arrangements (The Australian Charities and Not-for-Profit Commission (Consequential and Transitional) Act 2012), parts of which dealt with financial reporting. While the ACNC Act provided for financial and other reporting requirements, it left the specific requirements to be enacted through associated regulations. In January 2013, draft regulations covering financial reporting and governance matters were released for comment. Following a period of stakeholder consultations, the financial reporting and governance regulations were signed into law in June 2013. The main changes in the legislative process are detailed in Table 13.1.

Table 13.1 Main changes in the reporting requirements of the ACNC legislation from the 'First bill' to the 'Legislation and regulations'

Item	First bill	Revised bill and draft financial reporting regulations	Legislation and regulations
Scope	Charities and other NFPs	Only charities (with other NFPs to be progressively included over time)	Only charities (with other NFPs to be progressively included over time)
		Introduced a new category, that of basic religious charities, which are exempted from reporting financial information	Further refinement of the definition of a basic religious charity

Item	First bill	Revised bill and draft financial reporting regulations	Legislation and regulations
The nature of the reporting entity.	Entity	Entity of group. Group can report on other than an entity basis (i.e., according to the function performed)	Entity or group. Group can report on other than an entity basis (i.e., according to the function performed)
Composition of the annual information statement	No limiting criteria on composition of the information	Commissioner can only require information necessary to undertake recognised assessment activity	Commissioner can only require information necessary to undertake recognised assessment activity
Differential reporting	Size (per revenue) and status as a deductible gift recipient	Size (per revenue) only	Size (per revenue) only
Use of accounting standards	Financial statements to be prepared by applying all relevant accounting standards	No requirement for financial statements to be prepared by applying accounting standards Financial statements to prepare in accordance with (then) yet to be prescribed regulations	Regulations require application of the reporting entity concept Where the entity elects to prepare special purpose financial report, the regulations require the application of six specified standards Where there is a conflict between the accounting standards and the provisions of the ACNC Act to report on a group basis and/or a demand by the commissioner to require additional information to be reported, the ACNC Act prevails

In relation to the use of accounting standards, the requirement in the original bill for medium and large-sized entities to prepare general purpose financial statements was relaxed in the ACNC Act (through the associated regulations), with its requirement to apply the reporting entity concept. Thus, each charity would determine whether it would prepare a general purpose financial statement or special purpose financial statements. However, if the entity deemed that it was not a reporting entity and that its financial statements would be special purpose financial statements, the regulations required the application of six specified accounting standards: AASB 101, Presentation of Financial Statements; AASB 107, Statement of Cash Flows; AASB 108, Accounting Policies, Changes in Accounting Estimates and Errors; AASB 1031, Materiality; AASB 1048, Interpretation of Standards; AASB 1054, Australian Additional Disclosures.

The financial reporting regulations of the ACNC Act also provided for two exceptions to the requirement to apply the accounting standards: the first concerned joint and collective reporting and the second, situations where the commissioner used the power under the act to request further information. If, in either of these situations, there was any inconsistency with the accounting standards, the provisions of the ACNC Act prevail (Australian Charities and Not-for-Profits Commission Amendment Regulation 2013 (No. 3), s. 60.20). According to the explanatory materials associated with the financial reporting regulations, financial statements prepared through application of the joint and collective reporting requirements of the act may be inconsistent with AASB 10 Consolidated Financial Statements. Such a situation stands in contrast to the long-held policy of the Australian Accounting Standards Board to reject industry-specific accounting treatments (Commonwealth of Australia, 2013, p. 3).

While the ACNC Act came into operation on 3 December 2012, reporting requirements were subject to transitional arrangements such that the first annual information statement was not due until 31 December 2013 for entities with a year end of 31 December, and the first annual financial report was not due until 30 June 2014 for entities with a 30 June year-end. Furthermore, the first annual information statement only covered non-financial information such as corporate information and information about the entity's field of operation. Transitional arrangements for financial reports varied between independent schools and other charities and, for those other charities, the reporting requirements applicable to them prior to the commencement of the ACNC Act. Independent schools were required only to report under the ACNC Act what they were otherwise required to routinely report under the Schools Assistance Act 2008 to the Department of Education, Employment and Workplace Relations in order to acquit grants from the Commonwealth government until 2014–2015 (The Australian Charities and Not-for-Profit Commission (Consequential and Transitional) Act 2012, Schedule 1, s. 10). Such reports comprised a pro forma acquittal and an annual financial report in whatever form the school routinely adopted under its incorporating legislation, and any voluntary disclosures. (Anecdotal evidence provided to this writer from within the office of the regulator of school funding suggests that only one in three independent schools deemed that they were reporting entities and thus prepared general purpose financial statements.) For other entities that had reporting requirements under another Australian law, the ACNC Act allowed the commissioner to accept such reports as an annual financial report required by the ACNC Act for 2013–2014 (this period could be extended) (Commonwealth of Australia, 2013). In 2013, the commissioner invoked this authority. For entities that were not required, in 2012–2013, to prepare a financial report under another Australian law, the ACNC Act stipulated a set of particular summary financial reports be lodged for 2013–2014 (Australian Charities and Not-for-Profits Commission Amendment Regulation 2013 (No. 3), s. 60.30). Thus, with the exception of those charities that had no legal requirement to lodge a financial report in 2012–2013, Australian charities would not be required to change their financial reporting practices until June 2014 at the earliest, and for some, 2015.

In summary, while for the longer term some improvement in disclosure requirements for charities is likely, it is considerably less than was first proposed in the original bill, and in the majority of submissions that have been made to public inquiries and consultations over the past two decades, and, what has, in the views of many, been the benchmark for charity reporting: that administered by the Charity Commission of England and Wales, which includes the Application of Accounting and Reporting by Charities: Statement of Recommended Practice (Charity Commission, 2005). As such, the ambit of reporting is compliance rather than public accountability. For the short term, the transitional arrangements yield little meaningful improvement to charity reporting.

THE DEVELOPMENT OF AUSTRALIAN CHARITY REPORTING REQUIREMENTS: A REFLECTION AGAINST THE LITERATURE

The review of the literature cited earlier in this chapter highlighted the tension in charity reporting between acquitting individual accountabilities to external parties such as regulators, accreditation agencies and direct resource providers, and embracing a more proactive, holistic notion of a public accountability. Furthermore, the importance to all parties of striking an appropriate balance between the rights of those undertaking voluntary action and the rights of the community in the charity operates was also noted.

In tracing the development of Australia's first national regulation of charity reporting (albeit within a much wider regulatory regime), this chapter has evidenced the axis of public/private accountability to be central to the policy debate. For many stakeholders, charity accountability is essentially a public matter, and so answering the questions posed by Gray et al. (2006) goes to the heart of the organisation's mission, and exemplifies the position of Kearns (1996), as the following quote suggests:

> An Annual Report is much more than just a legal obligation for Mission Australia. It's a way of being accountable to our supporters, the people we help and the wider community.
>
> (Mission Australia, 2012)

Beginning with submissions to the Industry Commission Inquiry of 1993, we see arguments for public accountability running uninterrupted through to the consultation on the ACNC Bill. It has been argued that public accountability arises because of the nature of charities (more like government than private sector), and because of the direct funding from the public purse and indirect tax subsidies that charities receive. Examples of the former include the submission of the Brotherhood of St Laurence to the 1993 Inquiry by the Industry Commission (IC, 1995), where accountability is cast in moral dimensions, and the position of the AASB acknowledges the role that not-for-profits voluntarily assume and the necessary place they hold in the community (AASB, 2009). Some arguments for public accountability are cast as issues of wider policy issues (cf. AASB, 2009; Senate Standing Committee on Economics, 2008). Proactivity in acquitting accountabilities and taking responsibility for the dialogue is evidenced in the esteem given to PwC Transparency Awards by the sector (Johnson, 2012) and in submissions on the public record.

However, many arguments in favour of public accountability are based on more material criteria; that is, the direct funding from the public purse and indirect tax subsidies that charities receive (cf. Jobs Australia, 2001, p. 105). Others, while acknowledging the obligation of these charities to be accountable, argue that acquittal is satisfactorily achieved through more private mechanisms, such as meeting accreditation requirements, or accounting directly for each line item in a funding agreement (cf. Anglican Church Diocese of Sydney, 2012).

This chapter has also evidenced changes in how some stakeholders propose to best acquit public accountabilities. For example, in its submission to the 1993 Industry Commission Inquiry, the ICAA (as did others) proposed an accounting standard for charities; however, by 2012 it was satisfied that charity accountabilities could be acquitted through financial reports prepared by applying the reporting entity concept. Interestingly, the AASB, while maintaining its long-held policy of producing sector-neutral accounting standards, acknowledged that information needs of users of not-for-profit financial reports differ from those who use the reports of private sector entities, and has commenced a project aimed at producing a sector-specific accounting standard. It would seem though, that, on balance, the approach to charity reporting yielded by the recent reform process places greater emphasis on compliance than on public accountability.

POSTSCRIPT

The general election of September 2013 saw a change in government, with the incoming Coalition government committed to unwinding many of the reforms of 2001–2013. Specifically, it is committed to disbanding the ACNC and replacing it with a 'centre for excellence' that would focus more on education. Regulation of charities would be effected through the disparate system in operation prior to 2012. While the implementation of this policy has commenced (ProBono, 2014), it cannot be completed until after 1 July 2014 if, at that time, the composition of the Australian Senate is such that there is a majority of Senators in support of such change. Given that the transitional arrangements for reporting under the ACNC Act have effectively maintained the pre-2012 requirements for the present, it remains an open question as to whether the reforms of 2010–2012 effectively addressed two decades of concern.

REFERENCES

Accounting Standards Steering Committee. (1975). *The corporate report*. London.

Anglican Church Diocese of Sydney. (2011). *Submission to the scoping study for a national not-for-profit regulator January 2011*. Retrieved from http://archive.treasury.gov.au/contentitem.asp?NavId=066&ContentID=1983

Anglican Church Diocese of Sydney. (2012). *Submission to the Australian treasury on the draft ACNC bill January 2012*. Retrieved from http://www.treasury.gov.au/CONSULTATIONSANDREVIEWS/SUBMISSIONS/2011/AUSTRALIAN-CHARITIES-AND-NOT-FOR-PROFITS-COMMISSION-BILL/SUBMISSIONS

Association of Independent Schools of Western Australia. (2011). *Submission to the scoping study for a national not-for-profit regulator January 2011*. Retrieved from http://archive.treasury.gov.au/contentitem.asp?NavId=066&ContentID=1983

Australian Accounting Standards Board (AASB). (2009). *Project summary disclosures by not-for-profit entities AASB 23–24 September 2009*. Retrieved from www.aasb.gov.au

Australian Accounting Standards Board (AASB). (2012). *AASB service performance reporting project plan—as at 6 September 2012*. Retrieved from http://www.aasb.gov.au/admin/file/content102/c3/SPR_Summary_6_September_2012.pdf

Australian Bureau of Statistics (ABS). (2009). *Australian national accounts: Non-profit institutions satellite account, 2006–07*. Retrieved from http://www.abs.gov.au/AusStats/ABS@.nsf/MF/5256.0

Australian Catholic Bishops Conference. (2011). *Submission to the scoping study for a national not-for-profit regulator January 2011*. Retrieved from http://archive.treasury.gov.au/contentitem.asp?NavId=066&ContentID=1983

Australian Charities and Not-for-Profits Commission (ACNC). (2013a). *Background to reform*. Retrieved from www.acnc.gov.au

Australian Charities and Not-for-Profits Commission (ACNC). (2013b). *Background to the not-for-profit sector*. Retrieved from www.acnc.gov.au

Australian Council of Social Services. (2011). *Submission to the scoping study for a national not-for-profit regulator January 2011*. Retrieved from http://archive.treasury.gov.au/contentitem.asp?NavId=066&ContentID=1983

Australian Consumers Association. (2008). *The act of* giving. *Choice,* April, 12–20.

Australian Labor Party. (2007). *Let's move forward.* Canberra, AU.

Beilharz, P., Considine, M., & Watts, R. (1993). *Arguing about the welfare state.* North Sydney, AU: Allen and Unwin.

Bowen, C. (2009). *Productivity commission to review the contribution of the not-for-profit sector* [Media release], no. 0107. Retrieved from http://ministers.treasury.gov.au/DisplayDocs.aspx?doc=pressreleases/2009/017.htm&pageID 003&min=ceb&Year=&DocType=0

Brody, E. (2003). Accountability and public trust. In L. Salamon (Ed.), *The state of nonprofit America.* Washington, DC: Brookings Institution Press.

Cancer Council of NSW. (2012). *Annual report.* Retrieved from http://www.cancercouncil.com.au/54311/about-us/our-annual-reports-and-research-activity-reports/annual-report/cancer-council-nsw-wins-pwc-transparency-awards/

Charity Commission (2005) *Accounting and reporting by charities: Statement of recommended practice.* London: Charity Commission.

Chen, R. S. (1975). Social and financial stewardship. *Accounting Review, 50*(3), 533–543.

CHOICE. (2014). *About us.* Retrieved from http://www.choice.com.au/about-us.aspx

Choudhury, E., & Ahmed, S. (2002). The shifting meaning of governance: Public accountability and the third sector organizations in an emergent global regime. *International Journal of Public Administration, 25*(4), 561–588.

Commonwealth of Australia. (2001). *Report of the inquiry into the definition of charities and related organisations.* Canberra, AU.

Commonwealth of Australia. (2008, June 18). *Hansard, the Senate* (p. 2729).

Commonwealth of Australia. (2010). *Australia's future tax system report to the treasurer detailed analysis December 2009* (Vol. 2) . Canberra, AU.

Commonwealth of Australia. (2012). *Exposure draft: Australian charities and not-for-profits commission bill 2012, explanatory materials.* Retrieved from http://www.austlii.edu.au/cgi-bin/sinodisp/au/legis/cth/bill_em/acancb2012533/memo_2.html?stem=0&synonyms=0&query=australian%20charities%20draft%20bill%20explanatory%20memorandum%202012

Commonwealth of Australia. (2013). *Australian charities and not-for-profits commission amendment regulation 2013 (no. 3), explanatory materials.* Retrieved from http://www.austlii.edu.au/cgi-bin/sinodisp/au/legis/cth/num_reg_es/acancar 20133n124o2013804.html?stem=0&synonyms=0&query=Australian%20 Charities%20and%20Not%20for%20profits%20Commission%20Amendment%20Regulation%202013%20(No.%203),%20Explanatory%20Materials

Coy, D., Fischer, M., & Gordon, T. (2001). Public accountability: A new paradigm for college and university annual reports. *Critical Perspectives on Accounting, 12*(1), 1–31.

Cutt, J., & Murray, V. (2000). *Accountability and effectiveness in nonprofit organizations.* London: Routledge.

Dickey, B. (1986). *Rations, residence, resources.* Adelaide, AU: Wakefield Press.

Ferguson, A. (2005a, March 24). The $70-billion dollar sacred cow. *Business Review Weekly.* Retrieved from Factiva.

Ferguson, A. (2005b, March 24). Charity cases. *Business Review Weekly.* Retrieved from Factiva.

Ferguson, A. (2006, June 29). God's business. *Business Review Weekly.* Retrieved from Factiva.

Gray, R. Bebbington, J., & Collison, D. (2006). NGOs, civil society and accountability: Making the people accountable to capital. *Accounting, Auditing & Accountability Journal, 19*(3), 319–348.

Graycar, A., & Jamrozic, A. (1989). *How Australians live: Social policy in theory and practice.* South Melbourne, AU: Macmillan Australia.

Independent Schools Council of Australia. (2011). *Submission to the scoping study for a national not-for-profit regulator January 2011.* Retrieved from http://archive.treasury.gov.au/contentitem.asp?NavId=066&ContentID=1983

Industry Commission (IC). (1995). *Charitable organisations in Australia* (Report no. 45). Melbourne, AU: Australian Government Publishing Service.

Institute of Chartered Accountants in Australia (ICAA). (2003). *Review of not-for-profit financial and annual reporting.* Sydney.

Institute of Chartered Accountants in Australia (ICAA). (2006). *Not-for-profit sector reporting: A research project.* Sydney.

Institute of Chartered Accountants in Australia (ICAA). (2007). *Enhancing not-for-profit annual and financial reporting—best practice reporting.* Sydney.

Institute of Chartered Accountants in Australia (ICAA). (2013). *Enhancing not-for-profit annual and financial reporting—best practice reporting.* Sydney.

Jeavons, T. H. (1992). When the management is the message: Values in management practice in nonprofit organizations. *Nonprofit Management & Leadership, 2*(4), 403–417.

Jobs Australia. (2001). *Report of the inquiry into the definition of charities and related organisations.* Canberra, AU: Commonwealth of Australia.

Johnson, G. (2012). *Opportunity International, CCNSW top transparency awards.* Retrieved from http://www.fpmagazine.com.au/opportunity-internatio nal-ccnsw-top-transparency-awards-310208/

Kanter, R., & Summers, D. V. (1987). Doing well while doing good: Dilemmas of performance measurement in nonprofit organizations and the need for a multiple constituency approach. In W. W. Powell (Ed.), *The nonprofit sector: A research handbook.* New Haven, CT: Yale University Press.

Kearns, K. P. (1996). *Managing for accountability: Preserving the public trust in public and nonprofit organizations.* San Francisco: Jossey-Bass.

Lee, M. (2004). Public reporting a neglected aspect of nonprofit accountability. *Nonprofit Management and Leadership, 15*(2), 169–185.

Leslie, I. (2006). Sector neutrality. *Charter,* September, 35–36.Lyons, M. (2001). *The third sector in Australia.* Sydney: Allen and Unwin.

Master Builders Association. (2011). *Submission to the scoping study for a national not-for-profit regulator, January 2011.* Retrieved from http://archive.treasury. gov.au/contentitem.asp?NavId=066&ContentID=1983

McGregor-Lowndes,M.(2009). *Overview and themes of modernising charity law since 2001.* Paper presented at Modernising Charity Law Conference, Australian Centre for Philanthropy and Nonprofit Studies, Brisbane, AU. Retrieved from https://www.qut.edu.au/business/about/research-centres/australian-centre-for-philanthropy-and-nonprofit-studies/publications-and-resources/publications

Mission Australia. (2011). *Submission to the scoping study for a national not-for-profit regulator, January 2011.* Retrieved from http://archive.treasury.gov.au/cont entitem.asp?NavId=066&ContentID=1983

Mission Australia. (2012). *Annual Report.* Retrieved from https://www.mission australia.com.au/annual-report

Mulgan, R. (2000). Accountability: An ever-expanding concept? *Public Administration Review, 78*(3), 553–573.

Normanton, E. L. (1971). Public accountability and audit: A reconnaissance. In B. R. Smith & D. C. Hague (Eds.), *The dilemma of accountability in modern government: Independence versus control.* London: Macmillan.

ProBono. (2014). *ATO planning ACNC takeover.* Retrieved from http://www.probonoaustralia.com.au/news/2014/02/ato-planning-acnc-takeover?

utm_source Pro+Bono+Australia+-+email+updates&utm_campaign c422e073d5-news_27_22_27_2014&utm_medium email&utm_term 0_5ee68172fb-c422e07 3d5–146765493

Productivity Commission (PC). (2010). *Contribution of the not-for-profit sector.* Melbourne, AU: Commonwealth of Australia.

PwC. (2012). *PwC transparency awards 2012 jury report.* Retrieved from http://www.pwc.com.au/about-us/corporate-responsibility/assets/transparency/Transparency-Awards-Jury-Report-2012.pdf

Robbins, J. (1997). Playing a symphony or playing a market? A South Australian perspective on contracting for care. *Third Sector Review, 3*(Special issue), 225–249.

Rogan, L., & Moore, C. (1999). *Common cause.* Sydney: Australian Council of Social Services.

Saj, P. (2012). The influence of mandatory requirements on voluntary performance reporting by large multi-service community service organisation. *Third Sector Review, 18*(2), 139–169.

Senate Standing Committee on Economics. (2010). *Report: Inquiry into the tax laws amendment (public benefit test) bill 2010.* Canberra, AU: Australian Senate, Parliament House.

Simpkins, K. (2006). *A review of the policy of sector-neutral accounting standard-setting in Australia.* Canberra, AU: Financial Reporting Council.

Smith (family). (2008, September 2). *Submission to the senate standing committee on economics.* Retrieved from http://www.aph.gov.au/Parliamentary_Business/Committees/Senate/Economics/Completed%20inquiries/2008–10/charities_08/index

Senate Standing Committee on Economics. (2008). *Disclosure regimes for charities and not-for-profit organisations.* Canberra: Australian Senate, Parliament House.

Treasury. (2011). *Final report: Scoping study for a national regulator.* Canberra, AU: Commonwealth of Australia.

Woodward, S., & Marshall, J. (2004). *A better framework: Reforming not-for-profit regulation.* Melbourne, AU: Centre for Corporate Law and Securities Regulation.

Part IV

Issues in Performance Management and Risk

14 Conceptualising Performance in the Not-for-Profit Sector

A Tale of Two Theories

Basil Tucker

INTRODUCTION

Many of the themes in this book have directly or indirectly engaged with the issue of performance management and control in not-for-profit (NFP) organisations. This is clearly a fruitful area of research and one that makes important contributions to our body of knowledge in this area, because although the topic of management control has attracted increasing attention in the management accounting literature (see Otley, Broadbent, & Berry, 1995; Langfield-Smith, 1997, 2005, 2007; Chenhall, 2003; Merchant & Otley, 2007; Berry, Coad, Harris, Otley, & Stringer, 2009 for reviews of such research), its focus has been primarily directed towards for-profit organisations. While research on the similarities and differences between for-profit and NFPs is vast (Heinrich, 2000), the implications for how control is enacted within a NFP context have rarely been explicitly considered, and the contribution of management accounting research in informing this debate has been limited.

Implicit in studies of management control, irrespective of the ontological or epistemological frame of reference adopted, is that rather than an end in itself, control is more a means to achieving a particular end—that of enhanced performance. This contention is not controversial. For example, over three decades ago Otley and Berry argued, '. . . control can only exist when knowledge of outcomes is available; with no feedback on actual performance, improvement is possible only by chance' (1980, p. 236), and Langfield-Smith recognised that '. . . the adoption of certain controls might be in response to low (or high) organizational performance' (1997, p. 226). As the observations presented above suggest, this end is likely to be in some way tied to improving performance outcomes. In a for-profit context, such ends are (arguably) readily identifiable; for example, in the form of improved profits, appreciating share prices or capturing a greater proportion of market share. But in a NFP context, what is performance, and how might it be defined and operationalised?

Directing the attention of management control and performance research towards the NFP sector is important not only because of the considerable social and economic impact of this sector in Western economies[1], but also because the significance of management control and performance has been argued to be even greater in NFPs than in their for-profit counterparts (Parker, 2002; Anthony & Govindarajan, 2004). This argument emanates from two specific observations. First, funding agencies and government require increased accountability and transparency in evaluating the efficiency and effectiveness with which NFPs deliver their outcomes (Christensen & Mohr, 2003; Unerman & O'Dwyer, 2006; Parker, 2008; O'Dwyer & Unerman, 2008), resulting in demands for improved control in this sector generally (O'Dwyer & Unerman, 2008). Second, the need for NFPs to manage a diverse array of constituencies and stakeholders (Balser & McClusky, 2005; Chenhall, Hall, & Smith, 2010) brings with it an onus to accommodate multiple, complex, diverse and sometimes conflicting sets of goals and objectives (Herman & Renz, 1999; Brown & Iverson, 2004). The challenge in defining exactly what constitutes 'performance,' given this range of often-disparate goals and objectives, introduces to NFPs a degree of complexity in control efforts generally beyond that faced by for-profit organisations (Anthony & Govindarajan, 2004). The NFP sector, therefore, provides a unique vehicle for contributing to our understanding of 'performance,' and by extension, the ways in which control efforts may be subsequently designed, configured or used.

Two opposing views emerge from the NFP literature about how performance within this sector might be conceptualised. On the one hand, NFP commentators have argued that the characteristics of this sector, such as their unique governance structure, financial and legal status, distinct culture and goals based on social values make discussions about how to conceptualise and, by extension, how to improve organisational performance in NFPs more complex than that in for-profit organisations (Speckbacher, 2003; Moore, 2000; Herman & Renz, 1999). As Bradshaw suggests, '. . . what works in one setting, or at one point in time, may not work in another and that efficiency is related to the ongoing alignment of various contingencies' (2009, p. 62). With its emphasis on the diverse array of social, economic, operational and organisational variables and their influence on efficiency, this view is consistent with a contingency approach to defining the nature of organisational performance in NFPs, and offers a rich environment for testing and developing theory in this area.

In contrast, a recurrent observation appearing in the NFP literature is that the lines dividing for-profit and NFP organisations[2] are becoming increasingly blurred (Stone, Bigelow, & Crittenden, 1999; Herman & Renz, 1999; Speckbacher, 2003; Beck, Lengnick-Hall, & Lengnick-Hall, 2008). NFPs now operate in an environment where they compete for resources and are required to prove and improve their effectiveness. In response, NFP practitioners have progressively looked to private sector practices to improve efficiency and productivity (Beck et al., 2008; Lindenberg, 2001). This view is consistent with new institutional sociology (NIS) theory, which predicts that it is likely for NFPs to exhibit a high propensity to adopt for-profit approaches to conceptualising organisational performance as a direct response to isomorphic pressures (DiMaggio & Powell, 1991). From an institutional stance, it is therefore quite reasonable to expect that discernible differences in the conceptualisation of organisational performance between sectors would be insignificant (Ramanath, 2009).

These contrasting theoretical vantage points and their resulting paradoxical predictions on how organisational performance might be conceptualised within the NFP sector represents a tension which this chapter aims to confront. In broad terms, this chapter engages directly with the issue of conceptualising performance within a NFP environment, and reflects on these two conflicting theoretical perspectives that have informed our understanding of this concept as they may apply within NFP organisations.

The chapter is structured as follows. In the first section, the evolution of organisational performance as it has been viewed in for-profit organisations is briefly examined. This is followed by a reflection of how organisational performance has been treated in the NFP literature, and then, a comparison of the similarities and differences between the sectors in terms of their performance implications. The fourth section examines two theoretical lenses—contingency and institutional—through which organisational performance in NFPs has been commonly viewed in the management control literature. This leads to an evaluation of 'the best' vantage point from which NFP performance might be viewed. Finally, a conclusion which outlines the implications for both theory and practice and suggests avenues for future research is presented.

ORGANISATIONAL PERFORMANCE IN THE FOR-PROFIT SECTOR

The seminal theoretical work of Anthony (1965) has played a central role in the development of the management control literature, and by extension, how performance has been traditionally viewed in management accounting research. According to Anthony, control was defined as 'the process by which managers ensure that resources are obtained and used effectively and efficiently in the accomplishment of the organisation's objectives' (1965, p. 17). From this functionalist view of control, organisational performance was implicitly regarded as being primarily financially based. The role of management accounting was to monitor (predominantly) financially based metrics (such as revenue, cost and profits) so as to enable the correction of deviations from preset standards. Indeed, much empirical management accounting research has focused on variations of an array of such financial criteria as proxies for performance—for example, average annual growth in sales, growth in return on assets, growth in return on sales (Chenhall, 1997); revenues, expenses, profit margins and return on sales (Ittner &

Larcker, 1998); sales growth rate, operating cash flows, ROI/ROA and pre-tax net profit to sales (Moores & Yuen, 2001); ROI, sales volume and profits (Henri, 2006); overall profitability (Widener, 2007). Even with their concentration on financial effectiveness, it is clear that as different studies examine different aspects of performance, under different conditions and in different circumstances, comparisons of performance as presented in these studies should be made with caution. Findings are sensitive to the selection of different measures of performance, and therefore, conclusions drawn from this research need to be considered in this light.

In spite of the undisputed importance of such financial indicators as a reflection of organisational performance, it was recognised that financial results provided only one of many gauges of for-profit effectiveness, and that concentration solely on financial outcomes failed to provide information reflecting the full consequences of organisational activities (Kaplan & Norton, 1992; Ittner & Larcker, 1998; Ferreira & Otley, 2009). The advent of broader conceptualisations of performance (and frameworks for measuring performance) aimed to define costs and benefits beyond financial and operational terms by integrating insights from other disciplines, such as marketing, organisational behaviour, human resource management and strategy (Otley, 2008). This approach includes such approaches to conceptualisations of performance as the balanced scorecard (Kaplan & Norton, 1992), which measures performance from four different perspectives (financial, customer, internal business and learning and growth); 'triple bottom line' reporting, which recognises the economic, as well as environmental and community, impacts of organisational activity (Epstein & Birchard, 2000); and value-based reporting, which seeks to combine the reporting issues raised by economic, environmental, social, governance and empowerment frameworks (Ittner & Larcker, 1997). Despite the advent of these more contemporary approaches, it is clear that, notwithstanding the variety of models for examining organisational performance, there is still little consensus over what constitutes a valid set of performance criteria (Smith, 1998). The diversity in the way in which performance has been operationalised reflects the observation that the construct, 'performance,' remains 'an ambiguous term, and capable of no simple definition' (Otley, 1999, p. 364). This ambiguity suggests that if such a thing as an 'ideal' model exists upon which to conceptualise performance, it is likely to be contingent upon a range of considerations.

ORGANISATIONAL PERFORMANCE IN THE NFP SECTOR

It has been argued that organisational performance is more difficult to conceptualise in a NFP than in a for-profit organisation (Anthony & Govindarajan, 2004). This argument is centred around the legal constraint on NFPs on distributing profits, thereby effectively abolishing the profit motive as a primary objective of NFPs.

Profit is interpreted differently in for-profit and NFP organisations. A dominant goal of most for-profit organisations is to earn a profit, and in so doing, create wealth for its owners. The extent to which revenue exceeds expenditure reflects progress towards this goal. As a general rule, the larger the profit, the better the performance. In a NFP, however, a large profit may signal that the organisation is not providing the services that those who supplied resources had a right to expect. Clearly, long as well as short-term financial viability is a necessary goal, because NFPs cannot survive if over time their revenues are less than their expenses; an inability to generate sufficient cash flows to meet financial obligations will ultimately lead to insolvency, just as in a for-profit organisation. As noted by Casteuble (1997), NFPs may quite rightly claim that 'we might be not-for-profit but we are not-for-loss either.' Profit, however, is not and should not be the dominant goal in a NFP. Financial considerations can play an enabling or constraining role but will rarely be the primary objective of NFPs (Kaplan, 2001), and the overall effectiveness of such organisations can rarely be measured by this single quantitative metric (Brown, 2000).

Unlike for-profit organisations, the mission or goal of NFPs is typically to provide some sort of public service. Making the link between 'mission and measures' is a critical issue for performance management and applies to NFPs just as much as it does to public and for-profit organisations (Kaplan, 2001). However, in contrast to for-profit organisations, the problems addressed by NFPs have longer time horizons (Frumkin & Andre-Clarke, 2000), NFP missions typically possess a longer gestation period in comparison with for-profit organisations and how well or poorly a NFP is performing is usually only seen in time. This distinction based on time is important because it relates to the trade-off typically facing NFPs between short-term performance targets such as financial and operational efficiency, and long-term, mission-related policy effectiveness, stewardship responsibilities and the provision of services.

Another potentially important consideration facing NFPs in deliberating over how performance might be viewed is that the services they provide are often intangible, difficult to measure and sometimes conflicting (Forbes, 1998). This is due largely to the heterogeneous goals and needs of the variety of constituencies typically served by NFP organisations (Speckbacher, 2003). Such constituencies or stakeholders are numerous and diverse. They include funders, referral agencies, government officials, volunteers, clients, staff, the board of directors, the media and the general public. A multiple constituency perspective of organisational performance recognises this wide diversity of stakeholders or constituents who respectively define the criteria with which they evaluate a given NFP. Different constituencies are likely to use or to give different priorities to different criteria, making the possibility of a single measure of performance unlikely. In addition to financial considerations such as operating expense ratios, productivity measures, fundraising efficiency and the ability to acquire needed resources (Ritchie & Kolodinsky, 2003), non-financial criteria including quality of service provision, satisfaction of members/volunteers/staff, public image and programme/service effectiveness have been acknowledged as playing a pivotal role influencing performance (Kaplan, 2001).

As a result, there is broad agreement that, again as in for-profit organisations, no single conceptualisation of performance will work for NFPs (Sawhill & Williamson, 2001; Nobbie & Brudney, 2003; Balser & McClusky, 2005; Hodge & Piccolo, 2005; Herman & Renz, 2008; Doherty & Hoye, 2011), and that performance in a NFP context is best conceptualised through a multidimensional framework rather than through a single construct (Rojas, 2000). As Herman and Renz (2008) question, as with art, observers may know performance when they see it, but what do they look for? As with for-profit environments, for NFPs this is a vexed question to which definitive and conclusive answers are not readily apparent or unequivocally agreed upon.

A DIFFERENCE THAT MAKES NO DIFFERENCE IS NO DIFFERENCE?

From the preceding discussion, it appears as though many of the difficulties in conceptualising organisational performance are common to both NFP and for-profit sectors. Research on performance and effectiveness seems to support few specific conclusions and the academic study of organisational performance in for-profit organisations is about as inconclusive and muddled as it is for NFPs (Herman & Renz, 1999). Financial factors are clearly important in both sectors, but if the role of management accounting is to assist managers in the realisation of goals, it follows that the desired goals must be identified, and the information required to help achieve those goals be determined (Kelly & Alam, 2008).

It is fairly well established that the information required to inform organisations about how progress towards such goals is proceeding will include non-financial as well as financial indicators (Kaplan & Norton, 1992). For organisations operating in the for-profit sector, this has been recognised through an expansion of the way in which performance has been traditionally conceptualised, beyond solely the measurement and reporting of financial performance (Gray, Owen, & Adams, 1996; Otley, 1999). Similarly, in NFPs, organisational performance involves identifying, integrating and prioritising the concerns and goals of relevant stakeholders. This is not to say that the needs and requirements of stakeholders are not important to for-profit organisations. They are. For instance, recent corporate collapses such as Enron and WorldCom have called into question the adequacy of accounting-based performance metrics in protecting the interests of stakeholders (Unerman & O'Dwyer, 2010), and the growing area of social and environmental accounting (Durden, 2007), which is unequivocally directed towards the interests of stakeholders. Even so, the wider variety and heterogeneity of stakeholder constituencies in the NFP environment, and the diversity in their goals, expectations and requirements has been argued to introduce a level of complexity in the conceptualisation of performance in NFPs beyond that of for-profit organisations (Herman & Renz, 2008).

The fundamental question of how performance *should* be conceptualised within a NFP context nevertheless remains. Both institutional and contingency theories are well suited as theoretical frames of reference from which to examine organisational performance. The broad contention that there are no 'universally valid rules' of what constitutes organisational performance, and that the 'appropriate' conceptualisation of organisational performance will be influenced by, and needs to be matched to, the context within which NFPs operate, enhances the attractiveness of contingency explanations (Bradshaw, 2009). Institutional theory too is a sufficiently broad lens through which to view performance, and some empirical support vindicates this claim. In a synthesis of the results of studies investigating organisational performance in the NFP sector, Herman and Renz (2008) argue that more effective NFPs are more likely to use what are perceived to be 'best practices,' pointing to the importance of isomorphic pressures and institutional theory as a compelling framework for conceptualising organisational performance.

In many ways, contingency and institutional theory may be considered to represent two extremes of a theoretical spectrum. Tensions inevitably exist between interpretative approaches, such as institutional theory, and the positivist focus of contingency theory (Gupta, Dirsmith, & Fogarty, 1994). Although alternate theoretical vantage points can be brought to bear on an investigation of organisational performance in the NFP sector, the conflicting predictions offered by institutional and contingency theory engage directly with the debate that has occurred within the NFP literature about the propensity and relative merits of NFPs adopting for-profit approaches, based on the conflicting views of sectoral convergence as opposed to divergence. It is for this reason that these two theoretical positions have been selected in this enquiry, as lenses through which to more closely view organisational performance.

CONTRASTING THEORETICAL LENSES

Through the Institutional Lens—the Convergence View

The attention of both NFP researchers and practitioners over the past two decades has been progressively directed towards looking to private sector practices as potential avenues for NFP efficiency and productivity improvement (Lindenberg, 2001; Beck et al., 2008). NFPs are increasingly operating in an environment where they compete for resources and accordingly, are often required to demonstrate and improve their effectiveness (Rojas, 2000). This is particularly true as funding agencies and government require increased accountability in evaluating the efficiency and effectiveness with which NFPs deliver their outcomes (Gray, Bebbington, & Collison, 2006; Unerman & O'Dwyer, 2006; O'Dwyer & Unerman, 2008). Moreover, as outlined above, similar to profit-seeking firms, NFPs typically face the same economic pressures to survive (Clohesy, 2003; Beck et al., 2008) and in response, are increasingly looking towards implementing business-like models in order to enhance their efficiency and productivity (Shoham, Ruvio, Vigoda-Gadot, & Schwabsky, 2006). For example, management principles derived from the for-profit sector are frequently used by NFPs to guide their efforts in demonstrating accountability (Griggs, 2003; Herman & Renz, 1999; Parker, 1998) in response to growing expectations and requirements of stakeholders (Sowa, Selden, & Sandfort, 2004; Nobbie & Brudney, 2003; Speckbacher, 2003).

These trends are consistent with institutional theory, which posits that organisations seek internal and external legitimacy by engaging in similar activities, codifying the same practices, following approved procedures and developing comparable structures (Leiter, 2005, 2013; Herman & Renz, 2008). In terms of how organisational performance is conceptualised in NFPs, institutional theory predicts that NFPs adopt what (they perceive) they are required to adopt as a consequence of coercive pressures exerted by organisations on whom the organisation depends, mimetic pressures that encourage the imitation of other organisations and normative pressures that derive from professional organisations (DiMaggio & Powell, 1983). Such institutional pressures can 'proceed in the absence of evidence that they increase internal organizational efficiency' (DiMaggio & Powell, 1983, p. 153), and their adoption permits NFPs to achieve or maintain legitimacy, thereby demonstrating they are pursuing the 'right' objectives in the 'right' way.

The expectations and requirements of funding providers and other stakeholders as discussed above represent a central consideration for NFPs in determining what constitutes their effectiveness (Stone et al., 1999). In NFPs, measures of performance tend to focus on the activities specified in the organisation's mission, goals and objectives that are influenced by the collective expectations of numerous external constituencies (Herman & Renz, 1999). These performance expectations may be regarded as a form of coercive isomorphism, and from a practical perspective, their accommodation by NFPs is understandable; if NFPs adopt particular standards, targets or objectives as mandated by funders, or consistent with stakeholder requirements or expectations, then they are rewarded for doing so through an increase in resources.

Mimetic isomorphism might also provide an explanation of why NFPs adopt particular conceptualisations of performance, in that such conceptualisations signify 'a symbolic demonstration of managerial competence' (Mulhare, 1999, p. 323), a point reinforced by Herman and Renz, who state, 'keeping up with what is regarded as best practices is a sign of effective management and legitimises an NFP in the eyes of many of its stakeholders' (1999, p. 122). This form of isomorphism has some empirical support. NFP board members have been found to judge organisational effectiveness in relation to the extent of use of 'correct' management practices (Herman & Renz, 2008). Moreover, the extent to which NFPs 'follow suit' with for-profit concepts of performance, *because* such concepts are (perceived to be) 'best practice' in the for-profit sector, has also been identified (see Beck et al., 2008). These empirical studies point to an inclination by NFPs to imitate established views of effectiveness, grounded in the for-profit sector, particularly when there is substantial uncertainty about the methods for achieving outcomes (Parker, 2008), or when outcomes are difficult to measure (Herman & Renz, 1998).

Normative isomorphism (that is, the pressure to conform, stemming from the prevailing values, norms and accepted practices of professional or peer groups) (DiMaggio & Powell, 1983) may also influence NFPs' perceptions of what constitutes organisational performance. Although difficult to substantiate empirically, this claim can be inferred from the following line of argument. Strong, shared ideologies and forms of expression develop around certain occupations (Frumkin & Andre-Clark, 2000). Many NFP professionals, including managers, seek to bring a new rigor to their work and develop standards to measure performance (Stone et al., 1999). If senior managers or board members have previous private sector experience, an educational background (in business, accounting or commerce, for example) or are members of professional business, accounting or commercial associations, it is quite conceivable that this would influence their view on performance (Parker, 2008)—thereby linking performance in their NFP context with for-profit views of performance. This is not to say that such senior managers or board members would attempt to replicate for-profit perspectives, measures or frameworks of performance in their entirety, but almost certainly their conceptualisation of performance would be influenced to *some* extent with that of for-profit organisations.

From this discussion then, it is quite conceivable that one or more isomorphic pressures may influence NFP conceptualisations of organisational performance. These conceptualisations are based on sector-based similarities. By the same token, however, *differences* between the sectors are also likely to guide how performance is viewed in NFP organisations, and it is towards a consideration of the implications of these sector-based differences that the attention of this chapter is now directed.

Through the Contingency Lens—the Divergence View

'It is generally agreed that there is a conceptual separation and distinct differences between for-profit and NFP organisations and activities' (Lewis, 1998, p. 136). These differences stem from the unique character of NFP organisations, which has been well documented in the NFP literature (see Moore, 2000; Sawhill & Williamson, 2001; Brown & Iverson, 2004; Baruch & Ramalho, 2006; Beck et al., 2008). They include the unique culture prevalent within the NFP sector (Lindenberg, 2001; Lewis, 2002; Abraham, 2004); a lesser accessibility to crucial knowledge, skills, abilities and resources (Schneider, 2003; Lindenberg, 2001); the dependence on, but lack of control that NFPs have over resources (Stone et al., 1999); the need to manage a wide array of constituencies and stakeholders (Balser & McClusky, 2005) and to accommodate multiple, complex, diverse and sometimes conflicting sets of goals (Herman & Renz, 1999; Brown & Iverson, 2004).

These characteristics have been variously advanced to suggest the NFP sector is sufficiently unique so as to render many prescriptions for 'success' developed in the private sector either inappropriate, extremely difficult to apply or even detrimental (Beck et al., 2008). Moreover, it has been contended that the superimposition of for-profit practices on NFPs has not always produced the best solutions (Rojas, 2000; Moore, 2000), and their uncritical adoption may carry considerable risk (Bielefeld, 2006). Indeed, it has been argued that NFPs would be better served by the adoption of modified business practices (Brown & Iverson, 2004), or even a different model altogether (Lewis, 1998).

Directing attention to the differences between NFPs and for-profit organisations is consistent with a contingency theoretical orientation, which adopts the view that the appropriate conceptualisation of organisational performance will be influenced by the context within which it operates (Chenhall, 2003). That is, a contingency approach suggests that prescriptions developed in the for-profit sector cannot be assumed to be automatically transferable to a NFP environment. Rather, contingency theory aims to isolate and examine how contextual variables—in this case, sector-based differences—may influence the way in which organisational performance is viewed, defined and measured in a NFP context.

From the earlier discussion, three such differences appear to be of present particular challenges. First, although the need for consultation with the often wide range of constituencies—professionals, volunteers, members, multiple internal communities, multiple social lobby groups, professional and government organisations, sponsors and donors, service recipients and so on—is characteristic of the NFP sector (Abraham, 2004), the time-consuming and expensive nature of a consultative process with such stakeholders, with disparate and diverse goals (Mara, 2000; Hodge & Piccolo, 2005), is likely to pose practical difficulties in arriving at consensus about what constitutes performance. An example is succinctly illustrated by Parker (2001, 2002), who, in a study exploring the planning and control concepts and processes employed by the central offices of the Victorian Synod of the Uniting Church in Australia, found that despite providing 'an entirely rational approach to dealing with the complex array of social programs, stakeholders, external influences and resource constraints' (2002, p. 92) by permitting 'space and flexibility to assimilate and determine how best to respond to the myriad of issues arising from a complex web of stakeholders with whom they interact (2002, p. 354), consultation also carried with it appreciable downsides. These most notably included considerable uncertainty as to where final, decision-making authority lay, leading to a situation in which planning and control was reduced to a lowest common denominator—short-term, incremental planning decisions and protracted deliberations on crucial issues, resulting in delays in initiatives or responses to environmental change.

A second characteristic often cited as differentiating the NFP from the for-profit sector relates to the strong and distinctive organisational culture prevalent in many NFPs. The claim that this distinctive culture may very well be incongruous with private sector approaches to conceptualising performance has been voiced by a number of NFP researchers. For example, Herman and Renz (1999) pointed to organisational culture as an important factor differentiating NFPs from their for-profit and public sector counterparts. Baraldi (1998) reports 'soft' variables (perception, acceptance and organisational agreement) are crucial in NFPs. Abraham argued that in a sector that 'values informal relationships, voluntary participation and "niceness", the idea of accountability is somewhat alien' (2004, p. 1). Sawhill and Williamson (2001) noted the concept of accountability has traditionally been foreign to the NFP culture, and as observed by Lindenberg,

> nonprofit staff members clearly have different motivations for remaining in their chosen workplace. They have been willing to trade salary dollars for organizational participation and the satisfaction of working for a better world. They believe they have the right to be cynical about detailed analysis and data collection.
>
> (2001, p. 261)

NFPs often possess an 'ideological aversion' to view themselves as comparable to for-profit organisations, and the application of a corporate model, which emphasises a 'business mind-set,' immediately clashes with the philanthropic values of many NFPs, which stress community, cooperation and caring (Lindenberg, 2001). These commentaries are of particular relevance to the current chapter as if such sentiments are salient, they would almost certainly represent a restriction on the adoption and implementation of for-profit, grounded views of performance.

A final, sector-based difference between NFP and for-profit organisations is the relationship between supply of and demand for their services. For many NFPs, the concept of competition is rejected because their service market far outstrips organisational capabilities (Frumkin & Andre-Clarke, 2000). NFPs often feel that their service niche is secure (Brown & Iverson, 2004). This difference between the sectors may reflect a lack of recognition by NFPs of the need for, or importance of, a structured, rigorous approach to conceptualising performance—or at least one that demands the account-ability and fiscal reliance as necessarily exercised by for-profit organisations (Brown & Iverson, 2004).

. . . AND THE WINNER IS . . .?

Based on the discussion to date, the two contrasting theoretical lenses of contingency and institutional theory provide very different vistas about organisational performance as it may be conceptualised within a NFP con-text. On the one hand, contingency theory with its emphasis on sectoral differences between NFPs and for-profit organisations reflects a view that 'what works in business will not necessarily work in NFPs.' On the other hand, institutional theory focuses on the similarities between the sectors and advocates that NFPs will seek to emulate their for-profit cousins about what constitutes performance, in an effort to maintain or achieve legitimacy in the eyes of stakeholders and especially funders. What are we to make of this apparent conundrum, and which theoretical vantage point most accurately reflects how performance should be conceptualised in this important sector?

This chapter adopts the position that the former question is spurious, as it is predicated on the questionable assumption that any single theory is capable of producing exhaustive and universally valid conclusions about the 'real' world (Modell, 2009). If the adage of 'what you see depends on how you look' is correct, then the search for some singular and comprehensively valid 'theoretical truth' is likely to be a long one at best, but most probably futile. To the contrary, the importance of adopting a pluralistic theoretical approach has been recognised by numerous senior accounting scholars (for instance, van der Meer-Kooistra & Vosselman, 2012; Lukka, 2010; Malmi, 2010; Hopper & Hoque, 2006; Modell, 2005, 2009; Hopwood, 2002; Luft & Shields, 2002; Lukka & Mouritsen, 2002). Not least because being open to multiple theoretical perspectives enables sensitivity to variations in situ-ated meanings and potential explanations to be maintained (Modell, 2009), so that these meanings and explanations are not unwittingly suppressed by the mobilisation of particular theories and methods. Moreover, management accounting research informed by different theoretical perspectives has the potential to provide more nuanced and complete knowledge of management accounting in practice (Lukka & Mouritsen, 2002), enabling researchers to generate complementary conceptualisations, telling their 'story' in different ways (Ahrens & Dent, 1998). Insofar as the current conversation is concerned, the story unfolding is that both theoretical perspectives—contingency and institutional—have a valid role to play in identifying what forces may shape performance in NFPs, and most importantly, rather than be seen as diametrically opposed, may in fact be complementary.

Whereas contingency-based approaches are implicitly predicated on the assumption that rational managers are unlikely to adopt or use practices that do not assist in enhancing performance, an alternate view provided by an institutional frame of reference is that pressures to conform to accepted practices (such as how performance is conceptualised and operationalised) can be particularly powerful in NFPs (Tucker & Parker, 2014). Because the survival of such organisations depends primarily on the support of external constituents and only secondarily on actual effectiveness (Tucker, 2010), conforming to accepted social norms and external expectations is required to maintain organisational legitimacy, thereby strengthening support and ensuring continued funding (Chenhall et al., 2010). The adoption of such institutionally driven practices and their implementation in institutional settings is by no means axiomatic, however. In situations in which NFPs feel pressured to adapt to institutionalised expectations, they sometimes respond only superficially by appearing to adopt new structures, practices and approaches without necessarily implementing them (Meyer & Rowan, 1977). The scenario in which an organisation may sometimes exert conscious efforts to portray itself as conforming to institutionalised 'rules' while actually conducting 'business as usual' is known as 'decoupling,' and forms a central concept in institutional theory.

Decoupling need not necessarily be assumed to be automatically dysfunctional. It may build a desirable degree of flexibility and organisational slack that allows for rapid and adaptive organisational reactions to external environmental changes, while maintaining the support of key stakeholder groups and delivering ongoing services and socially approved outcomes (Meyer & Rowan, 1977). Parker (2001) termed this phenomenon as maintaining 'constructive ambiguity'; permitting creative and flexible responses to organisational ambiguity and change. More contemporaneous approaches to NIS (see Cornforth & Edwards, 1999; Lounsbury, 2008; Scott, 2008) recognise that organisations do not always blindly mimic or acquiesce in the face of institutional pressure. Rather, managers adopt a more conscious approach to making adoptive decisions than might be assumed by a simplistic assumption of mindless replication, and that decoupling may occur for brief or lengthy periods. Thus, the process of institutionalisation may exhibit twists and turns over time, occur via various routes and at different rates and need to respond to competing values and potentially conflicting practices (Dambrin, Lambert & Sponem, 2007). As such, it is highly likely that the ways in which performance is regarded within NFPs may be moderated or mediated by the influence of multiple factors, reflecting a product of complex processual interactions of social, political and institutional considerations—in addition to the rational economic goals of efficiency and effectiveness principally assumed by the adoption of a contingency approach (Tucker & Parker, 2014). Viewed in this light, contingency theory is represented in institutional theory with the implicit understanding that the symbolic or institutional world is simply another variant of the environment to which the organisation must adapt.

Thus, despite the conflicting explanations about how performance might be conceptualised within a NFP context, both contingency and institutional perspectives may be regarded as representing two sides of a coin, so to speak, each contributing to building a more complete understanding of how performance is and should be viewed within the NFP sector. Notwithstanding institutional reasons for adopting for-profit conceptualisations of performance, it is likely that contextual factors might mediate or moderate such conceptualisations. Such contingent factors relating to sectoral difference are able to be incorporated and assimilated within definitions, frameworks and measures of performance, thereby preventing the assignment of NFPs to an 'institutional prison' in their approach to conceptualising this construct.

In summary, to profess the 'superiority' of a particular theoretical stance would therefore be foolhardy. Whether or not isomorphic pressures equate to 'doing the right thing for the wrong reasons' (or vice-versa), or whether contingent factors significantly differentiate NFPs from their for-profit cousins is, it is argued, largely irrelevant. What *is* suggested is that these two theoretical vantage points are not implicitly incommensurate.

FROM CONCEPTUALISATION TO OPERATIONALISATION

The argument presented in this chapter to date is that the theoretical stances of contingency and institutional theory as alternate bases from which performance in NFPs may be viewed need not be inevitably regarded as representing polar opposites. Rather, they may each inform our understanding of how performance may be conceptualised in NFPs. Institutional theory on the one hand, provides insights into how a recognition of the need to gain legitimacy and signify compliance with the expectations of external stakeholders influences the way in which organisational performance may be conceptualised. On the other hand, contingency theory may be regarded as providing insights about the ways in which this view of performance may be adapted or augmented to accommodate additional contextual factors that may be either exogenous or endogenous to the NFP, and in particular, sectoral characteristics which delineate the NFP from its for-profit cousins.

For both NFP and management accounting researchers, and for NFP practitioners, how the abstract term, 'performance,' may be conceptualised is a necessary first step if organisational survival, financial stability and sustainability, outcomes assessment, programme evaluation and the propensity to 'make a difference' is to be understood. However, although definable in conceptual terms, the construct, performance, remains an abstraction in that it cannot be observed directly. For *practical* intents and purposes, it necessarily needs to be anchored to an observable reality and operationalised by means of indicators. To the researcher, as well as the practitioner, then, a more tangible means by which the nebulous concept of performance might be made more precise and specific would, in all likelihood, represent a logical next step in the quest to study and improve NFP effectiveness.

Operationalisation—the process of developing indicators or measures that accurately reflect or represent the observable manifestations of NFP performance—may also be informed by the theoretical conceptualisations imparted by institutional and contingency standpoints. These insights into how NFP performance might be both conceptualised and operationalised through the contrasting perspectives of NIS and contingency theories are illustrated in the conceptual framework, shown in Figure 14.1.

This framework aims to summarise the contributions that institutional and contingency views (on the horizontal axis) can make to conceptualising, as well as operationalising, performance (on the vertical axis). The northwestern quadrant reflects the influence that isomorphic forces, be they coercive, mimetic or normative, may have in shaping NFPs' views about what constitutes performance. Performance, as conceptualised from this vantage point, has much in common with the views held by for-profit, as well as public sector, organisations. In a sense, it represents constraints or 'hygiene factors' for many NFPs, in that although they may be essential for the continued and sustainable future of the organisation, they do not, in and of themselves, reflect the fundamental reason for the existence of the NFP. These 'hygiene factors' may be considered to relate to the 'business

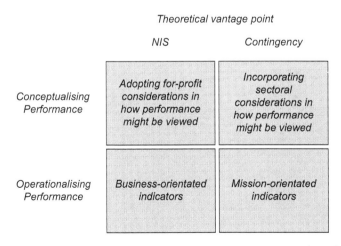

Figure 14.1 Contrasting theoretical perspectives on organisational performance: A conceptual framework (developed by the author)

orientation' of NFPs in that they reflect traditional for-profit measures and indicators of financial performance as presented in financial statements such as the balance sheet, income statement and cash-flow statement, for example. It is likely that importing such for-profit understandings relating to performance can meaningfully inform how effectiveness may be evaluated in NFPs, by preventing the need to 'reinvent the wheel' in attempts to develop performance indicators or metrics. The necessity of developing and incorporating such institutionally driven factors within the way in which performance may be operationalised from an institutional perspective is depicted by the southwestern quadrant of Figure 14.1. These considerations will typically relate to traditional financial ends (for example, profitability, liquidity, asset utilisation and capital investment), but also extend to more intangible outcomes (for example, skills, motivation, capabilities of employees and volunteers, client acquisition and retention, innovative products and services and information technology).

Assessing institutional factors, although important, however provides only a partial picture of performance, as the influence of additional contextual factors will almost certainly be only partially relevant to both the short as well as the longer-term effectiveness of the organisation. The northeastern quadrant of the framework reflects the argument advanced in this chapter that conforming to institutionally based expectations and requirements is, by itself, an inadequate basis for conceptualising performance in the NFP sector. It reflects the view that particular sectoral characteristics unique to the NFP environment will be pivotal in defining what constitutes 'performance,' and thus will need in some way to be incorporated within a NFP conceptualisation of performance. Irrespective of the service/client mix of the NFP, common to all organisations operating within this sector is the need to identify and address the diverse array of objectives and values typically embodied in their missions. The primacy of NFP missions in evaluating their effectiveness is, as we have seen, one of the most salient characteristics differentiating NFP and for-profit sectors. Such mission-related objectives and values, despite their variability, represent the inherent raison d'être of the NFP. It follows therefore that such mission-related criteria are likely to be paramount in any conversation about what may be regarded as essential performance outcomes. The necessity of incorporating mission in operationalising this contingency-based view of performance is represented in the southeastern quadrant of the framework, and is predicated on a view that assumes metrics directly reflecting the mission-related objectives and values will be necessary if measures of performance are to accurately reflect sectoral characteristics.

The bipolar dualism represented in Figure 14.1 is admittedly simplistic; clearly institutional considerations are not restricted solely to for-profit, commercial indicators of performance. In addition to the extent to which it presents itself as 'business-like,' the legitimacy of a NFP is also likely to be evaluated by how well the organisation is able to fulfil its mission. Similarly, a contingency perspective from which performance may be conceptualised is predicated upon an assumption that what works in one setting, or at one point in time, may not work in another, and that efficiency is related to the ongoing alignment of various contingencies. However, over time, established practices may very well become institutionalised and may not necessarily reflect the reality of changing circumstances in the NFP's strategic or operating environment. Nevertheless, the value of the framework lies in illustrating the contribution that both NIS and contingency theory may make to the challenges associated with conceptualising, as well as operationalising, performance. The message it seeks to convey is that individually, each theoretical perspective can provide quite insightful views of what performance is, and how it might be observed; yet in combination, institutional and contingency lenses can offer a more holistic insight into performance in what is a particularly challenging and complex sector.

CONCLUDING REFLECTIONS

Drawing on the discourse presented in the management accounting and NFP literatures, this chapter contributes to the debate about how organisational performance might be viewed in a NFP context. This was achieved by comparing and contrasting organisational performance through the lenses of institutional and contingency theory. In so doing, it provides much needed insights into the extent to which these quite different theoretical perspectives may be adopted by both management accounting and NFP practitioners. These insights have implications for theory and for practice.

Implications for Theory

From a theoretical perspective, the adoption of both institutional and contingency lenses to view how organisational performance might be conceptualised within a NFP environment should not overly concern researchers. The adoption of more than a single perspective from which phenomena may be interpreted and theorised helps to avoid the danger of seeing such phenomena as one would expect to see them (Marginson, 1999), and enables the development of more complete theoretical explanations, which might provide insights into the phenomena observed (Modell, 2005).

Theoretical triangulation involving both institutional and contingency theory as lenses through which to view the conceptualisation of performance suggests that contingent factors impinging and influencing NFPs can and should be incorporated within an institutional framework. Conversely, the transplantation of conceptualisations of contingency-based views of performance from the for-profit sector should incorporate the integration and assimilation of those distinctive sectoral characteristics of NFPs as suggested by an institutional standpoint. At the risk of embarking upon a somewhat esoteric (and controversial) digression, the pluralistic, theoretical stance advocated here bears some similarity with the recurring cultural, political, scientific and theological dispute about the origins of the Earth, humanity, life and the universe; the so-called creation-evolution debate. Both views in this debate focus on the same phenomenon, but in very broad terms; each view (arguably) seeks to address a fundamentally different question (creation focusing on 'why,' with evolution focusing on 'how'). Similarly, as presented here, institutional theory may very well address the question of *why* performance is conceptualised in a particular way, but the concern of contingency theory lies with *how* such conceptualisations need to be modified and adapted, given the particular mission of the NFP. As suggested at the commencement of this chapter, the role of management accounting research in informing this debate has, to date, been limited. Further research that seeks to explore the theoretical bases upon which views of NFP performance are grounded within different NFP industry contexts, over time and at different organisational levels, is likely to further advance our understanding of the complex nature of organisational performance in this sector.

Implications for Practice

The contentions of this chapter have three important implications for practitioners. First, the importance and value to NFPs of consciously identifying exactly what constitutes organisational performance or effectiveness is underlined. This involves a deliberate choice and warrants serious consideration by practitioners 'in the field.' Second, although conceptualisations should be specific, they must also be flexible, especially in where particular conceptions of performance are mandatorily imposed upon NFPs by funders. Once formed, NFPs must be prepared to rework and amend such conceptualisations incrementally in response to what they perceive to be important factors differentiating their particular organisation from for-profit organisations. Such potential contextual variables may very well include the range and diversity of stakeholders and constituencies who will require consultation, the distinctive culture of their organisation, the market position and, in particular, how resources are acquired and allocated amongst competing ends. At times, even full-scale abandonment of these conceptualisations may be necessary, depending on the predominance of institutional forces or contingency factors impinging upon their organisations. Third, for NFPs new to considering how performance should be defined, the importance of time horizons cannot be over-emphasised. Intangible NFP missions typically possess a longer gestation period in comparison with for-profit organisations, and how well or poorly a NFP is performing is usually only seen over a considerable period of time. Persistence in definition, as much as reflexivity, specificity and flexibility, is key to the realisation of realistic performance conceptualisations. Similar to most activities or processes, the quality is likely to improve the more it is done. NFPs reconsidering what constitutes performance should expect initial efforts to be somewhat off the mark, and procedures should be put in place to ensure that 'learning to define performance' is accomplished as efficiently as is possible—whichever tale is being told.

NOTES

1 For instance, in the UK over 22 million adults were involved in formal volunteering in the nonprofit sector in 2007, and the economic value of volunteering was estimated to be approximately £171 billion per year (UK Office for National Statistics, 2009). In 2006, there were over 1.25 million U.S. not-for-profit organisations with assets of $2.5 trillion (U.S. Internal Revenue Service, 2006). In Australia, there are over 58,000 nonprofit organisations, employing around 890,000 people (full-time equivalent), and 4.6 million volunteers, collectively contributing $58 billion to GDP (Australian Bureau of Statistics, 2009). The substantial scale of the NFP sector reflects its importance in assuming expanded roles as governments seek to provide social and other services in more flexible, cost-effective ways (Stone et al., 1999), and underscores the socio-political prominence of this sector and its contribution to Western economies (Lindenberg, 2001).

2 In this chapter, the term 'not-for-profit' encompasses organisations that are neither part of government nor in the for-profit business sector. Such organisations include associations, charities, clubs, cooperatives, mutuals, voluntary organisations, community groups and foundations. Among these organisations will be those that trade their products or services, thereby generating revenue through their activities. Thus, the term 'not-for-profit' does not mean that such institutions do not, or are not capable of making a profit in the generally accepted sense; rather, they do not exist *primarily* to generate profits and are non-profit distributing where they do make a profit. In the UK, such organisations are often generically labelled 'social enterprises.' In Australia, the term 'third sector' is more typically used to describe this broad range of organisations.

REFERENCES

Abraham, A. (2004, July 4–6). *A model of financial performance analysis adapted for nonprofit organisations*. Paper presented at the AFAANZ 2004 Conference Proceedings, Northern Territory, AU.

Ahrens, T. and Dent, J. F. (1998). Accounting and organizations: Realizing the richness of field research. *Journal of Management Accounting Research, 10*, 1–39.

Anthony, R. N. (1965). *Management planning and control systems: A framework for analysis*. Boston, MA: Harvard Business School Press.

Anthony, R. N., & Govindarajan, V. (2004). *Management control systems* (11th ed.). New York: McGraw-Hill/Irwin.

Australian Bureau of Statistics. (2009). *Not-for-profit organisations, Australia, Australian National Accounts 2006–07* (Cat. 8106.0). Canberra, AU.

Balser, D., & McClusky, J. (2005). Managing stakeholder relationships and non-profit organization effectiveness. *Nonprofit Management and Leadership, 15*(3), 295–315.

Baraldi, S. (1998). Management control systems in NPOs: An Italian survey. *Financial Accountability and Management, 14*(2), 141–164.

Baruch, Y., & Ramalho, N. (2006). Communalities and distinctions in the measurement of organizational performance and effectiveness across for-profit and nonprofit sectors. *Nonprofit and Voluntary Sector Quarterly, 35*(1), 39–65.

Beck, T. E., Lengnick-Hall, C. A., & Lengnick-Hall, M. L. (2008). Solutions out of context. Examining the transfer of business concepts to nonprofit organizations. *Nonprofit Management and Leadership, 19*(2), 153–171.

Berry, A. J., Coad, A. F., Harris, E. P., Otley, D. T., & Stringer, C. (2009). Emerging themes in management control: A review of recent literature. *The British Accounting Review, 41*(1), 2–20.

Bielefeld, W. (2006). Quantitative research for nonprofit management. *Nonprofit Management and Leadership, 16*(4), 395–409.

Bradshaw, P. (2009). A contingency approach to nonprofit governance. *Nonprofit Management and Leadership, 20*(1), 61–81.

Brown, W. A. (2000). *Understanding organizational configurations and models of board governance in nonprofit organizations.* Paper presented at the Association for Research on Nonprofit Organizations and Voluntary Action Annual Conference, New Orleans, LA, November 2004.

Brown, W. A., & Iverson, J. O. (2004). Exploring strategy and board structure in nonprofit organizations. *Nonprofit and Voluntary Sector Quarterly, 33*(3), 377–400.

Casteuble, T. (1997). Using financial ratios to assess performance. *Association Management, 49*(7), 29–36.

Chenhall, R. H. (1997). Reliance on manufacturing performance measures, total quality management and organizational performance. *Management Accounting Research, 8*(2), 187–206.

Chenhall, R. H. (2003). Management control systems design within its organizational context: Findings from contingency-based research and directions for the future. *Accounting, Organizations and Society, 28*(2/3), 127–168.

Chenhall, R. H., Hall, M., & Smith, D. (2010). Social capital and management control systems: A study of a non-government organization. *Accounting, Organizations and Society, 35*(8), 737–756.

Christensen, A. L., & Mohr, R. M. (2003). Not-for-profit annual reports: What do museum managers communicate. *Financial Accountability and Management, 19*(2), 139–158.

Clohesy, W. W. (2003). Fund-raising and the articulation of common goods. *Nonprofit and Voluntary Sector Quarterly, 32*(1), 128–140.

Cornforth, C., and Edwards, C. (1999). Board roles in the strategic management of non-profit organisations: Theory and practice. *Corporate Governance: An International Review, 7*(4), 346–362.

Dambrin, C., Lambert, C., & Sponem S. (2007). Control and change—Analysing the process of institutionalization. *Management Accounting Research, 18*(2), 172–208.

DiMaggio, P. J., & Powell, W. W. (1983). The iron cage revisited: Institutional isomorphism and collective rationality in organizational fields. *American Sociological Review, 48*(2), 147–160.

DiMaggio, P. J., & Powell, W. W. (1991). Introduction to the new institutionalism in organizational analysis. In P. DiMaggio & W. Powell (Eds.), *The new institutionalism in organizational analysis.* Chicago, IL: University of Chicago Press.

Doherty, A., & Hoye, R. (2011). Role ambiguity and volunteer board member performance in nonprofit sport organizations. *Nonprofit Management and Leadership, 22*(1), 107–128.

Durden, C. (2007). Towards a socially responsible management control system. *Accounting, Auditing & Accountability Journal, 21*(5), 671–694.

Epstein, M. J., & Birchard, B. (2000). *Counting what counts.* Cambridge, MA: Perseus Books.

Ferreira, A., & Otley, D. T. (2009). The design and use of performance management systems: An extended framework for analysis. *Management Accounting Research, 20*(4), 263–282.

Forbes, D. P. (1998). Measuring the unmeasurable: Empirical studies of nonprofit organization effectiveness from 1977 to 1997. *Nonprofit and Voluntary Sector Quarterly, 27*(2), 183–202.

Frumkin, P., & Andre-Clark, A. (2000). When missions, markets, and politics collide: Values and strategy in nonprofit human services. *Nonprofit and Voluntary Sector Quarterly, 29*(1), 141–163.

Gray, R., Bebbington, J., & Collison, D. (2006). NGOs, civil society, and accountability: Making the people accountable to capital. *Accounting, Auditing, and Accountability Journal, 19*(3), 319–348.

Gray, R., Owen, D., & Adams, C. (1996). *Accounting and accountability; changes and challenges in corporate social and environmental reporting.* London: Prentice-Hall.

Griggs, H. E. (2003). Corporatisation of the not-for-profit sector: Strategic planning and organisational performance in disability-based organisations. *International Journal of Disability, Development and Education, 50*(2), 197–220.

Gupta, P. P., Dirsmith, M. W., & Fogarty, T. J. (1994). Coordination and control in a government agency: Contingency and institutional theory perspectives on GAO audits. *Administrative Science Quarterly, 39*(2), 264–284.

Heinrich, C. J. (2000). Organizational form and performance: An empirical investigation of nonprofit and for-profit job-training service providers. *Journal of Policy Analysis and Management, 19*(2), 233–261.

Henri, J. F. (2006). Management control systems and strategy: A resource-based perspective. *Accounting, Organizations and Society, 31*(6), 529–558.

Herman, R. D., & Renz, D. O. (1998). Nonprofit organizational effectiveness: Contrasts between especially effective and less effective organizations. *Nonprofit Management and Leadership, 9*(1), 23–38.

Herman, R. D., & Renz, D. O. (1999). Theses on nonprofit organizational effectiveness. *Nonprofit and Voluntary Sector Quarterly, 28*(2), 107–125.

Herman, R. D., & Renz, D. O. (2008). Advancing nonprofit organizational effectiveness research and theory—nine theses. *Nonprofit Management and Leadership, 18*(4), 399–415.

Hodge, M. M., & Piccolo, R. (2005). Funding source, board involvement techniques, and financial vulnerability in nonprofit organizations. *Nonprofit Management and Leadership, 16*(2), 171–190.

Hopper, T., & Hoque, Z. (2006). Triangulation approaches to accounting research. In Z. Hoque (Ed.), *Methodological issues in accounting research. Theories, methods and issues.* London: Spiramus.

Hopwood, A. G. (2002). If only there were simple solutions, but there aren't: Some reflections on Zimmerman's critique of empirical management accounting research. *The European Accounting Review, 11*(4), 777–785.

Ittner, C. D., & Larcker, D. F. (1997). Quality strategy, strategic control systems, and organizational performance. *Accounting, Organizations and Society, 22*(3/4), 295–314.

Ittner, C. D., & Larcker, D. F. (1998). Innovations in performance measurement: Trends and research implications. *Journal of Management Accounting Research, 10*, 205–239.

Kaplan, R. S. (2001). Strategic performance measurement and management in nonprofit organizations. *Nonprofit Management and Leadership, 11*(3), 353–370.

Kaplan, R. S., & Norton, D. P. (1992). *The balanced scorecard.* Boston, MA: Harvard Business School Press.

Kelly, M., & Alam, M. (2008). Management accounting and the stakeholder value model. *Journal of Applied Management Accounting Research, 6*(1), 75–87.

Langfield-Smith, K. (1997). Management control systems and strategy: A critical review. *Accounting, Organizations and Society, 22*(2), 207–232.

Langfield-Smith, K. (2005). What do we know about management control systems and strategy? In C. S. Chapman (Ed.), *Controlling strategy: Management, accounting, and performance measurement* (pp. 62–85). Oxford: Oxford University Press.

Langfield-Smith, K. (2007). A review of quantitative research in management control systems and strategy. In C. S. Chapman, A. G. Hopwood, & M. D. Shields (Eds.), *Handbook of management accounting research—volume 2.* Oxford: Elsevier.

Leiter, J. (2005). Structural isomorphism in Australian nonprofit organizations. *VOLUNTAS: International Journal of Voluntary and Nonprofit Organizations, 16*, 1–31.

Leiter, J. (2013). An industry fields approach to isomorphism involving Australian nonprofit organizations. *VOLUNTAS: International Journal of Voluntary and Nonprofit Organizations, 24*, 1037–1070.

Lewis, D. (1998). Nongovernmental organizations, business, and the management of ambiguity. *Nonprofit Management and Leadership, 9*(2), 135–151.

Lewis, D. (2002). Organization and management in the third sector: Toward a cross-cultural research agenda. *Nonprofit Management and Leadership, 13*(1), 67–83.

Lindenberg, M. (2001). Are we at the cutting edge or the blunt edge? Improving NGO organizational performance with private and public sector strategic management frameworks. *Nonprofit Management and Leadership, 11*(3), 247–270.

Lounsbury, M. (2008). Institutional rationality and practice variation: New directions in the institutional analysis of practice. *Accounting, Organizations and Society, 33*, 349–361.

Luft, J., & Shields, M. D. (2002). Zimmerman's contentious conjectures: Describing the present and prescribing the future of empirical management accounting research. *The European Accounting Review, 11*(4),759–803.

Lukka, K. (2010). The roles and effects of paradigms in accounting research. *Management Accounting Research, 21*(2), 110–115.

Lukka, K., & Mouritsen, J. (2002). Homogeneity or heterogeneity of research in management accounting? *The European Accounting Review, 11*(4), 805–811.

Malmi, T. (2010). Reflections on paradigms in action in accounting research. *Management Accounting Research, 21*(2), 121–123.

Mara, C. M. (2000). A strategic planning process for a small non-profit organization: A hospice example. *Non-Profit Management and Leadership, 11*(2), 211–222.

Marginson, D.E.W. (1999). Beyond the budgetary control system: Towards a two-tiered process of management control. *Management Accounting Research, 10*(3), 203–230.

Merchant, K. A., & Otley, D. T. (2007). A review of the literature on control and accountability. In C. S. Chapman, A. G. Hopwood, & M. D. Shields (Eds.), *Handbook of management accounting research—volume 2.* Oxford: Elsevier.

Meyer, J. W., and Rowan, B. (1977). Institutionalized organizations: Formal structure as myth and ceremony. *American Journal of Sociology, 83*, 340–363.

Modell, S. (2005). Triangulation between case study and survey methods in management accounting research: An assessment of validity implications. *Management Accounting Research, 16*(2), 231–254.

Modell, S. (2009). In defence of triangulation: A critical realist approach to mixed methods research in management accounting. *Management Accounting Research, 20*(3), 208–221.

Moore, M. H. (2000). Managing for value: Organizational strategy in for-profit, nonprofit, and governmental organizations. *Nonprofit and Voluntary Sector Quarterly, 29*(1), 183–204.

Moores, K., & Yuen, S. (2001). Management accounting systems and organizational configuration: A life-cycle perspective. *Accounting, Organizations and Society, 26*(4/5), 351–389.

Mulhare, E. M. (1999). Mindful of the future: Strategic planning ideology and the culture of nonprofit management. *Human Organization, 58*(3), 323–330.

Nobbie, P. D., & Brudney, J. L. (2003). Testing the implementation, board performance, and organizational effectiveness of the policy governance model in nonprofit boards of directors. *Nonprofit and Voluntary Sector Quarterly, 32*(4), 571–595.

O'Dwyer, B., & Unerman, J. (2008). The paradox of greater NGO accountability: A case study of Amnesty Ireland. *Accounting, Organizations and Society, 33*(7–8), 801–824.

Otley, D. T. (1999). Performance management: A framework for management control systems research. *Management Accounting Research, 10*(4), 363–382.

Otley, D. T. (2008). Did Kaplan and Johnson get it right? *Accounting, Auditing & Accountability Journal, 21*(2), 229–239.

Otley, D. T., & Berry, A. J. (1980). Control, organization and accounting. *Accounting, Organizations and Society, 5*(2), 231–244.

Otley, D. T., Broadbent, J., & Berry, A. (1995). Research in management control: An overview of its development. *British Journal of Management, 6*, s31–s44.

Parker, L. D. (1998, July). Non-profit prophets: Strategy in non-commercial organisations. *Australian CPA, 68*, 50–52.

Parker, L. D. (2001). Reactive planning in a Christian bureaucracy. *Management Accounting Research, 12*(3), 321–356.

Parker, L. D. (2002). Budgetary incrementalism in a Christian bureaucracy. *Management Accounting Research, 13*(1), 71–100.

Parker, L. D. (2008). Boardroom operational & financial control: An insider view. *British Journal of Management, 19*(1), 65–88.

Ramanath, R. (2009). Limits to institutional isomorphism: Examining internal processes in NGO–government interactions. *Nonprofit and Voluntary Sector Quarterly, 38*(1), 51–76.

Ritchie, W. J., & Kolodinsky, R. W. (2003). Nonprofit organization financial performance measurement: An evaluation of new and existing financial performance measures. *Nonprofit Management and Leadership, 13*(4), 367–381.

Rojas, R. R. (2000). A review of models for measuring organizational effectiveness among for-profit and nonprofit organizations. *Nonprofit Management and Leadership, 11*(1), 97–104.

Sawhill, J., & Williamson, D. (2001). The erosion of the competitive advantage of strategic planning: A configuration theory and resources based view. *The McKinsey Quarterly, 2*, 96–107.

Schneider, J. A. (2003). Small, minority-based nonprofits in the information age. *Nonprofit Management and Leadership, 13*(4), 383–399.

Scott, W. R. (2008). Approaching adulthood: The maturing of institutional theory. *Theory and Society, 37*, 427–442.

Shoham, A., Ruvio, A., Vigoda-Gadot, E., & Schwabsky, N. (2006). Market orientations in the nonprofit and voluntary sector: A meta-analysis of their relationships with organizational performance. *Nonprofit and Voluntary Sector Quarterly, 35*(3), 453–476.

Smith, M. (1998). Measuring organisational effectiveness. *Management Accounting: Magazine for Chartered Management Accountants, 76*, 34–36.

Sowa, J. E., Selden, S. C., & Sandfort, J. R. (2004). No longer unmeasurable? A multidimensional integrated model of nonprofit organizational effectiveness. *Nonprofit and Voluntary Sector Quarterly, 33*(4), 711–728.

Speckbacher, G. (2003). The economics of performance management in nonprofit organizations. *Nonprofit Management and Leadership, 13*(3), 267–281.

Stone, M. M. , Bigelow, B., & Crittenden, W. (1999). Research on strategic management in nonprofit organizations. *Administration and Society, 31*(3), 378–424.

Tucker, B. P. (2010). Through which lens? Contingency and institutional approaches to conceptualising organisational performance in the not-for-profit sector. *Journal of Applied Management Accounting Research, 8*(1), 1–17.

Tucker, B. P., & Parker, L. D. (2014). In our ivory towers? The research-practice gap in management accounting: An academic perspective. *Accounting & Business Research, 44*(2), 104–143.

UK Office for National Statistics. (2009). *Blue book.* Retrieved 25 November 2009 from http://www.statistics.gov.uk/STATBASE/Product.asp?vlnk=1143

Unerman, J., & O'Dwyer, B. (2006). Theorising accountability for NGO advocacy. *Accounting, Auditing and Accountability Journal, 19*(3), 349–376.

Unerman, J., & O'Dwyer, B. (2010). *The relevance and utility of leading accounting research* (Research report 120). London: The Association of Chartered Certified Accountants.

U.S. Internal Revenue Service. (2006). *SOI tax stats—historical data tables* (Table 16). Nonprofit Charitable Organization and Domestic Private Foundation Information Returns, and Exempt Organization Business Income Tax Returns: Selected Financial Data, Expanded Version. Retrieved 1 December 2012 from http://www.irs.gov/taxstats/article/0,,id=75876,00.html

van der Meer-Kooistra, J., & Vosselman, E.G.J. (2012). Research paradigms, theoretical pluralism and the practical relevance of management accounting knowledge. *Qualitative Research in Accounting & Management, 9*(3), 245–264.

Widener, S. K. (2007). An empirical analysis of the levers of control framework. *Accounting Organizations and Society, 32*(7/8), 757–788.

15 Board Monitoring and the Balanced Scorecard in Nonprofits
Challenges in Realising Potential

Alan D. Hough, Myles McGregor-Lowndes and Christine M. Ryan

INTRODUCTION

Directors of nonprofits in most countries have legal responsibility for monitoring organisational performance (Brody, 2010), although there is typically little guidance on how this should occur. The balanced scorecard (BSC) (Kaplan & Norton, 1996, 2001) potentially provides boards with a monitoring tool (Kaplan & Norton, 2006; Lorsch, 2002). The BSC is intended to help integrate performance measurement, performance management and strategy implementation (Kaplan, 2009). The scorecard is balanced in that it should incorporate both financial and non-financial measures, external and internal perspectives, short and long-term objectives and both lagging and leading indicators. It is a relatively simple tool, but with potentially profound implications for directing board attention and subsequent action (Ocasio, 1997; Salterio, 2012).

The scorecard and the associated, recommended practices are based on normative expectations of rational behaviour, or 'cybernetic' (machine-like) assumptions (Hofstede, 1978; Swieringa & Weick, 1981). These assumptions are that managers and leaders engage in routines of setting goals, measuring achievements, comparing achievements to goals, providing feedback on variances and ensuring that variances are corrected. Despite both long-standing and recent challenges to these assumptions (Hofstede, 1978; Radin, 2006), they are the basis of all normatively promoted performance management systems.

The empirical evidence about the use of the scorecard in nonprofits is limited, and this chapter makes a contribution to this literature. Greiling (2010, p. 535) suggests that there are two generations of literature. The first generation consists of normative advocacy for the BSC's adoption. The second generation consists of case studies where the BSC has been adopted, often completed shortly after uptake. Many cases are recounted as 'success stories and challenges are only dealt with very briefly' (Greiling, 2010, p. 536). Examples of such studies include those of Kaplan and Norton (2001, 2004) and Stewart and Bestor (2000). There are a few studies taking a somewhat more considered approach (Gurd & Gao, 2008; Kaplan, 2001;

Manville, 2007). As Greiling states by way of summary, 'we cannot draw on a satisfying body of literature which empirically compares the experience [of] the balanced scorecard across nonprofit organisations' (2010, p. 538).

Similarly, the impact of the BSC on board-monitoring practices is under-researched. There are only five prior studies that reflect on the BSC and boards (Chang, Tung, Huang, & Yang, 2008; Craig & Moores, 2010; Inamdar & Kaplan, 2002; Kocakülâh & Austill, 2007; Manville, 2007). Of these, only two consider the impact on board monitoring, and then only incidentally. Both articles are based on single cases. Kocakülâh and Austill (2007) report on a single U.S. hospital group adopting and implementing the BSC. Although the article falls into the genre of a partial 'success story,' the authors note that the scorecard added to the number of data sources going to the board, with resulting confusion and concern for the directors because data was not synchronised across the various sources. Chang and colleagues' study (2008) of a Taiwanese nonprofit hospital is another 'success story,' with outcomes said to include the building of consensus between board and management about strategy, management's increased credibility with directors and improved timeliness in investment decision-making. To summarise, the literature on board monitoring and the BSC is scant. Nonetheless, these articles support the normative case for using the BSC as a board-monitoring tool. However, Salterio decries the general paucity of studies 'that examine real world BSC issues from a human information processing perspective' (2012, p. 467). More generally, there have been numerous calls for greater consideration of boardroom processes and practices (for example, Huse, 2007; Parker, 2008). Hence, our research question is: how does the availability of a BSC-type tool impact on board monitoring in nonprofit organisations? To the best of our knowledge, this is the first research-based publication dedicated to the issue of boards using the BSC for organisational monitoring. Further, the chapter extends the limited research evidence in relation to the use of the BSC in nonprofits.

Our research setting was five boards of small and medium-sized nonprofit health organisations in Queensland, Australia. All the organisations had a BSC-based external reporting tool imposed on them by their principal funder, namely the Department of Health (otherwise known as Queensland Health, or 'QH'). Thus, the research setting provided an unprecedented opportunity to examine intensively the scorecard's impact on board-monitoring practices. We find that the scorecard's potential as a board-monitoring tool was not realised in part due to the inertia of routines of CEO reporting and of board monitoring. By 'routines,' we mean the 'repetitive, recognizable patterns of interdependent actions, carried out by multiple actors' (Feldman & Pentland, 2003, p. 95).

The chapter proceeds by first providing background on the prescribed scorecard-type tool. The literature on organisational routines is then discussed. After outlining the research methods, the data are reported and then analysed. Conclusions and implications are discussed in the final section.

THE QUEENSLAND HEALTH PERFORMANCE FRAMEWORK
FOR THE NON-GOVERNMENT SECTOR

The QH balanced scorecard-tool for funded nonprofits was called the *Performance Framework for the Non-Government Sector* (Queensland Health, 2004b). The *Performance Framework* had its origins in a quality project concerning the external accountability and reporting of nonprofits funded by the Department (Queensland Health, 2002). Over time, the project developed a wider focus, including adopting the goal of enabling funded organisations to improve their service delivery (Queensland Health, 2003). A key aim of the project was to develop a *Performance Framework* based on the BSC (Queensland Health, 2003). The *Framework* was developed with the assistance of funded organisations; for example, 21 focus groups were conducted with funded organisations in the design of the *Framework* (Queensland Health, 2004a). There was a collaboratively run pilot project to test its application.

From July 2004, QH imposed on funded nonprofits a requirement to report against the *Framework* (Figure 15.1). The published aims of the *Framework* were to promote quality, to assist organisations in evaluating their services, to improve their service delivery and to promote accountability and transparency in management practice (Queensland Health, 2004b). There was an explicitly stated objective that organisations would use the *Performance Framework* to improve organisational performance (Queensland Health, 2004b). The *Framework* imposed a number of obligations on boards (called 'management committees'), including accountability for service efficiency, sustainability and quality.

Organisations were asked to lodge reports against the *Framework* (the 'performance reports') and service activity data each six months, and financial reports quarterly. The performance reports were to be signed off by the board (Queensland Health, 2004a), implying that the reports would be received, considered and authorised by the board.

Organisations were assisted to implement the *Framework* with workshops for organisations' staff and board representatives, publications and advice (Queensland Health, 2004a, 2004b). Before going to the research methods, it is necessary to examine the contribution of the literature on routines.

LEARNING FROM THE LITERATURE ON ROUTINES:
OSTENSIVE ASPECTS, PERFORMATIVE ASPECTS
AND ARTEFACTS

The work of boards might be considered to be a series of interlocking or 'nested' routines (Miner, Ciuchta, & Gong, 2008). Directors typically come together at specified intervals, usually follow an agenda which has

Focus Area	Objectives	Indicators
Perspective 1: Funded Service Delivery		
Service Types	1.1 The organisation delivers the services as agreed with Queensland Health.	1.1a The organisation describes its funded Service Types.
Service Statistics	1.2 Service and client data will provide Queensland Health with information to monitor an organisation's performance.	1.2a The organisation collects and reports direct service statistics to Queensland Health on a regular basis.
Perspective 2: Consumer and Community		
Consumer Focus	2.1 The organisation's consumers are satisfied with services delivered.	2.1a The organisation has a process for monitoring consumer satisfaction and improves its service according to the feedback collected.
		2.1b The organisation has a documented, advertised and accessible complaint mechanism
	2.2 The organisation ensure its consumers are aware of their rights and responsibilities and upholds those rights.	2.2a The organisation ensures workers inform consumers of their rights and responsibilities, and assist them to exercise those rights and meet their responsibilities.
		2.2b The organisation has systems in place to ensure the confidentiality, privacy and consent of consumers

Focus Area	Objectives	Indicators
Accessible Services	2.3 Services are provided with consideration for the target group's social and cultural needs and expectations.	2.3a The organisation develops strategies to ensure that its services are culturally appropriate and non-discriminatory to the target group.
	2.4 The organisation addresses physical and knowledge barriers that may prevent the target group from using its services.	2.4a The organisation addresses barriers to access its services by consumers, including hours of operation, publicising service availability, and service delivery location and environment.
Engagement and Participation	2.5 The organisation encourages participation by members of its target group and the broader community.	2.5a The organisation has a process in place to allow its consumers and representatives to the community to participate in service planning, delivery and evaluation.
Appropriate Services	2.6 The organisation plans its services in accordance with the needs of its target group.	2.6a The organisation develops and implements specialist activities that are appropriate to its target group's needs.
Collaboration	2.7 The organisation collaborates to enhance service delivery for its target group.	2.7a The Management Committee identifies priorities and documents how it will collaborate with other agencies to improve the health and well being of the target group.
		2.7b The organisation actively collaborates with other agencies to improve its service delivery.

(*Continued*)

Focus Area	Objectives	Indicators
Perspective 3: Continuous Quality Improvement		
Innovation and Learning.	3.1 The organisation is committed to ongoing development of its service activities and workers.	3.1a The organisation provides workers with opportunities for education and professional development.
		3.1b The organisation supports learning about best practice approaches to service delivery, management and operations
Workplace Health and Safety	3.2 The health and safety of all persons within the organisation is protected.	3.2a The organisation has a strategy to ensure safe management of work practices and physical and psychological aspects of the environment.
Risk Management	3.3 The organisation monitors organisational risks and controls these where possible.	3.3a The organisation develops, documents and implements a risk management process.
Evaluation	3.4 The organisation regularly evaluates its activities.	3.4a The organisation has developed valid systems or processes for evaluating and improving its service activities and outcomes.
		3.4b The organisation participates in research by other parties that relates to health services for the target group.

Focus Area	Objectives	Indicators
Perspective 4: Management and Resourcing		
Leadership and Governance	4.1 The Management Committee provides leadership and takes responsibility for ensuring that the organisation's achievements and services contribute to improving the health and well being of the target group.	4.1a The Management Committee meets its obligations under the Association Incorporation Act, including matters relating to corporate governance, financial administration and insurance.
		4.1b The Management Committee leads the identification of the organisation's service priorities and development of the service activity plan
Operational Management	4.2 The organisation's management is accountable for how services are delivered.	4.2a The organisation has an operational plan that clearly identifies its goals and strategies, and assign workers' responsibilities and accountabilities.
		4.2b Management involves the organisation's stakeholders in decision-making.
Efficient Use of Resources	4.3 Services are delivered to the target group with an efficient use of resources.	4.3a The organisation's human resource policies and practices comply with requirement of the Queensland Health Service Agreement and relevant legislation.
		4.3b The Management Committee is accountable for the efficiency of service delivery.

(*Continued*)

Focus Area	Objectives	Indicators
Sustainability	4.4 The Management Committee has identified ways to maintain or enhance the sustainability of the organisation.	4.4a The Management Committee addresses issues of sustainability and quality improvement in the organisation's strategic plan.
		4.4b Business cases are developed to assist the Management Committee with decisions that many significantly affect service delivery and resources.
Transparency and Accountability	4.5 The organisation is accountable to key stakeholders.	4.5a The organisation ensures that workers comply with the applicable codes of ethics, standards of practices and registration requirements.
		4.5b The Management Committee holds an appropriately convened Annual General Meeting and ensure that its Annual Report is distributed to key stakeholders.
		4.5c The organisation has a documented set of principles that guide the delivery of services to the target group, including clear eligibility guidelines.

Figure 15.1   The Queensland Health Performance Framework for the non-government sector (Pentland & Feldman, 2008, p. 241; reproduced with permission from Elsevier)

Source: Developed by the authors from Queensland Health 2004b, 23–24.

a standard format, receive reports that often have a common framework over successive meetings and follow common practices for monitoring, discussion and decision-making (Boardsource, 2010; Houle, 1997). Standard scripts are also readily observable—a script being 'a cognitive structure that specifies a typical sequence of occurrences in a given situation' (Ashford & Fried, 1988, p. 306). One example of a script would be a meeting chair asking the treasurer to present the financial reports, with the treasurer providing an analysis of the written reports and then recommending their adoption (Ashford & Fried, 1988; Gioia, 1986). Despite the potential utility of studying board routines, they have not been given fulsome attention in governance research, with only a handful of exceptions (Chait, Holland, & Taylor, 1996; Hendry & Seidl, 2003; Khurana & Pick, 2005; Ocasio, 1994, 1997, 1999; Smith, Dufour, & Erakovic, 2011).

Routines offer a number of potential benefits: assisting in informing group members, enabling sense-making, embodying organisational memory, especially procedural memory, assisting in organisational learning and informing expectations (Becker, 2008; Burns & Scapens, 2008; Parmigiani & Howard-Grenville, 2011; Weick, 1995). Routines can be one element of capabilities (Chalmers & Balan-Vnuk, 2013; Felin, Foss, Heimeriks, & Madsen, 2012; Parmigiani & Howard-Grenville, 2011), and hence mindfully performing appropriate routines can build board capabilities and potentially improve organisational effectiveness. However, routines can also have the disadvantages of fostering organisational inertia and 'mindless' enactment (Ashford & Fried, 1988; Parmigiani & Howard-Grenville, 2011; Schulz, 2008).

Management scholars—especially Feldman and Pentland—have advanced our understanding of routines by conceptualising them as having ostensive and performative aspects, supported by artefacts, as shown in Figure 15.2 (Feldman & Pentland, 2003; Miller, Pentland, & Choi, 2012; Pentland & Feldman, 2005, 2008; Quinn, 2011).

A routine's *ostensive* aspect is 'the idea' of the routine: the abstract concept or cognitive understanding of the routine (Feldman & Pentland, 2003, p. 102). For example, most readers can conceptualise a routine for hiring an employee as including steps such as shortlisting the best candidates,

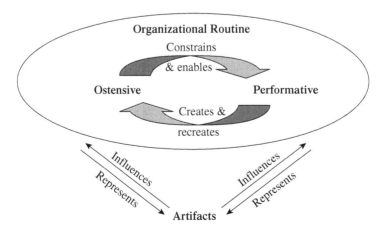

Figure 15.2   Organisational routines (Pentland & Feldman, 2008, p. 241; reprinted with permission from Elsevier)

interviewing the candidates, etc. In addition to a routine's ostensive aspect, there is a *performative* aspect of how it is enacted. This involves the 'specific actions of specific people at specific times' (Feldman & Pentland, 2003, pp. 101–102). For example, in a recruitment routine, it is the *actual performance* by known managers of shortlisting individual candidates (who might or might not be meritorious applicants), inviting them to interview on a specific day and place, etc. *Artefacts* sometimes play important roles in routines. They are 'the physical manifestations of the organizational routine' (Pentland & Feldman, 2005, p. 797) and can include written standard operating procedures, tools and software. In this study, the *Performance Framework* and the performance reports are potential artefacts in board-monitoring routines.

Sometimes a routine's performative aspect, the ostensive aspect and the associated artefacts are tightly coupled (e.g., a routine regulated by software). However, at other times, they are not. Any 'performance' involves 'actors' and hence human agency comes to the fore (Emirbayer & Mische, 1998; Howard-Grenville, 2005; Lazaric & Denis, 2005), including in the degree to which an artefact is used (Howard-Grenville, 2005; Parmigiani & Howard-Grenville, 2011; Pentland & Feldman, 2008, p. 244). Further, any one artefact should be appreciated in the context of the entire system of artefacts, for some and not others might be used (Cacciatori, 2012).

Although recent research has demonstrated that each occasion a routine is enacted can generate change in the routine, various mechanisms can perpetuate the routine's existing form; hence, the historic perception that routines involved inertia. Some of the potentially relevant mechanisms of perpetuation are: habits; priming through beginning a sequence; actor's mutual expectations; institutionalisation, in part because of perceived legitimacy; symbolism; formalisation; creating artefacts; commitment to prior effort, and all because a routine has many connections with other organisational processes (Gersick & Hackman, 1990; Howard-Grenville, 2005; Schulz, 2008; Weick, 1995). Schulz (2008) hypothesises that the likelihood that a routine is maintained depends on the intensity of the single mechanisms of perpetuation, the number of mechanisms in operation and the number of times a routine has been implemented.

What then do organisations do to overcome these inertial forces if they wish to create new patterns of interaction or modify existing ones? Developing the routine's ostensive side in order to influence the performative aspect is a key strategy, for the ostensive constrains and enables the performance. Pentland and Feldman observe that people involved in entities where interdependent action is critical, such as sports teams, firefighters and orchestras, 'get training, they practice together, they get feedback on their collective performance, and they practice together some more' (2008, p. 247). This argument finds support and elaboration in a range of settings (deHaven-Smith & Jenne, 2006; Edmondson, Bohmer, & Pisano, 2001; Moynihan & Lavertu, 2012).

Accordingly, we would argue that when adopting or imposing new monitoring tools such as the BSC, it should not be assumed that a new artefact's availability will change patterns of action (Pentland & Feldman, 2008), as there may be strong forces at work perpetuating the preexisting routines (Schulz, 2008). The BSC reports will be just one element in a system of artefacts (Cacciatori, 2012) and might well compete with other monitoring data for the time and attention of the board. As Miner et al. observe, 'achieving useful learning through changing mixes of routines presents considerable challenges' (2008, p. 174). Our next section sets out the research methods.

METHODS: SEEING WHAT PEOPLE DO, NOT MERELY WHAT THEY SAY THEY DO

Given that research on the BSC's impact on board monitoring is in its infancy, a multiple case design and qualitative method was an appropriate way of proceeding. The unique advantage of case studies is the ability to draw on a variety of evidence (Stake, 2000; Yin, 2003).

A list of nonprofits subject to the *Performance Framework* was obtained. To be eligible to be a case organisation, the nonprofits had to be legal entities in their own right, and have more than $100,000 in income. QH had to be their largest single funder, supplying at least one-third of revenue, to help minimise complexity due to different reporting regimes (Grønbjerg, 1993; Moxham & Boaden, 2007).

To select from among the potentially eligible organisations, a theory-driven sampling approach was attempted. Zald (1969) suggests that board-monitoring behaviours are significantly affected by organisational complexity, including size and programme complexity, and hence organisations of lower and higher complexity were selected. Organisational income was used as a proxy indicator of organisational size. Programme complexity was assessed having regard to information on the organisation's websites, data from a charity-rating agency and on the basis of the research team's personal knowledge. The enrolment of case organisations also embraced 'planned opportunism' (Pettigrew, 1990, p. 274): one of the first organisations approached was eager to participate, and was quickly enrolled. Importantly, it was confirmed on enrolment that the CEOs of all five case organisations intended to provide the performance reports as part of their board reporting.

Although the organisations will not be named to preserve their anonymity, some information can be provided. All the case organisations were member-based associations, with an elected board of directors. The organisations provided individual support and care, and/or health promotion services; however, none were hospitals. Some organisations were locally based, and others operated across Queensland. Three of the organisations had incomes of less than $500,000, and two significantly above. The organisations are referred to as Alpha, Bravo, Charlie, Delta and Echo, with the order reflecting ascending organisational size.

Each organisation was studied for between 12 and 14 months. Consistent with calls to use multiple sources of data about board behaviour (Heracleous, 2001), the study was informed by observation of board meetings, interviews with directors and CEOs and access to board documents (such as the performance reports, where provided to the board). Across the five organisations, 65 meetings were observed, involving more than 111 hours of observation. The lead author was a 'complete observer' (Jorgensen, 1989; Winkler, 1987). Given the timing of the research, the boards' reactions to the six-monthly performance reports could potentially be observed on three occasions. Hoque (2014) identifies that observation is a technique that has rarely been used in researching the impact of the BSC. However, it is a technique of obvious merit when trying to investigate how the BSC is used in practice. The second data source was the interviews. 50 directors (83.3% of directors) were interviewed, as were the five CEOs. Questions asked of directors about the performance reports would vary depending on whether the interviewee indicated they had, or had not, received the performance report, and were based around utility or potential utility of the reports. The third source of data was the documentary records of each organisation, such as agenda papers and meeting minutes.

The main analytical strategies were, first, within-case analysis to examine what occurred in each organisation, and, second, cross-case comparison. Langley comments that these strategies produce work of 'modest precision' in description, 'but much better than questionnaire research,' and that these strategies facilitate 'simple and moderately general' theorizing (1999, p. 696).

Having explained the research methods and analytical strategies, the chapter now explores the case boards' experiences. Contrary to normative assumptions that the BSC reports would be actively used, routines of reporting and monitoring proved to be formidable barriers.

THE EXPERIENCES OF THE CASE BOARDS AND DIRECTORS

In the case boards, various levels of routines could be observed. There were routines of CEO reporting (e.g., providing activity reports in writing to each meeting) and routines of board monitoring (e.g., the CEO reports being received and discussed). The potential routines of reporting and monitoring using the performance reports need to be appreciated as part of the CEOs and boards' broader routines; in particular, the performance reports need to be considered in the context of the broader system of artefacts used for performance reporting.

The Performance Reports and the Routines of CEO Reporting

We begin by considering the general CEO reporting routines, before moving on to consider the use of the performance reports where provided. On enrolment of the case organisations, it was explicitly affirmed that the CEO would be presenting the performance reports to their boards; by virtue of the research's timing and of the six-monthly reporting cycle, each board would receive the report on three occasions (at, or around, months 1, 7 and 12 or 13 of the period of observation). Table 15.1 reports on each board and its experiences. While there were board-monitoring routines, none of the case organisations had regularly occurring, formally structured opportunities for reviewing non-financial performance on a whole-of-organisation basis. Hence, reviewing the performance reports could have created such opportunities. However, the intended reporting did not occur in all organisations. In Alpha, Bravo and Delta, the performance reports were not provided by the CEOs to their board at any time (with the exception of asking the president to sign off the reports before submission to Queensland Health). In Charlie, the performance report was provided to all board members by email on the second occasion of reporting to QH, but not on the other occasions. In Echo, the reports were presented to the board on the second and third occasions of reporting only.

At interview, CEOs were asked about why they did not present, or did not always present, the reports to their boards as a whole. In Alpha, the CEO noted that the performance reports constituted a new process: 'we have to remember that it's been a new process and a lot of it has been learning the process.' It was obvious from what the CEO said and, in particular, the tone in which she spoke, that the interview was the first time she had realised the potential value of the performance reports to her board:

> The [board] would get a better understanding of what it is that staff and [consumers] do and [the] operational side of [Alpha]. And they also, when decisions are made [at the board], they're actually reminded of what the background of [Alpha] is, what it is we're trying to achieve, what we need to be achieving.
>
> (Alpha's CEO, second interview)

Bravo's CEO believed the reports had been circulated and it was only when asked to check did she discover that her belief was mistaken. The CEO believed that the reports would 'definitely' be useful for 'monitoring the overall work of the organisation and ensuring that it's meeting its commitment to funders,' while noting that 'some of the information is actually more relevant to the funder rather than to the organisation.'

In Charlie, the CEO realised during the second interview that the third report had not been circulated to the full board, and said that it should have been circulated as a formality. Charlie's CEO went on to explain that,

Table 15.1 Data sources and monitoring by the case boards

Org.	Board composition and service	Existing reporting artefacts to the board	Evidence of monitoring routines	Provision of performance reports	Evidence of monitoring with performance reports
Alpha	60% professionals or managers; 40% consumers Mean period of director service: 1.63 completed years	Financial: No written reports presented to board meetings at any time. (Written reports provided to the president and treasurer outside of the board meeting) Non-financial: Eight sources of performance data identified	Financial: Generalised oral reporting by treasurer or CEO with budget comparison. On occasions, some general questions or comments from directors Occasional favourable judgments expressed about financial performance by other directors Non-financial: Discussion of reports mainly about relevant action items identified by the CEO Six occasions on which judgments of performance expressed: all concerned particular aspects of performance rather than being holistic or integrated assessment	Not provided to board	Not used

Bravo	60% professionals or managers; 40% had administrative backgrounds Mean period of director service: 2.55 completed years	Financial: Written reports: Profit and Loss Statement (P&L), initially with previous year comparison, but moving to budget comparison at the board's request. P&L by funder. Balance Sheet. Cash disbursement journal Non-financial: Seven sources of performance data identified	Financial: Treasurer or financial officer would speak to the written reports, providing a very brief summary comment. Detailed discussion of proposed budget at one meeting Non-financial: Typically, directors would demonstrate their interest in the reports by asking detailed questions and/or sharing relevant information (e.g., related information from the external environment) 13 occasions when judgments of performance expressed, which were about aspects of organisational performance	Not provided to board	Not used

(Continued)

Table 15.1 (Continued)

Org.	Board composition and service	Existing reporting artefacts to the board	Evidence of monitoring routines	Provision of performance reports	Evidence of monitoring with performance reports
Charlie	70% professionals or managers; 30% from the target group served. Mean period of director service: 1.8 completed years	Financial: Written reports: P&L with budget comparison. Balance Sheet. Bank reconciliation report. Explanatory notes. Non-financial: Seven sources of performance data identified	Financial: CEO would speak to the reports. Non-financial: Before the reports were expanded, directors would typically ask few questions or make few comments in response to the reports. When the expanded reports were provided, directors spent more time discussing the reports 25 occasions when judgments of performance expressed, all but two about particular aspects of performance	Provided to board on second occasion of reporting to QH only. Provided by email as a draft, inviting comment on the draft	Some directors made suggestions by email on how the report might be strengthened. Report not discussed at a board meeting. Not a 'routine,' as behaviour was not repeated

Delta	90% professionals or managers	Financial: Written reports:	Financial: Treasurer would speak	Not provided to the board	Not used
		P&L with budget comparison.	to the written reports, usually with a reference to whether she was 'happy' (because a surplus existed that month) or 'grumpy' (because of a deficit). Routine of mid-year and end-of-year budget review also existed, which received considerable board attention		
	Mean period of director service: 4.7 completed years	Balance Sheet			
		Non-financial: 10 sources of performance data identified	Non-financial: Delta's board spent more time discussing CEO and staff reports than did other boards. Three directors had the habit of 'thinking out loud,' asking questions in response to reports and making comments to contextualise the information received		
			45 occasions when judgments of performance expressed, all but three about particular aspects of performance		

(Continued)

Table 15.1 (Continued)

Org.	Board composition and service	Existing reporting artefacts to the board	Evidence of monitoring routines	Provision of performance reports	Evidence of monitoring with performance reports
Echo	50% professionals or managers. Many directors represented different stakeholder groups Mean period of director service: 1.45 completed years	Financial: Written reports, customised to reflect the organisation's income and expenditure patterns, and including some Balance Sheet items Non-financial: Six sources of performance data identified, with detailed discussion of operations in these documents	Financial: Treasurer would speak to the written reports. There were rarely questions Non-financial: Typically, only a few questions or comments in response, often by a particular director 19 occasions when judgments of performance expressed, all but one about particular aspects of performance	Provided to the board on the second and third occasions of reporting to QH	On the second occasion of reporting to QH, the report was listed under the 'For noting' section of the agenda. No comments by directors On the third occasion of reporting, the report was again listed under the 'For noting' section of the agenda. The treasurer nonetheless briefly commented on the report, commending it to the board. No other director commented There were some comments regarding the performance reports made to the CEO outside of board meetings

although it was preferable the board had been provided with the report, 'it wouldn't be any different from what's been compiled separately over time, monthly for example, and provided to the board anyway.'

Delta's CEO did not provide the reports to the board as a whole and was equivocal about the reports' potential value to directors, stating they would be of value to some but not others. This perception was probably accurate: when interviewed, some of Delta's directors said they were not particularly interested in the more health-related information.

In Echo, the CEO provided the reports to her board on two occasions, and said this had been prompted by the research study, as she was aware it concerned boards and organisational performance. The reports were listed on the meetings' agendas as being 'For noting.'

To summarise, adding the performance reports to the existing sources of monitoring data going to the boards required a departure from the CEOs' routines of information gathering and presentation, and not all CEOs remembered to make that departure. Given the semi-regular nature of the reporting cycle, it required a conscious decision by a CEO to include the reports in the agenda papers.

It might be normatively assumed that even if CEOs forgot to provide the reports that directors—for example, chairs—would request the reports be presented as they were contractually required and would be submitted to the principal funder. At interview, four directors who said in retrospect that they would have preferred to see the reports offered reasons as to why they did not request them:

- They had not realised that the reports existed, at least in the case of one new director: 'being new . . . I probably don't have an expectation that we are even completing those formal reports' (Alpha director, interview).
- They expected the CEO to provide the reports: 'I would have thought that if those formal reports are taking place, why is the board not automatically getting them' (Alpha director, interview).
- They assumed that if QH continued to fund the organisation, the organisation must be meeting its performance criteria: 'it's almost like a naïve assumption on my part that they give us the funding, we've met the performance criteria' (Alpha director, interview).
- They had not been fully vigilant: 'I guess it's partly that I've been slack and partly that I've trusted the CEO and staff' (Charlie director, interview).

The existence of the opportunity to review the performance report was dependent on the agency of the actors in providing or requesting the foundational artefact. This simply did not occur in three of the five case organisations. Our case studies demonstrate that agency should not be assumed: clearly, the cybernetic view is under-socialised.

The Performance Reports and the Routines of Board Monitoring

In the two organisations where the boards were supplied the performance reports, there was no discernible impact other than that recorded in Table 15.1, and further discussed here. In Charlie organisation, on the second occasion of reporting to QH, the CEO said that three directors commented by email, suggesting additional information to include that would reflect favourably on the organisation. The report was not subsequently discussed at a board meeting.

In Echo, the second report to QH was presented to the next board meeting, under the 'For noting' section of the agenda, rather than the 'For discussion' section. Although the board's procedures allowed directors to move agenda items to ensure discussion, no director made this request. On the third occasion of reporting, there was a brief response from Echo's treasurer commending the report as 'well put together' and 'informative,' but there were no additional comments from other directors. At interview, Echo's directors were asked why they thought there was so little reaction to the performance reports at the board meetings. There was speculation that some colleagues had not read the reports. Other explanations included that the reports were presented for noting, some directors found the reports lengthy and difficult to absorb and on the third occasion of reporting, the report was part of 120 pages of agenda papers. One director said she had read the reports as she is 'obsessive' by nature, observing that she did not offer any comments because 'all the information is there that I needed, or that I felt that I needed to see.' Another director commented she had read the reports because of her 'analytical' focus, stating that she 'gets some satisfaction' when reading the reports 'that we've probably succeeded' in meeting QH's expectations.

In Echo, it was identified that 30% of directors had conversations with the CEO about the performance reports outside of meetings. For example, when interviewed, the president recalled discussing her perception that one report was 'patchy,' perceiving that the depth of content varied and the report needed to have more focus on health outcomes. Her concern was to promote the organisation to QH more effectively.

To summarise, what occurred fell far short of the creation of a routine in the cybernetic model. The reports were either not discussed at a meeting, or were only minimally discussed. While some directors had read the reports and evaluated (at some level) the information they contained, resulting suggestions were made for public relations reasons, rather than to improve organisational performance.

Directors' Perceptions of the Performance Reports

The themes among respondents who believed the performance reports were or would be useful are captured in Table 15.2.

These were clearly the dominant themes, with other points being mentioned by no more than three directors. An example of the positive regard for

Table 15.2 Example comments affirming the value of the performance reports

Summary	Examples
Reports informed the boards about compliance with the QH funding agreement (mentioned by 15 interviewees)	'that's the most critical report . . . to the major funder' (Bravo director, interview) 'It lets me see what the organisation is being judged against [by QH]' (Charlie director, interview)
Reports helped assess and demonstrate progress (nine interviewees)	'It's helpful in seeing where we're at in terms of making progress, what we need to achieve' (Alpha director, interview) 'I think it's good to quantify where our efforts are going' (Bravo director, interview)
Reports were formal or reliable (five interviewees)	'. . . it's a reliable indication of what's happening in the organisation, how it's working, because you got the hard evidence if you like, I guess, to back up what's happening (Charlie director, interview) 'They'll tell you very quickly if something is wrong' (Delta director, interview) 'And its honest as well. I've never doubted it' (Echo director, interview)

the performance reports comes from one of Echo's directors who strongly believed the reports were useful and said, 'they gave us a really good idea about what is happening with the organisation, where it is going, and what are the expectations about the [programmes] that we are undertaking . . . [The Report was] so informative, and really . . . you could read it and understand exactly what it was about.'

While there were positive remarks about the performance reports, there were also negative comments. The major themes of these comments are captured in Table 15.3.

To give an example of scepticism about the reports, one of Echo's directors, who was well qualified academically and who generally demonstrated diligence in her role, gave the performance reports a neutral rating and said, 'I personally rely on [the CEO's] ability to understand what the Health Department want and . . . how to collect that data . . . [The report is] big, it's sloppy, it's stuff we can't really change, staff seems very competent to do it.'

One notable phenomenon was the number of sceptical comments by directors who were current or former employees of QH; i.e., directors who had experience in both 'camps.' Some—but by no means all—of these

Table 15.3 Example comments critical of the performance reports

Summary	Examples
Reports were too detailed (mentioned by 12 interviewees)	'Quite tedious because there is so much of it' (Charlie director, interview)
	'I was bedazzled by the information they [QH] were seeking . . . Because it was so detailed and so many pages of it . . . I think they should have managed with less' (Delta director, interview—who had attended a QH training workshop on the *Performance Framework*)
Reports were bureaucratic in purpose or tone (11 interviews)	'. . . you're talking to bureaucrats, so you gotta do it in language of bureaucrats. I know this because I'm a bureaucrat' (Bravo Director, interview with the Director speaking in a derisive tone)
	'I work better informally than I do formally' (Charlie director, interview)
Reports merely provided information already available in other forms (six interviewees)	'. . . most of the information in the Report is likely to be in the CEO's monthly report (Alpha director, interview)
	Echo's CEO to the board: 'I will get sent to you the Performance Reports sent to Queensland Health. However, they are a bit dry and statistical. You will get a better sense of what is going on from the [staff reports]' (Observation notes, Echo board meeting, March 2005)
Reports were not required because directors trusted the CEO (five interviewees)	'It's partly that I've been slack and partly that I've trusted the CEO and staff' (Charlie director, interview)
	'think there's a proportion of board members who may not fully engage with those reports because they have trust and confidence in the staff team and from their informal observations' (Echo CEO, interview)
Reports were exercises in public relations with the funder (four interviewees)	'. . . there's more about what you don't write than what you write that's important . . .' (Bravo director, interview)
	'I tend to think [the performance reports] don't really give you a picture of what's really happening . . . I'm cynical enough to say it's good paperwork' (Delta director, interview)

Summary	Examples
Reports were more relevant to the funder than the organisation (including because the funder only provided part of the organisation's funding) (four interviewees)	'Some of the information is actually more relevant to the funder rather than to the organisation' (Bravo CEO, interview) The performance reports would be somewhat useful 'primarily because QH only part funds [the organisation. It] wouldn't give a full picture of how the organisation is going' (Bravo director, interview)
Reports were likely to have an overly technical health focus (four interviewees)	'Only the financial information would be of value to me because . . . I wouldn't have . . . a depth of understanding to appreciate the other information' (Alpha director, interview) 'I would attempt to read it, but I would walk away from it . . . I would let the professionals take what they want out of it' (Delta director, interview—who did not have a background in the technical aspects of the organisation's work)

interviewees were not convinced about the quality and appropriateness of the department's performance measurement practices. One director (deliberately not identified) commented that she reviewed the reports provided to QH Central Office in her employed role, commenting on 'how useless they can be sometimes . . . Why waste your life reading them if you don't have to?'

To sum up, boards did not use the performance reports in the cybernetic manner. The ostensive aspect of the proposed routine was not well developed, and the performative aspect—if it existed at all—was not enacted in a way consistent with cybernetic assumptions. The case studies demonstrate that reports based on the balanced scorecard—despite being promoted as superior sources of performance data—will not necessarily be so regarded by directors. In the next section, we extend the analysis to consider the challenges of modifying reporting and monitoring routines by using BSC-type reports.

DISCUSSION: THE CHALLENGES OF MODIFYING REPORTING AND MONITORING ROUTINES

We offer six plausible explanations for our findings. For some explanations, the links to the data presented so far will be readily apparent. For other explanations, it is necessary to reflect on the overall context. The first explanation is in this category.

First, we note the contextual challenges. Monitoring is not always motivating: as Chait, Holland, and Taylor note of the work of nonprofit boards, 'routine oversight is hardly engaging' (2005, p. 19). Further, there is limited oversight of boards: they are usually subject only to the indirect scrutiny, except when rare events such as court cases occur (Chait et al., 2005). Thus, boards do not usually have the benefit of feedback on a routine's enactment (Greve, 1998). A further contextual issue is the arguably symbolic nature of much board work—the meetings being 'a "sacred" territory within which ritual observance, not critical reflection, is required' (Hendry & Seidl, 2003, pp. 191–192). Consequently, information can be dealt with superficially; e.g., a report can be formally received without having been read. In this context, it is not surprising that the limited existing research on boards and monitoring demonstrates that directors of nonprofits tend to be 'reactive reviewers' rather than 'active users' of the information received (Harrow, Palmer, & Vincent, 1999; Hough, McGregor-Lowndes, & Ryan, 2014), and base their judgments of performance on professional background or personal circumstance (Miller, 2002).[1]

Second, the performance reports were an additional source of monitoring data competing with a preexisting system of artefacts (Cacciatori, 2012; Kocakülâh & Austill, 2007). As noted earlier, even the CEO of one organisation felt that the reports added nothing to already available information sources. Moreover, it is possible directors had already 'made sense' of organisational performance based on the existing information sources: 'People in organizations are talented at . . . making do with scraps of information, at translating equivocality into feasible alternatives, and at treating as sufficient whatever information is at hand' (Daft & Weick, 1984, p. 294). Formal occasions of judgment are not necessarily required as sense-making is ongoing; however, unless 'jarring' information is received, the existing understandings remain unchallenged (Hough et al., 2014; Weick, 1995). Hence, if the sense-making view is accurate, receiving the performance reports was likely to have little impact, unless the information they contained jarred with prior understandings.

Third, the semi-regular nature of the performance reports posed challenges. It required a conscious decision by the CEO each six months to provide the reports. This is a simple but important point, for without the reports being provided the cybernetic chain cannot commence. The semi-regular cycle of reporting also meant that, even if the performance reports were provided, the routine of using the reports would not be practiced frequently. Repeating the relevant pattern of behaviour is important to a routine's establishment and maintenance (and, indeed, repetition is required to be a routine). Meekings argues that, in his experience as a practitioner-academic, 'it typically takes around six periods of review to reach what might be termed the 'ah ha' point—the point at which people can connect the information they receive with the decisions they take, the actions they implement and the resulting outcomes' (2005, p. 217). If it is necessary to practice the new routine six times, this would require directors to receive and attend to the performance reports for up to three years before they properly appreciate and utilise them. As shown in Table 15.1, this is well beyond the average period of service of directors in four of the five case organisations.

Fourth, there is the challenge of modifying directors' monitoring routines in the face of significant inertial forces discussed earlier in the chapter. It *might* be that these forces could have been overcome through more extensive training and the provision of additional artefacts such as a script for discussing the performance reports. While the *Performance Framework* was supported by an extensive manual and some QH-provided training for directors, these did not extend to considering reporting and monitoring routines. Further, informal support was limited: QH, unlike other Queensland government departments funding nonprofits, did not have a system of field officers with the role of coaching and supporting the funded organisations. Nor were there learning opportunities of the type identified by Edmondson et al. (2001) or by Pentland and Feldman (2008) providing a chance to learn about the ostensive routine and to practice the performative. Especially in nonprofit boards, where board members are sometimes inexperienced in managerial discussions (as disclosed in Table 15.1), how to discuss a BSC-type report is not trivial. How might the performance reports be included in the agenda in a way to promote interactive use (compared to Echo, where the CEO listed the reports as 'For noting')? How might the discussion be commenced? What exactly does a board chair say and do to promote the interactive discussion of performance data (Simons, 1995; Tessier & Otley, 2012)? How is an appropriate tone of discussion promoted (deHaven-Smith & Jenne, 2006; Meyer, 2002; Moynihan, 2008)?

Fifth, we raise the possibility that QH imposition of the *Performance Framework* and reporting requirements might have adversely impacted on the use of the performance reports, at least for some directors. The *Performance Framework* project was initially focused on external accountability, and it might be that the later extension to internal purposes was perceived (possibly correctly) as an afterthought. It was also noteworthy that several directors were sceptical about QH Central Office initiatives, including directors who were current or former QH employees. This scepticism is understandable in the light of subsequent findings about the Minister and about the top level of the department (Lill, 2007; Queensland Public Hospitals Commission of Inquiry, 2005). The study of Moynihan and Lavertu (2012) of U.S. government agencies counterintuitively demonstrated that the involvement of the White House's Office of Management and Budget was a negative (although not statistically significant) predictor of information use. Similarly, Northcott and France (2005) identified that a barrier to the success of a BSC tool in New Zealand public hospitals was its imposition.

Perhaps a similar phenomenon was at work with QH's involvement in the *Performance Framework*?

The final explanation relates to the BSC's conceptual foundations. Kaplan (2009, 2012) has repeatedly stated that an organisation's BSC should be based on its unique circumstances, including its strategy. In his opinion, strategy must come first, measures second and generic measures should be avoided. The *Performance Framework*'s use of generic objectives and indicators arguably violates the BSC's conceptual underpinnings, which also might have limited the usefulness of the performance reports to the boards. Despite relatively extensive attempts to use BSC-type regimes for external accountability in different settings (for example, Griffiths, 2003; Northcott & France, 2005), it is arguable such regimes are a misapplication of the BSC concept. Given this context, it is perhaps predictable that some directors were concerned that the performance reports would be used to build organisational reputation with the external funder rather than be used for internal monitoring and control. Relatedly, the department's modification to the standard balanced scorecard structure might have reduced the utility of the performance reports by interfering with the line of sight between an organisation's strategy, objectives and financial and statistical performance measures.

However, three points should be made in relation to this last explanation. First, there is a degree of ambiguity in Kaplan's writing about whether the BSC can be used for external reporting, with acknowledgment that it might be used in this way in a public sector context at least (for example, Kaplan, 2012). Second, although the *Performance Framework* was imposed, the objectives and indicators were broad and based in the commonly expressed values of the case organisations and sector, with each organisation having discretion over the evidence it presented in the performance reports. Third, two CEOs explicitly stated that the reports could have assisted their boards in understanding their organisations and their work, despite the CEOs not providing them. This reinforces the importance of considering routines of reporting. We now turn to the chapter's contributions, limitations and implications.

CONTRIBUTIONS, LIMITATIONS, AND IMPLICATIONS

Given that the empirical research on the BSC and nonprofits is limited, and that the issue of boards and monitoring is scant, the chapter contributes to existing knowledge by providing empirical evidence on these topics. It is the first dedicated publication on the topic of board use of the BSC as a monitoring tool. While Kaplan and Norton suggest that BSC-type tools should result in improved understanding of organisational performance by boards, the evidence from this research is that they are no panacea. This research demonstrates there is a range of challenges in fostering the use of the BSC as a board-monitoring tool. Pentland and Feldman's insight that artefacts are not patterns of action is basic, but challenges many performance management programmes which assume that if artefacts are changed, behaviour will follow (Moynihan, 2008; Pentland & Feldman, 2008). Moynihan describes this as the 'if you build it, they will come' assumption: 'It assumes that the availability and quality of performance data are not just a necessary condition for use but also a sufficient one' (2008, p. 5). However, the enactment of most routines involves a level of human agency, and hence this assumption can be inaccurate. As a given artefact for performance monitoring is often just one component in an overall system of artefacts, actors have a choice as to which artefacts they use and to what extent. The artefact and the routine must be considered.

For practice, the data and analysis challenge assertions of the BSC's superiority as a monitoring tool. Funders, board members and CEOs might exercise caution about following heavily promoted, 'best-practice' models. However, the research should not be read as concluding that the BSC did not make a contribution to board monitoring (in some organisations and on the part of some directors) or that external reporting regimes cannot also benefit internal monitoring (Saj, 2012). More attention to implementation and routines might address some of these challenges, although perhaps not all.

The research is limited by the fact that the evidence is drawn from five organisations. Further, three occasions of potential experience might be insufficient to acquire competence in using the BSC as a monitoring tool (Meekings, 2005). The research is nonetheless useful because it points to the diverse challenges in modifying existing routines of reporting and monitoring.

The area is ripe with opportunities for further research. The chapter demonstrates the importance of extending our knowledge of boards and routines, an area in which research appears significantly underdeveloped given that board work involves numerous routines and given the recent 'practice' and 'process' turn in governance research (Huse, 2007). Despite the excellent foundations provided by Ocasio's work in the 1990s (Ocasio, 1994, 1997, 1999), there has been only limited governance research adopting a routine frame since. For example, there is limited research on varying routines to promote board effectiveness (although one notable exception is Chait et al., 1996).

Action research might explore whether there are ways to meet the challenges identified and to establish mindful routines using the BSC, particularly by building learning routines and a learning culture. Research might explore further whether the experiences of organisations which voluntarily adopt the BSC might be different to those on which it is imposed. Additionally, experimental designs might consider whether individual directors, and groups such as boards, are better able to monitor performance with the assistance of a tool like the BSC compared to other possible approaches, such as monitoring against a strategic plan.

Moynihan argues that '*the key challenge* for performance management is fostering performance information use' (2008, p. 190, emphasis added). He further argues that 'designers of performance management systems need to take routines to consider and discuss data as seriously as they do the routines to collect and disseminate data' (p. 178). While we recognise that Kaplan and Norton (1996, 2006) have made some contributions in this regard, we agree with Moynihan that there is much more to be done. The creation of routines and their mindful enactment is critical for successful use of the BSC by boards. We believe that this is an issue to which attention might increasingly be given, to the benefit of both theorizing and practice

NOTE

1   However, in more elaborate reporting regimes, directors report on portfolio areas and CEOs report against business plans and/or financial and non-financial key result areas and indicators (Parker, 2007, 2008).

REFERENCES

Ashford, B. E., & Fried, Y. (1988). The mindlessness of organizational behaviours. *Human Relations, 41*(4), 305–329.

Becker, M. C. (2008). *Handbook of organizational routines*. Cheltenham, UK: Edward Elgar.

Boardsource. (2010). *The handbook of nonprofit governance*. San Francisco: Jossey-Bass.

Brody, E. (2010). The board of nonprofit organizations: Puzzling through the gaps between law and practice—a view from the United States. In K. J. Hopt & T. Von Hippel (Ed.), *Comparative corporate governance of non-profit organizations* (pp. 481–530). Leiden, NL: Cambridge University Press.

Burns, J., & Scapens, R. W. (2008). Organizational routines in accounting. In M. C. Becker (Ed.), *Handbook of organizational routines* (pp. 87–106). Cheltenham, UK: Edward Elgar.

Cacciatori, E. (2012). Resolving conflict in problem-solving: Systems of artefacts in the development of new routines. *Journal of Management Studies, 49*(8), 1559–1585.

Chait, R. P., Holland, T. P., & Taylor, B. E. (1996). *Improving the performance of governing boards*. Phoenix, AR: Oryx Press.

Chait, R. P., Holland, T. P., & Taylor, B. E. (2005). *Governance as leadership: Reframing the work of nonprofit boards*. Hoboken, NJ: John Wiley & Sons.

Chalmers, D. M., & Balan-Vnuk, E. (2013). Innovating not-for-profit social ventures: Exploring the microfoundations of internal and external absorptive capacity routines. *International Small Business Journal, 31*(7), 785–810.

Chang, W. C., Tung, Y. C., Huang, C. H., & Yang, M. C. (2008). Performance improvement after implementing the balanced scorecard: A large hospital's experience in Taiwan. *Total Quality Management & Business Excellence, 19*(11), 1143–1154.

Craig, J., & Moores, K. (2010). Strategically aligning family and business systems using the balanced scorecard. *Journal of Family Business Strategy, 1*(2), 78–87.

Daft, R. L., & Weick, K. (1984). Toward a model of organizations as interpretation systems. *Academy of Management Review, 9*(2), 284–295.

deHaven-Smith, L., & Jenne, K. C. (2006). Management by inquiry: A discursive accountability system for large organizations. *Public Administration Review, 66*(1), 64–76.

Edmondson, A. C., Bohmer, R. M., & Pisano, G. P. (2001). Disrupted routines: Team learning and new technology implementation in hospitals. *Administrative Science Quarterly, 46*(4), 685–716.

Emirbayer, M., & Mische, A. (1998). What is agency? *American Journal of Sociology, 103*(4), 962–1023.

Feldman, M. S., & Pentland, B. S. (2003). Reconceptualizing organizational routines as a source of flexibility and change. *Administrative Science Quarterly, 48*(1), 94–118.

Felin, T., Foss, N. J., Heimeriks, K. H., & Madsen, T. L. (2012). Microfoundations of routines and capabilities: Individuals, processes, and structure. *Journal of Management Studies, 49*(8), 1351–1374.

Gersick, C. J., & Hackman, J. R. (1990). Habitual routines in task-performing groups. *Organizational Behavior and Human Decision Processes, 47*(1), 65–97.

Gioia, D. A. (1986). Symbols, scripts and sensemaking: Creating meaning in the organizational experience. In H. P. Sims, D. A. Gioia, & Associates (Eds.), *The thinking organization* (pp. 49–74). San Francisco: Jossey-Bass.

Greiling, D. (2010). Balanced scorecard implementation in German non-profit organisations. *International Journal of Productivity and Performance Management, 59*(6), 534–554.

Greve, H. R. (1998). Performance, aspirations and risky organizational change. *Administrative Science Quarterly, 43*(1), 58–86.

Griffiths, J. (2003). Balanced scorecard use is New Zealand government departments and Crown entities. *Australian Journal of Public Administration, 62*(4), 70–79.

Grønbjerg, K. A. (1993). *Understanding nonprofit funding: Managing revenues in social services and community development organizations.* San Francisco: Jossey-Bass.

Gurd, B., & Gao, T. (2008). Lives in the balance: An analysis of the balanced scorecard (BSC) in healthcare organisations. *International Journal of Productivity and Performance Management, 57*(1), 6–21.

Harrow, J., Palmer, P., & Vincent, J. (1999). Management information needs and perceptions in smaller charities: An exploratory study. *Financial Accountability & Management, 15*(2), 155–172.

Hendry, J., & Seidl, D. (2003). The structure and significance of strategic episodes: Social systems theory and the routine practice of strategic change. *Journal of Management Studies, 40*(1), 175–196.

Heracleous, L. (2001). What is the impact of corporate governance on organisational performance? *Corporate Governance: An International Review, 9*(3), 165–173.

Hofstede, G. (1978). The poverty of management control philosophy. *Academy of Management Review, 3*(3), 450–461.

Hoque, Z. (2014). 20 years of studies on the balanced scorecard: Trends, accomplishments, gaps and opportunities for future research. *British Accounting Review, 46*(1), 33–59.

Hough, A. D., McGregor-Lowndes, M., & Ryan, C. M. (2014). Board monitoring and judgement as processes of sensemaking. In C. Cornforth & W. A. Brown (Eds.), *Nonprofit governance: Innovative perspectives and approaches* (pp. 142–159). Abingdon, UK: Routledge.

Houle, C. O. (1997). *Governing boards: Their nature and nurture.* San Francisco: Jossey-Bass.

Howard-Grenville, J. A. (2005). The persistence of flexible organizational routines: The role of agency and organizational context. *Organization Science, 16*(6), 618–636.

Huse, M. (2007). *Boards, governance and value creation.* Cambridge, UK: Cambridge University Press.

Inamdar, N., & Kaplan, R. S. (2002). Applying the balanced scorecard in healthcare provider organizations. *Journal of Healthcare Management, 47*(3), 179–195.

Jorgensen, D. L. (1989). *Participant observation: A methodology for human studies.* Newbury Park, CA: Sage Publications.

Kaplan, R. S. (2001). Strategic performance measurement and management in nonprofit organizations. *Nonprofit Management and Leadership, 11*(3), 353–370.

Kaplan, R. S. (2009). Conceptual foundations of the balanced scorecard. In C. S. Chapman, A. G. Hopwood, & M. D. Shields (Eds.), *Handbook of management accounting research* (pp. 1253–1269). Amsterdam: Elsevier Science.

Kaplan, R. S. (2012). The balanced scorecard: Comments on balanced scorecard commentaries. *Journal of Accounting & Organizational Change, 8*(4), 539–545.

Kaplan, R. S., & Norton, D. P. (1996). *The balanced scorecard: Translating strategy into action.* Boston, MA: Harvard Business School Press.

Kaplan, R. S., & Norton, D. P. (2001). *The strategy-focused organization: How balanced scorecard companies thrive in the new business environment.* Boston, MA: Harvard Business School Press.

Kaplan, R. S., & Norton, D. P. (2004). *Strategy maps: Converting intangible assets into tangible outcomes.* Boston, MA: Harvard Business School Publishing.

Kaplan, R. S., & Norton, D. P. (2006). *Alignment: Using the balanced scorecard to create corporate synergies.* Boston, MA: Harvard Business School Press.

Khurana, R., & Pick, K. (2005). The social nature of boards. *Brooklyn Law Review, 70*(4), 1259–1285.

Kocakülâh, M. C., & Austill, A. D. (2007). Balanced scorecard application in the health care industry: A case study. *Journal of Health Care Finance, 34*(1), 72–99.

Langley, A. (1999). Strategies for theorizing from process data. *Academy of Management Review, 24*(4), 691–710.

Lazaric, N., & Denis, B. (2005). Routinization and memorization of tasks in a workshop: The case of the introduction of ISO norms. *Industrial and Corporate Change, 14*(5), 873–896.

Lill, J. *The Courier-Mail.* (2007, December 6). Nuttall hits fresh corruption charge. *The Courier-Mail,* 7.

Lorsch, J. W. (2002). Smelling smoke: Why boards of directors need the balanced scorecard. *Balanced Scorecard Report,* September–October, 9–11.

Manville, G. (2007). Implementing a balanced scorecard framework in a not for profit SME. *International Journal of Productivity and Performance Management, 56*(2), 162–169.

Meekings, A. (2005). Effective review meetings: The counter-intuitive key to successful performance measurement. *International Journal of Productivity and Performance Management, 54*(3), 212–220.

Meyer, M. W. (2002). Finding performance: The new discipline in management. In A. Neely (Ed.), *Business performance measurement: Theory and practice* (pp. 51–62). Cambridge, UK: Cambridge University Press.

Miller, J. L. (2002). The board as a monitor of organizational activity: The applicability of agency theory to nonprofit boards. *Nonprofit Management and Leadership, 12*(4), 429-450.

Miller, K. D., Pentland, B. T., & Choi, S. (2012). Dynamics of performing and remembering organizational routines. *Journal of Management Studies, 49*(8), 1536–1558.

Miner, A. S., Ciuchta, M. P., & Gong, Y. (2008). Organizational routines and organizational learning. In M. C. Becker (Ed.), *Handbook of organizational routines* (pp. 152–186). Cheltenham, UK: Edward Elgar.

Moxham, C., & Boaden, R. (2007). The impact of performance measurement in the voluntary sector: Identification of contextual and processual factors. *International Journal of Operations & Production Management, 27*(8), 826–845.

Moynihan, D. P. (2008). *The dynamics of performance management: Constructing information and reform*. Washington, DC: Georgetown University Press.

Moynihan, D. P., & Lavertu, S. (2012). Does involvement in performance management routines encourage performance information use? Evaluating GPRA and PART. *Public Administration Review, 72*(4), 592–602.

Northcott, D., & France, N. (2005). The balanced scorecard in New Zealand health sector performance management: Dissemination to diffusion. *Australian Accounting Review, 15*(3), 34–46.

Ocasio, W. (1994). *Boards as normative arenas: Corporate governance and the routines of CEO selection*. Working Paper. Cambridge: Massachusetts Institute of Technology Sloan School of Management.

Ocasio, W. (1997). Towards an attention-based view of the firm. *Strategic Management Journal, 18*(Summer special issue), 187–206.

Ocasio, W. (1999). Institutionalized action and corporate governance: The reliance on rules of CEO succession. *Administrative Science Quarterly, 44*(2), 384–416.

Parker, L. D. (2007). Board strategizing in professional associations: Processual and institutional perspectives. *Journal of Management Studies, 44*(8), 1454–1480.

Parker, L. D. (2008). Boardroom operational and financial control: An insider view. *British Journal of Management, 19*(1), 65–88.

Parmigiani, A., & Howard-Grenville, J. A. (2011). Routines revisited: Exploring the capabilities and practice perspectives. *Academy of Management Annals, 5*(1), 413–453.

Pentland, B. T., & Feldman, M. S. (2005). Organizational routines as a unit of analysis. *Industrial and Corporate Change, 14*(5), 793–815.

Pentland, B. T., & Feldman, M. S. (2008). Designing routines: On the folly of designing artifacts, while hoping for patterns of action. *Information and Organization, 18*(4), 235–250.

Pettigrew, A. (1990). Longitudinal field research on change: Theory and practice. *Organization Science, 1*(3), 267–292.

Queensland Health. (2002). *Measuring quality in the non-government health sector: Interim evaluation report*. Brisbane, AU: Queensland Health.

Queensland Health. (2003). *Measuring quality in the non-government health sector: Baseline evaluation report*. Brisbane, AU: Queensland Health.

Queensland Health. (2004a). Non-government organisation management committee information session. Brisbane, AU: Queensland Health.

Queensland Health. (2004b). *Performance framework for the non-government sector: User manual*. Brisbane, AU: Queensland Health.

Queensland Public Hospitals Commission of Inquiry. (2005). *Report*. Brisbane, AU: Queensland Government.

Quinn, M. (2011). Routines in management accounting research: Further exploration. *Journal of Accounting & Organizational Change, 7*(4), 337–357.

Radin, B. A. (2006). *Challenging the performance movement: Accountability, complexity and democratic values*. Washington, DC: Georgetown University Press.

Saj, P. (2012). The influence of mandatory requirements on voluntary performance reporting by large multi-service community service organisations. *Third Sector Review, 18*(2), 139–169.

Salterio, S. (2012). Balancing the scorecard through academic accounting research: Opportunity lost? *Journal of Accounting & Organizational Change, 8*(4), 458–474.

Schulz, M. (2008). Staying on track: A voyage to the internal mechanisms of routine reproduction. In M. C. Becker (Ed.), *Handbook of organizational routines* (pp. 228–255). Cheltenham, UK: Edward Elgar.

Simons, R. (1995). *Levers of control: How managers use innovative control systems to drive strategic renewal.* Boston, MA: Harvard Business School Press.

Smith, P., Dufour, Y., & Erakovic, L. (2011). Strategising and the routines of governance: An empirical analysis of practices in an international engineering consultancy firm. *Asia-Pacific Journal of Business Administration, 3*(2), 149–164.

Stake, R. E. (2000). Case studies. In N. K. Denzin & Y. S. Lincoln (Eds.), *Handbook of qualitative research* (pp. 435–454). Thousand Oaks, CA: Sage.

Stewart, L. J., & Bestor, W. E. (2000). Applying a balanced scorecard to health care organizations. *Journal of Corporate Accounting & Finance, 11*(3), 75–82.

Swieringa, R. J., & Weick, K. E. (1981). Interfaces between management accounting and organizational behavior. *Exchange: The Organizational Behavior Teaching Journal, 6*(3), 25–33.

Tessier, S., & Otley, D. (2012). A conceptual development of Simons' levers of control framework. *Management Accounting Research, 23*(3), 171–185.

Weick, K. E. (1995). *Sensemaking in organizations.* Thousand Oaks, CA: Sage Publications.

Winkler, J. T. (1987). The fly on the wall of the inner sanctum: Observing company directors at work. In G. Moyser & M. Wagstaff (Eds.), *Research methods for elite studies* (pp. 129–146). London: Unwin Hyman.

Yin, R. K. (2003). *Case study research: Design and methods.* Thousand Oaks, CA: Sage.

Zald, M. N. (1969). The power and functions of boards of directors: A theoretical synthesis. *American Journal of Sociology, 75*(1), 97–111.

16 Government Grants—an Abrogation or Management of Risks?

Debra Morris, Myles McGregor-Lowndes and Julie-Anne Tarr

INTRODUCTION

New public management (NPM), with its hands-on, private sector-style performance measurement, output control, parsimonious use of resources, disaggregation of public sector units and greater competition in the public sector, has significantly affected charitable and nonprofit organisations delivering community services (Hood, 1991; Dunleavy, 1994; George & Wilding, 2002). The literature indicates that nonprofit organisations under NPM believe they are doing more for less: while administration is increasing, core costs are not being met; their dependence on government funding comes at the expense of other funding strategies; and there are concerns about proportionality and power asymmetries in the relationship (Kerr & Savelsberg, 2001; Powell & Dowling, 2006; Smith & Lipsky, 1993; McGregor-Lowndes & Turnour, 2003; Lyons & Dalton, 2011; Smith, 2002, p. 175; Morris, 1999, 2000a). Government agencies are under increased pressure to do more with less, demonstrate value for money, measure social outcomes, not merely outputs and minimise political risk (Grant, 2008; McGregor-Lowndes, 2008). Government-community service organisation relationships are often viewed as 'uneasy alliances' characterised by the pressures that come with the parties' differing roles and expectations, and the pressures of funding and security (Productivity Commission, 2010, p. 308; McGregor-Lowndes, 2008, p. 45; Morris, 2000a).

Significant community services are now delivered to citizens through such relationships, often to the most disadvantaged in the community, and it is important for this to be achieved with equity, efficiently and effectively. On one level, the welfare state was seen as a 'risk management system' for the poor, with the state mitigating the risks of sickness, job loss and old age (Giddens, 1999), with the subsequent neoliberalist outlook shifting this risk back to households (Hacker, 2006). At the core of this risk shift are written contracts. Vincent-Jones (1999, 2006) has mapped how NPM is characterised by the use of written contracts for all manner of relations; e.g., regulation of dealings between government agencies, between individual citizens and the state, and the creation of quasi-markets of service providers and infrastructure partners. We take this lens of contracts to examine where risk falls in relation to the outsourcing of community services.

First we examine the concept of risk. We consider how risk might be managed and apportioned between governments and community service organisations (CSOs) in grant agreements, which are quasi-market transactions at best. This is informed by insights from the law and economics literature. Then, standard grant agreements covering several years in two jurisdictions—Australia and the United Kingdom—are analysed, to establish the risk allocation between government and CSOs. This is placed in the context of the reform agenda in both jurisdictions. In Australia this context is the nonprofit reforms built around the creation of a national charities regulator and red tape reduction. In the United Kingdom, the backdrop is the Third Way agenda with its compacts, succeeded by Big Society in a climate of austerity. These 'case studies' inform a discussion about who is best placed to bear and manage the risks of community service provision on behalf of government. We conclude by identifying the lessons to be learned from our analysis and possible pathways for further scholarship.

RISK AND ITS APPORTIONMENT

Risk is one of the pivotal concepts of Western market economies and its mastery defines a watershed in human history (Bernstein, 1996). Risk management is based on the notion that the future is more than a whim of the gods and one need not passively accept the 'fortunes' of nature. While one cannot always predict the future, rational risk-taking assists us in making choices for the better, rather than passively accepting consequences as fate. To choose to spread your investments over a managed portfolio of stocks, to take out insurance or to implement proportionate safety and prevention measures rather than consult a spiritualist, toss a coin or do nothing, are examples of this pivotal concept in action. It has become an underlying framework for analysing and organising market transactions in both stock markets and flea markets.

At a macro-societal level, risk has also been utilised to explain the shifting relationship of the state to citizens and business (Giddens, 1999; Quiggin, 2007; Hacker, 2006). The welfare state collectively manages, shares and reduces the risks of individuals to a wide range of social and economic factors (e.g. employment, health, accident, disability). On the other hand, the neoliberal state encourages risk-taking ideas and management of risks through market mechanisms by having the state step back in some areas, and step up in others; e.g., to protect businesses and directors from some forms of liability which may stifle risk-taking.

At another level, governments have adopted the concept of risk and its management to inform their administration of public resources and policy-making. For example, in Australia, this has been championed by Commonwealth and state government treasuries, audit offices and public accounts committees with a plethora of risk management guidance notes, checklists, reports, frameworks and implementation notes (e.g., Queensland Treasury, 1994; Management Advisory Board, 1996). This has found expression in arrangements for outsourcing of government procurements of goods and services, taking the form of contractual agreements which allocate risks between the parties.

Classic contractual theory has the terms of any contract being determined by a competitive process involving market forces for not only the price, but also other terms such as warranties, conditions, pre-estimation of damages and other remedies, for a defective exchange. Even where there may be a limited market for large infrastructure projects achieved in partnership with government, financiers of the private partners will only fund if they believe the transaction is feasible (Institution of Engineers & Australian Chamber of Commerce and Industry of Western Australia, 2001). The risk of adverse consequences in relation to the contract is routinely measured, priced and allocated. For example, if a government contracts for a box of pencils, then it might insist that all risk of the pencils not being 100% fit for purpose be borne by the seller. Consequently, the seller will price that risk and build that price into the transaction. The government may be able to negotiate a lower price if it agrees to bear and/or manage some of that risk itself, particularly if it can bear the risk at a lower cost than any other seller can.

Allocation of legal risk is a contested field. Some argue that the party who attracts some kind of fault for the injury should bear the costs—the traditional basis of tort law (Atiyah, 1970, p. 33). The common law looks for a duty, and a breach of that duty which causes the injury; the person who owes the duty and committed the breach may be made liable to compensate the injured party (for example, motorists who cause harm to other road users by failing to keep a proper lookout). Others have proposed no-fault liability where the costs of adverse risk consequences are spread over certain parties who benefit from the activity (e.g., third party motor vehicle insurance spreading the cost of personal injuries across all registered drivers, but not pedestrians) (Atiyah, 1970, p. 323). On another level, the state may spread the cost over all of society through taxpayer assumption of liability in a nationalised scheme (Atiyah, 1970, p. 360).

Calabresi (1961, 1970) argued that the efficient/optimal allocation of risk should be the economic and social objective pursued by the courts and governments. Acknowledged as one of the founding fathers of the law and economics movement, Calabresi elaborated on Ronald Coase's ideas and integrated them into the general law, particularly the law of torts. He suggested that risks should be allocated to the party who is best positioned to know about them and take precautions designed to avoid the event/accident. This is a search for the 'cheapest cost avoider.' For example, a person attempting to use an ATM late at night in an unlit shopping centre car park is attacked by criminals and suffers personal injury. Pursuant to the common law, the victim could sue those who directly caused the injuries and were at 'fault'—the criminals. However, most criminals (even if identifiable) do not have the resources to compensate their victims, so the victim is left to bear the loss. Among the many alternative solutions is a taxpayer-funded criminal compensation scheme which assesses the loss and pays compensation; or the private insurance market which provides insurance for such events. However, a Calabresi approach would look not only to compensation after the event (such as insurance) but a cost-effective mechanism to prevent or mitigate the risk. Calabresi maintained that this theory 'is just as applicable to charitable institutions as to profit making ones' (1961, p. 548). Using his argument, the shopping centre owner might be the cheapest cost avoider and therefore liable to compensate the victim's injury. The owner operates the car park to attract business to the shops and could pass on the injury costs as part of this business, spreading the loss over many thousands of customers. The proprietor also is in the best position to avoid the risk by providing lighting and other security measures to protect customers, and to decide the level at which such risk management strategies need to be implemented. The owner is a much better loss preventer and loss distributor than the individual (Luntz, 2001).

Historically, governments and their agencies have elected in many instances not to insure their risks, as a matter of policy. The policy reflects a de facto self-insurance approach whereby governments, based on size and revenue-raising capacity, are able to meet losses as and when they arise. It is a significant cost saving. In relation to procurement, governments have the negotiation 'weight' that enables them to allocate indemnification of risk to their suppliers within the constraints of the operating market, particularly those imposed by suppliers' financiers.

In a contractual context, this risk allocation is not unreasonable where the relative capacities of the parties are aligned and may further be justified having regard to transaction cost savings. However, an unreasonable or unbalanced allocation of risks under a contract, arising out of one party's inexperience or subordination, or the other party's stronger bargaining position, can introduce new risks to transacting that might not have arisen if more informed comprehension and allocation of risk were involved. It is, after all, difficult to create an effective mitigation strategy in circumstances where one party lacks the necessary capabilities to appreciate, manage or control the variables.

Governments' contractual negotiations with CSOs differ from commercial procurement in a number of ways. First, governments can use their monopsony power to impose a risk allocation on the contracting organisations which attempts to shift all possible risk to those organisations. Monopsony is a state in which demand comes from one source. It is analogous to a monopoly, but on the demand side, not the supply side. Second, CSOs have certain characteristics which often do not exist in commercial procurement markets:

1. Nonprofit CSOs generally cannot pass risk costs on, through prices to clients or consumers, because the services provided by these organisations are, in an economic sense, public goods which have free rider issues (Anheier, 2005, p. 117).
2. Even if they could pass on the costs, from an equity perspective it is often (but not always) inappropriate to pass costs to the beneficiaries, who are poor or disadvantaged and the objects of government benevolence in the first place.
3. It is also inappropriate to pass the actual primary cost of defaults in service delivery to beneficiaries, both from an equity perspective and ability to bear the loss (Anheier, 2005, p. 118).
4. CSOs have difficulty generating resources from their discretionary revenue streams such as philanthropic grants or donations for indirect expenses such as risk management, because of donors' unwillingness to fund indirect costs.
5. Ultimately, governments will probably bear the financial consequences of service failure through further reliance by the beneficiary on government welfare, safety net and support services.
6. Debt financiers' requirements carry great weight in the normal market as they force contractors to price risk. Debt financiers are generally absent from grant markets and governments can easily overlook the insurance costs and pricing of the risk for providing an indemnity by a CSO.
7. CSOs, particularly small volunteer organisations, are generally poorly equipped to negotiate sophisticated risk management strategies such as arranging their own insurance pools.

These issues are important in considering who is the most efficient loss preventer and distributor. A strategy of merely offloading risk to the weakest party with no preventive aspect may not be in the broader public interest. In terms of loss prevention, the beneficiaries are clearly not suited to being the sole loss preventers, given their general condition and financial resources. The primary financial loss is that legal liability is borne by government for the outsourcing of the services. This would presumably arise through some negligence or carelessness on the part of the government agency in their management of the outsourcing. It is clearly within the remit of government agencies to manage, through application of appropriate risk management prevention (rather than transfer) strategies. With its access to sophisticated self-financing insurance pools and taxes, government may be in the best position to be a loss distributor compared to a multitude of small and diverse nonprofit service providers, and impoverished clients receiving public goods. By comparison, nonprofit

374 Morris, McGregor-Lowndes and Tarr

community service enterprise has almost no access to dedicated private insurance pools.

APPROACH

The theory is compelling, but what is actually occurring in Australia and the United Kingdom in respect of risk allocation for community service contracts? Each jurisdiction is examined in turn, addressing a series of common lines of inquiry: first, to set the context, the nature of government funding of CSOs is examined; second, we identify and discuss reports from government agencies having authority to scrutinise such matters, to ascertain whether the issue of risk has been raised and any recommendation; third, we examine a selection of representative contracts over time, to identify shifts in the treatment of risk and how it is apportioned between the parties.

In Australia four contracts for major community service projects from large Commonwealth government departments were obtained. These were chosen because the departments have the largest total funding for, and number of agreements with, CSOs. The comparison benchmark is the Department of Finance and Deregulation's new grant conditions template, proposed for implementation across all federal grant agreements. It was specifically designed to address issues about contractual terms, which had been raised in various reports. The documents examined are:

- Australian Government, Department of Families, Housing, Community Service and Indigenous Affairs, Terms and Conditions—Standard Funding Agreement Version 2 April 2009 (the 2009 Agreement);
- Australian Government, Terms—Standard Funding Agreement 11 May 2011 (the 2011 Agreement);
- Australian Government, Department of Health and Aging, Terms and Conditions for Standard Funding Agreement, November 2012 (the 2012 Agreement);
- Australian Government, Department of Finance and Deregulation, Commonwealth Low-Risk Grant Agreement Template, Version 1 August 2013 (the 2013 Agreement).

Unlike Australia, 'standard contracts' are only recently available for examination in the UK. The study draws on a number of empirical projects looking at contracting between government and CSOs that involved the collection and examination of contracts from the contracting parties themselves, together with discussions of those contracts with the parties. Historically, commissioners have tended to consider these contracts to be private documents—in research undertaken by Morris (2001) one government agency would not give participating CSOs permission to release their contracts for the research. More recently, the British government has acknowledged the need for greater transparency across government procurement, so that public bodies and politicians can be held to account, and to achieve better value for public money. Standard contracts have now been produced and are generally available for examination. Three sets of contracts, involving significant government expenditures and CSOs, are identified as representative:

- National Health Service (NHS) Standard Contract 2013/14;
- The Standard Model Terms and Conditions for Department of Work and Pensions Services Contracts 2013;
- Business Innovation & Skills (BIS) Standard Terms and Conditions of Contract for the Purchase of Services 2011

A comparative approach examining contexts, recommended policy directions for the allocation of risk and the contractual terms over time is expected to inform our understanding of whether government is moving towards a more economically rational and sustainable allocation of contractual risk.

AUSTRALIA

All Australian governments have rapidly expanded outsourcing of services through grants, with the Commonwealth government leading the way. The exact size of government grants or even commercial procurement is unknown, but in 2007 about one-sixth of Commonwealth outlays ($40–$50 billion) was in the form of discretionary grants, having grown from $580 million in 2000 (Kelly, 2008, p. 36). The number of grants also grew in the same period, from fewer than 4,000 to over 49,000. In total, it is estimated that all Australian government contracting represents approximately 6.5% of gross domestic product (Seddon, 2013, p. 20). A large proportion of such grants, and probably a lesser amount in procurement, is allocated to Australian community organisations, which receive about one-third of all their funds from governments, to deliver community services (Productivity Commission, 2010, p. 72). In the seven years since 2000, the total government funding to the nonprofit sector increased from $10.1 billion to $25.5 billion (Productivity Commission, 2010, p. 300). Although the exact quantification of outsourced government services is unknown, it is clearly considerable, having grown rapidly.

Such rapid growth gives rise to foreseeable issues with increased political and financial risks, through poor grant administration on one side, and poor or non-performance on the other. As early as 1995, an Industry Commission report into charities expressed concerns about grant administration, describing government requirements as 'varied and ill-defined' (Industry Commission, 1995, p. 380). As outsourcing increased, Auditor-Generals' performance reports warned that departments needed to implement better command and control systems to track public funds flowing through CSOs to their intended beneficiaries or public purposes; and that governments needed to focus more on value for money and encourage more direct competition (Queensland Auditor-General, 1999; Legislative Assembly of Western Australia, Public Accounts Committee, 2000; Parliament of Victoria, Public Accounts and Estimates Committee, 2002; Grant, 2008; Australian Auditor-General, 2010a). Departments reacted to these criticisms contractually by introducing more prescriptive command and control conditions and greater reporting requirements in relation to accounting for both grant funds and performance. This has generally meant neither better service delivery nor meaningful accountability (Nowland-Foreman, 1998; McGuire & O'Neill, 2008), but higher compliance costs for CSOs (McGregor-Lowndes & Ryan, 2009). In 2010, the Productivity Commission (successor to the Industry Commission) re-examined the charities sector and identified many of the same issues that had been raised or predicted a decade and half earlier, noting that

> government [is] often perceived to be imposing 'unfair' terms and conditions that would not be considered appropriate or acceptable in dealing with for-profit providers.
>
> (2010, p. 340)

Specific concerns raised in its report were (Productivity Commission, 2010, p. 310):

- Failure of up to 70% of grants to be fully funded;
- Inappropriate transfer of risk and associated costs;
- The short-term nature of service agreements and contracts;
- Contractual and reporting requirements that are disproportionate to the level of government funding and risk involved;
- The government's use of express terms such as confidentiality clauses, or other punitive use of contract provisions;
- Service agreements being used to micromanage the provision of contracted services and probe into the management, operating methods and broader community activities of community organisations

In relation to risk in such agreements, the Productivity Commission concluded that poor risk management was leading to cost shifting, and that risk 'should be allocated to the party best able to bear it' and the focus should be 'on managing risk rather than seeking to eliminate it' (2010, p. 338). It recommended this be achieved by use of a risk management framework for community service outsourcing and a range of other principles to make the agreement and the actual relationship more appropriate. Broadly, it recommended that

- 'Australian governments should urgently review and streamline their tendering, contracting and acquittal requirements in the provision of services' (p. 348).
- Contracts be based on 'fair and reasonable terms and conditions' (p. 343).
- The Department of Finance and Deregulation 'should develop core principles to underpin all government service agreements and contracts in the human service area' (p. LII).

Alongside the Productivity Commission's very specific recommendations was a series of well-researched and prepared reports by agencies such as the Australian Auditor-General (2010a, 2010b) which sought to bring more mature practice and procedures to discretionary grant-making (see also Grant, 2008; Kelly 2008).

Each Australian state and territory developed a compact following the UK's example of necessitating a public commitment for government and the third sector to work together on specified common issues. Both Australian and UK compacts identified funding reforms as a significant issue for mutual attention. In the light of these developments, the Department of Finance and Deregulation recently produced revised guidelines for Commonwealth grants, providing a policy framework for Commonwealth government agencies' grant administration (Australian Department of Finance and Deregulation, 2013a). The guidelines represent a significant shift, recognising that government grant agreements should not suppress advocacy by CSOs on social issues and that information collected by the Australian Charities and Not-for-Profits Commission (ACNC) should not be requested again by agencies in the course of their operations. Importantly, the guidelines impose a risk-based approach for all grants, involving a risk assessment of the grant programme in proportion to the scale and risk profile of the granting activity (Australian Department of Finance and Deregulation, 2013a, p. 32). This follows a recommendation of the Productivity Commission that

> agency staff should ensure that the entity best placed to manage a specific risk is identified, the risks are assigned to that entity, and that they manage those risks. Identifying the entity best able to manage a risk and assigning that risk is an active process that should occur through all phases of grants administration.
>
> (Australian Department of Finance and Deregulation, 2013a, p. 33)

A model, low-risk grant agreement is being trialled with a risk assessment tool to determine the level of risk. The risks are categorised as those involving the granting activity (government agency's experience and capacity, scope and complexity of the grant), grantee risk (capacity, experience, accountability procedures, nature of industry) and project risk (nature, scope and range of funded activity, nature of beneficiaries and service standards) (Australian Department of Finance and Deregulation, 2013a, pp. 34–35).

Before examining the actual terms of the contract in relation to risk through indemnity and insurance provisions, some comments need to be made about how binding the model will be on agencies. The risk tool has an initial threshold and specifies that a low-risk agreement will be unsuitable if the grant involves real property, complex intellectual property rights or the grantee being located outside Australia. To apply, it then requires an assessment of risk as low, medium or high, based on the following criteria (Australian Department of Finance and Deregulation, 2013b):

- Amount of funding;
- Length of agreement;
- Nature of payments;
- Nature of activity;
- Consequence of grantee's failure to deliver grant outcome;
- Relationship with grantee;
- Nature of grantee industry or sector;
- Nature of any members of the public likely to be affected by the grant

If a majority of the answers are 'medium–high' or 'high' then the low-risk agreement may not be suitable. This affords agencies significant 'wriggle room,' as any agreement over one year is classed as medium risk, along with any grant that is likely 'to affect particular groups of the public directly' (Australian Department of Finance and Deregulation, 2013b), any involving multiple payments over more than one year, or anything other than a single activity aimed at a specific local community. Given that there is no effective review of an adverse decision, such criteria allow significant latitude to agencies to avoid the light-touch grant agreements. Further, an agency could decide to use a procurement framework, thereby circumventing the grant guidelines entirely. We now turn to examine trends in the allocation of risk by examining the selected mainstream agency contracts to community service organisations.

The 2009 and 2011 Agreements

These agreements unambiguously allocated risk to the party receiving funding from the Commonwealth. The recipient was required to indemnify the Commonwealth against 'all liability and losses, costs and expenses' (clause 20.1) and to have 'current and adequate insurance appropriate to the activity funded' (clause 21.1). Earlier agreements commonly specified the amount covered for any one event and classes of insurance. The only qualification upon the Commonwealth's right to an indemnity was provided in clause 20.4 whereby the party receiving funding was relieved of liability to indemnify the Commonwealth in proportion to the extent that the Commonwealth's own fault caused their loss.

The 2012 Agreement

This agreement is more nuanced to reflect the circumstances where liability will arise and acknowledges more explicitly certain limited qualifications upon the liability of the recipient of government funding. However, at its core is the central requirement that the recipient must indemnify the Commonwealth and its personnel against any loss or liability, loss of or damage to property or loss or expense incurred (clause 9.2.1). The agreement is more specific though as to the acts or omissions of the contracting party that will give rise to liability. The loss or liability must arise from: a breach of the contracting party's obligations or warranties under the agreement; from any act or omission where there was fault (including any negligent or other tortious or unlawful act or omission that gave rise to the liability, loss, damage or expense); or from acquisition or use of assets, real property, activity material or existing material (clause 9.2.1). The liability to indemnify the Commonwealth or its personnel is reduced in proportion to the extent that any negligent or other tortious or unlawful act or omission by the Commonwealth or its personnel contributed to the relevant liability, loss, damage or expense (clause 9.2.2). However, to the extent permitted by law, the contract endeavours to exclude the operation of any proportionate liability regime (clause 9.1.1).[1]

Insurance requirements are specified in clause 9.3 and the recipient of funding must take out and maintain all types and amounts of insurance necessary to cover the obligations under the agreement. A fact sheet accompanying the standard funding agreement explains that

> for low or moderate risk service providers, the department will neither dictate levels of insurance, nor sight insurance certificates. Nonetheless, appropriate levels of insurance should be held. For high and extreme risk service providers, the department will take a more active role in stipulating appropriate levels of insurance and sighting certificates.

Unfortunately, this is the only evidence in relation to this contract that the concerns of the Productivity Commission (2010, p. 310) as to risk transfer have had any impact—and then only to the extent that the monitoring of insurance arrangements for low to medium-risk organisations will be reduced. In all other respects the allocation of risk and liability remain unchanged.

The 2013 Agreement

As discussed above, the Commonwealth Department of Finance and Deregulation, which developed the whole of government grant guidelines, also developed a Low-Risk Grant Agreement Template with a risk tool to assist in deciding when it might be applicable. The central clauses relative to risk transfer and insurance are as follows:

The Grantee agrees to maintain adequate insurance for the duration of this Agreement and provide the Commonwealth with proof when requested (clause 15);

The Grantee indemnifies the Commonwealth, its officers, employees and contractors against any claim, loss or damage arising in connection with the Activity (clause 16.1);

The Grantee's obligation to indemnify the Commonwealth will reduce proportionately to the extent any act or omission involving fault on the part of the Commonwealth contributed to the claim, loss or damage (clause 16.2).

Clause 15 on insurance adopts the historical position of requiring grantees to 'agree to maintain adequate insurance' and to provide evidence of it on request. Clause 16 (indemnification requirements) similarly adopts the traditional position of mandating 'full indemnification of the Commonwealth, its officers, employees and contractors against any claim, loss or damage arising in connection with the Activity.' However, this is softened by a mitigating provision which, on its face, suggests a far more equitable and collaborative approach: 'A grantee's obligation . . . will reduce proportionally to the extent any act or omission involving fault on the part of the Commonwealth contributed to the claim, loss or damage.'

While reflective of the spirit of risk sharing and allocation outlined in the guidelines, this caveat represents legal recognition of differing state and federal proportionate liability statutes in relation to property damage, pure economic loss and misleading and deceptive conduct actions. These override historical common law precedent of joint and several liability between potential respondents to legal actions, replacing it instead with Court discretion to join and allocate liability to 'concurrent wrongdoers.' Accordingly, in states where contracting out of proportionate liability provisions is not permissible, this reflects existing law.

By contrast, in states where laws permit contracting out of proportionate liability, agencies attempting to take advantage of this additional indemnification capacity may generate two significant problems. First, grant agreements that contain contracting out provisions may unwittingly generate an insurance indemnity 'gap' in the event of litigation. Liability policies standardly exclude protection for contractually assumed liability that *would not ordinarily arise at law*. Accordingly if an insured assumes joint and several liability or an obligation to indemnify a claim otherwise able to be apportioned at law, the insured may be taking on a liability that, *but for* the contracting out, would not otherwise have existed. The grantee's cover would be limited to only that portion of the loss a court attributes to the insured; the Commonwealth's court-apportioned loss would not be indemnified and would have to be borne by the grantee. Given the relative sophistication necessary to consider this in the context of standard policies, this may not be understood by many CSOs.

Second, on public policy grounds, given the marked policy shift in loss and risk allocation that introduction of proportionate liability laws represents, agencies seeking to adhere to the spirit of best practice might be better advised to support this approach and not shed their liability. This avoids non-parity problems that grants to recipients in different states might otherwise occasion, and adheres best to the aspirational nature of the *Commonwealth Grant Guidelines*.

While this low-risk grant agreement template represents a step forward by improving and streamlining grant agreements and reporting processes associated with certain grants, there is no change to risk allocation as between the Commonwealth and grant recipients.

Summary

The guidelines in the Department of Finance and Deregulation (2013a) document seem sensibly to focus upon better-practice grants administration with an appropriate interest in understanding and managing risk. However there does appear still to be a disconnection between the principles being enunciated by the Department and earlier by the Productivity Commission, and the implementation of certain of those principles. In particular, we suggest that further attention should be devoted to risk allocation, having regard to the scale and risk profile of the granting activity and the grantee. Routinely allocating responsibility for indemnification and maintenance of insurance cover to the grantee is not necessarily the most effective or cost-efficient way to manage risk. Clearly the agencies referred to above understand and support this proposition, but the contractual documentation reviewed here does not correlate with this more evaluative and proportional approach. By contrast, the Victorian government appears to have adopted an approach which accords with these principles. It arranges insurance for its directly funded services in relation to those services (Victorian Department of Human Services, Corporate Resources Division, 2000). It is able to manage the appropriateness and fidelity of such insurance directly, and take advantage of its inherent attributes as a large and sophisticated insurance operative. It can also monitor the adverse events involving those it seeks to benefit with the provision of services.

UNITED KINGDOM

In the UK, government support through grants or contracts for CSOs totalled £14.2 billion in 2009–2010 (National Council for Voluntary Organisations, 2012), an increase of 56% in real terms from 2000. Much of this growth has been by way of contracting. Contract income was worth £11.2 billion in 2010–2011, a real increase of £6.7 billion (151%) since 2000–2001. Between 2003 and 2009, grants from government declined year-on-year by £2.5 billion. Between 2008 and 2011, the level remained roughly static in real terms: in 2010 it was worth £3 billion. Whilst 45% of income from government sources comes from central government and the National Health Service (NHS), 50% comes from local authorities and the remainder comes from European and international government sources.

An examination of National Council for Voluntary Organisations (NCVO) data (National Council for Voluntary Organisations, 2012), together with the consolidated accounts of more than 10,000 public sector entities—from central government, the devolved bodies and local councils, hospitals and schools (HM Treasury, 2012)—reveals that in 2010, central government contracts delivered by CSOs amounted to 5.6% of the £82 billion total. The sector accounted for a larger share of local government procurement at 9% (out of the total of £69 billion). Grants and subsidies from government totalled £68.4 billion in 2010, with the NCVO estimating that £3 billion (4.4% of the total) was received by CSOs.

As part of the 'Big Society' push (Morris, 2012), the Coalition government's public service reforms are intended to ensure that CSOs are able to realise even more opportunities to deliver public services. It has promised to work with the sector and commissioners of services in order to modernise commissioning, to ensure that the most effective and efficient charities, social enterprises, mutuals and cooperatives have a much greater involvement (HM Government, 2010b).

It is the case that many public functions previously carried out by the state are now undertaken by CSOs acting under contract, and the chances are that this will increase in the future. There are many benefits associated with this trend. CSOs have distinctive features that can provide significant benefit through (Knapp, Robertson, & Thomason, 1990):

- The provision of different or specialised services;
- Cost-effectiveness of provision;
- Flexibility and innovation;
- Advocacy;
- Citizen participation

Whilst the increased role of CSOs in public service delivery has its advantages, some have argued that CSOs risk their independence by becoming too immersed in the 'contract culture' (Morris, 2000a). In the 1990s the Labour Party, in opposition, committed itself to 'an independent and creative voluntary sector,' declaring that voluntary work was 'an expression of citizenship' and 'central to our vision of a stakeholder society' (Labour Party, 1997). In the *Compact on Relations Between Government and the Voluntary and Community Sector in England* (HM Government, 1998), these promises were laid out as a series of mutual undertakings between the government and the voluntary and community sector, which, in turn, formed the basis for developing codes of practice. The original *Compact*, launched in November 1998, was with the CSO sector in England, but parallel compacts have also been developed in other parts of the UK. The *Compact* sets out key principles and establishes a way of working to improve the relationship between government and CSOs for mutual advantage. It covers matters such as CSO involvement in policy design and consultation, funding arrangements (including grants and contracts), promoting equality, ensuring better involvement in delivering services and strengthening independence.

The joint foreword to the original, national *Compact*, by the then Home Secretary, Jack Straw, and Sir Kenneth Stowe (who chaired the voluntary and community sector's Working Group on Government Relations), expressed the commitment to carry the *Compact* forward, by encouraging the adoption of its principles and undertakings at a local level, where most voluntary and community sector activity takes place. As a result, there has been considerable work undertaken to develop compacts between the local voluntary and community sector and local governments and other local, public sector partners. In 2012, there were 182 local compacts in existence (Compact Voice, 2012); however, there is considerable local variation in the nature and scope of such agreements (Craig, Taylor, Szanto, & Wilkinson, 1999). Some merely replicate the national *Compact*. Others have been constructed specifically in response to local considerations, offering a means of supporting the development of the voluntary sector's capacity, so that independent but accountable CSOs can meet both their own aims and those of their statutory partners, thereby enhancing their contribution to the community.

There have been a number of versions of the national *Compact*, reflecting changes in the economic and social context in which it operates and in government's view of the role for the voluntary and community sector in implementing its policy agendas. The original version included a series of five supplementary 'Codes of Good Practice,' which were completed in 2005. It was replaced by the 'refreshed' *Compact* in December 2009 and, in turn, by the 'renewed' *Compact* in December 2010 (HM Government, 2010a). There are no longer any codes of good practice to accompany the *Compact*.

In 2007, in an attempt to ensure that the *Compact* was actually working in practice, the government launched the Office of the Commission for the Compact, a non-departmental public body sponsored by the Office of the Third Sector. The Commission sought to act as 'honest broker' between the *Compact* parties (Zimmeck, Rochester, & Rushbrooke, 2011, p. 5) and reported each year to parliament on its efforts to make *Compact* relations a reality rather than a paper exercise. Unfortunately, the Commission fell victim to the Coalition government's 'bonfire of the quangos' (Parkinson, 2010) and ceased to exist in March 2011. Responsibility for oversight of the *Compact* is now shared between the Office for Civil Society and Compact Voice.

Funding processes have been a particular stumbling block to the sector's greater participation in public service delivery, despite the *Compact*'s associated code of practice on funding (Commission for the Compact (UK), 2005). In 2002, a Treasury review of the sector's involvement in public services identified several important and commonplace weaknesses in funding processes, and made recommendations for improvement (HM Treasury, 2002). The aim of the review was to remove barriers and build capacity so as to maximise the distinctive contribution that CSOs bring to service delivery. The major concerns identified around funding were:

- Ensuring that the cost of contracts for services reflects the full cost of delivery, including any relevant part of the overhead costs;
- Streamlining the application system;
- End-loading of payment, with the CSOs bearing upfront risk;
- Moving to a more stable funding relationship, with longer contracts and longer-term partnerships;
- Creating a level playing field in competition for service delivery, particularly around value-added tax

A further National Audit Office report in 2005 examined the progress made by departments and other government funders, led by the Home Office, on improving the way that they fund the third sector to deliver public services (HM National Audit Office, 2005). One of its findings was that, whilst in the main the recommendations of the Treasury review had been implemented, further steps were needed to improve funding in practice. Too many contracts were placing excessive risk on providers, causing some organisations to reject opportunities to deliver services.

Interestingly, one of the recommendations from the 2005 National Audit Office report was that there should be a template contract developed, specifically for procurement from the third sector, suitable for adapting to special requirements. This has not happened. For example, in *Liverpool City Council's Corporate Procurement Strategy 2010–2014* (Liverpool City Council, 2010), it is stated,

> in line with the National Procurement Strategy, the Council wants to promote a sound commercial relationship with the third sector and will endeavour to remove barriers to entry for potential providers. Consideration will be given to extending opportunities for social enterprises and the not for profit sector in any appropriate procurement activity. However, contracting opportunities will be offered on a level playing field to all suppliers, regardless of the sector they operate in.

In terms of funding, the current *Compact* requires fair and effective funding and commissioning processes, with the sector involved in designing services. Funding should be allocated on a full cost recovery basis for more than one year. There should be proportionate monitoring, a fair balance of risk and three months' notice with reasons given when funding ends. In terms of risk, the *Compact* specifically states that the government undertakes to

> Discuss and allocate risks to the organisation(s) best equipped to manage them. Where prime contractors are used, ensure they adhere to the principles of this Compact in allocating risk. Ensure delivery terms and risks are proportionate to the nature and value of the opportunity.
>
> (HM Government, 2010a, para 3.9)

At a local level, where much of the contracting takes place, the city of Liverpool in the UK has a long history of voluntary activity, a large, dynamic and diverse voluntary, community and faith sector and a wide range of relationships with public sector organisations. There has been a local compact in Liverpool since 2002 and its most recent, 'refreshed' version, which was published for consultation in March 2013, contains the same terms regarding risk as the national compact (Liverpool City Council & Liverpool Charity and Voluntary Services, 2013, p. 12).

Whilst the compacts (both at the national and local level) are not legally binding documents—the provisions are generally too vague to be enforceable or to evidence intention to create a 'contract' as such—there is a legitimate expectation that the signatories will abide by their commitments. Recently, there has been a growing tendency to cite failure to abide by *Compact* commitments in cases seeking judicial review of decisions to reduce or discontinue funding arrangements between government and CSOs. In one case involving a local government compact, the judge stated, 'it seems to me that the compact was more than a wish list but less than a contract. It is a commitment of intent between the parties concerned' (R (Berry) v Cumbria County Council [2007] EWHC 3144 (Admin), [44]).

Analysis of Contracts: Early Evidence

The original *Compact* stated that '[the government undertakes to promote funding policies which] take account of the objectives of voluntary and community organisations and their need to operate efficiently and effectively' (HM Government, 1998, para 9.3). In terms of exposure to liability, however, early research looking at new deal contracts (Morris, 2001) found that there was significant potential for unacceptable exposure to liability in the complex contractual agreements that were examined. The *New Deal for 18–24 Year Olds* was a scheme in which CSOs featured heavily. Its aim was to help get young, unemployed people back into work through the provision of placements and training. The activity was potentially highly risky, with a strong likelihood of both the new dealers and the charity beneficiaries with whom they were working being vulnerable persons. Empirical research found that when one CSO attempted to amend a contract so as to limit its liability to the extent of its insurance cover, its pleas fell on deaf ears.

Employment services (the government agency contractor) was not prepared to take back any responsibility. The contract terms tended to be confusing, with less than half of the CSOs that were surveyed feeling confident that they had understood their contractual liabilities.

Empirical research by Morris (1999), again carried out before the *Compact* became a reality and at an early stage in the 'contract culture,' found that commissioners often used their greater bargaining power in contracts for service provision in order to impose terms on CSOs without sufficient negotiation. The resulting contracts often lacked mutuality, imposing the lion's share of the obligations upon charities. Further, the study found that inability to access appropriate advice compounded the inequality of bargaining problem for smaller, local organisations that did not have the backup of national support networks (Morris, 2000b). Indemnity clauses were common in the contracts examined, but only one of the contracts examined included a 'reverse' indemnity clause, providing that

> [the Purchasing Authority] will indemnify [the charity] against any liability, loss or claim or proceedings whatsoever arising:
>
> (a) out of breach by the Authority of its obligations under this Agreement; or
> (b) caused by any act or neglect of the Authority or any person for whom the Authority is responsible.
>
> (Morris, 1999, p. 38)

2011–2013 Contracts

Locating government contracts is easier now, with many posted online via government websites. It is comforting to discover that some limited progress seems to have been made, with terms generally slightly more balanced. It is difficult to ascertain whether this is as a result of the *Compact* and the other initiatives discussed above. These contracts apply to all types of providers, not just CSOs. Some examples will be considered.

National Health Service (NHS) Standard Contract 2013/14

This contract is used by NHS to commission acute, ambulance, community and mental health and learning disability services from all types of providers. It is also now used by clinical commissioning groups to commission community-based services. As well as including a comparable clause setting out the liability and indemnity position of the provider (in our case, the CSO), the 'General Conditions' in the *NHS Standard Contract 2013/14* include the following 'reverse' clause (clause 11.1):

11.1 Without affecting its liability for breach of any of its obligations under this Contract, each Commissioner will be severally liable to the Provider for, and must indemnify and keep the Provider indemnified against:

11.1.1 any loss, damages, costs, expenses, liabilities, claims, actions and/or proceedings (including the cost of legal and/or professional services) whatsoever in respect of:

11.1.1.1 any loss of or damage to property (whether real or personal); and 11.1.1.2 any injury to any person, including injury resulting in death; and 11.1.2 any Losses of the Provider, that result from or arise out of the Commissioner's negligence or breach of contract in connection with the performance of this Contract except insofar as that loss, damage or injury has been caused by any act or omission by or on the part of, or in accordance with the instructions of, the Provider, its employees or agents.

Symbolically, it is interesting that this clause comes *before* the comparable clause setting out the liability and indemnity position of the provider. Whilst its position in the contract has no legal impact, it may suggest some sensitivity towards the position of the provider.

There is no clause relating to contributory negligence, but, reading the two clauses which set out the liability and indemnity positions of both the commissioner and the provider, the same effect is achieved. In any event, the common law would support a contributory negligence 'defence' in any liability claim, should the circumstances allow it. It is also stated clearly (in clause 11.10) that there shall be no right to claim damages for indirect losses.

The provider is required to put appropriate indemnity arrangements in place, at its own cost (clause 11.5).

The Standard Model Terms and Conditions for Department of Work and Pensions Services Contracts 2013

This contract is used by the Department of Work and Pensions for all services contracts (including welfare to work services) where the anticipated contract value is over £10,000. The sharing of risk is more transparent in this contract, with a clear statement (clause G1.3) limiting the liability of the contractor where loss, etc. is caused by the negligence, wilful misconduct or breach of contractual obligations on the part of the authority (the government agency). There is the usual term requiring the provider to have insurance in place (clause G1.7), but this contract also has a clause (clause G1.5) limiting the liability of either party to a specified financial limit (to be inserted in the contract). It is also stated clearly that there shall be no liability for indirect loss (clause G1.6).

Business Innovation & Skills (BIS) Standard Terms and Conditions of Contract for the Purchase of Services 2011

BIS is the government department responsible for economic growth. It invests in skills and education to promote trade, boost innovation and help people to start and grow a business. BIS also protects consumers and reduces the impact of regulation. It purchases a wide variety of services. This standard contract imposes liability for indirect loss as a result of breach of contract, etc. by the provider (clause 14.1). It contains no 'reverse' indemnity clause, makes no mention of contributory negligence, but does limit the provider's liability to £2 million or twice the contract value, whichever is greater (clause 14.4). It also requires the provider to have insurance in place and specifies the minimum amounts of cover that must be purchased in relation to employers' liability, public liability and professional indemnity.

Summary

An examination of standard contracts from three government agencies shows some diversity in the way in which liability and risk are handled. Comparing these contracts to those examined in the empirical projects described above, it can be seen that contract terms have become slightly less onerous over the years. However, there is still little recognition of third sector providers and their specific needs. A new trend in public service commissioning in the United Kingdom is the use of 'payment by results' (PbR) contracts. Whilst this development has the potential to improve outcomes, it could also be regarded simply as a way of shifting risk away from the commissioner. A recent, evidence-based review of such contracts found that some contained wide indemnity clauses covering both direct and indirect losses, howsoever caused and without limit (Bates, Wells, and Braithwaite & National Council for Voluntary Organisations, 2013). More generally, it was found that excessive use of PbR, with its high financial risks for providers, could push CSOs that cannot bear the risk level out of public service provision completely. Previous government reviews and compact commitments appear to be having minimal impact in this area.

CONCLUSION

As governments progressively increase community services, while also altering the way in which they are delivered, it is critical for both fiscal responsibility to taxpayers and equity to the most vulnerable in society that service delivery processes are effective and efficient. Apportionment of risk is a key contractual provision and an important bargaining point in functioning markets. We have investigated the apportionment of financial risk through grant contracts in two jurisdictions, Australia and the United Kingdom, by examining the context of grants in both places and then comparing contractual terms over time, to assess the apportionment of risk.

In both jurisdictions, governments have embraced contracting out of what were once state-delivered community services, whereas, at the same time, significantly increasing expenditure. In Australia, the refinement of community service contracts has been pushed by pressures for greater accountability and political risks for non-delivery, and then pulled by the need to have a sustainable relationship with community service providers. On one side, those concerned with government fiscal accountability pushed for greater tracking of public funds and more conclusive evidence of outcome achievement. On the other side, Australia appeared to follow the UK's lead in developing compacts to improve relationships and cooperation between government and CSOs in response to CSOs' agitation for a better deal. However, it was the Productivity Commission report (2010) which finally prodded the Commonwealth government to reform CSO grant contracts.

The Department of Finance and Deregulation's grant guidelines (2013a) are a significant step forward in mitigating the race to boilerplate clauses easily obtained in a monopsony, but our analysis shows little improvement in the apportionment of risk between the parties. In any event, the low-risk grant template can easily be avoided by agencies because of its ambiguous nature and lack of review by affected parties.

In the United Kingdom the move from state provision of community services to NPM's outsourcing began before Australia's NPM had engaged properly. The UK is now actively looking beyond nonprofit organisations for community service delivery, being prepared to engage commercial firms as well. The *Compact* and its codes have played a more central role in the UK than in Australia, and have had some influence over the content and construction of funding agreements (HM Home Office, 1998, p. 2002). UK compacts are more dynamic and central, specifying the nature of the legal relationship, and supported by independent reviews of implementation and annual reports to Parliament (Lyons & Passey, 2006; HM National Audit Office, 2005).

However, the *Compact*'s strongest impact has not been in its ability to dictate favourable contract terms. Rather, it has helped to form more effective partnerships between government agencies and CSOs; e.g., being influential in the way that government agencies make decisions about funding and, in particular, decisions about funding cuts. So, as a result of the *Compact*, consultation exercises are sometimes more meaningful and, on occasion, more notice has been given to changes to funding arrangements (see, e.g., Compact Voice, 2012). There is still a long way to go, however, as the recent research on PbR contracts reveals. It appears that, like Australia, there has been some movement in the allocation of risk between government and CSOs, despite the recommendation of a contract template not being adopted. Progress appears to fall well short of a calculated response to the allocation of risk that would occur if market forces were at play.

As indicated by bodies in both the UK and Australia, a calculated and appropriate response would be to allocate risk to the party best able to finance and/or manage it. Governments have the attributes to manage risk far more efficiently and effectively than nonprofit CSOs, particularly small enterprises. Government agencies are reluctant to stop shifting risk to the other party in grant contracts, and over the years have only moved from this position marginally. It will be a matter for further research if the future brings greater participation by for-profit firms and the environment becomes more akin to a normal market. Perhaps then government will address the question of whether it can be more efficient by financing or managing the risk itself.

NOTE

1 Proportionate liability legislation was introduced into each Australian jurisdiction between 2002 and 2004 for claims involving economic loss and property damage; this new regime replaced the long-standing common law system of joint and several liabilities. The legislation had the effect that multiple defendants would, in general terms, only be potentially liable to pay for the loss they were responsible for causing. 'Deep pocket' defendants, such as professional advisers, would no longer face the prospect of becoming liable to pay the whole of a plaintiff's claim where their conduct contributed little to the loss suffered. These laws lack clarity and consistency across states and territories, posing a range of challenges to ensuring consistent results and contract terms, particularly for claims involving more than one jurisdiction. Given the nature of federally funded grants to a range of recipients across a range of jurisdictional borders, the inequities inherent in this are problematic for grantors and for the grantees and this complexity is compounded in jurisdictions where the courts are empowered to make independent determinations of liability to parties regardless of their contractually allocated indemnification status.

REFERENCES

Anheier, H. K. (2005). *Nonprofit organisations theory, management, policy*. New York: Routledge.
Atiyah, P. S. (1970). *Accidents, compensation and the law*. London: Weidenfeld and Nicholson.
Australian Auditor-General. (2010a). *Direct source procurement 2010–11* (Audit report no. 11). Canberra, AU: Australian National Audit Office.
Australian Auditor-General. (2010b). *Implementing better practice grants guide 2010–11*. Canberra, AU: Australian National Audit Office.
Australian Department of Finance and Deregulation. (2013a). *Commonwealth grant guidelines* (2nd ed.). Retrieved from http://www.finance.gov.au/financial-framework/financial-management-policy-guidance/grants/index.html
Australian Department of Finance and Deregulation. (2013b). *Commonwealth low-risk grant agreement risk tool*. Retrieved from http://www.finance.gov.au/financial-framework/financial-management-policy-guidance/grants/grant-agreement-template-project.html

Bates, Wells, and Braithtwaite, & National Council for Voluntary Organisations. (2013). *Payment by results contracts: A legal analysis of terms and process.* Retrieved from http://www.ncvo.org.uk/images/documents/practical_support/public_services/payment_by_results_contracts_a_legal_analysis_of_terms_and_process_ncvo_and_bwb_30_oct_2013.pdf

Bernstein, P. L. (1996). *Against the gods: The remarkable story of risk.* New York: John Wiley.

Calabresi, G. (1961). Some thoughts on risk distribution and the law of torts. *Yale Law Journal, 70,* 499–553.

Calabresi, G. (1970). *The cost of accidents: A legal and economic analysis.* New Haven, CT: Yale University Press.

Commission for the Compact (UK). (2005). *Funding and procurement: Compact code of good practice.* London: Commission for the Compact.

Compact Voice. (2012). *Impact report 2012.* London: Compact Voice. Retrieved from http://www.compactvoice.org.uk/resources/publications

Craig, G., Taylor, M., Szanto, C., & Wilkinson, M. (1999). Developing local compacts: Relationships between local public sector bodies and the voluntary and community sectors. York, UK: YPS.

Dunleavy, P. (1994). The globalization of public services production: Can government be "best in world"? *Public Policy & Administration, 9*(2), 36–64.

George, V., & Wilding, P. (2002). *Globalisation and human welfare.* London: Palgrave.

Giddens, A. (1999, April 7). *Runaway world.* BBC Reith Lectures. Retrieved from http://www.bbc.co.uk/programmes/p00gw9s1

Grant, P. (2008). *Strategic review of the administration of Australian government grant programs: Report no. 1.* Canberra, AU: Australian Department of Finance and Deregulation. Retrieved from http://www.finance.gov.au/publications/strategic-reviews/grants.html

Hacker, J. (2006). *The great risk shift: The assault on American jobs, families, health care, and retirement.* Oxford: Oxford University Press.

HM Government. (1998). *Compact on relations between government and the voluntary and community sector in England.* London: The Stationery Office. Retrieved from http://www.thecompact.org.uk

HM Government. (2010a). *The compact: The coalition government and civil society organisations working effectively in partnership for the benefit of communities and citizens in England.* London: The Stationery Office. Retrieved from http://www.thecompact.org.uk

HM Government. (2010b). *Building a stronger civil society. A strategy for voluntary and community groups, charities and social enterprises.* London: Office for Civil Society, Cabinet Office.

HM Home Office. (1998). *Compact guidance for public/voluntary sector partnerships: A proposed supplement to the funding code.* London: The Stationery Office.

HM National Audit Office. (2005). *Working with the third sector: Report by the comptroller and auditor-general* (HC 75 Session 2005–2006). London: The Stationery Office.

HM Treasury. (2002). *The role of the voluntary and community sector in service delivery: A cross cutting review.* London: The Stationery Office.

HM Treasury. (2012). *Whole of government accounts, year ended 31 March 2011.* London: The Stationery Office.

Hood, C. (1991). A public management for all seasons? *Public Administration, 69*(1), 3–19.

Industry Commission. (1995). *Charitable organisations in Australia* (Report no. 45). Melbourne: Australian Government Publishing Service.

Institution of Engineers, & Australian Chamber of Commerce and Industry of Western Australia. (2001). *Effective risk allocation in major projects: Rhetoric or reality?* Retrieved from http://www.ieaust.org.au/./policy/publications_by_year3.html

Kelly, J. (2008). *Strategic review of the administration of Australian government grant programs: Report no. 2.* Canberra, AU: Australian Department of Finance and Deregulation. Retrieved from http://www.finance.gov.au/publications/strategic-reviews/grants.html

Kerr, L., & Savelsberg, H. (2001). The community service sector in the era of the market model: Facilitators of social change or servants of the state? *Just Policy, 23,* 22–32.

Knapp, M., Robertson, E., & Thomason, C. (1990). Public money, voluntary action: Whose welfare? In H. K. Anheier & W. Seibel (Eds.), *The third sector: Comparative studies of nonprofit organisations* (pp. 183–218). Berlin: de Gruyter.

Labour Party. (1997). *Labour party manifesto.* London: Labour Party.

Legislative Assembly of Western Australia, Public Accounts Committee. (2000). *Accountability and not-for-profit organisations* (Report no. 49). Perth, AU: Legislative Assembly of Western Australia.

Liverpool City Council. (2010). *Liverpool city council's corporate procurement strategy 2010–2014.* Liverpool: Liverpool City Council.

Liverpool City Council, & Liverpool Charity and Voluntary Services. (2013). *Liverpool compact (refreshed 2013).* Liverpool: Liverpool City Council.

Luntz, H. (2001). Torts turnaround downunder. *Oxford University Commonwealth Law Journal, 1*(1), 95–106.

Lyons, M., & Dalton, B. (2011). Australia: A continuing love affair with the new public management. In S. D. Phillips & S. R. Smith (Eds.), *Governance and regulation in the third sector: International perspectives.* Oxford: Routledge.

Lyons, M., & Passey, A. (2006). Need public policy ignore the third sector? Government policy in Australia and the United Kingdom. *Australian Journal of Public Administration, 65*(3) 90–102.

Management Advisory Board, Australia. (1996). *Guidelines for managing risk in the Australian public service.* Canberra, AU: Australian Government Publishing Service.

McGregor-Lowndes, M. (2008). Is there something better than partnership? In J. Barraket (Ed.), *Strategic issues for the not-for-profit sector* (pp. 45–73). Sydney: UNSW Press.

McGregor-Lowndes, M., & Ryan, C. (2009). Reducing the compliance burden of non-profit organisations: Cutting red tape. *Australian Journal of Public Administration, 68,* 21–38.

McGregor-Lowndes, M., & Turnour, M. (2003). Recent developments in government community service relations: Are you really my partner. *Journal of Contemporary Issues in Business and Government, 9*(1), 31–42.

McGuire, L., & O'Neill, D. (2008). The report on government services: A new piece in the accountability matrix? In J. Barraket (Ed.), *Strategic issues for the not-for-profit sector* (pp. 236–262). Sydney: UNSW Press.

Morris, D. (1999). *Charities and the contract culture: Partners or contractors? Law and practice in conflict.* Liverpool: Charity Law Unit.

Morris, D. (2000a). Paying the piper: The "contract culture" as dependency culture for charities? In A. Dunn (Ed.), *The voluntary sector and the state and the law* (pp. 123–141). Oxford: Hart Publishing.

Morris, D. (2000b). Charities in the contract culture: Survival of the largest? *Legal Studies, 20*(3), 409–427.

Morris, D. (2001). *Charities and the new deal for young people.* Liverpool: Charity Law Unit.

Morris, D. (2012). Charities and the Big Society: A doomed coalition? *Legal Studies, 32*(1), 132–153.

National Council for Voluntary Organisations. (2012). *NCVO UK civil society almanac.* Retrieved from http://data.ncvo.org.uk/a/almanac13/almanac/databank/income-2/

Nowland-Foreman, G. (1998). Purchase of service contracting, voluntary organizations and civil society: Dissecting the goose that lays the golden eggs? *American Behavioral Scientist, 42,* 108–123.

Parkinson, J. (2010, October 17). Politicians' love/hate relationship with quangos. *BBC News.* Retrieved from http://web.archive.org/web/20101017023421/http://www.bbc.co.uk/news/uk-politics-11536323

Parliament of Victoria, Public Accounts and Estimates Committee. (2002). *Report on department of human services: Services agreements for community, health and welfare services* (Report no. 47). Melbourne: Parliament of Victoria.

Powell, D., & Dowling, B. (2006). New labour's partnerships: Comparing conceptual models with existing forms. *Social Policy & Society, 5*(2), 305–314.

Productivity Commission. (2010). *Contribution of the not-for-profit sector: Research report.* Melbourne: Productivity Commission.

Queensland Auditor-General. (1999). *Review of the administration of grants and subsidies* (Report no. 6 of 1998–99). Brisbane: Queensland Audit Office.

Queensland Treasury. (1994). *Guidelines on risk management and insurance.* Brisbane: Queensland Treasury.

Quiggen, J. (2007). *The risk society: Social democracy in an uncertain world.* Occasional Paper no. 2. Sydney: Centre for Policy Development.

Seddon, N. (2013). *Government contracts: Federal, state and local* (5th ed.). Sydney: Federation Press.

Smith, S. R. (2002). Social services. In L. M. Salamon (Ed.), *The state of nonprofit America* (p. 175). Washington, DC: Brookings Institution Press.

Smith, S. R., & Lipsky, M. (1993). *Nonprofits for hire: The welfare state in the age of contracting.* Cambridge, MA: Harvard University Press.

Victorian Department of Human Services, Corporate Resources Division. (2000). *Insurance guide for non-government organisations.* Melbourne: Victorian Department of Human Services.

Vincent-Jones, P. (1999). Competition and contracting in the transition from CCT to best value: Towards a more reflexive regulation? *Public Administration, 77*(2), 273–291.

Vincent-Jones, P. (2006). *The new public contracting: Regulation, responsiveness, relationality.* Oxford: Oxford University Press.

Zimmeck, M., Rochester, C., & Rushbrooke, B. (2011). *Use it or lose it: A summative evaluation of the compact.* London: Compact Commission.

17 Performing Civil Society

Chandana Alawattage, Danture Wickramasinghe and Anula Tennakoon

INTRODUCTION

Even though NGOs are said to be the means of strengthening the performance of civil societies, little attention has been paid to the ways in which this happens, and we know little about how civil societies give shape to forms of accountability that, in turn, trigger performance. This chapter explores how a particular developmental form of performance and accountability functioned in a civil society context. We use the term 'developmental accountability' to describe how social relations and practices in remote villages in Sri Lanka were organised into a participative mode of rural development based on 'folk Buddhist ideology.'[1]

To achieve this aim, we tell the story of Sarvodaya, the largest civil society organisation in Sri Lanka, and illustrate how the performance and accountabilities of civil society organisations are founded on the structural and ideological dynamics of the civil and political state. Our focus is specifically on the formative phase of Sarvodaya: we aim to explore how a particular social form of accountability functioned as a social movement without becoming a NGO. This gave shape to a performing civil society in which a particular development ideology and a civic structure framed the movement's accountability practices and relations—hence the term 'developmental accountability.'

Data for this chapter come from a research project undertaken for the third author's PhD, supplemented by the other two authors' subsequent field visits. These field visits were ethnographic in nature and involved lengthy interviews with Sarvodaya's past activists, present employees and beneficiaries; they included 40 informal conversations in four villages, as well as 21 semi-formal discussions with Sarvodaya Head Office managers and eight field-level workers. These ethnographic encounters helped us to construct an oral history of the Sarvodaya movement and to understand the particular modes of accountability and performance in the early phase of Sarvodaya's development. Sarvodaya has long been subjected to media coverage and literary explorations. Its history has been well documented in ethnographic writings (Bond, 2004; Kantowsky, 1980; Macy, 1985; Zadek,

1993; Zadek & Szabo, 1994), in the autobiographic writings of Ariyaratne (Ariyaratne, 1979, 1980, 1981, 1989, 1994, 2001) and in the self-reflections of Sarvodaya managers (for example, Perera, 1997). We triangulated our ethnographic data with a review of such secondary sources in order to theorise Sarvodaya's performance and accountability dimensions.

Sarvodaya is the largest and oldest NGO in Sri Lanka. It was founded in the late 1950s as a social movement associated with the post-independent reconstruction of the nation state. Since then it has undergone remarkable change and grown into a conglomerate of NGOs, each operating as a separate legal entity concentrating on a specialised field of development. Presently, this conglomerate consists of 11 independent legal entities with a massive organisational infrastructure and significant financial capital (see Table 17.1).

In this conglomerate catering to the 'development industry' in Sri Lanka, SEEDS and DDFC are dominant and fast growing while other social welfare and community development elements are in decline. Sarvodaya's primary focus now is neither on collective labour and the development of villages as self-reliant organisational entities for national development, nor on promoting a Buddhist ideology of spiritual development, as was the case in its early phase (see below). Instead, it has become a 'successful' operator running one of the largest microfinance enterprises in Sri Lanka.

Sarvodaya is now closer to neoliberal economic ideologies of individualistic, entrepreneurial development than to the traditional Buddhist ideology of community-based, collective development and well-being. Its accountability is functional and driven more by the economic efficiency, effectiveness and agency principles of global development capital than by a social form of accountability founded on the social structures and relations of rural villages. It is swiftly moving away from its original ideology of development and its basis in social capital. The amount of foreign aid it receives is in rapid decline and the existing donor-supported projects tend to concentrate on the rebuilding of the war-affected areas of the north, which draws in the majority of foreign aid to Sri Lanka. Nevertheless, it has a massive real estate asset base accumulated during the 'golden years,' and its survival and growth mostly depend on the property incomes generated from these assets, as well as on its new microfinance and banking businesses. Even the educational, training and consultancy services that Sarvodaya offers in rural areas are now offered on a 'cost recovery basis.' Matara regional centre, for example, survives on the property income from converting its real estate into a holiday resort. Traditional *shramadana* activities (see below) and other forms of community forums are almost non-existent in Sarvodaya's activity portfolio today.

However, the focus of this chapter is not the current mode of performance and accountability but Sarvodaya's formative period, when it focused on building 'performing villages.' We analyse how Sarvodaya as a social movement penetrated the social fabric of rural villages to transform them into a 'performing civil state'; that is, into a particular form of social

Table 17.1 Sarvodaya as a conglomerate of development capital

Entity	Operational activities
Sarvodaya Economic Enterprises Development Services (Guarantee) Limited (SEEDS)	Currently the primary operating entity of Sarvodaya, mainly concentrating on microfinance-based economic development activities. One of the leading microfinance providers in Sri Lanka. Operates as a limited liability company by guarantee and outlines its domain of activities as follows: 'As a microfinance practitioner, we offer a wide range of financial and non-financial services to poor, enterprising clients who have no access to credit to capitalize their micro and small enterprises through formal banks and financial institutions.' The total asset base of the company was 5,329 million Sri Lankan rupees as at 31 March 2011 (Annual Report, 2011).
Deshodaya Development Finance Company (DDFC)	Being the most recent addition (December 2012) to the Sarvodaya conglomerate, this was incorporated as a public limited liability company by shares and licensed by the Central Bank of Sri Lanka as a finance company. Similar to any other finance company in the country, its major activities involve savings, business and consumption loans, pawning and microfinance. The total asset base of the company was 3,732 million Sri Lankan rupees as at 31 March 2013 (Annual Report, 2013).
Lanka Jathika Sarvodaya Shramadana Sangamaya (Inc.)—Social Sector	This is the original Sarvodaya organisation, incorporated by a special parliamentary act (Act No. 16 of 1972). This act was passed to enable Sarvodaya to engage in economic activities both within and outside Sri Lanka; it mainly allows it to receive foreign aid and loans. As at March 2013, its total asset base was 1,216 million Sri Lankan rupees.
FUSION	The information and communication technology (ICT) arm of Sarvodaya. Engages in so-called e-empowerment of poor communities through ICT education, training and consultancy. Runs Sarvodaya's telecentres and village information centres, partly funded by foreign aid. Aims to be a self-sufficient, profit-earning social enterprise.

Entity	Operational activities
Sarvodaya Legal Services	Legal empowerment of communities and legal aid.
Sarvodaya Women's Movement	Ensuring gender equality through encouraging women's participation in development activities.
Sarvodaya Suwasetha	Social welfare arm of Sarvodaya, mainly concentrating on disaster relief and other welfare distribution activities.
Sarvodaya Shanthi Sena	Youth Brigade of Sarvodaya working towards developmental and peace attitudes among young people.
Sarvodaya Trust Fund	Recognition (through awards) of outstanding Sri Lankans who have contributed significantly to the promotion of humanity, peace and harmony.
A T Ariyaratne Charitable Trust	The spiritual empowerment arm of Sarvodaya. Has created and runs the Vishva Niketan International Peace Centre.
Sarvodaya Samodaya Services	Rehabilitation of drug addicts. Runs several centres across the country.

Source: Sarvodaya Annual Report 2012–13 (Sarvodaya, 2013), and various Sarvodaya websites.

accountability that needs to be understood as the antithesis of modern functional modes of NGO accountability.

The chapter is organised as follows. The next section provides a brief review of the accounting literature on NGO accountabilities in order to locate this work within the paradox debate of NGO accountability. This review is extended in the third section to highlight the importance of locating NGO accountabilities in micro-organisational/civil, societal and macro-political dynamics. Here we bring out the notion of the 'village' as a micro-organisational element of development accountability and performance. Section four comprises the main analysis in which we explore how a particular mode of development accountability and performance was constructed by drawing on a progressive ideology of 'protestant Buddhism' that incorporated both traditional Buddhist principles of spirituality and a liberal economic ideology of progress. In this section, we also demonstrate how performance and accountability were defined in three interrelated dimensions of social ideology, relations and practices. Finally, in the reflections and conclusions section, we relate our empirical and historical analysis to the notion of the nation state to re-emphasise the significance of macro-political dynamics in explaining the historical evolution of accountability and performance regimes.

NGO ACCOUNTABILITY: ORGANISATIONAL
VS CIVIL SOCIETAL ANALYSES

NGO accountability has become one of the key empirical and theoretical sites for accounting research. Some researchers are keen to explore how accounting can be instrumental in 'organising' and 'modernising' the spheres of social lives that fall beyond prototypical economic and public enterprises. Accountability research into NGOs and civil society movements has, thus, come to occupy a philanthropic position in making an 'accounting contribution' to the noble aims of these organisations. They wish to 'signify' accounting as an essential, modernising device in creating a 'fair' world of accountability and transparency. Others, especially those holding a 'critical' stance, are cautious about the rate at which NGOs are growing and the impact they make on democratic governance, especially in the peripheral nations, either for good or bad; they stress that these organisations must be accountable to a wider spectrum of stakeholders. They have explored the role of accounting in NGO accountability mechanisms (Ebrahim, 2003; O'Dwyer & Unerman, 2008), performance measurement and management control systems (Chenhall, Hall, & Smith, 2010), and the way in which the evolutionary dynamics of NGOs are shaped by accounting and calculative technologies (Lehman, 2007; O'Dwyer & Unerman, 2007).

However, we then encounter a paradox: the coexistence of contradictory forms of accountability in NGOs and the inability of NGOs to appreciate holistic and social forms of accountability together with functional forms, or colonisation of the social by the dominating functional forms (see Ebrahim, 2003; O'Dwyer & Unerman, 2007, 2008; O'Sullivan & O'Dwyer, 2009; Unerman & O'Dwyer, 2006b). Much of the literature on NGO accountability has been concerned with this paradox. For example, in the Irish section of Amnesty International (AI), O'Dwyer and Unerman (2008) observed a hierarchical conception of accountability that privileges a narrow range of powerful stakeholders and dominating accountability discourses and practices, despite a managerial preference for holistic accountability mechanisms. Similar managerial commitments to promote societal accountability through the creation of a virtual supra-organisational entity for accountability purposes have been observed in Ireland's Development Corporation (O'Dwyer & Unerman, 2007). Nevertheless, as they observe, the nature of the relationship between funding agencies and NGOs has never been supportive enough to realise these holistic desires. Ebrahim (2003) observes a similar difficulty in the developing world, and raises a concern about the importance of downward accountability. Some of the underlying issues have also been theorised either as having 'social capital' implications for management control (Chenhall et al., 2010) or as 'accounterability' (McKernan & McPhail, 2012).

In terms of the contesting nature of NGO accountability, two levels of empirical analysis have been carried out. First, at the organisational level,

the focus is on reporting procedures, the underlying organisational complexity of accountability and the multiplicity of power relations among
multiple stakeholders (for example, Ebrahim, 2003; O'Dwyer & Unerman,
2007, 2008; O'Dwyer, Unerman, & Bradley, 2005; Unerman & O'Dwyer,
2006a, 2006b). Here, researchers have explored NGO accountability procedures, practices and strategies to reveal how such accountability dimensions
are controlled by dominant stakeholder groups, especially donors, and they
have registered both dissatisfaction and empathy towards such dominance.
They call for NGO leadership to become 'more open and more knowledgeable about a broader, more holistic accountability conception' (O'Dwyer &
Unerman, 2008, p. 801). Perhaps due to the site-specific characteristics of
these case studies, such analyses have largely been confined to formal and
organisational processes that are in place to ensure communicative actions
between NGOs and their stakeholders; as a result, they are better at offering
managerial and organisational explanations for the accountability paradox.
For example, O'Dwyer and Unerman (2008) explain that managers' apathy
and inability to appreciate the trust that members place in professional staff
have played a critical role in constraining the development of a holistic form
of accountability in Amnesty Ireland. However, Gray, Kouhy, and Lavers
observe that such analysis represents the exercise of bourgeois perception,
and that it is confined to the 'relationships between the interest groups of
pluralism without explicit recognition of the way in which the forces of
the system (capitalism) construct the self-interests as group interests' (1995,
p. 53; see also Tinker, 1984).

The second level of analysis goes beyond managerial and organisational
parameters to examine the political contradictions that underlie accountability issues. Such research explores whether NGOs increasingly are becoming
vehicles for ideology rather than assistance; whether NGOs are doomed
to fail by the environment that made them necessary; whether NGOs can
truly fill a democratic vacuum (see Lehman, 2007); and how the craft of
accounting is articulated within a civil society context and the 'challenges
this may raise for such matters as the elusive nature of the "accounting
entity" and what constitutes appropriate reporting of performance' (Gray,
Bebbington, & Collison, 2006, p. 320). Such questions encourage us to
widen our analytical focus to the dynamics of the civil society within which
NGO accountability issues are embedded. Once NGOs are understood as
an accountability mechanism in the civil society, answers to the fundamental issues pertaining to NGO accountability lie in the structural contradictions in which they operate: the dialectics between the economy, polity and
civil society (see Lehman, 2007). So, as Lehman (2007) also argues, without
a full analysis of the democratic, dialectical and interpretive aspects of civil
society research, it is difficult to determine whether the accountability principles are satisfied (see also Cohen & Arato, 1992; Keane, 2003).

The present chapter falls within this civil society tradition, partly in
response to Lehman's observation that 'NGOs, as accountability mechanisms

in civil society, have been under-theorised' (2007, p. 648). By offering a historical account of a NGO, we offer a civil society perspective that reveals how societies are permeated with certain ideologies, which convey a pattern of social and political meanings and construct a particular form of accountability. Partly, we respond to calls by Gray (2002), Thomson and Bebbington (2005) and O'Dwyer and colleagues (O'Dwyer, 2005; O'Dwyer & Unerman, 2007, 2008; O'Dwyer et al., 2005; O'Sullivan & O'Dwyer, 2009; Unerman & O'Dwyer, 2006b) for richer, more in-depth case studies of how and why social forms of accounting emerge and evolve. This attempt, then, is not far from what Burchell, Clubb, Hopwood, Hughes, and Nahapiet (1980) famously articulated: it is an exploration of the ways in which accountability is ensnared in the social and institutional context of organisations.

ON NGO ACCOUNTABILITY AND CIVIL SOCIETY

Because of the boundary-spanning nature of NGOs—across the economy, civil society and the political state—their accountability is paradoxical. This paradox has to be identified in terms of the contradictions that arise between 'functional' and 'social' forms of accountabilities (see Ebrahim, 2003; O'Dwyer & Unerman, 2007, 2008; O'Sullivan & O'Dwyer, 2009; Unerman & O'Dwyer, 2006b). In this sense, the paradox is clear: the associated mechanisms for upward and downward accountability do not sit easily with each other. O'Dwyer and Unerman's (2008) exploration of this paradox in the Irish section of AI is interesting here. It was expected that accounting was constitutive in terms of maintaining better performance and delivery of accountability to all AI stakeholders, including victims of human rights violations. The managers at AI agreed this was essential, and they adopted a holistic accountability approach as opposed to narrowly defined functional accountability. However, they were concerned about the associated impracticalities of implementation that made such inspiration unrealistic. Here, leaning towards a functional tendency, O'Dwyer and Unerman highlight the 'absence, especially among senior managers, of knowledge about, or apparent desire to experiment with, more holistic forms of accountability' (2008, p. 819). Such views on NGO accountability, of course, offer an interesting explanation of the pragmatic difficulties involved in reconciling the functional and social forms of accountabilities, paying special attention to the programmatic and organisational dimensions of accountability. However, we believe that this accountability paradox has deeper structural contradictions, which need be understood at two distinct but interrelated levels: macro and micro.

By 'macro,' we mean here the historical dialectics among economy, society and polity. This is a particular structural premise that has long been fundamental to neo-Marxist analysis of organisational practices, especially

Gramscian analyses (see Alawattage & Wickramasinghe, 2008). 'Micro' practices and structures of accountability evolve as a result of the historical dialectics between polity, society and economy. Although such structural analyses have become somewhat outdated in the midst of more fashionable, post-structural trends in accounting academia, as our data reveal, such structural dynamics do explain the emergence of NGOs and their associated accountability structures and practices, especially in postcolonial contexts. Social movements stemming from macro-political dynamics provide enabling and constraining conditions for NGO accountability and performance. For example, the emergence of NGOs has often been related to the weakening polity and the erosion of democracy in the peripheral nations—hence the need for NGOs to meet this 'democratic gap' (Henderson, 1997; Kamat, 2004; Moore, 2006; Robinson, 1994, 1997). NGOs are said to represent the masses, responding to the needs of the poor and advocating for them on democratic and human rights matters. The pre-neoliberal state was criticised for its bureaucratic dysfunction, financial corruption, undue politicisation and lack of entrepreneurial and technological capacity. Thus, the NGO sector, seen as a Third Way, has come to promote democracy and social and economic development (Kamat, 2004). Furthermore, as Harvey (2005) argues, there is a dilemma contained within the state's need to be able to regulate market forces: on the one hand, although predisposed to authoritarianism, the state becomes unstable because of the conflict between market forces and the need to preserve nationalistic and democratic institutions; on the other, as Harvey observes, authoritarianism in market enforcement sits uneasily with the ideals of neoliberalism and becomes a way of diluting the ethos of neoliberalism itself. This is, Harvey continues, not a replacement of the capitalist state but rather a reconfiguration of state power by the introduction of an entity that opposes that power. Following the Gramscian idea of the state as uniting political and civil society, he shows that neoliberalism has created a civil society at the centre of opposition to conventional state power—hence the proliferation of the NGO as a civil society organisation (Harvey, 2005; Ohmae, 1995).

Such macro dynamics set the parameters for regimes of accountability, but it is the micro level that can empirically specify accountability practices and relations that characterise a particular accountability regime within a particular historical epoch. Accordingly, in this case study we focus on the notion of 'the village,' which, in the context of development discourse, is a 'real' organisational entity existing in a socio-political form, yet is subject to various modes of developmental planning, organising and controls. The village exists as the basic administrative unit—and as a basic centre of responsibility—of the government's administrative hierarchy, along with a set of officers and budget allocations from central and provincial governments. The village exists in various policy documents as the ultimate beneficiary of the rural development projects that are designed and funded by global development agencies. For example, microfinance funding projects are geared towards the development of a selected set of 'poorest villages' in the country. In addition, the village exists in social and political rhetoric not only as a 'place to be developed,' but also as a 'place of belonging': a living space to which groups and individuals attribute their belonging and identity. It is surprising, then, especially when we read through accounting and organisational studies of less-developed countries, to see that there is insufficient ontological emphasis placed on the 'village' as an organisational or social entity.

As we will illustrate later in the chapter, the village is the basic organisational unit from where 'developmental accountability' emerges and evolves and in which it is practised. Similar to the notions of 'nation state' or 'economy,' the village has become one of the key elements of the developmental state. The development of the village has become a normative goal to which individuals, groups and organisations are committed, and to which they contribute. In that sense, the village has become a 'heterotopian space' (Foucault, 1997) in which certain utopian development ideologies are embedded, realised and reflected back to the centre. It is a space in which the 'good old' is to be preserved, but within a global framework of modern, industrial and neoliberal ideologies. Thus, it is also a contested terrain. Above all, the village is a social space within which human activities and relations are organized, and accountabilities defined.

Accountabilities, in such a heterotopian space, need to be understood and defined in terms of contesting ideologies and social relations. At a mundane level, accountability involves giving and receiving 'accounts,' but it must be defined not only as the *process* of giving and receiving accounts, but also in relation to the social and political *conditions* on which such processes are based. Accountability, thus, refers to both the text and the context of accounts: that is, what is being accounted for, and how, as well as the underlying socio-political or structural rationales for the selection of methods, narratives and the particular social practices and rituals through which such exchanges are performed. This is a *totalising* concept where *communicative* actions (i.e., telling) collapse onto *performative* actions (i.e., doing) and become visible as a singular totality, while maintaining an ontological separateness from each other (see Munro, 1996). Such a performative conception of accountability can only be found in empirical sites through emic ethnographic accounts (that is, through the culturally particular, observable practices of giving and receiving accounts). These accounts encompass how accountability practices embed themselves in, and constitute, organisational and social performance; the structural and institutional parameters within which such practices are carried out; and how such mundane practices of accountability shape and reshape the structural parameters within which they are grounded. Accountability practices, then, entail not only the giving and the receiving of accounts, but also the dialectical relations that such practices hold in relation to the institutional and structural parameters of the civil society, which, in this case, is the village.

ON PERFORMING CIVIL SOCIETY IN A SRI LANKAN VILLAGE

Sri Lanka, the Village and Buddhist Ideology

Sri Lanka is a small island in the Indian Ocean, which underwent nearly 450 years of colonial rule from 1505, gained independence from the British in 1948 and embarked on a postcolonial development project from the 1950s. Despite a variety of development approaches that were tested, and notwithstanding their implications for the forms and practices of accounting, accountability and governance (Alawattage & Wickramasinghe, 2008), we focus here on the Sri Lankan village and Buddhist ideology—a local context in which an antithesis of present NGO accountability can be explored.

Independence did not produce significant change in the typical Sri Lankan village, which was still characterised by a pre-capitalist mode of production: its economic fabric and social stratification were institutionalised in terms of castes and extended families. The economy here was relatively self-sufficient in terms of basic needs, but infrastructure such as electricity, roads, railways, healthcare and education were far from being accessible. The village 'government' was organised around the extent of land ownership. Landlords maintained power over the subordinated tenant castes through feudalistic systems of domination where 'accounting' and 'performance measurements' for the appropriation of surplus value were embedded in cultural rituals. For example, rice harvesting was a communal ceremony in which the harvest was piled in an open place in order to determine the shares of the landlord, the temple and the farmers (Ryan, 1958). Even though the village enshrined social inequality, its pre-capitalist mode of production had persisted for centuries and continued after Independence. This village was not very different to what British official Charles Metcalfe described in relation to typical Indian villages in 1832—'little republics' that were 'almost independent of any foreign relations' (Macy, 1985).

What was different about the Sri Lankan village was that its governance mechanism had gained a moral authority through Sinhala peasant Buddhism (Bond, 2004; Ryan, 1958). The village temple had long been a physical space for the implementation of this moral authority while the monks mobilised Buddhist teaching in the maintenance of people's moral order. People had been warned that their economic and social status was what they brought from their previous lives based on their accumulated *karma*: they must accumulate good *karma* in the present life to become better in the next and to gain *nirvana*. These material circumstances, social relations and spiritual intents continued to reproduce the village governance structure in which aristocratic families and the Buddhist temple played a vital role (Bond, 2004).

As elaborated in the proceeding section, the Sarvodaya movement mobilised the traditional village as the centre from which to implement a form of development where traditional Buddhism was transformed into 'Protestant

Buddhism': the focus was on mobilising the rural mass for political and economic salvation and freedom, rather than for spiritual salvation in the next life. The rationality of this emerging movement was self-governance and the establishment of a particular mode of accountability towards the social and economic well-being of the village. The seeds for this development were gathered from the Ghandian movement in neighbouring India, which had led to a development discourse: 'a village-based society and polity was essential both for spiritual progress and for peace' (Bond, 2004, p. 46). In Sri Lanka, Sarvodaya tried to adopt the same ideas but using Buddhism to mobilise its four governing principles: sharing, virtuous speech, right livelihood and equality. The development mode that arose from this governing and accountability mechanism was termed 'Other Development' by Kantowsky (1980), who researched the village-based development model. In the next section, we elaborate on how this happened and how the associated accountability mechanism worked.

Performing Village and Developmental Accountability

The emergence of social organisations, such as NGOs, is necessitated and conditioned by the political circumstances of the time. Thus, the political backdrop to the formation of Sarvodaya was the postcolonial creation of the nation state. During the historical phase of searching for 'true independence' (according to the post-independence political rhetoric), the nation state was an articulation of contradictory political objectives. First, the political state was confronted with the task of 'organising and maintaining a modern political apparatus, that is a rationally conducted administration, a cadre of leaders grouped in the public form of a party system, and a machinery of public order' (Shils, 1963, p. 2). The main task was to indigenise the inherited apparatus of the colonial political state. Second, in contrast to the colonial state, the domain of postcolonial economic interests was not confined to colonial plantations: a large feudal society was awaiting capitalist penetration and modernisation. The economic progress and welfare of the neglected masses was prioritised by the post-independent electoral politics that emanated from universal franchise and the system of party politics. Third, in sharp contrast to these modernisation objectives, the new nation state was also concerned with upholding the dignity of its traditional cultures (Shils, 1963). This was where the notion of 'the village' became a central element of postcolonial 'developmentality,'[2] and it was conceived of as both the holder of traditional culture and the gateway to national development; hence, the village was to be preserved, on the one hand, in a cultural and spiritual sense, and to be developed, on the other, in a material sense.

Sarvodaya was the institutional articulation of such cultural-political objectives becoming a pragmatic 'social movement.'[3] In this sense, Sarvodaya's first '*shramadana*' (collective voluntary labour) camp was a historically significant event that brought together different social classes and strata into a unifying structure of accountability as a particular mode of modernising peripheral villages through Buddhist ideological practice. *Shramadana* was a social practice based upon the Buddhist doctrine of *dana* (philanthropic giving). As such, *shramadana* means the philanthropic giving of labour (*shrama*). When the Sarvodaya movement began in 1958, Dr A. T. Ariyaratne[4] organised a *shramadana* camp in the remote and destitute outcaste Kanatoluwa village. The aim of this first camp was, as Ariyaratne himself reflected,

> that the students [of Nalanda College Colombo] would understand and experience the true state of affairs that prevailed in the rural and poor urban areas . . . [and] develop a love for their people and utilize the education they received to find ways of building a more just and happier life for them.
>
> (Ariyaratne, 1981, p. 1)

As Ariyaratne (1981) explains further, students gained this understanding by experiencing village life first-hand: living in village huts, sharing meals, working side-by-side with villagers, sinking wells, constructing roads, planting gardens and talking until late at night in *village family gatherings*. Within a few years, hundreds of other schools had joined the practice of giving labour at weekend *shramadana* camps. The movement soon expanded beyond the school system and became a national rural development movement—the National Shramadana Movement, later, Sarvodaya. The movement, especially in this early stage before its transformation into a conglomerate of NGOs, integrated social classes and strata into a unifying structure of accountability and performance, embedded in a community-based religious ideology of development. Thus, a set of *performing villages* was created in the periphery (see Ariyaratne, 1981; Macy, 1985).

Here, the notion of *performance* has to be identified in an empirical sense in terms of three distinct, but interrelated, dimensions around which Sarvodaya 'organised' the villages: *ideologies, relations and practices* (see Figure 17.1). The ideological elements of performance relate to a 'higher order of worth,' to borrow the terminology of Boltanski and Thévenot (2006), which offers political and ethical justifications for the material practices and relations of performance. They embed certain utopian ideologies of 'just' and 'plentiful' worlds, as well as principles that define proper conduct and means of achieving such ideological elements of performance. Social relations and practices were legitimated as the means through which this higher order of worth was to be realised. Thus, revitalising the instrumentality of practices and relations in contributing towards the ideological elements reproduces social practices and relations.

Figure 17.1   Pillars of a performing village (Macy, 1985)

Performing Ideology

By the late 1960s Sarvodaya had grown from a work camp movement into a well-organised mass campaign for rural development. It had a unique, but well-articulated, development ideology, an active social coalition that provided the necessary social capital and a set of material practices to mobilise its development ideology. Through his reference to Buddhist spiritual principles and his charismatic leadership, his public speeches and writings and also charts and pictures posted at *shramadana* camps and village gatherings (see Figure 17.2 for an example of a chart), Ariyaratne articulated the ideological parameters of the Sarvodaya movement. This ideology was a 'postcolonial' infusion of two 'orders of worth.' First was the liberal, economic aspiration of economic growth and material development defined in terms of the economic, the political and the social. This encompassed economic empowerment by modernising the mode of production, political empowerment by widening the political participation of the rural mass and social empowerment through equality, solidarity, education and health. The

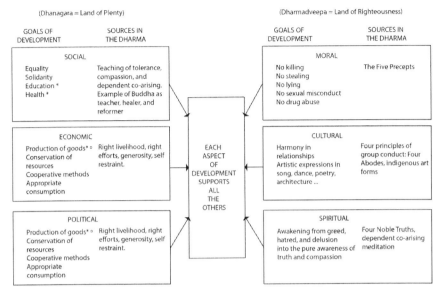

SARVODAYA DEFINITION OF DEVELOPMENT:
GOALS AND SOURCES

(Dhanagara = Land of Plenty)   (Dharmadveepa = Land of Righteousness)

| GOALS OF DEVELOPMENT | SOURCES IN THE DHARMA | | GOALS OF DEVELOPMENT | SOURCES IN THE DHARMA |

SOCIAL — Equality, Solidarity, Education*, Health* — Teaching of tolerance, compassion, and dependent co-arising. Example of Buddha as teacher, healer, and reformer

MORAL — No killing, No stealing, No lying, No sexual misconduct, No drug abuse — The Five Precepts

ECONOMIC — Production of goods*°, Conservation of resources, Cooperative methods, Appropriate consumption — Right livelihood, right efforts, generosity, self restraint.

CULTURAL — Harmony in relationships, Artistic expressions in song, dance, poetry, architecture ... — Four principles of group conduct: Four Abodes, indigenous art forms

POLITICAL — Production of goods*°, Conservation of resources, Cooperative methods, Appropriate consumption — Right livelihood, right efforts, generosity, self restraint.

SPIRITUAL — Awakening from greed, hatred, and delusion into the pure awareness of truth and compassion — Four Noble Truths, dependent co-arising meditation

EACH ASPECT OF DEVELOPMENT SUPPORTS ALL THE OTHERS

* Modern development goals usually limited to these
° Modern economic goals usually limited to these

Figure 17.2 Ideological apparatuses of Sarvodaya's performing village (Macy, 1985; © 1985 by Kumarian Press, used with permission of Lynne Rienner Publishers)

second order was drawn from religious aspirations of 'righteousness' as specifically defined in Buddhist precepts of well-being.

Communicating this ideology itself constitutes performance. Especially in the early stages of Sarvodaya, much time and effort was spent on practices through which Sarvodaya ideology was communicated to the rural masses. These included mass gatherings in the village temple and speeches given by Ariyaratne and other leaders of the Sarvodaya movement, including popular Buddhist monks and various other 'intellectuals' and 'nationalists.' In addition, this process included publication of booklets and posters. The relative success of such communicative practices was judged by the 'size of the crowd' attending mass rallies, and also by the number of people who volunteered to spread the Sarvodaya movement across the country. An example of communicative action as performance is reflected in the following thoughts from a Sarvodaya activist about his 'good old days' in the Sarvodaya movement:

I would say the 1960s and 70s were the best days of Sarvodaya ... we had thousands and thousands of followers gathering to each mega rally to listen to Ariyaratne and other wonderful speakers. It was the same as the mega rally of any political party but they did not talk politics.

Instead they talked of developing our villages on our own without the
support of government or any other international funding. It was about
self-reliance. . . . We had hundreds and hundreds of volunteers attending
our shramadana camps. We had them in hundreds and hundreds of villages all over the country. Not a cent paid to anybody; people just came
because they loved it and helped build their own villages, a road to their
village, a school building, some improvements to the temple, repairing
a water tank and so on. . . . Yes, you ask any old-timers, they would all
say that those were the best days because people did it on their own and
in big numbers, until it became a paid job not voluntary work anymore.

These mega rallies and meetings were performance, the outcome of which
was assumed to be the spread of Sarvodaya's *Boudya mathavadaya* (literally, *Buddhist ideology* of development). Despite the apparent difficulty of
producing clear 'measurements' of performance (as well as there being no
need to do so), these discursive activities were understood as the core of the
Sarvodaya movement, which was mainly defined as an ideological transformation of the nation. It was seen as a need to get the nation back on its
traditional Buddhist ideology of well-being (see Ariyaratne, 1981), which
refers to the quasi-religious and quasi-political character of the movement.
As such, translating postcolonial villages into an ideologically sound social
space was one of the key performances of the Sarvodaya movement.

PERFORMING RELATIONS

Such ideological performance was possible only by penetrating both the particular structure of social relations that characterised the traditional villages
and postcolonial politics. This included building cultural-political alliances
between power players in the traditional village landscape and 'national
intellectuals,' and also encompassed simultaneous micro and macro presence. At the macro level, the Sarvodaya Shramadana Movement quickly
found its way into a national forum of development through aligning with
various national-level, state-led development programmes, such as the Integrated Rural Development Programme. Alliance building with government
departments and officials, politicians and popular 'national intellectuals' has
been a key performance of Ariyaratne and other leaders. This was achieved
mainly through maintaining an apolitical development initiative that was
not aligned with party politics. Sarvodaya's presence in the national media
was positive and assisted by a national political alliance, the intention of
which was to build a postcolonial nation state.

More interesting, perhaps, was the set of micro social relations that
Sarvodaya tried to build within each village. These tapped into traditional
patronage and paternalistic power relations in villages, with the result that
the social relations articulated as accountability relations were founded on

the power relations of particular villages. The way in which this mundane level of accountability worked was explained by a Sarvodaya activist:

> It seems more like a business today . . . but those days, we never had any business or political motives. . . . When we approached a village, our first point of contact had mostly been the 'loku hamuduruwo' (head priest of the temple). Temples were often our meeting places. We reach other important people in the village through the temple. Sometimes, it was one of those other powerful people in the village who took us to the temple but the temple had always been the centre of building relationships. . . . We often started the work in the village with something to be done in the temple itself and then extended to other places like the village school, other common places like roads and public wells, and then even to repairing private properties of villagers in need. Often monks came and watched what we were doing in various places in the village and it was our sincere duty to make them informed. We would return to the temple every afternoon and often sleep in the banamaduwa (preaching hall). Not like today, no letters, no memos or written reports, but everybody gathered to the banamaduwa for Pawul Hamuwa (the name given to the evening gathering of everybody involved in shramadana activities) and had a productive discussion on what we did that day and what we were going to do next day. . . . Not much money involved at all; no business but simply shramadana; everybody saw what we were doing; and no worries of cheating, corruption or abuse.

Given its cultural significance and the commanding position of Buddhist monks in the village power structure, the temple had often been at the centre of the kinds of social relations that Sarvodaya started to reproduce. More than a mere gathering of people for traditional religious ceremonies and rituals, Sarvodaya was able to 'organise' what later came to be known as 'Sarvodaya Shramadana Societies' for each village. These were 'associations' with a cadre of officials committed to promoting Sarvodaya's idea of *gramodaya* (literally, village awakening). Each society in a village had such a cadre, which included Buddhist monks, notables and government officers (such as school headmasters, traditional Ayurvedic doctors, postmasters, police inspectors and regional government agents) as patrons. Active core office bearers were often young school leavers committed to the Sarvodaya movement. This society was organised into various subgroups targeting the development of specific activity areas, typically including a group for each of the following: preschool children, young people, mothers, farmers and adults (see Ariyaratne, 1981; Bond, 2004; Macy, 1985).

For example, Sarvodaya often organised preschool activities in the temple preaching hall, which were run by young women volunteers from the village. Later, especially when Sarvodaya began to receive foreign aid, these preschools were formalised, converting voluntary roles into permanent, salary-bearing employment opportunities with training provided by the Sarvodaya Head Office and other training centres. Such activity groups, especially the mother and the youth groups, provided peer communities that facilitated the awakening of members' political activism, and promoted an active set of community accountabilities and performances. The formation of such groups across many villages revitalised the collective power of the villagers who were performing these relations. Macy's ethnographic reflections on her experiences of working with such groups are an illustration of this point:

> I came to believe that . . . [Sarvodaya's] distinct contribution to grass-roots development lay in the way it combines physical work with . . . [village] meetings. . . . In shramadanas and their associated family gatherings, the community has an opportunity to come together, identify new leaders, and give a voice to people, such as women and young people, who had not previously participated in community decisions. These meetings help villagers overcome their sense of helplessness by realising their vast potential for self-development based on self-reliance, mutual cooperation, and the harnessing of local resources.
>
> (1985, p. 58)

Thus, the construction and maintenance of such development-oriented social relations themselves constituted performance. It was through the revitalisation of these social relations that Sarvodaya's practices and ideologies were to be grounded. The practical accountability implications of such performing relations are discussed in the next section.

PERFORMING PRACTICES

The central doctrine of Sarvodaya's performance in terms of day-to-day material practices was the notion of *shramadana*. In its traditional meaning *shramadana* involved philanthropic and voluntary labour, but this was no less 'organised' for being voluntary. As one of our interviewees reflected, a *shramadana* camp in any village involved a lot of 'organising':

> Yes, it involved a quite a big deal of organising and coordinating. What we normally did was to first identify some essential work in the village, especially something that needed immediate collective action; often it was something like building a water well and a tank, repairing a road or a bridge, or building a new classroom in the village school. That, however, varied depending on the village. Even before that you needed to get a set of people together to initiate the project and to do the necessary organising. . . . Then you needed to talk to all the important people and get their consent and support. It was important not to miss any such

important people; you needed to at least let them know that you were planning something like that, at least as a matter of courtesy or even not make any difficult enemies for you. . . . Yes, support meant lots of things, you needed people, lots of them in a shramadana, the bigger the number the better, because you could carry out a larger tasks or a number of them and it became a big shramadana. But then you needed to find tools, equipment, food and tea, and many other things. You needed to find the sponsorship from one or a few rich people for food and tea . . . After all, you had to keep an eye on everybody to make sure that there was nothing wrong going on. It was not easy to oversee everything when there were lots of people engaged in a shramadana. Everybody was not the same, there could be various issues among people and you had to make sure that everything went on smoothly. And, after all, they were volunteers. This was where you needed somebody like Buddhist monks or any other set of respected people behind all these. . . . it was fascinating work to organise a shramadana; you feel you are really doing something for the village.

Organising the *shramadana* was communal rather than 'organisational': that is, 'communal' was the organisational doctrine for such work. This communal apparatus of *shramadana* work derived not only from the collective and voluntary element of the labour involved but also from Sarvodaya's philosophy of self-reliance, which Ariyaratne outlined as follows:

> What are the resources of the have-nots? The capacity to think, to feel, to work. This shrama can either be exchanged for payment or be intelligently shared for common benefit. In the existing production relationships for mere survival one has to sell one's shrama, but to create a new non-exploitative relationship one has to learn the art and science of sharing it—of shramadana. Self-reliance cannot exist without sharing.
>
> (1980, p. 3)

In fact, there was a need to control and supervise the voluntary work, and our data reveal that this was achieved mainly through three different modes. First, there was a communally embedded, hierarchical mode of supervision in the form of paternalism and patronage, which worked as a system of accountability through rituals such as *pawul hamuwa*. Second, in such communal work settings, there was a community gaze within the work environment itself: 'work' was communally visible at the point of performance. Third, certain Buddhist religious ideals and precepts were incorporated into material practices pertaining to collective labour. For example, all participants of *shramadana* were expected to follow the 'four grounds of kindness' (*sanghavatthuni*) as guiding principles for collective behaviour: *dana* (generosity), *piyavajja* (kindly speech), *atthakariya* (useful conduct) and *samanaththa* (equality). These traditional Buddhist principles were not only viewed as the foundation of traditional village communal life but also as the antithesis of life in a modern colonial social order (see Bond, 2004). The aim was to infuse spirituality and materiality into a coherent social structure and set of accountability practices through which a performing village was to be constructed.

Performance of *shramadana* as communal work was understood and appreciated by a community (rather than measured and reported to an external party). As such, the giving and receiving of accounts was embedded in the relations of production, in communal rituals and ceremonies and in the social structure of the village. *Pawul hamuwa* was one example of such a ceremonial practice grounded in the communal power structure of the village. After the day's hard work of *shramadana*, people gathered in the temple preaching hall to reflect upon the process and the outcome of the day's work, and also to openly discuss their future *shramadana* plans. Such gatherings were often presided over by Buddhist monks and were intermingled with religious rituals and cultural shows that offered an opportunity to share ideas and skills, and to promote Sarvodaya's philosophy of self-reliance and trust. In this sense, *shramadana* was a particular mode of accountability in which a particular set of production relations were mobilised as relations of accountability, in order not only to coordinate and control the non-exploitative sharing of labour but also to promote a particular social ideology.

However, this *communal* form of accountability was never a hierarchy-free, participatory form of accountability, where everyone had equal status and the power to demand and provide accounts. Rather, it was structured according to the social hierarchy of the village. An individual's capacity to receive and provide accounts was always both facilitated and constrained by his/her symbolic capital (in terms of caste and official positions, for example) and economic capital (such as that held by the landed village aristocracy). Thus, who could *tell* and who should *listen* had never been free from structural prerogatives. Nevertheless, it is important to note that the *shramadana* movement did empower those at the bottom of social hierarchies, through their engagement in a national, political movement that had a localised presence in peripheral villages. The *shramadana* movement gave villagers a social space within which they could construct a political dialogue around both the political interests of an evolving, postcolonial nation state and the local development needs of the villages.

In this sense, accountability relations, which evolved through the *shramadana* movement, were not confined to the practice of giving and receiving accounts for the sake of organising work systems. They also provided for a far-reaching set of communicative actions through which a particular ideological discourse of development was constructed. This equates to what Gramsci called an 'agrarian bloc,' which was capable of encompassing the following: villagers' material interests in terms of better living standards, the political interests of nationalist/anti-colonial political movements that emanated from urban centres and the structural parameters of the village landscape (that is, patronage, paternalism and religious social order). These were brought under a unified structure and a set of mundane practices of accountability and cultural reproduction. In this context, mundane practices of giving and receiving accounts were driven by three distinct, but interrelated, political motives: (1) the goal of organising and executing the day-to-day practices of *shramadana*, through which the material needs of the villagers were identified and catered for; (2) the goal of reconstructing the village as a particular political space, through which the postcolonial, political interests of the nation state could be articulated; and (3) the goal of constructing Sarvodaya as a socio-political ideology that was grounded in self-reliance, sharing and non-exploitative production relations.

REFLECTIONS AND CONCLUSIONS

We have seen that Sarvodaya's accountability relations were manifested in a performing village within which both liberal economic and spiritual ideologies were mobilised to form a protestant folk Buddhism. On the one hand, liberal ideology was fortified with a set of development concepts that were discussed in terms of economic prosperity in the postcolonial struggle for economic and social emancipation. On the other, the spiritual principles of Buddhism were mobilised to discipline people in relation to ideal collective behaviour. Thus, Sarvodaya ideology and practices were seen as an alternative development path for collective emancipation, and the *shramadana* campaign was constructed as the performance regime of that development strategy. The set of mundane practices and relations generated by this campaign was an articulation of both liberal economic and local Buddhist ideologies within a project of building a postcolonial nation state as an antithesis to the colonial state. In this sense, the set of accountability relations and practices embraced by Sarvodaya was a result of the social movement of the protestant Buddhism of the 1950s, which infused a global, economic liberalism of development with local Buddhist traditions. The genesis and the nature of developmental accountability must thus be understood from this broader structural perspective, which drives us to pay attention to social movements as the historical root of the present NGO accountability paradox.

As we have observed, social movements are 'ideologically structured actions' (Zald, 2000) that open up the potential for NGO accountability analysis. Therefore, the formative phase of Sarvodaya can be conceived as a social movement that, while grounded in village power structures, was driven by two higher-order principles of development: economic liberalism and Buddhist spirituality. Although the early phase of this social movement was incoherent and ad hoc, later, it generated positions, rules, procedures and documents through which these two principles were translated into a set of tangible, material 'things,' practices and a hierarchy. This paved the way to extending the movement into a coherent civic organisation that came to be known as Lanka Jathika Sarvodaya Shramadana Sangamaya; it was incorporated by a parliamentary act and then evolved into a conglomerate of entities catering to the current neoliberal development industry in Sri Lanka.[5]

Nevertheless, in terms of understanding NGO accountability, the key message offered by this historical analysis is clear. Social movements and their subsequent evolution into rather formalised accountability structures and performance regimes are outcomes of historically specific and dialectically evolving sets of political circumstances encountered by nation states. Drawing on Gramsci's (Gramsci, 1971, 1978) definitions of state and civil society, what we mean by the term nation state here is not simply the political state, but the totality created by the dialectical interplay among civil society, political state and the economy—each of which offers competing, higher-order principles around which to organise the nation state depending on the political-economic circumstances of the time. It is, then, an overarching concept of nation, as an entity seeking to build coherence among its polity, economy and society. For example, as our data reveal, in the immediate aftermath of independence, nationalism was the overarching political principle around which a postcolonial nation state was to be built, and civil society (especially its micro-organisational unit—the traditional village) was given utmost priority in redefining the nation state. In that sense, the village was taken as the mundane entity around which the postcolonial economy, polity and society were all to be developed and administered. The village became the basic entity of development accountability and performance, and the coherence of economy, polity and society was to be achieved within this micro entity of development accountability and performance. Sarvodaya, supported at this time by both the political state and an emerging community of local and international donors, offered a pragmatic social movement to meet this end, and created a set of ideological, relational and practical apparatuses through which the village was to be organised, managed and developed as a collective entity of development accountability and performance.

Sarvodaya's current mode manifests a fundamentally different nation state, however, in which neoliberal economic and political ideology is the higher-order principle by which it organises its three spheres. In contrast to the supremacy of nationalism and nationalisation that held sway until the late 1970s, the current political state is driven by ideologies of globalisation and privatisation. When it comes to civil society and social development, the village no longer has primacy as a collective; individual entrepreneurs are instead valued in an idealised context of competitive markets. Thus, Sarvodaya's initial village ideology has now been replaced by a development ideology of neoliberal economic citizenship and entrepreneurship. In this regime of development accountability and performance, worth is no longer placed on the capacity of individuals and collectives to comply with traditional Buddhist rules of collective behaviour, or with liberal ideologies of emancipation through collective actions, but on individuals' capacity to compete with others and to become connected to global markets. This neoliberal economic doctrine of development is encapsulated in the notion of entrepreneurship, which is understood as the missing element of development among poor villagers (rather than villages). Hence, there is now a need for entrepreneurial development through microfinance—the objectives of which are financial inclusiveness, financial literacy, financial outreach and technological empowerment (known as 'e-empowerment' in Sarvodaya discourse).

Sarvodaya's current focus on microfinance and e-empowerment reflects this development logic of the neoliberal nation state. As was the case from its beginning, Sarvodaya still actively attempts to reform the peripheral rural landscape, but it now does so on the basis of this new neoliberal development ideology. To achieve this, and to survive over the longer term, the movement had to undergo reform, and it became a leading microfinance provider in Sri Lanka. The movement 'successfully' drew on the social capital that it had developed during its 'golden years.' Its success as a leading microfinance service provider is recognised and taken as an exemplary case because of its commendable achievements of financial inclusiveness (that is, incorporating hitherto excluded 'poor villagers' into the mainstream banking sector), financial outreach (taking banking to remote villages where mainstream banking is not available), financial literacy (teaching villagers financial basics, including bookkeeping, business management and entrepreneurship modules designed by the ILO and the World Bank) and e-empowerment (offering computing and mobile technologies to peripheral villages through telecentres, IT centres and IT training facilities). Above all, its own growth and development is conceptualised in terms of its strategic vision to become a 'mainstream banker,' which would make it a more significant player than would be possible if it remained a mere microfinance provider. And this is how development is now understood within this particular neoliberal development accountability and performance regime.

NOTES

1   There have been different forms of practices of Buddhism in Sri Lanka. We use this term 'folk Buddhist ideology' to describe how it is perceived and performed by people in rural villages. It is based more on people's beliefs, traditions and rituals than on the Buddhist philosophy articulated in canonical texts.

2   Here the term 'developmentality' is used vis-à-vis Foucault's (1997) 'governmentality' to mean a particular governmental apparatus in which development, though with contested meanings, has become an overarching political-economic theme in the organisation of the political state, economy

and civil society, especially in postcolonial nations. Thus, human efforts and aspirations are discursively 'organised' around ever-evolving and experimental conceptions of development goals and strategies.

3 'Social movement' flows from social movement theory developed in sociology and has been a popular topic in organisation theory since the 1970s (see McCarthy & Zald, 1977). Social movement is defined as 'ideologically structured action' (Zald, 2000) that can be mobilized in organisations, challenging their formal routines and actions.

4 The founder of the Sarvodaya movement, and a former science teacher at Nalanda College, a leading Buddhist establishment in Sri Lanka, which contributed to the development of nationalist political leadership in the country.

5 This subsequent *transition* of Sarvodaya from a nationalist social movement to a neoliberal economic agency of development is itself an interesting theoretical and empirical analysis, which, however, resides beyond the scope of this chapter.

REFERENCES

Alawattage, C., & Wickramasinghe, D. (2008). Appearance of accounting in a political hegemony. *Critical Perspectives on Accounting, 19*(3), 293–339.

Ariyaratne, A. T. (1979). *Sarvodaya and development.* Moratuwa, LK: Sarvodaya Press.

Ariyaratne, A. T. (1980, September). What is self reliance? *Dana,* 55–56.

Ariyaratne, A. T. (1981). *In search of development.* Moratuwa, LK: Sarvodaya Press.

Ariyaratne, A. T. (1989). *Collected works* (Vol. IV). Rathmalana, LK: Sarvodaya Vishva Lekha Press.

Ariyaratne, A. T. (1994). *Future directions of Sarvodaya.* Moratuwa, LK: Sarvodaya Press.

Ariyaratne, A. T. (2001). *Collected works* (2nd ed., Vol. I–VI). Rathmalana, LK: Sarvodaya Vishva Lekha Press.

Boltanski, L., & Thévenot, L. (2006). *On justification: Economies of worth.* Princeton, NJ: Princeton University Press.

Bond, G. D. (2004). *Buddhism at work: Community development, social empowerment and the Sarvodaya Movement.* Bloomfield, CT: Kumarian Press.

Burchell, S., Clubb, C., Hopwood, A., Hughes, J., & Nahapiet, J. (1980). The roles of accounting in organizations and society. *Accounting, Organizations and Society, 5*(1), 5–27.

Chenhall, R. H., Hall, M., & Smith, D. (2010). Social capital and management control systems: A study of a non-government organization. *Accounting, Organizations and Society, 35*(8), 737–756.

Cohen, J. L., & Arato, A. (1992). *Civil society and political theory.* Cambridge: Massachusetts Institute of Technology.

Ebrahim, A. (2003). Accountability in practice: Mechanisms for NGOs. *World Development, 31*(5), 813–829.

Foucault, M. (1997). Of other spaces: Utopias and heterotopias. In N. Leach (Ed.), *Rethinking architecture: A reader in cultural theory* (pp. 330–336). New York: Routledge.

Gramsci, A. (1971). *Selections from the prison notebooks of Antonio Gramsci.* New York: International Pubs.

Gramsci, A. (1978). *Selections from political writings (1921–1926): With additional texts by other Italian communist leaders.* London: Lawrence and Wishart.

Gray, R. (2002). The social accounting project and accounting organizations and society privileging engagement, imaginings, new accountings and pragmatism over critique? *Accounting, Organizations and Society, 27*(7), 687–708.

Gray, R., Bebbington, J., & Collison, D. (2006). NGOs, civil society and account-ability: Making the people accountable to capital. *Accounting, Auditing & Accountability Journal, 19*(3), 319–348.

Gray, R., Kouhy, R., & Lavers, S. (1995). Corporate social and environmental reporting: A review of the literature and a longitudinal study of UK disclosure. *Accounting, Auditing & Accountability Journal, 8*(2), 44–77.

Harvey, D. (2005). *A brief history of neoliberalism.* Oxford: Oxford University Press.

Henderson, K. M. (1997). Alternatives to imposed administrative reform: The NGOs. *International Journal of Public Sector Management, 10*(5), 353–364.

Kamat, S. (2004). The privatization of public interest: Theorizing NGO discourse in a neoliberal era. *Review of International Political Economy, 11*(1), 155–176.

Kantowsky, D. (1980). *Sarvodaya: The other development.* Bengaluru, IN: Vikas Publishing House.

Keane, J. (2003). *Global civil society?* Cambridge: Cambridge University Press.

Lehman, G. (2007). The accountability of NGOs in civil society and its public spheres. *Critical Perspectives on Accounting, 18*(6), 645–669.

Macy, J. (1985). *Dharma and development: Religion as resource in the Sarvodaya self-help movement* (Rev. ed.). West Hartford, CT: Kumarian Press.

McCarthy, J. D., and Zald, M. N. (1977) Resource mobilization and social move-ments: A partial theory. *American Journal of Sociology, 82*(6), 1212–1241.

McKernan, J. F., & McPhail, K. (2012). Accountability and accounterability. *Critical Perspectives on Accounting, 23*(3), 177–182.

Moore, M. (2006). Good government? (Introduction). *IDS Bulletin, 37*(4), 50–56.

Munro, R. (1996). Alignment and identity work: The study of accounts and account-ability. In R. Munro & J. Mouritsen (Eds.), *Accountability: Power, ethos and the technologies of managing* (pp. 3–19). London: International Thomson Business Press.

O'Dwyer, B. (2005). The construction of a social account: A case study in an over-seas aid agency. *Accounting, Organizations and Society, 30*(3), 279–296.

O'Dwyer, B., & Unerman, J. (2007). From functional to social accountability. *Accounting, Auditing & Accountability Journal, 20*(3), 446.

O'Dwyer, B., & Unerman, J. (2008). The paradox of greater NGO accountability: A case study of Amnesty Ireland. *Accounting, Organizations and Society, 33*(7–8), 801–824.

O'Dwyer, B., Unerman, J., & Bradley, J. (2005). Perceptions on the emergence and future development of corporate social disclosure in Ireland: Engaging the voices of non-governmental organisations. *Accounting, Auditing & Accountability Journal, 18*(1), 14–43.

Ohmae, K. (1995). *The end of the nation state: The rise of regional economies.* London: Harper Collins.

O'Sullivan, N., & O'Dwyer, B. (2009). Stakeholder perspectives on a financial sector legitimation process: The case of NGOs and the Equator Principles. *Accounting, Auditing & Accountability Journal, 22*(4), 553–587.

Perera, J. (1997). In unequal dialogue with donors: The experience of the Sarvodaya Shramadana Movement. In D. Hulme & M. Edwards (Eds.), *NGOs, states and donors: Too closer for comfort?* (pp. 156–167). London: Macmillan Press Ltd.

Robinson, M. (1994). Governance, democracy and conditionality: NGOs and the new policy agenda. In A. Clayton (Ed.), *Governance, democracy and condition-ality: What role for NGOs?* Oxford: INTRAC.

Robinson, M. (1997). Privatizing the voluntary sector: NGOs as public service contractors? In D. Hulme & M. Edwards (Eds.), *NGOs, states and donors: Too close for comfort?* Basingstoke, UK: Macmillan in association with Save the Children.

Ryan, B. F. (1958). *Sinhalese village.* Miami: University of Miami Press.

Sarvodaya. (2013). *Sarvodaya Annual Report 2012–13.* Retrieved from: http://www.sarvodaya.org/publications/annual-report-201213

Shils, E. (1963). On the comparative study of the new states: The quest for modernity in Asia and Africa. In C. Geertz (Ed.), *Old societies and new states* (pp. 1–26). London: The Free Press of Glencoe.

Thomson, I., & Bebbington, J. (2005). Social and environmental reporting in the UK: A pedagogic evaluation. *Critical Perspectives on Accounting, 16*(5), 507–533.

Tinker, A. (1984). Theories of the state and the state of accounting: Economic reductionism and political voluntarism in accounting regulation theory. *Journal of Accounting and Public Policy, 3*(1), 55–74.

Unerman, J., & O'Dwyer, B. (2006a). On James Bond and the importance of NGO accountability. *Accounting, Auditing & Accountability Journal, 19*(3), 305–318.

Unerman, J., & O'Dwyer, B. (2006b). Theorising accountability for NGO advocacy. *Accounting, Auditing & Accountability Journal, 19*(3), 305–318.

Zadek, S. (1993). The practice of Buddhist economics? Another view. *American Journal of Economics and Sociology, 52*(4), 433–445.

Zadek, S., & Szabo, S. (1994). *Valuing organisation: The case of Sarvodaya.* London: The New Economics Foundation.

Zald, M. N. (2000). Ideologically structured action: An enlarged agenda for social movement research. *Mobilization: An International Quarterly, 5*(1), 1–16.

Review Process

This volume is a peer-reviewed collection of chapters. Each submitted chapter has been subject to the following review process: (1) it has been reviewed by the editors for its suitability for further referencing, and (2) its final acceptance for publication has been subject to double and triple peer review.

The editors would like to thank the following reviewers for their constructive comments and suggestions on the chapters included in this book:

Manzurul Alam	Murdoch University, Australia
Michael S. Booth	Queensland University of Technology, Australia
David Brown	University Technology Sydney, Australia
Carolyn Fowler	Victoria University of Wellington, New Zealand
Les Hardy	Monash University, Australia
Tony Hines	Portsmouth University Business School, UK
Trevor Hopper	University of Sussex, UK
Alan D. Hough	Queensland University of Technology, Australia
Helen Irvine	Queensland University of Technology, Australia
Kerry Jacobs	University of New South Wales—Canberra, Australia
Stéphane Jaumier	Grenoble École de Management and Université Paris-Dauphine, France
Vassili Joannidès	Grenoble École de Management and Queensland University of Technology, Australia
Margaret Lightbody	University of Adelaide, Australia
Belinda Luke	Queensland University of Technology, Australia
Myles McGregor-Lowndes	Queensland University of Technology, Australia
Leslie S. Oakes	University of New Mexico, U.S.
Benjamin J. Pawson	Edinburgh International Science Festival, Scotland
Christine M. Ryan	Queensland University of Technology, Australia
Phil Saj	University of Adelaide, Australia
Rowena Sinclair	AUT University, Auckland
Carolyn Stringer	University of Otago, New Zealand

Editors

Zahirul Hoque Dr. Zahirul Hoque, PhD (Manchester), FCPA, FCMA is a Professor in Accounting at La Trobe University Business School, Melbourne, Australia. He has held positions at Deakin University; Charles Darwin University; Griffith University; Victoria University of Wellington; Dhaka University in Bangladesh; Nanyang Technological University in Singapore; American International University-Bangladesh; Babson College, U.S.; King Fahd University of Petroleum and Minerals, Saudi Arabia; University of Malaya, Malaysia and Sunway University, Malaysia. He is the founding Editor-in-Chief of the *Journal of Accounting & Organizational Change*. His research interests include management accounting and performance management, public sector accounting and management, accounting in developing economies, NGOs and nonprofits accounting, accountability and performance and interdisciplinary research on management control systems.

Lee Parker Professor Parker is a Professor in Accounting at RMIT University, Melbourne, Australia and at Royal Holloway, University of London. He has held previous university posts in Australasia, UK, North America and Asia. Joint Founding Editor of the internationally prominent, ISI-listed, interdisciplinary research journal, Accounting Auditing & Accountability Journal, Professor Parker's research has been published in over 200 articles and books on management and accounting internationally. Professor Parker is a qualitative, interdisciplinary researcher in strategic management, corporate governance, accounting and management history, social and environmental accountability, public and nonprofit sector accounting and qualitative and historical research methodology.

Contributors

Kamran Ahmed Dr. Kamran Ahmed is Professor of Accounting at La Trobe University, Australia. Professor Ahmed began his academic career in Australia in 1988 at the Australian National University, and later had academic appointments at Victoria University of Wellington and the University of New England prior to joining La Trobe University in 1999. His current research interests are corporate disclosure, corporate accounting policy choice, earnings management, international accounting harmonization, accounting and reporting practices in South Asia and microfinance reporting.

Zahir Ahmed Dr. Zahir Uddin Ahmed is a Senior Lecturer in Accounting at the Auckland University of Technology, New Zealand. He received his PhD in Management Accounting and Control from Manchester Business School, UK. He holds professional accountant membership of both CPA Australia and New Zealand Institute of Chartered Accountants (NZICA). His research interests include not-for-profit and NGO accountability and control, gender in management accounting and management accounting practice in developing countries.

Chandana Alawattage Dr. Chandana Alawattage has taught and researched management accounting at the University of Aberdeen Business School over the last eight years. Previously, he taught management accounting, organisational theory and economics at the University of Sri Jayewardenepura (Sri Lanka). He is the co-author of *Management Accounting Change: Approaches and Perspectives* (2007), a social theory-based management accounting text, and a Guest Editor of the special issue of 'Management Accounting in Less-Developed Countries' (2007) in *Journal of Accounting & Organizational Change*.

Oonagh B. Breen Dr. Oonagh B. Breen is a Senior Lecturer at the School of Law, University College Dublin where her teaching includes comparative charity law and policy. A graduate of UCD and Yale Law School and a qualified barrister, her research appraises the potential for the development of more structured legal relationships between the state and the nonprofit sector from the joint perspectives of regulation of the sector and facilitation of its work in a comparative context. A former Fulbright Scholar and holder of an Emerging Scholar Award from the Association of Research on Nonprofit Organizations and Voluntary Action (2006), Oonagh was awarded an ICNL/Cordaid Distinguished Research Award in 2008 for her work in the area of European regulation of charitable organization. Currently she is serving as a board member of the International Center for Not-for-Profit Law, Washington, DC, and of the International Advisory Board for the Model Nonprofit Law Project, Australia.

Evelyn Brody Evelyn Brody is Professor of Law at Chicago-Kent College of Law, Illinois Institute of Technology, and has spent semesters visiting at the University of Pennsylvania, Duke and New York University law schools. She previously worked in private practice and with the U.S. Treasury Department's Office of Tax Policy. For the American Law Institute's ongoing project on *Principles of the Law of Charitable Nonprofit Organizations*, Professor Brody has served as co-reporter (2001–2004), reporter (2004–2013) and consultant (from 2013). She is also an Affiliated Scholar with The Urban Institute's Center on Nonprofits and Philanthropy, for which she edited the multidisciplinary volume, *Property-Tax Exemption for Charities: Mapping the Battlefield* (Urban Institute Press, 2002), written book chapters and has assisted in organizing conferences on issues of law and philanthropy. A prolific author of law review articles and book chapters, Professor Brody serves as an advisory board member of Columbia Law School's Attorneys General Charities Law Project, and is a member of the Planned Giving Advisory Council of the Carter Center (Atlanta, Georgia).

Michael S. Booth Mr. Michael S. Booth is a PhD candidate in the School of Accountancy at Queensland University of Technology (QUT), Australia. Michael completed an MBus (research) in 2012. He teaches in the School of Accountancy and the School of Management at QUT. Before commencing studies at QUT he was a Senior Executive with the Australian Taxation Office.

Ciaran Connolly Ciaran Connolly is Professor of Financial Accounting at Queen's University Management School. Ciaran's main areas of research are in the fields of public services, particularly the financial and performance measurement aspects of the voluntary/charitable sector, and the public sector, where he has a particular focus on PPP/PFI contacts and accountability.

Ericka Costa Dr. Ericka Costa (PhD in Business Economics) is Assistant Professor of Accounting at the University of Trento (Italy) and Research

Fellow at EURICSE—European Research Institute of Cooperatives and Social Enterprises. She is a member of the EBEN, EAA, BAFA and CSEAR international networks. Her research interests are aimed at investigating social and environmental accounting and corporate social responsibility for nonprofit organizations specifically with regards to social enterprises.

Craig Furneaux Dr. Craig Furneaux is a Lecturer in the Australian Centre for Philanthropy and Nonprofit Studies. He is an ad hoc reviewer for a number of journals related to procurement, and nonprofit management, and is a member of the Academy of Management. His research examines performance management and accountability practices, procedural variations and public policy issues related to social procurement.

Trevor Hopper Trevor Hopper is Professor of Management Accounting at Sussex University, UK; Adjunct Professor at Victoria University of Wellington, New Zealand; and visiting Professor at Stockholm School of Economics, Sweden. Previously he was a cost accountant in industry, a Lecturer at Wolverhampton and Sheffield Universities and Professor at Manchester Business School. Professor Hopper was a Co-Editor of *British Accounting Review* and is the Associate Editor of the *Journal of Accounting & Organizational Change* and the Consulting Editor for the *Journal of Accounting in Emerging Economies*. He has co-edited eight books, including *A Handbook of Accounting in Developing Countries* (Elgar, 2012) and *Issues in Management Accounting* (Pearson, 2007, 3rd ed.). He received a Lifetime Achievement Award from the British Accounting Association and an Honorary Doctorate from Stockholm School of Economics.

Alan D. Hough Dr. Alan D. Hough completed his PhD in the Australian Centre for Philanthropy and Nonprofit Studies, School of Accountancy, at Queensland University of Technology. He has served as a CEO and board member of nonprofit organizations, as well as a consultant to nonprofit organizations and government. His previous work has been published in *Keeping Good Companies*, and a recent book chapter. His research interests are boards, performance management and sense-making.

Noel Hyndman Noel Hyndman is Professor of Management Accounting and Subject Leader (Accounting) at Queen's University Management School. His research interests include accounting, accounting change, reporting and governance in the third and public sectors. He is also a member of the joint SORP Committee of the Charity Commission (the regulator in England and Wales) and the Office of the Scottish Charity Regulator.

Helen Irvine Helen Irvine, MCom and PhD (University of Wollongong), is a Professor in the School of Accountancy at Queensland University of

Technology (QUT) Business School. Prior to joining QUT in 2008, Helen was at the University of Wollongong, and has been a Visiting Honorary Fellow there since 2011. Helen is a CPA, a member of the Taxation Institute of Australia, the Accounting Association of Australia and New Zealand (AFAANZ), its Special Interest Groups for Qualitative Research and Accounting History and is co-chair of the AFAANZ Public Sector and Not-for-Profit Special Interest Group. Helen is on the editorial boards of *Accounting, Auditing & Accountability Journal*, *Accounting History* and the *Australasian Accounting Business & Finance Journal*.

Stéphane Jaumier Stéphane Jaumier is a PhD candidate at Grenoble École de Management within the People, Organisations and Society Department, as well as at Université Paris-Dauphine within the MOST (Marchés-Organisations-Sociétés-Technologies) laboratory. He holds a Master's Degree in Engineering, a Master of Science in Finance and a Master of Philosophy. Before starting his PhD, he held various positions in logistics, management accounting and finance within companies in France and the Netherlands. His research interests include organisation theory, management control and accountability.

Vassili Joannidès Vassili Joannidès, PhD (Université Paris-Dauphine/Manchester) is Assistant Professor of management control and international relations at Grenoble École de Management and Queensland University of Technology School of Accountancy, as well as vice president and non-executive director of De Burg & Associés. His former positions were research equity analyst at Associés en Finance and due diligence officer at MCS & Associés in Paris. His research interests include management control and accountability, public sector management accounting, cultural issues in accounting, NGOs and nonprofits' accountability and interdisciplinary research on accountability.

Rakib Khan Dr. Rakib Khan is a Senior Lecturer in Accounting at Cambridge International College, Australia. He received his PhD in accounting from La Trobe University. His research interests include corporate disclosure, accountability and governance in NGOs in less developed economies.

Danielle McConville Danielle McConville is a Lecturer in Accounting at Queen's University Management School. A Chartered Accountant, her research interests are in performance reporting, governance and stakeholder engagement in the charity sector. Related to her research interests, she has been involved with a number of charity sector initiatives in the UK and Ireland.

Myles McGregor-Lowndes Myles McGregor-Lowndes OAM, PhD (Griffith University), MAdmin (Griffith University), BA/LLB (UQ) is a Professor in the QUT Business School and Director of The Australian Centre for Philanthropy and Nonprofit Studies (ACPNS). He is admitted as a solicitor of the Supreme Court of Queensland. He is a founding member of the ATO Charities Consultative Committee and the Australian Charities and Not-for-Profits Commission Advisory Board. He was part of the Productivity Commission's research team, examining the *Contribution of the Not-for-Profit Sector* and has been engaged to do research work for the Australian Treasury, Prime Minister and Cabinet, Board of Taxation, ATO, FaHCSIA and Arts Department. In June 2003, Professor McGregor-Lowndes was awarded a Medal of the Order of Australia (OAM) 'for service to the community by providing education and support in legal, financial and administrative matters to nonprofit organizations.'

Debra Morris Debra Morris is a Professor in Charity Law & Policy and Director of the Charity Law & Policy Unit, School of Law and Social Justice, University of Liverpool, UK. She has previously taught at Cayman Islands Law School where she was Assistant Director. She is the Editor of the *Charity Law & Practice Review* (Key Haven Publishers), the only specialized journal in this area in the UK. Her research interests include charity, property and employment law, with her specialism being in charity law. Her research has focused on many different aspects of charity law and regulation, ranging from the 'public benefit' test through to the regulation of fundraising. She has contributed to two of the leading texts on charity law, *Picarda: Law and Practice Relating to Charities* (4th ed.) (2010, Bloomsbury Professional) and *Tudor on Charities* (9th ed.) (2003, Sweet and Maxwell).

Leslie S. Oakes Leslie S. Oakes is an Associate Professor at the Anderson Schools of Management, University of New Mexico. She received her PhD in Business Administration-Accounting and her Masters Degree in Health Care Fiscal Management from the University of Wisconsin. Her research focuses on the social and historical role of accounting, primarily in community health and nonprofit organizations. She has published in *Accounting, Organizations and Society*, *Accounting, Auditing and Accountability Journal*, the *Accounting Review* and the *Administrative Science Quarterly*, among others. Dr. Oakes has actively supported the nonprofit community working with over 50 small and medium-sized organizations across New Mexico and the Navajo Nation. She has won awards for her research, community service and teaching.

Phil Saj Phil Saj is a Lecturer at the School of Accounting and Finance at the University of Adelaide, where he teaches courses in auditing and public sector and not-for-profit accountability. Phil's main research interests are accountability and governance of not-for-profit organisations. He has published on these topics in Australian and international journals, and has presented at professional and academic seminars. Phil has a long involvement with third sector organisations and is currently Treasurer of Australia, New Zealand Third Sector Research.

Benjamin J. Pawson Benjamin J. Pawson is a practicing fundraiser in the third sector in Scotland. He is currently a Development Officer for Edinburgh International Science Festival and was previously the Trusts and Corporate Fundraiser for Scottish Medical Nonprofit Chest Heart & Stroke Scotland. His research interests include fundraising strategy and innovation.

Christine M. Ryan Christine M. Ryan is an Adjunct Professor in the School of Accountancy at the Queensland University of Technology, Brisbane, Australia. Her research interests include nonprofit accounting standards setting, nonprofit accounting issues and corporate governance in nonprofit organisations. She is on the editorial boards of *Accounting, Auditing & Accountability Journal*, *Journal of Accounting & Organizational Change*, *Pacific Accounting Review* and *Accounting Research Journal*.

Neal Ryan Neal Ryan was the Pro Vice Chancellor of Research at Southern Cross University. He has published two books and over 90 journal articles and book chapters in discipline areas relating primarily to public policy, public management, technological change and management. He has been the recipient of 10 ARC grants, totalling more than $10 million. He has held an Executive Board position on the International Research Society for Public Management and Board positions on several major research consortiums such as CRCs. He currently holds Adjunct Professorial positions at Southern Cross University and Curtin University.

Julie-Anne Tarr Professor Julie-Anne Tarr has previously held professorial and senior administrative positions at Indiana University (Indianapolis), University of the South Pacific, University of Queensland and Bond University, in addition to roles as Director of the Litigation Reform Commission (Qld), COO of the Queensland Institute of Medical Research and Director of the Asia Pacific Law Institute (Bond University). She is a member of the Institute of Directors and sits on a number of commercial and not-for-profit boards. Her areas of expertise include insurance, risk management, contract and complex project management and structuring, in addition to not-for-profit sector contracting and governance. She has authored four monographs, two Titles of the Laws of Australia (Insurance, Insurance Contracts) and a range of law reform reports.

Anula Tennakoon Dr. Anula Tennakoon has earned BCom and MBA degrees from the Universities of Ruhuna and Colombo, Sri Lanka, respectively, and MRes and PhD degrees from the University of Bradford, UK. She is a Senior Lecturer at the University of Ruhuna, Sri Lanka, where she has taught management and accounting over the last 25 years. She continues researching issues in NGOs' management and accounting practices in developing countries.

Basil Tucker Basil Tucker, PhD (UniSA), MBA (Adelaide), BBus (SAIT), CPA is currently a Lecturer in the School of Commerce, UniSA Business School. He received his doctorate which investigated the relationship between management control and strategy in the not-for-profit sector in 2008. His research interests focus on the relevance of academic research, and, in particular, the research-practice 'gap' in management accounting and management control, how it supports and influences corporate strategy, how management control systems combine with informal modes of control and social network theory, and, in particular, how informal control is transmitted and maintained within organisations.

Matthew Turnour Dr. Matthew Turnour is a Senior Research Fellow of the Australian Centre for Philanthropy and Nonprofit Studies (ACPNS), School of Accountancy, Queensland University of Technology (QUT), and Managing Director of Neumann & Turnour Lawyers. His PhD thesis, entitled *Beyond Charity: Outlines of a Jurisprudence for Civil Society*, received an Outstanding Thesis Award at QUT. His other degrees include Bachelor of Economics, Bachelor of Laws and a Master of Arts by research. He is a Fellow of the Australian Institute of Company Directors and a Fellow of the Australian Institute of Management.

Danture Wickramasinghe Danture Wickramasinghe is Professor of Management Accounting at the University of Glasgow. He joined Glasgow after 19 years of research and teaching at the University of Manchester and one-and-a-half years at the University of Hull as Professor of Management Accounting and Director of the Centre for Accounting and Accountability Research. Previously, he taught management accounting and related subjects at the University of Colombo (Sri Lanka) and the University of Ruhuna (Sri Lanka), and had a visiting appointment at Paris-Dauphine University, France. He is the co-author of *Management Accounting Change: Approaches and Perspectives* (2007), a social theory-based management accounting text, Guest Editor of the special issue on Management Accounting in Less-Developed Countries (2007) in *Journal of Accounting & Organizational Change* and Co-Editor of *Handbook of Accounting and Development* (2012).

Index

Page numbers in **bold** indicate figures and tables